Algebra 1

An Incremental Development

Third Edition

Algebra 1

An Incremental Development

Third Edition

John H. Saxon, Jr.

SAXON PUBLISHERS, INC.

Algebra 1: An Incremental Development
Third Edition
Teacher's Edition

Printed in the United States of America.

ISBN: 1-56577-135-4

Editor: Smith Richardson
Pre-Press Manager: J. Travis Rose
Production Coordinator: Joan Coleman

Second printing: April 1998

┌─ *Reaching us via the Internet* ─┐
WWW: http://www.saxonpub.com
E-mail: info@saxonpub.com

Saxon Publishers, Inc.
2450 John Saxon Blvd.
Norman, OK 73071

Contents

Preface

This text is the third edition of the first book in the Saxon secondary school mathematics series. The series is comprised of three texts: *Algebra 1*, *Algebra 2*, and *Advanced Mathematics*. Together, these three books form an integrated treatment of secondary school mathematics. Topics from secondary school mathematics, including a full year of plane geometry, have been integrated throughout the three-book series.

The first edition of *Algebra 1*, published in the spring of 1981, was the first textbook published by Saxon Publishers (then called Grassdale Publishers), a company founded by John Saxon that same year. In fact, I first met John Saxon in 1980 as a 16-year-old high school student who was hired by him to help with the "dogwork" on his manuscript. When Mr. Saxon failed to find a publisher for his manuscript, he made the courageous move to publish the manuscript himself. The text became a classic and attracted many loyal and fervent adherents. The text underwent its first major revision in 1990. Lessons and problems covering geometry (basic geometric concepts like angle measure and classification of polygons, computations of perimeters and areas of irregularly-shaped regions, computations of volumes and surface areas of a variety of geometric solids, etc.) were added in the second edition.

The third edition continues the refinement and revision process of the *Algebra 1* textbook. It incorporates numerous changes suggested by classroom teachers. For example, one innovation is the addition of lesson reference numbers in the problem sets. Beneath each problem number in the problem sets is a number in parentheses; this number refers to the lesson where the concept or skill required to solve the problem is introduced. At the request of teachers, many new topics are discussed. Lessons on statistics (e.g., measures of central tendency, histograms, stem-and-leaf plots, box-and-whisker plots) have been added. Class projects that require the collection and analysis of data have been added to some problem sets. There is an increased emphasis on functions and the use of functional notation. Lessons on the graphs of functions (quadratic, cubic, square root, and absolute value) and on the translations and reflections of these graphs have been added. Finally, technology has been incorporated into the program as both the scientific calculator and the graphing calculator are used in some lessons.

Much of the early work on the textbook revision was done by John Saxon. Unfortunately, in October 1996, John Saxon passed away after a prolonged illness. The task of completing the revision rested largely with our experienced secondary math editor Smith Richardson. Smith had worked closely with John Saxon on the third edition revision as well as previous projects such as the second edition of *Advanced Mathematics*. To ensure the textbook would be revised according to schedule, Diana Stolfus, a long-time teacher of the Saxon program and user of both the first and second editions of *Algebra 1*, and I assisted in the work on the second half of this text. We tried to write in a style and manner consistent with John Saxon's and used as much as what he had written as possible.

The words that follow in the next two sections are those of John Saxon. They describe his pedagogical philosophy as well as a teaching method he suggests teachers employ in their classrooms. We suggest teachers also consult our *Upper Grades' Teacher's Resource Packet* (TRP). The TRP contains a discussion of classroom procedures successfully implemented by Saxon teachers as well as teaching tips and strategies. If you do not already have a TRP, please contact our company and we will send you a free copy.

philosophy This series of books is designed to teach students to be successful mathematical problem solvers. Students who have completed the series make high scores on problem-solving tests. Mathematical problem solving is simply the use of mathematical concepts in new situations. Teaching concepts is the first task. The best way to teach the concepts is to let the student work carefully designed problems that lead to use of productive thought patterns which utilize the concepts. Students do not grasp concepts quickly, and long-term practice is required at each hierarchical level. Whereas students understand slowly, they seem to forget quickly. The research of Benjamin Bloom has indicated that long-term practice beyond mastery is required to permit students to achieve what Bloom calls "automaticity." Bloom tells us that it is necessary to "overlearn" to achieve automaticity. When automaticity has been achieved, the student will be able to read a new problem, and the concept or concepts that are required to solve the problem will come automatically to mind. Long-term practice with the skills necessary to apply the concepts has allowed the student to automate these skills. Because concept recognitions and skill applications have been automated, the student's mind is freed from the lower-level mechanics of the problem, and the student can consider the problem at a higher cognitive level. When automaticity is achieved, the concepts are emblazoned in the long-term memory of the student and can be recalled when needed.

We have found that it is difficult to design problems that teach concepts and applications at the same time. In this book many word problems are designed so that the concept is the only real thing in the problem. For example, one ratio problem considers "the ratio of the erudite to the unlettered." If students protest that they don't know what the words mean, tell them it makes no difference. If these words bother students, they should use *eaters* and *uncles* or any two words that begin with *e* and *u*. If students learn to work word problems that contain unfamiliar words, they will not have trouble with chemistry problems containing words such as *sulfur dioxide* and *trinitrotoluene*. **If students learn the concepts, they can apply the concepts in any situation.** Books that try to teach applications and concepts at the same time often fail. **The teaching of the concepts must come first.**

Thus, the philosophy of this book is that students learn by doing and that students cannot fully learn a concept on the day it is introduced. This is the reason that the problem sets contain only three or four problems of the new kind and contain twenty-six or twenty-seven review problems. This emphasis on review allows students to practice every concept previously presented in every problem set. Some teachers who use the book for the first time remark that there are not enough problems of the new kind for students to "get it." They seem to forget that the students did not "get it" when they had 20 problems of the new kind and no review. Teachers have historically handed out review problem sets because the students were not "getting it." This book simply goes one step further and totally reverses the emphasis. We introduce the new concept with three or four problems with the realization that understanding will take time and that constant practice over a long period of time is the key ingredient of success.

We do not try for total understanding on the first day. **Since students learn by doing the problems repetitively, the teacher's overriding responsibility is to ensure that every student does every problem in every problem set.** If students work the problems, they will learn and they will understand. If students do not work the problems, they will not learn. It's that simple. The best way to ensure that students work the problems is to devote most of the class period to doing the homework.

After students have practiced a concept at one level for a period of time, another lesson on the concept is presented in which the concept is discussed at a higher cognitive level. This is the reason we say that the **incremental development** is not just distributed practice. The incremental development builds instead of just reviewing.

teaching procedure

The following recommended procedure has been used successfully by many teachers. Begin the class by projecting the answers to the previous problem set on the overhead so that students can mark their incorrect answers. Then collect the homework. **Do not answer questions at this time.** Every problem on last night's homework will be in the next homework problem set. Tell students to hold their questions until they begin to do the homework. Then explain the new topic thoroughly but briefly. Remember that the students will not grasp the concept totally on the first day. Then say, "Let's begin the homework now while we still have 40 minutes of class time. Begin with the problem that is hardest for you. If you need help, hold up your hand and I will help you." Suppose seven hands go up. You have five bright students. You must use them. Say "Mary help Frank and Roger help Susan. I will help you, Jimmy." The students who give help will benefit almost as much as the students who receive help. Then walk around the room for the rest of the period, giving help one-on-one and directing help as needed. We have found that this method permits every student to complete at least half of the homework problems in class, including every difficult problem. Thus students only have a few easy problems to do at home. If this procedure is followed, there will be no questions about tonight's homework at the beginning of class tomorrow because all the hard problems will have been completed in class today. This method gives you time to move through the classroom unhurriedly and to have the one-on-one contact with students that the lecture method of teaching does not permit.

Do not attempt to grade the homework. Thirty students with 30 problems each for five classes equals 4500 problems a day and 90,000 problems a month. It is impossible for a teacher to check 90,000 problems a month. However, the homework must be spot-checked to ensure that all problems have been completed and that all steps have been shown. We have found that 30 papers can be spot-checked and marked satisfactory or unsatisfactory in less than four minutes. This includes entries in the grade book. If one point is awarded for each satisfactory homework assignment, there will be four homework points available between two tests. Weight the test problems to total 96 points. Giving too much credit for homework is not a good practice. This is one way to do it. There are other ways to handle homework. Use what works for you.

acknowledgments

I thank editor Smith Richardson for completing the revision of this text in John Saxon's absence. I also thank Diana Stolfus for extensive help and for providing us the benefit of her wisdom and experience gained from many years in the classroom. I thank typesetter Lj Stephens for her very competent typesetting of the text. I thank editor Julie Webster for her very careful reading of the manuscript and her thoughtful suggestions. I thank artists John Chitwood, Chris Cope, Michael Lott, and Travis Southern for precisely and meticulously drawing the artwork required for the text. I thank our proofreaders for carefully reading the manuscript and working as well as checking the answers to the problems in the problem sets. I thank J. Travis Rose, pre-press manager, for overseeing the entire pre-press process, and Joan Coleman, production coordinator, for coordinating the manufacturing aspects of this revision process. Lastly, I thank the many, many Saxon teachers for their continued and abiding support of the Saxon program.

Frank Y. H. Wang, Ph.D.
President, Saxon Publishers, Inc.
Norman, Oklahoma

LESSON 1 *Addition and Subtraction of Fractions • Lines and Segments*

1.A

addition and subtraction of fractions

To add or subtract fractions that have the same denominators, we add or subtract the numerators as indicated below, and the result is recorded over the same denominator.

$$\frac{5}{11} + \frac{2}{11} = \frac{7}{11} \qquad \frac{5}{11} - \frac{2}{11} = \frac{3}{11}$$

If the denominators are not the same, it is necessary to rewrite the fractions so that they have the same denominators.

	PROBLEM	REWRITTEN WITH EQUAL DENOMINATORS	ANSWER
(a)	$\frac{1}{3} + \frac{2}{5}$	$\frac{5}{15} + \frac{6}{15}$	$\frac{11}{15}$
(b)	$\frac{2}{3} - \frac{1}{8}$	$\frac{16}{24} - \frac{3}{24}$	$\frac{13}{24}$

A **mixed number** is the sum of a whole number and a fraction. Thus the notation

$$13\frac{3}{5}$$

does not mean 13 multiplied by $\frac{3}{5}$ but instead 13 plus $\frac{3}{5}$.

$$13 + \frac{3}{5}$$

When we add and subtract mixed numbers, we handle the fractions and the whole numbers separately. In some subtraction problems it is necessary to borrow, as shown in (e).

	PROBLEM	REWRITTEN WITH EQUAL DENOMINATORS	ANSWER
(c)	$13\frac{3}{5} + 2\frac{1}{8}$	$13\frac{24}{40} + 2\frac{5}{40}$	$15\frac{29}{40}$
(d)	$13\frac{3}{5} - 2\frac{1}{8}$	$13\frac{24}{40} - 2\frac{5}{40}$	$11\frac{19}{40}$

		BORROWING	
(e)	$13\frac{3}{5} - 2\frac{7}{8}$	$13\frac{24}{40} - 2\frac{35}{40} = 12\frac{64}{40} - 2\frac{35}{40}$	$10\frac{29}{40}$

1

1.B
lines and segments

It is impossible to draw a mathematical line because a mathematical line is a **straight line** that has **no width** and **no ends.** To show the location of a mathematical line, we draw a pencil line and put arrowheads on both ends to emphasize that the mathematical line goes on and on in both directions.

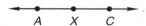

We can name a line by naming any two points on the line and using an overbar with two arrowheads. We can designate the line shown by writing $\overleftrightarrow{AX}$, $\overleftrightarrow{XA}$, $\overleftrightarrow{AC}$, $\overleftrightarrow{CA}$, $\overleftrightarrow{XC}$, or $\overleftrightarrow{CX}$.

A part of a line is called a **line segment.** A line segment contains the endpoints and all points between the endpoints. To show the location of a line segment, we use a pencil line with no arrowheads. We name a segment by naming the endpoints of the segment.

This is segment MC or segment CM. We can indicate that two letters name a segment by using an overbar with no arrowheads. Thus $\overline{MC}$ means segment MC. If we use two letters without the overbar, we designate the length of the segment. Thus MC is the length of $\overline{MC}$.

example 1.1   Add: $\dfrac{10}{11} - \dfrac{5}{6} + \dfrac{1}{3}$

solution   We begin by rewriting each fraction so that they have the same denominators. Then we add the fractions.

$$\frac{10}{11} - \frac{5}{6} + \frac{1}{3} = \frac{60}{66} - \frac{55}{66} + \frac{22}{66} \qquad \text{common denominators}$$

$$= \frac{5}{66} + \frac{22}{66} \qquad \text{added}$$

$$= \frac{27}{66} \qquad \text{added}$$

$$= \mathbf{\frac{9}{22}} \qquad \text{simplified}$$

example 1.2   Segment AC measures $10\frac{1}{4}$ units. Segment AB measures $4\frac{3}{7}$ units. Find BC.

solution   We need to know the length of segment BC. We know AC and AB. We subtract to find BC.

$$BC = AC - AB$$

$$= 10\frac{1}{4} - 4\frac{3}{7} \qquad \text{substituted}$$

$$= 10\frac{7}{28} - 4\frac{12}{28} \qquad \text{common denominators}$$

$$= 9\frac{35}{28} - 4\frac{12}{28} \qquad \text{borrowed}$$

$$= \mathbf{5\frac{23}{28}} \textbf{ units} \qquad \text{subtracted}$$

**problem set
1**

Add or subtract as indicated. Write answers as proper fractions reduced to lowest terms or as mixed numbers.

1. $\dfrac{1}{5} + \dfrac{2}{5}$

2. $\dfrac{3}{8} - \dfrac{2}{8}$

3. $\dfrac{4}{3} - \dfrac{1}{3} + \dfrac{2}{3}$

Different denominators:

4. $\dfrac{1}{3} + \dfrac{1}{5}$

5. $\dfrac{3}{8} - \dfrac{1}{5}$

6. $\dfrac{2}{3} - \dfrac{1}{8}$

7. $\dfrac{1}{13} + \dfrac{1}{5}$

8. $\dfrac{14}{15} - \dfrac{2}{3}$

9. $\dfrac{5}{9} + \dfrac{2}{5}$

10. $\dfrac{14}{17} - \dfrac{6}{34}$

11. $\dfrac{5}{13} + \dfrac{1}{26}$

12. $\dfrac{4}{7} - \dfrac{2}{5}$

13. $\dfrac{4}{7} + \dfrac{1}{8} + \dfrac{1}{2}$

14. $\dfrac{3}{5} + \dfrac{1}{8} + \dfrac{1}{8}$

15. $\dfrac{5}{11} - \dfrac{1}{6} + \dfrac{2}{3}$

Addition of mixed numbers:

16. $2\dfrac{1}{2} + 3\dfrac{1}{5}$

17. $7\dfrac{3}{8} + 6\dfrac{1}{3}$

18. $1\dfrac{1}{8} + 7\dfrac{2}{5}$

Subtraction with borrowing:

19. $15\dfrac{1}{3} - 7\dfrac{4}{5}$

20. $42\dfrac{3}{8} - 21\dfrac{3}{4}$

21. $22\dfrac{2}{5} - 13\dfrac{7}{15}$

22. $42\dfrac{1}{11} - 18\dfrac{2}{3}$

23. $78\dfrac{2}{5} - 14\dfrac{7}{10}$

24. $43\dfrac{1}{13} - 6\dfrac{5}{8}$

25. $21\dfrac{1}{5} - 15\dfrac{7}{13}$

26. $21\dfrac{2}{19} - 7\dfrac{7}{10}$

27. $43\dfrac{3}{17} - 21\dfrac{9}{10}$

28. The length of $\overline{AB}$ is $7\dfrac{1}{8}$ units. The length of $\overline{BC}$ is $5\dfrac{2}{7}$ units. Find AC.

29. DF is $42\dfrac{1}{7}$ units. EF is $24\dfrac{2}{11}$ units. Find DE.

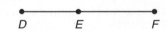

30. XZ is $12\dfrac{11}{16}$ units. XY is $3\dfrac{5}{8}$ units. Find YZ.

LESSON 2 *Angles • Polygons • Triangles • Quadrilaterals*

2.A
angles

If two lines cross, we say that the lines **intersect.** The place where the lines cross is called the **point of intersection.** Two lines in the same plane either intersect or do not intersect. If two lines in the same plane do not intersect, we say that the lines are **parallel lines.** The perpendicular distance between two parallel lines is everywhere the same.

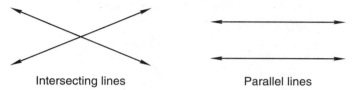

Intersecting lines   Parallel lines

If two lines make square corners at the point of intersection, we say that the lines are **perpendicular.** The angles made by perpendicular lines are called **right angles.** We can draw a little square at the point of intersection to indicate that all four angles formed are right angles. Two right angles form a **straight angle.** An angle smaller than a right angle is called an **acute angle.** An angle greater than a right angle but less than a straight angle is called an **obtuse angle.**

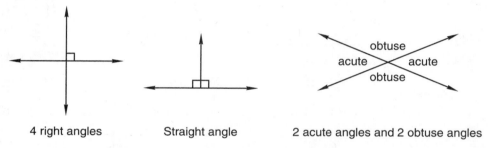

4 right angles   Straight angle   2 acute angles and 2 obtuse angles

If a right angle is divided into 90 parts, we say that each part has a measure of 1 degree. Thus, a right angle has a measure of 90 degrees, which can also be written as 90°. Two right angles form a straight angle. Thus, a straight angle has a measure of 180 degrees, which can also be written as 180°. Four right angles have a measure of 360 degrees, which can also be written as 360°. Thus, the measure of a circle is 360°:

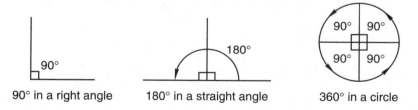

90° in a right angle   180° in a straight angle   360° in a circle

2.B
polygons

A **polygon** is a special kind of geometric figure. The word *polygon* is formed from the Greek roots *poly*, which means "more than one" or "many," and *gonon*, which means "angle." Thus, polygon literally means "more than one angle." Modern authors define polygons as simple, closed, flat geometric figures whose sides are line segments. The following are examples of figures that are not polygons.

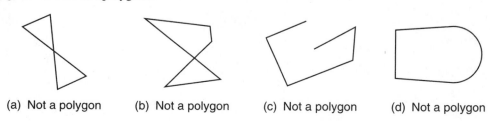

(a) Not a polygon   (b) Not a polygon   (c) Not a polygon   (d) Not a polygon

Figures (a) and (b) are not polygons because the line segments cross and therefore the figures are not simple figures. Figure (c) is not a polygon because it is not closed. Figure (d) is not a polygon because one of the "sides" is curved.

The following are examples of figures that are polygons:

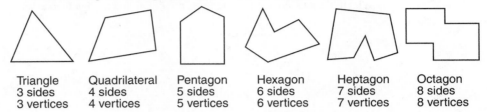

Triangle	Quadrilateral	Pentagon	Hexagon	Heptagon	Octagon
3 sides	4 sides	5 sides	6 sides	7 sides	8 sides
3 vertices	4 vertices	5 vertices	6 vertices	7 vertices	8 vertices

Each segment of a polygon is called a **side.** Each endpoint of a side is called a **vertex** of the polygon. The plural of vertex is **vertices. For each polygon, the number of sides is always equal to the number of vertices.**

Polygons are named according to the number of sides they have:

- The polygon with the fewest number of sides is the triangle.
- A polygon with 4 sides is called a *quadrilateral.*
- A polygon with 5 sides is called a *pentagon.*
- A polygon with 6 sides is called a *hexagon.*
- A polygon with 7 sides is called a *heptagon.*
- A polygon with 8 sides is called an *octagon.*
- A polygon with 9 sides is called a *nonagon.*
- A polygon with 10 sides is called a *decagon.*
- A polygon with 11 sides is called an *undecagon.*
- A polygon with 12 sides is called a *dodecagon.*

Some polygons of more than 12 sides have special names, but these names are not used often. Instead, we use the word *polygon* and tell the number of sides or use the number of sides with the suffix *-gon.* Thus, if a polygon has 42 sides, we would call it a polygon with 42 sides or a 42-gon. For easy reference, we list the names of special polygons in the following table.

Number of Sides	Name of Polygon	Number of Sides	Name of Polygon
3	Triangle	9	Nonagon
4	Quadrilateral	10	Decagon
5	Pentagon	11	Undecagon
6	Hexagon	12	Dodecagon
7	Heptagon	n	n-gon
8	Octagon		

concave and convex polygons

If a polygon has an indentation (a cave), the polygon is called a **concave polygon.** Any polygon that does not have an indentation is called a **convex polygon.** Any two points in the interior of a convex polygon can be connected by a line segment that does not cut a side of the polygon. This statement is not true for concave polygons. Most of the polygons that you will study will be convex polygons. In this book, when *polygon* is used it will mean *convex polygon* unless stated otherwise.

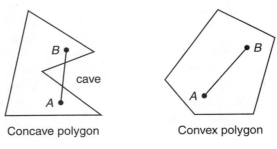

Concave polygon   Convex polygon

regular polygons
If all the sides of a polygon have the same length, the polygon is called an **equilateral polygon.** If all the angles of a polygon have the same measure, the polygon is called an **equiangular polygon.** Polygons in which all sides have the same length and all angles have the same measure are called **regular polygons.** In some of the following figures we use **tick marks** to denote sides whose lengths are equal and angles whose measures are equal.

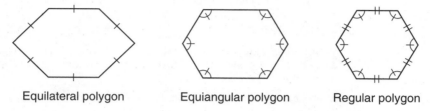

Equilateral polygon   Equiangular polygon   Regular polygon

The following are examples of polygons that are regular polygons.

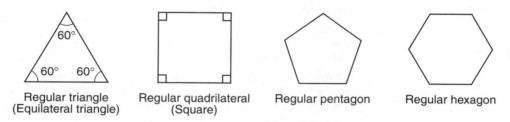

Regular triangle (Equilateral triangle)   Regular quadrilateral (Square)   Regular pentagon   Regular hexagon

A regular triangle is called an equilateral triangle. All the angles in an equilateral triangle are 60° angles. We remember that a quadrilateral is a polygon with four sides. A regular quadrilateral is a square.

2.C
triangles
We remember that the polygon with the fewest number of sides is the triangle. Triangles have three sides and three angles. **The sum of the measures of the three angles in any triangle is 180°.** Triangles can be classified according to the measures of their angles or according to the lengths of their sides.

If a triangle has a right angle, the triangle is a **right triangle.** If all angles have a measure less than 90°, the triangle is an **acute triangle.** If one angle has a measure greater than 90°, the triangle is an **obtuse triangle.** The Latin prefix *equi*- means "equal" and the Latin word *angulus* means "angle." We can put them together to form *equiangular*, which means "equal angles." An **equiangular triangle** is a triangle in which the measures of all angles are equal. Each angle in an equiangular triangle must have a measure of 60° because 3 × 60° equals 180°.

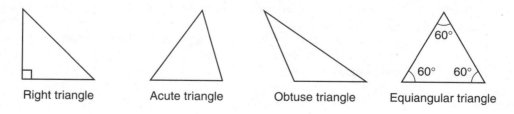

Right triangle   Acute triangle   Obtuse triangle   Equiangular triangle

Triangles are also classified according to the relative lengths of their sides. The Greek prefix *iso*- means "equal" and the Greek word *skelos* means "leg." We can put them together to form *isosceles*, which means "equal legs." An **isosceles triangle** is a triangle that has at least two sides of equal length. Since the Latin prefix *equi*- means "equal" and the Latin word *latus* means "side," we can put them together to form *equilateral*, which means "equal sides." An

equilateral triangle is a triangle in which the lengths of all sides are equal. If all the sides of a triangle have different lengths, the triangle is called a **scalene triangle.**

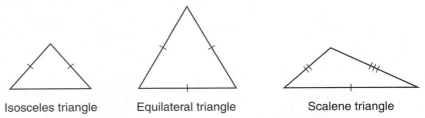

Isosceles triangle   Equilateral triangle   Scalene triangle

The lengths of the sides of a triangle and the measures of the angles opposite these sides are related. In any triangle, the angles opposite sides of equal lengths have equal measures. Also, the sides opposite angles of equal measures have equal lengths. We remember an isosceles triangle is a triangle that has at least two sides of equal length. The angles opposite these sides have equal measures. All three sides in an equilateral triangle have the same length. Since the angles opposite these sides have equal measures, an equilateral triangle is also an equiangular triangle. All three angles in an equiangular triangle have equal measures. Since the sides opposite these angles have equal lengths, an equiangular triangle is also an equilateral triangle. The scalene triangle has no equal sides, so no two angles have equal measures.

example 2.1   Find x.

solution   **The sum of the measures of the three angles in any triangle is 180°.** The two given angles have measures of 30° and 130°. The sum of the measures of these angles is 160°. Therefore, angle x must have a measure of 20° because

$$20 + 30 + 130 = 180$$

Therefore, $x = $ **20.**

example 2.2   Find x and y.

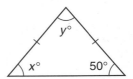

solution   The identical tick marks on two sides of the triangle tell us that these two sides have equal lengths. **In any triangle, the angles opposite sides of equal lengths have equal measures.** Therefore, angle x must have a measure of 50°. So, $x = $ **50.** The sum of the measures of the three angles must be 180°. So angle y must have a measure of 80° because

$$50 + 50 + 80 = 180$$

Therefore, $y = $ **80.**

example 2.3   Find x and y.

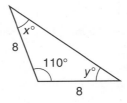

solution   The sum of the measures of the three angles must be 180°. The given angle has a measure of 110°, so the sum of the measures of angles *x* and *y* must be 70° because 180 − 110 = 70. Angles *x* and *y* must have equal measures because the sides opposite these angles have equal lengths. Since $\frac{70}{2} = 35$, angles *x* and *y* both have measures of 35°. Therefore, *x* = **35** and *y* = **35.**

2.D

quadrilaterals   We remember that a polygon with four sides is called a quadrilateral. We will discuss five different types of quadrilaterals. A **parallelogram** is a quadrilateral that has two pairs of parallel sides. A **trapezoid** is a quadrilateral that has exactly two parallel sides. A **rectangle** is a parallelogram with four right angles. A **rhombus** is an equilateral parallelogram. A **square** is a rhombus with four right angles.

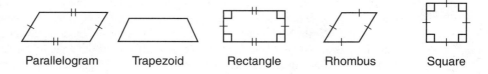

| Parallelogram | Trapezoid | Rectangle | Rhombus | Square |

practice   **a.** Find *x*.

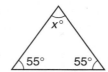

b. Find *x* and *y*.

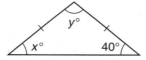

c. Find *x* and *y*.

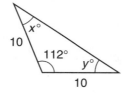

problem set 2

†1. What angles are formed by lines that are perpendicular?
(2)

2. What angle is formed by two right angles?
(2)

3. What is an acute angle?
(2)

4. What is an obtuse angle?
(2)

5. (a) What is the degree measure of a right angle?
(2)

　　(b) What is the degree measure of a straight angle?

　　(c) How many degrees are in a circle?

6. What do you call polygons in which all sides have the same length?
(2)

---

†The italicized numbers within parentheses below each problem number refer to the lesson in which concepts for that problem are discussed. These numbers are explained more fully in the preface.

7. What do you call polygons in which all angles have the same measure?
(2)

8. What do you call polygons in which all sides have the same length and all angles have
(2)   the same measure?

9. (a) What is a right triangle?
(2)

     (b) What is an acute triangle?

     (c) What is an obtuse triangle?

     (d) What is an equiangular triangle?

10. (a) What is an isosceles triangle?
(2)

     (b) What is an equilateral triangle?

     (c) What is a scalene triangle?

11. Find x.
(2)

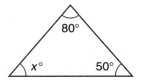

12. Find y.
(2)

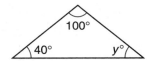

Add or subtract as indicated. Write answers as proper fractions reduced to lowest terms or as
mixed numbers.

13. $\dfrac{1}{3} + \dfrac{4}{9}$ **14.** $\dfrac{3}{5} + \dfrac{2}{7}$ **15.** $\dfrac{3}{4} - \dfrac{5}{12}$
(1)   *(1)*   *(1)*

16. $\dfrac{2}{3} + \dfrac{1}{15}$ **17.** $\dfrac{9}{14} - \dfrac{1}{2} + \dfrac{3}{7}$ **18.** $5\dfrac{1}{3} + 1\dfrac{1}{6}$
(1)   *(1)*   *(1)*

19. $3\dfrac{1}{8} + 4\dfrac{1}{2}$ **20.** $5\dfrac{2}{5} + 7\dfrac{7}{10}$ **21.** $9\dfrac{1}{3} + 3\dfrac{3}{5}$
(1)   *(1)*   *(1)*

22. $9\dfrac{3}{5} + 5\dfrac{2}{3}$ **23.** $23\dfrac{7}{10} - 14\dfrac{2}{5}$ **24.** $22\dfrac{2}{5} - 14\dfrac{4}{15}$
(1)   *(1)*   *(1)*

25. $8\dfrac{2}{5} - 5\dfrac{1}{3}$ **26.** $4\dfrac{2}{3} - 1\dfrac{5}{6}$ **27.** $14\dfrac{1}{2} - 12\dfrac{2}{3}$
(1)   *(1)*   *(1)*

28. The length of $\overline{AB}$ is $2\dfrac{1}{3}$ centimeters. The length of $\overline{BC}$ is $5\dfrac{2}{9}$ centimeters. Find AC.
(1)

29. PR is $16\dfrac{3}{4}$ meters. QR is $9\dfrac{7}{8}$ meters. Find PQ.
(1)

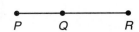

30. XZ is $10\dfrac{1}{5}$ units. XY is $4\dfrac{2}{3}$ units. Find YZ.
(1)

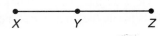

LESSON 3 *Perimeter • Circumference*

3.A
perimeter

The word **perimeter** comes from the Greek prefix *peri-*, which means "around," and the Greek word *metron*, which means "measure." Thus, perimeter means the measure around or the distance around.

example 3.1 Find the perimeter of this figure. All angles are right angles. Dimensions are in inches.

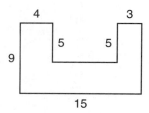

solution Several lengths are not given. Since all angles are right angles, we can determine the missing lengths. Since it is 15 inches across the bottom, it must be 15 inches across the top. The missing length on top is 8 inches because $4 + 3 + 8 = 15$. The height of the left-hand side is 9 inches, so the height of the right-hand side is 9 inches.

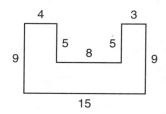

The perimeter is the distance around the figure, which equals the sum of the lengths of the straight sides of the figure.

$$\text{Perimeter} = (9 + 4 + 5 + 8 + 5 + 3 + 9 + 15) \text{ inches}$$

$$= \textbf{58 inches}$$

3.B
circumference

Every point on a circle is the same distance from the center of the circle. This distance is called the **radius** of the circle. The **diameter** of a circle is twice the length of the radius of the circle.

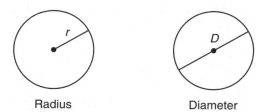

Radius   Diameter

We call the perimeter of a circle the **circumference** of the circle. Many ancients thought that the circle was the perfect geometric figure. They were especially interested in the relationship between the diameter of a circle and the circumference of the same circle. They found that it takes approximately 3.14 diameters to go all the way around a circle no matter how small or how large the circle is. The symbol ≈ means "approximately equals."

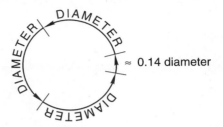

≈ 0.14 diameter

Now we know the exact number of times the diameter will go around a circle. This exact number is a number we call *pi* (pronounced "pie"). We use the symbol π to represent this number. To write π as a decimal number would require an infinite number of digits because π is an **irrational number.** A calculator gives a decimal approximation of π as

3.141592654

In this book, we will use 3.14 as an approximation for π when doing calculations that involve the number π. It takes π diameters to equal the circumference of a circle, and it takes 2π radii to equal the circumference of a circle.

Circumference = πD Circumference = $2\pi r$

Circumference of a circle = $\pi D = \pi(2r) = 2\pi r$

example 3.2   The radius of a circle is 3 centimeters. Find the circumference of the circle.

solution   The formula for the circumference of a circle of radius r is given by

$$\text{Circumference} = 2\pi r$$

Substituting 3 cm for r, we get

$$\text{Circumference} = 2\pi(3 \text{ cm})$$

$$= 2(3.14)(3 \text{ cm})$$

$$= \textbf{18.84 cm}$$

example 3.3   The circumference of a circle is 24 meters. Find the radius of the circle.

solution   The formula for the circumference of a circle of radius r is given by

$$\text{Circumference} = 2\pi r$$

Substituting 24 m for circumference, we get

$$24 \text{ m} = 2\pi r$$

$$24 \text{ m} = 2(3.14)r$$

$$24 \text{ m} = 6.28r$$

Solving for r, we get

$$r = \textbf{3.82 m}$$

example 3.4 Find the perimeter of this figure. Dimensions are in inches.

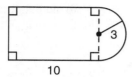

solution We begin by finding the missing lengths of the straight sides.

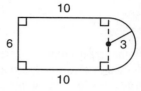

The perimeter is the distance around the figure, which equals the sum of the lengths of the
straight sides and the length of the semicircle (half of a circle).

$$\text{Perimeter} = 10 \text{ in.} + 6 \text{ in.} + 10 \text{ in.} + \frac{2\pi(3 \text{ in.})}{2}$$

$$= 26 \text{ in.} + \frac{2(3.14)(3 \text{ in.})}{2}$$

$$= 26 \text{ in.} + 9.42 \text{ in.}$$

$$= \mathbf{35.42 \text{ in.}}$$

example 3.5 Find the perimeter of this figure. Dimensions are in feet.

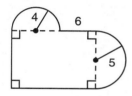

solution We begin by finding the missing lengths of the straight sides.

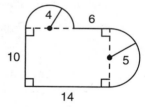

The perimeter is the distance around the figure, which equals the sum of the lengths of the
straight sides and the lengths of the two semicircles.

$$\text{Perimeter} = 14 \text{ ft} + 10 \text{ ft} + 6 \text{ ft} + \frac{2\pi(4 \text{ ft})}{2} + \frac{2\pi(5 \text{ ft})}{2}$$

$$= 30 \text{ ft} + \frac{2(3.14)(4 \text{ ft})}{2} + \frac{2(3.14)(5 \text{ ft})}{2}$$

$$= 30 \text{ ft} + 12.56 \text{ ft} + 15.7 \text{ ft}$$

$$= \mathbf{58.26 \text{ ft}}$$

practice **a.** The length of a rectangle is 10 centimeters. The width of the rectangle is 5 centimeters.
Find the perimeter of the rectangle.

b. The perimeter of a square is 12 meters. What is the length of one side of the square?

c. Find the perimeter of this figure. All angles are right angles. Dimensions are in kilometers.

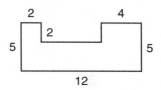

d. The radius of a circle is 5 inches. Find the circumference of the circle.

e. Find the perimeter of this figure. Dimensions are in feet.

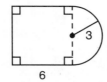

problem set 3

1. What is the sum of the measures of the three angles of any triangle?
(2)

2. (a) What are the measures of the angles of an equiangular triangle?
(2)
   (b) What are the measures of the angles of an equilateral triangle?

3. If two sides of a triangle have equal lengths, then what is true about the angles opposite those sides?
(2)

4. If two angles of a triangle have equal measures, then what is true about the sides opposite those angles?
(2)

5. What is the name of the quadrilateral that has two pairs of parallel sides?
(2)

6. What is the name of the quadrilateral that has exactly two parallel sides?
(2)

7. The length of a rectangle is 12 inches. The width of the rectangle is 8 inches. Find the perimeter of the rectangle.
(3)

8. The perimeter of a square is 16 feet. What is the length of one side of the square?
(3)

9. The radius of a circle is 6 centimeters. Find the circumference of the circle.
(3)

10. The diameter of a circle is 8 meters. Find the circumference of the circle.
(3)

Find the perimeter of each figure. Corners that look square are square. Dimensions are in inches.

11.
(3)

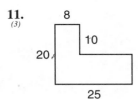

12.
(3)

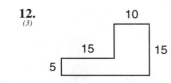

13.
(3)

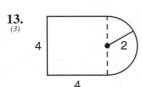

14.
(3)

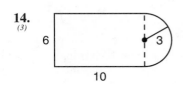

15. Find x.
(2)

16. Find y.
(2)

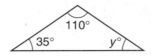

Add or subtract as indicated. Write answers as proper fractions reduced to lowest terms or as mixed numbers.

17. $\dfrac{1}{2} + \dfrac{5}{18}$ **18.** $\dfrac{11}{12} - \dfrac{3}{4}$ **19.** $\dfrac{8}{15} + \dfrac{2}{3} - \dfrac{1}{5}$
(1)   (1)   (1)

20. $5\dfrac{2}{3} + 1\dfrac{7}{12}$ **21.** $7\dfrac{5}{6} + 4\dfrac{1}{18}$ **22.** $6\dfrac{3}{5} + 14\dfrac{9}{10}$
(1)   (1)   (1)

23. $4\dfrac{7}{8} + 3\dfrac{3}{16}$ **24.** $5\dfrac{1}{8} + 8\dfrac{3}{7}$ **25.** $4\dfrac{3}{5} - 3\dfrac{4}{15}$
(1)   (1)   (1)

26. $15\dfrac{2}{3} - 4\dfrac{5}{11}$ **27.** $7\dfrac{5}{6} - 6\dfrac{11}{12}$ **28.** $33\dfrac{5}{8} - 7\dfrac{11}{16}$
(1)   (1)   (1)

29. The length of $\overline{AB}$ is $14\dfrac{1}{3}$ feet. The length of $\overline{BC}$ is $12\dfrac{2}{5}$ feet. Find AC.
(1)

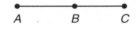

$$A \qquad B \qquad C$$

30. DF is $7\dfrac{2}{3}$ yards. EF is $4\dfrac{1}{2}$ yards. Find DE.
(1)

$$D \qquad E \qquad F$$

LESSON 4 *Review of Arithmetic*

4.A

numerals and numbers

A *number* is an idea. A *numeral* is a single symbol or a collection of symbols that we use to express the idea of a particular number.

The three drawings above all have the quality of *threeness*. The three children and the three pencils both bring to mind the idea of *three*. The drawing at the right also brings to mind the idea of *three*, although all the things in the drawing are not of the same kind.

If we wish to use a symbol to designate the idea of three, we could write any of the following:

$$\text{III}, \qquad 3, \qquad \dfrac{30}{10}, \qquad \dfrac{27}{9}, \qquad \dfrac{33}{11}, \qquad 2 + 1, \qquad 6 \div 2, \qquad 11 - 8$$

Each of these is a symbolic representation of the idea of three. Throughout the book, when we use the word *number*, we are describing the idea. We will use numerals to designate the numbers. But we will remember that none of the marks we make on paper are numbers because

A number is an idea!

Since the symbols

$$3 \quad \text{and} \quad \frac{30}{10}$$

are both numerals that represent the same number, we say that they have the same value. **Thus, the value of a numeral is the number represented by the numeral, and we see that the words *value* and *number* have the same meaning.**

4.B
natural or counting numbers

The system of numeration that we use to designate numbers is called the **decimal system.** It was invented by the Hindus of India, passed to their Arab neighbors, and finally transmitted to Europe circa A.D. 1200. The decimal system uses 10 symbols that we call *digits*. These digits are

$$0, \quad 1, \quad 2, \quad 3, \quad 4, \quad 5, \quad 6, \quad 7, \quad 8, \quad 9$$

We use these digits by themselves or in combination with one another to form the numerals that we use to designate decimal numbers.

We call the numbers that we use to count objects or things the *natural numbers* or the *counting numbers*. When we begin counting, we always begin with the number 1 and follow it with the number 2, etc.

$$1, \quad 2, \quad 3, \quad 4, \quad 5, \quad 6, \quad 7, \quad 8, \quad 9, \quad 10, \quad 11, \quad 12, \quad 13, \dots$$

It would not be natural to try to count by using numbers such as $\frac{1}{2}$ or 0 or $\frac{3}{4}$, so these numbers are not called natural or counting numbers. We designate the natural or counting numbers with the list above. The three dots after the number 13 indicate that this list continues without end.

4.C
real numbers

The numbers of arithmetic are zero and the positive real numbers. **We say that a *positive real number* is any number that can be used to describe a physical distance greater than zero.** Thus, all the numbers shown here

$$\frac{3}{4} \quad 0.000163 \quad 363 \quad 3\frac{3}{8} \quad 46 \quad \frac{11}{7} \quad 400.1623232323$$

are positive real numbers, for all of them can be used to describe physical distances when used with descriptive units such as inches, feet, yards, etc.

$$\frac{3}{4} \text{ mile} \quad 0.000163 \text{ yard} \quad 363 \text{ feet} \quad 3\frac{3}{8} \text{ meters}$$

$$46 \text{ inches} \quad \frac{11}{7} \text{ kilometers} \quad 400.1623232323 \text{ centimeters}$$

The number zero is not a **positive number,** but it can be used to describe a physical distance of no magnitude. Thus we say that zero is a **real number.** In addition to the positive numbers and zero, in algebra we use numbers that we call **negative numbers,** and these numbers are also called real numbers. The ancients did not understand or use negative numbers. A man could not own negative 10 sheep. If he owned any sheep at all, the number of sheep had to be designated by a number greater than zero. The ancients could subtract 4 from 6 and get 2, but they felt that it was impossible to subtract 6 from 4 because that would result in a number that was less than zero itself. To their way of thinking, this was clearly impossible.

While some might tend to agree with the ancients, to the modern mathematician, physicist, or chemist, the idea or concept of negative numbers does exist, and it is a useful concept. **We say that every positive real number has a negative counterpart, and we call these numbers the *negative real numbers*.** We must always use a minus sign when we designate a negative number, as we see here by writing a negative seven.

$$-7$$

We may use a plus sign to designate a positive number, as we see by writing positive seven.

$$+7$$

Or we may leave off the plus sign as we did in arithmetic and just write the numerical part with no sign.

$$7$$

We must remember that when we write a numeral with no sign, we designate a positive number. When we are talking about negative numbers as well as positive numbers, we say that we are talking about **signed numbers.** As we shall see later, the use of signed numbers will enable us to lump the operations of addition and subtraction into a single operation which we will call algebraic addition.

4.D
number lines

In the 1950s the so-called new math appeared, and among other things it introduced the **number line** at the elementary algebra level. The number line can be used as a graphic aid when discussing signed numbers, and it is especially useful when discussing the addition of signed numbers.

To construct a number line, we first draw a line and divide it into equal units of length. The units may be any length as long as they are all the same length.

Many books show small arrowheads on the ends of number lines to emphasize that the lines continue without end in both directions, as we show below. The arrowheads are not necessary and may be omitted. Now we choose a point on the line as our base point. We call this base point the **origin,** and we associate the number zero with this point.

0

Then we associate the positive real numbers with the points to the right of the origin and the negative real numbers with the points to the left of the origin.

$$-7 \quad -6 \quad -5 \quad -4 \quad -3 \quad -2 \quad -1 \quad 0 \quad 1 \quad 2 \quad 3 \quad 4 \quad 5 \quad 6 \quad 7$$

On the number line above we have indicated the location of zero, the counting numbers, and the negative counterpart of each counting number. As required, we can indicate the position of any real number by locating it in relation to the numbers shown. For example, on the number line below we indicate the position of $-1\frac{1}{2}$, $+\frac{3}{4}$, and $+2.6$ by placing a dot at the approximate location of each number.

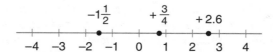

When we place a dot on the number line to indicate the location of a number, we say that we have *graphed* the number and that the dot is the graph of the number. Conversely, the number is said to be the coordinate of the point that we have graphed. We use the number line to tell if one number is greater than another number by saying that a number is *greater* than another number if its graph lies to the right of the graph

of the other number. Thus $\frac{3}{4}$ is greater than $-1\frac{1}{2}$ because the graph of $\frac{3}{4}$ lies to the right of the graph $-1\frac{1}{2}$. This topic will be discussed in considerable detail in later lessons.

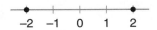

On the line above we have graphed +2 and –2. The number +2 (usually the + sign is omitted) lies 2 units to the right of the origin, and the number –2 lies 2 units to the left of the origin. Since the graphs of these numbers are equidistant from the origin but in opposite directions, it is sometimes helpful to think of each of these numbers as being the **opposite** of the other number. In this example, **we say that –2 is the opposite of 2 and that 2 is the opposite of –2.**

4.E
multiplication and division of fractions

Fractions are multiplied by multiplying the numerators to get the new numerator, and by multiplying the denominators to get the new denominator.

PROBLEM	SOLUTION
(a) $\dfrac{4}{3} \times \dfrac{7}{5}$	$\dfrac{4 \times 7}{3 \times 5} = \dfrac{28}{15} = 1\dfrac{13}{15}$

We divide fractions by inverting the divisor and then multiplying.

PROBLEM	INVERTING	SOLUTION
(b) $\dfrac{4}{3} \div \dfrac{15}{8}$	$\dfrac{4}{3} \times \dfrac{8}{15}$	$\dfrac{4 \times 8}{3 \times 15} = \dfrac{32}{45}$

If cancellation is possible, it is easier if we cancel before we multiply.

PROBLEM	CANCELLATION	SOLUTION
(c) $\dfrac{7}{3} \times \dfrac{30}{9}$	$\dfrac{7}{\cancel{3}_{1}} \times \dfrac{\cancel{30}^{10}}{9}$	$\dfrac{70}{9} = 7\dfrac{7}{9}$
(d) $\dfrac{3}{5} \times \dfrac{5}{6} \times \dfrac{21}{23}$	$\dfrac{\cancel{3}^{1}}{\cancel{5}_{1}} \times \dfrac{\cancel{5}^{1}}{\cancel{6}_{2}} \times \dfrac{21}{23}$	$\dfrac{21}{46}$

We change mixed numbers to improper fractions and then multiply or divide as indicated.

PROBLEM	IMPROPER FRACTION	SOLUTION
(e) $2\dfrac{1}{2} \times 5\dfrac{1}{3}$	$\dfrac{5}{\cancel{2}_{1}} \times \dfrac{\cancel{16}^{8}}{3}$	$\dfrac{40}{3} = 13\dfrac{1}{3}$
(f) $12\dfrac{1}{3} \div 2\dfrac{1}{6}$	$\dfrac{37}{\cancel{3}_{1}} \times \dfrac{\cancel{6}^{2}}{13}$	$\dfrac{74}{13} = 5\dfrac{9}{13}$
(g) $\dfrac{3\dfrac{1}{3}}{2\dfrac{1}{5}}$	$\dfrac{\dfrac{10}{3}}{\dfrac{11}{5}}$	$\dfrac{10}{3} \cdot \dfrac{5}{11} = \dfrac{50}{33} = 1\dfrac{17}{33}$

4.F
symbols of equality and inequality

We use the equals sign (=) to designate that two quantities are equal. Thus we can write

$$5 + 2 = 7$$

because the number represented by the notation 5 + 2 is the same number as that represented by the numeral 7. In the same way, we use the symbol ≠ to designate that two quantities are not equal. Thus we can write that

$$5 + 2 \neq 11$$

because 7 is not equal to 11.

4.G
basic operations

The four basic operations of arithmetic are also the basic operations of algebra. The operations are addition, subtraction, multiplication, and division. We will review these operations here and will restrict our discussion to the numbers of arithmetic, which are the positive real numbers and zero.

addition

When we wish to add two numbers to get a result, we use the plus sign (+) to indicate the operation of addition. We call each of the numbers an **addend,** and we call the result a **sum.**

$$2 + 3 = 5$$

In this example, we use the plus sign to indicate addition; we say that the numbers 2 and 3 are addends, and we say that 5 is the sum.

We note that the sum of zero and any particular real number is the particular real number itself.

$$4 + 0 = 4 \quad \text{and} \quad 15 + 0 = 15$$

subtraction

When we wish to subtract one number from another number, we use the minus sign (–) to indicate the operation of subtraction. We call the first number the **minuend;** the second number, the **subtrahend;** and the result, the **difference.**

$$9 - 5 = 4$$

In this example, 9 is the minuend, 5 is the subtrahend, and 4 is the difference.

multiplication

If two numbers are to be multiplied to achieve a result, each of the numbers is called a **factor** and the result is called a **product.** There are several ways to indicate the operation of multiplication.

$$4 \cdot 3 = 12 \quad 4(3) = 12 \quad (4) \cdot (3) = 12 \quad (4)(3) = 12 \quad 4 \times 3 = 12$$

In each of the five examples shown here, the notation indicates that 4 is to be multiplied by 3 and the result is 12. In algebra, we will avoid the last notation because the cross can be confused with the letter x, a symbol we will use for other purposes. In each of the above, we say that 4 and 3 are factors, and we say that 12 is the product.

We note that the product of a particular real number and the number 1 is the particular real number itself.

$$4 \cdot 1 = 4 \quad \text{and} \quad 15 \cdot 1 = 15$$

The number zero also has a unique multiplicative property. **The product of any real number and the number zero is the number zero.**

$$4 \cdot 0 = 0 \quad \text{and} \quad 15 \cdot 0 = 0$$

division   If one number is to be divided by another number to achieve a result, the first number is called the **dividend,** the second number is called the **divisor,** and the result is called the **quotient.**

$$\frac{10}{5} = 2 \qquad 10 \div 5 = 2$$

Both of the notations shown here indicate that 10 is to be divided by 5 and that the result is 2. We call 10 the dividend, call 5 the divisor, and say that the quotient is 2. When the indicated division is expressed in the form of a fraction such as $\frac{10}{5}$, we say that 10 is the **numerator** of the fraction and that 5 is the **denominator** of the fraction.

4.H
review of operations with decimal numbers

We must align the decimal points vertically when we add and subtract decimal numbers, as we show here.

$$\begin{array}{r} 1.005 \\ + \ 300.012 \\ \hline 301.017 \end{array}$$

example 4.1   Add 4.0016 and 0.02163.

solution   We remember to place the numbers so that the decimal points are aligned.

$$\begin{array}{r} 4.0016 \\ + \ 0.02163 \\ \hline \mathbf{4.02323} \end{array}$$

example 4.2   Subtract 0.02163 from 4.0016.

solution   Again we align the decimal points.

$$\begin{array}{r} 4.0016 \\ - \ 0.02163 \\ \hline \mathbf{3.97997} \end{array}$$

example 4.3   Multiply 4.06×0.016.

solution   We do not align the decimal points when we multiply.

$$\begin{array}{r} 4.06 \\ \times \ 0.016 \\ \hline 2436 \\ 406 \ \ \ \\ \hline \mathbf{0.06496} \end{array}$$

example 4.4   Divide 6.039 by 0.03.

solution   As the first step, we adjust the decimal points as necessary. Then we divide.

$$0.03\overline{)6.039} \qquad \begin{array}{r} \mathbf{201.3} \\ 3\overline{)603.9} \\ \underline{6} \ \ \ \ \\ 3 \ \ \\ \underline{3} \ \ \\ 9 \\ \underline{9} \end{array}$$

4.I
unit multipliers

If we multiply a number by a fraction that has a value of 1, we do not change the value of the number. We just change the numeral we use to represent the number. To write 5 with a denominator of 7, we multiply 5 by 7 over 7.

$$\frac{5}{1} \times \frac{7}{7} = \frac{35}{7}$$

The fraction 7 over 7 has a value of 1, so we have just multiplied 5 by 1. Thirty-five over 7 has a value of 5 and is just another way to write 5. The fractions

$$\frac{3 \text{ ft}}{1 \text{ yd}} \qquad \text{and} \qquad \frac{1 \text{ yd}}{3 \text{ ft}}$$

have units and are equal to 1 because 3 ft is another name for 1 yd. We call these fractions **unit multipliers.** We can use unit multipliers to change the units of a number.

4.J
conversions of length

In this section we will use unit multipliers to convert length measurements.

example 4.5   Use one unit multiplier to convert 32 feet to inches (1 ft = 12 in.).

solution   There are two unit multipliers that we can consider.

$$\frac{1 \text{ ft}}{12 \text{ in.}} \qquad \text{and} \qquad \frac{12 \text{ in.}}{1 \text{ ft}}$$

Let us try the first unit multiplier and see what happens.

$$\frac{32 \text{ ft}}{1} \times \frac{1 \text{ ft}}{12 \text{ in.}} = \frac{32 \text{ ft} \times 1 \text{ ft}}{12 \text{ in.}} = \frac{32 \text{ ft}^2}{12 \text{ in.}}$$

This answer is correct but is not what we want. Let us try the other unit multiplier.

$$\frac{32 \text{ ft}}{1} \times \frac{12 \text{ in.}}{1 \text{ ft}} = \mathbf{32(12) \text{ in.}}$$

We can cancel the ft on the bottom with the ft on top because ft over ft has a value of 1. Since we are not interested in a numerical answer, we will not do the multiplication.

example 4.6   Use one unit multiplier to convert 36 feet to miles (5280 ft = 1 mi).

solution   There are two unit multipliers that we may consider.

$$\frac{5280 \text{ ft}}{1 \text{ mi}} \qquad \text{and} \qquad \frac{1 \text{ mi}}{5280 \text{ ft}}$$

We will use the second unit multiplier because the feet on the bottom will cancel the feet on the top. We remember that the symbol ≈ means "approximately equals."

$$\frac{36 \text{ ft}}{1} \times \frac{1 \text{ mi}}{5280 \text{ ft}} = \frac{36}{5280} \text{ mi} \approx \mathbf{0.0068 \text{ mi}}$$

example 4.7   Use one unit multiplier to convert 47.25 inches to centimeters (1 in. = 2.54 cm).

solution   The inch is **defined** to be **exactly** 2.54 cm, so there are two unit multipliers that we may consider.

$$\frac{1 \text{ in.}}{2.54 \text{ cm}} \qquad \text{and} \qquad \frac{2.54 \text{ cm}}{1 \text{ in.}}$$

Since we have 47.25 inches, we will use the second unit multiplier because it has inches on the bottom, which will cancel inches on the top.

$$47.25 \text{ in.} \times \frac{2.54 \text{ cm}}{1 \text{ in.}} = \textbf{47.25(2.54) cm}$$

A numerical answer is not necessary, so we will leave the answer as it is.

example 4.8   Use one unit multiplier to convert 42 meters to centimeters (1 m = 100 cm).

solution   There are 100 centimeters in 1 meter. The two possible unit multipliers are

$$\frac{100 \text{ cm}}{1 \text{ m}} \quad \text{and} \quad \frac{1 \text{ m}}{100 \text{ cm}}$$

We will use the first unit multiplier because it has meters on the bottom.

$$\frac{42 \text{ m}}{1} \times \frac{100 \text{ cm}}{1 \text{ m}} = \textbf{4200 cm}$$

example 4.9   Use two unit multipliers to convert 42 feet to centimeters.

solution   Many people in the United States still use inches, feet, and miles to make measurements. The rest of the world uses centimeters, meters, and kilometers. Thus, U.S. engineers often find it necessary to convert from one system to another. The crossover point is the **exact relationship** 1 in. = 2.54 cm. We will convert feet to inches and then convert inches to centimeters.

$$42 \text{ ft} \times \frac{12 \text{ in.}}{1 \text{ ft}} \times \frac{2.54 \text{ cm}}{1 \text{ in.}} = \textbf{42(12)(2.54) cm}$$

We will not do the multiplication because a decimal answer is not required. We are interested in the method, not in an exact numerical answer.

example 4.10   Use two unit multipliers to convert 4 miles to inches.

solution   We will convert from miles to feet and then convert feet to inches.

$$4 \text{ mi} \times \frac{5280 \text{ ft}}{1 \text{ mi}} \times \frac{12 \text{ in.}}{1 \text{ ft}} = \textbf{4(5280)(12) in.}$$

The following table provides the basic equivalent measures.

TABLE OF EQUIVALENT MEASURES		
1 ft = 12 in.	1 yd = 3 ft	1 mi = 5280 ft
1 m = 100 cm	1 cm = 10 mm	1 km = 1000 m
	1 in. = 2.54 cm	

Problems to provide practice in operations with decimal numbers will appear in the problem sets. Do not use a calculator when working these problems.

practice   Perform operations as indicated. Do not use a calculator.

a. $4\frac{1}{2} \times 2\frac{4}{5}$ **b.** $3\frac{1}{4} \div 1\frac{3}{8}$

c. $47.123 + 8.416 + 705.4$ **d.** $800.62 - 75.88$

e. 47.05×6.42 **f.** $4.028 \div 0.04$

g. Use two unit multipliers to convert 75 feet to centimeters. (Go from feet to inches to centimeters.)

h. Use two unit multipliers to convert 450 inches to miles. (Go from inches to feet to miles.)

problem set 4

1. What is the difference between a number and a numeral?
(4)

2. (a) What do we call our system of numeration that we use to designate numbers?
(4)

(b) Who invented this system?

(c) List the digits that we use in this system.

3. (a) What numbers are called counting numbers?
(4)

(b) What numbers are called natural numbers?

4. The numbers of arithmetic are zero and the positive real numbers. How do we define positive real numbers?
(4)

5. (a) Define a rectangle.
(2)

(b) Define a rhombus.

(c) Define a square.

(d) Is every square also a rectangle?

6. Use one unit multiplier to convert 20 inches to centimeters (2.54 cm = 1 in.).
(4)

7. Use two unit multipliers to convert 25 feet to centimeters. (Go from feet to inches to centimeters.)
(4)

8. The length of a rectangle is 16 centimeters. The width of the rectangle is 9 centimeters. Find the perimeter of the rectangle.
(3)

9. The perimeter of a square is 24 meters. What is the length of one side of the square?
(3)

10. The radius of a circle is 8 inches. Find the circumference of the circle.
(3)

11. The diameter of a circle is 10 feet. Find the circumference of the circle.
(3)

Find the perimeter of each figure. Corners that look square are square. Dimensions are in centimeters.

12.
(3)

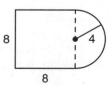

13.
(3)

14.
(3)

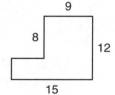

15.
(3)

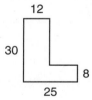

16. Find x.
(2)

Add, subtract, multiply, or divide as indicated:

17. $\dfrac{17}{24} - \dfrac{1}{4} - \dfrac{1}{8}$ (1)   **18.** $8\dfrac{1}{4} + 5\dfrac{3}{8}$ (1)   **19.** $8\dfrac{1}{4} - 5\dfrac{3}{8}$ (1)

20. $95\dfrac{1}{8} - 4\dfrac{13}{16}$ (1)   **21.** $\dfrac{4}{3} \times \dfrac{7}{2} \times \dfrac{9}{5}$ (4)   **22.** $4\dfrac{1}{2} \times 6\dfrac{2}{3}$ (4)

23. $4\dfrac{1}{2} \div 6\dfrac{2}{3}$ (4)   **24.** $\dfrac{14\frac{2}{3}}{3\frac{1}{4}}$ (4)   **25.** $6.0018 + 0.03121$ (4)

26. $8.0146 - 0.03251$ (4)   **27.** 16.04×3.46 (4)   **28.** $5.412 \div 0.123$ (4)

29. The length of $\overline{AB}$ is $3\frac{1}{2}$ meters. The length of $\overline{BC}$ is $10\frac{3}{8}$ meters. Find AC.   (1)

$$A \qquad B \qquad\qquad C$$

30. PR is $15\frac{2}{3}$ kilometers. PQ is $10\frac{1}{6}$ kilometers. Find QR.   (1)

$$P \qquad\qquad Q \qquad R$$

LESSON 5   Sets • Absolute Value • Addition of Signed Numbers

5.A

sets

We use the word **set** to designate a well-defined collection of numbers, objects, or things. We say that the individual objects or things that make up the set are the elements of the set or the members of the set. It is customary to designate a set by enclosing the members of the set within braces.

$$A = \{1, 2, 3, 4, 5\}$$

We have designated set A as the set whose members are the counting numbers 1 through 5 inclusive. We could also designate this set by placing a verbal phrase within the braces as

$$A = \{\text{counting numbers 1 through 5 inclusive}\}$$

or we could designate the members of this set by writing a sentence:

Set A is the set whose members are the counting numbers 1 through 5 inclusive.

Since we can designate which numbers are natural or counting numbers so that there is no doubt as to whether a number is or is not a natural or counting number, we say that these numbers constitute a set. Both *natural* and *counting* are names for the same set, and we normally use one name or the other. Thus we say

$$\text{Natural numbers} = \{1, 2, 3, 4, 5, \dots\}$$

The three dots indicate that the list of numbers continues without end.

If we include the number zero with the set of natural numbers, we say that we have designated the set of *whole numbers*.

$$\text{Whole numbers} = \{0, 1, 2, 3, 4, 5, \dots\}$$

We designate that the list of the members of the set of whole numbers continues without end by using the three dots after the last digit recorded. **Now if we include in our list the negative** of every member of the set of natural numbers, we have designated the set that we call the *integers*.

$$\text{Integers} = \{\ldots, -3, -2, -1, 0, 1, 2, 3, \ldots\}$$

The dots on each end indicate that the list continues without end in both directions.

5.B
absolute value

The number zero is neither positive nor negative and can be designated with the single symbol 0. Every other real number is either positive or negative and thus requires a two-part numeral. One of the parts is the plus or the minus sign, and the other part is the numerical part. If we look at the two numerals

$$+7 \quad \text{and} \quad -7$$

we note that the numerical part of each one is the same and that the numerals differ only in their signs. We can think of the numerical part as designating the quality of bigness of the number, and we use the words **absolute value** to describe this quality. **However, when we try to write the absolute value of one of these numbers by just writing the numerical part**

$$7$$

we find that we have written a positive number because we have agreed that a numeral written with no sign designates a positive number. Because of this agreement, we are forced to define the absolute value of any nonzero real number to be a positive number. We define the absolute value of zero to be zero. If we enclose a number[†] within vertical lines, we are designating the absolute value of the number. We will demonstrate this notation by designating the absolute value of zero, the absolute value of positive 7, and the absolute value of negative 7.

$$|0| = 0 \qquad \text{read "the absolute value of zero equals zero"}$$

$$|+7| = +7 \qquad \text{read "the absolute value of 7 equals 7"}$$

$$|-7| = +7 \qquad \text{read "the absolute value of } -7 \text{ equals 7"}$$

Since the plus sign in front of a positive number is customarily omitted, the above can be written without recording the plus signs:

$$|7| = 7 \qquad \text{read "the absolute value of 7 equals 7"}$$

$$|-7| = 7 \qquad \text{read "the absolute value of } -7 \text{ equals 7"}$$

Thus we have two rules for stating the absolute value of a real number.

1. The absolute value of zero is zero.

2. The absolute value of any nonzero real number is a positive number.

Here we designate the absolute value of zero and several other real numbers.

(a) $|0| = 0$ (b) $|-7.12| = 7.12$ (c) $|7.12| = 7.12$

(d) $|-5| = 5$ (e) $|5| = 5$ (f) $\left|\dfrac{3}{4}\right| = \dfrac{3}{4}$

[†]We really should use the word *numeral* here, but from now on we will often use the words *number* and *numeral* interchangeably because excessive attention to the difference between these words is counterproductive.

example 5.1   Simplify: (a) $|-5|$ (b) $|11 - 2|$ (c) $-|20 - 2|$

solution   (a) The absolute value of –5 is 5.

$$|-5| = \mathbf{5}$$

(b) First we simplify within the vertical lines:

$$|11 - 2| = |9|$$

The absolute value of 9 is 9.

$$|9| = \mathbf{9}$$

(c) Again we simplify within the vertical lines:

$$-|20 - 2| = -|18|$$

The absolute value of 18 is 18, but we want the opposite of this, so our answer is –18.

$$-|18| = \mathbf{-18}$$

5.C
addition of signed numbers

In arithmetic the minus sign always means to subtract, but in algebra we also use the minus sign to designate that a number is a negative number. This can be confusing at first, as we see if we look at the expression

$$3 - 2$$

and ask if the minus sign means to subtract or if it means that –2 is a negative number. It turns out that we will find the same answer with either thought process, but in algebra we normally prefer the second process in which we think of the negative sign as designating that –2 is a negative number. If we do this, we say that we are using algebraic addition.

To help explain the rules for algebraic addition, we will use diagrams drawn on a number line.

We will represent signed numbers with arrows and say that the arrows indicate directed numbers. We represent positive numbers with arrows that point to the right and negative numbers with arrows that point to the left. The length of each arrow corresponds to the absolute value of the number represented. For instance, +3 and –2 can be represented with the following arrows.

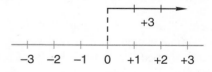

To use these arrows to add +3 and –2, we begin at the origin and draw the +3 arrow pointing to the right.

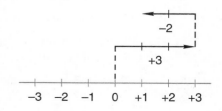

Then from the head of this arrow we draw the –2 arrow, which points to the left. The head of the –2 arrow is over +1 on the number line.

This a graphical solution to the problem

$$(+3) + (-2) = +1$$

Note that we obtain the same answer when we add signed numbers algebraically as we obtain when we use only the positive numbers of arithmetic and subtract!

$$3 - 2 = 1$$

It may seem that we are trying to turn an easy problem into a difficult problem, but such is not the case. **In algebra the operations of addition and subtraction are lumped together in the one operation of algebraic addition, and this enables a straightforward solution to problems that would be very confusing if the concepts of signed numbers and algebraic addition were not used.**

example 5.2   Use directed numbers and the number line to add +3 and –5.

solution

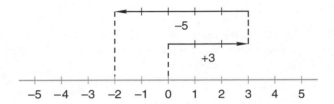

We begin at the origin and draw an arrow 3 units long that points to the right to represent the number +3. From the head of this arrow we draw an arrow 5 units long that points to the left to represent the number –5. The head of the second arrow is just above the number –2 on the number line. Thus we see that

$$(+3) + (-5) = \mathbf{-2}$$

example 5.3   Use directed numbers and the number line to add –5 and +3.

solution

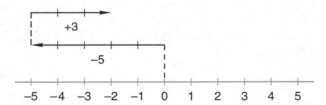

We will use the same arrows, but this time we will draw the –5 arrow first and then draw the +3 arrow. We note that again we get an answer of **–2.**

These examples demonstrate that we may exchange the order in which we add two numbers without changing the answer we get. The Latin word for "exchange" is *commutare*, so we call this peculiarity or property of real numbers the **commutative property for addition.**

COMMUTATIVE PROPERTY FOR ADDITION

The order in which two real numbers are added does not affect the sum. For example,

$$4 + 3 = 7 \quad \text{and} \quad 3 + 4 = 7$$

This property can be used to show that any number of numbers can be added in any order and the answer will be the same every time.

When the signed numbers to be added have the same sign, the arrows will point in the same direction, as we see in the next two examples.

example 5.4   Use directed numbers and the number line to add +2 and +1.

solution

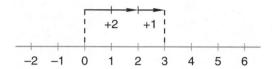

We see from the graph that the solution is +3.

$$(+2) + (+1) = \mathbf{+3}$$

example 5.5   Use directed numbers and the number line to add −2 and −1.

solution

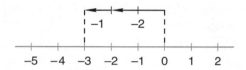

We see from the graph that the solution is −3.

$$(-2) + (-1) = \mathbf{-3}$$

The numbers to be added may also be exchanged when three or more numbers are being added. To demonstrate this we will add four signed numbers, and then exchange the order of the numbers and work the problem again. The sum will be the same.

example 5.6   Use directed numbers and the number line to add these numbers:

$$(-4) + (+2) + (-1) + (+5)$$

solution   We will use arrows and add the numbers in the order they are written.

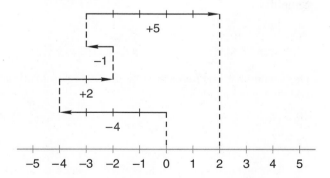

We begin at the origin and move 4 units to the left for −4, then 2 units to the right for +2, then 1 unit to the left for −1, and finally 5 units to the right for +5. We find that we end up directly above the number +2 on the number line. Thus

$$(-4) + (+2) + (-1) + (+5) = \mathbf{+2}$$

The answer will be the same regardless of the order in which we draw the arrows. To show this, we will work the problem again with the order of the numbers changed.

$$(-1) + (+2) + (-4) + (+5)$$

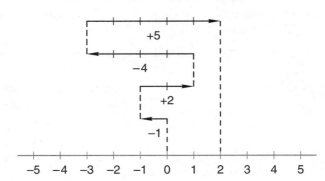

Again we find that the sum of the numbers is +2.

practice Simplify:

a. $|-4|$ **b.** $|4.2|$ **c.** $-|10 - 6|$ **d.** $-|-14 + 6|$

Draw a number line for each of the following problems and use directed numbers (arrows) to add the signed numbers.

e. $(+3) + (+2)$

f. $(-3) + (+2)$

g. $(-5) + (+2) + (-3) + (+3)$

problem set 5

1. (a) Use braces and digits to designate the set of natural numbers.
(5)

(b) Use braces and digits to designate the set of whole numbers.

(c) Use braces and digits to designate the set of integers.

2. What do we call the point on the number line with which we associate the number zero?
(4)

3. (a) What is the graph of a number?
(4)

(b) What is the coordinate of a point on the number line?

(c) How can we tell if one number is greater than another number?

Simplify:

4. $|-8|$ **5.** $|+8|$ **6.** $|-12|$
(5)   (5)   (5)

7. $-|15 - 5|$ **8.** $-|-15 + 5|$ **9.** $|12 - 30|$
(5)   (5)   (5)

Draw a number line for each of the following problems and use directed numbers (arrows) to add the signed numbers.

10. $(+3) + (-8)$ **11.** $(-1) + (+2)$
(5)   (5)

12. $(+4) + (+3)$ **13.** $(-4) + (+2) + (-4) + (+8)$
(5)   (5)

14. Use one unit multiplier to convert 28 centimeters to inches (2.54 cm = 1 in.).
(4)

15. Use two unit multipliers to convert 42 centimeters to feet. (Go from centimeters to inches to feet.)
(4)

16. The length of a rectangle is 22 inches. The width of the rectangle is 13 inches. Find the perimeter of the rectangle.
(3)

17. The radius of a circle is 10 feet. Find the circumference of the circle.
(3)

Find the perimeter of each figure. Corners that look square are square. Dimensions are in yards.

18.
(3)
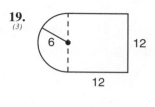

19.
(3)

20. Find *y*.
(2)

Add, subtract, multiply, or divide as indicated:

21. $6\frac{2}{3} + 7\frac{4}{9}$
(1)

22. $95\frac{1}{8} - 4\frac{13}{16}$
(1)

23. $4\frac{1}{2} \times 2\frac{2}{3}$
(4)

24. $4\frac{1}{2} \div 7\frac{3}{8}$
(4)

25. $\dfrac{7\frac{1}{8}}{4\frac{2}{5}}$
(4)

26. $23.0106 + 0.1094$
(4)

27. $48.2 - 13.34$
(4)

28. 8.08×0.120
(4)

29. $8.48636 \div 2.12$
(4)

30. *XZ* is $18\frac{2}{5}$ miles. *XY* is $6\frac{1}{15}$ miles. Find *YZ*.
(1)

LESSON 6   *Rules for Addition • Adding More Than Two Numbers • Inserting Parentheses Mentally • Definition of Subtraction*

6.A
rules for addition

In the preceding lesson we learned to add signed numbers by using a number line and arrows to represent the numbers. This procedure allows us to have a graphical picture of what we are doing. Unfortunately, this method is slow and time-consuming. We do not have time to go through the entire algebra course drawing number lines and arrows, so we must develop rules that will allow us to do algebraic addition quickly. We need two rules—one to use when the numbers to be added have the same signs and one to use when the numbers have different signs. In the following example we will draw two diagrams that will help us state the first rule.

example 6.1 Use directed numbers and the number line to add +1 and +3 algebraically, and use directed numbers and the number line to add −1 and −3 algebraically.

solution

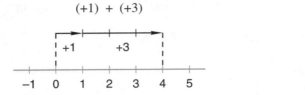 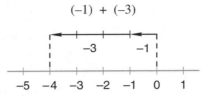

We see from these figures that

$$(+1) + (+3) = +4 \quad \text{and} \quad (-1) + (-3) = -4$$

Now we will generalize. **To add algebraically two signed numbers that have the same sign, we add the absolute values of the numbers and give the result the same sign as the sign of the numbers.**

Now we will use two examples in which numbers with different signs are added algebraically to help us state the second rule.

example 6.2   Use directed numbers and the number line to add –2 and +5 algebraically, and use directed numbers and the number line to add +2 and –5 algebraically.

solution

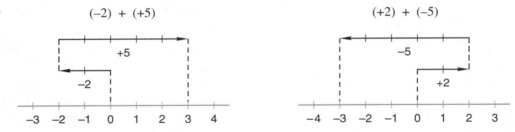

From the figure we see that the absolute value of each answer is 3 but that one of the answers is +3 and that one of the answers is –3.

$$(-2) + (+5) = +3 \qquad (+2) + (-5) = -3$$

In the first case, the number +5 had the larger absolute value and thus the sign of the result was positive. In the second case, the number –5 had the larger absolute value and thus the sign of the result was negative. In both cases, the absolute value of the answer was the difference in the absolute values of the numbers.

Now we will generalize. **To add algebraically two signed numbers that have opposite signs, we take the difference in the absolute values of the numbers and give to this result the sign of the original number whose absolute value is the greatest.**

When two numbers have the same absolute value but different signs, their sum is zero. For instance, the sum of (–5) and (+5) is zero.

$$(-5) + (+5) = 0$$

We say that –5 is the opposite of +5 and that +5 is the opposite of –5. **Every real number except zero has an opposite, and the sum of any real number and its opposite is zero. Another name for the opposite of a number is the additive inverse of the number, so we can also say that the sum of any real number and its additive inverse is zero.**

Test your understanding of the rules by covering the answers to the following problems and seeing if your answers are the same.

(a) $(+7) + (-3) = +4$ (b) $(+2) + (+6) = +8$

(c) $(-7) + (-3) = -10$ (d) $(-2) + (-8) = -10$

(e) $(-7) + (+3) = -4$ (f) $(-2) + (+8) = +6$

(g) $(-4) + (-1) = -5$ (h) $(+2) + (-8) = -6$

6.B
adding more than two numbers

We have noted that signed numbers may be added in any order and the answer will not change. Some people add from left to right, and others begin by first adding numbers that have the same sign.

example 6.3   Add: $(-5) + (4) + (-3) + (+2)$

solution   This time we will add from left to right.

$$(-5) + (4) + (-3) + (+2) \qquad \text{original problem}$$
$$(-1) + (-3) + (+2) \qquad \text{added } (-5) \text{ and } (4)$$
$$(-4) + (+2) \qquad \text{added } (-1) \text{ and } (-3)$$
$$-2 \qquad \text{added } (-4) \text{ and } (+2)$$

example 6.4   Add: $(-3) + (+2) + (-2) + (+4)$

solution   We see that we have two negative numbers and two positive numbers. As the first step, we will add (-3) to (-2) and $(+2)$ to $(+4)$ and then add these sums.

$$(-3) + (+2) + (-2) + (+4) \qquad \text{original problem}$$
$$(-5) + (+6) \qquad \text{added } (-3) \text{ to } (-2) \text{ and } (+2) \text{ to } (+4)$$
$$+1 \qquad \text{added } (-5) \text{ to } (+6)$$

6.C
inserting parentheses mentally

Most signed number problems are written without parentheses enclosing the signed numbers. We must insert the parentheses mentally before we can add. **We will let the sign preceding the number designate whether the number is a positive number or a negative number, and we will mentally insert a plus sign in front of each number to indicate algebraic addition.** If we use this process,

$$4 - 3 + 2 \qquad \text{can be read as} \qquad (+4) + (-3) + (+2)$$

and

$$-6 - 3 - 2 + 5 \qquad \text{can be read as} \qquad (-6) + (-3) + (-2) + (+5)$$

Thus, to simplify an expression such as

$$-4 + 2 - 3 - 3 - 2 + 6$$

we mentally enclose each of the numbers in parentheses, insert the extra plus signs, and then add.

$$(-4) + (+2) + (-3) + (-3) + (-2) + (+6) = -4$$

Care must be used to avoid associating the signs with the wrong numbers. If the mental parentheses are not used, some would incorrectly read the original expression from right to left as "6 plus 2 minus 3," etc. Guard against this.

example 6.5   Simplify: $-4 - 3 + 2 - 4 - 3 - 2$

solution   We mentally enclose each number in parentheses and use plus signs so that we can read the problem as

$$(-4) + (-3) + (+2) + (-4) + (-3) + (-2)$$

Now we add the numbers and get a sum of -14.

$$(-4) + (-3) + (+2) + (-4) + (-3) + (-2) = \mathbf{-14}$$

example 6.6   Simplify: $-2 + 11 - 4 + 3 - 2$

solution   We mentally enclose the numbers in parentheses and add algebraically to get a sum of +6.

$$(-2) + (+11) + (-4) + (+3) + (-2) = \textbf{+6}$$

example 6.7   Simplify: $(-4) + |-2| + 3 - 7 - 2$

solution   We mentally insert parentheses so that the problem reads as follows:

$$(-4) + (|-2|) + (+3) + (-7) + (-2)$$

Now we simplify and get an answer of -8.

$$(-4) + (+2) + (+3) + (-7) + (-2) = \textbf{-8}$$

6.D
definition of subtraction

As we have seen, if we use algebraic addition, we can handle minus signs without using the word *subtraction*. We let the signs tell whether the numbers are positive or negative, and we mentally insert parentheses and extra plus signs as necessary. Thus the subtraction problem on the left

$$7 - 4 = 3 \qquad 7 + (-4) = 3$$

can be turned into the algebraic addition problem on the right. A definition of algebraic subtraction does exist, however, and some people prefer to use it rather than using mental parentheses. The result is exactly the same, but the definition uses the word *subtraction*. To subtract algebraically, we change the sign of the subtrahend and add.

$$7 - 4 = 3 \qquad 7 + (-4) = 3$$

The formal definition of the operation of algebraic subtraction is as follows.

ALGEBRAIC SUBTRACTION

If a and b are real numbers, then

$$a - b = a + (-b)$$

where $-b$ is the opposite of b.

Thus there are two thought processes that may be used to simplify expressions that contain minus signs such as

$$7 - 4$$

Since we prefer to consider that the minus sign designates a negative number, we will emphasize algebraic addition in this book and will avoid the use of the word *subtraction*.

practice   Use parentheses to enclose each number or expression and its sign. Then insert plus signs between the parentheses. Then add to get a sum.

   a. $-5 - 2 + 7 - 6$ **b.** $-4 - |-2| - 6 + (-5)$

   c. $-|-8| - 3 + 5 - 11$ **d.** $-8 + |-6| - |5| - 7$

problem set 6

   1. State the rule for adding two numbers whose signs are alike.
   (6)

   2. State the rule for adding two numbers whose signs are different.
   (6)

   3. What property of addition states that the order in which two real numbers are added does
   (5) not affect the sum?

4. (a) What do we call the answer to an addition problem?
(4)

   (b) What do we call the answer to a subtraction problem?

   (c) What do we call the answer to a multiplication problem?

   (d) What do we call the answer to a division problem?

Simplify:

5. $|-5|$ **6.** $-|10 - 7|$ **7.** $|3 - 6|$
(5)   (5)   (5)

Draw a number line for each of the following problems and use directed numbers (arrows) to add the signed numbers.

8. $(+4) + (-5)$ **9.** $(+1) + (-3) + (+4) + (-2)$
(5)   (5)

10. Use one unit multiplier to convert 34 meters to centimeters (100 cm = 1 m).
(4)

11. Use two unit multipliers to convert 6 miles to inches. (Go from miles to feet to inches.)
(4)

12. The perimeter of a square is 36 centimeters. What is the length of one side of the square?
(3)

13. The diameter of a circle is 14 meters. Find the circumference of the circle.
(3)

Simplify:

14. $(+3) + (-14)$ **15.** $(-3) + (-14)$
(6)   (6)

16. $(-5) + (4) + (-3) + (+8)$ **17.** $(-3) + (+2) + (-2) + |-2|$
(6)   (6)

Use parentheses to enclose each number and its sign. Then insert plus signs between the parentheses. Then add to get a sum.

18. $-2 + 11 - 4 + 3 - 8$ **19.** $-5 - 11 + 20 - 14 + 5$
(6)   (6)

20. $-4 - 3 + 2 - 4 - 3 - 8$ **21.** $7 - 3 + 2 - 11 + 4 - 5 + 3$
(6)   (6)

Use parentheses to enclose each number or expression and its sign. Then insert plus signs between the parentheses. Then add to get a sum.

22. $-7 + (-8) + 3$ **23.** $-7 + (-3) + 4 - 3 + (-2)$
(6)   (6)

24. $-4 - 2 + (+8) + |-5|$ **25.** $+|-2 - 3| - 4 + (-8)$
(6)   (6)

Find the perimeter of each figure. Corners that look square are square. Dimensions are in kilometers.

26.
(3)

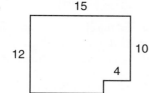

27.
(3)

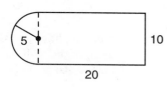

28. Find x.
(2)

29. Simplify: $\dfrac{21}{5} \times \dfrac{15}{7} \times \dfrac{4}{9}$
(4)

30. AC is $25\frac{3}{4}$ inches. BC is $20\frac{1}{20}$ inches. Find AB.
(1)

LESSON 7   *The Opposite of a Number • Simplifying More Difficult Notations*

7.A
the opposite of a number

We can use the thought "opposite of a number" to help us understand and simplify expressions such as $-(-2)$, $-[-(-2)]$, $-\{-[-(2)]\}$, etc. We begin by graphing the number 2 and the number –2.

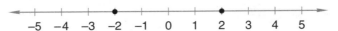

From the figure we see that the number –2 lies on the **opposite** side of the origin from 2 and is exactly the same distance from the origin. Thus we can think of +2 as being the **opposite of** –2, and –2 as being the opposite of +2. Often it is helpful to read a negative sign as "the opposite of." If we use this wording, it is easy to locate $-(-2)$, for we read this as "the opposite of the opposite of 2." Well, the opposite of 2 is –2, and the opposite of that must be 2 itself.

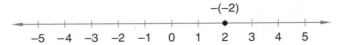

Thus 2 and $-(-2)$ are different numerals or symbols for the same number. If this is true, then where does $-[-(-2)]$ lie? We can read this as "the opposite of the opposite of the opposite of 2."

If we begin at 2, we can find the opposite of 2 at –2. Then the opposite of the opposite of 2 is back on the right-hand side, so the opposite of the opposite of the opposite of 2 is on the left-hand side and is another way to write –2. Of course, we could go on forever with this process, but we will not.

7.B
simplifying more difficult notations

Complicated expressions such as

$$-(-4) + (-2) + [-(-6)]$$

can be simplified by using algebraic addition and the concept of opposites. We begin by noting that algebraic addition of three numbers is indicated. We emphasize this by enclosing the numbers that are to be added and writing plus signs between the enclosures.

$$\boxed{-(-4)} + \boxed{+(-2)} + \boxed{+[-(-6)]}$$

The number in the first enclosure is +4, in the second is –2, and in the third is +6. So we can write

$$(+4) + (-2) + (+6) = 8$$

example 7.1   Simplify: $-(+4) - (-5) + 5 - (-3) + (-6)$

solution   This problem indicates addition of five numbers.

$$\boxed{-(+4)} + \boxed{-(-5)} + \boxed{(+5)} + \boxed{-(-3)} + \boxed{+(-6)}$$

We simplify within each enclosure and add algebraically.

$$(-4) + (+5) + (+5) + (+3) + (-6) = \mathbf{3}$$

example 7.2   Simplify: $-(-3) - [-(-2)] + [-(-3)]$

solution We see three numbers are to be added. We begin by enclosing each number and inserting the necessary plus signs.

$$\boxed{-(-3)} \ + \ \boxed{-[-(-2)]} \ + \ \boxed{+[-(-3)]}$$

Now we simplify within each enclosure and then add.

$$(+3) + (-2) + (+3) = \mathbf{4}$$

example 7.3 Simplify: $-(-4) + (-2) - [-(-6)]$

solution This time we will picture the enclosures mentally but we will not write them down. If we do this, we can simplify the given expression as

$$(+4) + (-2) + (-6) = \mathbf{-4}$$

example 7.4 Simplify: $-(+4) - (-5) + 5 - (-3) + (-6)$

solution This time we will not even use parentheses but will write the simplification directly as

$$-4 + 5 + 5 + 3 - 6 = \mathbf{3}$$

It might take a lot of practice to become adept in doing simplifications such as this one. Do not get discouraged if you find these problems troublesome.

practice Use the concept of opposites and algebraic addition to simplify the following. Use additional plus signs and brackets as required.

    a. $-(-3) - (-4)$ **b.** $+(-5) + [-(-6)]$

    c. $-(+6) - (-8) + 7 - (-3) + (-5)$ **d.** $-(-3) - [-(-4)] + [-(-6)]$

problem set 7

1. (6,7) (a) What is the opposite of 2?

    (b) What is the opposite of -2?

    (c) What is the sum of a real number and its opposite?

2. (6) What is another name for the opposite of a number?

3. (5) (a) Designate the set of natural numbers.

    (b) Designate the set of whole numbers.

    (c) Designate the set of integers.

Use the concept of opposites to simplify:

4. (7) $-(+4)$ **5.** (7) $-(-4)$

6. (7) $-[-(-4)]$ **7.** (7) $-\{-[-(-4)]\}$

8. (4) Use one unit multiplier to convert 2200 centimeters to meters (100 cm = 1 m).

9. (4) Use two unit multipliers to convert 3000 inches to miles. (Go from inches to feet to miles.)

10. (3) The length of a rectangle is 32 inches. The width of the rectangle is 16 inches. Find the perimeter of the rectangle.

11. (3) The radius of a circle is 12 feet. Find the circumference of the circle.

Use the concept of opposites and algebraic addition to simplify the following. Use additional plus signs and brackets as required.

12. (7) $+7 - (-3) + (-2)$ **13.** (7) $-3 + (-2) - (-3)$

14. (7) $-(-3) - [-(-4)] - 2 + 7$ **15.** (7) $-2 - (-3) - \{-[-(-4)]\}$

16. (7) $-(-2) - |-2|$ **17.** (7) $-|-10| - (-10)$

18. $-3 - (-3) + |-3|$
(7)

19. $-2 - [-(-6)] + |-5|$
(7)

20. $-|-3 - 2| - (-3) - 2 - 5$
(7)

21. $|-2 - 5 - 7| - (-4)$
(7)

Find the perimeter of each figure. Corners that look square are square. Dimensions are in yards.

22.
(3)

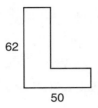

62
50

23.
(3)

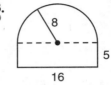

8
5
16

24. Find x.
(2)

60°
$x°$

Add, subtract, multiply, or divide as indicated:

25. $5\frac{1}{2} + 7\frac{3}{8} - 1\frac{1}{4}$
(1)

26. $1\frac{3}{5} \times 12\frac{1}{2}$
(4)

27. $4\frac{1}{4} \div 3\frac{2}{5}$
(4)

28. $0.00143 + 0.012 + 443.6 + 0.0007$
(4)

29. 3.628×0.0404
(4)

30. The length of $\overline{XY}$ is $16\frac{2}{3}$ centimeters. The length of $\overline{YZ}$ is $5\frac{5}{6}$ centimeters. Find XZ.
(1)

X Y Z

LESSON 8 *Area*

8.A
the concept of area

The **area** of a closed figure is the number of square units contained in the figure. A **square unit** is a square having sides that measure one unit in length. Any shape that fills a closed figure without overlapping can be used to measure area, but the square is used because of its simplicity.

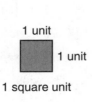

1 unit
1 unit
1 square unit

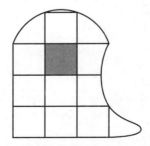

Closed figure with irregular boundary

For many closed figures with irregular boundaries, we must "break up" some of the square units to fill the figure. Therefore, it is not uncommon to have closed figures whose areas contain fractional square units. We can see that counting square units is not the easiest or the best way to find the area of a closed figure. Therefore, in the following sections we will develop formulas for computing the areas of some common geometrical figures.

8.B
areas of rectangles and squares

On the left we show a rectangle whose length is 4 units and whose width is 2 units.

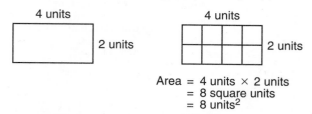

Area = 4 units × 2 units
= 8 square units
= 8 units^2

On the right we see that it takes 8 square units to fill the rectangle. Therefore, the area of the rectangle is 8 square units which equals the length of the rectangle times the width of the rectangle. From this we see that the area of a rectangle equals the length times the width.

$$\text{Area of a rectangle } = \text{ length } \times \text{ width}$$

A square is a rectangle so the area formula for a rectangle also applies to a square. The length and width of a square are the same, so the area of a square is equal to the square of the length of a side.

$$\text{Area of a square } = \text{ (length of a side)}^2$$

Areas are always measured in square units. Some common units of area are the square centimeter (cm^2) and the square meter (m^2). It is important to remember that *units* are used for length and *square units* are used for area.

example 8.1   Find the area of this figure. All angles are right angles. Dimensions are in centimeters.

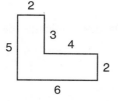

solution   We will divide the figure into rectangles and find the area of each of the rectangles. Then we will add the areas. We show two different ways to work this problem.

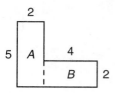

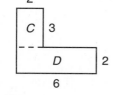

Area A = 2 cm × 5 cm = 10 cm^2
Area B = 4 cm × 2 cm = $\underline{\ \ 8\text{ cm}^2}$
18 cm^2

Area C = 2 cm × 3 cm = $\ \ 6$ cm^2
Area D = 6 cm × 2 cm = $\underline{12\text{ cm}^2}$
18 cm^2

example 8.2   Find the area of the shaded portion of this figure. All angles are right angles. Dimensions are in meters.

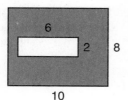

solution   The area of the shaded portion of the figure equals the area of the large rectangle minus the area of the small rectangle.

$$\text{Area} = \text{area of large rectangle} - \text{area of small rectangle}$$

$$= (10 \text{ m})(8 \text{ m}) - (6 \text{ m})(2 \text{ m})$$

$$= 80 \text{ m}^2 - 12 \text{ m}^2$$

$$= \textbf{68 m}^2$$

8.C

areas of triangles

The **altitude,** or **height,** of a triangle is the perpendicular distance from either the base of the triangle or an extension of the base to the opposite vertex. Any one of the three sides can be designated as the base.

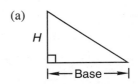 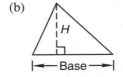 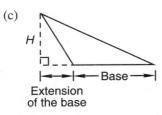

The altitude can (a) be one of the sides of the triangle, (b) fall inside the triangle, or (c) fall outside the triangle. When the altitude falls outside the triangle, we have to extend the base so that the altitude can be drawn. This extension of the base is not part of the length of the base. The area of any triangle equals one half the product of the base and the height.

$$\text{Area of a triangle} = \frac{\text{base} \times \text{height}}{2}$$

example 8.3   Find the areas of these triangles. Dimensions are in inches.

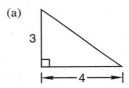 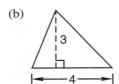 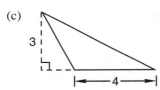

solution   The base of each triangle is 4 in. and the height of each triangle is 3 in. Thus, all the triangles have the same area.

$$\text{Area} = \frac{B \times H}{2} = \frac{4 \text{ in.} \times 3 \text{ in.}}{2} = \textbf{6 in.}^2$$

example 8.4   Find the area of this right triangle. Dimensions are in feet.

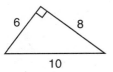

solution   Any one of the three sides of the right triangle can be designated as the base. We will not choose the side of length 10 ft as the base because it would be too difficult to find the height. We can choose either of the two remaining sides as the base. The other side then becomes the height.

$$\text{Area} = \frac{1}{2}BH = \frac{1}{2}(6 \text{ ft})(8 \text{ ft}) = \textbf{24 ft}^2$$

example 8.5   Find the area of this figure. Corners that look square are square. Dimensions are in yards.

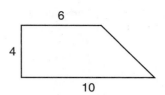

solution   First we divide the figure into a rectangle and a right triangle.

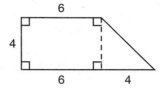

The area of the figure equals the sum of the areas of the rectangle and the right triangle.

$$\text{Area} = \text{area of rectangle} + \text{area of right triangle}$$

$$= (6 \text{ yd})(4 \text{ yd}) + \frac{1}{2}(4 \text{ yd})(4 \text{ yd})$$

$$= 24 \text{ yd}^2 + 8 \text{ yd}^2$$

$$= \mathbf{32 \ yd^2}$$

8.D

areas of circles

We remember that the radius of a circle is the distance from the center of the circle to any point on the circle. The area of a circle equals πr^2, where r is the length of the radius of the circle.

Area $= \pi r^2$

$$\boxed{\text{Area of a circle } = \pi r^2}$$

example 8.6   The radius of a circle is 3 centimeters. Find the area of the circle.

solution   The formula for the area of a circle of radius r is given by

$$\text{Area} = \pi r^2$$

Substituting 3 cm for r, we get

$$\text{Area} = \pi(3 \text{ cm})^2$$

$$= (3.14)(9 \text{ cm}^2)$$

$$= \mathbf{28.26 \ cm^2}$$

example 8.7   The area of a circle is 25 square meters. Find the radius of the circle.

solution   The formula for the area of a circle of radius r is given by

$$\text{Area} = \pi r^2$$

Substituting 25 m^2 for area, we get

$$25 \text{ m}^2 = \pi r^2$$

$$25 \text{ m}^2 = (3.14)r^2$$

$$7.96 \text{ m}^2 = r^2$$

Solving for r, we get

$$r = \mathbf{2.82 \text{ m}}$$

example 8.8   Find the area of this figure. Lines that look parallel are parallel. Dimensions are in inches.

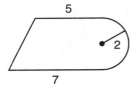

solution   First we divide the figure into a right triangle, a rectangle, and a semicircle (half of a circle).

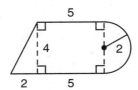

The area of the figure equals the sum of the areas of the right triangle, the rectangle, and the semicircle.

Area = area of right triangle + area of rectangle + area of semicircle

$$= \frac{1}{2}(2 \text{ in.})(4 \text{ in.}) + (5 \text{ in.})(4 \text{ in.}) + \frac{\pi(2 \text{ in.})^2}{2}$$

$$= 4 \text{ in.}^2 + 20 \text{ in.}^2 + \frac{(3.14)(2 \text{ in.})^2}{2}$$

$$= 24 \text{ in.}^2 + 6.28 \text{ in.}^2$$

$$= \mathbf{30.28 \text{ in.}^2}$$

These problems are arithmetic problems. A calculator can be used to help with the arithmetic. **We remember that in this book, we will use 3.14 as an approximation for π when doing calculations that involve the number π.**

8.E

areas of parallelograms and trapezoids   There is a formula for the area of a parallelogram. There is also a formula for the area of a trapezoid. These formulas are hard to remember because they are used so seldom. The easiest way to find the areas is to divide the figures into two triangles as we show in the following examples.

example 8.9   Find the area of this parallelogram. Dimensions are in centimeters.

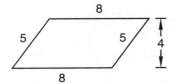

solution A diagonal of a parallelogram divides the figure into two triangles whose areas are equal. The base of each triangle is 8 cm and the height of each triangle is 4 cm.

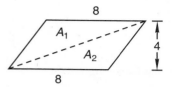

The area of the parallelogram equals the sum of the areas of the two triangles.

$$\text{Area} = A_1 + A_2$$

$$= \frac{1}{2}(8 \text{ cm})(4 \text{ cm}) + \frac{1}{2}(8 \text{ cm})(4 \text{ cm})$$

$$= 16 \text{ cm}^2 + 16 \text{ cm}^2$$

$$= \mathbf{32 \text{ cm}^2}$$

example 8.10 Find the area of this trapezoid. Dimensions are in meters.

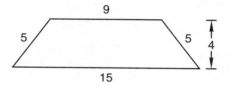

solution A diagonal of a trapezoid divides the figure into two triangles. The base of one triangle is 9 m and the base of the other triangle is 15 m. The height of each triangle is 4 m.

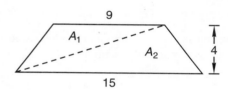

The area of the trapezoid equals the sum of the areas of the two triangles.

$$\text{Area} = A_1 + A_2$$

$$= \frac{1}{2}(9 \text{ m})(4 \text{ m}) + \frac{1}{2}(15 \text{ m})(4 \text{ m})$$

$$= 18 \text{ m}^2 + 30 \text{ m}^2$$

$$= \mathbf{48 \text{ m}^2}$$

practice **a.** Find the area of this figure. All angles are right angles. Dimensions are in inches.

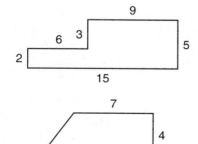

b. Find the area of this figure. Corners that look square are square. Dimensions are in feet.

c. The radius of a circle is 5 centimeters. Find the area of the circle.

d. Find the area of this figure. Corners that look square are square. Dimensions are in meters.

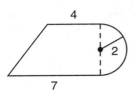

problem set 8

1. (6,7)   (a)   What is the opposite of $\frac{1}{2}$?

       (b)   What is the opposite of $-\frac{1}{2}$?

       (c)   What is the sum of a real number and its opposite?

2. (6)   What is another name for the opposite of a number?

3. (2)   What angles are formed by lines that are perpendicular?

4. (2)   What angle is formed by two right angles?

5. (4)   Use two unit multipliers to convert 36 feet to centimeters. (Go from feet to inches to centimeters.)

6. (4)   Use two unit multipliers to convert 44 inches to meters. (Go from inches to centimeters to meters.)

7. (3)   The perimeter of a rectangle is 30 centimeters. The length of the rectangle is 10 centimeters. Find the width of the rectangle.

8. (8)   The length of a rectangle is 5 meters. The width of the rectangle is 4 meters. Find the area of the rectangle.

9. (3)   The radius of a circle is 3 inches. Find the circumference of the circle.

10. (8)   The radius of a circle is 4 feet. Find the area of the circle.

Use the concept of opposites and algebraic addition to simplify the following. Use additional plus signs and brackets as required.

11. (7) $-(-4) + (-2) - (-3)$

12. (6) $-3 + (-3) + (-6) - 2$

13. (6) $-7 + 3 - 2 - 5 + (-6)$

14. (7) $5 - 3 - (-2) - [-(-3)]$

15. (7) $-|-2| - (-2)$

16. (7) $-|-2| + |2| - (-2)$

17. (6) $7 - 4 - 5 + 12 - 2 - |-2|$

18. (7) $|-4 - 3| - 2 + 7 - (-3)$

19. (7) $5 - |-2 + 5| - (-3) + 2$

20. (7) $4 - 3 - (-2) - |12 - 3 + 4|$

Find the perimeter of each figure. Corners that look square are square. Dimensions are in yards.

21. (3)

22. (3)

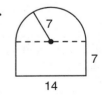

Find the area of each figure. Dimensions are in centimeters.

23. (8)

24. (8)

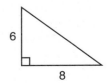

25. Find y.
(2)

Add, subtract, multiply, or divide as indicated:

26. $8\frac{1}{18} - 2\frac{1}{6} - 4\frac{1}{3}$
(1)

27. $3\frac{2}{3} \times 1\frac{4}{5} \times 2\frac{3}{11}$
(4)

28. $4.016 + 0.984$
(4)

29. $\dfrac{0.0832}{4.16}$
(4)

30. PR is $33\frac{1}{3}$ meters. PQ is $5\frac{5}{6}$ meters. Find QR.
(1)

LESSON 9 *Rules for Multiplication of Signed Numbers • Inverse Operations • Rules for Division of Signed Numbers • Summary*

9.A

rules for multiplication of signed numbers

The sum of three 2s is 6. Also the sum of two 3s is 6.

$$2 + 2 + 2 = 6 \qquad 3 + 3 = 6$$

We can get the same results from multiplication by writing

$$3 \cdot 2 = 6 \qquad \text{or} \qquad 2 \cdot 3 = 6$$

because multiplication is just a shorthand notation for repeated addition of the same numeral. Thus, if we wish to use the number line to explain the multiplication of $3 \cdot 2$, we can do it two ways. We can show the sum of two 3s or the sum of three 2s.

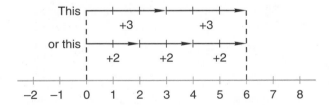

Now let us find the product of 2 and –3 on the number line. We can obtain the same answer by adding two –3s.

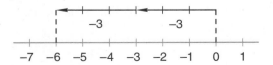

Thus we see that

$$(-3) + (-3) = -6 \qquad \text{so} \qquad 2 \cdot (-3) = -6$$

But now if we attempt to use the number line to show –3 times 2 by trying to draw –3 arrows that are +2 units long, we find that the task is impossible. We do not know how to draw –3 arrows because any number of arrows we draw will be a number greater than or equal to 1.

The number line was a useful graphic aid in understanding the concept of signed numbers and their algebraic addition but is of less help when discussing the multiplication or division of signed numbers, so we will not try to use it further for this purpose. Instead we will state the rules for multiplication and division of signed numbers and show some examples.

The three rules for multiplication of signed numbers are the following:

1. The product of two positive real numbers is a positive real number whose absolute value is the product of the absolute values of the two numbers. The following examples demonstrate this rule:

     (a) $(+3)(+4) = 12$ (b) $2(9) = 18$ (c) $4 \cdot 5 = 20$

2. The product of two signed real numbers that have opposite signs is a negative real number whose absolute value is the product of the absolute values of the two numbers. The following examples demonstrate this rule:

     (a) $(-2)(4) = -8$ (b) $6(-2) = -12$ (c) $(-3)(5) = -15$

3. The product of two negative real numbers is a positive real number whose absolute value is the product of the absolute values of the two numbers. The following examples demonstrate this rule:

     (a) $-2(-3) = 6$ (b) $(-5)(-3) = 15$ (c) $-4(-5) = 20$

9.B
inverse operations

If one operation will *undo* another operation, the two operations are called *inverse operations*. If we take a particular number and then add and subtract the same number, the result is the particular number itself. For example, if we begin with the number 7 and add 3 and then subtract 3, the result is 7.[†]

$$7 + 3 - 3 = 7$$

Thus addition and subtraction are inverse operations.

Multiplication and division are also inverse operations. If we multiply 7 by 2 and then divide by 2, the result is 7.

$$\frac{7 \cdot 2}{2} = 7$$

There has been no change since dividing by 2 *undoes* the effect of multiplying by 2.

Since multiplication and division are inverse operations, our rules for the multiplication and division of signed numbers must be stated in such a way that these operations are inverse operations.

9.C
rules for division of signed numbers

The four rules for division of signed numbers are the following:

1. If one positive real number is divided by another positive real number, the quotient is a positive real number whose absolute value is the quotient of the absolute values of the original numbers. The following examples demonstrate this rule:

     (a) $\dfrac{6}{3} = 2$ (b) $\dfrac{8}{2} = 4$ (c) $\dfrac{12}{4} = 3$

[†]Now we use algebraic addition instead of subtraction.

2. If a negative real number is divided by a positive real number, the quotient is a negative real number whose absolute value is the quotient of the absolute values of the original numbers. The following examples demonstrate this rule:

(a) $\dfrac{-6}{2} = -3$ (b) $\dfrac{-10}{5} = -2$ (c) $\dfrac{-12}{3} = -4$

3. If a positive real number is divided by a negative real number, the quotient is a negative real number whose absolute value is the quotient of the absolute values of the original numbers. The following examples demonstrate this rule:

(a) $\dfrac{6}{-2} = -3$ (b) $\dfrac{10}{-5} = -2$ (c) $\dfrac{12}{-3} = -4$

4. If one negative real number is divided by another negative real number, the quotient is a positive real number whose absolute value is the quotient of the absolute values of the original numbers. The following examples demonstrate this rule:

(a) $\dfrac{-6}{-3} = 2$ (b) $\dfrac{-8}{-2} = 4$ (c) $\dfrac{-12}{-4} = 3$

9.D
summary

We can consolidate all we have learned about the multiplication and division of signed numbers into two rules:

1. *Like signs.* **The product or the quotient of two signed numbers that have the same sign is a positive number whose absolute value is the absolute value of the product or the quotient of the absolute values of the original numbers.**

2. *Unlike signs.* **The product or the quotient of two signed numbers that have opposite signs is a negative number whose absolute value is the absolute value of the product or the quotient of the absolute values of the original numbers.**

We can state the rules above in a less rigorous but more easily remembered way if we say

---

IN BOTH MULTIPLICATION AND DIVISION

1. *Like* signs $\xrightarrow{yield}$ a positive number.

2. *Unlike* signs $\xrightarrow{yield}$ a negative number.

---

practice

Simplify the following expressions by using the rules for multiplication and division of signed numbers.

a. $-4(2)$ **b.** $3(-2)$ **c.** $-4(+3)$ **d.** $(-3)(-5)$

e. $\dfrac{4}{2}$ **f.** $\dfrac{-6}{3}$ **g.** $\dfrac{8}{-4}$ **h.** $\dfrac{-16}{-2}$

problem set 9

1. (a) Is the product or the quotient of two signed numbers that have the same sign a positive number or a negative number?

(b) Is the product or the quotient of two signed numbers that have opposite signs a positive number or a negative number?

2. (a) What is the additive inverse of 3?
(6,7)

(b) What is the additive inverse of –3?

(c) What is the sum of a real number and its additive inverse?

3. What is another name for the additive inverse of a number?
(6)

Simplify the following expressions by using the rules for multiplication and division of signed numbers.

4. (2)(5)   **5.** –5(+2)   **6.** 5(–2)
(9)   (9)   (9)

7. (–3)(–5)   **8.** –(2)(–3)   **9.** $\dfrac{6}{3}$
(9)   (9)   (9)

10. $\dfrac{-18}{3}$ **11.** $\dfrac{8}{-4}$ **12.** $\dfrac{-16}{-2}$
(9)   (9)   (9)

13. Use two unit multipliers to convert 320 centimeters to feet. (Go from centimeters to
(4)   inches to feet.)

14. Use two unit multipliers to convert 65 meters to inches. (Go from meters to centimeters
(4)   to inches.)

15. The perimeter of a rectangle is 40 inches. The width of the rectangle is 8 inches. Find the
(3)   length of the rectangle.

16. The area of a square is 9 square feet. What is the length of one side of the square?
(8)

17. The radius of a circle is 5 yards. Find the area of the circle.
(8)

Use the concept of opposites and algebraic addition to simplify the following. Use additional plus signs and brackets as required.

18. –6 – 4 – (3) – (–3) + 3   **19.** –6 + (–3) – [–(–2)] + 7
(7)   (7)

20. –|–6| – [–(–2)] + 5   **21.** –7 – 4 – (–3) + |–3|
(7)   (7)

22. –3 + (–3) – (–5) – |7| **23.** –|–5 + 3 – 2| + 2
(7)   (6)

Find the perimeter of each figure. Corners that look square are square. Dimensions are in centimeters.

24.
(3)

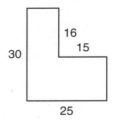

25.
(3)

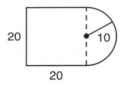

Find the area of each figure. Dimensions are in meters.

26.
(8)

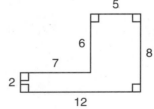

27.
(8)

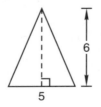

Simplify:

28. 52.3 – 15.26   **29.** 4.03 × 0.220
(4)   (4)

30. AC is $20\frac{5}{12}$ kilometers. BC is $6\frac{1}{4}$ kilometers. Find AB.
(1)

LESSON 10   *Division by Zero* • *Exchange of Factors in Multiplication* • *Conversions of Area*

10.A

division by zero

The operation of division is the inverse operation of the operation of multiplication, for division is defined as the process that will *undo* multiplication. Thus if $3 \times 2 = 6$, it is necessary that

$$\frac{6}{3} = 2 \quad \text{and} \quad \frac{6}{2} = 3$$

We will now use the same thought process to try to decide what the result will be if we divide a nonzero number by zero. We will use the example of 6 divided by 0.

$$\frac{6}{0} = ?$$

Since we say that division *undoes* multiplication, the multiplication that is to be undone by the above division must be

$$6 = ? \cdot 0$$

But the product of zero and any real number is zero—it is not 6. There is no number that we can substitute for ? so that the product of ? and 0 equals 6. Therefore, we say that since the multiplication does not exist that is to be undone by the division, the expression

$$\frac{6}{0}$$

has no meaning, or is **undefined.** A similar reasoning process is used to show that we cannot divide zero by zero, and we say that zero divided by zero is **indeterminate** rather than saying it is undefined. Thus indicated divisions such as

$$\frac{0}{0} \qquad \frac{142}{0} \qquad \frac{6}{0} \qquad \frac{-5}{0}$$

have no meaningful simplifications.

example 10.1   Evaluate: (a) $\dfrac{4 - 2 - 2}{13}$ (b) $\dfrac{13}{4 - 2 - 2}$

solution   (a) First we simplify the numerator.

$$\frac{4 - 2 - 2}{13} = \frac{0}{13} = \mathbf{0}$$

Zero over 13 is read as "zero thirteenths" and has a value of **zero. If the bottom of a fraction is not zero and the top is zero, the fraction equals zero.**

(b) $\dfrac{13}{4 - 2 - 2} = \dfrac{13}{0} = ?????$

The expression 13 over 0 has no meaning and thus has no value. **It does not have a value of infinity. It does not have a value of zero. The expression is undefined.**

10.B
exchange of factors in multiplication

In Lesson 5, we noted that we can change the order in which signed numbers are added without changing the answer. This is called the commutative property for addition. Now we note that the order of multiplying signed numbers does not affect the answer. This is called the **commutative property for multiplication.**

COMMUTATIVE PROPERTY FOR MULTIPLICATION

The order in which two real numbers are multiplied does not affect the product. For example,

$$4 \cdot 3 = 12 \quad \text{and} \quad 3 \cdot 4 = 12$$

The order in which signed numbers are multiplied does not affect the value of the product! This property can be used to show that any number of numbers can be multiplied in any order and the answer will be the same every time.

example 10.2   Find the product: $-4(3)(-6)(-2)$

solution

$$-4(3)(-6)(-2) \qquad \text{given}$$
$$-12(-6)(-2) \qquad \text{multiplied } -4 \text{ by } 3$$
$$72(-2) \qquad \text{multiplied } -12 \text{ by } -6$$
$$\mathbf{-144} \qquad \text{multiplied } 72 \text{ by } -2$$

In the first step, we multiplied -4 by 3 to get -12. In the second step, we multiplied -12 by -6 to get $+72$, which we multiplied by -2 to get the final result of -144.

example 10.3   Find the product: $-6(-2)(3)(-4)$

solution

$$-6(-2)(3)(-4) \qquad \text{given}$$
$$12(3)(-4) \qquad \text{multiplied } -6 \text{ by } -2$$
$$36(-4) \qquad \text{multiplied } 12 \text{ by } 3$$
$$\mathbf{-144} \qquad \text{multiplied } 36 \text{ by } -4$$

example 10.4   Find the product: $-6(-4)(3)(-2)$

solution

$$-6(-4)(3)(-2) \qquad \text{given}$$
$$24(3)(-2) \qquad \text{multiplied } -6 \text{ by } -4$$
$$72(-2) \qquad \text{multiplied } 24 \text{ by } 3$$
$$\mathbf{-144} \qquad \text{multiplied } 72 \text{ by } -2$$

In each of the three preceding examples, the same factors were multiplied, but the order of multiplication was different. The product was -144, however, regardless of the order of the factors.

10.C

conversions of area

In this section we will use unit multipliers to convert area measurements.

example 10.5   Use two unit multipliers to convert 44 square inches to square centimeters.

solution   We will write 44 in.^{2} as 44 in. · in. Therefore, we have

$$44 \cancel{\text{in.}} \cdot \cancel{\text{in.}} \times \frac{2.54 \text{ cm}}{1 \cancel{\text{in.}}} \times \frac{2.54 \text{ cm}}{1 \cancel{\text{in.}}} = \mathbf{44(2.54)(2.54)cm^2}$$

example 10.6   Use four unit multipliers to convert 125 square centimeters to square feet.

solution   We will write 125 cm^2 as 125 cm · cm. Therefore, we have

$$125 \cancel{\text{cm}} \cdot \cancel{\text{cm}} \times \frac{1 \cancel{\text{in.}}}{2.54 \cancel{\text{cm}}} \times \frac{1 \cancel{\text{in.}}}{2.54 \cancel{\text{cm}}} \times \frac{1 \text{ ft}}{12 \cancel{\text{in.}}} \times \frac{1 \text{ ft}}{12 \cancel{\text{in.}}} = \frac{125}{(2.54)(2.54)(12)(12)} \text{ ft}^2$$

practice   Simplify:

a. $\dfrac{-3 - 2}{-2 + 8 - 6}$

b. $\dfrac{-8 + 6 + 2}{8 - 4 - 4}$

c. $-(-4)(-1)(-4)$

d. $2(-6)(10)(-2)$

e.   Use two unit multipliers to convert 44 square miles to square feet.

f.   Use two unit multipliers to convert 3500 square centimeters to square meters.

problem set 10

1.   What property of multiplication states that the order in which two real numbers are
(10)   multiplied does not affect the product?

2.   (a)   What operation is the inverse operation of addition?
(9)
     (b)   What operation is the inverse operation of subtraction?

     (c)   What operation is the inverse operation of multiplication?

     (d)   What operation is the inverse operation of division?

3.   (a)   What is the additive inverse of $\frac{1}{3}$?
(6,7)
     (b)   What is the additive inverse of $-\frac{1}{3}$?

     (c)   What is the sum of a real number and its additive inverse?

4.   What is another name for the additive inverse of a number?
(6)

Simplify:

5. $-2(3)(4)$
(10)

6. $-4(3)(-2)$
(10)

7. $4(-3)(-4)$
(10)

8. $\dfrac{-2 + 3}{4 - 5 + 3}$
(10)

9. $\dfrac{4 + 7 - 6}{2 + 7 - 3}$
(10)

10. $\dfrac{-3 + 6 - 1}{-2 + 4 - 2}$
(10)

11.   Use one unit multiplier to convert 50 inches to centimeters.
(4)

12. Use two unit multipliers to convert 48 square inches to square centimeters.
(10)

13. The perimeter of a rectangle is 28 centimeters. Two of the sides are each 9 centimeters
(3) long. What is the length of each of the other two sides?

14. The length of a rectangle is 15 meters. The width of the rectangle is 8 meters. Find the
(8) area of the rectangle.

15. The diameter of a circle is 16 inches. Find the circumference of the circle.
(3)

16. The radius of a circle is 6 feet. Find the area of the circle.
(8)

Simplify:

17. $\dfrac{-8}{2}$
(9)

18. $\dfrac{9}{-3}$
(9)

19. $3 - (-4) + (-3) - (-4)$
(7)

20. $-[-(-4)] - (-3) + 2$
(7)

21. $-|-3 - 2| + (-5)$
(6)

22. $-\{-[-(-2)]\} - |-4 - 2|$
(7)

23. $3 - |-2 - 3| + (-6) - (-3)$
(7)

24. Find the perimeter of this figure. All
(3) angles are right angles. Dimensions
are in yards.

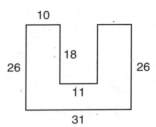

Find the area of each figure. Dimensions are in centimeters.

25.
(8)

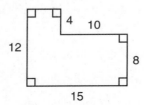

26.
(8)

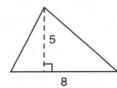

27.
(8)

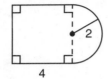

Simplify:

28. $\dfrac{3\frac{3}{5}}{2\frac{7}{10}}$
(4)

29. $0.008484 \div 0.0028$
(4)

30. The length of $\overline{XY}$ is $3\frac{8}{21}$ meters. The length of $\overline{YZ}$ is $3\frac{2}{7}$ meters. Find XZ.
(1)

LESSON *11*   *Reciprocal and Multiplicative Inverse • Order of Operations • Identifying Multiplication and Addition*

11.A
reciprocal and multiplicative inverse

If one fraction is the inverted form of another fraction, each of the fractions is said to be the **reciprocal** of the other fraction.

$$\frac{2}{3} \qquad \text{is the reciprocal of} \qquad \frac{3}{2}$$

$$\frac{3}{2} \qquad \text{is the reciprocal of} \qquad \frac{2}{3}$$

$$-\frac{4}{11} \qquad \text{is the reciprocal of} \qquad -\frac{11}{4}$$

$$-\frac{11}{4} \qquad \text{is the reciprocal of} \qquad -\frac{4}{11}$$

Since numbers such as 4 can also be written in a form such as $\frac{4}{1}$, these numbers also have reciprocals.

$$\frac{1}{4} \qquad \text{is the reciprocal of} \qquad 4$$

$$4 \qquad \text{is the reciprocal of} \qquad \frac{1}{4}$$

$$-5 \qquad \text{is the reciprocal of} \qquad -\frac{1}{5}$$

$$-\frac{1}{5} \qquad \text{is the reciprocal of} \qquad -5$$

The number zero does not have a reciprocal because if we try to write the reciprocal of zero we get

$$\frac{1}{0} \qquad \text{(meaningless)}$$

which we say is a meaningless notation because division by zero is undefined. **Zero is the only real number that does not have a reciprocal.** The reciprocal of a number is often called the **multiplicative inverse** of the number.

DEFINITION OF RECIPROCAL OR MULTIPLICATIVE INVERSE

For any nonzero real number a, the reciprocal, or multiplicative inverse, of the number is $\frac{1}{a}$.

If a number is multiplied by its reciprocal (its multiplicative inverse), the product is the number 1. Thus

$$4 \cdot \frac{1}{4} = 1 \qquad -5 \cdot \frac{1}{-5} = 1 \qquad \text{and} \qquad -\frac{1}{13} \cdot (-13) = 1$$

This simple fact is of great importance and will be very useful in the solutions of equations, a topic that will be discussed in later lessons.

11.B
order of operations

If we wish to compute the value of

$$4 + 3 \cdot 2$$

we have a problem. It appears that there are two possible solutions.

(a) $4 + 3 \cdot 2$

Here we will first multiply 3 by 2 to get

$$4 + 6$$

and then add to get 10.

$$4 + 6 = 10$$

(b) $4 + 3 \cdot 2$

Here we will first add 4 and 3 to get 7

$$7 \cdot 2$$

and then multiply to get 14.

$$7 \cdot 2 = 14$$

We worked the problem two ways and got two different answers. **Neither way is necessarily more correct than the other, but since there are two possible ways to work the problem, mathematicians have found it necessary to agree on one way so that everyone will get the same answer. They have agreed to do the multiplications first and then to do the additions.** Thus, to simplify an expression such as

$$4 \cdot 3 + 5 - 6 + 4 - 3 \cdot 5 + 6 - 4 \cdot 2$$

we will use a two-step process. First we will perform all the multiplications and get

$$12 + 5 - 6 + 4 - 15 + 6 - 8$$

Now we will do the algebraic additions.

$17 - 6 + 4 - 15 + 6 - 8$	added 12 and 5
$11 + 4 - 15 + 6 - 8$	added 17 and -6
$15 - 15 + 6 - 8$	added 11 and 4
$0 + 6 - 8$	added 15 and -15
-2	added 6 and -8

example 11.1 Simplify: $4 \cdot 3 + 2 + (-3)5$

solution We perform the multiplications first and get

$$12 + 2 - 15$$

which we now add algebraically.

$$12 + 2 - 15 = \mathbf{-1}$$

example 11.2 Simplify: $-5(2) - 3 + 6(3)$

solution We perform the two multiplications first

$$-10 - 3 + 18$$

and now add to get **5**.

example 11.3 Simplify: $4 \cdot 3 - 2 \cdot 5 + 6 - 5 \cdot 2$

solution

$12 - 10 + 6 - 10$	performed multiplications
-2	added algebraically

11.C

identifying multiplication and addition

When confronted with an expression such as

$$4 - 3(5) - 7(-6) - (4)(-5)$$

the beginner often has difficulty telling whether quantities are to be added or multiplied. There is an easy way to identify indicated multiplication. **If there is no + or − sign between symbols, multiplication is indicated.** Let us simplify the expression above from left to right by first performing the indicated multiplications. The first place where there is no sign between the symbols is between the 3 and the parentheses enclosing the 5. The second place is between the 7 and the parentheses enclosing the −6, and the third place is between the parentheses enclosing both the 4 and the −5.

$$4 - 3(5) - 7(-6) - (4)(-5)$$

The places where multiplication is indicated are designated by arrows. If we perform the indicated multiplications, we have

$$4 - 15 - (-42) - (-20)$$

Now we can simplify this expression and add.

$$4 - 15 + 42 + 20 = 51$$

practice Simplify. Remember that multiplication is done before addition.

a. $6 \cdot 3 - 4(5)(6)$

b. $3 \cdot 5 + 2 + 4(-2)$

c. $2 \cdot 4 - 3 \cdot 2 - 7 + 5 \cdot 2$

d. $13 - 4(-5) - 3(10)$

problem set 11

1.
(11)
(a) What is the reciprocal of 2?

(b) What is the reciprocal of −2?

(c) What is the product of any nonzero real number and its reciprocal?

2. What is another name for the reciprocal of a number?
(11)

3. Which real number does not have a reciprocal and why?
(11)

4. Is the product of two negative numbers always a positive number?
(9)

5. What is an acute angle?
(2)

6. What is an obtuse angle?
(2)

7. Use one unit multiplier to convert 25 meters to centimeters.
(4)

8. Use two unit multipliers to convert 40 square meters to square centimeters.
(10)

9. The perimeter of a square is 49 inches. What is the length of one side of the square?
(3)

10. The area of a square is 16 square feet. What is the length of one side of the square?
(8)

11. The diameter of a circle is 14 yards. Find the area of the circle.
(8)

Simplify. Remember that multiplication is done before addition.

12. $6 - 8 + 2(3)$
(11)

13. $-2 - 3(+6)$
(11)

14. $3 - 2 \cdot 4 + 3 \cdot 2$
(11)

15. $-3(-2)(-3) - 2$
(11)

16. $-4(-3) + (-2)(-5)$
(11)

17. $-2 - 2(-2) + (-2)(-2)$
(11)

18. $(-5) - (-5) + 2(-2) + 4$
(11)

19. $-3 - (-2) + (-3) - 2(-2)$
(11)

20. $(-2)(-2)(-2) - |-8|$
(11)

21. $-(-5) + (-2) + (-5)|-3|$
(11)

22. $4 + |-3 - 1| + (-3) - (-2)$
(7)

23. $3(-2) - |-3 + 6| + 9 - 7(-2)$
(11)

24. $\dfrac{-3 + 5}{4 - 6 + 5}$
(10)

25. $\dfrac{-6 + 4 + 2}{-2 + 5 + 3}$
(10)

26. Find the perimeter of this figure. Cor-
(3)   ners that look square are square.
      Dimensions are in centimeters.

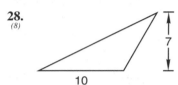

Find the area of each figure. Dimensions are in meters.

27.
(8)

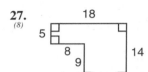

28.
(8)

29. Find the area of the shaded portion of
(8)   this figure. All angles are right angles.
      Dimensions are in inches.

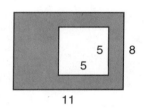

30. AB is $8\frac{3}{10}$ feet. AC is $26\frac{1}{2}$ feet. Find BC.
(1)

LESSON 12   *Symbols of Inclusion • Order of Operations*

12.A
symbols of inclusion

In Lesson 11 we found that the simplification of

$$4 + 3 \cdot 2$$

is 10 because we have agreed to do the multiplication first and then do the addition. So,

$$4 + 3 \cdot 2 = 4 + 6 = 10$$

Parentheses, brackets, braces, and bars are all called **symbols of inclusion,** and can be used to help us emphasize the meaning of our notation. Using these symbols, the notation above could be written in any of the following ways:

(a) $4 + (3 \cdot 2)$ (b) $4 + [3 \cdot 2]$ (c) $4 + \{3 \cdot 2\}$ (d) $4 + \overline{3 \cdot 2}$

Each of the notations emphasizes that 3 is to be multiplied by 2 and that 4 is to be added to this product. A further benefit of the use of symbols of inclusion is that a nonstandard order of operations can be indicated. For example, we can use parentheses to indicate that 4 is to be added to 3 and the result multiplied by 2 by writing

$$2(3 + 4) \quad \text{or} \quad (3 + 4)2$$

While braces and bars can be used as indicated on the previous page, we normally reserve the use of braces to indicate a set, and bars are most often used as fraction lines, as shown here.

$$\frac{4 + (3 \cdot 2)}{5(2 - 3)} = \frac{4 + 6}{5(-1)} = \frac{10}{-5} = -2$$

The parentheses in the numerator are used to emphasize that 4 is to be added to the product of 3 and 2, and the parentheses in the denominator are used to designate that 5 is to be multiplied by the algebraic sum of 2 and –3.

12.B

order of operations

To simplify numerical expressions that contain symbols of inclusion, we begin by simplifying within the symbols of inclusion. Then we simplify the resulting expression, remembering that multiplication is performed before addition.

example 12.1   Simplify: $4(3 + 2) - 5(6 - 3)$

solution   First we will simplify within the parentheses.

$$4(5) - 5(3) \qquad \text{simplified within parentheses}$$
$$20 - 15 \qquad \text{multiplied}$$
$$\mathbf{5} \qquad \text{added algebraically}$$

example 12.2   Simplify: $-3(2 - 3 + 5) - 6(4 + 2) - 3$

solution   First we simplify within the parentheses, then multiply, and finish by adding.

$$-3(4) - 6(6) - 3 \qquad \text{simplified within parentheses}$$
$$-12 - 36 - 3 \qquad \text{multiplied}$$
$$\mathbf{-51} \qquad \text{added algebraically}$$

example 12.3   Simplify: $-2(-3 - 3)(-2 - 4) - (-3 - 2) + 3(4 - 2)$

solution   We begin by simplifying within the parentheses.

$$-2(-6)(-6) - (-5) + 3(2) \qquad \text{simplified within parentheses}$$
$$-72 + 5 + 6 \qquad \text{multiplied}$$
$$\mathbf{-61} \qquad \text{added algebraically}$$

When the expression is in the form of a fraction, we begin by simplifying both the numerator and the denominator. Then we have our choice of dividing or leaving the result in the form of a fraction.

example 12.4   Simplify: $\dfrac{5(-5 + 3) + 7(-5 + 9) + 2}{(4 - 2) + 3 + 5}$

solution   First we will simplify the numerator and the denominator.

$$\frac{5(-2) + 7(4) + 2}{2 + 3 + 5} \qquad \text{simplified within parentheses}$$

$$\frac{-10 + 28 + 2}{2 + 3 + 5} \qquad \text{multiplied}$$

$$\frac{20}{10} \qquad \text{added algebraically}$$

$$\mathbf{2} \qquad \text{divided}$$

example 12.5   Simplify: $\dfrac{-3(4 - 2) - (-5)}{4 - (3)(-3)}$

solution   First we will simplify the numerator and the denominator.

$$\dfrac{-3(2) + 5}{4 - (3)(-3)}$$ simplified within parentheses

$$\dfrac{-6 + 5}{4 + 9}$$ multiplied

$$\dfrac{-1}{13}$$ added algebraically

$$-\dfrac{1}{13}$$ this does not divide evenly, and we will leave it in fractional form

practice   Simplify:

a. $(-3 - 2)(-4 - 1)$

b. $(6 - 2) - (4 - 6)$

c. $-5(-3 - 3) + 2(1 - 3)$

d. $\dfrac{-3(10 - 8) - (-4)}{4 - 3(-3) - 13}$

problem set 12

1. (11) (a)   What is the reciprocal of $\frac{1}{2}$?

(b)   What is the reciprocal of $-\frac{1}{2}$?

(c)   What is the product of any nonzero real number and its reciprocal?

2. (11)   What is another name for the reciprocal of a number?

3. (11)   Which real number does not have a reciprocal and why?

4. (6)   Is the sum of a positive number and a negative number always a negative number?

5. (2) (a)   What is the degree measure of a right angle?

(b)   What is the degree measure of a straight angle?

(c)   How many degrees are in a circle?

6. (4)   Use two unit multipliers to convert 80 feet to centimeters.

7. (10)   Use two unit multipliers to convert 12 square feet to square inches.

8. (8)   The area of a rectangle is 18 square centimeters. The length of the rectangle is 6 centimeters. Find the width of the rectangle.

9. (3)   The circumference of a circle is 6π meters. Find the radius of the circle.

Simplify:

10. (12) $(-4 + 7) + (-3 - 2)$

11. (12) $(-3 - 2) - (-6 + 2)$

12. (12) $(-2 - 2)(-3 - 4)$

13. (12) $4(8 + 4) + 7(10 - 8)$

14. (12) $5(9 + 2) - (-4)(5 + 1)$

15. (12) $-3(-6 - 2) + 3(-2 + 5)$

16. (12) $-2(-5 - 7) - 3(-8 + 2)$

17. (12) $(-3 - 2)(-2)(-2 - 2)$

18. (12) $(6 - 2)(-3 - 5) - (-5)$

19. (11) $-8 - 4 - (-2) - (+2)(-3)$

20. (12) $\dfrac{1}{4}(8 - 4) - 5(8 - 2) - 2$

21. (12) $5(12 + 2) - 6(-3 + 8) - (2 + 3)$

22. $(2 - 3)(-8 + 2) + |-3 + 5|$
(12)

23. $-|-2 - 5 + 3|(5 - 2)$
(12)

24. $4 - \dfrac{(+12)}{(-3)} + 2$
(12)

25. $\dfrac{-4(5 - 2) - (-8)}{3 - (-3)(3)}$
(12)

26. Find the perimeter of this figure. Cor-
(3)   ners that look square are square.
       Dimensions are in kilometers.

Find the area of each figure. Corners that look square are square. Dimensions are in inches.

27.
(8)

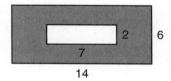

28.
(8)

29. Find the area of the shaded portion of
(8)   this figure. All angles are right angles.
       Dimensions are in feet.

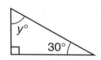

30. Find y.
(2)

LESSON 13   *Multiple Symbols of Inclusion • More on Order of Operations • Products of Signed Numbers*

13.A

**multiple
symbols of
inclusion**

Often we encounter expressions such as

$$-3[(-2 - 4) - 3] - 2$$

where symbols of inclusion are within other symbols of inclusion. We simplify these expressions by beginning with the innermost symbol of inclusion and working our way out. Here we will simplify within the parentheses and then within the brackets.

$-3[(-6) - 3] - 2$	simplified within parentheses
$-3[-9] - 2$	simplified within brackets
$27 - 2$	multiplied
25	added

example 13.1   Simplify: $4\{2[(-3-2)(-7+4)-5]\}-2$

solution   We will begin on the inside with the parentheses and work our way out.

$$4\{2[(-5)(-3)-5]\}-2 \qquad \text{simplified within parentheses}$$

$$4\{2[10]\}-2 \qquad \text{simplified within brackets}$$

$$4\{20\}-2 \qquad \text{simplified within braces}$$

$$80-2 \qquad \text{multiplied}$$

$$\mathbf{78} \qquad \text{added}$$

example 13.2   Simplify: $\dfrac{-3\{[(-2-3)][-2]\}}{-3(4-2)}$

solution   First we will simplify the numerator and the denominator. Then we will divide as the last step.

$$\frac{-3\{[(-5)][-2]\}}{-3(2)} \qquad \text{simplified within parentheses}$$

$$\frac{-3\{10\}}{-3(2)} \qquad \text{simplified within braces}$$

$$\frac{-30}{-6} \qquad \text{multiplied}$$

$$\mathbf{5} \qquad \text{divided}$$

13.B

more on order of operations

In the discussion of the order of operations in Lesson 11 we said that mathematicians have agreed that when they write

$$4 \cdot 3 + 2$$

the **multiplication should be done first** and then the addition.

$$12 + 2 \qquad \text{multiplied}$$

$$14 \qquad \text{added}$$

We did not discuss division because if symbols of inclusion are properly used, the order in which division is to be performed is apparent.

If we write

$$\frac{4 \cdot 3 + 2}{-7 + 5}$$

we find the value of the numerator and the value of the denominator and then divide.

$$\frac{14}{-2} = -7$$

If the following problem is encountered, however,

$$4 + \frac{14}{2} - 3 \cdot 6$$

the notation clearly indicates that only 14 is to be divided by 2, and if we do this first, we get

$$4 + 7 - 3 \cdot 6$$

Now we do the multiplication and conclude with algebraic addition.

$$4 + 7 - 18$$

$$11 - 18$$

$$-7$$

At this point in an algebra book, however, it is customary to give a rule for finding the number represented by

$$6 + 3 \cdot 6 \div 2 - 6 \cdot 2$$

The rule is to perform the operations from left to right in the following order:

1. Multiplication and division
2. Algebraic addition

First we will go through the problem from **left to right,** performing the multiplications and divisions **in the order in which they are encountered.**

$6 + 3 \cdot 6 \div 2 - 6 \cdot 2$	original problem
$6 + 18 \div 2 - 6 \cdot 2$	multiplied 3 times 6
$6 + 9 - 6 \cdot 2$	divided 18 by 2
$6 + 9 - 12$	multiplied 6 times 2

Now we go through the problem again from left to right, performing the algebraic additions as they are encountered.

$6 + 9 - 12$	from above
$15 - 12$	added 6 and 9
3	added 15 and −12

If symbols of inclusion had been properly used, instead of stating the problem as

$$6 + 3 \cdot 6 \div 2 - 6 \cdot 2$$

the problem would have been written as follows:

$$6 + \frac{(3 \cdot 6)}{2} - (6 \cdot 2)$$

and here the method of solution is clearly indicated. We simplify within the parentheses as the first step.

$6 + \dfrac{18}{2} - 12$	simplified within parentheses
$6 + 9 - 12$	divided 18 by 2
$15 - 12$	added 6 and 9
3	added 15 and −12

We will use symbols of inclusion to include the use of a bar as a fraction line when stating problems. Thus problems such as the one just discussed will not be encountered again in this book.

13.C

**products of
signed
numbers**

Let us review the concept of the opposite of a number by watching the pattern that develops here.

	READ AS	WHICH IS
2	2	2
–2	the opposite of 2	–2
–(–2)	the opposite of the opposite of 2	2
–[–(–2)]	the opposite of the opposite of the opposite of 2	–2
–{–[–(–2)]}	the opposite of the opposite of the opposite of the opposite of 2	2

The expressions in the left-hand column are all equivalent expressions for 2 or for –2. If we look at the right-hand column, we see that every time an additional (–) is included in the left-hand expression, the right-hand expression changes sign.

A similar alternation in sign occurs whenever a particular number is multiplied by a negative number. For instance,

$$-2 = -2$$

$$(-2)(-2) = +4$$

$$(-2)(-2)(-2) = -8$$

$$(-2)(-2)(-2)(-2) = +16$$

$$(-2)(-2)(-2)(-2)(-2) = -32$$

The numbers on the right have different absolute values, but they *alternate in sign*. We note that

The product of **two** negative factors is **positive.**

The product of **three** negative factors is **negative.**

The product of **four** negative factors is **positive.**

The product of **five** negative factors is **negative.**

Without proof, we will generalize these observations.

1. **The product of an even number of negative real numbers is a positive
   real number.**
2. **The product of an odd number of negative real numbers is a negative
   real number.**

We can use these observations to determine the sign of the product of several signed numbers. Let us consider

$$(4)(-3)(-4)(-2)(11) = ?$$

Here we have +4 and +11 as two of the five factors. Since multiplication by a positive number does not affect the sign of the product, we will not consider these numbers. The other three factors are negative. We can look at the rules stated previously and see that the sign of the product of three negative numbers is negative. Thus our answer can be expressed as

$$-(4 \cdot 3 \cdot 4 \cdot 2 \cdot 11) = -1056$$

example 13.3 Determine the signs of the following products and give the reasons. Do not do the multiplications.

(a) $(-4)(-3)(2)(+5)(+6)$

(b) $(3)(+2)(6)$

(c) $(-3)(-2)(6)(4)(-2)$

(d) $(-3)(-2)(-5)(-7)(-2)$

(e) $(-3)(-4)(-2) + 2(-3)$

solution

		SIGN	REASON
(a)	$(-4)(-3)(2)(+5)(+6)$	**positive**	Even number of negative factors
(b)	$(3)(+2)(6)$	**positive**	No negative factors
(c)	$(-3)(-2)(6)(4)(-2)$	**negative**	Odd number of negative factors
(d)	$(-3)(-2)(-5)(-7)(-2)$	**negative**	Odd number of negative factors
(e)	$(-3)(-4)(-2) + 2(-3)$	?	Rule does not apply, as this is an indicated *sum*. We will do the problem in three steps.
	1. $(-3)(-4)(-2)$	negative	Odd number of negative factors
	2. $2(-3)$	negative	Odd number of negative factors
	3. $-(3)(4)(2) - (2)(3)$	**negative**	Algebraic sum of two negative numbers is a negative number

practice Simplify:

a. $3\{2[(-4-3)(-8-2)-4]\}$

b. $\dfrac{-3\{[(-4-1)3]-5\}}{2(4-7)}$

c. $(-2)(-2)(-3)(-3)$

d. $-\{-[-(-2)]\}$

e. Is the following product a positive number or negative number? Do not multiply. Give the reason.

$$4(-3)(5)(-4)(-3)(-7)(-21)(5)(14)(-5)(-8)$$

problem set 13

1. (13) Is the product of 5 negative numbers and 2 positive numbers a positive number or a negative number?

2. (11) (a) What is the multiplicative inverse of 3?

(b) What is the multiplicative inverse of –3?

(c) What is the product of any nonzero real number and its multiplicative inverse?

3. (11) What is another name for the multiplicative inverse of a number?

4. (11) Which real number does not have a multiplicative inverse and why?

5. (2) What do you call polygons in which all sides have the same length?

6. (4) Use two unit multipliers to convert 60 miles to inches.

7. (10) Use two unit multipliers to convert 125 square miles to square feet.

8. (8) The area of a rectangle is 35 square centimeters. The width of the rectangle is 5 centimeters. Find the length of the rectangle.

9. The diameter of a circle is 6 meters. Find the area of the circle.
(8)

Simplify:

10. $-[-(-2)]$
(7,13)

11. $-\{-[-(-3)]\}$
(7,13)

12. $(-3 - 2) - (5 + 2)$
(12)

13. $(-3 + 5)(2 - 3)$
(12)

14. $-2(-6 - 3) + \dfrac{0}{5}$
(12)

15. $-2 + (-2) - (-4)5$
(11)

16. $-3 - (2) + (-2) - (-3)(-2)$
(11)

17. $-5(-3 - 2) + (-2) - (-3 - 4)$
(12)

18. $(-2)(-3)(-4 + 2) - (3 + 1)$
(12)

19. $-2 - (-2) - |-2|(2)$
(12)

20. $\dfrac{-6}{-10} + (-3)(-2) + 3|-4 - 2|$
(13)

21. $(-7) - [-(-2)]5$
(13)

22. $-3 - [-(-2)] + (-3)(5)$
(13)

23. $\dfrac{-2(-6) - 2}{-3 + (-7 + 2)}$
(12)

24. $\dfrac{4 + 2 - 3(2)}{3(2) - 6}$
(10)

25. Find the perimeter of this figure. All
(3) angles are right angles. Dimensions
are in inches.

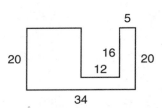

Find the area of each figure. Corners that look square are square. Dimensions are in feet.

26.
(8)

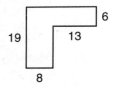

27.
(8)

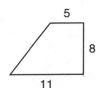

28.
(8)

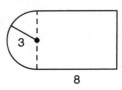

29. Find the area of the shaded portion of
(8) this rectangle. Dimensions are in yards.

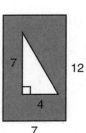

30. *EF* is $4\frac{2}{15}$ miles. *DF* is $15\frac{4}{5}$ miles. Find *DE*.
(1)

LESSON 14   *Evaluation of Algebraic Expressions*

In Lesson 4, we said that a **number** is an **idea** and that when we wish to write down something to represent this **idea,** we use a **numeral.** If we wish to bring to mind the number 7, we could write any of the following:

$$7 \qquad \frac{14}{2} \qquad 4 + 3 \qquad \frac{-21}{-3} \qquad 2 + 2 + 2 + 1$$

We call each of these notations a **numerical expression** or just a **numeral.** Every numerical expression represents only one number and we call this number the **value** of the expression. Each of the numerical expressions shown above has a **value** of 7.

In algebra we often use letters to represent numbers. When letters as well as numbers are used in an expression, we do not call the expression a numerical expression but we call it by the more general name of **algebraic expression** or **mathematical expression.** These words are used to describe expressions that contain only numbers or only letters or contain both numbers and letters.

If we write the algebraic expression

$$4 + x$$

the algebraic expression has a **value** that depends on the value that we assign to x. If we give x a value of 5, then the algebraic expression has a value of 9 because

$$4 + 5 = 9$$

If we give x a value of 11, then the algebraic expression has a value of 15 because

$$4 + 11 = 15$$

Because the value assigned to x can be changed or varied, we call letters such as x **variables.** We also call the letters **unknowns** since they represent unknown or unspecified numbers. The numeral 4 in this example does not change value and has a constant value of 4. For this reason the symbol that we use to denote a number is called a **constant.**

When we use variables in algebraic expressions, the notations that we use to indicate the operations of division and algebraic addition are the same as the notations that we use to indicate the division and algebraic addition of real numbers. The notation for the multiplication of variables is sometimes slightly different. We can denote that we wish to multiply 4 by the variable x by writing any of the following:

(a) $4x$ (b) $4(x)$ (c) $(4)(x)$ (d) $4 \cdot x$ (e) $(4) \cdot (x)$

The notations (b) through (e) are the same as the notations that we use for real number multiplication, but the notation shown in (a) is different from the real number notation.

$\qquad\qquad 4x \qquad$ indicates that 4 is to be multiplied by the value of x

whereas

$\qquad\qquad 45 \qquad$ does not indicate that 4 is to be multiplied by 5, but instead
$\qquad\qquad\qquad$ is a numeral that represents the number 45

Thus the algebraic expression xym indicates that the values of x, y, and m are to be multiplied. If we give x a value of 1, y a value of 2, and m a value of 3, the value of the algebraic expression xym can be found.

$$1 \cdot 2 \cdot 3 = 6$$

If we write the algebraic expression

$$4x + mx$$

we indicate that 4 is to be multiplied by the value of x and that the value of m is to be multiplied by the value of x and that the two products are to be added. If we give x a value of 3 and m a value of 5, then we can find the value of the algebraic expression.

$$4 \cdot 3 + 5 \cdot 3$$
$$12 + 15 \quad = 27$$

Thus the value of the algebraic expression when x equals 3 and m equals 5 is 27.

If we give x the value of 2 and m the value of 6, then the algebraic expression will have a different value.

$$4x + mx = 4 \cdot 2 + 6 \cdot 2 = 8 + 12 = 20$$

In this case, the value of the algebraic expression is 20.

It is of **utmost importance** to note that in the first case, when we gave x a value of 3, the value of x everywhere in the algebraic expression was 3. When we gave x a value of 2, the value of x everywhere in the algebraic expression was 2. **While the values assigned to variables may change or be changed, under any set of conditions the value assigned to a particular variable in an algebraic expression is the same value throughout the algebraic expression. Also, when we begin solving equations and working problems, we must remember that the value assigned to any particular variable under any set of conditions must be the same value regardless of where the particular variable appears in the equation or the problem.**

example 14.1   Find the value of: xmp if $x = 4$, $m = 5$, and $p = 2$

solution   We replace x with 4, m with 5, and p with 2.

$$xmp = 4 \cdot 5 \cdot 2 = 20 \cdot 2 = \mathbf{40}$$

example 14.2   Evaluate (find the value of): $4yz - 5$ if $y = 2$ and $z = 10$

solution   We replace y with 2 and z with 10 and then simplify.

$$4yz - 5 = 4(2)(10) - 5 = 80 - 5 = \mathbf{75}$$

example 14.3   Evaluate: $y - z$ if $y = -2$ and $z = -6$

solution   We replace y with -2 and $-z$ with $+6$ since $-z$ represents the opposite of z.

$$y - z = -2 + 6 = \mathbf{+4}$$

example 14.4   Evaluate: $-a - b - ab$ if $a = -3$ and $b = -4$

solution   The value of a is -3, so the opposite of a is 3. The value of b is -4, so the opposite of b is 4. Finally, $ab = 12$ and the opposite of this is -12. Thus, we get -5 for an answer.

$$3 + 4 - 12 = \mathbf{-5}$$

example 14.5   Evaluate: $-x - (-a + b)$ if $x = 2$, $a = -4$, and $b = -6$

solution   Some people find that it is helpful to replace each variable with parentheses. Then the proper number is written inside the parentheses.

$$-(\ ) - [-(\ ) + (\ )] \qquad \text{replaced variables with parentheses}$$
$$-(2) - [-(-4) + (-6)] \qquad \text{numbers inserted}$$

The first entry can be read as the opposite of 2, or –2. Inside the brackets we have –(–4), read "the opposite of the opposite of 4," which is 4 itself. The last entry inside the brackets is +(–6), read "plus the opposite of 6," which is the same as –6. Thus we have

$$-2 - (4 - 6) = -2 - (-2) = -2 + 2 = \mathbf{0}$$

example 14.6   Evaluate: $x - y(-a + x)$ if $x = -2$, $y = +3$, and $a = -4$

solution   We will replace each variable with parentheses.

$$(\ ) - (\ )[-(\ ) + (\ )]$$ replaced variables with parentheses

$$(-2) - (+3)[-(-4) + (-2)]$$ numbers inserted

$$= -2 - (3)(4 - 2) = -2 - (3)(2)$$ simplified

$$= -2 - 6 = \mathbf{-8}$$ simplified

example 14.7   Evaluate: $-(m + x)(-a + mx)$ if $m = 2$, $x = -3$, and $a = -4$

solution   We will replace each variable with parentheses.

$$-[(\ ) + (\ )][-(\ ) + (\ )(\ )]$$ replaced variables with parentheses

$$-[(2) + (-3)][-(-4) + (2)(-3)]$$ numbers inserted

$$= -(2 - 3)[4 + (-6)] = -(-1)(4 - 6)$$ simplified

$$= -(-1)(-2) = -(2) = \mathbf{-2}$$ simplified

example 14.8   Evaluate: $-xa(x - a) + a$ if $a = -2$ and $x = 4$

solution   We will replace each variable with parentheses.

$$-(\ )(\ )[(\ ) - (\ )] + (\ )$$ replaced variables with parentheses

$$-(4)(-2)[(4) - (-2)] + (-2)$$ numbers inserted

$$= -(-8)(4 + 2) - 2 = 8(6) - 2$$ simplified

$$= 48 - 2 = \mathbf{46}$$ simplified

practice   Evaluate:

a. $x - xy$ if $x = -2$ and $y = 3$

b. $a - (ab - a)$ if $a = -4$ and $b = -2$

c. $x - ab(a - b)$ if $x = -3$, $a = -2$, and $b = -4$

d. $-xa(a + x) + x$ if $x = -4$ and $a = -2$

problem set 14   **1.** What is the difference between a numerical expression and an algebraic expression?
(14)

2. What do we mean by the value of an expression?
(14)

3. (a) What is a variable of an algebraic expression?
(14)
     (b) What is an unknown of an algebraic expression?

4. Is the product of 6 negative numbers and 5 positive numbers a positive number or a
(13)   negative number?

5. What do you call polygons in which all angles have the same measure?
(2)

6. Use two unit multipliers to convert 300 inches to meters.
(4)

7. Use two unit multipliers to convert 100 square yards to square feet.
(10)

8. The area of a rectangle is 44 square inches. The length of one side is 11 inches. What is
(8) the length of the other side?

9. The circumference of a circle is 8π feet. Find the radius of the circle.
(3)

Evaluate:

10. $xm - 2m$ if $x = -2$ and $m = -3$
(14)

11. $ma - m - a$ if $m = -2$ and $a = -4$
(14)

12. $2abc - 3ab$ if $a = 2$, $b = -3$, and $c = 4$
(14)

13. $-x(a + b)$ if $x = 4$, $a = -3$, and $b = -5$
(14)

14. $-a + b + ab$ if $a = -5$ and $b = -2$
(14)

15. $x - y(a - x)$ if $x = -3$, $y = 4$, and $a = 4$
(14)

16. $-(m - x)(a - mx)$ if $m = 3$, $x = -4$, and $a = -2$
(14)

17. $-xa(x + a) - a$ if $a = -4$ and $x = 2$
(14)

18. $-xy - (-x + y)$ if $x = -3$ and $y = -4$
(14)

Simplify:

19. $-2(-1 - 4)(5 - 6) + 3$
(12)

20. $-4 - [-(-5)] + |-6|$
(13)

21. $-|-3|(2 - 5) - [-(-3)]$
(13)

22. $-2[-3(-2 - 5)(3)]$
(13)

23. $\dfrac{-2[-(-3)]}{(-2)(-4 + 3)}$
(13)

24. $\dfrac{(-5 - 2) + (-3 - 2)}{-3 - (-2)}$
(12)

25. Find the perimeter of this figure. Cor-
(3) ners that look square are square. Dimensions are in yards.

Find the area of each figure. Corners that look square are square. Dimensions are in centimeters.

26.
(8)

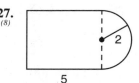

27.
(8)

28. Find the area of the shaded portion of
(8) this figure. Dimensions are in meters.

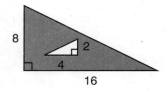

29. Find x.
₍₂₎

30. Simplify: $\dfrac{0.0612}{1.02}$
₍₄₎

LESSON 15 *Surface Area*

Geometric figures that have three dimensions are called **geometric solids.** Geometric solids whose sides are at right angles to the bases are called **right geometric solids** or just **right solids.** The "top" and the "bottom" of a right solid are called the **bases** of the right solid and are identical geometric figures. If the bases of a right solid are polygons, the right solid is called a **right prism.**

The **surface area** of a geometric solid is the total area of all the exposed surfaces of the geometric solid. In this lesson, we will learn how to compute the surface area of right solids.

example 15.1   Find the surface area of this right rectangular prism. Dimensions are in centimeters.

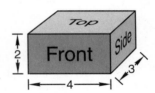

solution   A right rectangular prism has six faces that are rectangles. It has a top and a bottom, a front and a back, and two sides. The areas of the top and the bottom are equal. The area of the front equals the area of the back, and the areas of the two sides are equal. The surface area of the right rectangular prism is equal to the sum of the areas of the six faces.

$$
\begin{aligned}
\text{Area of top} \quad &= 4\,\text{cm} \times 3\,\text{cm} = 12\,\text{cm}^2 \\
\text{Area of bottom} \quad &= 4\,\text{cm} \times 3\,\text{cm} = 12\,\text{cm}^2 \\
\text{Area of front} \quad &= 4\,\text{cm} \times 2\,\text{cm} = 8\,\text{cm}^2 \\
\text{Area of back} \quad &= 4\,\text{cm} \times 2\,\text{cm} = 8\,\text{cm}^2 \\
\text{Area of side} \quad &= 3\,\text{cm} \times 2\,\text{cm} = 6\,\text{cm}^2 \\
\text{Area of side} \quad &= 3\,\text{cm} \times 2\,\text{cm} = \underline{6\,\text{cm}^2} \\
\text{Surface area} \quad &= \text{Total} \qquad\quad = \mathbf{52\ cm^2}
\end{aligned}
$$

example 15.2   Find the surface area of this right triangular
prism. Dimensions are in meters.

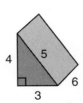

solution A right triangular prism has five faces. It has two faces that are right triangles and three faces that are rectangles. The surface area of the right triangular prism is equal to the sum of the areas of the five faces.

$$\text{Area of one end} = \frac{3 \text{ m} \times 4 \text{ m}}{2} = 6 \text{ m}^2$$

$$\text{Area of one end} = \frac{3 \text{ m} \times 4 \text{ m}}{2} = 6 \text{ m}^2$$

$$\text{Area of bottom} = 3 \text{ m} \times 6 \text{ m} = 18 \text{ m}^2$$

$$\text{Area of back} = 4 \text{ m} \times 6 \text{ m} = 24 \text{ m}^2$$

$$\text{Area of front} = 5 \text{ m} \times 6 \text{ m} = \underline{30 \text{ m}^2}$$

$$\text{Surface area} = \text{Total} = \mathbf{84 \text{ m}^2}$$

example 15.3 A right circular cylinder has a radius of 4 inches and a height of 10 inches, as shown. Find the surface area of the right circular cylinder.

solution The right circular cylinder has two equal bases that are circles. So the area of a base is the area of a circle.

$$\text{Area of one base} = \pi r^2 = (3.14)(4 \text{ in.})^2 = 50.24 \text{ in.}^2$$

We define the **lateral surface area** of a right circular cylinder to be the area of the curved surface between the bases. **The lateral surface area of a right circular cylinder is equal to the perimeter of a base times the height.** We can see this if we think of the right circular cylinder as a tin can that we can cut down the dotted line and then press flat. When we do this we get a rectangle.

 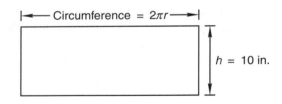

The length of the rectangle is the perimeter of a base of the right circular cylinder. We note that the perimeter of a base is the circumference of a circle. The height of the rectangle is the height of the right circular cylinder. The lateral surface area of the right circular cylinder is the area of the rectangle which is equal to the perimeter of a base times the height. Therefore, we have

$$\text{Lateral surface area} = (\text{perimeter of a base})(\text{height})$$

$$= (\text{circumference})(\text{height})$$

$$= 2\pi rh$$

$$= 2(3.14)(4 \text{ in.})(10 \text{ in.})$$

$$= 251.2 \text{ in.}^2$$

The surface area of a right circular cylinder is equal to the areas of the two equal bases added to the lateral surface area.

$$\text{Surface area} = \text{base area} + \text{base area} + \text{lateral surface area}$$

$$= 50.24 \text{ in.}^2 + 50.24 \text{ in.}^2 + 251.2 \text{ in.}^2$$

$$= \mathbf{351.68 \text{ in.}^2}$$

example 15.4　A base of the right solid 10 feet high is shown. Find the surface area of the right solid. Dimensions are in feet.

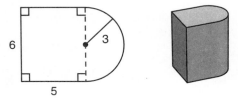

solution　The right solid has two equal bases. The area of a base equals the sum of the areas of the rectangle and the semicircle.

$$\text{Area of one base} = \square + D$$

$$= (5 \text{ ft} \times 6 \text{ ft}) + \frac{\pi(3 \text{ ft})^2}{2}$$

$$= 30 \text{ ft}^2 + \frac{(3.14)(3 \text{ ft})^2}{2}$$

$$= 30 \text{ ft}^2 + 14.13 \text{ ft}^2$$

$$= 44.13 \text{ ft}^2$$

We define the **lateral surface area** of a right solid to be the area of the surface between the bases. **The lateral surface area of a right solid is equal to the perimeter of a base times the height.** We can see this if we cut the right solid down the dotted line and then press flat. When we do this we get a rectangle.

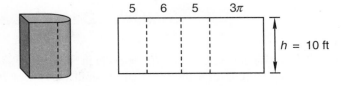

The length of the rectangle is the perimeter of a base of the right solid. The perimeter of a base is equal to the sum of the lengths of the straight sides and the length of the semicircle.

$$\text{Perimeter of a base} = 5 \text{ ft} + 6 \text{ ft} + 5 \text{ ft} + \frac{2\pi(3 \text{ ft})}{2}$$

$$= 5 \text{ ft} + 6 \text{ ft} + 5 \text{ ft} + 3\pi \text{ ft}$$

$$= 16 \text{ ft} + 3(3.14) \text{ ft}$$

$$= 25.42 \text{ ft}$$

The height of the rectangle is the height of the right solid. The lateral surface area of the right solid is the area of the rectangle which is equal to the perimeter of a base times the height. Therefore, we have

$$\text{Lateral surface area} = (\text{perimeter of a base})(\text{height})$$

$$= (25.42 \text{ ft})(10 \text{ ft})$$

$$= 254.2 \text{ ft}^2$$

The surface area of a right solid is equal to the areas of the two equal bases added to the lateral surface area.

$$\text{Surface area} = \text{base area} + \text{base area} + \text{lateral surface area}$$

$$= 44.13 \text{ ft}^2 + 44.13 \text{ ft}^2 + 254.2 \text{ ft}^2$$

$$= \mathbf{342.46 \text{ ft}^2}$$

practice   **a.** Find the surface area of this right rectangular prism. Dimensions are in inches.

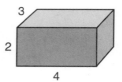

b. Find the surface area of this right triangular prism. Dimensions are in feet.

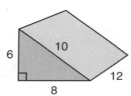

c. A right circular cylinder has a radius of 20 centimeters and a length of 200 centimeters, as shown. Find the surface area of the right circular cylinder.

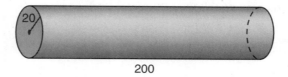

d. A base of the right solid 10 meters high is shown. Find the surface area of the right solid. Dimensions are in meters. (Remember that the lateral surface area of a right solid is equal to the perimeter of a base times the height.)

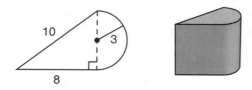

problem set   **1.** (a) What do we call the total area of all exposed surfaces of a geometric solid?
15   (15)
                 (b) How do you find the lateral surface area of any right solid?

2.
(11)
(a) What is the multiplicative inverse of $\frac{1}{3}$?

(b) What is the multiplicative inverse of $-\frac{1}{3}$?

(c) What is the product of any nonzero real number and its multiplicative inverse?

3. What is another name for the multiplicative inverse of a number?
(11)

4. Which real number does not have a multiplicative inverse and why?
(11)

5. Use two unit multipliers to convert 112 feet to centimeters.
(4)

6. Use two unit multipliers to convert 60 square kilometers to square meters.
(10)

7. The area of a rectangle is 72 square centimeters. The length of one side is 6 centimeters.
(8)   What is the length of the other side?

8. The length of the base of a right triangle is 12 meters. The height of the right triangle is
(8)   9 meters. Find the area of the right triangle.

9. The diameter of a circle is 16 kilometers. Find the area of the circle.
(8)

Evaluate:

10. $a - ab$ if $a = 2$ and $b = -3$
(14)

11. $xy - 3y$ if $x = 2$ and $y = 4$
(14)

12. $2ab - 3abc$ if $a = -1$, $b = 2$, and $c = 3$
(14)

13. $-x(a - b)$ if $x = -2$, $a = 3$, and $b = -1$
(14)

14. $-x - (-a + b)$ if $x = 3$, $a = -2$, and $b = 4$
(14)

15. $(x - y)(y - x)$ if $x = -2$ and $y = 3$
(14)

16. $(-x) + (-y)$ if $x = -3$ and $y = 2$
(14)

17. $-c - (p - c)$ if $p = -5$ and $c = 2$
(14)

18. $(a - x)(ma - x)$ if $a = -3$, $x = -4$, and $m = 5$
(14)

Simplify:

19. $-2(-6 - 1 - 2) - (-2 + 7)$
(12)

20. $-|-11| + (-3)|-3 + 5|$
(12)

21. $-3(-3)(-2 - 5 + |-11|)$
(12)

22. $-3\{[(-5 - 2)](-1)\}$
(13)

23. $\dfrac{-4 - (-1 - 3)}{-7 - (-9 + 2)}$
(10)

24. $\dfrac{3(-5 + 2) + 6(-4 + 10) - 2}{(10 - 2) + 7 + 5}$
(12)

25. Find the perimeter of this figure. All
(3)   angles are right angles. Dimensions
are in inches.

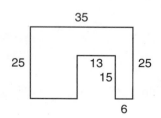

26. Find the area of this figure. Corners
(8)   that look square are square. Dimensions are in feet.

Simplify:

27. $-2\frac{2}{3} + 2\frac{3}{5}$
(1)

28. $\dfrac{4\frac{2}{3}}{-3\frac{1}{9}}$
(4)

29. The length of $\overline{PQ}$ is $5\frac{1}{3}$ yards. The length of $\overline{QR}$ is $8\frac{5}{12}$ yards. Find PR.
(1)

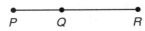

30. Find the surface area of this right rec-
(15) tangular prism. Dimensions are in centimeters.

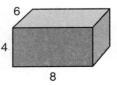

LESSON 16 *More Complicated Evaluations*

The procedures discussed in Lesson 14 are also used to evaluate more complicated expressions. The use of parentheses, brackets, and braces is often helpful in preventing mistakes. We will use all of these symbols of inclusion in the following examples.

example 16.1 Evaluate: $-a[-a(p - a)]$ if $p = -2$ and $a = -4$

solution We use parentheses, brackets, and braces as required.

$$-(\ \ )\big\{-(\ \ )[(\ \ ) - (\ \ )]\big\}$$

Now we will insert the numbers inside the parentheses.

$$-(-4)\big\{-(-4)[(-2) - (-4)]\big\}$$

Lastly, we simplify.

$$4\{4[2]\} = 4\{8\} = \mathbf{32}$$

example 16.2 Evaluate: $ax[-a(a - x)]$ if $a = -2$ and $x = -6$

solution This time we will not use parentheses. We will replace a with -2, $-a$ with 2, x with -6, and $-x$ with 6.

$$12[2(-2 + 6)]$$

Now we simplify, remembering to begin with the innermost symbol of inclusion.

$$12[2(-2 + 6)] = 12[2(4)] = 12[8] = \mathbf{96}$$

example 16.3 Evaluate: $-b[-b(b - c) - (c - b)]$ if $b = -4$ and $c = -6$

solution We replace b with -4, $-b$ with 4, c with -6, and $-c$ with 6.

$$4[4(-4 + 6) - (-6 + 4)]$$

Now we simplify, remembering to begin within the innermost symbols of inclusion and to multiply before adding.

$$4[4(2) - (-2)] = 4[8 + 2] = 4[10] = \mathbf{40}$$

practice   Evaluate:

    a. $-a[-a(p - a)]$ if $p = -4$ and $a = 2$

    b. $pa[-p(-a)]$ if $p = -2$ and $a = -4$

    c. $-x[-x(x - a) - (a - x)]$ if $x = -2$ and $a = -5$

problem set   **1.** Is the product of 4 positive numbers and 7 negative numbers a positive number or a
16   ₍₁₃₎ negative number?

    2. (a) What do we call the answer to an addition problem?
    ₍₄₎
        (b) What do we call the answer to a subtraction problem?

        (c) What do we call the answer to a multiplication problem?

        (d) What do we call the answer to a division problem?

    3. What do you call polygons in which all sides have the same length and all angles have
    ₍₂₎ the same measure?

    4. Use one unit multiplier to convert 100 centimeters to inches.
    ₍₄₎

    5. Use two unit multipliers to convert 152 square centimeters to square inches.
    ₍₁₀₎

    6. The length of a rectangle is 31 inches. The width of the rectangle is 11 inches. Find the
    ₍₃₎ perimeter of the rectangle.

    7. The length of a rectangle is 17 feet. The width of the rectangle is 13 feet. Find the area
    ₍₈₎ of the rectangle.

    8. The radius of a circle is 9 yards. Find the area of the circle.
    ₍₈₎

Evaluate:

    9. $x - xy$ if $x = -2$ and $y = -3$
    ₍₁₄₎

    10. $x(x - y)$ if $x = -2$ and $y = -3$
    ₍₁₄₎

    11. $(x - y)(y - x)$ if $x = 2$ and $y = -3$
    ₍₁₄₎

    12. $(x - y) - (x - y)$ if $x = -2$ and $y = 3$
    ₍₁₄₎

    13. $-xa(x - a)$ if $a = -2$ and $x = 4$
    ₍₁₄₎

    14. $(-x + a) - (x - a)$ if $x = -4$ and $a = 5$
    ₍₁₄₎

    15. $(p - x)(a - px)$ if $a = -3$, $p = 2$, and $x = -4$
    ₍₁₄₎

    16. $-a[-a(x - a)]$ if $a = -2$ and $x = 3$
    ₍₁₆₎

    17. $-a[(-x - a) - (x - y)]$ if $a = -3$, $x = 4$, and $y = -5$
    ₍₁₆₎

Simplify:

    18. $-3(-1 - 2)(4 - 5) + 6$ **19.** $-2 + (-3) - |-5 + 2|3$
    ₍₁₂₎   ₍₁₂₎

    20. $4[2(3 - 2) - (6 - 4)]$ **21.** $-2(-4) - \left\{-[-(-6)]\right\}$
    ₍₁₃₎   ₍₁₃₎

    22. $\dfrac{3(-2) - 5}{-3(-2)}$ **23.** $\dfrac{-3(-6 - 2) + 5}{-3(-2 + 1)}$
    ₍₁₂₎   ₍₁₂₎

    24. Find the perimeter of this figure. Cor-
    ₍₃₎ ners that look square are square.
        Dimensions are in miles.

25. Find the area of this right triangle.
(8) Dimensions are in centimeters.

26. Find the area of the shaded portion of
(8) this rectangle. Dimensions are in
meters.

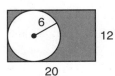

27. Find y.
(2)

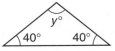

Simplify:

28. $1\dfrac{7}{12} + 5\dfrac{5}{6} - 4\dfrac{2}{3}$
(1)

29. $2\dfrac{2}{5} \times 11\dfrac{2}{3}$
(4)

30. Find the surface area of this right trian-
(15) gular prism. Dimensions are in kilometers.

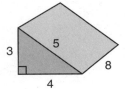

LESSON 17 *Factors and Coefficients • Terms • The Distributive Property*

17.A

factors and coefficients

If the form in which variables and constants are written in an expression indicates that the variables and constants are to be multiplied, we say that the expression is an **indicated product.** If we write

$$4xy$$

we indicate that 4 is to be multiplied by the product of x and y. Each of the symbols is said to be a factor of the expression. Any one factor of an expression or any product of factors of an expression can also be called the **coefficient** of the rest of the expression. Thus, in the expression $4xy$ we can say that

(a) 4 is the coefficient of xy $4(xy)$

(b) x is the coefficient of $4y$ $x(4y)$

(c) y is the coefficient of $4x$ $y(4x)$

(d) xy is the coefficient of 4 $xy(4)$

(e) $4y$ is the coefficient of x $4y(x)$

(f) $4x$ is the coefficient of y $4x(y)$

As mentioned earlier, the value of a product is not affected by the order in which the multiplication is performed, so we may arrange the factors in any order without affecting the value of the expression. Note that we change the order at will in (a) through (f) above.

If the coefficient is a number as in (a) above, we call it a **numerical coefficient,** and if the coefficient consists entirely of variables or letters as in (b), (c), and (d) above, we call it a **literal coefficient.** We need to speak of numerical coefficients so often that we usually drop the adjective *numerical* and use the single word *coefficient*. Thus, in the following expressions

$$4xy \qquad -15pq \qquad 81xmz$$

4 is the coefficient of *xy*, −15 is the coefficient of *pq*, and 81 is the coefficient of *xmz*.

17.B
terms

A **term** is an algebraic expression that

1. Consists of a single variable or constant.
2. Is the indicated product or quotient of variables and/or constants.
3. Is the indicated product or quotient of expressions that contain variables and/or constants.

$$4 \qquad x \qquad 4x \qquad \frac{4xy(a + b)}{p} \qquad \frac{3x + 2y}{m}$$

All the expressions above can be called **terms.** The first two are terms because they consist of a single symbol. The third is a term because it is an indicated product of symbols. The fourth and fifth are terms because they are considered to be indicated quotients even though the numerator of the fourth term is an indicated product and the numerator of the fifth term is an indicated sum. **A term is thought of as a single entity that represents or has the value of one particular number.** The word *term* is very useful in allowing us to identify or talk about the parts of a larger expression. For instance, the expression

$$x + 4xym - \frac{6p}{y + 2} - 8$$

is an expression that has four terms. We can speak of a particular term of this expression, say the third term, without having to write out the term in question. The terms of an expression are numbered from left to right, beginning with the number 1. Thus, for the expression above

The first term is +*x*.   The third term is $-\dfrac{6p}{y + 2}$.

The second term is +4*xym*.   The fourth term is −8.

If we consider that the sign preceding a term indicates addition or subtraction, then the sign is not a part of the term. In this book, we prefer to use the thought of algebraic addition, and thus, most of the time we will consider the sign preceding a term to be a part of the term. But we must be careful.

Let us look at the third term in the expression we are considering.

$$-\frac{6p}{y + 2}$$

If *p* and *y* are given values such that $\frac{6p}{y + 2}$ is a negative number, then $-\frac{6p}{y + 2}$ will be positive. For example, if *p* is equal to −4 and *y* is equal to 1, then the expression has a value of +8.

$$-\frac{6p}{y + 2} = -\frac{6(-4)}{1 + 2} = -(-8) = +8$$

17.C
the distributive property

We have noted that the order of adding two real numbers does not change the answer. Also, the order of multiplying two real numbers does not change the answer. We call these two properties or peculiarities of real numbers the **commutative property for addition** and the **commutative property for multiplication.**

Now we will discuss another property of real numbers that is of considerable importance, the **distributive property of real numbers.** If we write

$$4(5 - 3)$$

we indicate that we are to multiply 4 by the algebraic sum of the numbers 5 and –3. A property (or peculiarity) of real numbers permits the value of this product to be found two different ways.

$$
\begin{array}{cc}
4(5 - 3) & 4(5 - 3) \\
4(2) & 4 \cdot 5 + 4(-3) \\
8 & 20 - 12 \\
 & 8
\end{array}
$$

On the left, we first added 5 and –3 to get 2, and then multiplied by 4 to get 8. On the right, we first multiplied 4 by both 5 and –3, and then added the products 20 and –12 to get 8. Both methods of simplifying the expression led to the same result. **We call this property or peculiarity of real numbers the** *distributive property* **because we get the same result if we distribute the multiplication over the algebraic addition.**[†]

DISTRIBUTIVE PROPERTY

For any real numbers a, b, c,

$$a(b + c) = ab + ac$$

It is possible to extend the distributive property so that the extension is applicable to the indicated product of a number or a variable and the algebraic sum of any number of real numbers or variables.

EXTENSION OF THE DISTRIBUTIVE PROPERTY

For any real numbers a, b, c, d, …,

$$a(b + c + d + \cdots) = ab + ac + ad + \cdots$$

---

example 17.1   Use the distributive property to find the value of $4(6 - 2 + 5 - 7)$.

solution   We begin by multiplying 4 by each of the terms within the parentheses, and then we add the resultant products.

$$4(6 - 2 + 5 - 7) = 4(6) + 4(-2) + 4(5) + 4(-7)$$

$$= 24 - 8 + 20 - 28 = \mathbf{8}$$

[†]Note that while multiplication can be distributed over addition, the reverse is not true, for addition cannot be distributed over multiplication. For example,

$$2 + (3 \cdot 5) \neq (2 + 3) \cdot (2 + 5)$$

because $17 \neq 35$

example 17.2   Use the distributive property to expand $mn(x + y + 2p)$.

solution   We will multiply mn by each of the terms within the parentheses.

$$mn(x + y + 2p) = mnx + mny + 2mnp$$

example 17.3   Use the distributive property to expand $(x - 3y + xz)mp$.

solution   The order is different, but we use the same procedure. Thus, mp is multiplied by each term within the parentheses.

$$(x - 3y + xz)mp = mpx - 3ymp + mpxz$$

example 17.4   Use the distributive property to expand $-3(2x - 4)$.

solution   **This can be read two ways! The first way is to read it as the opposite of $3(2x - 4)$.** Since $3(2x - 4)$ can be expanded as

$$3(2x - 4) = 6x - 12$$

we can write the opposite of this as

$$-6x + 12$$

The second way is to multiply -3 by both $2x$ and -4 and write the result as an algebraic sum. If we do this, we get the same answer.

$$-3(2x - 4) = -6x + 12$$

practice   **a.**   Evaluate $4(5 - 3)$ by adding and then multiplying.

b.   Evaluate $4(5 - 3)$ by multiplying and then adding.

c.   Use the letters a, b, and c and parentheses to write the distributive property.

d.   When we multiply first, we say we are using the distributive property. Use the distributive property to evaluate $4(6 - 2 + 5 - 7)$.

Expand by using the distributive property:

e. $2m(xy - 3p)$ **f.** $xy(a + b - 2c)$

problem set 17   **1.** *(17)*   What is a coefficient of an expression?

2. *(17)*   (a)   What is a numerical coefficient of an expression?

(b)   What is a literal coefficient of an expression?

3. *(5)*   What property of addition states that the order in which two real numbers are added does not affect the sum?

4. *(10)*   What property of multiplication states that the order in which two real numbers are multiplied does not affect the product?

5. *(4)*   Use one unit multiplier to convert 250 centimeters to meters.

6. *(10)*   Use two unit multipliers to convert 5000 square centimeters to square meters.

7. *(3)*   The perimeter of a square is 64 centimeters. What is the length of one side of the square?

8. *(8)*   The area of a square is 25 square meters. What is the length of one side of the square?

9. The length of the base of an isosceles triangle is 6 inches. The height of the isosceles
(8) triangle is 8 inches. Find the area of the isosceles triangle.

Evaluate by using the distributive property:

10. $-7(-8 + 3)$
(17)

11. $5(-3 - 6)$
(17)

Expand by using the distributive property:

12. $mx(ab - b)$
(17)

13. $-4y(d + cx)$
(17)

14. $(a + bc)2x$
(17)

15. $3a(x + 2y)$
(17)

Evaluate:

16. $-a(a - b)$ if $a = -2$ and $b = -7$
(14)

17. $(x - y) - (y - x)$ if $x = -2$ and $y = -4$
(14)

18. $x - 2a(-a)$ if $x = 4$ and $a = -3$
(14)

19. $-x(a - xa)$ if $x = -4$ and $a = -3$
(14)

20. $-y[-ay - (xy)]$ if $a = -2$, $x = 2$, and $y = -3$
(16)

Simplify:

21. $4[(2 - 4) - (6 - 3)]$
(13)

22. $-[-(-3)] - 2(-2) + (-3)$
(13)

23. $-|-2| + (-3) - 3 - (-4 - 2)$
(12)

24. $-5(-2)(-2 - 3) - (-|-2|)$
(13)

25. $\dfrac{3 - (-2)(4)}{5 - (-3)}$
(12)

26. $\dfrac{3 + 7(-3)}{-6 - 2(-3)}$
(10)

27. Find the perimeter of this figure. All
(3) angles are right angles. Dimensions
are in feet.

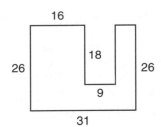

28. Find the area of this figure. Corners
(8) that look square are square. Dimensions are in yards.

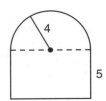

29. AB is $4\frac{1}{2}$ miles. BC is $2\frac{3}{8}$ miles. CD is $5\frac{1}{8}$ miles. Find AD.
(1)

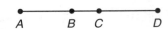

30. A right circular cylinder has a radius
(15) of 2 centimeters and a height of 4 centimeters, as shown. Find the surface
area of the right circular cylinder.

LESSON 18 *Like Terms • Addition of Like Terms*

18.A

like terms Like terms are terms that have the same variables in the same form or in equivalent forms so that the terms (excluding numerical coefficients) **represent the same number regardless of the nonzero values assigned to the variables.** Let us look at the indicated sum of terms

$$4xmp - 2pmx + 6mxp$$

Now whether terms are **like terms** or not does not depend on the signs of the terms or on the values of the numerical coefficients. So we will not consider the + and − signs or the numbers 4, 2, and 6. We just need to know if

$$xmp, \quad pmx, \quad \text{and} \quad mxp$$

are in the same form or equivalent forms and if each expression represents the same number regardless of the nonzero values that are assigned to the variables. We state the following:

1. They are in equivalent forms, for they have the same variables in the form of an indicated product, and the order of multiplication of the factors does not affect the value of the product.
2. They represent the same number regardless of the nonzero values assigned to the variables.

We will not attempt to prove the second statement but will demonstrate it with one set of values for the variables. If we let $x = 4$, $m = 2$, and $p = 6$, we have

xmp	pmx	mxp
$4 \cdot 2 \cdot 6$	$6 \cdot 2 \cdot 4$	$2 \cdot 4 \cdot 6$
48	48	48

Thus, $4xmp$, $-2pmx$, and $6mxp$ are like terms because the variables represent the same number regardless of the nonzero real number replacements used for the variables.

18.B

addition of like terms The extension of the distributive property of Lesson 17 can be rewritten as

$$ba + ca + da + \cdots = (b + c + d + \cdots)a$$

We note that a is a common factor of each of the terms on the left and is written outside the parentheses on the right. If we look at the indicated sum of terms

$$4xmp - 2pmx + 6mxp$$

we see that the factor xmp is a factor of all three terms and can be treated in the same manner as the a factor on the left side of the statement or restatement of the distributive property.

Thus we can write the sum of three terms as a product of $(4 - 2 + 6)$ and xmp, as shown here.

$$4xmp - 2pmx + 6mxp = (4 - 2 + 6)xmp = 8xmp$$

The factors of the three variables in the expression $8xmp$ can be written in any order without changing the *value* of the expression. Thus, any of the following would be equally acceptable.

$$8xmp \qquad 8xpm \qquad 8mxp \qquad 8mpx \qquad 8pmx \qquad 8pxm$$

The above is a rather detailed approach to justify the following statement:

To add like terms, we algebraically add the numerical coefficients.

Thus to add

$$4xmp - 2pmx + 6mxp$$

we simply add the numerical coefficients 4, –2, and +6 to get $8xmp$.

$$4xmp - 2pmx + 6mxp = 8xmp$$

example 18.1   Simplify by adding like terms: $3x + 5 - xy + 2yx - 5x$

solution   The first term and the fifth term are like terms, and the third term and the fourth term are like terms. If we add these terms, we get

$$-2x + xy + 5$$

example 18.2   Simplify by adding like terms: $3xy + 2xyz - 10yx - 5yzx$

solution   The first term and the third term are like terms and may be added. Also, the second term and the fourth term are like terms and may be added. If we add these terms, we get

$$-7yx - 3xyz$$

example 18.3   Simplify by adding like terms: $4 + 7mxy + 5 + 3yxm - 15$

solution   We add like terms and get

$$-6 + 10mxy$$

example 18.4   Simplify by adding like terms: $3x - x - y + 5 - 2y - 3x - 10 - 8y$

solution   We add the x terms, the y terms, and the numbers and get

$$-x - 11y - 5$$

example 18.5   Simplify by adding like terms: $-3 + xmy - y - 5 + 8ymx - 3y - 14$

solution   We add the y terms, the xmy terms, and the numbers in any order and get

$$-22 - 4y + 9myx$$

Of course, the letters myx could be in any order.

practice   Simplify by adding like terms:

   a. $-2xy + 3x + 4 - 4yx - 2x$ **b.** $2xyz + 3xy - 5zyx$

   c. $3yac - 2ac + 6acy$ **d.** $4 - x - 2xy + 3x - 7yx$

problem set   1. What is a term of an algebraic expression?
18 $^{(17)}$

          2. When can terms of an algebraic expression be called like terms?
          $^{(18)}$

          3. Which of the following terms are like terms?
          $^{(18)}$
          (a) $2xmp$ (b) xmy (c) $-4pmx$ (d) $3mxp$

          4. Use the letters a, b, and c and parentheses to write the distributive property.
          $^{(17)}$

          5. Use two unit multipliers to convert 1500 centimeters to feet.
          $^{(4)}$

          6. Use two unit multipliers to convert 1250 square inches to square feet.
          $^{(10)}$

          7. The perimeter of a rectangle is 76 inches. The length of the rectangle is 22 inches. Find
          $^{(3)}$ the width of the rectangle.

8. The diameter of a circle is 18 feet. Find the area of the circle.
(8)

Simplify by adding like terms:

9. $3xyz + 2zxy - 7zyx + 2xy$ (18)

10. $4x + 3 - 2xy - 5x - 7 + 4yx$ (18)

Expand by using the distributive property:

11. $(4 + 2y)x$ (17)

12. $3x(y - 2m)$ (17)

13. $2p(xy - 3k)$ (17)

Evaluate:

14. $-a(x - a)$ if $a = -3$ and $x = 6$ (14)

15. $-x - (-a)(a - x)$ if $x = -2$ and $a = 4$ (14)

16. $-p(-x) - px$ if $p = -3$ and $x = 4$ (14)

17. $-x(-y) - xy$ if $x = 3$ and $y = -2$ (14)

18. $(-a)(b)(-a + b)$ if $a = 6$ and $b = -3$ (14)

Simplify:

19. $-6 - 2(-3)(-1) - 5(3 - 2 - 2)$ (12)

20. $-\{3(-2)(-4 + 2) - [3 - (-2)]\}$ (13)

21. $-4 - (-2) - [-(-2)] - |-3|$ (13)

22. $-3 - 2(-4 + 7) - 5 - |-2 - 5|$ (12)

23. $\dfrac{-2(-3 + 7)}{(-2)(-3)}$ (12)

24. $\dfrac{-2 - 2(3) + 10}{3 - (-2)(-3)}$ (12)

25. Find the perimeter of this figure. Corners that look square are square. Dimensions are in yards.
(3)

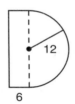

12

6

26. Find the area of this isosceles triangle. Dimensions are in centimeters.
(8)

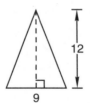

12

9

27. Find the area of the shaded portion of this right triangle. Dimensions are in meters.
(8)

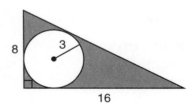

8   3

16

Simplify:

28. 0.304×12.5 (4)

29. $\dfrac{0.09338}{0.046}$ (4)

30. Find the surface area of this right rectangular prism. Dimensions are in inches.
(15)

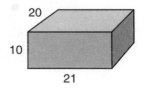

20

10

21

LESSON 19   *Exponents • Powers of Negative Numbers • Roots • Evaluation of Powers*

19.A

exponents

Often we find it necessary to indicate that a number is to be used as a factor a given number of times. For instance, if we wish to indicate that 5 is to be used as a factor seven times, we could write $5 \cdot 5 \cdot 5 \cdot 5 \cdot 5 \cdot 5 \cdot 5$. This is a cumbersome expression and mathematicians have developed a sort of mathematical shorthand called **exponential notation** that allows the expression to be written more concisely. The exponential notation for 5 used as a factor seven times is 5^7, read **"five to the seventh."** The general form of the expression is x^n, which indicates that x is to be used as a factor n times and is read **"x to the nth."**

> DEFINITION OF EXPONENTIAL NOTATION
>
> $$\underbrace{x \cdot x \cdot x \cdot \cdots \cdot x}_{n \text{ factors}} = x^n$$

In this definition, the letter x represents a real number and is called the **base** of the expression. The letter n represents a positive integer and is called the **exponent.**

For example,

$$x^4 = x \cdot x \cdot x \cdot x \qquad \text{The base is } x \text{ and the exponent is 4.}$$
$$(-4)^3 = (-4)(-4)(-4) \qquad \text{The base is } (-4) \text{ and the exponent is 3.}$$
$$\left(\frac{1}{3}\right)^4 = \left(\frac{1}{3}\right)\left(\frac{1}{3}\right)\left(\frac{1}{3}\right)\left(\frac{1}{3}\right) \qquad \text{The base is } \frac{1}{3} \text{ and the exponent is 4.}$$

The value of an exponential expression is called a **power** of the base.

$$2^4 = (2)(2)(2)(2) = 16$$

The value of 2 used as a factor four times is 16. **We say that the fourth power of 2 is 16.** We find it convenient to sometimes use the word *power* to name the exponent. To do this, we would say that the expression

$$2^4$$

represents 2 raised to the **fourth power.**

19.B

powers of negative numbers

When a positive number is raised to a positive power, the result is always a positive number.

example 19.1   Simplify: (a) 3^2 (b) 3^3 (c) 3^4 (d) -3^4

solution   Each of these notations tells us that +3 is the base. The exponents 2, 3, and 4 tell us to use 3 as a factor twice, three times, and four times.

(a) $3^2 = (3)(3) = \mathbf{9}$

(b) $3^3 = (3)(3)(3) = \mathbf{27}$

(c) $3^4 = (3)(3)(3)(3) = \mathbf{81}$

(d) We must be careful here because -3^4 means the opposite of 3^4 and not $(-3)^4$.

$$-3^4 = -(3)(3)(3)(3) = \mathbf{-81}$$

When a negative number is raised to an even power, the result is always positive; and when a negative number is raised to an odd power, the result is always negative, as demonstrated in the next example.

example 19.2   Simplify: (a) $(-3)^2$ (b) $(-3)^3$ (c) $(-3)^4$ (d) $-(-3)^4$

solution   The first three are straightforward.

(a) $(-3)^2 = (-3)(-3) = \mathbf{9}$

(b) $(-3)^3 = (-3)(-3)(-3) = \mathbf{-27}$

(c) $(-3)^4 = (-3)(-3)(-3)(-3) = \mathbf{81}$

(d) Be careful here. We want the opposite of $(-3)^4$.

$$-(-3)^4 = -(-3)(-3)(-3)(-3) = \mathbf{-81}$$

example 19.3   Simplify: $-3^3 - (-3)^2 + (-2)^2$

solution   Be careful with the first term.

$$-3^3 - (-3)^2 + (-2)^2 = -(3)(3)(3) - (-3)(-3) + (-2)(-2)$$
$$= -27 - 9 + 4$$
$$= \mathbf{-32}$$

example 19.4   Simplify: $-2^2 - 4(-3)^3 - 2(-2)^2 - 2$

solution -2^2 is -4, $(-3)^3$ is -27, and $(-2)^2$ is 4, so we get

$$-2^2 - 4(-3)^3 - 2(-2)^2 - 2 = -4 - 4(-27) - 2(4) - 2$$
$$= -4 + 108 - 8 - 2$$
$$= \mathbf{94}$$

19.C

roots

If we use 3 as a factor twice, the result is 9. Thus, 3 is the positive square root of 9. We use a **radical sign** to indicate the root of a number.

$$(3)(3) = 9 \qquad \text{so} \qquad \sqrt{9} = 3$$

If we use 3 as a factor three times, the result is 27. Thus, 3 is the positive cube root of 27.

$$(3)(3)(3) = 27 \qquad \text{so} \qquad \sqrt[3]{27} = 3$$

If we use 3 as a factor four times, the result is 81. Thus, 3 is the positive fourth root of 81.

$$(3)(3)(3)(3) = 81 \qquad \text{so} \qquad \sqrt[4]{81} = 3$$

If we use 3 as a factor five times, the result is 243. Thus, 3 is the positive fifth root of 243.

$$(3)(3)(3)(3)(3) = 243 \qquad \text{so} \qquad \sqrt[5]{243} = 3$$

Because $(-3)(-3)$ equals $+9$, we say that -3 is the negative square root of 9. Because $(-3)(-3)(-3)(-3)$ equals $+81$, we say that -3 is the negative fourth root of 81. **If n is an even number, every positive real number has a positive nth root and a negative nth root. We use the radical sign to designate the positive even root.** To designate the negative even root, we also use a minus sign.

$$\sqrt{9} = 3 \qquad -\sqrt{9} = -3 \qquad \sqrt[4]{81} = 3 \qquad -\sqrt[4]{81} = -3$$

The number under the radical sign is called the **radicand,** and the little number that designates the root is called the **index.** If n is an odd number, every positive number has exactly one positive real nth root. Also, every negative number has exactly one negative real nth root.

$$\sqrt[3]{27} = 3 \qquad \sqrt[3]{-27} = -3$$

In this book, we will consider even roots of positive numbers and odd roots of both positive and negative numbers. Even roots of negative numbers will be discussed in the next book in this series.

example 19.5 Simplify: (a) $\sqrt{64}$ (b) $\sqrt[4]{16}$ (c) $\sqrt[3]{-27}$ (d) $-\sqrt{81}$

solution (a) The notation $\sqrt{64}$ designates the positive number which used as a factor twice has a product of 64. The answer is **8** because 8 times 8 equals 64. The notations $\sqrt[2]{64}$ and $\sqrt{64}$ both designate the positive square root of 64. If the index is not written, it is understood to be 2.

$$\sqrt{64} = \mathbf{8}$$

(b) The fourth root of 16 is 2 because

$$\sqrt[4]{16} = \mathbf{2} \qquad \text{because} \qquad (2)(2)(2)(2) = 16$$

(c) Every real number has exactly one real nth root, where n is odd.

$$\sqrt[3]{-27} = \mathbf{-3} \qquad \text{because} \qquad (-3)(-3)(-3) = -27$$

(d) The square root of 81 is 9. We want the opposite of this.

$$-\sqrt{81} = \mathbf{-9}$$

19.D

evaluation of powers

Evaluation of expressions with exponents is straightforward when the replacements of the variables are all positive numbers. To evaluate

$$yx^2m^3$$

with $y = 3$, $x = 4$, and $m = 2$, we proceed as follows:

$$(3)(4)^2(2)^3 = (3)(16)(8) = \mathbf{384}$$

We must be careful, however, when the expressions contain minus signs or when some replacement values of the variables are negative numbers.

example 19.6 If $a = -2$, what is the value of each of the following?

(a) a^2 (b) $-a^2$ (c) $-a^3$ (d) $(-a)^3$

solution (a) a^2 means a times a, or $(-2)(-2) = \mathbf{+4.}$

(b) $-a^2$ asks for the opposite of a^2, or $-(-2)(-2) = \mathbf{-4.}$

(c) $-a^3$ means the opposite of a times a times a, or $-(-2)(-2)(-2) = \mathbf{+8.}$

(d) $(-a)^3$ means $(-a)(-a)(-a) = (2)(2)(2) = \mathbf{+8.}$

example 19.7 Evaluate: x^2z^3y if $x = 2$, $z = 3$, and $y = -2$

solution We replace x with 2, z with 3, and y with -2.

$$(2)^2(3)^3(-2) = (4)(27)(-2) = \mathbf{-216}$$

example 19.8   Evaluate: $pm^2 - z^3$ if $p = 1$, $m = -4$, and $z = -2$

solution   We replace p with 1, m with -4, and z with -2.

$$(1)(-4)^2 - (-2)^3 = (1)(16) - (-8) = 16 + 8 = \mathbf{24}$$

practice   Simplify:

   a. $(-2)^2$ **b.** -2^2 **c.** $-3^3 - (-2)^2 - 2^2$

   d. $\sqrt[3]{-64}$ **e.** $(-3)^3 + \sqrt[3]{-27}$ **f.** $-3^2 - \sqrt[3]{-8} - \sqrt{16}$

Evaluate:

   g. $x^2 z^3 y$ if $x = -3$, $z = -2$, and $y = -2$

   h. $b^2 - 4ac$ if $b = -4$, $a = -3$, and $c = -5$

problem set 19

1. *(18)*   What kinds of terms may be added in an algebraic expression?

2. *(13)*   Is the product of 7 positive numbers and 6 negative numbers a positive number or a negative number?

3. *(2)*   (a)   What is a right triangle?

      (b)   What is an acute triangle?

      (c)   What is an obtuse triangle?

      (d)   What is an equiangular triangle?

4. *(4)*   Use two unit multipliers to convert 10,000 inches to miles.

5. *(10)*   Use two unit multipliers to convert 15,000 square feet to square miles.

6. *(8)*   The area of a rectangle is 92 square centimeters. The length of the rectangle is 23 centimeters. Find the width of the rectangle.

7. *(8)*   The length of the base of a scalene triangle is 9 meters. The height of the scalene triangle is 14 meters. Find the area of the scalene triangle.

Simplify:

8. *(19)* $(-4)^2$ **9.** *(19)* -4^2 **10.** *(19)* $-2^2 + (-2)^2$

11. *(19)* $-3^2 - (-3)^2$ **12.** *(19)* $\sqrt[3]{8}$ **13.** *(19)* $\sqrt[3]{-8}$

Evaluate:

14. *(19)* $x^2 y^3 z$ if $x = 3$, $y = -2$, and $z = 4$

15. *(19)* $-x^2 - y^3$ if $x = -3$ and $y = -2$

Simplify by adding like terms:

16. *(18)* $xym - 3ymx - 4xmy - 3my + 2ym$ **17.** *(18)* $a - 3 - 7a + 2a - 6ax + 4xa - 5$

Expand by using the distributive property:

18. *(17)* $x(4 - ap)$ **19.** *(17)* $(5p - 2c)4xy$ **20.** *(17)* $4k(2c - a + 3m)$

Evaluate:

21. *(14)* $-x(a - 3x) + x$ if $a = 3$ and $x = 4$

22. *(14)* $-(a - x)(x - a)$ if $a = -5$ and $x = 3$

23. *(16)* $-a[(x - a) + (2x + a)]$ if $a = -4$ and $x = 3$

Simplify:

24. *(12)* $-3(4 - 3) - 3 - |-3|$ **25.** *(10)* $\dfrac{8 + 2 - 3(2)}{3(2) - 6}$

26. Find the perimeter of this figure. All
(3) angles are right angles. Dimensions
are in kilometers.

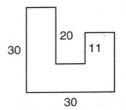

27. Find the area of this figure. Corners
(8) that look square are square. Dimensions are in inches.

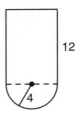

Simplify:

28. $9\frac{2}{15} - 3\frac{1}{5} - 3\frac{1}{3}$
(1)

29. $12.16608 \div 3.04$
(4)

30. Find the surface area of this right trian-
(15) gular prism. Dimensions are in feet.

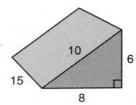

LESSON 20　Volume

In Lesson 15 we defined a **geometric solid** as a geometric figure that has three dimensions.
The **volume** of a geometric solid is the number of cubic units contained in the geometric solid.
A **cubic unit** is a cube having edges that measure one unit in length. A **cube** is a geometric
solid that has six identical square faces.

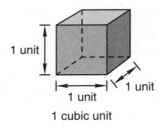

Volumes are always measured in cubic units. Some common units of volume are the cubic
centimeter $\left(cm^3\right)$ and the cubic meter $\left(m^3\right)$. It is important to remember that *units* are used
for length, *square units* are used for area, and *cubic units* are used for volume.

When we discuss volume, it is helpful to think of sugar cubes. We can visualize volume by mentally stacking sugar cubes. In the left-hand figure we have a rectangle that measures 3 cm by 2 cm. It has an area of 6 cm².

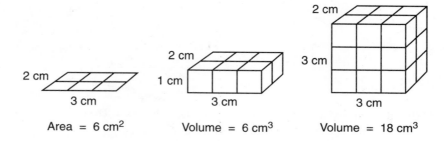

In the center figure we have placed a 1-cubic-centimeter sugar cube on each square. There are 6 cubes, so we say that the volume is 6 cm³. In the right-hand figure we have stacked the cubes three deep. There are 18 cubes, so we say that the volume is 18 cm³. From this we can induce that the volume equals the number of cubes on the bottom layer times the number of layers. We can extend this process to determine the volume of any right solid. We remember that geometric solids whose sides are at right angles to the bases are called **right solids.** The "top" and the "bottom" of a right solid are called the **bases** of the right solid and are identical geometric figures. If the bases of a right solid are polygons, the right solid is called a **right prism.** The volume of a right solid is equal to the number of cubes that we can place on the bottom layer (area of a base) times the number of layers (height of the right solid).

VOLUME OF A RIGHT SOLID

The volume of a right solid is equal to the area of a base times the height.

---

example 20.1   A base of the right prism is the isosceles triangle shown. The height of the right prism is 6 cm. Find the volume of the right prism.

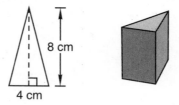

solution   First we find the area of a base of the right prism. Since a base of the right prism is a triangle, the area of a base can be easily computed.

$$\text{Area of a base} = \frac{1}{2}(4 \text{ cm})(8 \text{ cm}) = 16 \text{ cm}^2$$

The volume of a right prism is equal to the area of a base times the height. Therefore, we have

$$\text{Volume} = (\text{area of a base})(\text{height})$$

$$= \left(16 \text{ cm}^2\right)(6 \text{ cm})$$

$$= \mathbf{96 \text{ cm}^3}$$

example 20.2   A base of the right prism 8 meters high is shown. Find the volume of the right prism. Dimensions are in meters.

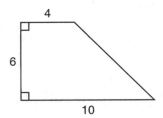

solution   First we find the area of a base of the right prism. The area of a base equals the sum of the areas of the rectangle and the right triangle.

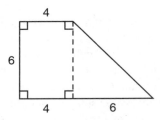

$$\text{Area of a base} = (4 \text{ m})(6 \text{ m}) + \frac{1}{2}(6 \text{ m})(6 \text{ m})$$

$$= 24 \text{ m}^2 + 18 \text{ m}^2$$

$$= 42 \text{ m}^2$$

The volume of a right prism is equal to the area of a base times the height. Therefore, we have

$$\text{Volume} = (\text{area of a base})(\text{height})$$

$$= \left(42 \text{ m}^2\right)(8 \text{ m})$$

$$= \mathbf{336 \text{ m}^3}$$

example 20.3   A base of the right solid 10 kilometers high is shown. Find the volume of the right solid. Dimensions are in kilometers.

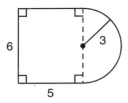

solution   First we find the area of a base of the right solid. The area of a base equals the sum of the areas of the rectangle and the semicircle.

$$\text{Area of a base} = \square + D$$

$$= (5 \text{ km} \times 6 \text{ km}) + \frac{\pi(3 \text{ km})^2}{2}$$

$$= 30 \text{ km}^2 + \frac{(3.14)(3 \text{ km})^2}{2}$$

$$= 30 \text{ km}^2 + 14.13 \text{ km}^2$$

$$= 44.13 \text{ km}^2$$

The volume of a right solid is equal to the area of a base times the height. Therefore, we have

$$\text{Volume} = (\text{area of a base})(\text{height})$$

$$= (44.13 \text{ km}^2)(10 \text{ km})$$

$$= \mathbf{441.3 \text{ km}^3}$$

example 20.4   A right circular cylinder has a radius of 6 inches and a height of 11 inches, as shown. Find the volume of the right circular cylinder.

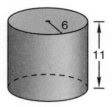

solution   First we find the area of a base of the right circular cylinder. Since a base of the right circular cylinder is a circle, the area of a base can be easily computed.

$$\text{Area of a base} = \pi(6 \text{ in.})^2 = 36\pi \text{ in.}^2$$

The volume of a right solid is equal to the area of a base times the height. Therefore, we have

$$\text{Volume} = (\text{area of a base})(\text{height})$$

$$= (36\pi \text{ in.}^2)(11 \text{ in.})$$

$$= 396\pi \text{ in.}^3$$

$$= 396(3.14) \text{ in.}^3$$

$$= \mathbf{1243.44 \text{ in.}^3}$$

example 20.5   A base of the right solid has an area of 52 ft^2. The height of the right solid is 15 ft. Find the volume of the right solid.

solution   The volume of a right solid is equal to the area of a base times the height. Therefore, we have

$$\text{Volume} = (\text{area of a base})(\text{height})$$

$$= (52 \text{ ft}^2)(15 \text{ ft})$$

$$= \mathbf{780 \text{ ft}^3}$$

practice   **a.**   A base of the right solid 10 inches high is shown. Find the volume of the right solid. Dimensions are in inches.

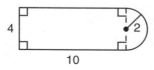

b. A right circular cylinder has a radius of 6 feet and a length of 20 feet, as shown. Find the volume of the right circular cylinder.

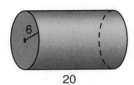

20

c. A base of the right solid has an area of 50 cm². The height of the right solid is 12 cm. Find the volume of the right solid.

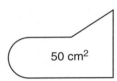 

50 cm²

problem set 20

1. Which of the following terms are like terms?
(18)

(a) $-3xym$ (b) $2xyp$ (c) $5xyk$ (d) $4myx$

2. Is the sum of a positive number and a negative number always a positive number?
(6)

3. (a) Designate the set of natural numbers.
(5)

   (b) Designate the set of whole numbers.

   (c) Designate the set of integers.

4. Use two unit multipliers to convert 50 meters to inches.
(4)

5. Use two unit multipliers to convert 600 square feet to square yards.
(10)

6. The perimeter of a rectangle is 110 inches. The width of the rectangle is 14 inches. Find the length of the rectangle.
(3)

7. The circumference of a circle is 10π feet. Find the radius of the circle.
(3)

Simplify:

8. $3^2 + (-3)^2$ **9.** $-2^2 + (-4)^2$ **10.** $-2^3 + (-2)^3$
(19)   *(19)*   *(19)*

11. $-(-3)^2 - (-2)^3$ **12.** $\sqrt[3]{-27}$ **13.** $(-3)^3 - \sqrt[3]{-27}$
(19)   *(19)*   *(19)*

Evaluate:

14. xz^2y^3 if $x = 2$, $z = -3$, and $y = -2$
(19)

15. $a^2 - b^2a$ if $a = -2$ and $b = 3$
(19)

Simplify by adding like terms:

16. $5 - x + xy - 3yx - 2 + 2x$ **17.** $-3pxk + pkx - 3kpx - kp - 3kx$
(18)   *(18)*

Expand by using the distributive property:

18. $-3(-x - 4)$ **19.** $(4 - 2p)4x$ **20.** $2x(a - 3p + 2)$
(17)   *(17)*   *(17)*

Evaluate:

21. $-p(-a + 2p) + p$ if $p = -3$ and $a = 2$
(14)

22. $k(ak - 4a) + k$ if $k = -3$ and $a = 2$
(14)

23. $a(x - a) + |x|$ if $a = -2$ and $x = -3$
(14)

Simplify:

24. $2[-3(-2 - 4)(3 - 2)]$ **25.** $\dfrac{(-4)(-3 + 7)(-1)}{(7 - 4 - 1)(2 - 3)}$
(13)   *(12)*

26. Find the perimeter of this figure. Cor-
_(3)_ ners that look square are square.
Dimensions are in centimeters.

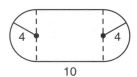

27. Find the area of this scalene triangle.
_(8)_ Dimensions are in meters.

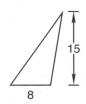

28. Find the area of the shaded portion of
_(8)_ this rectangle. Dimensions are in kilometers.

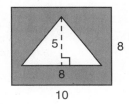

29. WX is $5\frac{1}{2}$ inches. XY is $12\frac{3}{10}$ inches. YZ is $3\frac{2}{5}$ inches. Find WZ.
_(1)_

30. A base of the right solid has an area of 45 ft^2. The height of the right solid is 10 ft. Find
_(20)_ the volume of the right solid.

LESSON 21   *Product Rule for Exponents • Addition of Like Terms with Exponents*

21.A
product rule for exponents

The product rule for exponents can be deduced from the definition of exponential notation. We know that

	(a) 3^5	means	$3 \cdot 3 \cdot 3 \cdot 3 \cdot 3$
and thus	(b) $3^2 \cdot 3^3$	means	$(3 \cdot 3) \cdot (3 \cdot 3 \cdot 3)$, or 3^5
and also	(c) $3 \cdot 3^4$	means	$(3) \cdot (3 \cdot 3 \cdot 3 \cdot 3)$, or 3^5

We see that when we multiply exponentials whose bases are the same, the exponent of the product is obtained by adding the exponents of the factors. Thus,

(a) $x^5 \cdot x^7 \cdot x^2 = x^{14}$ (b) $5^2 \cdot 5^3 \cdot 5^2 = 5^7$

(c) $p^5 \cdot p^{12} = p^{17}$ (d) $4^2 \cdot 4^3 \cdot 4^{25} = 4^{30}$

We call this rule the **product rule for exponents** and give the formal definition as follows:

PRODUCT RULE FOR EXPONENTS

If m and n are real numbers and $x \neq 0$, then

$$x^m \cdot x^n = x^{m+n}$$

We can use this rule to help simplify expressions that contain exponents.

example 21.1 Simplify: $x^2 y^2 x^5 y^3$

solution Since rearranging the order of the factors of a product does not change the value of the product, we may write $x^2 y^2 x^5 y^3$ as

$$x^2 x^5 y^2 y^3 = x^7 y^5$$

example 21.2 Simplify: $x^2 y^3 m^5 x^3 y^2$

solution First we rearrange the factors and then we simplify.

$$x^2 x^3 y^2 y^3 m^5 = x^5 y^5 m^5$$

Now we define the notation x^1.

DEFINITION

$$x^1 = x$$

This says that x means the same thing as x^1 and that x^1 means the same thing as x. **If any variable or constant is written without an exponent, it is understood to have an exponent of 1.** Thus,

$$5^1 \text{ equals } 5, \qquad 7^1 \text{ equals } 7, \qquad \text{and} \qquad x^1 \text{ equals } x$$

example 21.3 Simplify: $xyy^2 x^3$

solution First we rearrange the letters. Then we simplify, remembering that x means x^1 and y means y^1.

$$xx^3 yy^2 = x^4 y^3$$

example 21.4 Simplify: $m^3 pmxm^2 x^3 p^5$

solution We rearrange and simplify to get the result.

$$m^3 mm^2 xx^3 pp^5 = m^6 x^4 p^6$$

We note that there are six ways that this result can be written:

$$m^6 x^4 p^6 \qquad m^6 p^6 x^4 \qquad x^4 m^6 p^6 \qquad x^4 p^6 m^6 \qquad p^6 m^6 x^4 \qquad p^6 x^4 m^6$$

Because the order of factors does not affect the product, all six of these answers are equally correct and none is preferred. In mathematics, preference is reserved to the individual. There is no requirement to alphabetize the variables.

21.B

addition of like terms with exponents

In the previous section we noted that we multiply exponential expressions with like bases by adding the exponents. The task of adding like terms that contain exponents appears similar, but the rule is different. When we add like terms that contain exponents, we do not add the exponents. Thus

$$3x^2 + 2x^2 = 5x^2$$

and does not equal $5x^4$. Addition and multiplication are often confused, so we discuss them in the same lesson so that we can point out the difference.

When we add, we can only add like terms. We recall that letters stand for unspecified numbers and that the order of multiplication of real numbers can be changed. This means that

$$x^2yp^5 \qquad \text{and} \qquad p^5x^2y$$

are like terms, and that

$$xy^2p^5 \qquad \text{and} \qquad y^2xp^5$$

are like terms because the literal factors of the terms are the same.

example 21.5 Simplify by adding like terms: $x^2yp^5 + 2xy^2p^5 + 3p^5x^2y - 7y^2xp^5$

solution The first and third terms are like terms, and the second and fourth terms are also like terms. We add the numerical coefficients of these terms and get

$$\mathbf{4x^2yp^5 - 5xy^2p^5}$$

example 21.6 Simplify by adding like terms: $2m^3xy^2p + 3pxy^2m^3 - 10xy^2m^3p + yx^2m^3p$

solution The first three terms are like terms and may be added.

$$\mathbf{-5xy^2m^3p + yx^2m^3p}$$

example 21.7 Simplify by adding like terms: $2x^2y + 3yx^2 + x^2y^2 - x^2y - 4x^2y^2$

solution The first, second, and fourth terms are like terms and so are the third and fifth terms. Thus we add the first, second, and fourth terms and the third and fifth terms to obtain

$$\mathbf{4x^2y - 3x^2y^2}$$

practice Simplify:

   a. $xyx^4x^3y^5$ **b.** $x^3xy^2y^5x^7mm$

Simplify by adding like terms:

   c. $2x^2y^3 + xy - 8y^3x^2 - 5yx$ **d.** $x^6y + yx^6 + 3xy - 5xy^6$

problem set 21

1. Is the product of 13 negative numbers and 10 positive numbers a positive number or a negative number?
(13)

2. Use the letters a, b, and c and parentheses to write the distributive property.
(17)

3. (a) What is an isosceles triangle?
(2)

   (b) What is an equilateral triangle?

   (c) What is a scalene triangle?

4. Use two unit multipliers to convert 366 centimeters to feet.
(4)

5. Use two unit multipliers to convert 5000 square meters to square kilometers.
(10)

6. The area of a rectangle is 95 square centimeters. The width of the rectangle is
(8)   5 centimeters. Find the length of the rectangle.

7. The radius of a circle is 10 meters. Find the area of the circle.
(8)

Simplify:

8. x^2yyyx^3yx
(21)

9. $xm^2xm^3x^3m$
(21)

10. $ky^2k^3k^2y^5$
(21)

11. $a^2ba^2b^3ab^4$
(21)

Simplify by adding like terms:

12. $4xyz - 3yz + zxy$
(18)

13. $7 - 3k - 2k + 2kx - xk + 8$
(18)

14. $3ab^2 - 2ab + 5b^2a - ba$
(21)

15. $x^2 - 3yx + 2yx^2 - 2xy + yx$
(21)

Expand by using the distributive property:

16. $5(2 - 4p)$
(17)

17. $x(3p - 2y)$
(17)

18. $(3 - 2b)a$
(17)

Evaluate:

19. $(a - x)(x - a)$ if $a = -3$ and $x = 4$
(14)

20. $m(x - m) - |x|$ if $m = -3$ and $x = -4$
(14)

21. $x^2 - y^2$ if $x = -3$ and $y = -2$
(19)

Simplify:

22. $-5 - (-5)^2 - 3 + (-2)$
(19)

23. $-3^2 - 2^2 - (-3)^3 - \sqrt[3]{-8}$
(19)

24. $\dfrac{3 - [-(-3)]}{-(-2)}$
(13)

25. $\dfrac{5(-6 + 4) + 7(-3 + 9)}{(5 - 3) + 6}$
(12)

26. Find the perimeter of this figure. All
(3)   angles are right angles. Dimensions
      are in inches.

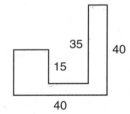

27. Find the area of this figure. Dimen-
(8)   sions are in feet.

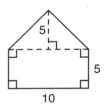

Simplify:

28. $\dfrac{-1\frac{3}{4}}{2\frac{1}{3}}$
(9)

29. $(0.004)(0.012)$
(4)

30. A right circular cylinder has a radius
(15)   of 3 yards and a length of 10 yards, as
      shown. Find the surface area of the
      right circular cylinder.

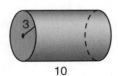

LESSON 22   *Review of Numerical and Algebraic Expressions • Statements and Sentences • Conditional Equations*

22.A
review of numerical and algebraic expressions

Each of the following expressions

$$\text{(a) } 4 \qquad \text{(b) } 6 + 3 \qquad \text{(c) } 4(2 + 3) \qquad \text{(d) } \frac{7(8 + 4)}{5 + 2}$$

is called a **numerical expression** because it consists of **a meaningful arrangement of numerals and symbols that designate specific operations.** Every numerical expression represents a particular number, and we say that this number is the **value** of the expression. The **values** of expressions (a), (b), (c), and (d) are 4, 9, 20, and 12, respectively.

We use the words **algebraic expression** to describe **numerical expressions** and also to describe expressions that contain variables.

$$\text{(e) } 6 \qquad \text{(f) } x + 4 \qquad \text{(g) } x^2 - 6 \qquad \text{(h) } x(x + 4)$$

Each of the expressions shown in (e) through (h) is an algebraic expression. The value of expression (e) is 6, but the values of expressions (f), (g), and (h) depend on the value that we assign to the variable x. If we assign to x the value of 3, then the values of expressions (f), (g), and (h) are 7, 3, and 21, respectively.

22.B
statements and sentences

If we wish to make a statement that certain quantities are equal or not equal, we can do so by writing a grammatical **sentence** in English.

(a) The number of peaches equals the number of apples.

(b) The number of peaches does not equal the number of apples.

(c) The number of peaches is greater than the number of apples.

(d) The number of peaches is less than the number of apples.

If we use the variables

$$N_p \qquad \text{and} \qquad N_a$$

to represent the number of peaches and the number of apples, and if we use the symbols

=	to mean	equal
≠	to mean	not equal
>	to mean	greater than (read left to right)
<	to mean	less than (read left to right)

we can make the same statements by writing algebraic sentences.

$$\text{(a) } N_p = N_a$$
$$\text{(b) } N_p \neq N_a$$
$$\text{(c) } N_p > N_a$$
$$\text{(d) } N_p < N_a$$

We see that all four are called statements or sentences but only the first one, (a), uses the equals sign. This algebraic statement is called an **equation.** The other three statements, (b), (c), and (d), do not use the equals sign and are called **inequalities.** We will discuss equations here and hold the topic of inequalities for a later lesson.

22.C

conditional
equations

An *equation* is an algebraic statement consisting of two algebraic expressions connected by an equals sign. Thus all the following are statements and all are also equations.

(a) $4 = 3 + 1$ (b) $4 + x = 2 + 2 + x$ (c) $4 = 6$

(d) $4 + x = 6 + x$ (e) $x + 4 = 8$

Equations are not always true equations, as we see here. Two of these equations are true equations and two are false equations, and the truth or falsity of one of them depends on the number we use as a replacement for x in the equation.

(a) This is a true equation because 4 does equal the sum of 3 and 1.

(b) This is a true equation regardless of the number we use as a replacement for x. We will demonstrate this by replacing x with –3 and then by replacing x with +7.

WITH (–3)	WITH (+7)
(b) $4 + (-3) = 2 + 2 + (-3)$	(b) $4 + (+7) = 2 + 2 + (+7)$
$4 - 3 = 4 - 3$	$4 + 7 = 4 + 7$
$1 = 1$ True	$11 = 11$ True

(c) This is a false equation because 4 is not equal to 6.

(d) This is a false equation regardless of the number we use as a replacement for x. We will demonstrate this by replacing x with –3 and then by replacing x with +7.

WITH (–3)	WITH (+7)
(d) $4 + (-3) = 6 + (-3)$	(d) $4 + (+7) = 6 + (+7)$
$4 - 3 = 6 - 3$	$4 + 7 = 6 + 7$
$1 = 3$ False	$11 = 13$ False

(e) We call this equation a **conditional equation** because its truth or falsity is conditioned by the number used as a replacement for x. If we use –2 as the replacement for x, we get a false equation; but if we use 4 as the replacement for x, we get a true equation.

WITH (–2)	WITH (4)
(e) $(-2) + 4 = 8$	(e) $(4) + 4 = 8$
$-2 + 4 = 8$	$4 + 4 = 8$
$2 = 8$ False	$8 = 8$ True

Replacement values of the variable that turn the equation into a true equation are called *solutions* of the equation or *roots* of the equation and are said to satisfy the equation. Thus in the equation

$$x + 4 = 8$$

we say that the number 4 is a **solution** or **root** of the equation, and we also say that the number 4 **satisfies** the equation.

example 22.1   Does –2 or +5 satisfy the equation $x^2 = -5x - 6$?

solution   First we try –2.

$$(-2)^2 = -5(-2) - 6 \qquad \text{replaced } x \text{ with } -2$$

$$4 = 10 - 6 \qquad \text{simplified}$$

$$4 = 4 \qquad \text{True}$$

Now we try +5.

$$(5)^2 = -5(5) - 6 \qquad \text{replaced } x \text{ with } 5$$
$$25 = -25 - 6 \qquad \text{simplified}$$
$$25 = -31 \qquad \text{False}$$

Thus **–2 is a solution** and **+5 is not a solution.**

example 22.2 Is –2 or +5 a root of the equation $x^2 - 3x = 10$?

solution First we try –2.

$$(-2)^2 - 3(-2) = 10 \qquad \text{replaced } x \text{ with } -2$$
$$4 + 6 = 10 \qquad \text{simplified}$$
$$10 = 10 \qquad \text{True}$$

Now we try +5.

$$(5)^2 - 3(5) = 10 \qquad \text{replaced } x \text{ with } 5$$
$$25 - 15 = 10 \qquad \text{simplified}$$
$$10 = 10 \qquad \text{True}$$

Thus, both –2 and +5 are solutions or roots to the given equation, and we say that **both –2 and +5 satisfy this equation.**

practice **a.** Does –2 or 2 satisfy the equation $x - 2 = 0$?

b. Is –2 or –5 a root of the equation $x^2 + 7x = -10$?

problem set 22

1.
(22) (a) What is an equation?

(b) What is a conditional equation?

2.
(22) What do we call the replacement values of the variable that turn an equation into a true equation?

3.
(18) Which of the following terms are like terms?

(a) $-aby$ (b) $8yba$ (c) $3abm$ (d) $-6bya$

4.
(4) Use one unit multiplier to convert 72 inches to centimeters.

5.
(10) Use two unit multipliers to convert 55 square meters to square centimeters.

6.
(3) The perimeter of a rectangle is 124 centimeters. Two of the sides are each 45 centimeters long. What is the length of each of the other two sides?

7.
(8) The area of a circle is 4π square meters. Find the radius of the circle.

8.
(22) Does –1 or 1 satisfy the equation $x - 1 = 0$?

9.
(22) Is –3 or 2 a root of the equation $x^2 - x = 12$?

Simplify:

10.
(21) $x^2xxy^2xy^3$

11.
(21) $a^2aba^3b^2a^5$

12.
(21) $p^2m^5ypp^3my^2$

13.
(21) $4p^2x^2kpx^3k^2k$

Simplify by adding like terms:

14. $-8 - py + 2yp + 4 - y$
(18)

15. $m + 4 + 3m - 6 - 2m + mc - 4mc$
(18)

16. $xy - 3xy^2 + 5y^2x - 4xy$
(21)

17. $-3x^2ym + 7x - 5ymx^2 + 16x$
(21)

Expand by using the distributive property:

18. $a(3x - 2)$
(17)

19. $4xy(5 - 2a)$
(17)

20. $2x(4a + b - 3m)$
(17)

Evaluate:

21. $cy(cx - y)$ if $x = -3$, $y = 3$, and $c = -2$
(14)

22. $|x - a| - a(-x)$ if $x = 4$ and $a = 3$
(14)

23. $a - b(a^2 - b)$ if $a = -2$ and $b = 3$
(19)

Simplify:

24. $(-3)^3 + (-2)^3 - |-2|$
(19)

25. $-3^2 - (-2)^2 + \sqrt[3]{-27}$
(19)

26. Find the perimeter of this figure. Cor-
(3) ners that look square are square.
Dimensions are in kilometers.

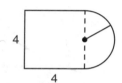

27. Find the area of this figure. All angles
(8) are right angles. Dimensions are
in inches.

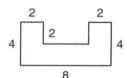

28. Find the area of the shaded portion of
(8) this right triangle. Dimensions are
in feet.

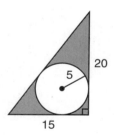

29. Find x.
(2)

30. A base of the right prism is the isosceles triangle shown. The height of the right prism is
(20) 10 in. Find the volume of the right prism.

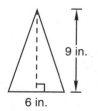

LESSON 23   *Equivalent Equations • Additive Property of Equality*

23.A
equivalent equations

Two equations are said to be equivalent if *every* solution of either one of the equations is also a solution of the other equation.

(a) $x + 6 = 9$ (b) $x + 10 = 13$

The two equations shown are equivalent equations, for the number 3 will satisfy both equations and 3 is the only number that will satisfy either equation.

23.B
additive property of equality

If we begin with the true statement that

$$2 = 2$$

and add +4 to both sides of the equality, we get the true statement that 6 equals 6.

$2 + 4 = 2 + 4$ $4 + 2 = 4 + 2$

$6 = 6$ $6 = 6$

On the left we placed the 4s after the 2s and on the right we placed the 4s before the 2s. We note that both procedures yield the same result. We emphasize this fact in the formal definition given in the box by writing the definition twice, the second time with the order of the addends reversed.

ADDITIVE PROPERTY OF EQUALITY

If a, b, and c are any real numbers and if $a = b$, then

$a + c = b + c$ and also $c + a = c + b$

The additive property of equality can be used to find the solution of conditional equations such as

$$x + 4 = 6$$

This equation is a conditional equation and is neither true nor false because no value has been assigned to x, so the additive property of equality does not apply. Thus we must hedge a little. We assume that some real number exists that when substituted for x will make the equation a true equation. We further assume that x in the equation represents this number. Now we have assumed that

$$x + 4 \text{ equals } 6$$

is a true statement, and thus we can use the additive property of equality. We will use the additive property of equality to eliminate the +4 that is now on the left side with x. We will add −4 to both sides of the equation.

$x + 4 = 6$	original equation
$\underline{-4 \quad -4}$	added −4 to both sides
$x + 0 = 2$	
$x = 2$	

Now since we made an assumption to permit the use of the additive property of equality, we must check our solution in the original equation.

$$x + 4 = 6 \qquad \text{original equation}$$

$$(2) + 4 = 6 \qquad \text{substituted 2 for } x$$

$$6 = 6 \qquad \text{True}$$

Since using the number 2 for x in the equation makes the equation a true equation, we say that the number 2 is a solution or root of the equation and that the number 2 satisfies the equation. It can be shown that the use of the additive property of equality will not change the numbers that satisfy the equation, so we say that the use of the additive property of equality results in an equation that is an **equivalent equation** to the original equation.

> If the same quantity is added to both sides of an equation, the resulting equation will be an **equivalent equation** to the original equation, and thus every solution of one of these equations will also be a solution of the other equation.

The rule says that we may add the same quantity to both sides of an equation, but it does not specify a particular format to be used, and one format is usually just as acceptable as another. Below are shown three possible formats for the problem worked previously.

(a)
$$\begin{array}{rcl} x + 4 &=& 6 \\ -4 &=& -4 \\ \hline x &=& 2 \end{array}$$

(b)
$$\begin{array}{rcl} x + 4 &=& 6 \\ -4 & & -4 \\ \hline x &=& 2 \end{array}$$

(c)
$$\begin{array}{rcl} x + 4 + (-4) &=& 6 + (-4) \\ x + 0 &=& 2 \\ x &=& 2 \end{array}$$

In (a) we added -4 to both sides of the equation and placed an equals sign between the -4s to *emphasize* that they are equal. In (b) we added -4 to both sides of the equation but omitted the equals sign since it is unnecessary. In (c) we added the -4s on the same line with the rest of the numbers and variables. This form is adequate for very simple problems such as this one but is less desirable for more complicated problems. By the end of the book, one should be able to perform this calculation mentally, without writing anything down, so that none of these formats will be necessary.

example 23.1   Solve: $x - 3 = 12$

solution   To solve the equation, we want to isolate x on one side of the equals sign. We can do this if we eliminate the -3. Thus we will add $+3$ to both sides of the equation.

$$\begin{array}{rcl} x - 3 &=& 12 \\ +3 & & +3 \\ \hline x &=& \mathbf{15} \end{array}$$

This same procedure can be used when the equation contains fractions or mixed numbers, as we see in the next two examples.

example 23.2   Solve: $x + \dfrac{1}{4} = -\dfrac{3}{8}$

solution   To isolate x we must eliminate the $\frac{1}{4}$. Thus, we add $-\frac{1}{4}$ to both sides of the equation.

$$\begin{array}{rcl} x + \dfrac{1}{4} &=& -\dfrac{3}{8} \\ -\dfrac{1}{4} & & -\dfrac{1}{4} \\ \hline x &=& -\dfrac{3}{8} - \dfrac{1}{4} \quad \longrightarrow \quad x = -\dfrac{5}{8} \end{array}$$

example 23.3   Solve: $k + 2\frac{1}{3} = \frac{2}{9}$

solution   This time we add $-2\frac{1}{3}$ to both sides of the equation and then simplify the result.

$$k + 2\frac{1}{3} = \frac{2}{9}$$

$$\underline{\quad -2\frac{1}{3} \qquad -2\frac{1}{3} \quad}$$

$$k \qquad = \quad \frac{2}{9} - 2\frac{1}{3} \quad \rightarrow \quad k = \frac{2}{9} - \frac{21}{9} \quad \rightarrow \quad k = -\frac{19}{9}$$

practice   Solve:

a. $x + 5 = 17$ **b.** $k - 27 = -38$

c. $x - \frac{1}{2} = \frac{3}{8}$ **d.** $d + 4\frac{1}{7} = 3\frac{1}{6}$

problem set 23

1. What does "solve an equation" mean?
(23)

2. What are equivalent equations?
(23)

3. What is the sum of the measures of the three angles of any triangle?
(2)

4. Use one unit multiplier to convert 150 meters to centimeters.
(4)

5. Use two unit multipliers to convert 116 square inches to square centimeters.
(10)

6. The area of a rectangle is 209 square inches. The length of one side is 19 inches. What is the length of the other side?
(8)

7. The area of a circle is 9π square feet. Find the radius of the circle.
(8)

Solve:

8. $x - 4 = 10$ **9.** $x + \frac{1}{5} = -\frac{1}{10}$ **10.** $x + 1\frac{1}{4} = -\frac{5}{8}$
(23)   (23)   (23)

11. Does -2 or 2 satisfy the equation $x + 2 = 0$?
(22)

12. Is -2 or 3 a root of the equation $x^2 - 2x = 3$?
(22)

Simplify:

13. $x^2 y m^5 x^2 y^4$ **14.** $x^3 y^2 m y x m$ **15.** $x x x^2 y y y^3 x y$
(21)   (21)   (21)

Simplify by adding like terms:

16. $-4 + 7x - 3x - 5 + 2x - 4x$ **17.** $p^2 xy - 3yp^2 x + 2xp^2 y - 5$
(18)   (21)

Expand by using the distributive property:

18. $4x(a + 2b)$ **19.** $(2x + 4)3$ **20.** $4px(my - 3ab)$
(17)   (17)   (17)

Evaluate:

21. $x(x - y) - y$ if $x = -2$ and $y = 3$
(14)

22. $(a - b)(b - x)$ if $x = 2$, $a = 3$, and $b = -3$
(14)

23. $x^3 - a(a - b)$ if $x = -2$, $a = 3$, and $b = 3$
(19)

Simplify:

24. $-3^2 - (-3)^2 + \sqrt[5]{32}$ **25.** $\dfrac{-3 - 4(4) - 6}{10 + (-5)(-4)}$
(19)   (12)

26. Find the perimeter of this figure. Cor-
⁽³⁾ ners that look square are square.
Dimensions are in yards.

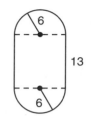

27. Find the area of this figure. Dimen-
⁽⁸⁾ sions are in centimeters.

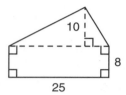

Simplify:

28. $3\frac{3}{7} \times 3\frac{1}{16}$
⁽⁴⁾

29. $\dfrac{3\frac{1}{5}}{-2\frac{2}{15}}$
⁽⁹⁾

30. Find the surface area of this right rec-
⁽¹⁵⁾ tangular prism. Dimensions are in
meters.

LESSON 24   *Multiplicative Property of Equality*

To demonstrate the **multiplicative property of equality,** we will begin with the true equation

$$2 = 2 \qquad \text{true}$$

and multiply both sides of the equation by 3.

$$3 \cdot 2 = 3 \cdot 2$$

The result is the true equation that 6 equals 6.

$$6 = 6 \qquad \text{still true}$$

The formal statement of the multiplicative property of equality in the box below is made twice to emphasize the fact that the order of the factors does not affect the product.

MULTIPLICATIVE PROPERTY OF EQUALITY

If a, b, and c are any real numbers and if

$$a = b,$$

then

$$ca = cb \qquad \text{and also} \qquad ac = bc$$

It is possible to use the multiplicative property of equality to prove that multiplying or dividing every term on both sides of an equation by the same nonzero number does not change the solution(s) to the equation. This means that the new equation is an equivalent equation to the original equation.

> If **every term** on both sides of an equation is multiplied or divided by the same nonzero quantity, the resulting equation will be an equivalent equation to the original equation, and thus every solution of one of these equations will be a solution of the other equation.

We can use this rule with either of two thought processes to solve equations such as

$$4x = 12$$

The first way is to remember that division by 4 will undo multiplication by 4 because division and multiplication are inverse operations. Thus, we solve by dividing both sides of the equation by 4.

$$4x = 12 \quad \longrightarrow \quad \frac{4x}{4} = \frac{12}{4} \quad \longrightarrow \quad x = 3$$

The second way is to remember that the product of 4 and its reciprocal is 1. To solve by using this thought, we will multiply both sides of the equation by $\frac{1}{4}$, which is the reciprocal of 4.

$$4x = 12 \quad \longrightarrow \quad \frac{1}{4} \cdot 4x = \frac{1}{4} \cdot 12 \quad \longrightarrow \quad x = 3$$

Both of the preceding thought processes are correct and either one can be used at any time.

example 24.1   Solve: $5x = 20$

solution   We can solve by (a) multiplying both sides of the equation by $\frac{1}{5}$, or by (b) dividing both sides of the equation by 5.

$$\text{(a)} \quad \frac{1}{5} \cdot 5x = \frac{1}{5} \cdot 20 \qquad \text{(b)} \quad \frac{5x}{5} = \frac{20}{5}$$

$$x = \mathbf{4} \qquad\qquad\qquad x = \mathbf{4}$$

example 24.2   Solve: $\frac{2}{5}x = 7$

solution   We can solve by (a) multiplying both sides of the equation by $\frac{5}{2}$, or by (b) dividing both sides of the equation by $\frac{2}{5}$.

$$\text{(a)} \quad \frac{5}{2} \cdot \frac{2}{5}x = \frac{5}{2} \cdot 7 \qquad \text{(b)} \quad \frac{\frac{2}{5}x}{\frac{2}{5}} = \frac{7}{\frac{2}{5}}$$

$$x = \frac{\mathbf{35}}{\mathbf{2}} \qquad\qquad x = 7 \cdot \frac{5}{2} \quad \longrightarrow \quad x = \frac{\mathbf{35}}{\mathbf{2}}$$

     Many beginning algebra students would prefer to write the preceding answer as the mixed number $17\frac{1}{2}$. Both forms of the answer are equally correct, but we prefer the improper fraction $\frac{35}{2}$ to the mixed number $17\frac{1}{2}$ because the improper fraction is easier to use. Suppose the instructions in this problem had been to solve and then multiply the answer by $\frac{11}{4}$. If we had written the answer as the mixed number $17\frac{1}{2}$, we would have to change it back to the improper fraction $\frac{35}{2}$ before the multiplication could be performed. Instructors at this level and in higher courses usually prefer the improper fraction to the mixed number.

example 24.3   Solve: $2\frac{1}{4}x = 3$

solution   We can undo multiplication by $2\frac{1}{4}$ by dividing both sides of the equation by $2\frac{1}{4}$,

$$2\frac{1}{4}x = 3 \quad \longrightarrow \quad \frac{2\frac{1}{4}x}{2\frac{1}{4}} = \frac{3}{2\frac{1}{4}} \quad \longrightarrow \quad x = \frac{3}{\frac{9}{4}} \quad \longrightarrow \quad x = \frac{12}{9} = \frac{4}{3}$$

or by rewriting $2\frac{1}{4}$ as the improper fraction $\frac{9}{4}$ and then multiplying both sides of the equation by $\frac{4}{9}$, which is the reciprocal of $\frac{9}{4}$.

$$\frac{9}{4}x = 3 \quad \longrightarrow \quad \frac{4}{9} \cdot \frac{9}{4}x = \frac{4}{9} \cdot 3 \quad \longrightarrow \quad x = \frac{4}{3}$$

example 24.4   Solve: $\frac{x}{3} = 9$

solution   We can undo division by 3 by multiplying both sides of the equation by 3. Thus, we multiply both sides of the equation by 3 and cancel.

$$3 \cdot \frac{x}{3} = 9 \cdot 3 \qquad \text{and thus} \qquad x = \mathbf{27}$$

We can also use the concept of inverse operations when x is divided by a fraction or a mixed number.

example 24.5   Solve: (a) $\dfrac{x}{2\frac{1}{2}} = 7$ (b) $\dfrac{p}{\frac{3}{2}} = 4\frac{1}{3}$

solution   (a) We can undo division by $2\frac{1}{2}$ by multiplying both sides of the equation by $2\frac{1}{2}$.

$$\frac{x}{2\frac{1}{2}} = 7 \quad \longrightarrow \quad \frac{2\frac{1}{2}x}{2\frac{1}{2}} = 7 \cdot 2\frac{1}{2} \quad \longrightarrow \quad x = 7 \cdot \frac{5}{2} \quad \longrightarrow \quad x = \frac{35}{2}$$

(b) We can undo division by $\frac{3}{2}$ by multiplying both sides of the equation by $\frac{3}{2}$.

$$\frac{p}{\frac{3}{2}} = 4\frac{1}{3} \quad \longrightarrow \quad \frac{\frac{3}{2}p}{\frac{3}{2}} = 4\frac{1}{3} \cdot \frac{3}{2} \quad \longrightarrow \quad p = \frac{13}{3} \cdot \frac{3}{2} = \frac{13}{2}$$

practice   Solve:

   a. $\frac{3}{5}x = 27$ **b.** $3\frac{1}{5}y = 32$ **c.** $\dfrac{x}{\frac{1}{4}} = 20$ **d.** $\dfrac{x}{2\frac{1}{4}} = 5$

problem set 24

   1.   Is the product of 16 negative numbers and 11 positive numbers a positive number or a
(13)   negative number?

   2.   Which of the following terms are like terms?
(18)

     (a) $-4xyk$ (b) $-4xyz$ (c) $7zyx$ (d) $7zyk$

3. (a) What are the measures of the angles of an equiangular triangle?
₍₂₎

(b) What are the measures of the angles of an equilateral triangle?

4. Use two unit multipliers to convert 280 miles to inches.
₍₄₎

5. Use two unit multipliers to convert 45 square feet to square inches.
₍₁₀₎

6. The length of the base of a right triangle is 24 centimeters. The height of the right triangle
₍₈₎ is 18 centimeters. Find the area of the right triangle.

7. The circumference of a circle is 12π meters. Find the radius of the circle.
₍₃₎

Solve:

8. $x + 5 = 7$
₍₂₃₎

9. $y - 3 = 2$
₍₂₃₎

10. $x - \dfrac{1}{4} = \dfrac{7}{8}$
₍₂₃₎

11. $y - \dfrac{1}{2} = -2\dfrac{1}{2}$
₍₂₃₎

12. $x + \dfrac{1}{2} = 2\dfrac{1}{5}$
₍₂₃₎

13. $2x = 20$
₍₂₄₎

14. $3x = 4\dfrac{1}{2}$
₍₂₄₎

15. $\dfrac{x}{3} = 5$
₍₂₄₎

16. $\dfrac{x}{\frac{1}{2}} = 4$
₍₂₄₎

17. Does –5 or 5 satisfy the equation $x - 5 = 0$?
₍₂₂₎

Simplify:

18. $m^2xyp^2x^3y^5$
₍₂₁₎

19. $3p^2xxypp^3xy^2$
₍₂₁₎

Simplify by adding like terms:

20. $a + 3 - 2a - 5a + 5 - a$
₍₁₈₎

21. $-3x^2ym + 5myx^2 - 2my^2x$
₍₂₁₎

22. Use the distributive property to expand $(3a - 5p)xy$.
₍₁₇₎

Evaluate:

23. $(-x)^3 - y$ if $x = -2$ and $y = 4$
₍₁₉₎

24. $a^3 - (a - b) + |a - b|$ if $a = -2$ and $b = 3$
₍₁₉₎

Simplify:

25. $-2\{-5(-3 + 4) - [3 - (-4)]\}$
₍₁₃₎

26. $(-2)^3 - (-2)^2 - 5 + \sqrt[3]{-64}$
₍₁₉₎

27. Find the perimeter of this figure. All
₍₃₎ angles are right angles. Dimensions
are in kilometers.

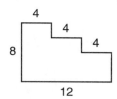

28. Find the area of this figure. All angles
₍₈₎ are right angles. Dimensions are in
inches.

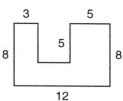

29. Find the area of the shaded portion of
₍₈₎ this isosceles triangle. Dimensions are
in feet.

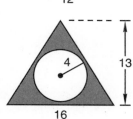

30. A base of the right solid has an area of 95 cm². The height of the right solid is 16 cm.
(20) Find the volume of the right solid.

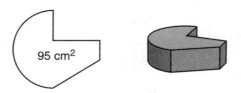

LESSON 25 *Solution of Equations*

In Lessons 23 and 24, we were introduced to the two rules for solving equations. These are two of the most important rules in algebra. In order to emphasize this fact, they are repeated here in boldface.

1. **The same quantity can be added to both sides of an equation without changing the answers[†] to the equation.**
2. **Every term on both sides of an equation can be multiplied or divided by the same nonzero quantity without changing the answers to the equation.**

In many equations, it is necessary to use both of these rules to find the solution. We will always use the addition rule first and then the multiplication/division rule. We do this because we are undoing a normal order of operations problem. To demonstrate, we will begin with the number 4, multiply by 3, and then add –2 for a result of 10.

$$3(4) - 2 = 10$$

Now, to undo what we have done and get back to 4, we must undo the addition of –2 first and then undo the multiplication. **This is the reason that in solving equations, we reverse the normal order of operations and undo addition first and then undo multiplication or division.** We demonstrate this procedure by replacing 4 with x in the above expression and getting the equation $3x - 2 = 10$. Now we solve to find that x equals 4.

$$3x - 2 = 10 \qquad \text{replaced 4 with } x$$
$$\underline{ +2 \quad +2} \qquad \text{added 2 to both sides}$$
$$3x \quad\;\; = 12$$

$$\frac{\cancel{3}x}{\cancel{3}} = \frac{12}{3} \;\longrightarrow\; x = 4 \qquad \text{divided both sides by 3}$$

example 25.1   Solve: $4x + 5 = 17$

solution   We must use the addition rule to eliminate the +5 and then use the multiplication/division rule to eliminate the 4. We always use the addition rule first.

$$4x + 5 = 17 \qquad \text{original equation}$$
$$\underline{ -5 \quad -5} \qquad \text{added } -5 \text{ to both sides}$$
$$4x \quad\;\; = 12$$

$$\frac{4x}{4} = \frac{12}{4} \;\longrightarrow\; x = \mathbf{3} \qquad \text{divided both sides by 4}$$

[†]We remember that the answers to an equation are formally called the solutions or roots of the equation.

example 25.2   Solve: $-5m + 6 = 8$

solution   To isolate m, we must first eliminate the 6 and then eliminate the -5.

$$\begin{array}{rl} -5m + 6 = 8 & \text{original equation} \\ \underline{-6\ \ -6} & \text{added } -6 \text{ to both sides} \\ \text{(a)}\quad -5m = 2 \end{array}$$

Now we complete the solution by dividing both sides of the equation by -5.

$$\frac{-5m}{-5} = \frac{2}{-5} \quad \longrightarrow \quad m = -\frac{2}{5}$$

Dividing by a negative number sometimes leads to errors. In this problem, division by a negative number can be avoided by mentally multiplying both sides of equation (a) by -1. This changes the signs on both sides.

$$-5m = 2 \quad \xrightarrow{\text{mentally multiplying both sides by } -1} \quad 5m = -2$$

Now we can finish by dividing both sides of the equation by $+5$.

$$\frac{5m}{5} = \frac{-2}{5} \quad \longrightarrow \quad m = -\frac{2}{5} \qquad \text{divided both sides by 5}$$

example 25.3   Solve: $-7k - 4 = -21$

solution   We begin by adding $+4$ to both sides of the equation.

$$\begin{array}{rl} -7k - 4 = -21 & \text{original equation} \\ \underline{+4+4} & \text{added 4 to both sides} \\ -7k = -17 \end{array}$$

Now we change the signs by mentally multiplying both sides of the equation by -1 and get

$$7k = 17$$

We finish by dividing both sides of the equation by $+7$.

$$\frac{7k}{7} = \frac{17}{7} \quad \longrightarrow \quad k = \frac{17}{7} \qquad \text{divided both sides by 7}$$

example 25.4   Solve: $-11p + 5 = 17$

solution   We first eliminate the $+5$ and then the -11.

$$\begin{array}{rl} -11p + 5 = 17 & \text{original equation} \\ \underline{-5-5} & \text{added } -5 \text{ to both sides} \\ -11p = 12 \end{array}$$

$$11p = -12 \qquad\qquad\qquad\qquad \text{multiplied both sides by } -1$$

$$\frac{11p}{11} = \frac{-12}{11} \quad \longrightarrow \quad p = -\frac{12}{11} \qquad \text{divided both sides by 11}$$

example 25.5   Solve: $\dfrac{1}{5}m - \dfrac{1}{2} = \dfrac{3}{4}$

solution   We first eliminate the $-\frac{1}{2}$.

$$\begin{array}{rl} \dfrac{1}{5}m - \dfrac{1}{2} = \dfrac{3}{4} & \text{original equation} \\[2mm] \underline{\phantom{\dfrac{1}{5}m}+\dfrac{1}{2}\ \ +\dfrac{1}{2}} & \text{added } \dfrac{1}{2} \text{ to both sides} \\[2mm] \dfrac{1}{5}m = \dfrac{5}{4} \end{array}$$

Now we finish by multiplying both sides of the equation by $\frac{5}{1}$.

$$\frac{5}{1} \cdot \frac{1}{5}m = \frac{5}{4} \cdot \frac{5}{1} \qquad \text{multiplied both sides by } \frac{5}{1}$$

$$m = \frac{25}{4}$$

example 25.6   Solve: $0.4x - 0.2 = -0.16$

solution   We first add $+0.2$ to both sides of the equation and then we divide both sides of the equation by 0.4.

$$
\begin{array}{ll}
0.4x - 0.2 = -0.16 & \text{original equation} \\
\underline{+0.2 \quad +0.2} & \text{added 0.2 to both sides} \\
0.4x \qquad = -0.04 &
\end{array}
$$

Now we divide both sides of the equation by 0.4.

$$\frac{\cancel{0.4}x}{\cancel{0.4}} = \frac{0.04}{0.4} \quad \longrightarrow \quad x = \mathbf{0.1} \qquad \text{divided both sides by 0.4}$$

practice   Solve:

a. $\dfrac{2}{5}x - \dfrac{3}{10} = \dfrac{1}{2}$ 　　　　　　　**b.**　$2\dfrac{1}{4}x + \dfrac{3}{7} = \dfrac{5}{14}$

c. $1.2 = -1.4 + 20x$ 　　　　　　　　　**d.**　$0.7x - 0.4 = 0.16$

problem set 25

1.
(18)
Which of the following terms are like terms?

　(a)　$5mnp$ 　　　(b)　$-mnk$ 　　　(c)　$3mny$ 　　　(d)　$-10npm$

2.
(9)
(a)　What operation is the inverse operation of addition?

(b)　What operation is the inverse operation of subtraction?

(c)　What operation is the inverse operation of multiplication?

(d)　What operation is the inverse operation of division?

3.
(4)
Use one unit multiplier to convert 508 centimeters to inches.

4.
(10)
Use two unit multipliers to convert 15,000 square centimeters to square meters.

5.
(3,8)
The area of a square is 9 cm^2. Find the perimeter of the square.

Solve:

6. $x - 5 = 3$ 　　　**7.** $x + \dfrac{1}{2} = \dfrac{2}{3}$ 　　　**8.** $x + 3\dfrac{1}{3} = 5$
(23)　　　　　　　　(23)　　　　　　　　　　　(23)

9. $4x = 2\dfrac{2}{3}$ 　　　**10.** $2x + 3 = 11$ 　　　**11.** $3x - 4 = 10$
(24)　　　　　　　　(25)　　　　　　　　　　(25)

12. $-2x - 2 = 10$ 　　　**13.** $\dfrac{1}{8}m - \dfrac{1}{4} = \dfrac{3}{4}$ 　　　**14.** $0.5x - 0.2 = 0.15$
(25)　　　　　　　　　(25)　　　　　　　　　　　　(25)

15.
(23)
(a)　What value of x satisfies the equation $x + 2 = 3$?

(b)　What value of x satisfies the equation $x + 5 = 6$?

(c)　Are the solutions of both equations the same?

(d)　Given your answer to part (c), are the two equations equivalent?

16.
(22)
Is -2 or 4 a root of the equation $x^2 - 2x = 8$?

Simplify:

17. $x^2kxk^2x^2ykx^2$
(21)

18. $aaa^3bxa^2b^3abx^4$
(21)

Simplify by adding like terms:

19. $6c - 6 - 2c - 5 - 3c + 7$
(18)

20. $a^2xx + a^2x^2 - 3x^2aa$
(21)

21. Use the distributive property to expand $4x(2y - 3 + 2a)$.
(17)

Evaluate:

22. $-b(b - a)$ if $a = -2$ and $b = 1$
(14)

23. $a(a^3 - b) - b$ if $a = -2$ and $b = 3$
(19)

Simplify:

24. $-3^2 + (-3)^3 - 4 - \sqrt[3]{27}$
(19)

25. $\dfrac{20 - 8 + (-6)(-2)}{8(-5) + 10}$
(12)

26. Find the perimeter of this figure. Corners that look square are square. Dimensions are in meters.
(3)

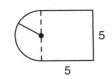

27. Find the area of this figure. Corners that look square are square. Dimensions are in kilometers.
(8)

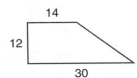

28. Find y.
(2)

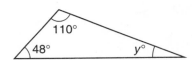

29. Simplify: $\dfrac{0.0636}{3.18}$
(4)

30. Find the surface area of this right triangular prism. Dimensions are in inches.
(15)

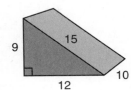

LESSON 26 More Complicated Equations

Often we will encounter equations that have variables on both sides of the equation. When this occurs, we will begin the solution by using the addition rule to eliminate the variable on one side or the other. It makes no difference which side we choose, as we will demonstrate by working the first problem both ways.

example 26.1   Solve: $3x - 4 = 5x + 7$

solution   We begin by eliminating the variable on the right-hand side by adding $-5x$ to both sides.

$$
\begin{array}{ll}
3x - 4 = 5x + 7 & \text{original equation} \\
\underline{-5x \qquad\;\; -5x} & \text{added } -5x \text{ to both sides} \\
-2x - 4 = \qquad 7 &
\end{array}
$$

We finish by adding $+4$ and then dividing by -2.

$$
\begin{array}{ll}
-2x - 4 = 17 & \\
\underline{+4 \quad +4} & \\
-2x \quad\;\; = 11 \;\rightarrow\; \dfrac{-2x}{-2} = \dfrac{11}{-2} \;\rightarrow\; x = -\dfrac{\mathbf{11}}{\mathbf{2}} & \text{added 4 to both sides} \\
& \text{divided by } -2
\end{array}
$$

example 26.2   Solve: $3x - 4 = 5x + 7$

solution   This time we begin by eliminating the variable on the left-hand side by adding $-3x$ to both sides.

$$
\begin{array}{ll}
3x - 4 = 5x + 7 & \text{original equation} \\
\underline{-3x \qquad\;\; -3x} & \text{added } -3x \text{ to both sides} \\
-4 = 2x + 7 &
\end{array}
$$

Now we finish by adding -7 and dividing by 2. We will get $-\frac{11}{2}$, the same answer that we got in the last example.

$$
\begin{array}{ll}
-4 = 2x + 7 & \\
\underline{-7 \qquad\;\; -7} & \\
-11 = 2x \;\rightarrow\; -\dfrac{11}{2} = \dfrac{2x}{2} \;\rightarrow\; x = -\dfrac{\mathbf{11}}{\mathbf{2}} & \text{added } -7 \text{ to both sides} \\
& \text{divided by 2}
\end{array}
$$

In many problems we must begin by simplifying on both sides by adding like terms.

example 26.3   Solve: $3x + 2 - x + 4 = -5 - x - 4$

solution   We begin by adding like terms on both sides of the equation to get

$$2x + 6 = -9 - x$$

This time we decide to eliminate the x term on the right-hand side, so we add $+x$ to both sides.

$$
\begin{array}{ll}
2x + 6 = -9 - x & \text{added like terms} \\
\underline{+x \qquad\qquad +x} & \text{added } x \text{ to both sides} \\
3x + 6 = -9 &
\end{array}
$$

Now we can finish by adding -6 to both sides and then dividing both sides by 3.

$$
\begin{array}{ll}
3x + 6 = \;\; -9 & \\
\underline{-6 \quad\; -6} & \\
3x \qquad = -15 \;\rightarrow\; \dfrac{3x}{3} = -\dfrac{15}{3} \;\rightarrow\; x = \mathbf{-5} & \text{added } -6 \text{ to both sides} \\
& \text{divided by 3}
\end{array}
$$

example 26.4   Solve: $k + 3 - 4k + 7 = 2k - 5$

solution   We will begin by adding like terms on both sides of the equation to get

$$-3k + 10 = 2k - 5$$

Next, we eliminate the $-3k$ on the left-hand side by adding $+3k$ to both sides and then finish the solution.

$$
\begin{array}{rl}
-3k + 10 = 2k - 5 & \text{added like terms} \\
\underline{+3k \qquad\quad +3k} & \text{added } 3k \text{ to both sides} \\
10 = 5k - 5 & \\
\underline{+5 \qquad +5} & \text{added 5 to both sides} \\
15 = 5k & \\
\\
\dfrac{15}{5} = \dfrac{5k}{5} & \text{divided both sides by 5} \\
\\
k = \mathbf{3} &
\end{array}
$$

example 26.5   Solve: $-7n + 3 + 2n = 4n - 5 + n$

solution   We begin by simplifying and then eliminating the $5n$ term on the right-hand side.

$$
\begin{array}{rl}
-5n + 3 = 5n - 5 & \text{simplified both sides} \\
\underline{-5n \qquad\quad -5n} & \text{added } -5n \text{ to both sides} \\
-10n + 3 = -5 & \\
\underline{-3 \quad -3} & \text{added } -3 \text{ to both sides} \\
-10n = -8 & \\
\\
10n = 8 & \text{multiplied both sides by } (-1)
\end{array}
$$

$$\frac{10n}{10} = \frac{18}{10} \quad \longrightarrow \quad n = \mathbf{\frac{4}{5}} \qquad \text{divided each side by 10 and}$$
$$\text{simplified answer}$$

Note that we used four steps in solving this equation. The steps were:

1. **Simplify by adding like terms.**
2. **Eliminate the variable on one side.**
3. **Eliminate the constant term on the side with the variable.**
4. **Solve for the variable.**

Check the order of these steps in the next problem.

example 26.6   Solve: $2x - 5 + 7x = 5 + 3x + 10$

solution   After we simplify, we will eliminate the $3x$ term on the right-hand side.

$$
\begin{array}{rl}
9x - 5 = 3x + 15 & \text{simplified} \\
\underline{-3x \qquad -3x} & \text{added } -3x \text{ to both sides} \\
6x - 5 = 15 & \\
\underline{+5 \quad +5} & \text{added 5 to both sides} \\
6x = 20 & \\
\\
\dfrac{6x}{6} = \dfrac{20}{6} & \text{divided both sides by 6} \\
\\
x = \mathbf{\dfrac{10}{3}} & \text{simplified answer}
\end{array}
$$

practice Solve:

a. $3m - 7m = 8m - 6$

b. $5 - 6p = 9p - 7 + 8p - 3 + 2p$

c. $2x + 3x + 4x - 5 = 2 + 3 + 4x$

d. $3p + 7 - (-3) = p + (-2)$

**problem set
26**

1.
(13)
Is the product of 8 positive numbers and 15 negative numbers a positive number or a negative number?

2.
(5)
(a) Designate the set of natural numbers.

(b) Designate the set of whole numbers.

(c) Designate the set of integers.

3.
(4)
Use one unit multiplier to convert 1000 centimeters to meters.

4.
(10)
Use two unit multipliers to convert 525 square centimeters to square inches.

5.
(8)
The length of the base of an isosceles triangle is 15 inches. The height of the isosceles triangle is 12 inches. Find the area of the isosceles triangle.

6.
(8)
The area of a circle is 16π square feet. Find the radius of the circle.

Solve:

7.
(23)
$k - \dfrac{2}{3} = 3\dfrac{1}{3}$

8.
(24)
$7x = 49$

9.
(24)
$2\dfrac{1}{2}x = \dfrac{3}{7}$

10.
(25)
$3x - 4 = 7$

11.
(25)
$-3y + \dfrac{1}{2} = \dfrac{5}{7}$

12.
(25)
$0.4x - 0.3 = -0.14$

13.
(26)
$3x - 2 = 6x + 4$

14.
(26)
$2x + x + 3 = x + 2 - 5$

15.
(26)
$-m - 6m + 4 = -2m - 5$

16.
(23)
(a) What value of x satisfies the equation $x - 4 = 6$?

(b) What value of x satisfies the equation $x - 2 = 8$?

(c) Are the solutions of both equations the same?

(d) Given your answer to part (c), are the two equations equivalent?

17.
(22)
Does -7 or 7 satisfy the equation $x + 7 = 0$?

Simplify:

18.
(21)
$m^2 y^5 m y y^3 m^3$

19.
(21)
$k^5 m m m^2 k^2 m^2 k^3 a a^2$

Simplify by adding like terms:

20.
(18)
$a - ax + 2xa - 3a - 3$

21.
(21)
$a^2 bc + 2bc - bca^2 + 5ca^2 b - 3cb$

22.
(17)
Use the distributive property to expand $4(7 - 3x^2)$.

Evaluate:

23.
(14)
$x(y - a) + a(y - x)$ if $x = -3$, $y = 2$, and $a = -1$

24.
(19)
$a(-a^2 + b) - |b - a|$ if $a = -2$ and $b = 4$

Simplify:

25.
(12)
$-4(-3 + 2) - 3 - (-4) - |-3 + 2|$

26.
(19)
$-3^2 - (-3)^3 + (-2) - \sqrt[3]{-125}$

27.
(3)
Find the perimeter of this figure. All angles are right angles. Dimensions are in miles.

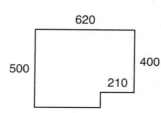

28. Find the area of this right triangle.
(8) Dimensions are in centimeters.

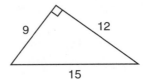

29. AB is $4\frac{2}{3}$ meters. BC is $5\frac{1}{4}$ meters. CD is $9\frac{1}{12}$ meters. Find AD.
(1)

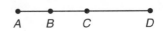

30. A right circular cylinder has a radius
(20) of 2 kilometers and a height of 6 kilometers, as shown. Find the volume of
the right circular cylinder.

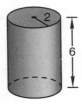

LESSON 27   *More on the Distributive Property • Simplifying Decimal Equations*

27.A
more on the distributive property

Remember that we can simplify expressions such as

$$4(2 + 7)$$

by adding first or by using the distributive property and multiplying first.

ADDING FIRST	MULTIPLYING FIRST
$4(2 + 7)$	$4(2 + 7)$
$4(9)$	$8 + 28$
36	36

Thus far, we have restricted our use of this property to expanding simple expressions such as $4p(x + 3y)$.

$$4p(x + 3y) = 4px + 12py$$

In the following examples, we will use the distributive property to expand expressions that are more complicated. We remember that in each case the expression on the outside is multiplied by every term inside the parentheses.

example 27.1 Use the distributive property to expand $xy\left(y^2 - x^2z\right)$.

solution The xy is multiplied by y^2 and also by $-x^2z$.

$$xy\left(y^2 - x^2z\right) = (xy)\left(y^2\right) + (xy)\left(-x^2z\right)$$

$$= xy^3 - x^3yz$$

example 27.2   Use the distributive property to expand $4xy^3(x^4y - 5x)$.

solution $4xy^3$ is to be multiplied by both x^4y and $-5x$.

$$4xy^3(x^4y - 5x) = (4xy^3)(x^4y) + (4xy^3)(-5x)$$
$$= 4x^5y^4 - 20x^2y^3$$

example 27.3   Use the distributive property to expand $(ay - 4y^5)2x^2y$.

solution   It is not necessary to write down two steps. We can do the multiplication in our head if we are careful.

$$(ay - 4y^5)2x^2y = 2ax^2y^2 - 8x^2y^6$$

example 27.4   Use the distributive property to expand $8m^2x(5m^3x - 3x^5 + 2x)$.

solution   This time $8m^2x$ must be multiplied by all three terms inside the parentheses.

$$8m^2x(5m^3x - 3x^5 + 2x) = (8m^2x)(5m^3x) + (8m^2x)(-3x^5) + (8m^2x)(2x)$$
$$= 40m^5x^2 - 24m^2x^6 + 16m^2x^2$$

27.B

simplifying decimal equations

Finding the solutions of equations such as

$$0.4 + 0.02m = 4.6 \qquad \text{and} \qquad 0.002k + 0.02 = 4.02$$

can be facilitated if we begin by multiplying every term on both sides of the equation by the power of 10 that will make every decimal coefficient an integer. The value of the smallest decimal number in the problem often determines whether we multiply by 10 or 100 or 1000 or 10,000, etc.

example 27.5   Solve: $0.4 + 0.02m = 4.6$

solution   The smallest decimal number in the problem is 0.02. We can convert 0.02 to 2 if we multiply by 100. Thus, we will multiply every term on both sides of the equation by 100 and then solve.

$0.4 + 0.02m = 4.6$	original equation
$40 + 2m = 460$	multiplied every term by 100
$2m = 420$	added -40 to both sides
$m = 210$	divided both sides by 2

example 27.6   Solve: $0.002k + 0.02 = 4.02$

solution   This time, the smallest decimal number is 0.002, so we will use 1000 as our multiplier.

$0.002k + 0.02 = 4.02$	original equation
$2k + 20 = 4020$	multiplied every term by 1000
$2k = 4000$	added -20 to both sides
$k = 2000$	divided both sides by 2

practice   Expand by using the distributive property:

  a. $xy^2(y^2p - p)$ **b.** $(xy - x)2xy$

  c. $3xp^3(p^5 - x^2p^8)$ **d.** $2x^2m^2(m^2 - 4m)$

Solve:

e. $0.08x - 0.1 = 16.7$

f. $0.7m + 0.6m = 3.4$

problem set 27

1. Which of the following terms are like terms?
(18)

    (a) $-7cba$ (b) $7cbd$ (c) $-2abc$ (d) $5bca$

2. If two sides of a triangle have equal lengths, then what is true about the angles opposite
(2) those sides?

3. Use two unit multipliers to convert 63,400 inches to miles.
(4)

4. Use two unit multipliers to convert 5800 square inches to square feet.
(10)

5. The perimeter of a square is 12 cm. Find the area of the square.
(3,8)

Solve:

6. $x - \dfrac{1}{4} = \dfrac{5}{8}$
(23)

7. $1\dfrac{1}{2}y = 6\dfrac{3}{4}$
(24)

8. $\dfrac{x}{3\dfrac{1}{2}} = 4$
(24)

9. $\dfrac{1}{2}x + \dfrac{3}{4} = -\dfrac{3}{8}$
(25)

10. $0.02m + 0.2 = 1.4$
(27)

11. $0.4x - 0.2 = -0.12$
(27)

12. $5x - 3 - 2 = 3x - 2 + x$
(26)

13. $x + 3 - 5 - 2x = x - 3 - 7x$
(26)

14. $m + 4m - 2 - 2m = 2m + 2 - 3$
(26)

15. (a) What value of x satisfies the equation $x + 3 = 2$?
(23)

    (b) What value of x satisfies the equation $x + 5 = 4$?

    (c) Are the solutions to both equations the same?

    (d) Given your answer to part (c), are the two equations equivalent?

16. Is -3 or 1 a root of the equation $x^2 + 2x = 3$?
(22)

Simplify:

17. $p^2xyy^2x^2yx^2x$
(21)

18. $3p^2x^4yp^5xxyy^2$
(21)

Simplify by adding like terms:

19. $-4x + x^2 - 3x - 5 + 7x^2$
(21)

20. $xyp^2 - 4p^2xy + 5xp^2y - 7yxp^2$
(21)

21. Use the distributive property to expand $4x^2(ax - 2)$.
(27)

Evaluate:

22. $(a - b) + (-a)^2$ if $a = -3$ and $b = 6$
(19)

23. $-(-p)^2 + (p - x)$ if $p = -2$ and $x = 5$
(19)

Simplify:

24. $-3^2 - 3(3^2 - 4) - \sqrt[4]{16} - |-7 + 2|$
(19)

25. $\dfrac{-6 - (-2 - 3) + 1}{4 - (-3) - 7}$
(10)

26. Find the perimeter of this figure. All
(3) angles are right angles. Dimensions
are in meters.

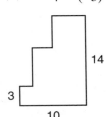

27. Find the area of this figure. Dimen-
(8) sions are in kilometers.

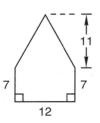

28. Find the area of the shaded portion of
(8) this rectangle. Dimensions are in
inches.

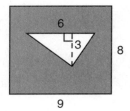

29. Find x and y.
(2)

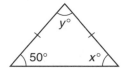

30. A right circular cylinder has a radius
(15) of 4 feet and a height of 7 feet, as
shown. Find the surface area of the
right circular cylinder.

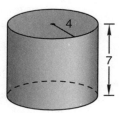

LESSON 28 *Fractional Parts of Numbers • Functional Notation*

28.A

**fractional
parts of
numbers**

When we multiply a number by a fraction, we say that the result is a fractional part of the number. If we multiply $\frac{7}{8}$ by 48, we get 42. We say this mathematically by writing

$$\frac{7}{8} \times 48 = 42$$

and if we use words we say that

(seven eighths)   (of 48)   (is 42)

We can generalize this problem into an equation that has three parts.

$$(F) \times (\text{of}) = (\text{is})$$

The letter F stands for "fraction," and the words *of* and *is* associate the parts of the statement as we note in the following examples. We will use the variable WN to represent "what number" and WF to represent "what fraction." We will avoid the use of the meaningless variable x.

example 28.1 $\dfrac{3}{4}$ of what number is 69?

solution   In this problem, the fraction is $\frac{3}{4}$, the word *of* associates with "what number" (*WN*), and the word *is* associates with 69. We make these replacements and get.

$$(F) \times (\text{of}) = (\text{is}) \quad \longrightarrow \quad \left(\dfrac{3}{4}\right) \times (WN) = 69$$

We can undo multiplication by $\frac{3}{4}$ by multiplying by $\frac{4}{3}$. Thus we solve by multiplying both sides of the equation by $\frac{4}{3}$.

$$\dfrac{4}{3} \cdot \dfrac{3}{4} WN = 69 \cdot \dfrac{4}{3} \quad \longrightarrow \quad WN = \mathbf{92}$$

example 28.2   What fraction of 40 is 24?

solution   This time the fraction is unknown, *of* associates with 40, and *is* associates with 24. We make these replacements. Then to solve, we divide both sides of the equation by 40.

$$(F) \times (\text{of}) = (\text{is}) \quad \longrightarrow \quad (WF)(40) = (24) \quad \longrightarrow \quad \dfrac{WF \cdot \cancel{40}}{\cancel{40}} = \dfrac{24}{40} \quad \longrightarrow \quad WF = \mathbf{\dfrac{3}{5}}$$

example 28.3 $2\dfrac{1}{2}$ of 240 is what number?

solution   This time the fraction is written as the mixed number $2\frac{1}{2}$. We see that *of* associates with 240 and *is* with "what number" (*WN*). We make these substitutions and solve by multiplying $2\frac{1}{2}$ and 240.

$$(F) \times (\text{of}) = (\text{is}) \quad \longrightarrow \quad \left(2\tfrac{1}{2}\right)(240) = WN \quad \longrightarrow \quad WN = \mathbf{600}$$

28.B
functional notation

We will begin our study of **functions** by introducing **functional notation.** The algebraic expression

$$x + 2$$

has exactly one value for any real number that we choose as a replacement for x. If we replace x with 5, the expression has a value of 7, and for x values of 0 and –75, the expression has the values 2 and –73, respectively, as we show here.

when $x = 5$	when $x = 0$	when $x = -75$
$(5) + 2 = 7$	$(0) + 2 = 2$	$(-75) + 2 = -73$

If an expression in which the only variable is x has exactly one value for any value of x we call the expression a **function of x.** Since $x + 2$ has only one value for any replacement value of x, we can say that $x + 2$ is a function of x. If we write an equation where y equals $x + 2$

$$y = x + 2$$

we can say that y is a function of x. If x is replaced with 5, 0, and –75, in that order, we get values of y of 7, 2, and –73, respectively, as we show here.

when $x = 5$	when $x = 0$	when $x = -75$
$y = x + 2$	$y = x + 2$	$y = x + 2$
$y = (5) + 2$	$y = (0) + 2$	$y = (-75) + 2$
$y = 7$	$y = 2$	$y = -73$

Mathematicians have found it convenient to use $f(x)$ in the equation instead of using y. We read the following equation

$$f(x) = x + 2$$

by saying "f of x equals $x + 2$." This form uses what we call *functional notation*. We do not have to restrict ourselves to the letter f. We can use any letter in the alphabet instead of f and can use other symbols such as Greek letters. Suppose we have the three equations

$$y = x + 7 \qquad y = x^2 - 2 \qquad y = 2x^3 - 3$$

If we ask someone to find the value of y when x equals -3, they will not know which equation to use. So let us use functional notation to identify the functions and write:

$$f(x) = x + 7 \qquad g(x) = x^2 - 2 \qquad h(x) = 2x^3 - 3$$

which we read as "f of x equals $x + 7$," "g of x equals $x^2 - 2$," and "h of x equals $2x^3 - 3$." Now we have named the functions the f function, the g function, and the h function. If we are asked to find $h(-3)$, we are asked to find the value of the h function when x is replaced with -3.

$$
\begin{array}{ll}
h(x) = 2x^3 - 3 & h \text{ function} \\
h(-3) = 2(-3)^3 - 3 & \text{replaced } x \text{ with } -3 \\
h(-3) = 2(-27) - 3 & \text{simplified} \\
h(-3) = -57 & \text{simplified}
\end{array}
$$

In this example we can see three benefits of using functional notation. The first line identified the h function as $2x^3 - 3$. In the next two lines, $h(-3)$ tells us that we have replaced x with -3, and in the last line we see that the value of the h function when x is replaced with -3 is -57. We read this line by saying "h of -3 equals -57."

In essence, a functional notation problem is exactly the same as the evaluation problems we have been doing. To demonstrate, we will state the problem two ways, as we show in the following examples.

example 28.4 Evaluate: $x(x^2 - 3x)$ if $x = 2$

solution We find the answer by replacing x everywhere with 2.

$$
\begin{array}{ll}
x(x^2 - 3x) & \text{expression} \\
= 2[(2)^2 - 3(2)] & \text{replaced } x \text{ with 2} \\
= 2(4 - 6) & \text{simplified} \\
= 2(-2) & \text{simplified} \\
= -4 & \text{simplified}
\end{array}
$$

example 28.5 If $f(x) = x(x^2 - 3x)$, find $f(2)$.

solution This problem is the same problem as the evaluation problem in example 28.4. We just restated this problem by using functional notation. We read this example by saying "if f of x equals $x(x^2 - 3x)$, find f of 2." We find the answer by replacing x everywhere with 2.

$$
\begin{array}{ll}
f(x) = x(x^2 - 3x) & f \text{ function} \\
f(2) = 2[(2)^2 - 3(2)] & \text{replaced } x \text{ with 2} \\
f(2) = 2(4 - 6) & \text{simplified} \\
f(2) = 2(-2) & \text{simplified} \\
f(2) = -4 & \text{simplified}
\end{array}
$$

example 28.6   Evaluate: $x^2(2x - 1)$ if $x = -2$

solution   We find the answer by replacing x everywhere with –2.

$$x^2(2x - 1) \qquad \text{expression}$$
$$= (-2)^2[2(-2) - 1] \qquad \text{replaced } x \text{ with } -2$$
$$= 4(-4 - 1) \qquad \text{simplified}$$
$$= 4(-5) \qquad \text{simplified}$$
$$= \mathbf{-20} \qquad \text{simplified}$$

example 28.7   If $g(x) = x^2(2x - 1)$, find $g(-2)$.

solution   This problem is the same problem as the evaluation problem in example 28.6. We just restated this problem by using functional notation. We read this example by saying "if g of x equals $x^2(2x - 1)$, find g of –2." We find the answer by replacing x everywhere with –2.

$$g(x) = x^2(2x - 1) \qquad g \text{ function}$$
$$g(-2) = (-2)^2[2(-2) - 1] \qquad \text{replaced } x \text{ with } -2$$
$$g(-2) = 4(-4 - 1) \qquad \text{simplified}$$
$$g(-2) = 4(-5) \qquad \text{simplified}$$
$$g(-2) = \mathbf{-20} \qquad \text{simplified}$$

practice   **a.** $\dfrac{4}{3}$ of what number is 64?   **b.** $3\dfrac{1}{5}$ of what number is 48?

         c.   What fraction of 60 is 48?   **d.** $4\dfrac{1}{2}$ of 220 is what number?

         e.   If $f(x) = x^2 - 3$, find $f(-1)$.   **f.**   If $g(x) = x(x^2 - 3)$, find $g(2)$.

problem set 28

1.
(13)
Is the product of 17 positive numbers and 17 negative numbers a positive number or a negative number?

2.
(2)
If two angles of a triangle have equal measures, then what is true about the sides opposite those angles?

3.
(4)
Use two unit multipliers to convert 3938 inches to meters.

4.
(10)
Use two unit multipliers to convert 200 square kilometers to square meters.

5.
(8)
The area of a circle is 25π square inches. Find the diameter of the circle.

6. $\dfrac{2}{5}$ of what number is 40?   **7.**   What fraction of 30 is 25?
(28)   (28)

8. If $f(x) = x + 1$, find $f(2)$.   **9.**   If $g(x) = 2x + 1$, find $g(-1)$.
(28)   (28)

Solve:

10. $3x = 18$ **11.** $2x - 3 = -9$ **12.** $\dfrac{1}{5}x + \dfrac{1}{2} = 2\dfrac{1}{10}$
(24)   (25)   (25)

13. $0.05x - 0.3 = 1.8$
(27)

14. $x - 2 - 2x = 3 - x + 4x$
(26)

15. $3y - y + 2y - 5 = 7 - 2y + 5$
(26)

16. (a) What value of x satisfies the equation $x - 7 = -1$?
(23)

(b) What value of x satisfies the equation $x - 3 = 3$?

(c) Are the solutions of both equations the same?

(d) Given your answer to part (c), are the two equations equivalent?

17. Does -10 or 10 satisfy the equation $x - 10 = 0$?
(22)

Simplify:

18. $y^5 x^2 y^3 yxy^2$
(21)

19. $m^2 myy^2 m^3 ym$
(21)

Simplify by adding like terms:

20. $pc - 4cp + c - p + 7pc - 7c$
(18)

21. $xym^2 + 3xy^2 m - 4m^2 xy + 5mxy^2$
(21)

22. Use the distributive property to expand $x^2 y(x^3 - xyz^3)$.
(27)

Evaluate:

23. $p(a) - xp(-a)$ if $p = -2$, $a = 3$, and $x = 4$
(14)

24. $x^3 y(x - y)$ if $x = -3$ and $y = 1$
(19)

Simplify:

25. $-4(-7 + 5)(-2) - |-2 - 5|$
(12)

26. $-3^2 + (-2)^3 - \sqrt[4]{81}$
(19)

27. Find the perimeter of this figure. Cor-
(3) ners that look square are square.
Dimensions are in feet.

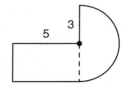

28. Find the area of this figure. Corners
(8) that look square are square. Dimensions are in miles.

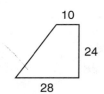

29. Find x.
(2)

30. A base of the right prism is the isosceles triangle shown. The height of the right prism is
(20) 12 cm. Find the volume of the right prism.

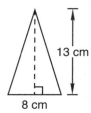 

LESSON 29 *Negative Exponents* • *Zero Exponents*

29.A

negative exponents

It is convenient to have an alternative way to write the reciprocal of an exponential expression. Here we show an alternative way to write 1 over 5^2 and 1 over 5^{-2}.

$$\frac{1}{5^2} = 5^{-2} \qquad \frac{1}{5^{-2}} = 5^2$$

In the formal definition we will use x and n to represent the base and the exponent.

DEFINITION OF x^{-n}

If n is any real number and x is any real number that is not zero, then

$$\frac{1}{x^n} = x^{-n}$$

(a) $\dfrac{1}{3^4} = 3^{-4}$ (b) $7^{-2} = \dfrac{1}{7^2}$ (c) $\dfrac{1}{5^{-8}} = 5^8$ (d) $6^{-3} = \dfrac{1}{6^3}$

In (a) we moved 3^4 from the denominator to the numerator and **changed the sign of the exponent** from plus to minus. In (b) we moved 7^{-2} from the numerator to the denominator and **changed the sign of the exponent** from minus to plus. In (c) we moved 5^{-8} from the denominator to the numerator and **changed the sign of the exponent** from minus to plus. In (d) we moved 6^{-3} from the numerator to the denominator and **changed the sign of the exponent** from minus to plus. The formal definition of x^{-n} is stated in the box above. We will now state the definition informally.

A number or a variable that is written as an exponential expression can be written in reciprocal form if the sign of the exponent is changed.

If the exponent is positive, the exponent is negative in the reciprocal form. If the exponent is negative, the exponent is positive in the reciprocal form.

example 29.1 Simplify: 3^{-2}

solution The negative exponent is meaningless as an operation indicator. Thus the first step in the solution is to write 3^{-2} in reciprocal form and change the negative exponent to a positive exponent.

$$3^{-2} = \frac{1}{3^2}$$

Now we can complete the simplification because a positive exponent is an operation indicator because 3^2 means $3 \cdot 3$.

$$3^{-2} = \frac{1}{3^2} = \frac{1}{3 \cdot 3} = \mathbf{\frac{1}{9}}$$

example 29.2   Simplify: $\dfrac{1}{3^{-3}}$

solution   Again, as the first step we write the expression in reciprocal form so that the negative exponent can be changed to a positive exponent.

$$\frac{1}{3^{-3}} = 3^3$$

Now 3^3 is meaningful as $3 \cdot 3 \cdot 3,$ and 3^3 equals 27, so

$$\frac{1}{3^{-3}} = 3^3 = 3 \cdot 3 \cdot 3 = \mathbf{27}$$

example 29.3   Simplify: $(-3)^{-2}$

solution   We first change the negative exponent to a positive exponent by writing the exponential expression in reciprocal form.

$$(-3)^{-2} = \frac{1}{(-3)^2} = \frac{\mathbf{1}}{\mathbf{9}}$$

We have defined negative exponents so that their use will not conflict with the use of the product rule, which is repeated here.

> PRODUCT RULE FOR EXPONENTS
>
> If m and n are real numbers and $x \neq 0$, then
>
> $$x^m \cdot x^n = x^{m+n}$$

When the bases are the same, we multiply exponential expressions by adding the exponents. This is true even if some of the exponents are negative numbers.

(a) $x^{-5}x^2 = x^{-3}$ (b) $y^7y^5y^{-2} = y^{10}$ (c) $p^{10}p^{-15} = p^{-5}$

example 29.4   Simplify: $x^4m^2x^{-2}m^{-5}$

solution   We first change the order of multiplication

$$x^4x^{-2}m^2m^{-5}$$

and then add the exponents of the exponential expressions whose bases are the same.

$$\mathbf{x^2m^{-3}}$$

example 29.5   Simplify: $x^{-2}y^{-6}y^5x^4zxz^5$

solution   We change the orders of the factors and add the exponents of the exponential expressions that have the same bases to get

$$x^{-2}x^4xy^{-6}y^5zz^5 = \mathbf{x^3y^{-1}z^6}$$

29.B

zero exponents

We know that a nonzero number divided by itself equals 1. For instance,

$$1 = \frac{4^2}{4^2}$$

We can simplify this expression by moving the 4^2 on the bottom to the top and changing the exponent from 2 to –2. Then we multiply 4^2 by 4^{-2} and get 4^0.

$$1 = \frac{4^2}{4^2} = 4^2 \cdot 4^{-2} = 4^0$$

Now, 4^0 must equal 1 because 4^2 divided by 4^2 equals 1. In the same way, we see that any nonzero quantity raised to the zero power must have a value of 1.

$$(x + y + z^2)^0 = 1 \qquad (pm)^0 = 1 \qquad (px^{-4})^0 = 1$$

Each of the above has a value of 1 if the expression in parentheses does not have a value of zero. Zero raised to the zero power has no meaning.

DEFINITION

If x is any real number that is not zero, then

$$x^0 = 1$$

---

example 29.6 Simplify the following expressions: (a) $x^2y^5y^{-2}x^{-2}$ (b) $m^5b^2mb^{-2}$

solution (a) $x^2y^5y^{-2}x^{-2} = y^3x^0 = \mathbf{y^3}$ (because $x^0 = 1$ if $x \neq 0$)

(b) $m^5b^2mb^{-2} = m^6b^0 = \mathbf{m^6}$ (because $b^0 = 1$ if $b \neq 0$)

Since we must not use the expression 0^0, it is necessary in problems such as (a) and (b) to assume that the variable with the zero exponent is not zero. Further, in the problem sets, we will assume a nonzero value for any variable that has zero for its exponent.

example 29.7 Use the distributive property to expand $x^5y^0z(p^{-3}z^0 - 4x^{-5}z^{-1})$.

solution We choose to begin by simplifying x^5y^0z and $p^{-3}z^0$, remembering that $y^0 = 1$ and that $z^0 = 1$. Now we have

$$x^5z(p^{-3} - 4x^{-5}z^{-1})$$

We finish by doing the two multiplications and get

$$x^5zp^{-3} - 4x^0z^0 = \mathbf{x^5zp^{-3} - 4}$$

example 29.8 Use the distributive property to expand $x^{-2}y^{-2}(x^2y^2 + 4x^4y^2)$.

solution We do the two multiplications and get

$$x^{-2}y^{-2}x^2y^2 + x^{-2}y^{-2}4x^4y^2$$

Now we simplify by remembering that both x^0 and y^0 equal 1.

$$x^0y^0 + 4x^2y^0 = (1)(1) + 4x^2(1) = \mathbf{1 + 4x^2}$$

example 29.9 Simplify: (a) 2^0 (b) -2^0 (c) $(-2)^0$

solution Any expression (except 0) raised to the zero power has a value of 1. Thus the answer to both (a) and (c) is **1**. The expression in (b) asks for the value of the opposite of 2^0. The answer to (b) is **–1**.

practice Simplify:

a. $\dfrac{1}{2^{-3}}$ b. $(-4)^{-2}$ c. $\dfrac{1}{(-3)^{-2}}$

d. 8^0 e. -8^0 f. $(-3)^0$

g. $\left(p + m + k^2\right)^0$ h. $x^{-3}y^{-8}y^5x^4zx^2z^5$ i. $x^6y^{-3}x^2y^3$

j. Use the distributive property to expand $2x^{-2}y^3\left(x^2y - 3x^{-1}y^{-3}\right)$.

problem set 29

1. Which of the following terms are like terms?
(18)

    (a) $6pcy$ (b) $-5ycp$ (c) $-5yck$ (d) $6pck$

2. What is the name of the quadrilateral that has two pairs of parallel sides?
(2)

3. Use two unit multipliers to convert 500 feet to centimeters.
(4)

4. Use two unit multipliers to convert 180 square yards to square feet.
(10)

5. The area of a square is 16 in.^{2}. Find the perimeter of the square.
(3,8)

Simplify:

6. 2^{-2} **7.** $\dfrac{1}{4^{-2}}$ **8.** 3^0
(29)   (29)   (29)

9. $2\frac{1}{4}$ of what number is 72? **10.** $3\frac{1}{8}$ of 72 is what number?
(28)   (28)

11. If $f(x) = 2x - 1$, find $f(3)$. **12.** If $g(x) = 3x + 2$, find $g(-2)$.
(28)   (28)

Solve:

13. $-x = 3$ **14.** $\dfrac{y}{2\frac{1}{3}} = 6$ **15.** $\dfrac{1}{4}x + \dfrac{1}{2} = \dfrac{7}{8}$
(24)   (24)   (25)

16. $0.002k + 0.04 = 2.04$ **17.** $3x + 5 - x = x + 5$
(27)   (26)

18. $3m - 2 - m = -2 + m - 5$
(26)

Simplify:

19. $x^5m^2x^{-3}m^{-4}$ **20.** $a^3b^{-4}a^{-3}b^6$
(29)   (29)

21. Simplify by adding like terms: $4x^2yp - 7px^2y + 3ypx^2 - 4$
(21)

Expand by using the distributive property:

22. $x^2y^3(3xy - 5y)$ **23.** $x^{-2}y\left(x^2y + 2x^3y^0\right)$
(27)   (29)

Evaluate:

24. $4x(a + x)(-x)$ if $x = -3$ and $a = 2$
(14)

25. $a^2 - (a + b) - \left|-a^3\right|$ if $a = -2$ and $b = 3$
(19)

26. Simplify: $\dfrac{2^2 - 3^2 - 4^2}{(-3)^2}$
(19)

27. Find the perimeter of this figure. All angles are right angles. Dimensions are in feet.
(3)

28.
(8)
Find the area of this figure. Dimensions are in miles.

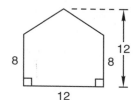

29.
(8)
Find the area of the shaded portion of this scalene triangle. Dimensions are in centimeters.

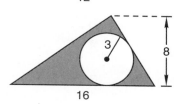

30.
(15)
Find the surface area of this right rectangular prism. Dimensions are in meters.

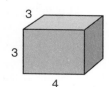

LESSON 30   *Algebraic Phrases • Decimal Parts of a Number*

30.A

algebraic phrases

In algebra we learn to answer verbal questions by turning these questions into algebraic equations. Then we solve the equations to get the desired answers. The equations that we write contain algebraic phrases that have the same meanings as the verbal phrases used in the questions. There are several keys to writing these phrases. The word *sum* means that things are added, and the word *product* means that things are multiplied. Seven more than, or increased by 7, means to add 7; while 7 less than, or decreased by 7, means to subtract 7. If we use N to represent an unknown number, then we will use $-N$ to represent the opposite of the unknown number. In the same way, twice a number would be represented by $2N$, and 5 times the opposite of a number would be represented by $5(-N)$. If we write the sum of twice a number and negative 10 as $2N - 10$, we would write 7 times this sum by writing $7(2N - 10)$. Cover the answers in the right-hand column below and see if you can write the algebraic phrase that is indicated.

The sum of a number and 7	$N + 7$
Seven less than a number	$N - 7$
The opposite of a number decreased by 5	$-N - 5$
The sum of the opposite of a number and -5	$-N - 5$
The product of twice a number and 8	$8(2N)$
The sum of twice a number and -5	$2N - 5$
Five times the sum of twice a number and -5	$5(2N - 5)$
Six times the sum of twice the opposite of a number and -8	$6[2(-N) - 8]$
The product of 7 and the sum of a number and 10	$7(N + 10)$
The sum of 3 times a number and -4, multiplied by 5	$5(3N - 4)$
The sum of -10 and 6 times the opposite of a number	$6(-N) - 10$

30.B

decimal parts of a number

Many people call decimal numbers *decimal fractions* because terminating decimal numbers can be written as fractions. For example,

$$\text{(a)} \quad 28.6132 = \frac{286{,}132}{10{,}000} \qquad \text{(b)} \quad 0.000463 = \frac{463}{1{,}000{,}000}$$

We have been working problems concerning fractional parts of a number by using the relationship

$$(F) \times (\text{of}) = (\text{is})$$

We can solve statements about decimal parts of a number by using the slightly different relationship

$$(D) \times (\text{of}) = (\text{is})$$

where D stands for the decimal (decimal fraction) part of the number and *of* and *is* have the same meanings as before.

example 30.1   0.32 of what number is 24.32?

solution   We will use

$$(D) \times (\text{of}) = (\text{is})$$

We replace D with 0.32, *of* with *WN*, and *is* with 24.32 and then solve.

$$0.32WN = 24.32 \quad \longrightarrow \quad \frac{0.32\,WN}{0.32} = \frac{24.32}{0.32} \quad \longrightarrow \quad WN = \mathbf{76}$$

example 30.2   What decimal part of 42 is 26.04?

solution   In $(D) \times (\text{of}) = (\text{is})$, we replace D with *WD*, *of* with 42, and *is* with 26.04. Then we solve.

$$WD(42) = 26.04 \quad \longrightarrow \quad \frac{WD(42)}{42} = \frac{26.04}{42} \quad \longrightarrow \quad WD = \mathbf{0.62}$$

example 30.3   0.42 of 86 is what number?

solution   This time 0.42 replaces D and 86 replaces *of*. Then we multiply to find *WN*.

$$(0.42)(86) = WN \quad \longrightarrow \quad WN = \mathbf{36.12}$$

practice   In practice problems a–d, write the algebraic phrases that correspond to the word phrases.

a.   Five times the sum of 3 times a number and –5.

b.   The product of 3 and the sum of a number and –50.

c.   The sum of 5 times a number and –13.

d.   Three times the sum of the opposite of a number and negative 7.

e.   0.16 of what number is 10.24?

f.   What decimal part of 80 is 60?

g.   0.48 of 8 is what number?

problem set 30

1. $_{(13)}$ Is the product of 18 negative numbers and 20 positive numbers a positive number or a negative number?

2. $_{(2)}$ What is the name of the quadrilateral that has exactly two parallel sides?

3. $_{(4)}$ Use two unit multipliers to convert 10,000 feet to centimeters.

4. $_{(10)}$ Use two unit multipliers to convert 135 square miles to square feet.

5. $_{(8)}$ The area of a circle is 36π square centimeters. Find the diameter of the circle.

Write the algebraic phrases that correspond to these word phrases.

6. $_{(30)}$ The sum of 5 times a number and –8.

7. $_{(30)}$ Three times the sum of the opposite of a number and –7.

8. $_{(30)}$ 0.18 of what number is 4.68?

9. $_{(30)}$ What decimal part of 60 is 45?

Simplify:

10. $_{(29)}$ $(-3)^{-2}$

11. $_{(29)}$ $\dfrac{1}{(-3)^{-3}}$

12. $_{(29)}$ -3^0

13. $_{(28)}$ $3\frac{1}{4}$ of what number is 91?

14. $_{(28)}$ $\frac{7}{3}$ of 42 is what number?

15. $_{(28)}$ If $f(x) = 3x - 5$, find $f(-2)$.

16. $_{(28)}$ If $g(x) = 4x + 2$, find $g(2)$.

Solve:

17. $_{(25)}$ $3x - 7 = 42$

18. $_{(24)}$ $\dfrac{3}{4}y = 4\dfrac{7}{8}$

19. $_{(25)}$ $\dfrac{1}{2}x + \dfrac{1}{2} = 2\dfrac{1}{5}$

20. $_{(27)}$ $0.03x - 0.6 = 2.4$

21. $_{(26)}$ $7p - 15 = 4p - 5 + p$

Simplify:

22. $_{(29)}$ $x^{-5}y^5 axy^3 a^{-3}$

23. $_{(29)}$ $m^2 p^{-4} m^{-2} p^6$

24. $_{(21)}$ Simplify by adding like terms: $5m^2x^2y - 2x^2m^2y + 8m^2y^2x$

25. $_{(29)}$ Use the distributive property to expand: $x^{-4}y^0\left(x^4 - 3y^2x^5p^0\right)$

Evaluate:

26. $_{(14)}$ $-c(ac - a)$ if $a = -3$ and $c = 4$

27. $_{(19)}$ $-n(n - m) - |m^2|$ if $n = -4$ and $m = 3$

28. $_{(3)}$ Find the perimeter of this figure. Corners that look square are square. Dimensions are in meters.

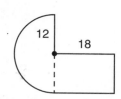

29. $_{(8)}$ Find the area of this right triangle. Dimensions are in kilometers.

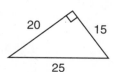

30. $_{(20)}$ A right circular cylinder has a radius of 4 inches and a length of 10 inches, as shown. Find the volume of the right circular cylinder.

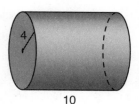

LESSON *31* *Equations with Parentheses*

When equations contain parentheses, we begin by eliminating the parentheses. If the parentheses are preceded by a number, we use the distributive property. We multiply the number by every term inside the parentheses and discard the parentheses.

example 31.1   Solve: $2(3 - b) = b - 5$

solution   As the first step, we will use the distributive property on the left-hand side to expand $2(3 - b)$. Then we will complete the solution.

$$
\begin{array}{lll}
2(3 - b) = & b - 5 & \text{original equation} \\
6 - 2b = & b - 5 & \text{used distributive property} \\
\underline{+ 2b \quad} & \underline{+ 2b} & \text{added } 2b \text{ to both sides} \\
6 \quad = & 3b - 5 & \\
\underline{+5 \quad} & \underline{+5} & \text{added 5 to both sides} \\
11 \quad = & 3b \; \rightarrow \; b = \dfrac{11}{3} & \text{divided both sides by 3}
\end{array}
$$

example 31.2   Solve: $3(1 + 2x) + 7 = -4(x + 2)$

solution   This equation has parentheses on both sides. Thus we begin by using the distributive property on the left-hand side and again on the right-hand side to eliminate both sets of parentheses.

$$
\begin{array}{lll}
3(1 + 2x) + 7 = -4(x + 2) & & \text{original equation} \\
3 + 6x + 7 = -4x - 8 & & \text{used distributive property} \\
10 + 6x = -4x - 8 & & \text{added like terms} \\
\underline{+ 4x \qquad +4x \quad} & & \text{added } 4x \text{ to both sides} \\
10 + 10x = -8 & & \\
\underline{-10 \qquad\qquad -10} & & \text{added } -10 \text{ to both sides} \\
10x = -18 & & \\
x = -\dfrac{18}{10} \; \rightarrow \; x = -\dfrac{9}{5} & & \text{divided both sides by} \\
& & \text{10 and simplified}
\end{array}
$$

In this problem, we used all of the five steps that we will use to solve equations. Sometimes one of the steps is not necessary, as in example 31.1 above where addition of like terms was not required. If the variable is x, the five steps are:

1. **Eliminate parentheses.**
2. **Add like terms on both sides.**
3. **Eliminate x on one side or the other.**
4. **Eliminate the constant term.**
5. **Eliminate the coefficient of x.**

example 31.3   Solve: $15(4 - 5x) = 16(4 - 6x) + 10$

solution   As the first step, we will use the distributive property as required on both sides of the equation.

$$15(4 - 5x) = 16(4 - 6x) + 10 \qquad \text{original equation}$$

$$60 - 75x = 64 - 96x + 10 \qquad \text{used distributive property}$$

$$
\begin{aligned}
60 - 75x &= 74 - 96x && \text{added like terms}\\
+ 96x & \qquad + 96x && \text{added } 96x \text{ to both sides}\\
\hline
60 + 21x &= 74 \\
-60 & \qquad -60 && \text{added } -60 \text{ to both sides}\\
\hline
21x &= 14
\end{aligned}
$$

$$x = \frac{14}{21} \quad \rightarrow \quad x = \frac{2}{3} \qquad \begin{array}{l}\text{divided both sides by}\\ \text{21 and simplified}\end{array}$$

In the preceding three examples we began by using the distributive property. To solve the next two problems, we need to have two rules for eliminating parentheses preceded by a plus sign or a minus sign. The rules are:

1. **When parentheses are preceded by a plus sign, both the parentheses and the sign may be discarded, as demonstrated here.**

$$+(-4 + 3x) = -4 + 3x$$

2. **When parentheses are preceded by a minus sign, both the minus sign and the parentheses may be discarded if the signs of all terms within the parentheses are changed. This rule is used because the minus sign indicates the negative of, or the opposite of, the quantity within the parentheses.**

$$-(x - 3y + 6 - k) = -x + 3y - 6 + k$$

example 31.4   Solve: $12 - (2x + 5) = -2 + (x - 3)$

solution   As the first step we drop the parentheses, remembering that if the parentheses are preceded by a minus sign, we must change all signs inside the parentheses.

$$12 - 2x - 5 = -2 + x - 3$$

Now we simplify on both of sides of the equation

$$7 - 2x = x - 5$$

and solve for x

$$
\begin{aligned}
7 - 2x &= \quad x - 5 \\
+5 + 2x & \quad +2x + 5 && \text{added } 5 + 2x \text{ to both sides}\\
\hline
12 &= \quad 3x \\
\frac{12}{3} &= \frac{3x}{3} \quad \rightarrow \quad x = 4 && \begin{array}{l}\text{divided both sides by}\\ \text{3 and simplified}\end{array}
\end{aligned}
$$

example 31.5   Solve: $-(4y - 17) + (-y) = (2y - 1) - (-y)$

solution   Again we remember that when we discard parentheses preceded by a minus sign, the signs of all terms within the parentheses are changed.

$$-4y + 17 + -y = 2y - 1 + y$$

First we add like terms and then we solve.

$$-5y + 17 = 3y - 1 \qquad \text{added like terms}$$
$$\underline{+5y + 1 \qquad +5y + 1} \qquad \text{added } 5y + 1 \text{ to both sides}$$
$$18 = 8y$$
$$\frac{18}{8} = \frac{8y}{8} \longrightarrow y = \frac{9}{4} \qquad \begin{array}{l}\text{divided both sides by}\\ \text{8 and simplified}\end{array}$$

practice   Solve:

a. $-3(2 - c) = c - 2$

b. $-(6c - 5) = 4(7c - 8) + 3$

c. $-(7 - 9)z - 6z = 8(-6 + 2)$

problem set   **1.** Which of the following terms are like terms?
31   (21)

(a) abc^2 (b) $-2ab^2c$ (c) $-3c^2ba$ (d) $-3a^2bc$

2. (a) Define a rectangle.
(2)

(b) Define a rhombus.

(c) Define a square.

(d) Is every square also a rectangle?

3. Use two unit multipliers to convert 20 meters to inches.
(4)

4. Use two unit multipliers to convert 1800 square meters to square kilometers.
(10)

5. The perimeter of a square is 20 in. Find the area of the square.
(3,8)

Write the algebraic phrases that correspond to these word phrases.

6. Seven times the sum of a number and –5.
(30)

7. Seven less than twice the opposite of a number.
(30)

8. The sum of 7 times a number and –51.
(30)

9. A number is multiplied by 4 and this product decreased by 15.
(30)

10. 0.21 of what number is 7.98?   **11.** 0.32 of 62 is what number?
(30)   (30)

Simplify:

12. 2^{-4} **13.** $\dfrac{1}{3^{-2}}$ **14.** $(-4)^0$
(29)   (29)   (29)

15. What fraction of 60 is 42?
(28)

16. $5\frac{1}{3}$ of 120 is what number?
(28)

17. If $f(x) = -2x + 3$, find $f(3)$.
(28)

Solve:

18. $5k - 4 = -30$ **19.** $3\frac{1}{3}x - \frac{1}{2} = 5$
(25)   (25)

20. $0.002k + 0.02 = 2.06$ **21.** $3(p - 2) = p + 7$
(27)   (31)

22. $2(3x - 5) = 7x + 2$
(31)

23. Is –1 or 4 a root of the equation $x^2 + 5x = -4$?
(22)

24. Simplify by adding like terms: $xmp^{-2} - 4p^{-2}xm + 6p^{-2}mx - 5mx$
(21)

Expand by using the distributive property:

25. $p^0x^{-1}(x - 2x^0)$ **26.** $y^0x^{-4}(x^4 - 5y^4x^4)$
(29)   (29)

Evaluate:

27. $-a^2 - 3a(a - b)$ if $a = -2$ and $b = -1$
(19)

28. $-c(ac - a^0)$ if $a = -3$ and $c = 4$
(29)

29. Find the perimeter of this figure. Cor-
(3)   ners that look square are square.
      Dimensions are in feet.

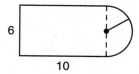

30. A base of the right solid has an area of 58 cm². The height of the right solid is 15 cm.
(20)   Find the volume of the right solid.

LESSON 32   *Word Problems*

To solve word problems, we look for statements in the problems that describe equal quantities. Then we use algebraic phrases and equals signs to write equations that make the same statements of equality. We will begin by solving problems that contain only one statement of equality. These problems require that we write only one equation. Later, we will encounter problems that contain more than one statement of equality. These problems will require more than one equation for their solution.

We will avoid the use of the letters x and y in writing these equations. We will try to use variables whose meaning is easy to remember. The problems in this lesson discuss some unknown number. We will use the letter N to represent the unknown number.

example 32.1   The sum of twice a number and 13 is 75. Find the number.

solution   We will use N to represent the unknown number. **The word *is* means "equal to." Thus, the sum of twice a number and 13 equals 75.**

$$2N + 13 = 75 \qquad \text{equation}$$

We can solve this equation by adding –13 to both sides and then dividing both sides by 2.

$$
\begin{array}{rcl}
2N + 13 & = & 75 \qquad \text{equation} \\
-13 & & -13 \qquad \text{added } -13 \text{ to both sides} \\
\hline
2N & = & 62 \\
\\
N & = & \mathbf{31} \qquad \text{divided both sides by 2}
\end{array}
$$

Solutions to word problems should always be checked to see if they really do solve the problem.

$$2(31) + 13 = 75 \;\longrightarrow\; 62 + 13 = 75 \;\longrightarrow\; 75 = 75 \qquad \text{Check}$$

example 32.2   Find a number such that 13 less than twice the number is 137.

solution   We will use N to represent the unknown number. Then twice the unknown number is $2N$ and 13 less than that is $2N - 13$.

$$\begin{array}{ll} 2N - 13 = 137 & \text{equation} \\ \underline{+\ 13\quad +13} & \text{added 13 to both sides} \\ 2N\qquad = 150 & \\ \\ N = \mathbf{75} & \text{divided both sides by 2} \end{array}$$

$$2(75) - 13 = 137 \ \longrightarrow\ 150 - 13 = 137 \ \longrightarrow\ 137 = 137 \qquad \text{Check}$$

example 32.3   Find a number such that if 5 times the number is decreased by 14, the result is twice the opposite of the number.

solution   If we use N for the number, then $2(-N)$ will represent twice the opposite of the number.

$$\begin{array}{ll} 5N - 14 = 2(-N) & \text{equation} \\ \\ 5N - 14 = -2N & \text{multiplied} \\ \underline{2N + 14\qquad 2N + 14} & \text{added } 2N + 14 \text{ to both sides} \\ 7N\quad = \qquad\quad 14 & \\ \\ N = \mathbf{2} & \text{divided both sides by 7} \end{array}$$

$$5(2) - 14 = 2(-2) \ \longrightarrow\ 10 - 14 = -4 \ \longrightarrow\ -4 = -4 \qquad \text{Check}$$

example 32.4   Find a number which decreased by 18 equals 5 times its opposite.

solution   Again we use N for the number and $-N$ for its opposite.

$$\begin{array}{ll} N - 18 = 5(-N) & \text{equation} \\ \\ N - 18 = -5N & \text{multiplied} \\ \underline{5N + 18\qquad 5N + 18} & \text{added } 5N + 18 \text{ to both sides} \\ 6N\quad = \qquad\quad 18 & \\ \\ N = \mathbf{3} & \text{divided both sides by 6} \end{array}$$

$$3 - 18 = 5(-3) \ \longrightarrow\ 3 - 18 = -15 \ \longrightarrow\ -15 = -15 \qquad \text{Check}$$

example 32.5   We get the same result if we multiply a number by 3 *or* if we multiply the number by 5 and then add 2. Find the number.

solution   The statement of the problem leads to the following equation.

$$\begin{array}{ll} 3N = \ \ 5N + 2 & \text{equation} \\ \underline{-5N\quad -5N} & \text{added } -5N \text{ to both sides} \\ -2N = \qquad\ 2 & \\ \\ N = \mathbf{-1} & \text{divided both sides by } -2 \end{array}$$

$$3(-1) = 5(-1) + 2 \ \longrightarrow\ -3 = -5 + 2 \ \longrightarrow\ -3 = -3 \qquad \text{Check}$$

practice   **a.**   Four times a number decreased by 8 equals 92. Find the number. Check your answer.

b.   If the product of 4 and a number is decreased by 12, the result is twice the opposite of the number. Find the number. Check your answer.

problem set 32

1. ₍₁₅₎ (a) What do we call the total area of all exposed surfaces of a geometric solid?

(b) How do you find the lateral surface area of any right solid?

2. ₍₅₎ (a) The set {1, 2, 3, …} represents what set of numbers?

(b) The set {0, 1, 2, 3, …} represents what set of numbers?

(c) The set {…, –3, –2, –1, 0, 1, 2, 3, …} represents what set of numbers?

3. ₍₄₎ Use two unit multipliers to convert 1828 centimeters to feet.

4. ₍₁₀₎ Use two unit multipliers to convert 57 square feet to square yards.

5. ₍₃₎ The circumference of a circle is 14π centimeters. Find the diameter of the circle.

6. ₍₃₂₎ The sum of twice a number and 17 is 55. Find the number.

7. ₍₃₂₎ Find a number such that 16 less than twice the number is 84.

8. ₍₃₀₎ What decimal part of 25 is 1.25?

Simplify:

9. ₍₂₉₎ $(-5)^{-2}$

10. ₍₂₉₎ $\dfrac{1}{(-4)^{-3}}$

11. ₍₂₉₎ -5^0

12. ₍₂₈₎ $2\frac{1}{9}$ of what number is 76?

13. ₍₂₈₎ If $g(x) = -5x - 4$, find $g(-5)$.

Solve:

14. ₍₂₅₎ $2\frac{1}{2}x - 5 = 15$

15. ₍₂₅₎ $2\frac{1}{4}k + \dfrac{1}{4} = \dfrac{1}{8}$

16. ₍₂₇₎ $0.025x + 0.03 = 1.03$

17. ₍₃₁₎ $3p - 4 - 6 = -2(p - 5)$

18. ₍₃₁₎ $-(x - 3) - 2(x - 4) = 7$

19. ₍₂₃₎ (a) What value of x satisfies the equation $2x - 1 = 7$?

(b) What value of x satisfies the equation $3x + 5 = -7$?

(c) Are the solutions of both equations the same?

(d) Given your answer to part (c), are the two equations equivalent?

20. ₍₂₁₎ Simplify by adding like terms: $k^2p^{-4}y - 5k^2yp^{-4} + 2yk^2p^{-4} - 5k^2yp^{-4}$

Expand by using the distributive property:

21. ₍₂₉₎ $2x^{-2}y^0\left(x^2y^0 - 4x^{-6}y^4\right)$

22. ₍₂₉₎ $\left(x^2 - 4x^5y^{-5}\right)3p^0x^{-2}$

Evaluate:

23. ₍₂₉₎ $-a^3\left(a^0 - b\right)$ if $a = -2$ and $b = 4$

24. ₍₂₉₎ $x\left(x^0 - y\right)(y - 2x)$ if $x = -3$ and $y = 5$

Simplify:

25. ₍₁₉₎ $-3^2 + (-3)^3 - 3^0 - |-3 - 3|$

26. ₍₁₃₎ $\dfrac{-3[5(-2 - 1) - (6 - 3)]}{2(-3 - 4)}$

27. ₍₈₎ Find the area of this parallelogram. Dimensions are in meters.

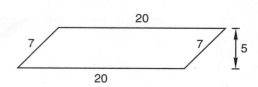

28. Simplify: $\dfrac{0.09338}{-0.046}$
(9)

29. *PS* is $14\frac{2}{5}$ kilometers. *QR* is $4\frac{3}{10}$ kilometers. *RS* is $3\frac{1}{2}$ kilometers. Find *PQ*.
(1)

$$P \qquad Q \quad R \quad S$$

30. A base of the right prism 10 inches high is shown. Find the surface area of the right prism.
(15) All angles are right angles. Dimensions are in inches. (Remember that the lateral surface area of a right prism is equal to the perimeter of a base times the height.)

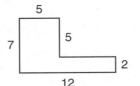

LESSON 33   *Products of Prime Factors • Statements About Unequal Quantities*

33.A

products of prime factors

The number 6 can be composed by multiplying the two counting numbers 3 and 2.

$$3 \cdot 2 = 6$$

Because 6 can be composed by multiplying two counting numbers that are both greater than 1, we say that 6 is a **composite number.** The number 35 is also a composite number because it can be composed as the product of the counting numbers 5 and 7.

$$5 \cdot 7 = 35$$

The number 1 must be one of the factors if we wish to compose 17 by multiplying.

$$17 \cdot 1 = 17$$

The number 1 must also be a factor if we wish to compose either 3 or 11 or 23.

$$1 \cdot 3 = 3 \qquad 1 \cdot 11 = 11 \qquad 1 \cdot 23 = 23$$

Since these numbers can be composed only if 1 is one of the factors, we do not call these numbers composite numbers. We call them **prime numbers.**

A prime number is a counting number greater than 1 whose only counting number factors are 1 and the number itself.

The number 12 can be written as a product of integral factors in four different ways.

(a) $12 \cdot 1$ (b) $4 \cdot 3$ (c) $2 \cdot 6$ (d) $2 \cdot 2 \cdot 3$

In (a), (b), and (c), one of the factors is not a prime number, but in (d) all three of the factors are prime numbers. **A prime factor is a factor that is a prime number.** To find the prime factors of a counting number, we divide by prime numbers, as we see in the following examples.

example 33.1   Express 80 as a product of prime factors.

solution   We will divide by prime numbers.

$$\frac{80}{2} = 40 \qquad \frac{40}{2} = 20 \qquad \frac{20}{2} = 10 \qquad \frac{10}{2} = 5$$

Using the five factors we have found, we can express 80 as a product of prime factors as **2 · 2 · 2 · 2 · 5.**

example 33.2   Express 147 as a product of prime factors.

solution   147 is not divisible by 2 or by 5, so let us try 3.

$$\frac{147}{3} = 49 \qquad \text{and} \qquad \frac{49}{7} = 7$$

So 147 expressed as a product of prime factors is **3 · 7 · 7.**

33.B

statements about unequal quantities

Often a word problem makes a statement about quantities that differ by a specified amount. Thus, the statement tells us that the quantities are not equal, and our task is to write an equation about quantities that are equal. To perform this task, we must add as required so that both sides of the equation represent equal quantities.

example 33.3   Twice a number is 42 less than −102. Find the number.

solution   **We must be careful because the problem tells us about things that are not equal. We begin by writing an equation that we know is incorrect.**

$$2N = -102 \qquad \text{incorrect}$$

The problem said that $2N$ was 42 less than −102, so we must add 42 to $2N$ or we must add −42 to −102.

Adding 42 to $2N$			Adding −42 to −102	
$2N + 42 = -102$	correct		$2N = -102 - 42$	correct
$\underline{\quad -42 \qquad -42}$			$2N = -144$	
$2N \qquad = -144$			$N = \mathbf{-72}$	
$N = \mathbf{-72}$				

We remember that solutions to word problems should always be checked to see if they really do solve the problem.

$$2(-72) + 42 = -102 \quad \longrightarrow \quad -144 + 42 = -102 \quad \longrightarrow \quad -102 = -102 \qquad \text{Check}$$

example 33.4   Five times a number is 72 greater than the opposite of the number. Find the number.

solution   **This statement is tricky because it describes quantities that are unequal. As the first step in writing the desired equation, we will write an equation that we know is incorrect.**

$$5N = -N \qquad \text{incorrect}$$

This equation is incorrect because $5N$ is really 72 greater than $-N$. We can make the equation correct by adding -72 to $5N$ or by adding 72 to $-N$.

ADDING -72 TO $5N$	or	ADDING $+72$ TO $-N$

$$5N - 72 = -N \qquad\qquad 5N = -N + 72$$
$$\underline{N + 72 \qquad N + 72} \qquad\qquad \underline{N \qquad\quad N}$$
$$6N \qquad = \qquad 72 \qquad\qquad 6N = \qquad\quad 72$$

$$N = \mathbf{12} \qquad\qquad\qquad N = \mathbf{12}$$

$$5(12) - 72 = -12 \;\longrightarrow\; 60 - 72 = -12 \;\longrightarrow\; -12 = -12 \qquad \text{Check}$$

example 33.5 If the sum of twice a number and -14 is multiplied by 2, the result is 12 greater than the opposite of the number. Find the number.

solution **Again we begin by writing an equation that we know is incorrect.**

$$2(2N - 14) = -N \qquad \text{incorrect}$$

We know that the left-hand side of the equation is greater by 12. We can write a correct equation by adding -12 to the left-hand side of the equation or by adding $+12$ to the right-hand side of the equation.

ADDING -12 TO THE LEFT SIDE	or	ADDING $+12$ TO THE RIGHT SIDE

$$2(2N - 14) - 12 = -N \qquad\qquad 2(2N - 14) = -N + 12$$

$$4N - 28 - 12 = -N \qquad\qquad 4N - 28 = -N + 12$$

$$5N = 40 \qquad\qquad\qquad 5N = 40$$

$$N = \mathbf{8} \qquad\qquad\qquad\qquad N = \mathbf{8}$$

$$2(2 \cdot 8 - 14) - 12 = -8 \;\longrightarrow\; 2(2) - 12 = -8 \;\longrightarrow\; -8 = -8 \qquad \text{Check}$$

example 33.6 Five times a number is 21 less than twice the opposite of the number. What is the number?

solution **Again we begin by writing an equation that we know is incorrect.**

$$5N = 2(-N) \qquad \text{incorrect}$$

We know that the left-hand side of the equation is 21 less than the right-hand side of the equation. We can write a correct equation by adding 21 to the left-hand side of the equation.

$$5N + 21 = 2(-N) \qquad\qquad \text{added 21 to } 5N$$

$$5N + 21 = -2N \qquad\qquad \text{multiplied}$$
$$\underline{2N - 21 \qquad\quad 2N - 21} \qquad\qquad \text{added } 2N - 21 \text{ to both sides}$$
$$7N \qquad = \qquad -21$$

$$N = \mathbf{-3} \qquad\qquad \text{divided both sides by 7}$$

$$5(-3) + 21 = 2(3) \;\longrightarrow\; -15 + 21 = 6 \;\longrightarrow\; 6 = 6 \qquad \text{Check}$$

practice **a.** Find a number such that 8 times the number is 36 greater than the opposite of the number. Check your answer.

b. If the sum of a number and 6 is multiplied by 2, the result is 10 greater than the number. Find the number. Check your answer.

Write the following numbers as products of prime factors:

c. 108

d. 400

problem set 33

1. (13) Is the product of 21 negative numbers and 23 positive numbers a positive number or a negative number?

2. (2) If two sides of a triangle have equal lengths, then what is true about the angles opposite those sides?

3. (4) Use two unit multipliers to convert 9140 centimeters to feet.

4. (10) Use two unit multipliers to convert 28,000 square feet to square miles.

5. (3,8) The area of a rectangle is 24 cm^2. The length of the rectangle is 8 cm. Find the perimeter of the rectangle.

6. (32) Find a number such that if 3 times the number is decreased by 15, the result is twice the opposite of the number.

7. (33) Twice a number is 36 less than –104. Find the number.

Write the following numbers as products of prime factors:

8. (33) 60

9. (33) 105

10. (30) 1.025 of 50 is what number?

Simplify:

11. (29) 2^{-3}

12. (29) $(-3)^{-3}$

13. (29) $(-6)^0$

14. (28) $2\frac{5}{8}$ of 32 is what number?

15. (28) If $h(x) = -9x - 3$, find $h(3)$.

Solve:

16. (25) $\frac{5}{8}x - 3 = \frac{1}{2}$

17. (25) $\frac{1}{8}y + 10 = 14\frac{1}{4}$

18. (27) $0.005p + 1.4 = 0.005$

19. (31) $k + 4 - 5(k + 2) = 3k - 2$

20. (31) $x - 4(x - 3) + 7 = 6 - (x - 4)$

21. (21) Simplify by adding like terms: $-3x^{-2}y^2x^5 + 6x^3y^{-2}y^4 - 3x^3y^2 + 5x^2y^3$

Expand by using the distributive property:

22. (29) $2x^{-2}(x^{-2}y^0 + x^2y^5p^0)$

23. (29) $(4p^{-2} - 3x^{-3}p^5)p^2x^0$

Evaluate:

24. (29) $m - (-m)(m^0 - a)$ if $m = -2$ and $a = 3$

25. (19) $a^3x - |x^3|$ if $a = -3$ and $x = -2$

Simplify:

26. (29) $-2(-3) - (-4)^0(-3)|-5 - 2|$

27. (19) $(-2)^3 - (-2)^2 - 5 + \sqrt[3]{-64}$

28. (8) Find the area of this trapezoid. Dimensions are in meters.

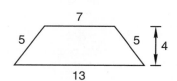

29. In this figure, the radius of the small
(8) circle is 10 inches and the radius of the
big circle is 16 inches. Find the area of
the shaded portion of this figure.

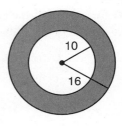

30. Find x and y.
(2)

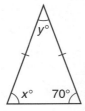

LESSON 34 *Greatest Common Factor*

The number 210 has four prime number factors, as shown here.

$$2 \cdot 3 \cdot 5 \cdot 7 = 210$$

We call factors that are numbers **numerical factors.** Some expressions have factors that are
letters, and some expressions have both numbers and letters as factors, as does $210xy^2z^3$.

$$210xy^2z^3 = 2 \cdot 3 \cdot 5 \cdot 7 \cdot x \cdot y \cdot y \cdot z \cdot z \cdot z$$

We call the letter factors **literal factors,** and we use the words **algebraic factor** as a general
term to describe factors that are either numbers or letters or both numbers and letters.

DEFINITION

The greatest common factor (GCF) of two or more terms is
the product of all prime algebraic factors common to every
term, each to the highest power that it occurs in all of the
terms.

The expression $6x^2y^2m^2 + 3xy^3m^2 + 3x^3y^2$ can be written as

$$2 \cdot 3 \cdot x \cdot x \cdot y \cdot y \cdot m \cdot m + 3 \cdot x \cdot y \cdot y \cdot y \cdot m \cdot m + 3 \cdot x \cdot x \cdot x \cdot y \cdot y$$

Now only the first term has 2 as a factor, so 2 is not a part of the greatest common factor. Each
term has 3 as a factor at least once, so 3 is a factor of the greatest common factor of all
the terms.

$$3$$

Each term has x as a factor at least once in every term, so x is a factor of the GCF.

$$3x$$

In the same way, y is used as a factor at least twice in every term, so the greatest common factor of the three given terms is

$$3xy^2$$

The variable m is not included because it is not a factor of the third term of the original expression.

example 34.1   Find the greatest common factor of $8z^4m^2p - 12z^3m^4p^2$.

solution   The greatest common factor of the expression is $4z^3m^2p$.

example 34.2   Find the greatest common factor of $4x^2y^3z - 8y^2xz^3$.

solution   The GCF is $4xy^2z$.

example 34.3   Find the greatest common factor of $16x^2yp^3 - 4x^3y^2p + 2x^2y^2p^{15}$.

solution   The GCF is $2x^2yp$.

practice   Find the greatest common factor:

    a. $6x^2y^3m - 14xy^5m^2 + 24x^{10}y^6m^4$

    b. $5a^2b^2c^2 + 60a^3b^3c^3 - 30a^4b^4c^4$

    c. $12xy^5p - 16x^6y^2p^{16} + 28x^3yp^5$

problem set 34

1. Which of the following terms are like terms?
(21)

    (a) $6xy$ (b) $-2x^3yx^{-1}$ (c) $2x^3x^{-2}y$ (d) $6xxx^{-1}y^3y^{-1}$

2. What number do you get when you divide the circumference of a circle by the diameter
(3) of the circle?

3. Use three unit multipliers to convert 85,000 inches to kilometers. (Go from inches to
(4) centimeters to meters to kilometers.)

4. Use four unit multipliers to convert 3200 square inches to square meters. (Use two unit
(10) multipliers to go from square inches to square centimeters and two unit multipliers to go from square centimeters to square meters.)

5. The radius of a circle is 12 inches.
(3,8)

    (a) Find the circumference of the circle.

    (b) Find the area of the circle.

6. Find a number which decreased by 24 equals 3 times its opposite.
(32)

7. Six times a number is 56 greater than the opposite of the number. Find the number.
(33)

Write the following numbers as products of prime factors:

8. 90   **9.** 216
(33)   (33)

10. 0.125 of what number is 5.25?
(30)

Simplify:

11. $(-5)^{-3}$ **12.** $\dfrac{1}{(-5)^{-2}}$ **13.** -8^0
(29)   (29)   (1)

14. What fraction of $2\frac{1}{4}$ is $\frac{3}{4}$?
(28)

15. If $f(x) = 7 - 2x$, find $f(2)$.
(28)

Solve:

16. $3\dfrac{1}{2} + 2\dfrac{1}{4}x = 1\dfrac{1}{4}$ **17.** $0.3 + 0.06x = 6.9$
(25)   (27)

18. $8 - k + 2(4 - 2k) = k + 2k$ **19.** $3(x - 2) + (2x + 5) = x + 7$
(31)   (31)

Find the greatest common factor:

20. $4ab^2c^4 - 2a^2b^3c^2 + 6a^3b^4c$ **21.** $5x^2y^5m^2 - 10xy^2m^2 + 15x^2y^4m^2$
(34)   (34)

22. Simplify by adding like terms: $3xy - 2x^2yx^{-1} + 5x^3x^{-2}y^3y^{-2} + 5xxxx^{-2}y$
(21)

Expand by using the distributive property:

23. $4x^{-3}y^2(x^3y^{-2} - 2x^4y^{-2})$ **24.** $(y^{-5} - 2y^7x^5)x^0y^5$
(29)   (29)

Evaluate:

25. $-x^0 - a(x - 2a)$ if $x = -5$ and $a = 3$
(29)

26. $a^2 - a^3 - a^4$ if $a = -2$
(19)

Simplify:

27. $-3^2 + (-3)^3 - 3^0 - |-3 - 3|$ **28.** $\dfrac{-7(-4 - 6)}{-(-4) - [-(-6)]}$
(29)   (13)

29. Find the perimeter of this figure. All
(3)   angles are right angles. Dimensions
are in feet.

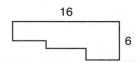

30. A base of the right prism 6 centimeters high is shown. Find the volume of the right prism.
(20)   All angles are right angles. Dimensions are in centimeters.

LESSON 35   *Factoring the Greatest Common Factor • Canceling*

35.A

factoring the greatest common factor

When we use the distributive property, we change an expression from a product to a sum. The expression $2a(x + c)$ tells us to multiply $2a$ by $x + c$. If we do this multiplication, we get the algebraic sum $2ax + 2ac$.

$$2a(x + c) = 2ax + 2ac$$

If we reverse the process and write $2ax + 2ac$ as the product of the two factors $2a$ and $(x + c)$, we say that we are factoring.

Factoring is the process of writing an indicated sum as a product of factors.

example 35.1   Factor the greatest common factor of $2ax + 2ac$.

solution   We will factor in three steps. The first step is to write two empty parentheses to indicate a product.

$$(\quad)(\quad)$$

The second step is to write the greatest common factor of the terms in the first parentheses.

$$(2a)(\quad)$$

The third step is to write the proper terms in the second parentheses so that $2a$ times these terms gives us $2ax + 2ac$.

$$(2a)(x + c)$$

And since the first parentheses are not necessary, the answer can be written as

$$\mathbf{2a(x + c)}$$

example 35.2   Factor the greatest common factor of $a^3x^2m^2 + a^2xm^3 - a^4x^3m^2$.

solution   We want to write this sum as a product. We begin by writing two sets of parentheses.

$$(\quad)(\quad)$$

In the first parentheses we want to write the greatest common factor of all three terms. To find this greatest common factor, we will write the three terms as products of individual factors.

$$a^3x^2m^2 + a^2xm^3 - a^4x^3m^2$$

$$a \cdot a \cdot a \cdot x \cdot x \cdot m \cdot m + a \cdot a \cdot x \cdot m \cdot m \cdot m - a \cdot a \cdot a \cdot a \cdot x \cdot x \cdot x \cdot m \cdot m$$

Look at the a's. Each term has at least two a's, so a^2 is part of the greatest common factor.

$$(a^2\quad)(\quad)$$

Each term has at least one x, so x is a part of the greatest common factor.

$$(a^2x\quad)(\quad)$$

Finally, each term has at least two m's, so m^2 is a part of the greatest common factor. No other factors are common to all three terms.

$$(a^2xm^2)(\quad)$$

Now, the first entry in the second parentheses must be ax because $a^2xm^2(ax) = a^3x^2m^2$, the first term in the original expression.

$$(a^2xm^2)(ax\quad)$$

The second entry in the second parentheses must be m because $a^2xm^2(m) = a^2xm^3$, the second term in the original expression.

$$(a^2xm^2)(ax + m\quad)$$

The last entry in the second parentheses must be $-a^2x^2$ because $a^2xm^2(-a^2x^2) = -a^4x^3m^2$, the third entry in the original expression. The desired factored expression is $\mathbf{a^2xm^2(ax + m - a^2x^2)}$ because

$$(a^2xm^2)(ax + m - a^2x^2) = a^3x^2m^2 + a^2xm^3 - a^4x^3m^2$$

example 35.3   Factor $4a^3b^4z^3 + 2a^2bz^4$.

solution   We want to write this sum as a product. We begin by writing two sets of parentheses.

$$(\qquad)(\qquad)$$

In the first parentheses we want to write the greatest common factor of the two terms. To find this greatest common factor, we will write the two terms as products of individual factors.

$$4a^3b^4z^3 + 2a^2bz^4$$

$$2 \cdot 2 \cdot a \cdot a \cdot a \cdot b \cdot b \cdot b \cdot b \cdot z \cdot z \cdot z + 2 \cdot a \cdot a \cdot b \cdot z \cdot z \cdot z \cdot z$$

Each term has at least one 2, two a's, one b, and three z's as factors. Thus the greatest common factor is $2a^2bz^3$, so we write

$$(2a^2bz^3)(\qquad)$$

The first term in the second parentheses is $2ab^3$ because $2a^2bz^3(2ab^3) = 4a^3b^4z^3$, the first term in the original expression.

$$(2a^2bz^3)(2ab^3\qquad)$$

The second term in the second parentheses is z because $2a^2bz^3(z) = 2a^2bz^4$, the second term in the original expression. Now

$$\mathbf{2a^2bz^3\left(2ab^3 + z\right)}$$

is our answer because

$$2a^2bz^3(2ab^3 + z) = 4a^3b^4z^3 + 2a^2bz^4$$

example 35.4   Factor the greatest common factor of $6a^2x^2 + 2a^3x^3 + 4a^4x^3$.

solution   The greatest common factor is $2a^2x^2$.

$$(2a^2x^2)(\qquad)$$

The entry in the second parentheses is

$$(3 + ax + 2a^2x)$$

because

$$\mathbf{2a^2x^2\left(3 + ax + 2a^2x\right) = 6a^2x^2 + 2a^3x^3 + 4a^4x^3}$$

example 35.5   Factor the greatest common factor of $3m^3xy^2 + m^2y$.

solution   The answer is $\mathbf{m^2y(3mxy + 1)}$ because

$$m^2y(3mxy + 1) = 3m^3xy^2 + m^2y$$

35.B

canceling   We have been solving equations by using the fact that multiplication and division are inverse operations because they "undo" one another. If we want to solve the equation

$$4x = 20$$

we see that x is multiplied by 4. To undo multiplication by 4, we must divide by 4. If we divide one side of an equation by 4, we must also divide the other side of the equation by 4.

$$\frac{\cancel{4}x}{\cancel{4}} = \frac{20}{4} \quad \rightarrow \quad x = 5$$

On the left, we say that we have canceled the 4s. Some people prefer to say that 4 over 4 is "reduced to 1" instead of saying "canceled" because the use of these words helps to prevent canceling when canceling is not permissible. For instance, the 4s cannot be canceled in the following expression because addition and division are not inverse operations and do not undo one another.

$$\frac{x + \cancel{4}}{\cancel{4}} = x + 1 \qquad \text{incorrect}$$

In this problem nothing "reduces to 1." However, the following expression can be simplified by canceling

$$\frac{\cancel{4}(x + 1)}{\cancel{4}}$$

because multiplication by 4 and division by 4 undo each other. We can see that 4 over 4 "reduces to 1."

$$\frac{4(x + 1)}{4} = x + 1$$

Cancellation or reduction to 1 is possible when the numerator and the denominator contain one or more common factors. In the expression being discussed, we remember that the 4 in the denominator can be written as $4 \cdot 1$. Thus, both the numerator and denominator have 4 as a factor.

example 35.6   Simplify: (a) $\dfrac{4(a - 3)}{4}$ (b) $\dfrac{3(x - 2)}{x - 2}$

solution   (a) Here the common factor is 4, and 4 over 4 equals 1.

$$\frac{\cancel{4}(a - 3)}{\cancel{4}} = a - 3$$

(b) Here the common factor is $x - 2$, and $x - 2$ over $x - 2$ equals 1.

   We will assume in all problems of this type that the denominator does not equal zero.

$$\frac{3\cancel{(x - 2)}}{\cancel{x - 2}} = 3$$

example 35.7   Simplify: $\dfrac{3p + 3}{3}$

solution   We cannot simplify in this form because the numerator is not a product. However, if we factor $3p + 3$, we see that we can cancel because both the numerator and the denominator will have 3 as a factor.

$$\frac{\cancel{3}(p + 1)}{\cancel{3}} = p + 1$$

example 35.8   Simplify: $\dfrac{3x - 9x^2}{3x}$

solution   If we factor out a $3x$ on top, we can cancel the $3x$ in the numerator and the $3x$ in the denominator.[†]

$$\frac{3x - 9x^2}{3x} \qquad \text{original expression}$$

$$= \frac{3x(1 - 3x)}{3x} \qquad \text{factored out } 3x$$

$$= \mathbf{1 - 3x} \qquad \text{canceled } 3x \text{ above and below}$$

example 35.9   Simplify: $\dfrac{5x - 25x^2}{5xy}$

solution   If we factor out a $5x$ on top, we can cancel the $5x$ in the numerator and the $5x$ in the denominator.

$$\frac{5x - 25x^2}{5xy} \qquad \text{original expression}$$

$$= \frac{5x(1 - 5x)}{5x(y)} \qquad \text{factored out } 5x$$

$$= \frac{\mathbf{1 - 5x}}{\mathbf{y}} \qquad \text{canceled } 5x \text{ above and below}$$

practice   Factor the greatest common factor:

   a. $15a^2z^8 - 35z^5a$ **b.** $2a^2b^2 + 2a^3b^2 + 2a^3b^6$

Simplify (factor if necessary):

   c. $\dfrac{4 - 4x}{4}$ **d.** $\dfrac{7x - 49x^2}{7x}$

**problem set
35**

1. (a) What do we call the total area of all exposed surfaces of a geometric solid?
$^{(15)}$

    (b) How do you find the lateral surface area of any right solid?

2. Use three unit multipliers to convert 6 feet to meters. (Go from feet to inches to
$^{(4)}$ centimeters to meters.)

3. Use four unit multipliers to convert 20 square feet to square centimeters. (Use two unit
$^{(10)}$ multipliers to go from square feet to square inches and two unit multipliers to go from square inches to square centimeters.)

4. The perimeter of a rectangle is 32 cm. The length of the rectangle is 10 cm. Find the area
$^{(3,8)}$ of the rectangle.

5. We get the same result if we multiply a number by 4 or if we multiply the number by 7
$^{(32)}$ and then add 9. Find the number.

6. If the sum of twice a number and -12 is multiplied by 2, the result is 11 greater than the
$^{(33)}$ opposite of the number. Find the number.

[†] Note the use of the words *factor out*. This phrase is meaningful even though some authorities insist that it is redundant and that the single word *factor* will suffice. However, this slight redundancy is not harmful, especially since it is a natural redundancy.

Write the following numbers as products of prime factors:

7. 160
(33)

8. 294
(33)

9. What decimal part of 36 is 20.88?
(30)

Simplify:

10. 2^{-4}
(29)

11. $\dfrac{1}{3^{-3}}$
(29)

12. $3\frac{1}{5}$ of $3\frac{1}{8}$ is what number?
(28)

13. If $g(x) = -3 + 6x$, find $g(-2)$.
(28)

Solve:

14. $4\frac{1}{2}y - \dfrac{1}{6} = 1\frac{1}{3}$
(25)

15. $0.8m + 0.4m = 4.8$
(27)

16. $3(-k - 4) + 6 = k + 7$
(31)

17. $x - 4 - 2x + 5 = 3(2x - 4)$
(31)

18. Is -1 or 3 a root of the equation $x^2 - 4x = -3$?
(22)

Factor the greatest common factor:

19. $3x^4y^2p - 6x^2y^5p^4$
(35)

20. $6a^3x^2m^5 + 2a^4x^5m^5 + 4a^2x^2m$
(35)

Simplify (factor if necessary):

21. $\dfrac{4x + 4}{4}$
(35)

22. $\dfrac{4x - 16x^2}{4x}$
(35)

23. Simplify by adding like terms: $3x^2xyy^3y^{-1} + 2x^2xyyy - 4x^{-2}yx^5y^2 + 7x^2$
(21)

Expand by using the distributive property:

24. $p^0x^2y(x^3y^{-1} - 3x^5y^{-2})$
(29)

25. $(p^5y^5 - y^{-5})p^0y^5$
(29)

Evaluate:

26. $a^2 - a^3 - a^4$ if $a = -1$
(19)

27. $x(y - xy^0)$ if $x = -2$ and $y = 4$
(29)

28. Find the area of this figure. Dimen-
(8) sions are in meters.

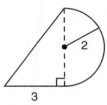

29. Simplify: $-3^2 + (-6)^0 - \sqrt[4]{16} + |2 - 7|$
(29)

30. A base of the right prism 15 inches high is shown. Find the surface area of the right prism.
(15) All angles are right angles. Dimensions are in inches. (Remember that the lateral surface area of a right prism is equal to the perimeter of a base times the height.)

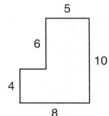

LESSON 36 *Distributive Property of Rational Expressions that Contain Positive Exponents • Minus Signs and Negative Exponents*

36.A

distributive property of rational expressions that contain positive exponents

Two fractions are multiplied by multiplying the numerators to form the new numerator and by multiplying the denominators to form the new denominator. For example,

$$\frac{2}{3} \cdot \frac{5}{7} = \frac{10}{21}$$

Since variables stand for unspecified real numbers, all the rules for real numbers also apply to variables. Thus fractions that contain variables are multiplied by using the same rule.

$$\frac{mx}{4y} \cdot \frac{ax}{2y} = \frac{amx^2}{8y^2}$$

The distributive property of real numbers is also applicable to expressions that contain fractions. Expressions that contain fractions are often called **rational expressions.** We can expand the following rational expression by multiplying x over y by both of the terms inside the parentheses.

$$\frac{x}{y}\left(\frac{a}{y} - b\right) = \frac{xa}{y^2} - \frac{xb}{y}$$

example 36.1 Use the distributive property to expand $\dfrac{x^2}{y^2}\left(\dfrac{x^2}{y} - \dfrac{3y^3}{m}\right)$.

solution Two multiplications are indicated. We multiply $\frac{x^2}{y^2}$ by $\frac{x^2}{y}$ and then multiply $\frac{x^2}{y^2}$ by $\frac{-3y^3}{m}$. This gives

$$\frac{x^2 x^2}{y^2 y} - \frac{x^2 3y^3}{y^2 m}$$

Lastly, we simplify both terms and get

$$\frac{x^4}{y^3} - \frac{3yx^2}{m}$$

example 36.2 Use the distributive property to expand $\dfrac{m}{z}\left(\dfrac{axp}{mk} - 2m^4 p^4\right)$.

solution Again we will use two steps. First, we multiply and then we simplify.

$$\frac{maxp}{zmk} + \frac{m}{z}\left(-2m^4 p^4\right) = \frac{axp}{zk} - \frac{2m^5 p^4}{z}$$

example 36.3 Use the distributive property to expand $\dfrac{ab}{c^2}\left(\dfrac{xab}{c} + 2bx - \dfrac{4}{c^2}\right)$.

solution The fraction $\frac{ab}{c^2}$ must be multiplied by all three terms inside the parentheses. We do this and get

$$\frac{xa^2 b^2}{c^3} + \frac{2ab^2 x}{c^2} - \frac{4ab}{c^4}$$

36.B
minus signs and negative exponents

Expressions that contain both minus signs and negative exponents can be troublesome. **A minus sign in front of an expression indicates the opposite of the expression, whereas a negative exponent has a meaning that is entirely different.**

(a) 4^2 (b) 4^{-2} (c) -4^2

(d) $(-4)^2$ (e) -4^{-2} (f) $(-4)^{-2}$

The notations in (a) and (b) are easy to simplify because in each of these we have a positive number raised to a power.

(a) $4^2 = \mathbf{16}$ (b) $4^{-2} = \dfrac{1}{4^2} = \dfrac{\mathbf{1}}{\mathbf{16}}$

The notations in (c) and (d) often give difficulty because of the problem caused by the minus sign in front of the 4. When the minus sign is not enclosed in parentheses as in (c),

$$-4^2$$

it is helpful to cover up the minus sign with a fingertip. If we cover the minus sign in -4^2, we get

$$4^2$$

Now we raise 4 to the second power and get

$$16$$

Now we move our fingertips and uncover the minus sign. We see that the result is

$$\mathbf{-16}$$

From this we see that -4^2 is read as the "opposite of" 4 squared and is not read as the "opposite of 4" squared. The notation in (d) is "the opposite of 4" squared

$$(-4)^2$$

If we try to cover up the minus sign with a fingertip, we cannot because the minus sign is "protected" by the parentheses.

$$(-4)^2$$

This reminds us that (-4) is to be used as a factor twice.

$$(-4)^2 = (-4)(-4) = \mathbf{+16}$$

The notations in (e) and (f) are similar to the two we have just discussed. They are

(e) -4^{-2} and   (f) $(-4)^{-2}$

The minus sign in (e) is "unprotected," so we can cover it with a fingertip.

$$4^{-2}$$

Now we simplify 4^{-2} as

$$4^{-2} = \frac{1}{4^2} = \frac{1}{16}$$

We finish by removing the fingertip and finding that the answer is negative one sixteenth.

$$-\frac{1}{16}$$

The minus sign in (f) is "protected" by the parentheses. Thus, the simplification is

$$(-4)^{-2} = \frac{1}{(-4)^2} = \frac{1}{(-4)(-4)} = \frac{\mathbf{1}}{\mathbf{16}}$$

practice   Expand by using the distributive property:

a. $\dfrac{x^2}{y}\left(\dfrac{x^2}{y} - \dfrac{3y^2}{m}\right)$ **b.** $\dfrac{am}{b^2}\left(\dfrac{xm}{ab} - 3ab + \dfrac{6m}{b^2}\right)$

Simplify:

c. -4^{-2} **d.** $\dfrac{1}{-4^{-2}}$ **e.** $-(-4)^{-3}$ **f.** $\dfrac{1}{-(-4)^{-3}}$

problem set
36

1. Which of the following terms are like terms?

$_{(21)}$ (a) $2a^2b^2$ (b) $5aaaa^{-1}b^{-1}b^4$ (c) $-5aab^2b^{-1}$ (d) $2a^2bbb$

2. If two angles of a triangle have equal measures, then what is true about the sides opposite
$_{(2)}$ those angles?

3. Use three unit multipliers to convert 80 yards to centimeters. (Go from yards to feet to
$_{(4)}$ inches to centimeters.)

4. Use four unit multipliers to convert 36 square yards to square inches. (Use two unit
$_{(10)}$ multipliers to go from square yards to square feet and two unit multipliers to go from
   square feet to square inches.)

5. The diameter of a circle is 18 centimeters.
$_{(3,8)}$
   (a) Find the circumference of the circle.

   (b) Find the area of the circle.

6. Find a number which decreased by 21 equals twice the opposite of the number.
$_{(32)}$

7. Seven times a number is 18 less than twice the opposite of the number. Find the number.
$_{(33)}$

8. Write 250 as a product of prime factors.
$_{(33)}$

Simplify:

9. -2^{-2} **10.** $\dfrac{1}{-2^{-2}}$
$_{(36)}$ $_{(36)}$

11. $2\frac{5}{8}$ of what number is 14?
$_{(28)}$

12. If $h(x) = -4 - 7x$, find $h(-3)$.
$_{(28)}$

Solve:

13. $-5\dfrac{1}{2} + 2\dfrac{2}{5}p = 7\dfrac{1}{4}$ **14.** $m - 0.4m + 1.5 = 5.7$
$_{(25)}$ $_{(27)}$

15. $x - (3x - 2) + 5 = 2x + 4$ **16.** $-p - 4 - (2p - 5) = 4 + 2(p + 3)$
$_{(31)}$ $_{(31)}$

Factor the greatest common factor:

17. $4a^2xy^4p - 6a^2x^4$ **18.** $3a^2x^4y^6 + 9ax^2y^4 - 6x^4a^2y^5z$
$_{(35)}$ $_{(35)}$

Simplify (factor if necessary):

19. $\dfrac{2 - 6x}{2}$ **20.** $\dfrac{9x^2 - 3x}{3x}$
$_{(35)}$ $_{(35)}$

21. Simplify by adding like terms: $2x^4y^{-3} - 3x^2x^2y^{-7}y^4 + 6x^3xy^{-1}y^{-3} + x^2x^2y^{-3}y^{-1}$
$_{(21)}$

Expand by using the distributive property:

22. $3x^4y^2\left(xy^{-4} - 3x^{-4}y^5\right)$ **23.** $\dfrac{x}{z}\left(\dfrac{15y}{x} - \dfrac{4x}{y}\right)$
$_{(29)}$ $_{(36)}$

Evaluate:

24. $k^3 - k(a)^2$ if $k = -3$ and $a = 2$
$_{(19)}$

25. $m(a^0 - ma)(-m) + |m^2 - 2|$ if $m = 2$ and $a = -4$
$_{(29)}$

Simplify:

26. $-3^3 - 3^2 - (-3)^4 - \left| -3^2 - 3 \right|$ **27.** $\dfrac{-5(-5-4)}{-2^0(-8-1)}$
(19)   (29)

28. Find the perimeter of this figure. All
(3) angles are right angles. Dimensions
are in meters.

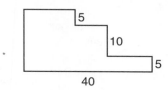

29. Find the area of the shaded portion of
(8) this circle. The radius of the circle is
4 inches. Dimensions are in inches.

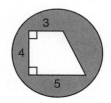

30. Find y.
(2)

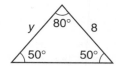

LESSON 37   *Inequalities • Greater Than and Less Than • Graphical Solutions of Inequalities*

37.A
inequalities We use the symbols

$$\neq \qquad > \qquad <$$

to designate that quantities are not equal, and we say that these symbols are symbols of
inequality. They can be read from left to right or from right to left. We read

$$4 \neq 5$$

from left to right as "4 is not equal to 5," or from right to left as "5 is not equal to 4." The
symbols > and < are inequality symbols and are also called *greater than/less than symbols.*
The small or pointed end is read as "less than" and the big or open end is read as "greater than."
When we read, we read only one end of the symbol, the end that we come to first. Thus we read

$$4 > 2$$

from left to right as "4 is greater than 2," or from right to left as "2 is less than 4." If the sign
is combined with an equals sign, only one of the conditions must be met. We read

$$4 \geq 2 + 2$$

from left to right as "4 is greater than or equal to 2 plus 2," or from right to left as "2 plus 2 is
less than or equal to 4." This combination symbol is also called an *inequality symbol* although
half of it is an equals sign.

Inequalities can be false inequalities, true inequalities, or conditional inequalities.

(a) $4 + 2 \le 3$ (b) $x + 2 \ge x$ (c) $x < 4$

Inequality (a) is false, (b) is true, and the truth or falsity of (c) depends on the replacement value used for the variable. If a number that we use as a replacement for the variable makes the inequality a true inequality, we say that the number is a **solution of the inequality** and say that the number **satisfies the inequality.** If the number that we use as a replacement for the variable makes the inequality a false inequality, then the number is not a solution of the inequality and does not satisfy the inequality. Since more than one number will often satisfy a given inequality, there is often more than one solution to the inequality.

> We call the **set of numbers** that will satisfy a given equation or inequality the **solution set** of the equation or inequality.

37.B
greater than and less than

Zero is a real number and can be used to describe a distance of zero. Any other number that can be used to describe a physical distance is a positive real number, and the opposite of each of these numbers is a negative real number.

We use the number line to help us picture the way real numbers are ordered (arranged in order) and to help us define what we mean by *greater than*. On this number line we have graphed 2 and 4.

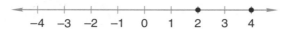

We remember that one number is greater than another number if its graph is to the right of the graph of the other number. Since the graph of 4 is to the right of the graph of 2, we say that 4 is greater than 2.

Using the same definition, we can say that -1 is greater than -4 because the graph of -1 is to the right of the graph of -4.

In the following section the small arrows will not be drawn on the ends of the number line because these arrows can be confused with the arrows drawn to indicate the solutions to the problems.

37.C
graphical solutions of inequalities

We can use the number line to display the graph or the picture of the solution to many problems.

example 37.1   Draw a number line and graph the solution of $x > 2$.

solution   This inequality is read from left to right as *x* **is greater than 2.** Thus we are asked to show the location on the number line of all real numbers that are greater than 2. We draw an arrow to designate these numbers.

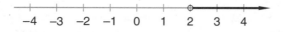

The open circle at 2 indicates that 2 is not a part of the solution because 2 is not greater than 2.

example 37.2   Draw a number line and graph the solution of $x \leq 2$.

solution   This inequality is read from left to right as **x is less than or equal to 2.** Thus we are asked to show the location on the number line of all real numbers that are less than or equal to 2.

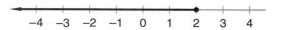

The locations of the numbers that satisfy the condition are indicated by the heavy line. The solid circle at 2 indicates that the number 2 is a part of the solution of $x \leq 2$.

example 37.3   Write an inequality that describes this graph.

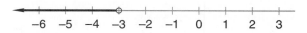

solution   The graph indicates all real numbers that are less than −3, so the inequality is

$$x < -3$$

practice   **a.**   Draw a number line and graph the solution of $x \leq 5$.

b.   Write an inequality that describes this graph.

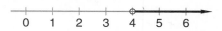

problem set 37

1. (32)   Zollie had a secret number. She found that the sum of 3 times her number and 70 equaled −50. What was her number?

2. (33)   If the product of 3 and a number is increased by 7, the result is 23 greater than the number. Find the number.

3. (4)   Use three unit multipliers to convert 17 miles to centimeters. (Go from miles to feet to inches to centimeters).

4. (10)   Use four unit multipliers to convert 200 square miles to square inches. (Use two unit multipliers to go from square miles to square feet and two unit multipliers to go from square feet to square inches.)

5. (3,8)   The area of a rectangle is 54 in.^{2}. The length of one side of the rectangle is 9 in. Find the perimeter of the rectangle.

6. (37)   Draw a number line and graph the solution of $x > 3$.

7. (37)   Write an inequality that describes this graph.

8. (33)   Write 360 as a product of prime factors.

Simplify:

9. (36) $-(-2)^{-2}$

10. (36) $\dfrac{1}{-(-2)^{-2}}$

11. (30)   What decimal part of 0.42 is 0.00504?

12. (28)   If $f(x) = x^2 + 1$, find $f(3)$.

Solve:

13.
(25) $-\dfrac{1}{3} + 2\dfrac{1}{2}p = 3$

14.
(27) $-n + 0.4n + 1.8 = -4.2$

15.
(31) $-3m - 3 + 5m - 2 = -(2m + 3)$

16.
(31) $x - 3(x - 2) = 7x - (2x + 5)$

17.
(25)
  (a) What value of x satisfies the equation $\frac{1}{2}x + 2 = 4\frac{1}{2}$?

  (b) What value of x satisfies the equation $\frac{1}{4}x - 2 = -3\frac{1}{4}$?

  (c) Are the solutions of both equations the same?

  (d) Given your answer to part (c), are the two equations equivalent?

Factor the greatest common factor:

18.
(35) $12a^2x^5y^7 - 3ax^2y^2$

19.
(35) $15a^5x^4y^6 + 3a^4x^3y^7 - 9a^2x^6y$

Simplify (factor if necessary):

20.
(35) $\dfrac{2x + 6}{2}$

21.
(35) $\dfrac{4x^2 - 4x}{4x}$

22.
(21) Simplify by adding like terms: $3xxy^2x^{-2} - 2xx^{-1}yy + 5y^2 - 6x^2 - 4x^2xxx^{-2}$

Expand by using the distributive property:

23.
(29) $(x^3y^0 - p^0x^2y^4)x^{-3}$

24.
(36) $\dfrac{ax}{c^2}\left(\dfrac{b^4}{xk} - 2b^2\right)$

Evaluate:

25.
(29) $a^2 - a^0(a - ab)$ if $a = -3$ and $b = 5$

26.
(29) $-k - kp^0 - (-pk^2)$ if $k = -3$ and $p = 2$

Simplify:

27.
(29) $2^2 - 2^3 - (-3)^2 + \sqrt[4]{81}$

28.
(29) $\dfrac{-(-3 + 7) + 4^0}{(-2)(3 - 5)}$

29.
(3) Find the perimeter of this figure. Corners that look square are square. Dimensions are in centimeters.

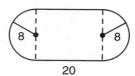

30.
(20) A base of the right prism 8 meters high is shown. Find the volume of the right prism. All angles are right angles. Dimensions are in meters.

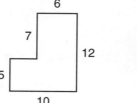

LESSON 38 *Ratio Problems*

When we write the numbers 3 and 4 separated by a fraction line as

$$\frac{3}{4}$$

we say that we have written the fraction three fourths. Another name for a fraction is **ratio,** and we can also say that we have written the ratio of 3 to 4. All of the following ratios designate the same number and thus are equal ratios.

$$\frac{3}{4} \qquad \frac{6}{8} \qquad \frac{300}{400} \qquad \frac{15}{20} \qquad \frac{27}{36} \qquad \frac{111}{148}$$

An equation or statement in which two ratios are equal is called a **proportion.** Thus, we can say that

$$\frac{3}{4} = \frac{15}{20}$$

is a proportion. We note that the cross products of equal ratios are equal, as shown.

$$\frac{3}{4} \underset{3\,\cdot\,20}{\overset{4\,\cdot\,15}{\times}} \frac{15}{20} \qquad\qquad 4 \cdot 15 = 3 \cdot 20$$
$$60 = 60 \qquad \text{True}$$

We can solve proportions that contain an unknown by setting the cross products equal and then dividing to complete the solution. To solve

$$\frac{7}{5} = \frac{91}{g}$$

we first set the cross products equal

$$7g = 5 \cdot 91$$

and then finish by dividing both sides by 7.

$$\frac{7g}{7} = \frac{5 \cdot 91}{7} \quad \longrightarrow \quad g = \frac{455}{7} \quad \longrightarrow \quad g = 65$$

When we set the cross products equal, we say that we have cross multiplied.

example 38.1   Solve: $\dfrac{4}{m} = \dfrac{21}{5}$

solution   We begin by setting the cross products equal.

$$4 \cdot 5 = 21m$$

Now we finish by dividing both sides by 21.

$$\frac{4 \cdot 5}{21} = \frac{21m}{21} \quad \longrightarrow \quad m = \frac{20}{21}$$

We use proportions and cross multiplication to solve ratio word problems. In these problems, we wish to maintain a constant ratio between two things. We will use meaningful variables to represent the things and avoid the meaningless variables x, y, and z.

example 38.2   The ratio of pigs to goats in the barnyard was 7 to 5. If there were 91 pigs, how many goats were there?

solution   We first note that we are comparing pigs and goats. Either one may be on top. If it is on top on one side, it must also be on top on the other side. We will demonstrate this by working the problem two ways.

$$\text{(a)} \quad \frac{P}{G} = \frac{P}{G} \qquad \text{(b)} \quad \frac{G}{P} = \frac{G}{P}$$

Now we read the problem and find that the ratio of pigs to goats was 7 to 5. So on the left-hand side of both equations, we replace P with 7 and G with 5.

$$\text{(a)} \quad \frac{7}{5} = \frac{P}{G} \qquad \text{(b)} \quad \frac{5}{7} = \frac{G}{P}$$

Now we read the problem again and find that there were 91 pigs. Thus, we can replace P in both equations with 91.

$$\text{(a)} \quad \frac{7}{5} = \frac{91}{G} \qquad \text{(b)} \quad \frac{5}{7} = \frac{G}{91}$$

We solve both of these proportions the same way—by cross multiplying and then dividing both sides by 7.

$$7G = 5 \cdot 91 \quad \rightarrow \quad 7G = 455 \quad \rightarrow \quad \frac{7G}{7} = \frac{455}{7} \quad \rightarrow \quad G = \mathbf{65}$$

example 38.3   In the same barnyard, the ratio of chickens to ducks was 9 to 4, and there were 108 chickens. How many ducks were there?

solution   Either chickens or ducks may go on top. We decide to put the ducks on top, so we write

$$\frac{D}{C} = \frac{D}{C}$$

The ratio of chickens to ducks was 9 to 4, so on the left we replace C with 9 and D with 4.

$$\frac{4}{9} = \frac{D}{C}$$

Finally, we replace C on the right with 108, and finish by cross multiplying and then dividing both sides by 9.

$$\frac{4}{9} = \frac{D}{108} \quad \rightarrow \quad 9D = 4 \cdot 108 \quad \rightarrow \quad \frac{9D}{9} = \frac{4 \cdot 108}{9} \quad \rightarrow \quad D = \mathbf{48}$$

practice   a.   The ratio of neophytes to masters at the tryout was 7 to 2. If there were 714 neophytes, how many masters were there?

   b.   The crowd in the Belgrade town square was made up of Croats and Serbs in the ratio of 5 to 9. If there were 18,000 Serbs, how many Croats were there?

problem set   1.   In a picaresque novel about the Spanish Main, the ratio of rascals to good guys was 13
38   (38)   to 5. If 600 were good guys, how many rascals were in the novel?

   2.   If the product of 5 and a number is increased by 8, the result is −42. What is the number?
   (32)

3. Twice the sum of 3 times a number and 60 is 155 greater than the opposite of the number.
(33) Find the number.

4. Is the product of 25 positive numbers and 29 negative numbers a positive number or a
(13) negative number?

5. Use three unit multipliers to convert 49 meters to feet. (Go from meters to centimeters to
(4) inches to feet.)

6. The area of a circle is 36π cm^2.
(3,8)
    (a) Find the radius of the circle.

    (b) Find the circumference of the circle.

7. Draw a number line and graph the solution of $x < 2$.
(37)

8. Write an inequality that describes this graph.
(37)

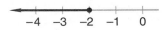

-4 -3 -2 -1 0

Simplify:

9. $(-6)^{-2}$
(36)

10. -5^{-2}
(36)

11. What fraction of $3\frac{3}{4}$ is $22\frac{1}{2}$?
(28)

12. If $g(x) = x^2 - 2$, find $g(-2)$.
(28)

Solve:

13. $3\frac{1}{2}k + \frac{3}{4} = -\frac{7}{8}$
(25)

14. $0.3k + 0.85k - 2 = 2.6$
(27)

15. $2(3p - 2) - (p + 4) = 3p$
(31)

16. $3(x - 2) - (2x + 5) = -2x + 10$
(31)

Factor the greatest common factor:

17. $4a^2x^3y^5 - 8a^4x^2y^4$
(35)

18. $6a^2xm^6 - 18a^5x^3m^5$
(35)

Simplify (factor if necessary):

19. $\dfrac{3x - 9}{3}$
(35)

20. $\dfrac{5x^2 - 25x}{5x}$
(35)

21. Simplify by adding like terms: $xy - 3yx + 7x^3y^2x^{-2}y^{-1} - 2x^2yy^5y^{-4}y^{-1}x^{-1}$
(21)

Expand by using the distributive property:

22. $3x^0y^{-3}(4y^3z - 7x^2)$
(29)

23. $\dfrac{ax}{c^2}\left(\dfrac{ax^2}{c} - \dfrac{3c^2a}{x^3}\right)$
(36)

Evaluate:

24. $k^2 - k^3(km^0)$ if $k = -3$ and $m = 2$
(29)

25. $-n(n^0 - m) - |2 - m^2|$ if $n = -4$ and $m = -2$
(29)

Simplify:

26. $-3^3 - 3^2 - (-3)^2 - |-2^2|$
(19)

27. $\dfrac{-4(3^0 - 6)(-2)}{-4 - (-3)(-2) - 5}$
(29)

28. Find the area of this figure. Dimen-
(8) sions are in meters.

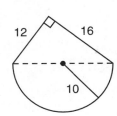

12   16

10

29. WZ is $8\frac{3}{4}$ inches. WX is $2\frac{1}{3}$ inches. YZ is $3\frac{1}{2}$ inches. Find XY.
(1)

30. Find the surface area of this right trian-
(15) gular prism. Dimensions are in feet.

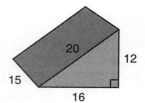

LESSON 39   *Trichotomy Axiom • Negated Inequalities •*
Advanced Ratio Problems

39.A
trichotomy axiom

Johnny wrote a number on a piece of paper. Then he turned the paper over and wrote a number on the other side. There are exactly three possibilities.

1. The second number is less than the first number.

2. The second number is the same number as the first number.

3. The second number is greater than the first number.

While this is seemingly self-evident, it is not trivial. Mathematicians recognize that this property of real numbers reveals that the real numbers are an ordered set. Since this property has three parts, we give it the name **trichotomy.**[†]

> TRICHOTOMY AXIOM
>
> For any two real numbers a and b, exactly one of the following is true:
>
> $$a < b \qquad a = b \qquad a > b$$

39.B
negated inequalities

Symbols of inequality can be negated by drawing a slash through the symbol. We read

$$\text{(a)} \quad x \not> 10$$

from left to right as "x is not greater than 10." There are only three possibilities under the trichotomy axiom, and if x is not greater than 10, then it must be less than or equal to 10. So we can say the same thing by writing

$$\text{(b)} \quad x \le 10$$

[†] From the Greek *trikha* meaning "in three parts."

In the same way, if we write

$$\text{(c) } x \not\geq 6$$

which says that x is not greater than or equal to 6, then x must be less than 6 because that is the only other possibility. Thus, both (c) and (d) make the same statement.

$$\text{(d) } x < 6$$

example 39.1   Draw a number line and graph the solution of $x \not< 2$.

solution   This negated inequality is read from left to right as **x is not less than 2.** If x is not less than 2, then x has to be greater than or equal to 2. Thus, the solution is the graph of $x \geq 2$.

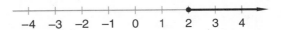

The solid circle at 2 indicates that the number 2 is a part of the solution of $x \geq 2$.

example 39.2   Write both an inequality and a negated inequality that describe this graph.

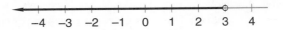

solution   The graph indicates all real numbers that are less than 3. These are the real numbers that are not greater than or equal to 3.

$$x < 3 \qquad \text{means the same thing as} \qquad x \not\geq 3$$

39.C
advanced ratio problems

Some ratio problems are difficult because key information is hidden by the way the problem is worded. If we are told that the ratio of red marbles to blue marbles is 5 to 7, we would write

$$\frac{R}{B} = \frac{5}{7}$$

Now if we are told that we have a total of 156 marbles and are asked for the number of marbles that are red, we would have difficulty because there is no place for the total in the equation we have written. If we use the following four-step procedure, we can work any ratio problem with ease because this method will produce three useful equations.

1. Write the information given to include the total.
2. Use the cover-up method to write three equations.
3. Reread the problem to determine which equation to use.
4. Substitute in the selected equation and solve the problem.

example 39.3   The ratio of red marbles to blue marbles is 5 to 7. If there are 156 marbles in the bag, how many marbles are red?

solution   **Step 1.**   Write all the information to include the total. If 5 are red and 7 are blue, the total is 12.

$$R = 5$$
$$B = 7$$
$$T = 12$$

Step 2. Write all the implied equations. In this problem there are three implied equations. We can recognize the equations if we cover part of the information with a finger, as we show here.

$$B = 7$$
$$T = 12$$
(a) $\dfrac{B}{T} = \dfrac{7}{12}$

$$R = 5$$
$$T = 12$$
(b) $\dfrac{R}{T} = \dfrac{5}{12}$

$$R = 5$$
$$B = 7$$
(c) $\dfrac{R}{B} = \dfrac{5}{7}$

Step 3. Now we reread the question. It says we have 156 total and asks for the number that are red. This tells us to use equation (b) because the variables in this equation are R and T.

$$\text{(b)} \quad \dfrac{R}{T} = \dfrac{5}{12}$$

Step 4. Now we substitute 156 for T and solve for R.

$$\dfrac{R}{156} = \dfrac{5}{12} \quad \longrightarrow \quad 12R = 5 \cdot 156 \quad \longrightarrow \quad \dfrac{12R}{12} = \dfrac{5 \cdot 156}{12} \quad \longrightarrow \quad R = \mathbf{65}$$

example 39.4 The ratio of fish to crabs in the sea cave was 13 to 4. If there were 119 fish and crabs in the sea cave, how many were fish?

solution **The first step is very important.** If we record the information to include the total, the equations can be written by inspection.

$$F = 13$$
$$C = 4$$
$$T = 17$$

From this we can write the three equations.

(a) $\dfrac{C}{T} = \dfrac{4}{17}$ (b) $\dfrac{F}{T} = \dfrac{13}{17}$ (c) $\dfrac{F}{C} = \dfrac{13}{4}$

Now we reread the question. It says we have 119 total and asks for the number of fish. This tells us to use equation (b) because the variables in this equation are F and T. Now we substitute 119 for T and solve for F.

$$\dfrac{F}{119} = \dfrac{13}{17} \quad \longrightarrow \quad 17F = 13 \cdot 119 \quad \longrightarrow \quad \dfrac{17F}{17} = \dfrac{13 \cdot 119}{17} \quad \longrightarrow \quad F = \mathbf{91}$$

practice   **a.** The team played 65 games. If the ratio of wins to losses was 3 to 2, how many games did the team win?

   b. The ratio of hard problems to easy problems was 23 to 7. How many easy problems were there if the total number of problems was 930?

    c. Draw a number line and graph the solution of $x \not\geq 2$.

    d. Write both an inequality and a negative inequality that describe this graph.

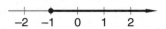

problem set
39

1. When the smoke cleared, the ratio of believers to skeptics was 15 to 7. If there were
(38) 105 believers, how many skeptics were there?

2. The ratio of white marbles to black marbles is 7 to 10. If there are 136 marbles in the bag,
(39) how many marbles are white?

3. If the product of 6 and a number is decreased by 5, the result is -35. What is the number?
(32)

4. If the product of 5 and a number is increased by 9 and this sum multiplied by 3, the result
(33) is 11 greater than the opposite of the number. Find the number.

5. Use three unit multipliers to convert 300 kilometers to inches.
(4)

6. The perimeter of a rectangle is 56 cm. The length of one side of the rectangle is 18 cm.
(3,8) Find the area of the rectangle.

7. Draw a number line and graph the solution of $x < 1$.
(37)

8. Draw a number line and graph the solution of $x \not> 1$.
(39)

9. Write 450 as a product of prime factors.
(33)

10. Which of the following terms are like terms?
(21)
    (a) $3x^4x^{-2}y^0$ (b) $-3x^2x^{-2}y$ (c) $-4x^0y^0y^3y^{-2}$ (d) $4x^0y^4y^{-2}$

Simplify:

11. $(-7)^0$
(29)

12. $\dfrac{1}{-3^{-2}}$
(36)

13. If $h(x) = 2 - x^2$, find $h(4)$.
(28)

Solve:

14. $-\dfrac{7}{8} + 2\dfrac{3}{4}x = \dfrac{1}{2}$
(25)

15. $0.1p - 0.2p + 2 = -4.6$
(27)

16. $5(x - 2) - (-x + 3) = 7$
(31)

17. $-5(p - 4) - 3(-2 - p) = p - 2$
(31)

Factor the greatest common factor:

18. $3x^2y^3z^5 - 9xy^6z^6$
(35)

19. $4x^2y - 12xy^2 + 24x^3y^3$
(35)

Simplify (factor if necessary):

20. $\dfrac{7x + 7}{7}$
(35)

21. $\dfrac{9x - 3x^2}{3x}$
(35)

22. Simplify by adding like terms: $3x^4x^{-3}y^0 + xy^0y^{-2}y^2 - 7x^3x^{-2}x^0y^0$
(21)

Expand by using the distributive property:

23. $\left(y^{-5} + 3x^5y^2\right)x^0y^5$
(29)

24. $\left(\dfrac{a^2}{x} - \dfrac{2x}{a}\right)\dfrac{4x^2}{a}$
(36)

Evaluate:

25. $m^2 - \left(m - p^0\right)$ if $m = 2$ and $p = -2$
(29)

26. $a^2b^0 - (a - b) - \left|a^3\right|$ if $a = -2$ and $b = -1$
(29)

Simplify:

27. $3^2 - 3^3 - 3^0 + |-3^0|$
(29)

28. $\dfrac{4(-2-3) - 4^0}{-2(-4+6) - 3}$
(29)

29. Find the perimeter of this figure. Cor-
(3)   ners that look square are square.
      Dimensions are in meters.

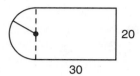

20

30

30. A base of the right prism is the scalene triangle shown. The height of the right prism is
(20) 15 in. Find the volume of the right prism.

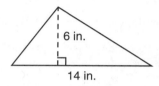

6 in.

14 in.

LESSON 40 *Quotient Rule for Exponents • Distributive Property of Rational Expressions that Contain Negative Exponents*

40.A

quotient rule for exponents

Let us review our rules and definitions for exponents.

DEFINITION:	$\underbrace{x \cdot x \cdot x \cdot \,\cdots\, \cdot x}_{n \text{ factors}} = x^n$
PRODUCT RULE:	If x is not zero, then $x^m \cdot x^n = x^{m+n}$
DEFINITION:	$x^1 = x$
DEFINITION:	If x is not zero, then $x^{-n} = \dfrac{1}{x^n}$
DEFINITION:	If x is not zero, then $x^0 = 1$

The **quotient rule for exponents** is really an extension of the next-to-last definition above that says if n is any real number and x is any real number that is not zero, then $x^{-n} = \frac{1}{x^n}$. If we wish to multiply

$$x^5 \qquad \text{times} \qquad \frac{1}{x^2}$$

we can use the definition of x^{-n} to write $\frac{1}{x^2}$ as x^{-2} and then multiply by using the product rule.

$$x^5 \cdot \frac{1}{x^2} = x^5 \cdot x^{-2} = x^{5-2} = x^3$$

The quotient rule permits the same procedure in just one step.

QUOTIENT RULE FOR EXPONENTS

If m and n are real numbers and $x \neq 0$, then

$$\frac{x^m}{x^n} = x^{m-n} = \frac{1}{x^{n-m}}$$

example 40.1   Simplify (write the answer with the x in the numerator): $\dfrac{x^6}{x^4}$

solution   We know that we can move the x^4 from the denominator to the numerator if we change the sign of the 4 from plus to minus.

$$\frac{x^6}{x^4} = x^6 x^{-4} = x^{6-4} = \boldsymbol{x^2}$$

If we use the quotient rule, we can omit the first step and write

$$\frac{x^6}{x^4} = x^{6-4} = \boldsymbol{x^2}$$

example 40.2   Simplify (write the answer with the x in the denominator): $\dfrac{x^6}{x^4}$

solution   We know that we can move the x^6 from the numerator to the denominator if we change the sign of the 6 from plus to minus.

$$\frac{x^6}{x^4} = \frac{1}{x^4 x^{-6}} = \frac{1}{x^{4-6}} = \boldsymbol{\frac{1}{x^{-2}}}$$

If we use the quotient rule, we can omit the first step and write

$$\frac{x^6}{x^4} = \frac{1}{x^{4-6}} = \boldsymbol{\frac{1}{x^{-2}}}$$

example 40.3   Simplify: $\dfrac{x^6}{x^{-4}}$

solution   We will work the problem twice. The first time we will simplify the expression so that the x is in the numerator and the second time we will simplify the expression so that the x is in the denominator.

(a) We will use the quotient rule to simplify so that the x is in the numerator.

$$\frac{x^6}{x^{-4}} = x^{6+4} = \boldsymbol{x^{10}}$$

(b) This time we will use the quotient rule to simplify so that the x is in the denominator.

$$\frac{x^6}{x^{-4}} = \frac{1}{x^{-4-6}} = \boldsymbol{\frac{1}{x^{-10}}}$$

example 40.4   Simplify: $\dfrac{x^{-a}}{x^b}$

solution   We will work the problem twice. The first time we will simplify the expression so that the x is in the numerator and the second time we will simplify the expression so that the x is in the denominator.

(a) We will use the quotient rule to simplify so that the x is in the numerator.

$$\frac{x^{-a}}{x^b} = x^{-a-b}$$

(b) This time we will use the quotient rule to simplify so that the x is in the denominator.

$$\frac{x^{-a}}{x^b} = \frac{1}{x^{b+a}}$$

The two answers shown in (a) and (b) are **equivalent expressions,** which means that they have the same value no matter which nonzero real number is used as a replacement for x. Since they are equivalent expressions, neither expression can be designated as the preferred answer because the preference of one person will not necessarily be the same as the preference of another person.

example 40.5   Simplify: $\dfrac{x^{-5}y^6z}{z^{-3}y^2x}$

solution   We will find four equivalent expressions for this expression.

(a) $x^{-6}y^4z^4$ (b) $\dfrac{1}{x^6y^{-4}z^{-4}}$ (c) $\dfrac{y^4z^4}{x^6}$ (d) $\dfrac{x^{-6}}{y^{-4}z^{-4}}$

Answer (a) is written with all variables in the numerator; (b) has all variables in the denominator; (c) has all exponents positive; and (d) has all exponents negative. No one of these forms is more correct than another. We will emphasize this by using different forms for the answers in the back of the book unless the problem states otherwise.

40.B
distributive property of rational expressions that contain negative exponents

In the preceding four problem sets, we have used the distributive property to expand expressions that contain fractions, such as

$$\frac{x}{y^2}\left(\frac{x^2}{y} - \frac{4y^3}{x^2}\right)$$

In this lesson, we will do the same expansions, but now we will also consider rational expressions that contain negative exponents.

example 40.6   Use the distributive property to expand. Write the answer with all exponents positive.

$$\frac{4x^{-2}}{y^4}\left(y^4x^2 - \frac{3x^4}{y^{-2}}\right)$$

solution   We will use two steps. First we use the distributive property to multiply.

$$\frac{4x^{-2}}{y^4}\left(y^4x^2 - \frac{3x^4}{y^{-2}}\right) = \frac{4x^{-2}y^4x^2}{y^4} - \frac{12x^{-2}x^4}{y^4y^{-2}}$$

Now we simplify and write the answer with all exponents positive.

$$4 - \frac{12x^2}{y^2}$$

example 40.7 Use the distributive property to expand. Write the answer with all variables in the numerator.

$$x^{-2}y\left(\frac{y^4}{x^2} - \frac{x^4}{y^2}\right)$$

solution Again we will use two steps. First we use the distributive property to multiply.

$$x^{-2}y\left(\frac{y^4}{x^2} - \frac{x^4}{y^2}\right) = \frac{x^{-2}yy^4}{x^2} - \frac{x^{-2}yx^4}{y^2}$$

Now we simplify and write the answer with all variables in the numerator.

$$x^{-4}y^5 - x^2y^{-1}$$

example 40.8 Use the distributive property to expand. Write the answer with all variables in the denominator.

$$\frac{k^2b}{p^{-2}}\left(\frac{ab^{-1}}{k^2} - \frac{4p^2}{b}\right)$$

solution Again we will use two steps. First we use the distributive property to multiply.

$$\frac{k^2b}{p^{-2}}\left(\frac{ab^{-1}}{k^2} - \frac{4p^2}{b}\right) = \frac{k^2bab^{-1}}{p^{-2}k^2} - \frac{4p^2k^2b}{p^{-2}b}$$

Now we simplify and write the answer with all variables in the denominator.

$$\frac{1}{a^{-1}p^{-2}} - \frac{4}{p^{-4}k^{-2}}$$

practice Simplify. Write the answers with all variables in the numerator.

a. $\dfrac{x^{-6}y^4z^5}{x^{-6}y^5z^2}$

b. $\dfrac{m^4p^3z^{10}d}{m^{-2}p^4z^{-6}d^{-2}}$

Expand by using the distributive property. Write the answers with all variables in the numerator.

c. $\dfrac{z^{-3}}{m}\left(\dfrac{x^4}{m^2} - \dfrac{3z}{m}\right)$

d. $\left(\dfrac{m^{-5}}{w^4x} - \dfrac{cw^2}{x^3m}\right)\dfrac{m^{-2}}{3cm}$

problem set 40

1. (38) The ratio of good guys to malefactors was 13 to 6. If there were 78 good guys, how many malefactors were there?

2. (39) The ratio of gaudy scarves to tawdry scarves was 7 to 11. If there were 2520 scarves in the pile, how many were merely gaudy?

3. (32) Jay and Bill found that 4 times the sum of a number and −6 equaled 20. What was the number?

4. (33) If the sum of 4 times a number and 6 is multiplied by 3, the result is 5 greater than the opposite of the number. Find the number.

5. (10) Use four unit multipliers to convert 30 square meters to square inches.

6. (39) Write both an inequality and a negated inequality that describe this graph.

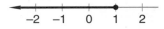

7. (21) Which of the following terms are like terms?

(a) $6xxx^3y^2x^{-2}$ (b) $7x^2yyy^0x^{-1}$ (c) $-6xxx^0y^3y^0$ (d) $-7x^2x^{-1}y^3y^{-1}y^0$

Simplify:

8. $-(-3)^{-3}$
(36)

9. $\dfrac{1}{-(-3)^{-3}}$
(36)

10. 1.05 of 0.043 is what number?
(30)

11. If $f(x) = -x^2 + 5$, find $f(5)$.
(28)

Solve:

12. $\dfrac{3}{4} + \dfrac{1}{2}x + 2 = 0$
(25)

13. $1.3p + 0.3p - 2 = 1.2$
(27)

14. $p - 3(p - 4) = 2 + (2p + 5)$
(31)

15. $2(5 - x) - (-2)(x - 3) = -(3x - 4)$
(31)

Factor the greatest common factor:

16. $4a^2xy^4p - 6a^2x^4$
(35)

17. $3a^2x^4y^6 + 9ax^2y^4 - 6x^4a^2y^5z$
(35)

Simplify (factor if necessary):

18. $\dfrac{6x - 36x^2}{6x}$
(35)

19. $\dfrac{4xy + 16xy^2}{4xy}$
(35)

Simplify. Write the answers with all variables in the numerator.

20. $\dfrac{x^3y^2}{xy^4}$
(40)

21. $\dfrac{x^3y^{-3}z}{z^5x^2y}$
(40)

Expand by using the distributive property. Write the answers with all variables in the numerator.

22. $\dfrac{m^{-2}}{b}\left(\dfrac{b^2}{m^3} - \dfrac{4am^2}{b^4}\right)$
(40)

23. $\left(\dfrac{x^{-4}}{a^3} - \dfrac{a^3}{x}\right)\dfrac{a^{-3}}{x}$
(40)

24. Simplify by adding like terms: $-3x^2x^0xy^2 + 2x^3yy^0y^{-3}y^4 + 5x^3x^{-6}y^0y^3y^{-5}$
(21)

Evaluate:

25. $a(b^0 - ab)$　　　if $a = 3$ and $b = -5$
(29)

26. $(m - x^2)x - |m - x|$　　　if $m = -3$ and $x = -2$
(19)

Simplify:

27. $-3^3 - 2^2 - 4^3 - |-2^2 - 2|$
(19)

28. $\dfrac{-3^2 + 4^2 + 3^3}{2(-5 + 2) - 3^0}$
(29)

29. Find the area of the shaded portion of
(8)　　this figure. Dimensions are in centi-
　　　meters.

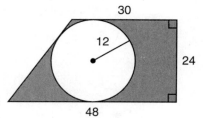

30. Find x and y.
(2)

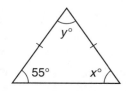

LESSON *41*   *Addition of Like Terms in Rational Expressions • Two-Step Problems*

41.A

addition of like terms in rational expressions

Sometimes it is difficult to determine if terms in a rational expression are like terms. For instance, if we look at the rational expression

$$\frac{bx}{x^3 y^{-2}} - 3by^2 x^{-2} + \frac{4y^2}{bx^2}$$

it is rather difficult to see that two of the terms are like terms and thus may be added. If each of the terms is written in the same form, however, it is easy to identify like terms. Let us write each of the three terms with all exponents positive.

$$\frac{by^2}{x^2} - \frac{3by^2}{x^2} + \frac{4y^2}{bx^2}$$

We see that the first two terms are like terms and may be added. The last term is different and thus cannot be added.

$$\frac{by^2}{x^2} - \frac{3by^2}{x^2} + \frac{4y^2}{bx^2} = -\frac{2by^2}{x^2} + \frac{4y^2}{bx^2}$$

Now we will work the problem again by first writing the original terms so that all exponents are negative.

$$\frac{x^{-2}}{b^{-1} y^{-2}} - \frac{3x^{-2}}{b^{-1} y^{-2}} + \frac{4b^{-1} x^{-2}}{y^{-2}} = -\frac{2x^{-2}}{b^{-1} y^{-2}} + \frac{4b^{-1} x^{-2}}{y^{-2}}$$

Again we see that the first two terms are like terms and may be added. To see if terms are like terms, we can put them in any form we wish as long as we use the same form for every term. However, many people feel more comfortable with all exponents positive.

example 41.1   Simplify by adding like terms: $\dfrac{bx}{x^3 y^{-2}} - 3by^2 x^{-2} + \dfrac{4y^2}{b^{-1} x^2}$

solution   To help us identify like terms, we will rewrite each term so that all exponents are positive.

$$\frac{by^2}{x^2} - \frac{3by^2}{x^2} + \frac{4by^2}{x^2}$$

We see that all three terms are like terms and can be added by adding the numerical coefficients.

$$\frac{by^2}{x^2} - \frac{3by^2}{x^2} + \frac{4by^2}{x^2} = \frac{2by^2}{x^2}$$

example 41.2   Simplify by adding like terms: $\dfrac{a^{-3} b}{b^{-3}} + \dfrac{2b^4}{a^3}$

solution   We begin by writing each term with all exponents positive.

$$\frac{b^4}{a^3} + \frac{2b^4}{a^3}$$

Now we see that the terms are like terms and can be added by adding the numerical coefficients.

$$\frac{b^4}{a^3} + \frac{2b^4}{a^3} = \frac{3b^4}{a^3}$$

example 41.3   Simplify by adding like terms: $\dfrac{7a^{-3}b^2}{c^{-1}} - \dfrac{5b^2}{a^3c^{-1}} + \dfrac{3b^2}{a^3c}$

solution   We begin by writing each term with all exponents positive.

$$\frac{7cb^2}{a^3} - \frac{5cb^2}{a^3} + \frac{3b^2}{a^3c}$$

Now we see that the first two terms are like terms and may be added. The third term is different and thus cannot be added.

$$\frac{7cb^2}{a^3} - \frac{5cb^2}{a^3} + \frac{3b^2}{a^3c} = \mathbf{\frac{2cb^2}{a^3}} + \mathbf{\frac{3b^2}{a^3c}}$$

41.B

two-step problems   Some problems require two steps for their solution. The answer for the first step is used in the second step.

example 41.4   If $x + 3 = 7$, what is the value of $x - 8$?

solution   First we solve $x + 3 = 7$ to find x.

$$\begin{array}{rl} x + 3 = 7 & \text{original equation} \\ \underline{-3 \quad -3} & \text{added } -3 \text{ to both sides} \\ x \quad\;\; = 4 & \end{array}$$

Now we use 4 for x to find the value of $x - 8$.

$$\begin{array}{ll} x - 8 & \text{expression} \\ 4 - 8 & \text{substitution} \\ \mathbf{-4} & \text{simplified} \end{array}$$

example 41.5   If $x - 5 = 7$, what is the value of $x + 4$?

solution   First we solve $x - 5 = 7$ to find x.

$$\begin{array}{rl} x - 5 = 7 & \text{original equation} \\ \underline{\quad 5 \quad\; 5} & \text{added 5 to both sides} \\ x \quad\;\; = 12 & \end{array}$$

Now we use 12 for x to find the value of $x + 4$.

$$\begin{array}{ll} x + 4 & \text{expression} \\ 12 + 4 & \text{substitution} \\ \mathbf{16} & \text{simplified} \end{array}$$

practice   Simplify by adding like terms. Write the answers with all variables in the numerator.

   a. $x^{-2}y + \dfrac{3y}{x^2} - 5xy$

   b. $\dfrac{a^{-8}b^2}{b^{-9}} - \dfrac{4b^{11}}{a^8} + \dfrac{6b^{11}}{a^8b^5}$

   c. If $x + 7 = 2$, what is the value of $x + 3$?

   d. If $x - 6 = 4$, what is the value of $x - 5$?

problem set 41

   1.
   (38)   The ratio of brigands to highway robbers skulking in the shadows was 15 to 9. If 75 brigands were skulking in the shadows, how many highway robbers were there?

   2.
   (33)   If the product of a number and -3 is reduced by 5, the result is 25 less than twice the opposite of the number. Find the number.

3. (a) The set $\{1, 2, 3, \ldots\}$ represents what set of numbers?
₍₅₎

(b) The set $\{0, 1, 2, 3, \ldots\}$ represents what set of numbers?

(c) The set $\{\ldots, -3, -2, -1, 0, 1, 2, 3, \ldots\}$ represents what set of numbers?

4. Use three unit multipliers to convert 40 meters to feet.
₍₄₎

5. The area of a circle is 25 in.^{2}.
_(3,8)

(a) Find the radius of the circle.

(b) Find the circumference of the circle.

6. Draw a number line and graph the solution of $x > 1$.
₍₃₇₎

7. Draw a number line and graph the solution of $x \not< 1$.
₍₃₉₎

8. Write 270 as a product of prime factors.
₍₃₃₎

9. If $g(x) = -x^2 - 10$, find $g(-4)$.
₍₂₈₎

Solve:

10. $3\dfrac{3}{4}n - \dfrac{9}{16} = 2\dfrac{1}{4}$
₍₂₅₎

11. $0.3 + 0.06p + 0.02 - 0.02p = 4$
₍₂₇₎

12. $-x - 2(-x - 3) = -4 - x$
₍₃₁₎

13. $3(-2x - 2 - 3) - (-x + 2) = -2(x + 1)$
₍₃₁₎

14. If $x + 4 = 6$, what is the value of $x - 7$?
₍₄₁₎

Factor the greatest common factor:

15. $3x^2y^5p^6 - 9x^2y^4p^3 + 12x^2yp^4$
₍₃₅₎

16. $2x^2y^2 - 6y^2x^4 - 12xy^5$
₍₃₅₎

Simplify (factor if necessary):

17. $\dfrac{5xy + 20xy^2}{5xy}$
₍₃₅₎

18. $\dfrac{k^2x - k^3x}{k^2x}$
₍₃₅₎

Simplify. Write the answers with all variables in the denominator.

19. $\dfrac{x^2y^5}{x^4y^{-3}}$
₍₄₀₎

20. $\dfrac{x^{-4}y^{-3}p^2}{x^{-5}yp^4}$
₍₄₀₎

Expand by using the distributive property. Write the answers with all variables in the denominator.

21. $\dfrac{x^{-2}}{y}\left(\dfrac{xz}{y} - \dfrac{1}{y^{-4}}\right)$
₍₄₀₎

22. $\left(\dfrac{a}{b} - \dfrac{2b}{a}\right)\dfrac{a^{-2}}{b^{-2}}$
₍₄₀₎

23. Simplify by adding like terms: $x^2y^2y^{-2}pp^0 - 4xxy^0p - 3x^4x^{-2}yy^{-1}p$
₍₂₁₎

24. Simplify by adding like terms. Write the answer with all variables in the numerator.
₍₄₁₎

$$\dfrac{m^2}{y^2} - \dfrac{3y^{-2}}{m^{-2}}$$

Evaluate:

25. $b - \left(-c^0\right) - b^3$ if $b = -2$ and $c = 4$
₍₂₉₎

26. $k^3 - (k - c)|k - c|$ if $k = -2$ and $c = 3$
₍₁₉₎

Simplify:

27. $\dfrac{1}{4^{-2}} - \sqrt[3]{-27}$
₍₂₉₎

28. $\dfrac{-3^2 + 4^2 - 5(4 - 2)}{3^0(5 - 2)}$
₍₂₉₎

29. Find the area of this figure. Dimen-
 (8) sions are in feet.

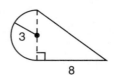

30. A right circular cylinder has a length
 (15) of 12 centimeters and a radius of
 2 centimeters, as shown. Find the surface area of the right circular cylinder.

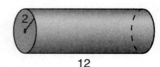

LESSON 42 *Solving Multivariable Equations*

When we are asked to solve an equation in one unknown, such as

$$12 + 4x - 3 + 4 - 2x = 6x - 3 - 2 + 5x$$

we are asked to simplify both sides and to finally write the equation with x all by itself on one side and a number on the other side. When we do this, we say that we have **isolated x** on one side of the equation. When we have isolated x in this problem, we get

$$x = 2$$

If an equation contains more than one variable and we are asked to solve the equation for one of the variables, our task is the same as that described above. **We are asked to rearrange the equation so that the designated variable is the sole member of one side of the equation (either side).** In the following problems, however, the other side of the equation will contain variables as well as numbers.

example 42.1 Solve for y: $6y - x + z = 4$

solution We will begin the process of isolating y by eliminating $-x$ and z on the left-hand side of the equation.

$$
\begin{array}{ll}
\begin{array}{l}
6y - x + z = 4 \\
\underline{\quad + x - z \qquad + x - z} \\
6y \qquad\quad = 4 + x - z
\end{array}
& \begin{array}{l}
\text{original equation} \\
\text{added } x - z \text{ to both sides}
\end{array}
\end{array}
$$

Now we complete the isolation of y by dividing every term by 6.

$$\frac{6y}{6} = \frac{4}{6} + \frac{x}{6} - \frac{z}{6} \qquad \text{divided both sides by 6}$$

$$y = \frac{2}{3} + \frac{x}{6} - \frac{z}{6} \qquad \text{simplified}$$

example 42.2 Solve for y: $4x - 2y + 2 = y - 4$

solution The first step is to eliminate the y term on one side or the other. We choose to eliminate the $-2y$ on the left-hand side of the equation, so we add $2y$ to both sides of the equation.

$$
\begin{array}{ll}
\begin{array}{l}
4x - 2y + 2 = \quad y - 4 \\
\underline{\quad + 2y \qquad\quad + 2y} \\
4x \qquad + 2 = \quad 3y - 4
\end{array}
& \begin{array}{l}
\text{original equation} \\
\text{added } 2y \text{ to both sides}
\end{array}
\end{array}
$$

Now we have all the y's on the right-hand side of the equation. To isolate y on the right-hand side of the equation, we must eliminate the -4 and the 3 that are on the right-hand side of the equation. To eliminate the -4, we add 4 to both sides of the equation.

$$\begin{array}{ll} 4x + 2 = 3y - 4 & \text{equation} \\ \underline{ + 4 + 4} & \text{added 4 to both sides} \\ 4x + 6 = 3y & \end{array}$$

Now we complete the isolation of y by dividing every term by 3.

$$\frac{4x}{3} + \frac{6}{3} = \frac{3y}{3} \qquad \text{divided both sides by 3}$$

$$y = \frac{4}{3}x + 2 \qquad \text{simplified}$$

example 42.3   Solve for p: $4p + 2a - 5 = 6a + p$

solution   We begin by eliminating the p on the right-hand side of the equation.

$$\begin{array}{ll} 4p + 2a - 5 = 6a + p & \text{original equation} \\ \underline{-p -p} & \text{added } -p \text{ to both sides} \\ 3p + 2a - 5 = 6a & \end{array}$$

Now we eliminate the $2a$ and -5 on the left-hand side of the equation.

$$\begin{array}{ll} 3p + 2a - 5 = 6a & \text{equation} \\ \underline{ - 2a + 5 -2a + 5} & \text{added } -2a + 5 \text{ to both sides} \\ 3p = 4a + 5 & \end{array}$$

Now we complete the isolation of p by dividing every term by 3.

$$\frac{3p}{3} = \frac{4a}{3} + \frac{5}{3} \qquad \text{divided both sides by 3}$$

$$p = \frac{4}{3}a + \frac{5}{3} \qquad \text{simplified}$$

example 42.4   Solve for x: $5y + x - 2y - 4 + 3x = 0$

solution   We will begin by adding like terms. Then we will eliminate the $3y$ and the -4 on the left-hand side of the equation by adding $-3y + 4$ to both sides of the equation.

$$\begin{array}{ll} 3y + 4x - 4 = 0 & \text{added like terms} \\ \underline{-3y + 4 = -3y + 4} & \text{added } -3y + 4 \text{ to both sides} \\ 4x = -3y + 4 & \end{array}$$

Now we complete the isolation of x by dividing every term by 4.

$$\frac{4x}{4} = \frac{-3y}{4} + \frac{4}{4} \qquad \text{divided both sides by 4}$$

$$x = -\frac{3}{4}y + 1 \qquad \text{simplified}$$

example 42.5   Solve for y: $4y + 6x - 4 = 2$

solution   Since only one term contains a y, we begin by moving all other terms to the right-hand side of the equation.

$$\begin{array}{ll} 4y + 6x - 4 = 2 & \text{original equation} \\ \underline{ - 6x + 4 = +4 - 6x} & \text{added } 4 - 6x \text{ to both sides} \\ 4y = 6 - 6x & \end{array}$$

Now we complete the isolation of y by dividing every term by 4.

$$\frac{4y}{4} = \frac{6}{4} - \frac{6x}{4} \qquad \text{divided both sides by 4}$$

$$y = \frac{3}{2} - \frac{3}{2}x \qquad \text{simplified}$$

practice   **a.** Solve for y: $8y - 13x - 8 = 4$

b. Solve for p: $8p + 3w = w - 15 - 2p$

problem set   **1.** War Eagle spied a total of 1428 antelope and wildebeests grazing on the savannah. If the
42   (39)   ratio of antelope to wildebeests was 9 to 5, how many antelope were there?

2. If the sum of twice a number and -3 is multiplied by 4, the answer is 28. Find the number.
(32)

3. Is the product of 30 positive numbers and 33 negative numbers a positive number or a
(13)   negative number?

4. Use four unit multipliers to convert 58 square centimeters to square feet.
(10)

5. The area of a square is 25 cm². Find the perimeter of the square.
(3,8)

6. Write both an inequality and a negated inequality that describe this graph.
(39)

7. $5\frac{7}{10}$ of what number is $9\frac{1}{2}$?
(28)

8. If $h(x) = -2x^2 + 3$, find $h(3)$.
(28)

Solve:

9. $2\frac{1}{3}x + 5 = 19$ **10.** $0.4k + 0.4k - 0.02 = 4.02$
(25)   (27)

11. $3p - 2(p - 4) = 7p + 6$ **12.** $4(x - 2) - 4x = -(3x + 2)$
(31)   (31)

13. If $x - 6 = 3$, what is the value of $x + 2$?
(41)

Solve for y:

14. $3x + 2y = 5 - y$ **15.** $-2y + 6y - x - 4 = 0$
(42)   (42)

Factor the greatest common factor:

16. $4x^2m^5y - 2x^4m^3y^3$ **17.** $4m^2x^5 - 2m^2x^2 + 6m^5x^2$
(35)   (35)

Simplify (factor if necessary):

18. $\dfrac{3xy - 9x^2y^2}{3xy}$ **19.** $\dfrac{x^2ym + xym}{xym}$
(35)   (35)

Simplify. Write the answers with all exponents positive.

20. $\dfrac{x^5y^5mm^{-2}}{xx^3y^{-3}m^4}$ **21.** $\dfrac{x^2xyp^{-5}}{p^{-3}p^{-4}y^{-4}}$
(40)   (40)

22. Expand by using the distributive property. Write the answer with all exponents positive.
(40)

$$x^2z^{-2}\left(\frac{x^4z^{-4}}{x} - \frac{3z^2}{x^2}\right)$$

23. Simplify by adding like terms: $5yxx^0p^2 - p^2y^2y^{-1}x + 2p^2p^0yx - 3p^2y^2y^{-1}x$
(21)

24. Simplify by adding like terms. Write the answer with all variables in the denominator.
(41)

$$\frac{3x^{-2}x^3y}{y^{-4}} - 2xy^5$$

Evaluate:

25. $x(x^0 - y) + |xy|$ if $x = -2$ and $y = 5$
(29)

26. $k^3 - (k - c)$ if $k = -2$ and $c + 2 = 6$
(41)

Simplify:

27. $\dfrac{1}{-3^{-2}} - \sqrt[3]{8}$
(36)

28. $\dfrac{-3^2 - (-3)^3 - 3}{-3(-3)(+3)}$
(19)

29. Find the perimeter of this figure. Cor-
(3) ners that look square are square.
Dimensions are in meters.

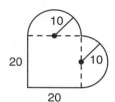

30. A right circular cylinder has a radius
(20) of 10 inches and a height of 20 inches,
as shown. Find the volume of the right
circular cylinder.

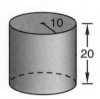

LESSON 43   *Least Common Multiple • Least Common Multiples of Algebraic Expressions*

43.A

least common multiple

If we are given the numbers

4,   5,   and   8

and are asked to find the **smallest number that is evenly divisible by each of the numbers,** a reasonable guess would be the product of the numbers, which is 160, because we know that each of the numbers will divide 160 evenly.

$$\frac{160}{4} = 40 \qquad \frac{160}{5} = 32 \qquad \frac{160}{8} = 20$$

But 160 is not the smallest number that is evenly divisible by the three numbers. The number 40 is.

$$\frac{40}{4} = 10 \qquad \frac{40}{5} = 8 \qquad \frac{40}{8} = 5$$

We call the smallest number that can be divided evenly by each of a group of specified numbers the least common multiple (LCM) of the specified numbers.

We can find the LCM of some numbers by making mental calculations, but it is nice to have a special procedure to use if some of the numbers are large numbers. The procedure is as follows:

1. Write each number as a product of prime factors.
2. Compute the LCM by using every factor of the given numbers as a factor of
    the LCM. Use each factor the greatest number of times it is a factor in any of
    the numbers.

To demonstrate this procedure, we will find the LCM of

18, 81, and 500

First we write each number as a product of prime factors.

$$18 = 2 \cdot 3 \cdot 3 \qquad 81 = 3 \cdot 3 \cdot 3 \cdot 3 \qquad 500 = 2 \cdot 2 \cdot 5 \cdot 5 \cdot 5$$

Now we find the LCM by using the procedure in Step 2. The number 2 is a factor of both 18 and 500. It appears twice in 500, so it will appear twice in the LCM.

$$2 \cdot 2$$

The number 3 is a factor of both 18 and 81. It appears four times in 81, so it will appear four times in the LCM.

$$2 \cdot 2 \cdot 3 \cdot 3 \cdot 3 \cdot 3$$

The number 5 is the other factor. It appears three times in 500, so it will appear three times in the LCM. Thus, the LCM is

$$\text{LCM} = 2 \cdot 2 \cdot 3 \cdot 3 \cdot 3 \cdot 3 \cdot 5 \cdot 5 \cdot 5 = 40{,}500$$

Therefore, 40,500 is the smallest number that is evenly divisible by each of the three numbers 18, 81, and 500.

example 43.1   Find the least common multiple (LCM) of 8, 15, and 100.

solution   First we write each number as a product of prime factors.

$$8 = 2 \cdot 2 \cdot 2 \qquad 15 = 3 \cdot 5 \qquad 100 = 2 \cdot 2 \cdot 5 \cdot 5$$

To compute the LCM, we use each factor the greatest number of times it is a factor in any of the numbers. The number 2 is a factor of both 8 and 100. It appears three times in 8, so it will appear three times in the LCM.

$$2 \cdot 2 \cdot 2$$

The number 3 is a factor of 15. It appears once in 15, so it will appear once in the LCM.

$$2 \cdot 2 \cdot 2 \cdot 3$$

The number 5 is a factor of both 15 and 100. It appears two times in 100, so it will appear two times in the LCM. Thus, the LCM is

$$\text{LCM} = 2 \cdot 2 \cdot 2 \cdot 3 \cdot 5 \cdot 5 = \mathbf{600}$$

Therefore, 600 is the smallest number that is evenly divisible by each of the three numbers 8, 15, and 100.

example 43.2   Find the least common multiple (LCM) of 30, 75, and 80.

solution   First we write each number as a product of prime factors.

$$30 = 2 \cdot 3 \cdot 5 \qquad 75 = 3 \cdot 5 \cdot 5 \qquad 80 = 2 \cdot 2 \cdot 2 \cdot 2 \cdot 5$$

To compute the LCM, we use each factor the greatest number of times it is a factor in any of the numbers. The number 2 is a factor of both 30 and 80. It appears four times in 80, so it will appear four times in the LCM.

$$2 \cdot 2 \cdot 2 \cdot 2$$

The number 3 is a factor of both 30 and 75. It appears once in 30 and once in 75, so it will appear once in the LCM.

$$2 \cdot 2 \cdot 2 \cdot 2 \cdot 3$$

The number 5 is a factor of 30, 75, and 80. It appears twice in 75, so it will appear twice in the LCM. Thus, the LCM is

$$\text{LCM} = 2 \cdot 2 \cdot 2 \cdot 2 \cdot 3 \cdot 5 \cdot 5 = \mathbf{1200}$$

Therefore, 1200 is the smallest number that is evenly divisible by each of the three numbers 30, 75, and 80.

example 43.3   Find the least common multiple (LCM) of 560, 588, and 1250.

solution   First we write each number as a product of prime factors.

$$560 = 2 \cdot 2 \cdot 2 \cdot 2 \cdot 5 \cdot 7 \qquad 588 = 2 \cdot 2 \cdot 3 \cdot 7 \cdot 7 \qquad 1250 = 2 \cdot 5 \cdot 5 \cdot 5 \cdot 5$$

To compute the LCM, we use each factor the greatest number of times it is a factor in any of the numbers. The number 2 is a factor of 560, 588, and 1250. It appears four times in 560, so it will appear four times in the LCM.

$$2 \cdot 2 \cdot 2 \cdot 2$$

The number 3 is a factor of 588. It appears once in 588, so it will appear once in the LCM.

$$2 \cdot 2 \cdot 2 \cdot 2 \cdot 3$$

The number 5 is a factor of both 560 and 1250. It appears four times in 1250, so it will appear four times in the LCM.

$$2 \cdot 2 \cdot 2 \cdot 2 \cdot 3 \cdot 5 \cdot 5 \cdot 5 \cdot 5$$

The number 7 is a factor of both 560 and 588. It appears twice in 588, so it will appear twice in the LCM. Thus, the LCM is

$$\text{LCM} = 2 \cdot 2 \cdot 2 \cdot 2 \cdot 3 \cdot 5 \cdot 5 \cdot 5 \cdot 5 \cdot 7 \cdot 7 = \mathbf{1{,}470{,}000}$$

Therefore, 1,470,000 is the smallest number that is evenly divisible by each of the three numbers 560, 588, and 1250.

43.B
least common multiples of algebraic expressions

The least common multiple is most often encountered when it is used as the least common denominator. If we are asked to add the fractions

$$\frac{1}{4} + \frac{5}{8} + \frac{7}{12}$$

we rewrite each of these fractions as a fraction whose denominator is 24, which is the least common multiple of 4, 8, and 12.

$$\frac{6}{24} + \frac{15}{24} + \frac{14}{24} = \frac{35}{24}$$

In Lesson 44 we will discuss the method of adding algebraic fractions such as

$$\frac{b}{15a^2b} + \frac{c}{10ab^3}$$

To prepare for this lesson, we will practice finding the least common multiple of algebraic expressions.

example 43.4   Find the least common multiple (LCM) of $15a^2b$ and $10ab^3$.

solution   We begin by writing the expressions as products of factors whose exponents are 1.

$$15a^2b = 3 \cdot 5 \cdot a \cdot a \cdot b \qquad 10ab^3 = 2 \cdot 5 \cdot a \cdot b \cdot b \cdot b$$

To compute the LCM, we use each factor the greatest number of times it is a factor in any of the expressions. Thus, the LCM is

$$LCM = 2 \cdot 3 \cdot 5 \cdot a \cdot a \cdot b \cdot b \cdot b = \mathbf{30a^2b^3}$$

example 43.5   Find the least common multiple (LCM) of $4x^2m$ and $6x^3m$.

solution   We begin by writing the expressions as products of factors whose exponents are 1.

$$4x^2m = 2 \cdot 2 \cdot x \cdot x \cdot m \qquad 6x^3m = 2 \cdot 3 \cdot x \cdot x \cdot x \cdot m$$

To compute the LCM, we use each factor the greatest number of times it is a factor in any of the expressions. Thus, the LCM is

$$LCM = 2 \cdot 2 \cdot 3 \cdot x \cdot x \cdot x \cdot m = \mathbf{12x^3m}$$

example 43.6   Find the least common multiple (LCM) of $12x^2am^2$ and $14x^3am^4$.

solution   The LCM of 12 and 14 is 84. The most that x, a, and m are used as factors in any of the expressions is three times, once, and four times, respectively. Thus, the LCM is

$$LCM = \mathbf{84x^3am^4}$$

practice   Find the least common multiple (LCM) of:

   a.   14, 20, and 30   **b.**   75, 120, and 315

   c. $4a^3b^4$ and $6a^{10}b^2$ **d.** $12x^4y^2m^3$ and $20x^6ym^3$

problem set 43

1. (38) The ratio of idle onlookers to serious spectators in the crowd was 6 to 17. If there were 136 serious spectators, how many idle onlookers were in the crowd?

2. (33) If a number is multiplied by 7 and this product is increased by 7, the result is 1 less than 9 times the number. What is the number?

3. (4) Use three unit multipliers to convert 500 centimeters to yards.

4. (37) Draw a number line and graph the solution of $x \geq 1$.

5. (39) Draw a number line and graph the solution of $x \nleq 1$.

6. (28) If $f(x) = -3x^2 + 7$, find $f(-3)$.

Solve:

7. (25) $\dfrac{1}{2} + \dfrac{3}{8}x - 5 = 10\dfrac{1}{2}$ 8. (27) $0.02x - 4 - 0.01x - 2 = -6.3$

9. (31) $2p - 5(p - 4) = 2p + 12$ 10. (31) $x - 5x + 4(x - 2) = 3x - 8$

11. (41) If $x - 4 + 2x = 8$, what is the value of $x + 3$?

Solve for y:

12. (42) $x + 3y - 4 = 0$ 13. (42) $4 + 2x + 2y - 3 = 5$

Find the least common multiple (LCM) of:

14. (43) 12, 16, and 50   15. (43) $4a^2b^2$ and $8a^3b$

Factor the greatest common factor:

16. (35) $6k^5m^2 - 2mk^3 - mk$ 17. (35) $x^4y^2m - x^3y^3m^2 + 5x^6y^2m^2$

Simplify (factor if necessary):

18.
(35)
$$\frac{4px^2 - 8px}{px}$$

19.
(35)
$$\frac{x^2y - xy}{xym}$$

Simplify. Write the answers with all exponents negative.

20.
(40)
$$\frac{x^5yx^{-7}y^2}{x^4yy^3x^3}$$

21.
(40)
$$\frac{x^{-2}y^{-6}m}{x^5y^5m^{-4}}$$

22.
(40)
Expand by using the distributive property. Write the answer with all exponents negative.

$$m^{-2}z^4\left(m^2z^{-4} - \frac{3m^6z}{z^4}\right)$$

23.
(21)
Simplify by adding like terms: $-x^3x^{-3}ym^2 + 6yy^0m^2x^0 - 3x^2y^2y^{-1}m^2 + 9yxxm^2$

24.
(41)
Simplify by adding like terms. Write the answer with all exponents positive.

$$\frac{3m^{-1}y^2}{m^{-2}} - \frac{5m^2y^2}{x^2} + \frac{my^2}{m^{-1}x^2}$$

Evaluate:

25.
(41)
$|m| - (m - x)$ if $m + 3 = -2$ and $x = 3$

26.
(41)
$|x| - x(y)(-x)$ if $x = -2$ and $y + 4 = 8$

Simplify:

27.
(29)
$$\frac{1}{4^{-3}} - \sqrt[5]{-32}$$

28.
(29)
$$\frac{-2^0(-5 - 7)(-3) - |-4|}{-2[-(-6)]}$$

29.
(8)
Find the area of this parallelogram. Dimensions are in inches.

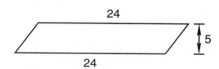

30.
(15)
A base of the right solid 10 feet high is shown. Find the surface area of the right solid. Dimensions are in feet. (Remember that the lateral surface area of a right solid is equal to the perimeter of a base times the height.)

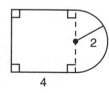

LESSON *44* *Addition of Rational Expressions with Equal Denominators • Addition of Rational Expressions with Unequal Denominators*

If we add one eleventh to two elevenths, we get three elevenths.

$$\frac{1}{11} + \frac{2}{11} = \frac{1+2}{11} = \frac{3}{11}$$

This is a demonstration of the rule for adding fractions whose denominators are the same.

RULE FOR ADDING FRACTIONS WITH EQUAL DENOMINATORS

Fractions with equal denominators are added by adding the numerators algebraically and recording the sum over a single denominator.

Here is another demonstration of the rule for adding fractions with equal denominators. This rule also applies if the fractions are rational expressions with equal denominators.

$$\frac{5}{a+6} + \frac{a+b}{a+6} + \frac{2}{a+6}$$

We see that the denominators are the same, so we can add the numerators and record the sum over a single denominator.

$$\frac{5}{a+6} + \frac{a+b}{a+6} + \frac{2}{a+6} = \frac{5+a+b+2}{a+6} = \frac{7+a+b}{a+6}$$

example 44.1 Add: $\dfrac{4}{2x^2+y} - \dfrac{6ax}{2x^2+y}$

solution The denominators are the same, so we can add the numerators.

$$\frac{4}{2x^2+y} - \frac{6ax}{2x^2+y} = \mathbf{\frac{4-6ax}{2x^2+y}}$$

example 44.2 Add: $\dfrac{5}{a^2+7y} - \dfrac{3}{a^2+7y} + \dfrac{z}{a^2+7y}$

solution The denominators are the same, so we can add the numerators.

$$\frac{5}{a^2+7y} - \frac{3}{a^2+7y} + \frac{z}{a^2+7y} = \frac{5-3+z}{a^2+7y} = \mathbf{\frac{2+z}{a^2+7y}}$$

example 44.3 Add: $\dfrac{5x+7}{5a^2x} - \dfrac{3x-2}{5a^2x}$

solution The denominators are the same, so we can add the numerators.

$$\frac{5x+7}{5a^2x} - \frac{3x-2}{5a^2x} = \frac{5x+7-3x+2}{5a^2x} = \mathbf{\frac{2x+9}{5a^2x}}$$

44.B

addition of rational expressions with unequal denominators

There are three rules of algebra that some people believe are more important than all the rest of the rules put together. Two of them are the addition rule for equations and the multiplication rule for equations. We have used these, and they are restated very informally here:

1. **The same quantity can be added to both sides of an equation.**
2. **Every term on both sides of an equation can be multiplied (or divided[†]) by the same quantity.**

The other important rule is that

3. **The denominator and numerator of a fraction can be multiplied by the same quantity.[†]**

This theorem is usually called the *fundamental theorem of fractions* or the *fundamental theorem of rational expressions*. We will call it the **denominator-numerator same-quantity rule** because this name is more meaningful. We use the **denominator-numerator same-quantity rule** for adding fractions or rational expressions with unequal denominators.

DENOMINATOR-NUMERATOR SAME-QUANTITY RULE

The denominator and the numerator of a fraction may be multiplied by the same nonzero quantity without changing the value of the fraction.

We cannot find the sum of

$$\frac{1}{4} + \frac{1}{2}$$

in this form because the denominators are not the same. But if we use the **denominator-numerator same-quantity rule** and multiply both the numerator and the denominator of $\frac{1}{2}$ by 2, we get $\frac{2}{4}$, which is an equivalent fraction for $\frac{1}{2}$.

$$\frac{1}{4} + \frac{1}{2} = \frac{1}{4} + \frac{1(2)}{2(2)}$$

Now the fractions may be added for they both have denominators of 4.

$$\frac{1}{4} + \frac{2}{4} = \frac{3}{4}$$

If the fractions to be added have different denominators, the procedure shown here can be used to rewrite the fractions as equivalent fractions that have the same denominators.

example 44.4   Add: $\frac{3}{4} + \frac{2}{b}$

solution   We will use the **denominator-numerator same-quantity rule** and a three-step procedure to rewrite the fractions as equivalent fractions that have the same denominators.

[†]Except zero.

(a) As the first step, we write the fraction lines with the proper sign between them:

$$— + —$$

(b) As the second step, we write the least common multiple of the denominators as the new denominators. When the least common multiple is used in this fashion, we call it the **least common denominator.**

$$\frac{}{4b} + \frac{}{4b}$$

(c) The first two steps were automatic. We used no theorems or rules. Now we use the **denominator-numerator same-quantity rule.** We have multiplied the denominator 4 of the first fraction by b to get $4b$, so we must also multiply the numerator 3 by b to get the new numerator of $3b$.

$$\frac{3b}{4b} + \frac{}{4b}$$

We have multiplied the denominator b of the second fraction by 4 to get $4b$, so we must also multiply the numerator 2 by 4 to get the new numerator of 8.

$$\frac{3b}{4b} + \frac{8}{4b}$$

Now the fractions have the same denominators and can be added.

$$\frac{3b}{4b} + \frac{8}{4b} = \frac{3b + 8}{4b}$$

example 44.5   Add: $\dfrac{4}{b} + \dfrac{1}{c} + \dfrac{1}{2}$

solution   (a) $— + — + —$ write the fraction lines

(b) $\dfrac{}{2bc} + \dfrac{}{2bc} + \dfrac{}{2bc}$ use the LCM as the new denominator of every term

(c) $\dfrac{8c}{2bc} + \dfrac{2b}{2bc} + \dfrac{bc}{2bc} = \dfrac{8c + 2b + bc}{2bc}$ find the new numerators and add

example 44.6   Add: $\dfrac{5}{x} + \dfrac{x}{b} + \dfrac{a}{c}$

solution   (a) $— + — + —$ write the fraction lines

(b) $\dfrac{}{xbc} + \dfrac{}{xbc} + \dfrac{}{xbc}$ use the LCM as the new denominator of every term

(c) $\dfrac{5bc}{xbc} + \dfrac{x^2c}{xbc} + \dfrac{axb}{xbc} = \dfrac{5bc + x^2c + axb}{xbc}$ find the new numerators and add

example 44.7   Add: $\dfrac{m}{c^3} + \dfrac{4}{c^2} - 6$

solution   When a term does not have a denominator, a good first step is to write a denominator of 1.

$$\frac{m}{c^3} + \frac{4}{c^2} - \frac{6}{1}$$ insert denominator

Now we use three steps to complete the process.

(a) $\dfrac{}{} + \dfrac{}{} - \dfrac{}{}$ write the fraction lines

(b) $\dfrac{}{c^3} + \dfrac{}{c^3} - \dfrac{}{c^3}$ use the LCM as the new denominator of every term

(c) $\dfrac{m}{c^3} + \dfrac{4c}{c^3} - \dfrac{6c^3}{c^3} = \dfrac{m + 4c - 6c^3}{c^3}$ find the new numerators and add

example 44.8   Add: $\dfrac{p}{4} - \dfrac{a}{2} + \dfrac{c}{b}$

solution   (a) $\dfrac{}{} - \dfrac{}{} + \dfrac{}{}$ write the fraction lines

(b) $\dfrac{}{4b} - \dfrac{}{4b} + \dfrac{}{4b}$ use the LCM as the new denominator of every term

(c) $\dfrac{pb}{4b} - \dfrac{2ab}{4b} + \dfrac{4c}{4b} = \dfrac{pb - 2ab + 4c}{4b}$ find the new numerators and add

example 44.9   Add: $\dfrac{a}{c^2} + \dfrac{3}{4c^3} + \dfrac{m}{3c^4}$

solution   (a) $\dfrac{}{} + \dfrac{}{} + \dfrac{}{}$ write the fraction lines

(b) $\dfrac{}{12c^4} + \dfrac{}{12c^4} + \dfrac{}{12c^4}$ use the LCM as the new denominator of every term

(c) $\dfrac{12ac^2}{12c^4} + \dfrac{9c}{12c^4} + \dfrac{4m}{12c^4} = \dfrac{12ac^2 + 9c + 4m}{12c^4}$ find the new numerators and add

practice   Add:

a. $\dfrac{4m - 2}{3m + 2} + \dfrac{6m - 4}{3m + 2}$ **b.** $\dfrac{9}{xy^3 + m} - \dfrac{7ap}{xy^3 + m}$

c. $\dfrac{x}{m^3} + \dfrac{1}{c^3} + \dfrac{a}{m^4}$ **d.** $\dfrac{m}{p^2} + \dfrac{3}{p^3} - 4$

problem set 44

1.
(39)   The ratio of poseurs to outright frauds was 14 to 3. If they totaled 2244, how many were poseurs?

2.
(32)   Isaac and Gottfried found that 9 times the sum of a number and −3 equaled 36. What was the number?

3.
(10)   Use four unit multipliers to convert 170 square inches to square yards.

4.
(3,8)   The perimeter of a square is 52 in. Find the area of the square.

5.
(39)   Write both an inequality and a negated inequality that describe this graph.

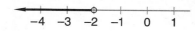

6.
(33)   Write 168 as a product of prime factors.

7.
(28)   If $g(x) = x(x + 1)$, find $g(-4)$.

Solve:

8.
(25) $\dfrac{1}{4} + \dfrac{2}{5}x + 1 = 2\dfrac{1}{4}$

9.
(27) $0.004m - 0.001m + 0.002 = -0.004$

10.
(31) $3(-x - 4) = 2x + 3(x - 5)$

11.
(31) $5p - 6(2p + 1) = -4p - 2$

12.
(41) If $x + 3 - 4x = 12$, what is the value of $2x - 1$?

Solve for y:

13.
(42) $3y - 2x - 7 = 0$

14.
(42) $3x - 3y + 4 = y - 4$

Find the least common multiple (LCM) of:

15.
(43) 8, 30, and 75

16.
(43) $4w^2y^3$ and $6wy^2$

Add:

17.
(44) $\dfrac{2x + m}{3x^2m} + \dfrac{x + 3m}{3x^2m}$

18.
(44) $\dfrac{3}{a} + \dfrac{1}{b} + \dfrac{1}{3}$

19.
(35) Factor the greatest common factor of $8x^5y^2z - 16x^2y^2z^2 - xyz$.

20.
(35) Simplify (factor if necessary): $\dfrac{5x^2y^2 - 25x^3y^3}{x^2y^2}$

Simplify. Write the answers with all variables in the numerator.

21.
(40) $\dfrac{p^5p^{-4}z^2}{z^{-5}zp^3}$

22.
(40) $\dfrac{akp^2p^4}{a^{-3}a^5p^5k^4}$

23.
(40) Expand by using the distributive property. Write the answer with all variables in the numerator.

$$\left(\dfrac{m^2}{y^{-1}} + 4m^5y^6 \right)m^{-2}y$$

24.
(41) Simplify by adding like terms. Write the answer with all exponents negative.

$$4aaxxy^{-3} - \dfrac{2a^2x^2}{y^3} - \dfrac{a^3x^2}{ay^3}$$

Evaluate:

25.
(41) $x - \left(-y^0\right) - y^2$ if $x - 3 = 2$ and $y = -2$

26.
(36) $m - 3m^{-2}$ if $m = -3$

Simplify:

27.
(36) $\dfrac{1}{(-4)^{-3}} - \sqrt[3]{64}$

28.
(10) $\dfrac{-(2 - 5) - (-3 - 6)}{-2^0(-4)(-2) + (-3)^0(-1)(-8)}$

29.
(8) Find the area of the shaded portion of this parallelogram. Dimensions are in feet.

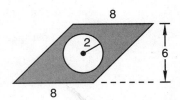

30.
(1) AD is $10\dfrac{7}{18}$ miles. AB is $2\dfrac{1}{3}$ miles. BC is $4\dfrac{2}{9}$ miles. Find CD.

LESSON 45 *Range, Median, Mode, and Mean*

Every discipline has unusual words that have simple meanings. English teachers will say that the word "buzz" is an example of onomatopoeia because it sounds like what it means. They will also say that the words "sum" and "some" are homophones because they sound the same but have different meanings. Mathematics also has unusual words whose meanings are simple. For example, when speaking about a series of measurements we use the mathematical terms **range, median, mode,** and **mean** to describe the numerical difference between the least and greatest measurement, the middle measurement, the measurement that appears the most frequently, and the average of the measurements, respectively.

To show how these terms are used, we use a real-life example. Let us say that the veterinarian weighed the first five dogs. Their weights in pounds were 10, 30, 8, 14, and 30, respectively. Then the veterinarian weighed the next six dogs. Their weights in pounds were 4, 15, 4, 8, 15, and 18, respectively. On the left below, we arrange the first set of numbers in order from the least to the greatest, and on the right below, we show the second set of numbers arranged in order from the least to the greatest.

Range	Range
8, 10, 14, 30, 30	4, 4, 8, 15, 15, 18
Range is 30 − 8 = 22	Range is 18 − 4 = 14

We note that the set of numbers on the left above ranges from 8 lb to 30 lb, so we say that the **range** of this set of numbers is 30 minus 8, or 22. The set of numbers on the right above ranges from 4 lb to 18 lb, so we say that the **range** of this set of numbers is 18 minus 4, or 14.

The median of a four-lane highway is the strip of grass or concrete that is in the middle of the highway. The word *median* comes to us from the Latin word *medius*, which means "middle." We also use the word **median** to name the middle number in a set of numbers that are arranged in order from the least to the greatest. The set of numbers on the left below has an odd number of members (5), so it has a middle number, or median, which is 14.

Median   Median

8, 10, 14, 30, 30   4, 4, 8, 15, 15, 18

Median is 14   Median is $\dfrac{8 + 15}{2} = 11.5$

The set of numbers on the right above has an even number of members (6), so there is no middle number. We say that the median of this set of numbers is the average of the two middle numbers, which is 11.5, as we show.

The French word for "fashion" is *mode*, which comes from the Latin word *modus*. We use the word **mode** in data analysis to describe the number in a set of numbers that appears more than any other number and thus, is more fashionable. The number 30 appears more times than any other number in the set of numbers on the left below, so the mode of this set is the number 30.

8, 10, 14, 30, 30   4, 4, 8, 15, 15, 18

Mode is 30   Modes are 4 and 15

The set of numbers on the right has two modes—4 and 15. A bicycle has two wheels because *bi* means "two." Thus, we say that the set of numbers on the right above is **bimodal** because it has two modes.

The average of a set of numbers is also called the **mean.** The average of a set of numbers is the sum of the numbers divided by the number of numbers in the set. We compute the mean of each set of numbers as shown below.

$$\text{Mean} = \frac{8 + 10 + 14 + 30 + 30}{5} = \frac{92}{5} = 18.4$$

$$\text{Mean} = \frac{4 + 4 + 8 + 15 + 15 + 18}{6} = \frac{64}{6} = 10.67$$

We use the word **statistics** to describe the mathematics used in the collection, organization, and interpretation of numerical data. A statistic can be a single measurement, but most often refers to a parameter such as range, median, mode, or mean that is obtained from the numerical data. We call the median, mode, and mean **measures of central tendency,** for these statistics can sometimes help us to understand how a set of measurements is grouped about a central point.

Suppose three measurements are

8, 10, and 11

The median (middle number) is 10 and the mean (average) is 9.67. Since both the median and the mean are close in value, they are considered meaningful statistics for this set of measurements. Since no one of the numbers occurs more frequently than the others, there is no mode.

example 45.1 A freight company receives a shipment of eight cats and one cow. Their weights in pounds are 2, 3, 2, 2, 3, 2, 4, 3, and 800, respectively. Find the (a) range, (b) median, (c) mode, and (d) mean of the weights.

solution We begin by arranging the weights in order from least to greatest.

2, 2, 2, 2, 3, 3, 3, 4, 800

(a) The weights range from 2 to 800, so the range of the weights is the difference of these numbers, which is **798.**

(b) The median of this set of numbers is **3** since this is the middle number when the set of numbers is arranged in order from least to greatest.

(c) The mode of this set of numbers is **2** since it appears more often than any other number.

(d) To find the mean, we divide the sum of the numbers by the number of numbers.

$$\text{Mean} = \frac{2 + 2 + 2 + 2 + 3 + 3 + 3 + 4 + 800}{9} = \frac{821}{9} = \textbf{91.22}$$

example 45.2 The scores on the test were 86, 93, 60, 66, 95, 83, 85, and 78. Find the (a) range, (b) median, (c) mode, and (d) mean of the test scores.

solution We begin by arranging the test scores in order from least to greatest.

60, 66, 78, 83, 85, 86, 93, 95

(a) The test scores range from 60 to 95, so the range of the test scores is the difference of these numbers, which is **35.**

(b) There are eight numbers, so there is no middle number. The median is the number halfway between 83 and 85, which is **84.**

(c) No number appears more often than any other number, so there is **no mode.**

(d) To find the mean, we divide the sum of the numbers by the number of numbers.

$$\text{Mean} = \frac{60 + 66 + 78 + 83 + 85 + 86 + 93 + 95}{8} = \frac{646}{8} = \textbf{80.75}$$

example 45.3   The mean of five numbers is 10. Four of the numbers are 2, 8, 11, and 14. Find the fifth number.

solution   We know that the mean is 10 and there are five numbers, so we can write the following equation:

$$\frac{\text{(sum of the five numbers)}}{5} = 10$$

$$\frac{2 + 8 + 11 + 14 + x}{5} = 10$$

$$35 + x = 50$$

$$x = \mathbf{15}$$

practice   **a.**   Find the range, median, mode, and mean of the following numbers:

$$3, 8, 7, 4, 9, 10, 12, 9$$

b.   The scores on the test were 81, 79, 96, 66, 81, 70, 89, 80, and 92. Find the range, median, mode, and mean of the test scores.

c.   The mean of four numbers is 8. Three of the numbers are 2, 4, and 7. Find the fourth number.

problem set   **1.**   The ratio of those who stayed awake to those who dozed was 5 to 18. If 125 stayed
45   (38)   awake, how many dozed?

2.   Every discipline has key words that many neophytes find difficult to remember. Three
(45)   key words in statistics are *median*, *mode*, and *mean*. Mnemonics are often helpful. We suggest the "median in the middle," the "fashionable mode," and the "mean old average." Find the range, median, mode, and mean of the following numbers:

$$5, 6, 9, 6, 12, 8, 7$$

3.   Use three unit multipliers to convert 80,500 centimeters to miles.
(4)

4.   The area of a circle is 36 cm^2.
(3,8)

(a)   Find the radius of the circle.

(b)   Find the circumference of the circle.

5.   Draw a number line and graph the solution of $x < 3$.
(37)

6.   Draw a number line and graph the solution of $x \not\geq -2$.
(39)

7.   If $h(x) = x(x - 10)$, find $h(5)$.
(28)

Solve:

8. $\dfrac{1}{3} + \dfrac{5}{12}x - 2 = 6\dfrac{2}{3}$ **9.** $0.004k - 0.002 + 0.002k = 4$
(25)   (27)

10. $7(x - 3) - 6x + 4 = 2 - (x + 3)$ **11.** $5p - 4p - (p - 2) = 3(p + 4)$
(31)   (31)

12.   If $x - 4 + 2x - 5 = 6$, find the value of $3x - 2$.
(41)

Solve for y:

13. $3x + 2y = 5$ **14.** $2x - 5y + 4 = 0$
(42)   (42)

Find the least common multiple (LCM) of the following:

15.   18, 27, and 45   **16.** $8a^4m^2x$ and $12a^3m^3x$
(43)   (43)

Add:

17. $\dfrac{4x + 2}{3a^2m} - \dfrac{x - 1}{3a^2m}$ **18.** $\dfrac{5}{x} + \dfrac{1}{y} + \dfrac{1}{4}$
(44)   (44)

19. Factor the greatest common factor of $3a^2b^4c^5 - 6a^2b^6c^6$.
₍₃₅₎

20. Simplify (factor if necessary): $\dfrac{k^4p - 2k^5p^2}{k^4p}$
₍₃₅₎

Simplify. Write the answers with all variables in the denominator.

21. $\dfrac{k^5m^2}{k^7m^{-5}}$
₍₄₀₎

22. $\dfrac{a^2bc^{-2}c^5}{a^2b^{-3}a^2c^3}$
₍₄₀₎

23. Expand by using the distributive property. Write the answer with all variables in the
₍₄₀₎ denominator.

$$\frac{x^{-2}p^0}{y^4}\left(\frac{x^2}{p^4} - x^4p^6\right)$$

24. Simplify by adding like terms. Write the answer with all variables in the numerator.
₍₄₁₎

$$xy^2 - \frac{3xy}{y^{-1}} + \frac{2x^0y^2}{x^{-1}} - \frac{4x^2}{y^2} + 2x^2y^{-2}$$

Evaluate:

25. $|x - y| + |y - x|$ if $x = 2$ and $y = 5$
₍₁₄₎

26. $xa - a(x^{-2} - xa)$ if $x = 3$ and $a = -1$
₍₂₉₎

Simplify:

27. $\dfrac{1}{-(-3)^{-3}} - \sqrt[3]{-27}$
₍₃₆₎

28. $\dfrac{-4\left[(-2 + 5) - (-3 + 8^0)\right]}{-2^0|5 - 1|}$
₍₂₉₎

29. Find the perimeter of this parallelo-
₍₃₎ gram. Dimensions are in meters.

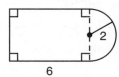

$5\frac{2}{7}$

$2\frac{3}{14}$

$5\frac{2}{7}$

30. A base of the right solid 8 inches high is shown. Find the volume of the right solid.
₍₂₀₎ Dimensions are in inches.

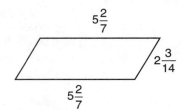

2

6

LESSON *46* *Conjunctions*

If we wish to designate the numbers that are greater than 5, we can write

$$x > 5$$

If we wish to designate the numbers that are less than 10, we can write

$$x < 10$$

If we wish to designate the numbers that are greater than 5 and that are also less than 10, we can write either of the following:

$$x > 5 \text{ and } x < 10 \qquad \text{or} \qquad 5 < x < 10$$

Both of these notations mean the same thing and designate the numbers that are between 5 and 10. We use the word **conjunction** to describe a statement of two conditions, both of which must be met. Thus, both of the above statements are conjunctions. In the concise notation on the right, we note that the symbols point in the same direction. They always do, as we see when we reverse both the symbols and the numbers to make the same statement another way.

$$10 > x > 5$$

But we must be careful when we write conjunctions because

$$10 < x < 5$$

designates the numbers that are greater than 10 and are also less than 5. Of course, there are no numbers that fall into this category.

example 46.1   Draw a number line and graph the solution of $5 < x < 10$.

solution   This conjunction designates the numbers between 5 and 10.

example 46.2   Draw a number line and graph the solution of $-2 < x \le 4$.

solution   This conjunction asks for the graph of the numbers between -2 and 4. Note that the symbol $<$ excludes -2 and that the symbol $\le$ includes 4 in the solution set.

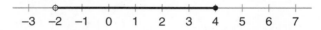

example 46.3   Write a conjunction that describes this graph.

solution   The graph shows the numbers that are greater than or equal to -5 and less than 0. We write this conjunction as

$$-5 \le x < 0$$

example 46.4   Write the conjunction that designates the numbers that are greater than -1 and less than or equal to 5.

solution   The conjunction is $-1 < x \le 5$.

practice **a.** Draw a number line and graph the solution of $-5 < x \le 4$.

b. Draw a number line and graph the solution of $-7 < x < -2$.

c. Write a conjunction that describes this graph.

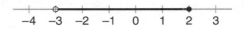

d. Write a conjunction that designates the numbers that are greater than or equal to -2 and less than 5.

problem set 46

1. If the sum of twice a number and -7 is increased by 8, the result is 16 greater than the opposite of the number. What is the number?
(33)

2. The scores on the test were 92, 72, 83, 64, 98, 83, 94, 89, and 78. Find the range, median, mode, and mean of the test scores.
(45)

3. Use four unit multipliers to convert 42,000 square inches to square miles.
(10)

4. The area of a rectangle is 221 in.^{2}. The width of the rectangle is 13 in. Find the perimeter of the rectangle.
(3,8)

5. Write both an inequality and a negated inequality that describe this graph.
(39)

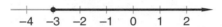

6. Draw a number line and graph the solution of $-3 < x < 2$.
(46)

7. What decimal part of 41.25 is 2.475?
(30)

8. If $f(x) = x(6 - x)$, find $f(-5)$.
(28)

Solve:

9. $\dfrac{2}{3} - \dfrac{4}{9}x + 1 = 2\dfrac{7}{9}$
(25)

10. $0.06 + 0.06x = -0.042$
(27)

11. $5x - 4(2x - 2) = 5 - x$
(31)

12. If $3x - 4 + x - 6 = 10$, find the value of $2x - 4$.
(41)

Solve for y:

13. $5x + 4 = 3y$
(42)

14. $2y - 5 - x = 0$
(42)

Find the least common multiple (LCM) of the following:

15. 45, 75, and 125
(43)

16. $5x^5y^3z$ and $6x^3y^4z^2$
(43)

Add:

17. $\dfrac{7}{x^2 + y} - \dfrac{4}{x^2 + y} + \dfrac{3}{x^2 + y}$
(44)

18. $\dfrac{a}{4d^2} + \dfrac{5}{d} + \dfrac{b}{d^3}$
(44)

19. Factor the greatest common factor of $3x^2yz - 4zyx^2 + 2xyz^2$.
(35)

20. Simplify (factor if necessary): $\dfrac{a^3b - 2a^2b^2}{a^2b}$
(35)

Simplify. Write the answers with all exponents positive.

21. $\dfrac{m^4p^5}{p^{-3}m^6}$
(40)

22. $\dfrac{xxx^3y^5y^{-2}}{x^{-3}yy^{-6}}$
(40)

23.
(40) Expand by using the distributive property. Write the answer with all exponents positive.

$$\left(\frac{a^2}{x^{-1}} - 4a^6x^4\right)\frac{a^{-2}}{x}$$

24.
(41) Simplify by adding like terms. Write the answer with all variables in the denominator.

$$4m^2y^{-2} - \frac{2mmy^{-2}}{x} + \frac{3m^2x^{-1}}{y^2} - 3mmyy^{-3}$$

Evaluate:

25.
(14) $|x - y| - |y - x|$ if $x = 5$ and $y = 2$

26.
(36) $-a^{-3}(a - a^2x)$ if $a = -2$ and $x = 4$

Simplify:

27.
(19) $-2^4 + \dfrac{1}{-(-2)^3} + \sqrt[3]{64}$

28.
(29) $\dfrac{-2\left[(-3 + 2)(-3 + 5^0)\right]}{|-4 - 1| - (-6)^0}$

29.
(8) Find the area of this trapezoid. Dimensions are in feet.

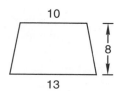

30.
(15) A base of the right solid 30 centimeters high is shown. Find the surface area of the right solid. Dimensions are in centimeters. (Remember that the lateral surface area of a right solid is equal to the perimeter of a base times the height.)

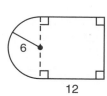 

LESSON 47   *Percents Less Than 100* • *Percents Greater Than 100*

47.A

percents less than 100

We have been working problems about fractional and decimal parts of numbers by using one of the following equations:

(a) $(F) \times (\text{of}) = \text{is}$ or   (b) $(D) \times (\text{of}) = \text{is}$

The percent equation is exactly the same as (a) except that the fraction has a denominator of 100. *Centum* is the Latin word for 100, and thus percent literally means "by the 100." We often use the symbol % to represent the word *percent*. The percent equation is

(c) $\dfrac{P}{100} \times \text{of} = \text{is}$ which can also be written as   (d) $\dfrac{P}{100} = \dfrac{\text{is}}{\text{of}}$

The part identified by the word *of* is often called the **base,** and the part identified by the word *is* is called the **percentage.** If we use these words, we get equation (e). In equation (f) $\frac{P}{100}$ is called the **rate.**

$$\text{(e)} \quad \frac{P}{100} \times \text{base} = \text{percentage} \qquad \text{(f)} \quad \text{rate} \times \text{base} = \text{percentage}$$

All four equations produce the same result. We prefer equation (c) because it is just like equation (a), which we have used for fractional parts of numbers. However, your teacher may prefer one of the other forms. Many teachers like equation (d) because this form can be explained using the concepts and vocabulary of ratios. Others prefer equation (e) or equation (f) because these forms are used almost exclusively in the business world. The four equations (c), (d), (e), and (f) are not different equations but different forms of the same equation. Each form has advantages and disadvantages. None is perfect. Some people find equation (c) to be the most difficult to solve. The ratio form, equation (d), is almost never used except in beginning algebra classes. Equation (f) does not use percent as such but uses rate, which is percent divided by 100. We find that it is best to pick one equation and stick with it. If you do not like equation (c), use another.

To solve word problems about percent, it is necessary to be able to visualize the problem. We will begin to work on achieving this visualization by drawing diagrams of percent problems after we work the problems. **Learning to draw these diagrams is very important.**

example 47.1   Twenty percent of what number is 15? Work the problem and then draw a diagram of the problem.

solution   We will use equation (c) and use 20 for *percent*, *WN* for *what number*, and 15 for *is*.

$$\frac{P}{100} \times \text{of} = \text{is} \quad \longrightarrow \quad \frac{20}{100} \cdot WN = 15$$

We will solve by multiplying both sides by $\frac{100}{20}$.

$$\frac{\cancel{100}}{\cancel{20}} \cdot \frac{\cancel{20}}{\cancel{100}} WN = 15 \cdot \frac{100}{20} \quad \longrightarrow \quad WN = \frac{1500}{20} \quad \longrightarrow \quad WN = \mathbf{75}$$

The "before" diagram is 75, which represents 100 percent. The "after" diagram shows that 15 is 20 percent. Thus the other part must be 60, which is 80 percent.

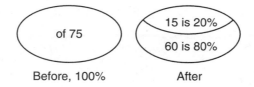

Before, 100%   After

example 47.2   What percent of 140 is 98? Work the problem and then draw a diagram of the problem.

solution   We will use equation (c) and use *WP* for *what percent*, 140 for *of*, and 98 for *is*.

$$\frac{P}{100} \times \text{of} = \text{is} \quad \longrightarrow \quad \frac{WP}{100} \cdot 140 = 98$$

We will solve by multiplying both sides by $\frac{100}{140}$.

$$\frac{\cancel{100}}{\cancel{140}} \cdot \frac{WP}{\cancel{100}} \cdot \cancel{140} = 98 \cdot \frac{100}{140} \quad \longrightarrow \quad WP = \frac{9800}{140} \quad \longrightarrow \quad WP = \mathbf{70\%}$$

The diagrams show that 140, or 100 percent, was divided into two parts. One part is 42, which is 30 percent, and the other part is 98, which is 70 percent.

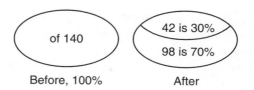

Before, 100%   After

example 47.3   Fifteen percent of 300 is what number? Work the problem and then draw a diagram of the problem.

solution   We will use equation (c) and use 15 for *percent*, 300 for *of*, and *WN* for *what number*.

$$\frac{P}{100} \times \text{of} = \text{is} \quad \longrightarrow \quad \frac{15}{100} \cdot (300) = WN$$

We multiply to solve and get

$$\frac{4500}{100} = WN \quad \longrightarrow \quad WN = \mathbf{45}$$

The diagrams show that 300, or 100 percent, was divided into two parts. One part is 45, which is 15 percent, and the other part is 255, which is 85 percent.

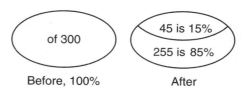

Before, 100%   After

47.B

percents greater than 100

When a problem discusses a quantity that increases, the final quantity is greater than the initial quantity. If we let the initial quantity represent 100 percent, the final percent will be greater than 100. This means that the "after" diagram representing the final quantity will be larger than the "before" diagram. **The "after" diagrams in this book will not be drawn to scale.**

To demonstrate, we will work three problems of this type. We will finish each problem by drawing diagrams that give a visual representation of the problem.

example 47.4   What number is 160 percent of 60? Work the problem and then draw a diagram of the problem.

solution   We will use equation (c) and substitute 160 for *P*, 60 for *of*, and *WN* for *is*.

$$\frac{P}{100} \times \text{of} = \text{is} \quad \longrightarrow \quad \frac{160}{100} \cdot (60) = WN \quad \longrightarrow \quad \frac{9600}{100} = WN \quad \longrightarrow \quad WN = \mathbf{96}$$

Thus, our diagrams show a "before" of 60 and an "after" of 96, which is 160 percent of 60.

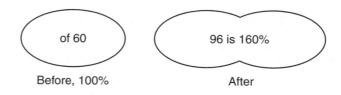

Before, 100%   After

example 47.5   If 75 is increased by 150 percent, what is the result? Work the problem and then draw a diagram of the problem.

solution   **We must be careful here. Seventy-five is the original number and is 100 percent. If we increase the percentage by 150 percent, the final percentage will be 250 percent.** We can restate the problem as follows: 250 percent of 75 is what number? We will use equation (c) and substitute 250 for *P*, 75 for *of*, and *WN* for *is*.

$$\frac{P}{100} \times of = is \quad \longrightarrow \quad \frac{250}{100} \times 75 = WN \quad \longrightarrow \quad 2.5 \times 75 = WN$$

$$WN = \mathbf{187.5}$$

Thus, our diagrams show a "before" of 75 and an "after" of 187.5, which is 250 percent of 75.

Before, 100%   After

example 47.6   What percent of 90 is 306? Work the problem and then draw a diagram of the problem.

solution   We will use equation (c) and substitute *WP* for *P*, 90 for *of*, and 306 for *is*.

$$\frac{P}{100} \times of = is \quad \longrightarrow \quad \frac{WP}{100} \cdot 90 = 306$$

We will solve by multiplying both sides by $\frac{100}{90}$.

$$\frac{\cancel{100}}{\cancel{90}} \cdot \frac{WP}{\cancel{100}} \cdot \cancel{90} = 306 \cdot \frac{100}{90} \quad \longrightarrow \quad WP = \frac{30,600}{90} \quad \longrightarrow \quad WP = \mathbf{340\%}$$

Thus, our diagrams show a "before" of 90 and an "after" of 306, which is 340 percent of 90.

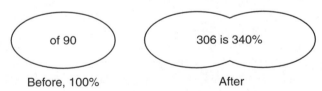

Before, 100%   After

practice   Work each problem and then draw a diagram for each problem.

   a.   Twenty percent of what number is 800?

   b.   What number is 18% of 360?

   c.   What number is 270 percent of 80?

   d.   If 20 is increased by 90 percent, what is the result?

problem set 47

   1.
   (39)   The defense budget was spent on halberds and other armor in the ratio of 2 to 19. If the total budget was 84,000 farthings, how much went for halberds?

   2.
   (45)   The mean of three numbers is 10. Two of the numbers are 4 and 7. Find the third number.

   3.
   (4)   Use three unit multipliers to convert 42 feet to meters.

   4.
   (3,8)   The circumference of a circle is 16π cm.

      (a)   Find the radius of the circle.

      (b)   Find the area of the circle.

5. Twenty percent of what number is 18? Work the problem and then draw a diagram of the
(47) problem.

6. What number is 140 percent of 70? Work the problem and then draw a diagram of the
(47) problem.

7. Draw a number line and graph the solution of $-3 < x \le 2$.
(46)

8. If $g(x) = -x(1 - x)$, find $g(10)$.
(28)

Solve:

9. $2\frac{1}{3}k - 4 = 17$
(25)

10. $-4.2 + 0.02x - 0.4 = 0.03x$
(27)

11. $-2^0 - |-3| - 2^2 - (3 - x) = -(-3)^3$
(31)

12. If $5x - 9 + x - 3 = 6$, find the value of $9 - 3x$.
(41)

Solve for y:

13. $2x + 4y = 6$
(42)

14. $5x - 3y + 5 = 2y - 5$
(42)

Find the least common multiple (LCM) of the following:

15. 18, 35, and 40
(43)

16. 2, c^2, and c^3
(43)

Add:

17. $\dfrac{a}{b} + \dfrac{c^2 - a}{b} + \dfrac{4}{b}$
(44)

18. $\dfrac{4}{a} + \dfrac{c}{4a} + 5$
(44)

19. Factor the greatest common factor of $5x^2y^5m^2 - 10x^4y^2m^3$.
(35)

20. Simplify (factor if necessary): $\dfrac{4a^2x - ax^2y}{ax}$
(35)

Simplify. Write the answers with all exponents negative.

21. $\dfrac{x^2xyy^{-4}}{x^4y^{-5}}$
(40)

22. $\dfrac{mm^2p^3y^{-3}}{m^{-3}m^{-2}p^{-3}y^4}$
(40)

23. Expand by using the distributive property. Write the answer with all exponents negative.
(40)

$$\frac{x^{-2}}{y^{-3}}\left(\frac{x^2}{y^3} - \frac{ax^3}{y^{-4}}\right)$$

24. Simplify by adding like terms. Write the answer with all exponents positive.
(41)

$$5m^2k^5 - \frac{3m^3k^6}{mk} - 4mmk^6k^{-1} + \frac{3m^2m^0}{k^{-5}}$$

Evaluate:

25. $-x - |xa|(x^0 - a)$ if $x = -2$ and $a = -3$
(29)

26. $a^{-2}(2a - a^{-3})$ if $a = -3$
(36)

Simplify:

27. $\dfrac{1}{-3^{-3}} - (-5)^0 + \sqrt[5]{32}$
(36)

28. $\dfrac{-2^2\left[(-4 - 6^0)(5 - 3^0)\right]}{|-6| - [-(-2)]}$
(29)

29. Find the perimeter of this trapezoid.
(3) Dimensions are in meters.

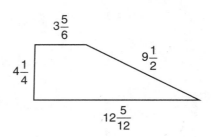

30. A base of the right solid 7 inches high is shown. Find the volume of the right solid.
(20) Dimensions are in inches.

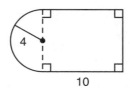 

LESSON 48 *Polynomials • Degree • Addition of Polynomials*

48.A
polynomials Thus far we have encountered expressions such as

(a) $\dfrac{x^{-3} + m}{x}$ 　　　　(b) $\dfrac{2y}{x^3}$ 　　　　(c) $4a^{-2}x + m^3$

(d) rt^{n-2} 　　　　(e) 4 　　　　(f) $-4a^2$

(g) $7x^2 + 2$ 　　　　(h) $4x^2y$ 　　　　(i) $7y^3 + 3y + 2$

All of these expressions are called **algebraic expressions** or **mathematical expressions** and are individual terms or indicated sums of terms. The more complicated algebraic expressions as shown in (a) through (d) have no special names and are just called **terms** or **algebraic expressions.** The simple algebraic expressions as shown in (e) through (i) occur so often and are so useful that we give these algebraic expressions a special name: **polynomial.** It is unfortunate that we use such an intimidating word to describe the simplest kind of algebraic expression. We should think "simplenomial" when we see the word *polynomial.*

A polynomial in one variable is one term or a sum of individual terms each of which has the form

$$ax^n$$

where **a is a real number** and **n is a whole number,** such as the following:

(a) $4x^2$ 　　　　(b) $-x^3$ 　　　　(c) $-1.414x^{32}$

(d) $2x^4$ 　　　　(e) $-7x$ 　　　　(f) -7

Each of the six algebraic expressions meets all three of the requirements for being called a polynomial:

    1. Each algebraic expression is in the form ax^n.
    2. The numerical coefficient of each algebraic expression, a, is a real number.
    3. The exponent of the variable, n, is a positive integer or it is the number zero.

The last polynomial shown, -7, can be thought of as being $-7x^0$, which is the same as -7 if x has a value other than zero because we remember that **any nonzero quantity raised to the zero power has a value of 1!**

We refresh our memories with the following examples:

$$(-15)^0 = 1 \qquad \left(\frac{75}{14}\right)^0 = 1 \qquad x^0 = 1 \qquad (x + y)^0 = 1 \qquad (x, \ x + y \neq 0)$$

Thus, since x^0 equals 1 if x is not zero, we can write

$$-7x^0 = -7(1) = -7$$

A **polynomial of one term** is called a **monomial,** so each of the six algebraic expressions in (a) through (f) on the previous page can be called a polynomial or may be described by using the more restrictive name of monomial.

A **polynomial of two terms** is called a **binomial,** and a **polynomial of three terms** is called a **trinomial.** Thus each of the following

$$\text{(a)} \ 4 + x \qquad \text{(b)} \ p^{15} - 4p \qquad \text{(c)} \ -y^{10} + 3y$$

can be described by using either the word *polynomial* or the word *binomial*. The following algebraic expressions

$$\text{(a)} \ x^2 + 2x + 4 \qquad \text{(b)} \ y^{14} - 1.6y^2 + 4 \qquad \text{(c)} \ m^4 + 2m - 1.6$$

can be called either polynomials or trinomials. Indicated sums of more than three monomial terms have no special names and are just called polynomials. Thus we can call any of the following algebraic expressions a polynomial.

$$\text{(a)} \ -14.2 \qquad \text{(b)} \ \frac{7}{2} \qquad \text{(c)} \ 4x^2 \qquad \text{(d)} \ 6x^2 + 4$$

$$\text{(e)} \ x^4 - 3x^2 + 2x \qquad \text{(f)} \ -7x^{15} + 2x^3 - 5x^2 + 6x + 4$$

Algebraic expressions (a) and (b) are polynomials because the exponent of the understood variable is the number zero.

$$\text{(a)} \ -14.2m^0 = -14.2 \qquad \text{(b)} \ \frac{7}{2}y^0 = \frac{7}{2}$$

Although algebraic expressions (c), (d), and (e) are all polynomials, they can also be called a monomial, a binomial, and a trinomial, in that order. The last algebraic expression, (f), is a polynomial because each term in the indicated sum is a monomial. This algebraic expression does not have a more restrictive name.

DEFINITION OF A POLYNOMIAL IN ONE UNKNOWN

A polynomial in one unknown is an algebraic expression of the form

$$4x^{15} + 2x^{14} - 3x^{10} + \cdots + 2x + 2$$

where the coefficients are real numbers, x is a variable, and the exponents are whole numbers.

Thus none of the following algebraic expressions is a polynomial.

$$\text{(a)} \ 4x^{-3} \qquad \text{(b)} \ \frac{-6x + y}{z} \qquad \text{(c)} \ -15y^{-5}$$

The algebraic expressions (a) and (c) have real number coefficients, but the exponent of the variable is not a whole number. Algebraic expression (b) is not a polynomial because it is not in the required form of ax^n.

DEFINITION OF A POLYNOMIAL IN ONE OR MORE UNKNOWNS

A polynomial in one or more unknowns is an algebraic expression having only terms of the form $ax^n y^m z^p...$, where the coefficient a is a real number and the exponents $n, m, p, ...$, are whole numbers.

Thus the general definition of a polynomial has the same restrictions that are given by the definition of a polynomial in one unknown, namely:

1. The numerical coefficients of the individual terms must be **real numbers.**
2. The exponents of the variables must be **whole numbers.**

The following can therefore be called polynomials in more than one variable.

$$\text{(a)} \ xyz^2m \qquad \text{(b)} \ 4x^{15}ym^3 + pq^5 \qquad \text{(c)} \ -11x^2p^4 + 2$$

48.B

degree The **degree of a term** of a polynomial is the sum of the exponents of the variables in the term.

$$4x^3, \ 6xym, \ 2x^2y \qquad \text{are third-degree terms}$$
$$4x^2m^3, \ 3y^5, \ 2xypmz \qquad \text{are fifth-degree terms}$$

The **degree of a polynomial** is the same as the degree of its highest-degree term.

$$3x^2 + xyz + m \qquad \text{is a third-degree polynomial because the degree of its}$$
$$\text{highest degree term } (xyz) \text{ is } 3$$

$$4x^5 + yx^3 + 2x^2 + 2 \qquad \text{is a fifth-degree polynomial because the degree of its}$$
$$\text{highest degree term } \left(4x^5\right) \text{ is } 5$$

Polynomials are usually written in descending powers of one of the variables. The polynomials

$$x^5 - 3x^4 + 2x^2 - x + 5$$
$$x^4m + x^3m^2 - 2xm^5 - 6$$
$$-2xm^5 + x^3m^2 + x^4m - 6$$

are written in descending powers of a particular variable. The first two polynomials are written in descending powers of x. The third polynomial is the same polynomial as the second but is written in descending powers of m instead of descending powers of x.

48.C

addition of polynomials Since polynomials are composed of individual terms, the rule for adding polynomials is the same rule that we use for adding terms—**like terms may be added.**

example 48.1 Add. Write the answer in descending order of the variable.

$$\left(x^3 + 3x^2 + 2\right) + \left(2x^3 + 4\right)$$

solution   We remember that we can discard parentheses preceded by a plus sign without changing the signs of the terms therein.

$$(x^3 + 3x^2 + 2) + (2x^3 + 4) = x^3 + 3x^2 + 2 + 2x^3 + 4$$
$$= 3x^3 + 3x^2 + 6$$

example 48.2   Add. Write the answer in descending order of the variable.

$$(3x^4 - 2x^2 + 3) - (x^4 - 2x^3 + x^2)$$

solution   When we discard the parentheses in this problem, we remember to **change the sign of every term in the second parentheses** because the second parentheses are preceded by a minus sign.

$$(3x^4 - 2x^2 + 3) - (x^4 - 2x^3 + x^2) = 3x^4 - 2x^2 + 3 - x^4 + 2x^3 - x^2$$
$$= 2x^4 + 2x^3 - 3x^2 + 3$$

example 48.3   Add. Write the answer in descending order of the variable.

$$(3x^3 + 2x^2 - x + 4) - (x^2 - 7x - 5)$$

solution   The first parentheses can be removed with no change to the terms inside, but because the second parentheses are preceded by a minus sign, we must **change the sign of all terms therein** when we remove these parentheses.

$$(3x^3 + 2x^2 - x + 4) - (x^2 - 7x - 5) = 3x^3 + 2x^2 - x + 4 - x^2 + 7x + 5$$
$$= 3x^3 + x^2 + 6x + 9$$

practice   Add. Write the answers in descending order of the variable.

a. $-(3x^5 + 6x^4 - 7x^3 - 5) + (x^5 - x^4 + 3x^2 - 2x - 8)$

b. $(3x^2 + x^4 - 6x + 2) - (15x^4 + 2x^3 - 6x^2 + 5x - 3)$

problem set 48

1.
(32)
Courtney and Kristofer thought of the same number. They multiplied the number by 3 and then increased the product by 5 for a final result of −55. What number were they thinking of?

2.
(45)
Find the range, median, mode, and mean of the following numbers:

$$8, 11, 5, 7, 11, 2, 12, 4$$

3.
(10)
Use six unit multipliers to convert 28,000 square inches to square kilometers.

4.
(3,8)
The perimeter of a rectangle is 66 in. The width of the rectangle is 11 in. Find the area of the rectangle.

5.
(47)
What percent of 160 is 88? Work the problem and then draw a diagram of the problem.

6.
(47)
If 25 is increased by 140 percent, what is the result? Work the problem and then draw a diagram of the problem.

7.
(46)
Write a conjunction that describes this graph.

8.
(33)
Write 315 as a product of prime factors.

9.
(28)
If $h(x) = \dfrac{1}{x}$, find $h(4)$.

Solve:

10.
(25)
$-4\dfrac{3}{4} + 3\dfrac{3}{5}x = 13\dfrac{1}{4}$

11.
(27)
$0.2p + 2.2 + 2.2p = 4.36$

12.
(31)
$(-2)^3(-x - 4) - |-4| = -2(x + 7^0)$

13. If $x + 3 = 4$, find the value of $x^2 - 19$.
(41)

14. Solve for y: $6y + x - 4y - 6 + 5x = 0$
(42)

15. Find the least common multiple (LCM) of 8, 36, and 75.
(43)

Add:

16. $\dfrac{1}{3} + \dfrac{2}{5} + \dfrac{3}{10}$
(1)

17. $\dfrac{a}{x} + \dfrac{b}{c^2 x^2} + d$
(44)

18. Add. Write the answer in descending order of the variable:
(48)

$$\left(4x^3 + x^2 + 3\right) + \left(x^3 + 2x^2 + 1\right)$$

19. Factor the greatest common factor of $4x^2 y^5 p^2 - 3x^5 y^4 p^2$.
(35)

20. Simplify (factor if necessary): $\dfrac{x^3 y^2 k - x^2 yk}{x^2 yk}$
(35)

Simplify. Write the answers with all variables in the numerator.

21. $\dfrac{xx^{-3} y^5 x^0}{x^2 y^{-3} xy^2}$
(40)

22. $\dfrac{kp^2 k^{-1} p^{-3} p^{-4}}{k^2 pp^2 k^{-5}}$
(40)

23. Expand by using the distributive property. Write the answer with all variables in the numerator.
(40)

$$\left(\dfrac{x^2}{yp^{-4}} - \dfrac{x^2 y}{p^{-4}}\right)\dfrac{x^{-2}}{y^4 p}$$

24. Simplify by adding like terms. Write the answer with all exponents negative.
(41)

$$\dfrac{7my^0}{ym^0} - \dfrac{3m^2 y}{my^2} - \dfrac{5m^{-3} m^4}{y^{-3} y^4} + \dfrac{2ymm}{my^2}$$

Evaluate:

25. $x - y^2\left(x^0 - y\right)$ if $x = -2$ and $y + 1 = 4$
(41)

26. $-p^{-2} - \left(p^2 - x\right)$ if $p = -3$ and $x + 2 = 4$
(41)

Simplify:

27. $-\dfrac{1}{(-4)^{-2}} - \sqrt[3]{-27}$
(36)

28. $\dfrac{(-6)^0\left[\left(-4 - 2^0\right) + \left(9 - 2^2\right)\right]}{|-2| - |-6|}$
(29)

29. Find the area of the shaded portion of this trapezoid. Dimensions are in feet.
(8)

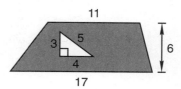

30. Find x and y.
(2)

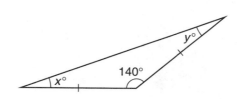

LESSON 49   *Multiplication of Polynomials*

We remember that we use the distributive property

$$a(b + c) = ab + ac$$

when we multiply a monomial by a binomial. The expression on the outside of the parentheses is multiplied by both terms inside the parentheses.

example 49.1   Multiply. Write the answer in descending order of the variable.

$$4x(x^2 - 2)$$

solution   We must multiply $4x$ by x^2 and by -2. Then we sum the products.

$$4x(x^2 - 2) = 4x(x^2) + 4x(-2) = \mathbf{4x^3 - 8x}$$

To develop a general procedure for multiplying two polynomials, we will use the distributive property to multiply

$$(a + b)(c + d)$$

The notation $(a + b)(c + d)$ tells us that $(a + b)$ is to be multiplied by c and that $(a + b)$ is also to be multiplied by d and that the two products are to be summed.

$$(a + b)(c + d) = (a + b)c + (a + b)d$$

Now we use the distributive property again to multiply $(a + b)$ by c

$$(a + b)c = ac + bc$$

and to multiply $(a + b)$ by d

$$(a + b)d = ad + bd$$

and the products are summed.

$$(a + b)(c + d) = (a + b)c + (a + b)d$$
$$= ac + bc + ad + bd$$

This has been a rather involved development to illustrate the following rule.

RULE FOR MULTIPLYING POLYNOMIALS

To multiply one polynomial by a second polynomial, each term of the first polynomial is multiplied by each term of the second polynomial and then the products are summed.

---

example 49.2   Multiply. Write the answer in descending order of the variable.

$$(4x + 5)(3x - 2)$$

solution   The notation indicates that $4x$ is to be multiplied by both $3x$ and -2

$$4x(3x - 2) = 12x^2 - 8x$$

and that $+5$ is to be multiplied by both $3x$ and -2

$$+5(3x - 2) = 15x - 10$$

and that the products are to be added algebraically.

$$(4x + 5)(3x - 2) = 12x^2 - 8x + 15x - 10 = \mathbf{12x^2 + 7x - 10}$$

We can also do the multiplication if the binomials are written one above the other, as we show in the following examples. Either one may be on top.

example 49.3   Multiply. Write the answer in descending order of the variable.

$$(4x + 2)(x - 5)$$

solution   We begin writing the binomials one above the other.

$$\begin{array}{r} 4x + 2 \\ \underline{x - 5} \end{array}$$

Now, the x of $x - 5$ is multiplied by both terms of $4x + 2$, and the products are recorded.

$$\begin{array}{r} 4x + 2 \\ \underline{x - 5} \\ 4x^2 + 2x \end{array} \qquad \text{product of } x \text{ and } 4x + 2$$

Now, the -5 of $x - 5$ is multiplied by both terms of $4x + 2$, and the products are recorded so that like terms (if any) are recorded below like terms to facilitate addition.

$$\begin{array}{r} 4x + 2 \\ \underline{x - 5} \\ 4x^2 + 2x \\ \underline{- 20x - 10} \\ 4x^2 - 18x - 10 \end{array} \qquad \begin{array}{l} \text{product of } x \text{ and } 4x + 2 \\ \text{product of } -5 \text{ and } 4x + 2 \\ \text{sum of the products} \end{array}$$

The product $-20x$ was recorded below the term $+2x$. There was no constant in the first product for -10 to be recorded below, so -10 was written out to the right.

example 49.4   Multiply. Write the answer in descending order of the variable.

$$(4x + 2)(3x - 5)$$

solution   We will use the vertical format to multiply.

$$\begin{array}{r} 4x + 2 \\ \underline{3x - 5} \\ 12x^2 + 6x \\ \underline{- 20x - 10} \\ 12x^2 - 14x - 10 \end{array} \qquad \begin{array}{l} \text{product of } 3x \text{ and } 4x + 2 \\ \text{product of } -5 \text{ and } 4x + 2 \\ \text{sum of the products} \end{array}$$

example 49.5   Multiply. Write the answer in descending order of the variable.

$$(3x + 2)^2$$

solution   When we write $(3x + 2)^2$, we mean $3x + 2$ times $3x + 2$. We will use the vertical format to multiply.

$$\begin{array}{r} 3x + 2 \\ \underline{3x + 2} \\ 9x^2 + 6x \\ \underline{+ 6x + 4} \\ 9x^2 + 12x + 4 \end{array} \qquad \begin{array}{l} \text{product of } 3x \text{ and } 3x + 2 \\ \text{product of } 2 \text{ and } 3x + 2 \\ \text{sum of the products} \end{array}$$

This same procedure can be used if one or both algebraic expressions have three or more terms. Each term in one algebraic expression is multiplied by every term in the other algebraic expression and the products are then summed algebraically. The next example illustrates the procedure for multiplying a binomial by a trinomial.

example 49.6 Multiply. Write the answer in descending order of the variable.

$$(4x - 2)(x^2 + x + 4)$$

solution We will multiply both $4x$ and -2 by all three terms in the second parentheses. This will give us six products. Then we simplify by adding the like terms.

$$(4x - 2)(x^2 + x + 4) = 4x^3 + 4x^2 + 16x - 2x^2 - 2x - 8$$
$$= 4x^3 + 2x^2 + 14x - 8$$

practice Multiply. Write the answers in descending order of the variable:

   a. $(5x + 3)(2x - 4)$ **b.** $(5x - 6)^2$ **c.** $(3x - 1)(x^2 - 2x + 3)$

problem set 49

1. The village was polyglot. If the ratio of bilingual denizens to trilingual denizens was 14 to 3 and the denizens totaled 3400, how many were trilingual?
(39)

2. The scores on the test were 71, 89, 62, 71, 94, 97, 71, 78, 67, and 85. Find the range, median, mode, and mean of the test scores.
(45)

3. Use four unit multipliers to convert 10,000 feet to kilometers. (Go from feet to inches to centimeters to meters to kilometers.)
(4)

4. The diameter of a circle is 22 in.
(3,8)
   (a) Find the circumference of the circle.
   (b) Find the area of the circle.

5. Twenty-five percent of 200 is what number? Work the problem and then draw a diagram of the problem.
(47)

6. What percent of 80 is 208? Work the problem and then draw a diagram of the problem.
(47)

7. Write a conjunction that designates the numbers that are greater than -3 and less than or equal to 6.
(46)

8. What fraction of $5\frac{5}{8}$ is $2\frac{1}{4}$?
(28)

9. If $f(x) = -\dfrac{1}{x}$, find $f(5)$.
(28)

Solve:

10. $\dfrac{1}{5} + \dfrac{3}{25}x - 3 = 2\dfrac{3}{5}$ **11.** $0.04x + 0.2 - 0.4x = 0.38$
(25)   *(27)*

12. $(-2)^3(-x - 4) - |-2| - 3^2 = -2(x - 4) - x$
(31)

13. If $x + 4 = 3$, find the value of $x^2 - 11$.
(41)

14. Find the least common multiple (LCM) of b^3, b^2c, and b^2c^2.
(43)

Add:

15. $\dfrac{3}{4} + \dfrac{2}{5} - \dfrac{3}{20}$ **16.** $\dfrac{ad}{4d^3} + \dfrac{8}{d} + \dfrac{mx}{d^4}$
(1)   *(44)*

17. Add. Write the answer in descending order of the variable:
(48)

$$(2x^4 - x^2 + 5) - (x^4 - x^3 + 2x^2)$$

Multiply. Write the answers in descending order of the variable:

18. $(2x + 3)(x - 2)$ **19.** $(2x + 1)^2$
(49)   *(49)*

20. Factor the greatest common factor of $8m^3x^2y^4p - 4m^2xpm$.
(35)

Simplify. Write the answers with all variables in the denominator.

21. $\dfrac{m^2 xy m^3 x^{-5}}{yy^{-4} m^{-3} x^2}$
(40)

22. $\dfrac{x^2 y^{-2} m^{-5} y^0}{xxy^2 y^{-5} x^{-3}}$
(40)

23. Expand by using the distributive property. Write the answer with all variables in the denominator.
(40)

$$\frac{x^{-1}}{y}\left(\frac{y}{x} - \frac{3xy^{-5}}{p^6}\right)$$

24. Simplify by adding like terms. Write the answer with all variables in the numerator.
(41)

$$\frac{x^2 y}{p^{-3}} - \frac{4x^2 p^3}{y^{-1}} - \frac{2xp}{y^{-1} p^2} - \frac{5y}{p^{-3} x^{-2}}$$

Evaluate:

25. $-p^2 - p^{-3}(xp^0)$ if $p = -2$ and $x + 2 = -2$
(41)

26. $-x - x^{-2} - xy^{-2}$ if $x + 1 = -1$ and $y = 2$
(41)

Simplify:

27. $\dfrac{1}{-(-3)^{-2}} - \sqrt[3]{-64}$
(36)

28. $-2\left[(-4 - 3^0)(5 - 2) - (-6)\right] - \sqrt[3]{-125}$
(29)

29. Find the area of this figure. Corners
(8)   that look square are square. Dimensions are in feet.

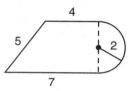

30. A right circular cylinder has a radius
(15) of 8 yards and a height of 12 yards, as
shown. Find the surface area of the
right circular cylinder.

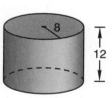

LESSON 50   *Polynomial Equations • Ordered Pairs • Cartesian Coordinate System*

50.A

polynomial equations

In Lesson 48, we noted that the **degree of a term** of a polynomial is the sum of the exponents of the variables of the term. Thus

$$2x^3 \qquad \text{is a third-degree term}$$

$$x \qquad \text{is a first-degree term}$$

$$xyz \qquad \text{is a third-degree term}$$

Also, we said that the **degree of a polynomial** is the same as the degree of its highest-degree term. Thus

$$x^3 + xy + m \qquad \text{is a third-degree polynomial}$$

$$2x + 4y \qquad \text{is a first-degree polynomial}$$

$$2x \qquad \text{is a first-degree polynomial}$$

If two polynomial expressions are connected by an equals sign, we call the equation a **polynomial equation. The degree of a polynomial equation is the same as the degree of its highest-degree term.** Thus

$$x^4 - 3x^2 + 2 = 0 \qquad \text{is a fourth-degree polynomial equation}$$

$$xyz + y = 4 \qquad \text{is a third-degree polynomial equation}$$

$$y = 2x + 4 \qquad \text{is a first-degree polynomial equation}$$

There is an infinite number of pairs of values of x and y that are solutions to any first-degree polynomial equation in two variables. We will use the equation

$$y = 2x + 4$$

to investigate. If we assign a value to x, the equation will then indicate the value of y that is paired with the assigned value of x. For instance, if we assign to x a value of 2, then

$$y = 2(2) + 4 \quad \longrightarrow \quad y = 8$$

the paired value of y is 8. If we give x a value of 2 and y a value of 8 in the original equation, we find that these values of x and y satisfy the equation and are solutions to the equation because the replacement of the variables by these numbers makes the equation a true statement.

$$y = 2x + 4 \qquad \text{equation}$$

$$8 = 2(2) + 4 \qquad \text{replaced } x \text{ with 2 and } y \text{ with 8}$$

$$8 = 4 + 4 \qquad \text{simplified}$$

$$8 = 8 \qquad \text{True}$$

If, in the original equation, we give x a value of -5, then

$$y = 2(-5) + 4 \quad \longrightarrow \quad y = -10 + 4 \quad \longrightarrow \quad y = -6$$

we find that the paired value of y is -6. Thus the pair of values $x = -5$ and $y = -6$ will also satisfy the equation, for the use of both of these numbers in the original equation in place of x and y will cause the equation to become a true equation, as shown here.

$$y = 2x + 4 \qquad \text{equation}$$

$$-6 = 2(-5) + 4 \qquad \text{replaced } x \text{ with } -5 \text{ and } y \text{ with } -6$$

$$-6 = -10 + 4 \qquad \text{simplified}$$

$$-6 = -6 \qquad \text{True}$$

We can replace x with any real number and use the equation to find the value of y that the equation pairs with this value of x.

In both of the foregoing examples we **assigned** a value to the variable x. The variable x, to which we assign a value, is called the **independent variable.** We see that, in each case, the value of y **depends** on the value that we assigned to x. Therefore, in our examples, we call the variable y the **dependent variable.** We could have assigned a value to y and then used the equation to find the corresponding value of x, in which case y would be the independent variable and *x* would be the dependent variable. **It is customary, however, to use the letter *x* to designate the independent variable and to use the letter *y* to designate the dependent variable. To avoid confusion, we will follow this custom in this book.**

50.B
ordered pairs

In the preceding section, we found that, given the equation

$$y = 2x + 4$$

if we let $x = 2$ and $y = 8$, this pair of values of *x* and *y* will make the equation a true equation. Also, the pair of values $x = -5$ and $y = -6$ will make the equation a true equation. Since writing $x = 2$ and $y = 8$ and writing $x = -5$ and $y = -6$ is rather cumbersome, it is customary to write just (2, 8) and (−5, −6), **with the *x* value always designated by the first number in the parentheses and the *y* value always designated by the second number.** Since the numbers are written in order with *x* first and *y* second, we designate this notation as an **ordered pair** of *x* and *y*. The general form of an ordered pair of *x* and *y* is (x, y). If two other variables are used instead of *x* and *y*, it is necessary to designate which variable will be represented by each of the entries in the parentheses. If the variables *m* and *p* are to be used and we wish to write the *m* value first, we could designate this at the outset by making a statement about the ordered pair (m, p). **It is important to remember that in ordered pairs of *x* and *y*, the first number will always designate the value of *x* and the second number will always designate the value of *y*.**

50.C
Cartesian coordinate system

In Lesson 37 we learned that the solution of an equation or inequality in one variable can be presented in graphical form on a single number line, as we show here.

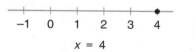   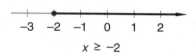

The graphical solution to equations or inequalities that contain two variables cannot be displayed on a single number line. We must have one number line for one of the variables and another number line for the other variable. We draw the *x* number line horizontally and the *y* number line vertically, and we let the number lines intersect at right angles at the origin of both number lines. The positive values of *x* are located to the right of the origin on the *x* number line, and the positive values of *y* are located above the origin on the *y* number line. The *x* number line is called the **x axis,** or **horizontal axis,** and the *y* number line is called the **y axis,** or **vertical axis.**

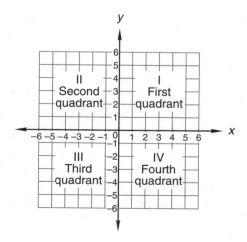

The figure on the previous page shows that the two number lines divide the plane into four *quarters*, or *quadrants*. The quadrants are named the **first quadrant, second quadrant, third quadrant,** and **fourth quadrant,** as shown. The figure in its entirety is called a system of **Cartesian coordinates** or a **Cartesian coordinate system** after the famous seventeenth-century French philosopher and mathematician René Descartes. It is also called a **rectangular coordinate system** and is sometimes called a **coordinate plane.**

When we use a single number line to graph the solution to an equation in one variable such as $x = 2$ (below), we call the mark we make on the number line the **graph** of the point; conversely, we call the number the **coordinate** of the point on the line designated by the graph. The point is defined to be without size, and thus the graph is not the point but denotes the location of the point.

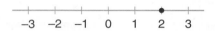

Since a rectangular coordinate system has two number lines, **it is necessary to associate with every point on a rectangular coordinate system two numbers or coordinates.** These numbers designate the location of the point. The following figure shows the graphs of four points. Written by each point is the ordered pair of values of x and y that we associate with the point; these numbers are the x and y coordinates of the point. **The number written first is always the x coordinate of the point and is called the *abscissa* of the point.** This number denotes the measure of the distance of the point to the right (+) or left (−) of the vertical axis. **The number written second is always the y coordinate of the point and is called the *ordinate* of the point.** This number denotes the measure of the distance of the point above (+) or below (−) the horizontal axis.

example 50.1 Graph these ordered pairs of x and y on a rectangular coordinate system:

(a) $(3, 3)$ (b) $(-4, 0)$ (c) $(0, -3)$ (d) $(4, -2)$

solution In the rectangular coordinate system below we place four dots, one to mark the location of each point.

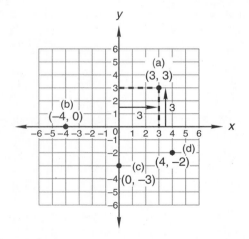

In the first quadrant we show the graph of the point $(3, 3)$, which is **3 units to the right** of the y axis and thus has an **x coordinate of +3.** The point is also **3 units above** the x axis and thus has a **y coordinate of +3.** The next point, $(-4, 0)$, is located 4 units to the left of the y axis and thus has an x coordinate of −4. The point is no units above or below the x axis (it is on the x axis) and thus has a y coordinate of 0. The exact positions of the other two points shown are designated by the ordered pairs $(0, -3)$ and $(4, -2)$. Thus we see that the location of every point on the coordinate plane can be designated by stating the x and y coordinates of the point.

We have seen that a point on a number line is without size and that the graph of a point is not the point but only denotes the location of the point. In the same way, a point in a rectangular coordinate system is without size, and the graph of the point is not the point but designates the location of the point.

practice   Graph these ordered pairs of x and y on a rectangular coordinate system:

     a. $(-6, -7)$ **b.** $(4, -5)$

problem set 50

1. Madeline and Vivian found that the sum of -3 and 4 times the opposite of a number is 27 larger than the number. What is the number?
₍₃₃₎

2. The mean of four numbers is 9. Three of the numbers are 5, 8, and 13. Find the fourth number.
₍₄₅₎

3. Use six unit multipliers to convert 15 square kilometers to square inches.
₍₁₀₎

4. Eighty percent of what number is 1120? Work the problem and then draw a diagram of the problem.
₍₄₇₎

5. What number is 170 percent of 40? Work the problem and then draw a diagram of the problem.
₍₄₇₎

6. Draw a number line and graph the solution of $-5 \le x < 1$.
₍₄₆₎

7. Write 1155 as a product of prime factors.
₍₃₃₎

8. If $g(x) = -\dfrac{1}{x}$, find $g(-6)$.
₍₂₈₎

Solve:

9. $\dfrac{2}{7} - \dfrac{1}{14}x + 2 = 3\dfrac{1}{14}$ **10.** $0.3z - 0.02z + 0.2 = 1.18$
₍₂₅₎   ₍₂₇₎

11. $(-2)^3(-k - |-3|) - (-2) - 2k = k - 3^2$
₍₃₁₎

12. Solve for p: $7p + 3w = w - 12 - 3p$
₍₄₂₎

13. Find the least common multiple (LCM) of x, c^2x^2, and cdx.
₍₄₃₎

Graph these ordered pairs of x and y on a rectangular coordinate system:

14. $(-3, 4)$ **15.** $(-1, -3)$
₍₅₀₎   ₍₅₀₎

Add:

16. $\dfrac{3}{7} + \dfrac{8}{9} - \dfrac{1}{3}$ **17.** $\dfrac{4}{x^2} + \dfrac{6}{2x^3} - \dfrac{3}{4x^4}$
₍₁₎   ₍₄₄₎

18. Add. Write the answer in descending order of the variable:
₍₄₈₎

$$\left(2x^5 + x^3 + 4x - 1\right) - \left(x^5 + 2x^3 - x + 2\right)$$

Multiply. Write the answers in descending order of the variable:

19. $(2x - 1)^2$ **20.** $(x + 1)\left(x^2 - 2x + 3\right)$
₍₄₉₎   ₍₄₉₎

21. Simplify (factor if necessary): $\dfrac{3x^4 - 3x^2}{3x^2}$
₍₃₅₎

22. Simplify (write the answer with all exponents positive): $\dfrac{x^{-4}yy^{-3}x^0x^2}{x^{-3}y^3y^2x^{-4}}$
₍₄₀₎

23. Expand by using the distributive property. Write the answer with all exponents positive.
₍₄₀₎

$$\left(\dfrac{ax^{-5}}{y^{-2}} + \dfrac{4x^3}{ay^2}\right)\dfrac{x^5}{ay^2}$$

24. Simplify by adding like terms. Write the answer with all variables in the denominator.
(41)

$$\frac{m^2 x x^0}{y^{-1}} - \frac{3m^2 y}{x^{-1} y^0} + 5mmyx - \frac{4x^2 y m^2}{x}$$

Evaluate:

25. $-x(x - y^0)|y|$ if $x + 2 = 1$ and $y + 3 = -1$
(41)

26. $ab^0(a^{-3} - b^{-2})$ if $a = -2$ and $b = \sqrt[3]{8}$
(41)

27. Simplify: $\dfrac{1}{-4^{-2}} - |-2| - \sqrt[5]{-243}$
(36)

28. Find the perimeter of this figure.
(3) Dimensions are in centimeters.

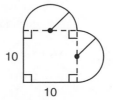

29. Find the area of the rectangle in square
(8) inches. The tick marks show that the length is 32 inches and the width is 1 foot.

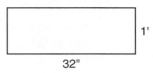

30. A base of the right solid 12 meters high is shown. Find the volume of the right solid.
(20) Dimensions are in meters.

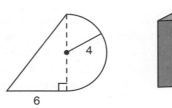

LESSON 51   *Graphs of Linear Equations • Graphs of Vertical and Horizontal Lines*

51.A

graphs of linear equations

If we use a rectangular coordinate system to graph the ordered pairs that satisfy a first-degree polynomial equation in two variables, we find that the graph is the graph of a straight line. For this reason, we call a first-degree polynomial equation in one or more variables a **linear equation.** The following equations are examples of linear equations in two variables

$$y - 2x + 1 = 0 \qquad x - 4 = -2y \qquad x + y = 0$$

for the graph of each of the equations is a straight line.

To graph a linear equation in two variables, we need to know only two ordered pairs of x and y that satisfy the equation since only two points are needed to determine the graph of a line. But since the topic is a new one, in the examples we will learn how to find two or more ordered pairs of x and y that lie on the line.

example 51.1   Graph: $y = 2x - 1$

solution   We begin by making a table and choosing convenient values for x. The values chosen for x should not be too close together. Also, they should not be so large that they will graph off our coordinate system. Numbers such as 0, 2, –2, 3, and –3 usually work well.

x	0	2	–2	3	–3
y					

Now we will use the numbers 0, 2, –2, 3, and –3, one at a time, as replacement values for x in the equation $y = 2x - 1$ to find the paired values of y.

WHEN $x = 0$	WHEN $x = 2$	WHEN $x = -2$	WHEN $x = 3$	WHEN $x = -3$
$y = 2(0) - 1$	$y = 2(2) - 1$	$y = 2(-2) - 1$	$y = 2(3) - 1$	$y = 2(-3) - 1$
$y = -1$	$y = 3$	$y = -5$	$y = 5$	$y = -7$

Next, we complete the table by entering the values of y that the equation has paired with the chosen values of x.

x	0	2	–2	3	–3
y	–1	3	–5	5	–7

Thus we have found five ordered pairs of x and y that satisfy the equation and therefore lie on the graph of the equation. These ordered pairs are (0, –1), (2, 3), (–2, –5), (3, 5), and (–3, –7). In the next figure we have graphed the points designated by these ordered pairs and have connected them with a straight line. The point (–3, –7) was not graphed since this point fell outside the borders of our coordinate system.

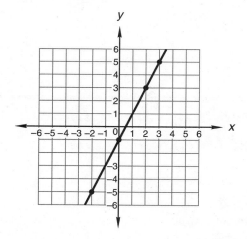

Since a line (straight line) in mathematics is defined to be infinite in length, we have graphed only a segment of the line, or a line segment. Also, we remember that a mathematical line has no width, and since the line we have drawn has a width that can be measured, it is not a mathematical line but is a **graph of a mathematical line** and indicates the location of the mathematical line in question.

example 51.2   Graph: $y = -\dfrac{1}{2}x + 2$

solution   We begin by making a table and choosing convenient values for x.

x	0	2	-2
y			

Now we find the values of y that the equation $y = -\frac{1}{2}x + 2$ pairs with the chosen values of x.

WHEN $x = 0$ WHEN $x = 2$ WHEN $x = -2$

$y = -\dfrac{1}{2}(0) + 2$ $y = -\dfrac{1}{2}(2) + 2$ $y = -\dfrac{1}{2}(-2) + 2$

$y = 2$ $y = 1$ $y = 3$

Next, we complete the table by entering the values of y that the equation has paired with the chosen values of x.

x	0	2	-2
y	2	1	3

We finish by graphing the points and drawing the line through the points.

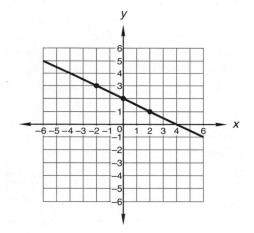

example 51.3   Graph: $y = -x$

solution   We begin by making a table and choosing convenient values for x.

x	0	3	-3
y			

Now we find the values of y that the equation $y = -x$ pairs with the chosen values of x.

WHEN $x = 0$ WHEN $x = 3$ WHEN $x = -3$

$y = -(0)$ $y = -(3)$ $y = -(-3)$

$y = 0$ $y = -3$ $y = 3$

Next, we complete the table by entering the values of y that the equation has paired with the chosen values of x.

x	0	3	-3
y	0	-3	3

We finish by graphing the points and drawing the line through the points.

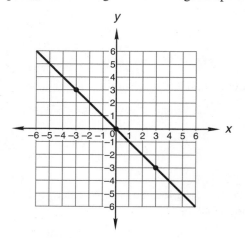

51.B

**graphs of
vertical and
horizontal
lines**

In the previous section, we graphed the following equations:

$$y = 2x - 1 \qquad y = -\frac{1}{2}x + 2 \qquad y = -x$$

We note that each of these equations has both an x term and a y term. We also note that none of the graphs was a vertical line or a horizontal line. **Some equations of a straight line contain either an x term or a y term but not both an x term and a y term, and the graph of these equations is either a vertical line or a horizontal line.**

The graph of every vertical line on the coordinate plane has the form

$$x = h$$

where h is the value of the x coordinate of any point on the vertical line. Note that h can be a positive number, a negative number, or zero.

The graph of every horizontal line on the coordinate plane has the form

$$y = k$$

where k is the value of the y coordinate of any point on the horizontal line. Note that k can be a positive number, a negative number, or zero.

example 51.4   Graph: $x = -2$

solution   This equation places no restriction on the y coordinates of the points on the line. It tells us that the x coordinate of every point on the line is -2 regardless of the y coordinate of the point. Note that each point graphed has an x coordinate of -2.

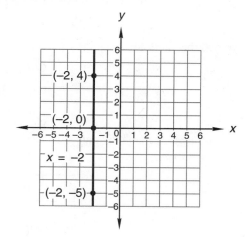

example 51.5   Graph: $y = 4$

solution   This equation tells us that the y coordinate of every point on the line is 4. On the line, we indicate three points. Note that each of these points has a y coordinate of 4.

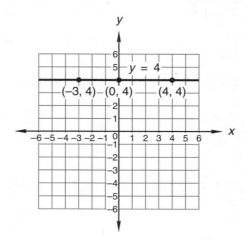

example 51.6   Graph $y = 2x$ and $y = 2$ on the same rectangular coordinate system.

solution   These equations are often confused. The equation $y = 2$ is the equation of a horizontal line, while the equation $y = 2x$ is not.

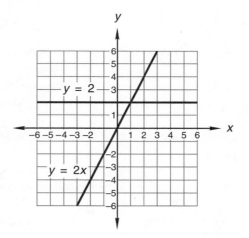

practice   Graph these equations on a rectangular coordinate system:

a. $y = -x + 1$ **b.** $y = -\dfrac{1}{3}x + 2$

c. $x = 3$ **d.** $y = -4$

**problem set
51**

1.
(39)   At the Mardi Gras ball the guests roistered and rollicked until the wee hours. If the ratio of roisterers to rollickers was 7 to 5 and 1080 were in attendance, how many were rollickers?

2.
(45)   Find the range, median, mode, and mean of the following numbers:

8, 23, 15, 6, 28, 4, 18, 15, 14

3.
(4)   Use four unit multipliers to convert 10 kilometers to feet. (Go from kilometers to meters to centimeters to inches to feet.)

4. The circumference of a circle is 20 cm.
(3,8)

    (a) Find the radius of the circle.

    (b) Find the area of the circle.

5. What percent of 8300 is 996? Work the problem and then draw a diagram of the problem.
(47)

6. If 72 is increased by 130 percent, what is the result? Work the problem and then draw a
(47) diagram of the problem.

7. Draw a number line and graph the solution of $x \not\le 3$.
(39)

8. If $h(x) = \dfrac{1}{x}$, find $h\left(-\dfrac{1}{2}\right)$.
(28)

Solve:

9. $-1\dfrac{2}{9} + 2\dfrac{1}{5}p = -\dfrac{1}{3}$
(25)

10. $0.4x - 0.02x + 1.396 = 0.598$
(27)

11. $3x - [-(-2)]x + (-3)(x + 2) = 5x + (-7)$
(31)

12. If $x + 9 = 3$, find the value of $-x^2 + 4$.
(41)

13. Find the least common multiple (LCM) of $4x^2$, yx^2, and $8m^3x^2$.
(43)

Graph these equations on a rectangular coordinate system:

14. $y = x - 3$
(51)

15. $x = 2$
(51)

Add:

16. $\dfrac{4}{x^2} + \dfrac{c}{4x^3} + m$
(44)

17. $\dfrac{1}{2a^3} + \dfrac{3}{4ab^2} + \dfrac{c}{8a^2b^2}$
(44)

18. Add. Write the answer in descending order of the variable:
(48)

$$\left(3x^4 - 2x^3 - x - 2\right) + \left(x^4 + x^3 - 4x + 5\right)$$

Multiply. Write the answers in descending order of the variable:

19. $(2x + 4)(5x - 3)$
(49)

20. $(x + 3)^2$
(49)

21. Factor the greatest common factor of $4k^2pz - 6k^3p^2z^5 - 2k^2p^2z^2 - 4kp$.
(35)

22. Simplify (write the answer with all exponents negative): $\dfrac{x^3y^{-4}p^0y^4p^2}{x^4xx^{-7}y^2p^4}$
(40)

23. Expand by using the distributive property. Write the answer with all exponents negative.
(40)

$$\dfrac{x^{-4}}{y^4}\left(\dfrac{x^{-4}}{y^4} - \dfrac{x^2}{ay^2}\right)$$

24. Simplify by adding like terms. Write the answer with all exponents positive.
(41)

$$\dfrac{x^2y}{p^{-3}} - \dfrac{4x^2p^3}{y^{-1}} - \dfrac{2xp}{y^{-1}p^{-2}} - \dfrac{5y}{p^{-3}x^{-2}}$$

Evaluate:

25. $-|xa|\left(a - xa^0\right)$ if $a + 2 = -1$ and $x + 1 = 2$
(41)

26. $x^0y\left(y^{-2} - x^{-3}\right)$ if $x = -2$ and $y = \sqrt[3]{-8}$
(41)

27. Simplify: $27(-3)^{-3} - 5^2 - \sqrt[3]{-125}$
(36)

28. Find the area of the right triangle in
$_{(8)}$ square inches. The tick marks show
that the base is 80 inches and the
height is 5 feet.

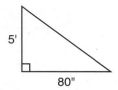

29. Find the area of this figure. Dimen-
$_{(8)}$ sions are in inches.

30. A right circular cylinder has a radius
$_{(15)}$ of 24 feet and a height of 20 feet, as
shown. Find the surface area of the
right circular cylinder.

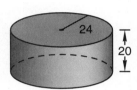

LESSON 52   *More on Addition of Rational Expressions with Unequal Denominators • Overall Average*

52.A

**more on
addition of
rational
expressions
with unequal
denominators**

Possibly the most useful rule in algebra is the **denominator-numerator same-quantity rule.**
Because this rule is so important, we will write it again here.

> DENOMINATOR-NUMERATOR SAME-QUANTITY RULE
>
> The denominator and the numerator of a fraction may be
> multiplied by the same nonzero quantity without changing
> the value of the fraction.

In this lesson we will use the denominator-numerator same-quantity rule for adding more
complicated rational expressions with unequal denominators.

example 52.1   Add: $\dfrac{a}{x} + \dfrac{b}{x + y}$

solution   If the denominator of a term in an addition problem is in the form of a sum, this sum must be
a factor of the least common multiple of the denominators. The least common multiple of the
denominators is $x(x + y)$, and we will use this expression as the new denominator. We will
use the **denominator-numerator same-quantity rule** to find the new numerators.

$$\frac{}{x(x + y)} + \frac{}{x(x + y)}$$

The original denominator of the first term was x, and it has been multiplied by $(x + y)$, so the original numerator a must also be multiplied by $(x + y)$.

$$\frac{a(x + y)}{x(x + y)} + \frac{}{x(x + y)}$$

The original denominator of the second term was $x + y$, and it has been multiplied by x, so the original numerator b must also be multiplied by x. Then we add the numerators.

$$\frac{a(x + y)}{x(x + y)} + \frac{xb}{x(x + y)} = \frac{a(x + y) + xb}{x(x + y)}$$

There are many equally correct forms of the answer. We may multiply out in either the numerator or the denominator or both. Thus all three of the following forms are correct:

$$\frac{ax + ay + xb}{x(x + y)} \qquad \frac{a(x + y) + xb}{x^2 + xy} \qquad \frac{ax + ay + xb}{x^2 + xy}$$

Since all the forms are correct, no one form is preferred. In mathematics, preference is reserved to the individual.

example 52.2 Add: $\dfrac{4x + a}{a + b} + \dfrac{c}{x}$

solution We begin by writing the fraction lines with the new denominators. Then we find the new numerators and add.

$$\frac{}{x(a + b)} + \frac{}{x(a + b)}$$

$$\frac{x(4x + a)}{x(a + b)} + \frac{c(a + b)}{x(a + b)} = \frac{4x^2 + ax + ca + cb}{x(a + b)}$$

We could multiply $x(a + b)$ in the denominator, but we decide to leave it in this more concise form.

example 52.3 Add: $\dfrac{a + b}{x} + \dfrac{c}{m} + d$

solution We begin by writing the fraction lines with the new denominators. Then we find the new numerators and add.

$$\frac{}{mx} + \frac{}{mx} + \frac{}{mx}$$

$$\frac{m(a + b)}{mx} + \frac{cx}{mx} + \frac{dmx}{mx} = \frac{m(a + b) + cx + dmx}{mx}$$

We could multiply $m(a + b)$ in the numerator, but we decide to leave it as it is.

example 52.4 Add: $\dfrac{a}{b + c} - x + \dfrac{d + m}{k}$

solution We begin by writing the fraction lines with the new denominators. Then we find the new numerators and add.

$$\frac{}{k(b + c)} - \frac{}{k(b + c)} + \frac{}{k(b + c)}$$

$$\frac{ka}{k(b + c)} - \frac{xk(b + c)}{k(b + c)} + \frac{(d + m)(b + c)}{k(b + c)} = \frac{ka - xk(b + c) + (d + m)(b + c)}{k(b + c)}$$

Again we choose not to use the distributive property, and we leave the answer in the more concise form.

52.B

overall average

The average of the averages is seldom the overall average. Suppose the average of the first six numbers is 8 and the average of the next four numbers is 10. If we find the average of the averages, we add 8 to 10 and divide by 2.

$$\text{Average of the averages } = \frac{8 + 10}{2} = 9$$

This is the average of the averages but is not the overall average. The overall average is

$$\text{Overall average } = \frac{\text{sum of all the numbers}}{\text{number of numbers}}$$

The average of the first six numbers is 8, so the sum of the first six numbers is 6×8, or 48. The average of the next four numbers is 10, so the sum of the next four numbers is 4×10, or 40. The number of numbers is $6 + 4 = 10$, so the correct overall average is

$$\text{Overall average } = \frac{(6 \times 8) + (4 \times 10)}{6 + 4} = \frac{48 + 40}{10} = 8.8$$

example 52.5   The average of the first 90 numbers was 4. The average of the next 10 numbers was 6. What was the overall average?

solution   **The overall average is the sum of all the numbers divided by the number of numbers.**

$$\text{Overall average } = \frac{(4 \times 90) + (10 \times 6)}{90 + 10} = \frac{360 + 60}{100} = \mathbf{4.2}$$

The overall average is much closer to the average of the first group than to the average of the second group because the first group had 90 numbers and the second group had only 10 numbers.

practice   Add:

a. $\dfrac{x}{y} - b + \dfrac{c + d}{m}$

b. $\dfrac{5b + c}{a + b} - \dfrac{x}{b} + c$

c.   The average of the first 5 weights was 10 pounds. The average of the next 10 weights was 25 pounds. What was the overall average of all the weights?

problem set 52

1.
(33)   Kacey and Starr found that if 3 times a number is decreased by 5 and this difference is doubled, the result is 14 less than twice the number. What is the number?

2.
(52)   The average of the first 6 weights was 15 pounds. The average of the next 14 weights was 30 pounds. What was the overall average of all the weights?

3.
(10)   Use six unit multipliers to convert 70 square feet to square meters.

4.
(47)   Sixteen percent of 4200 is what number? Work the problem and then draw a diagram of the problem.

5.
(47)   What percent of 50 is 700? Work the problem and then draw a diagram of the problem.

6.
(39)   Draw a number line and graph the solution of $x \ngtr -4$.

7.
(30)   What decimal part of 7 is 14.14?

8.
(28)   If $f(x) = -\dfrac{1}{x}$, find $f\left(-\dfrac{2}{3}\right)$.

Solve:

9.
(25) $2\dfrac{1}{5}x - \dfrac{1}{3} = -15$

10.
(31) $0.2k - 4.21 - 0.8k = 2(-k + 0.1)$

11.
(31) $-2[(-k - 3)(-2) - 3] = (-3 - 3k)(-2)^3 - 3^2$

12. Solve for p: $5p + a - 10 = p - 5a$
(42)

13. Find the least common multiple (LCM) of 21, 24, and 60.
(43)

Graph these equations on a rectangular coordinate system:

14. $y = -2x + 4$ **15.** $y = 3$
(51)   *(51)*

Add:

16. $\dfrac{4}{a^2b^2} - \dfrac{c}{ad} - \dfrac{m}{a^3b}$ **17.** $\dfrac{2x + a}{a + b} + \dfrac{d}{x}$
(44)   *(52)*

18. Add. Write the answer in descending order of the variable:
(48)
$$(3x^3 - x^2 + 2x + 5) - 2(x^3 + 2x^2 - x - 3)$$

Multiply. Write the answers in descending order of the variable:

19. $(5x - 3)^2$ **20.** $(x + 1)(5x^2 + 12x + 7)$
(49)   *(49)*

21. Simplify (factor if necessary): $\dfrac{6xay - 24xay^2}{6xay}$
(35)

22. Simplify (write the answer with all variables in the numerator): $\dfrac{m^2 p^4 x^{-2} x^2 x^0 p^6}{m^2 p^{-4} x^0 p^0 x^2}$
(40)

23. Expand by using the distributive property. Write the answer with all variables in the
(40) numerator.
$$\frac{x}{y^{-1}}\left(\frac{x}{y} - \frac{3x^2}{xy}\right)$$

24. Simplify by adding like terms. Write the answer with all exponents negative.
(41)
$$\frac{3x^2 y^{-2}}{m^5} - \frac{3x^2 y^2}{m^5} - \frac{4xx^3 m^{-5}}{x^2 y^2} + \frac{6m^{-5}}{x^{-2} y^{-2}}$$

Evaluate:

25. $|x - y||y - x|$ if $x = -3$ and $y + 1 = -3$
(41)

26. $p^{-2}(a^{-5} - y)$ if $p = 2$, $y = -4$, and $a = \sqrt[3]{-1}$
(41)

27. Simplify: $\dfrac{8(-2)^{-3} - 27(-3)^{-3}}{|3| - |-3|}$
(10)

28. Find the perimeter of this figure. Cor-
(3) ners that look square are square.
Dimensions are in centimeters.

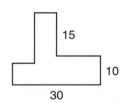

29. Find the area of the isosceles triangle
(8) in square inches. The tick marks show
that the base is 4 feet and the height is
20 inches.

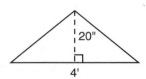

30. A base of the right solid 30 meters high is shown. Find the volume of the right solid.
(20) Dimensions are in meters.

LESSON 53   *Power Rule for Exponents* • *Conversions of Volume*

53.A

power rule for exponents

In some of the previous problem sets there have been problems whose solutions have required the use of one or more of the following definitions and theorems.

DEFINITION: $\underbrace{x \cdot x \cdot x \cdot x \cdots x}_{m \text{ factors}} = x^m$ (*m* is a natural number)

PRODUCT RULE: $x^m \cdot x^n = x^{m+n}$ $(x \neq 0)$

DEFINITION: $x^1 = x$

DEFINITION: $x^{-n} = \dfrac{1}{x^n}$ $(x \neq 0)$

DEFINITION: $x^0 = 1$ $(x \neq 0)$

QUOTIENT RULE: $\dfrac{x^m}{x^n} = x^{m-n} = \dfrac{1}{x^{n-m}}$ $(x \neq 0)$

To complete the list of rules for exponents, we will introduce the **power rule for exponents,** which is a logical extension of the first definition listed above. By using this definition, we can show that *x* is to be used as a factor three times by writing x^3 as

$$x \cdot x \cdot x = x^3 \qquad \text{or} \qquad (x)^3$$

If we wish to show that x^5 should be used as a factor three times, we could write

$$x^5 \cdot x^5 \cdot x^5 = \left(x^5\right)^3$$

Since $x^5 \cdot x^5 \cdot x^5$ equals x^{15}, then $\left(x^5\right)^3$ must also equal x^{15}.

$$\left(x^5\right)^3 = x^{15}$$

Thus, when an exponential expression is raised to a power, we simplify by multiplying the exponents. We call this rule the power rule for exponents.

POWER RULE FOR EXPONENTS

If *m* and *n* are real numbers and $x \neq 0$, then

$$\left(x^m\right)^n = x^{mn}$$

We demonstrate some examples of the power rule for exponents below.

(a) $\left(a^5\right)^2 = a^{10}$ (b) $\left(x^{-4}\right)^{-2} = x^8$ (c) $\left(m^{-2}\right)^4 = m^{-8}$

(d) $\left(p^{-7}\right)^{-7} = p^{49}$ (e) $\left(x^3\right)^5 = x^{15}$ (f) $\left(m^k\right)^2 = m^{2k}$

The use of the power rule for exponents in expressions such as those above usually gives little trouble, but the use of this rule to simplify expressions such as $\left(2x^5y^2z\right)^3$ is more complicated. We know that the notation indicates that $2x^5y^2z$ is to be used as a factor three times because 3 is the exponent of the whole expression.

$$\left(2x^5y^2z\right)\left(2x^5y^2z\right)\left(2x^5y^2z\right)$$

Since the order of multiplication of factors of a product does not affect the value of the product, we will rearrange the order of multiplication to get

$$2 \cdot 2 \cdot 2 \cdot x^5 \cdot x^5 \cdot x^5 \cdot y^2 \cdot y^2 \cdot y^2 \cdot z \cdot z \cdot z$$

which could be written by the use of the product rule for exponents as

$$2^3x^{15}y^6z^3 \qquad \text{which equals} \qquad 8x^{15}y^6z^3$$

To obtain the same result by using the power rule for exponents,

$$\left(2x^5y^2z\right)^3$$

we would have to multiply the exponent of each factor of the given term by 3 or raise each factor of the given term to the third power.

$$\left(2x^5y^2z\right)^3 = (2)^3\left(x^5\right)^3\left(y^2\right)^3(z)^3 = 8x^{15}y^6z^3$$

This is clear to the mathematician from the notation that $\left(x^m\right)^n = x^{mn}$, but it is sometimes not clear to the student at this level. Therefore, we will state it as follows: **To raise a term that contains no indicated additions to a given power, the exponent indicating the power is multiplied by the exponent of every factor of the numerator and the denominator** (if there is one) **of the term.** For example,

(a) $\left(\dfrac{3x^{-2}y^5}{z^4}\right)^{-2} = \dfrac{3^{-2}x^4y^{-10}}{z^{-8}} = \dfrac{x^4y^{-10}}{9z^{-8}}$

(b) $\left(2a^{-2}b^2z^{-10}\right)^{-5} = 2^{-5}a^{10}b^{-10}z^{50} = \dfrac{a^{10}b^{-10}z^{50}}{32}$

(c) $\left(\dfrac{4xy}{m^{-2}}\right)^2 = \dfrac{4^2x^2y^2}{m^{-4}} = \dfrac{16x^2y^2}{m^{-4}}$ (d) $\left(\dfrac{3xy^{-2}}{p^5}\right)^{-2} = \dfrac{3^{-2}x^{-2}y^4}{p^{-10}} = \dfrac{x^{-2}y^4}{9p^{-10}}$

(e) $\left(\dfrac{3x^0y}{k^4}\right)^3 = \dfrac{3^3y^3}{k^{12}} = \dfrac{27y^3}{k^{12}}$ (f) $\left(\dfrac{2^0x^{-2}y^4}{z}\right)^{15} = \dfrac{x^{-30}y^{60}}{z^{15}}$

53.B
conversions of volume

In this section we will use unit multipliers to convert volume measurements.

example 53.1 Use three unit multipliers to convert 180 cubic feet to cubic inches.

solution We will write 180 ft^3 as 180 ft · ft · ft. Therefore, we have

$$180\, \cancel{ft} \cdot \cancel{ft} \cdot \cancel{ft} \times \frac{12 \text{ in.}}{1\, \cancel{ft}} \times \frac{12 \text{ in.}}{1\, \cancel{ft}} \times \frac{12 \text{ in.}}{1\, \cancel{ft}} = 180(12)(12)(12) \text{ in.}^3$$

example 53.2 Use six unit multipliers to convert 800 cubic centimeters to cubic feet.

solution We will write 800 cm^3 as 800 cm · cm · cm. Therefore, we have

$$800\, \cancel{cm} \cdot \cancel{cm} \cdot \cancel{cm} \times \frac{1\, \cancel{in.}}{2.54\, \cancel{cm}} \times \frac{1\, \cancel{in.}}{2.54\, \cancel{cm}} \times \frac{1\, \cancel{in.}}{2.54\, \cancel{cm}} \times \frac{1 \text{ ft}}{12\, \cancel{in.}} \times \frac{1 \text{ ft}}{12\, \cancel{in.}} \times \frac{1 \text{ ft}}{12\, \cancel{in.}}$$

$$= \frac{800}{(2.54)(2.54)(2.54)(12)(12)(12)} \text{ ft}^3$$

practice Simplify. Write the answers with all variables in the numerator.

a. $\left(\dfrac{3^0\,y^{-2}z^5}{x^3}\right)^{-3}$

b. $\left(\dfrac{x^2y^{-2}}{3m^4k}\right)^{-2}\left(\dfrac{y^{-2}m}{x^3k}\right)^2$

c. Use three unit multipliers to convert 75 cubic inches to cubic centimeters.

d. Use six unit multipliers to convert 28 cubic meters to cubic inches.

1. When Oberon and Titania assembled the little people, they found that the pixies and leprechauns were in a ratio of 3 to 13. If there were 6816 in all, how many were pixies?
(39)

2. The average weight of the first 3 students was 135 pounds. The average weight of the next 97 students was 163 pounds. What was the overall average weight of all 100 students?
(52)

3. Use three unit multipliers to convert 50 cubic inches to cubic centimeters.
(53)

4. Sixty-five percent of what number is 260? Work the problem and then draw a diagram of the problem.
(47)

5. What number is 190 percent of 30? Work the problem and then draw a diagram of the problem.
(47)

6. Write both an inequality and a negated inequality that describe this graph.
(39)

7. Write 990 as a product of prime factors.
(33)

8. If $g(x) = x^{-1}$, find $g\left(-\dfrac{3}{5}\right)$.
(28)

Solve:

9. $3\dfrac{1}{8}p + 2\dfrac{1}{4} = \dfrac{1}{6}$
(25)

10. $-(-3)^3 - |-2| - 2^2 - (-k - 3) = -4^2 - (3k - 4)$
(31)

11. If $x + 1 = 4$ and $y - 2 = 3$, find the value of $x^2 - y^2$.
(41)

12. Find the least common multiple (LCM) of $2c^2$, $4c^3$, and $3c^4$.
(43)

Graph these equations on a rectangular coordinate system:

13. $y = \dfrac{1}{3}x - 3$ **14.** $x = -1$
(51)   (51)

Add:

15. $\dfrac{m}{p^2 k} - \dfrac{4a}{3pk} + \dfrac{6}{5pk^2}$ **16.** $\dfrac{a}{b + c} - \dfrac{4x}{b^2}$
(44)   (52)

17. Add. Write the answer in descending order of the variable:
(48)
$$\left(7x^5 + 4x^2 - 2x\right) - 2\left(3x^4 + 2x^2 + x - 4\right)$$

Multiply. Write the answers in descending order of the variable:

18. $(x + 3)(3x - 4)$ **19.** $(2x + 7)(2x - 7)$
(49)   (49)

20. Factor the greatest common factor of $9k^2 bm^4 - 3kb^4 m^2 + 12kb^3 m^3$.
(35)

Simplify. Write the answers with all variables in the numerator.

21. $\left(x^2 y^{-3} z^{-1}\right)^2$ **22.** $\left(\dfrac{xy^{-3}}{m^4}\right)^{-2}$
(53)   (53)

23. Expand by using the distributive property. Write the answer with all variables in the denominator.
(40)
$$\left(\dfrac{x^2 m^2}{3} - \dfrac{5x^5 p^0}{m^{-4}}\right)\dfrac{3x^{-2} y^0}{m^2}$$

24. Simplify by adding like terms. Write the answer with all variables in the numerator.
(41)
$$\dfrac{xx^0}{y} - \dfrac{3x^2 x^{-1} y^2}{x^0 y^3} + \dfrac{2x^2}{xy^2} - \dfrac{4xxy^{-1}}{xyy^0}$$

Evaluate:

25. $x^{-3} - x^{-2} - x^{-1}$ if $x + 3 = 1$
(41)

26. $|a + b||a - b|$ if $a = \sqrt[4]{16}$ and $b + 1 = -2$
(41)

27. Simplify: $\dfrac{1}{(-2)^{-3}} + \dfrac{1}{2^{-3}} + \sqrt[3]{27}$
(36)

28. Find the perimeter of this figure in meters. Corners that look square are square.
(3)

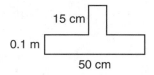

29. Find the area of this figure. Dimensions are in inches.
(8)

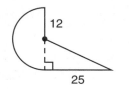

30. Find the surface area of this right rectangular prism. Dimensions are in feet.
(15)

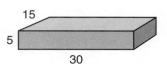

LESSON 54 *Substitution Axiom • Simultaneous Equations • Solving Simultaneous Equations by Substitution*

54.A
substitution axiom

Since Lesson 14 we have been finding the value of a particular expression that contains variables by assigning a value to each variable. Thus the value of

$$\frac{x^2 y}{p} \qquad \text{when } x = 2, \ y = 4, \text{ and } p = -1 \text{ is} \qquad \frac{(2)^2(4)}{(-1)} = \frac{16}{-1} = -16$$

To do this we have been using what is usually called the **substitution axiom.**

The substitution axiom is stated in different ways by different authors. Three statements of this axiom that are frequently used follow:

SUBSTITUTION AXIOM

1. Changing the numeral by which a number is named in an expression does not change the value of the expression.
2. For any numbers a and b, if $a = b$, then a and b may be substituted for each other.
3. If $a = b$, then a may replace b or b may replace a in any statement without changing the truth or falsity of the statement.

Definition 1 seems to apply only to individual expressions. Definition 2 is general enough but not sufficiently specific. Definition 3 seems to apply only to statements and not to individual expressions. **We will use the definition below to state formally and exactly the thought that if two expressions have equal value, it is permissible to use either expression.**

SUBSTITUTION AXIOM

If two expressions a and b are of equal value, $a = b$, then a may replace b or b may replace a in any expression without changing the value of the expression. Also, a may replace b or b may replace a in any statement without changing the truth or falsity of the statement. Also, a may replace b or b may replace a in any equation or inequality without changing the solution set of the equation or inequality.

Thus the substitution axiom applies to expressions, equations, and inequalities. We have already been using this axiom to evaluate expressions as shown in the problem worked at the beginning of this section. Now we will use the substitution axiom to solve a system of first-degree linear equations in two unknowns.

54.B
simultaneous equations

If we consider the two equations

$$\text{(a)}\ 2x - y = 1 \qquad \text{and} \qquad \text{(b)}\ x = -3y + 11$$

we see that $(3, 5)$ is a solution to equation (a) and that $(5, 2)$ is a solution to equation (b).

(a)	(b)
$2x - y = 1$	$x = -3y + 11$
$2(3) - (5) = 1$	$5 = -3(2) + 11$
$6 - 5 = 1$	$5 = -6 + 11$
$1 = 1 \qquad$ True	$5 = 5 \qquad$ True

But neither $(3, 5)$ nor $(5, 2)$ is a solution to both equations at the same time or simultaneously. If we need one solution that will satisfy two or more equations, we call the equations a **system of simultaneous equations.** We can designate that two or more equations form a system of simultaneous equations by stating so in words or by using a brace, as shown here.

$$\begin{cases} 2x - y = 1 \\ x = -3y + 11 \end{cases}$$

54.C
solving simultaneous equations by substitution

We can find the common solution to a system of two first-degree simultaneous equations in two unknowns by using the substitution axiom.

example 54.1   Use substitution to solve for x and y: $\begin{array}{l}\text{(a)} \\ \text{(b)}\end{array}\begin{cases} 2x - y = 1 \\ x = -3y + 11 \end{cases}$

solution   **First we must assume that a unique ordered pair of real numbers exists which will satisfy both of these equations and that x and y in the equations represent these real numbers.** If our assumption is correct, we can find the value of the members of this unique ordered pair. If our assumption is incorrect, the attempted solution will degenerate into an expression involving real numbers that may be true or false. Examples are $1 = 2$ or $4 + 2 = 6$ or $0 = 0$.[†]

Now, since both equations are assumed to be true equations and also since x in both equations stands for the number that will satisfy both equations, we can **replace the variable x in equation (a) with the equivalent expression for x given by equation (b).**

$2x - y = 1$	equation (a)
$2(-3y + 11) - y = 1$	replaced x with $-3y + 11$
$-6y + 22 - y = 1$	multiplied
$-7y + 22 = 1$	added like terms
$-7y = -21$	added -22 to both sides
$y = 3$	divided both sides by -7

We have found that the y value of the desired ordered pair is 3. Now we may find the value of x by substituting the number 3 for y in either of the original equations.

In Equation (a)	In Equation (b)
$2x - y = 1$	$x = -3y + 11$
$2x - (3) = 1$	$x = -3(3) + 11$
$2x - 3 = 1$	$x = -9 + 11$
$2x = 4$	$x = 2$
$x = 2$	

Thus the ordered pair of x and y that will satisfy both equations is **(2, 3).**

example 54.2 Use substitution to solve for x and y: $\begin{cases} 2x + 3y = -13 \\ y = x - 6 \end{cases}$

solution The bottom equation states that y equals $x - 6$. Therefore, in the top equation we will replace y with $x - 6$ and solve for x.

$2x + 3y = -13$	top equation
$2x + 3(x - 6) = -13$	replaced y with $x - 6$
$2x + 3x - 18 = -13$	multiplied
$5x = 5$	simplified
$x = 1$	divided both sides by 5

Now the paired value for y may be found by replacing x with 1 in either of the original equations.

Top Equation	Bottom Equation
$2x + 3y = -13$	$y = x - 6$
$2(1) + 3y = -13$	$y = (1) - 6$
$2 + 3y = -13$	$y = 1 - 6$
$3y = -15$	$y = -5$
$y = -5$	

Thus the solution is the ordered pair **(1, -5).**

[†] To be discussed in Lesson 81.

example 54.3   Use substitution to solve for x and y: $\begin{cases} 3x + 2y = 3 \\ x = 3y - 10 \end{cases}$

solution   The bottom equation states that x equals $3y - 10$. Therefore, in the top equation we will replace x with $3y - 10$ and solve for y.

$$3x + 2y = 3 \qquad \text{top equation}$$

$$3(3y - 10) + 2y = 3 \qquad \text{replaced } x \text{ with } 3y - 10$$

$$9y - 30 + 2y = 3 \qquad \text{multiplied}$$

$$11y = 33 \qquad \text{simplified}$$

$$y = 3 \qquad \text{divided both sides by 11}$$

Now the paired value for x may be found by replacing y with 3 in either of the original equations.

TOP EQUATION	BOTTOM EQUATION
$3x + 2(3) = 3$	$x = 3(3) - 10$
$3x + 6 = 3$	$x = 9 - 10$
$3x = -3$	$x = -1$
$x = -1$	

Thus the solution is the ordered pair **(−1, 3)**.

example 54.4   Use substitution to solve for x and y: $\begin{cases} -x - 2y = 4 \\ y = -3x + 8 \end{cases}$

solution   The bottom equation states that y equals $-3x + 8$. Therefore, in the top equation we will replace y with $-3x + 8$ and solve for x.

$$-x - 2y = 4 \qquad \text{top equation}$$

$$-x - 2(-3x + 8) = 4 \qquad \text{replaced } y \text{ with } -3x + 8$$

$$-x + 6x - 16 = 4 \qquad \text{multiplied}$$

$$5x = 20 \qquad \text{simplified}$$

$$x = 4 \qquad \text{divided both sides by 5}$$

Now we can replace x with 4 in either of the original equations to find the value of y.

TOP EQUATION	BOTTOM EQUATION
$-x - 2y = 4$	$y = -3x + 8$
$-(4) - 2y = 4$	$y = -3(4) + 8$
$-4 - 2y = 4$	$y = -12 + 8$
$-2y = 8$	$y = -4$
$y = -4$	

Thus the solution is the ordered pair **(4, −4)**.

example 54.5   Use substitution to solve for x and y: $\begin{cases} 2x + 3y = 5 \\ x = y \end{cases}$

solution   The bottom equation states that x equals y. Therefore, in the top equation we will replace x with y and solve for y.

$$2x + 3y = 5 \qquad \text{top equation}$$

$$2(y) + 3y = 5 \qquad \text{replaced } x \text{ with } y$$

$$5y = 5 \qquad \text{simplified}$$

$$y = 1 \qquad \text{divided both sides by 5}$$

and since $x = y$ $\qquad\qquad x = 1$

Thus the solution is the ordered pair **(1, 1)**.

practice   Use substitution to solve for x and y:

a. $\begin{cases} 2x + 3y = 24 \\ x = 4y - 10 \end{cases}$

   b. $\begin{cases} y = x + 7 \\ x + 2y = -16 \end{cases}$

problem set 54

1. If twice a number is increased by 5 and this sum is multiplied by -3, the result is -57.
(32)   What is the number?

2. The average of Brendan's first two tests was 90. The average of his next eight tests was 95.
(52)   What was his overall average?

3. Use three unit multipliers to convert 140 cubic centimeters to cubic inches.
(53)

4. What percent of 860 is 43? Work the problem and then draw a diagram of the problem.
(47)

5. If 76 is increased by 140 percent, what is the result? Work the problem and then draw a
(47)   diagram of the problem.

6. Draw a number line and graph the solution of $-4 < x \le 3$.
(46)

7. If $h(x) = -x^{-1}$, find $h\left(\dfrac{2}{5}\right)$.
(28)

Solve:

8. $-(0.2 - 0.4z) - 0.4 = z - 1.47$
(31)

9. $-\left[-|-3|(-2 - m) - 4\right] = -2[(-3 - m) - 2m]$
(31)

Use substitution to solve for x and y:

10. $\begin{cases} 2x + y = 7 \\ x = -3y + 11 \end{cases}$
(54)

11. $\begin{cases} 2x + 3y = 4 \\ y = 2x + 4 \end{cases}$
(54)

12. Find the least common multiple (LCM) of 15, 175, and 225.
(43)

Graph these equations on a rectangular coordinate system:

13. $y = 3x - 4$
(51)

14. $y = -3$
(51)

Add:

15. $\dfrac{x}{mc} + \dfrac{b}{c} - \dfrac{2}{kc^2}$
(44)

16. $\dfrac{4}{x - y} - \dfrac{3}{y}$
(52)

17. Add. Write the answer in descending order of the variable:
(48)

$$\left(-2x^3 + 4x^2 - x + 1\right) - \left(x^2 - 6x - 3\right)$$

Multiply. Write the answers in descending order of the variable:

18. $(4x - 2)^2$
(49)

19. $(x + 1)(x^2 - 2x + 5)$
(49)

20. Simplify (factor if necessary): $\dfrac{3ap^2m - 6ap^2m^2}{3ap^2m}$
(35)

Simplify. Write the answers with all variables in the denominator.

21. $\left(2^0 a^{-3} b^4 z^2\right)^{-4}$
(53)

22. $\left(\dfrac{3^0 x^{-5} y^2}{z^2}\right)^5$
(53)

23. Expand by using the distributive property. Write the answer with all exponents positive.
(40)

$$\frac{x^2 y^0 p}{m^{-2}} \left(\frac{p^{-3} m^2}{k} - \frac{p^0 p m^2}{x^2} \right)$$

24. Simplify by adding like terms. Write the answer with all variables in the denominator.
(41)

$$a^2 k^2 y^{-1} - \frac{4k^2}{a^{-2} y} + \frac{2k^2 a}{a^{-1} y} - \frac{6k^{-4}}{k^2 y}$$

Evaluate:

25. $a^{-3} - a(x - a)$ if $a = -2$ and $2x + 8 = 16$
(41)

26. $x^2 - xy^{-2} - (-y)^{-2}$ if $x = 3$ and $2y - 5 = -11$
(41)

27. Simplify: $\dfrac{1}{-2^{-3}} - \dfrac{1}{(-3)^{-3}} + \dfrac{1}{4^{-3}} + \sqrt[3]{64}$
(36)

28. Find the perimeter of this figure. Cor-
(3) ners that look square are square. Dimensions are in centimeters.

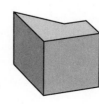

29. Find the area of this figure in square
(8) meters. Corners that look square are square.

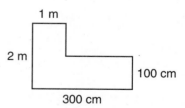

30. A base of the right prism 20 meters high is shown. Find the volume of the right prism.
(20) Dimensions are in meters.

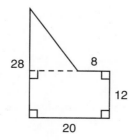

LESSON 55 *Complex Fractions • Division Rule for Complex Fractions*

55.A

complex fractions

To review the **denominator-numerator same-quantity rule,** we will begin with the number 5. Then if we multiply 5 by 2 and divide by 2, the answer is 5

$$5 = \frac{5 \cdot 2}{2} = \frac{10}{2}$$

because $\frac{10}{2}$ is another way to write 5. We have changed the numeral, but the number it represents is unchanged because 2 over 2 has a value of 1. This is why we can multiply the denominator and the numerator of a fraction by any nonzero number without changing the value of the fraction.

Fractions of fractions are called **complex fractions.** We will simplify complex fractions by multiplying the numerator and the denominator by the same quantity.

$$\frac{\frac{a}{b}}{\frac{c}{d}} \qquad \begin{pmatrix} b \neq 0 \\ c \neq 0 \\ d \neq 0 \end{pmatrix}^{\dagger}$$

If we multiply the denominator of this complex fraction by the reciprocal of the denominator, we obtain a product of 1 because we remember that the product of a number and the reciprocal of the same number is the number 1.

$$\frac{c}{d} \cdot \frac{d}{c} = \frac{cd}{dc} = 1$$

But if we wish to multiply the denominator of the fraction by its reciprocal, which is $\frac{d}{c}$, we must also multiply the numerator by $\frac{d}{c}$ so that the value of the original expression will not be changed.

$$\frac{\frac{a}{b}}{\frac{c}{d}} = \frac{\frac{a}{b} \cdot \frac{d}{c}}{\frac{c}{d} \cdot \frac{d}{c}} = \frac{\frac{ad}{bc}}{\frac{cd}{dc}} = \frac{\frac{ad}{bc}}{1} = \frac{ad}{bc}$$

We have simplified the original fraction by multiplying both the denominator and the numerator by the **reciprocal of the denominator.**

example 55.1 Simplify: $\dfrac{\dfrac{a}{b}}{c}$ $(b, c \neq 0)$

solution We multiply both the denominator and the numerator by $\frac{1}{c}$, which is the reciprocal of the denominator c.

$$\frac{\frac{a}{b}}{c} = \frac{\frac{a}{b} \cdot \frac{1}{c}}{\frac{c}{1} \cdot \frac{1}{c}} = \frac{\frac{a}{bc}}{\frac{c}{c}} = \frac{\frac{a}{bc}}{1} = \frac{a}{bc}$$

---

† If neither b, c, nor d equals zero, the denominator cannot equal zero. We provide this notation to ensure the reader that we are not implying that division by zero is permissible.

example 55.2   Simplify: $\dfrac{\dfrac{1}{c}}{\dfrac{1}{b}}$ $(c, b \neq 0)$

solution   We multiply both the denominator and the numerator by b, which is the reciprocal of the denominator $\frac{1}{b}$.

$$\frac{\dfrac{1}{c}}{\dfrac{1}{b}} = \frac{\dfrac{1}{c} \cdot \dfrac{b}{1}}{\dfrac{1}{b} \cdot \dfrac{b}{1}} = \frac{\dfrac{b}{c}}{1} = \frac{b}{c}$$

example 55.3   Simplify: $\dfrac{a}{\dfrac{1}{c}}$ $(c \neq 0)$

solution   We multiply both the denominator and the numerator by c, which is the reciprocal of the denominator $\frac{1}{c}$.

$$\frac{a}{\dfrac{1}{c}} = \frac{\dfrac{a}{1} \cdot \dfrac{c}{1}}{\dfrac{1}{c} \cdot \dfrac{c}{1}} = \frac{\dfrac{ac}{1}}{1} = ac$$

example 55.4   Simplify: $\dfrac{\dfrac{a}{x}}{\dfrac{b}{a + x}}$ $(x, b, \ a + x \neq 0)$

solution   We multiply both the denominator and the numerator by $\frac{a + x}{b}$, which is the reciprocal of the denominator $\frac{b}{a + x}$.

$$\frac{\dfrac{a}{x}}{\dfrac{b}{a + x}} = \frac{\dfrac{a}{x} \cdot \dfrac{a + x}{b}}{\dfrac{b}{a + x} \cdot \dfrac{a + x}{b}} = \frac{a(a + x)}{xb}$$

55.B

division rule for complex fractions

The rule for dividing fractions is sometimes stated as follows: **To divide one fraction by another fraction, invert the fraction in the denominator and multiply.** If we use this rule to simplify

$$\frac{\dfrac{m}{n}}{\dfrac{x}{y}}   (n, x, y \neq 0)$$

the solution is

$$\frac{m}{n} \cdot \frac{y}{x} = \frac{my}{nx}$$

If we use the denominator-numerator same-quantity rule to perform the same simplification, we obtain

$$\frac{\dfrac{m}{n}}{\dfrac{x}{y}} = \frac{\dfrac{m}{n} \cdot \dfrac{y}{x}}{\dfrac{x}{y} \cdot \dfrac{y}{x}} = \frac{my}{nx}$$

This procedure yields the same result as that obtained by using the rule for dividing fractions, but hopefully we have some understanding of what we did and can justify our procedure.

Many algebraic manipulations can be justified by one of the following:

1. **The denominator-numerator same-quantity rule.**
2. **The multiplicative property of equality.**
3. **The additive property of equality.**

We will remember to justify our algebraic manipulations by one of these three rules whenever possible.

practice Simplify:

a. $\dfrac{\frac{x}{m}}{d}$

b. $\dfrac{\frac{1}{r}}{\frac{1}{z}}$

c. $\dfrac{\frac{n}{a}}{\frac{b}{d}}$

d. $\dfrac{\frac{w}{1}}{w + c}$

problem set 55

1. $_{(39)}$ At the prestidigitator's banquet, the ratio of real magicians to charlatans was 7 to 2. If there were 324 at the banquet, how many were real magicians?

2. $_{(52)}$ The average of the first 5 numbers was 200. The average of the second 20 numbers was 400. What was the overall average of the numbers?

3. $_{(53)}$ Use six unit multipliers to convert 24,000 cubic inches to cubic yards.

4. $_{(47)}$ Thirty-eight percent of 700 is what number? Work the problem and then draw a diagram of the problem.

5. $_{(47)}$ What percent of 18 is 27? Work the problem and then draw a diagram of the problem.

6. $_{(46)}$ Draw a number line and graph the solution of $0 \le x < 4$.

7. $_{(28)}$ If $f(x) = \dfrac{1}{x^2}$, find $f(-2)$.

Solve:

8. $_{(25)}$ $\dfrac{1}{3} + 5\dfrac{1}{3}k + 3\dfrac{2}{9} = 0$

9. $_{(31)}$ $-[-(-k)] - (-2)(-2 + k) = -k - (4k + 3)$

Simplify:

10. $_{(55)}$ $\dfrac{\frac{m}{n}}{z}$

11. $_{(55)}$ $\dfrac{m + 1}{\frac{n}{d}}$

Use substitution to solve for x and y:

12. $_{(54)}$ $\begin{cases} 3x + 2y = 7 \\ x = 7 - 3y \end{cases}$

13. $_{(54)}$ $\begin{cases} x + 2y = -6 \\ y = 3x + 4 \end{cases}$

14. $_{(43)}$ Find the least common multiple (LCM) of $2x^2$, $4x^2y$, and $8x^3p$.

Graph these equations on a rectangular coordinate system:

15. $_{(51)}$ $y = 2x + 2$

16. $_{(51)}$ $x = -1\dfrac{1}{2}$

Add:

17.
(44) $\dfrac{3}{2x^2y} - \dfrac{ab}{4x^3y} - c$

18.
(52) $\dfrac{a}{x^2} - \dfrac{m}{x+y}$

19.
(48) Add. Write the answer in descending order of the variable:
$$-(4x^5 + x^3 - 5x + 2) + (x^5 - 2x^3 - 3x + 3)$$

20.
(49) Multiply. Write the answer in descending order of the variable: $(4x - 2)(3x + 5)$

21.
(35) Factor the greatest common factor of $x^2ym - 4x^2ym^3 + 2x^4y^3m^6$.

Simplify. Write the answers with all exponents positive.

22.
(53) $\left(2x^2y^{-2}z\right)^{-2}(xy)^4$

23.
(53) $\left(\dfrac{3x^{-3}y^4z^3}{p^5}\right)^{-3}$

24.
(40) Expand by using the distributive property. Write the answer with all exponents negative.
$$\left(\dfrac{p^{-3}m^2}{k} - \dfrac{p^0pm^2}{x^2}\right)\dfrac{x^2y^0p}{m^2}$$

25.
(41) Simplify by adding like terms. Write the answer with all exponents positive.
$$mx^0x - \dfrac{3m^0}{m^{-1}x^{-1}} + \dfrac{4m^2m^{-1}x}{m^2xx} + \dfrac{5m^2x^{-1}}{mx^{-2}}$$

26.
(41) Evaluate: $(xa - a)\left(-a^{-4}x\right)$ if $a = -3$ and $2x - 5 = 9$

27.
(36) Simplify: $\dfrac{1}{-2^{-4}} + |-4||-4| - \sqrt[3]{125}$

28.
(3) Find the perimeter of this figure in meters. Corners that look square are square.

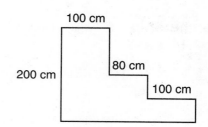

29.
(8) Find the area of this parallelogram. Dimensions are in inches.

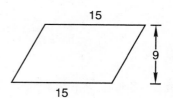

30.
(15) Find the surface area of this right triangular prism. Dimensions are in feet.

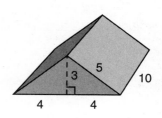

LESSON 56 *Finite and Infinite Sets • Membership in a Set • Rearranging Before Graphing*

56.A
finite and infinite sets

The words **finite** and **infinite** are basic words and are difficult to define. The word *finite* implies the thought of bounded or limited, while the word *infinite* implies the thought of unbounded or without limit. Thus when we say that a set has a finite number of members, we are describing a set such as

$$\{6, 7, 8, 9, 10\}$$

in which the list of the members has an end. **A set with a finite number of members is called a finite set.**

When we say that a set has an infinite number of members, we are describing a set such as

$$\{1, 2, 3, 4, 5, \ldots\}$$

in which the list of the members of the set continues without end. **Sets that have an infinite number of members are called infinite sets.**

Some authors define a finite set as a set whose members could be counted if we could live the number of lifetimes necessary to do the counting. Thus the set that has

$$63{,}072{,}000{,}000{,}000{,}000$$

members is a finite set because we could count the members of this set if we counted for one billion years at two counts per second (not considering leap years).

If we use the same definition, the set

$$\{1, 2, 3, 4, \ldots\}$$

is an infinite set because we could never count the number of members of this set since the list has no end.

56.B
membership in a set

If we have the numbers

$$0, 0, 0, 0, 0, 0, 1, 1, 1, 1, 2, 2, 2, 2$$

and wish to designate these numbers as members of a set B, we would write

$$B = \{0, 1, 2\}$$

which is read "B is the set whose members are the numbers 0, 1, and 2." **Note that each of the numbers is listed only once.** Thus, if we have the set

$$D = \{0, 1, 2, 3, 4\}$$

we have said that the set consists of 0, or any number of 0s; also the set consists of 1s, 2s, 3s, and 4s, but not necessarily just one 1 and one 2 and one 3 and one 4.

example 56.1   Represent the following numbers as being members of set K:

$$1, 0, 2, 1, 0, 5, 7, 4, 5, 7$$

solution   We list each number only once. The order in which the numbers are listed is unimportant.

$$K = \{0, 1, 2, 4, 5, 7\}$$

example 56.2   Represent the following numbers as being members of set L:

$$7, 15, 0, 1, 15, 0, 8, -13, 42$$

solution   We list each number only once. The order in which the numbers are listed is unimportant.

$$L = \{7, 15, 0, 1, 8, -13, 42\}$$

We use the symbols

$$\in \qquad \text{and} \qquad \notin$$

to designate that a particular symbol or number is a member of a given set or is not a member of the given set.

$$0 \in L \qquad 23 \notin L$$

We would read the above as "zero is a member of set L" and "23 is not a member of set L."

example 56.3   Given the sets $A = \{0, 1, 3, 5\}$, $B = \{0, 4, 6, 7\}$, and $C = \{1, 2, 3, 5, 7\}$, are the following statements true or false?

(a) $5 \in A$ (b) $4 \in C$ (c) $5 \notin B$

solution   (a) $5 \in A$ **True,** because 5 is a member of set A.

(b) $4 \in C$ **False,** because 4 is not a member of set C.

(c) $5 \notin B$ **True,** because 5 is not a member of set B.

example 56.4   Given the sets $L = \{0, 1, 2, 3\}$, $M = \{5, 6, 7\}$, and $N = \{0, 1\}$, are the following statements true or false?

(a) $6 \in L$ (b) $0 \in N$

solution   (a) **False,** because 6 is not a member of set L.

(b) **True,** because 0 is a member of set N.

56.C

rearranging   Often we encounter linear equations that have not been solved for y. Graphing these equations
before   is easier if we first rearrange them by solving for y.
graphing

example 56.5   Graph: $3x + 2y = 4$

solution   We first solve for y by adding $-3x$ to both sides of the equation and then dividing both sides of the equation by 2.

$$
\begin{array}{ll}
3x + 2y = 4 & \text{original equation} \\
\underline{-3x \qquad\qquad -3x} & \text{added } -3x \text{ to both sides} \\
2y = 4 - 3x &
\end{array}
$$

$$y = 2 - \frac{3}{2}x \qquad \text{divided both sides by 2}$$

$$y = -\frac{3}{2}x + 2 \qquad \text{order of terms changed}$$

Now we make a table and choose convenient values for x.

x	0	2	−2
y			

Now we find the values of y that the equation $y = -\frac{3}{2}x + 2$ pairs with the chosen values of x.

WHEN $x = 0$	WHEN $x = 2$	WHEN $x = -2$
$y = -\frac{3}{2}(0) + 2$	$y = -\frac{3}{2}(2) + 2$	$y = -\frac{3}{2}(-2) + 2$
$y = 2$	$y = -1$	$y = 5$

Now we complete the table, graph the points, and draw the line.

x	0	2	-2
y	2	-1	5

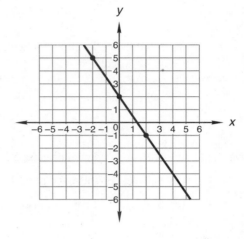

example 56.6   Graph: $y - x = 0$

solution   We first solve for y by adding x to both sides of the equation.

$$\begin{array}{ll} y - x = 0 & \text{original equation} \\ \underline{+\ x\ \ \ \ +\ x} & \text{added } x \text{ to both sides} \\ y = x & \end{array}$$

Now we make a table and choose convenient values for x.

x	0	3	-3
y			

Now we find the values of y that the equation $y = x$ pairs with the chosen values of x.

WHEN $x = 0$	WHEN $x = 3$	WHEN $x = -3$
$y = 0$	$y = 3$	$y = -3$

Now we complete the table, graph the points, and draw the line.

x	0	3	-3
y	0	3	-3

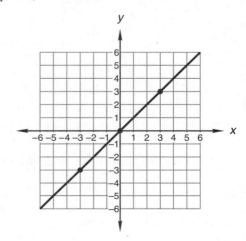

practice

a. Represent the following numbers as being members of set K:

$$3, 1, 0, 5, 0, 9, 5$$

b. Given the sets $A = \{0,\ 2,\ 4\}$, $B = \{0,\ 1,\ 5,\ 6\}$, and $C = \{1,\ 3,\ 4,\ 6\}$, are the following statements true or false?

    (a) $5 \in B$ (b) $5 \notin C$ (c) $0 \in A$ (d) $3 \notin C$

c. Graph the following equation on a rectangular coordinate system: $2x - 3y = 6$

problem set 56

1.
(33) Averi and Rachel found that if the product of 3 and a number was increased by 13, the result was 12 less than twice the opposite of the number. What was their number?

2.
(53) Use six unit multipliers to convert 30 cubic yards to cubic inches.

3.
(56) Represent the following numbers as being members of set K:

$$2, 4, 2, 0, 6, 0, 10, 8$$

4.
(56) Given the sets $A = \{1,\ 3,\ 5\}$, $B = \{0,\ 2,\ 4,\ 6\}$, and $C = \{1,\ 2,\ 3,\ 4\}$, are the following statements true or false?

    (a) $0 \in A$ (b) $1 \notin B$ (c) $2 \in C$ (d) $3 \notin A$

5.
(3,8) The area of a circle is 100 cm^2.

    (a) Find the radius of the circle.   (b) Find the circumference of the circle.

6.
(47) Caitlin and Jacqueline found that 40 percent of their number equaled 22. What was their number? Work the problem and then draw a diagram of the problem.

7.
(47) What number is 180 percent of 55? Work the problem and then draw a diagram of the problem.

8.
(46) Write a conjunction that describes this graph.

9.
(28) If $g(x) = \dfrac{1}{x^2}$, find $g\left(-\dfrac{1}{3}\right)$.

10.
(31) Solve: $-3(-2 - x) - 3^2 - |-2| = -(-2x - 3)$

11.
(41) If $-x - 11 = -9$ and $a + 1 = 1$, find the value of $x^2 - 2a$.

Simplify:

12.
(55)
$$\dfrac{\dfrac{am}{n}}{\dfrac{x}{dc}}$$

13.
(55)
$$\dfrac{\dfrac{x}{c}}{x + y}$$

Use substitution to solve for x and y:

14.
(54)
$$\begin{cases} 2x - 2y = 18 \\ x = 6 - 2y \end{cases}$$

15.
(54)
$$\begin{cases} 3x - y = 4 \\ y = 6 - 2x \end{cases}$$

Graph these equations on a rectangular coordinate system:

16.
(51) $y = -\dfrac{1}{2}x + 4$

17.
(56) $3y + 2x = 3$

Add:

18.
(44) $\dfrac{4}{2x^2} - \dfrac{3}{4x^2 p} + \dfrac{2a}{8x^3 p}$

19.
(52) $\dfrac{m}{b(b + c)} - \dfrac{k}{b}$

20.
(48) Add. Write the answer in descending order of the variable:

$$4(x^2 - 3x + 5) - 2(x^2 - 2x - 4) - (x^2 - 3x + 3)$$

21. Multiply. Write the answer in descending order of the variable: $(3 - x)^2$
(49)

Simplify. Write the answers with all exponents negative.

22. $\left(5x^{-3}y^{-2}\right)^2\left(x^0y^{-1}\right)^{-4}$
(53)

23. $\left(\dfrac{x^2y^{-1}m^{-3}}{2p^{-4}}\right)^3$
(53)

24. Expand by using the distributive property. Write the answer with all variables in the
(40) numerator.

$$\frac{x^{-4}y}{p^2}\left(\frac{y^{-1}}{x^4} + \frac{2x^{-4}p^{-2}}{y^{-1}}\right)$$

25. Simplify by adding like terms. Write the answer with all exponents negative.
(41)

$$\frac{xyz^0}{z} - \frac{7x^2y^2}{xyz} + \frac{2x^3x^{-2}yz^{-2}}{z^{-1}x^0} + \frac{5xy^{-1}y^0}{zy^{-2}}$$

26. Evaluate: $|x|\left(y^{-4} - y^{-3} - y^{-2}\right)$ if $3x + 8 = -10$ and $y = \sqrt[3]{-1}$
(41)

27. Simplify: $-\left\{3\left(-3 \times 2^0\right)[-(3 - 2)(-2)] - |-4|\right\} + \sqrt[3]{64}$
(29)

28. Find the area of this figure in square
(8) centimeters.

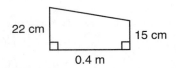

22 cm   15 cm

0.4 m

29. Find x and y.
(2)

$y°$

$x°$ 65°

30. A base of the right prism 11 meters high is shown. Find the volume of the right prism.
(20) Dimensions are in meters.

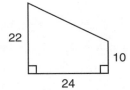

22

10

24

LESSON 57   *Addition of Algebraic Expressions with Negative Exponents*

We have learned to simplify algebraic expressions by adding like terms and to add abstract fractions by finding a common denominator. A common denominator of the two terms on the left below is x^3m^2y and the numerator we get when we add the two terms with this common denominator is $axm^2 + by$, as we show.

$$\frac{a}{x^2y} + \frac{b}{x^3m^2} = \frac{axm^2 + by}{x^3m^2y}$$

When we are asked to simplify algebraic expressions such as

$$ax^{-1} + y^{-1}$$

the method of attack is not immediately apparent.

example 57.1   Add (write the answer with all exponents positive): $ax^{-1} + y^{-1}$

solution   First we rewrite the expression so that all exponents are positive. Then we add the fractions.

$ax^{-1} + y^{-1}$	original expression
$= \dfrac{a}{x} + \dfrac{1}{y}$	new form
$= \dfrac{ay}{xy} + \dfrac{x}{xy}$	common denominator
$= \dfrac{ay + x}{xy}$	added

example 57.2   Add (write the answer with all exponents positive): $ay^{-1}x + bz$

solution   First we rewrite the expression so that all exponents are positive. Then we add the fractions.

$ay^{-1}x + bz$	original expression
$= \dfrac{ax}{y} + bz$	new form
$= \dfrac{ax}{y} + \dfrac{bzy}{y}$	common denominator
$= \dfrac{ax + bzy}{y}$	added

example 57.3   Add (write the answer with all exponents positive): $a^{-2}xy^{-1} + az^{-1}$

solution   First we rewrite the expression so that all exponents are positive. Then we add the fractions.

$a^{-2}xy^{-1} + az^{-1}$	original expression
$= \dfrac{x}{a^2 y} + \dfrac{a}{z}$	new form
$= \dfrac{xz}{a^2 yz} + \dfrac{a^3 y}{a^2 yz}$	common denominator
$= \dfrac{xz + a^3 y}{a^2 yz}$	added

practice   Add. Write the answers with all exponents positive.

a. $ax^{-1} - by^{-2}$ **b.** $a^{-3}xy^{-1} - bx^{-2}$

problem set 57

1.   Leonardo and Michelangelo turned out paintings whose areas were in the ratio of 14 to 13. During the period in question, the total area of their paintings was 1080 square units. How many square units were painted by Leonardo?
(39)

2.   The first ten cows down the chute weighed 790 kg, 832 kg, 745 kg, 804 kg, 804 kg, 745 kg, 810 kg, 760 kg, 740 kg, and 745 kg, respectively. Find the range, median, mode, and mean of the weights.
(45)

3.   Use three unit multipliers to convert 8400 cubic inches to cubic feet.
(53)

4. Represent the following numbers as being members of set L:
(56)

$$-3, 1, 3, -1, -3, 7, 1, -7, -5, 5$$

5. Given the sets $A = \{0, 2, 4\}$, $B = \{5, 6, 7\}$, and $C = \{0, 3, 6, 9\}$, are the following
(56) statements true or false?

    (a) $1 \notin A$ (b) $5 \in B$ (c) $6 \notin C$ (d) $4 \in B$

6. What percent of 180 is 36? Work the problem and then draw a diagram of the problem.
(47)

7. Write a conjunction that designates the numbers that are greater than or equal to -4 and
(46) less than or equal to 2.

8. If $h(x) = -\dfrac{2}{x^2}$, find $h(-2)$.
(28)

9. Solve: $0.02 + 0.02x - 0.4 - 0.4x = 3.116$
(27)

Simplify:

10. $\dfrac{\frac{1}{a}}{x}$
(55)

11. $\dfrac{\frac{b}{c}}{\frac{1}{a+b}}$
(55)

Use substitution to solve for x and y:

12. $\begin{cases} x + y = 6 \\ x = 9 - 2y \end{cases}$
(54)

13. $\begin{cases} 5x - 3y = 6 \\ y = 2x + 3 \end{cases}$
(54)

Graph these equations on a rectangular coordinate system:

14. $y = -3x - 2$
(51)

15. $4y + 8x = 12$
(56)

Add:

16. $4 - \dfrac{7}{a} + \dfrac{a+b}{a^2}$
(44)

17. $\dfrac{a}{x^2 y} + 4a - \dfrac{m}{x+y}$
(52)

Add. Write the answers with all exponents positive.

18. $xy^{-1} + az$
(57)

19. $x^{-1} + ay^{-1}$
(57)

20. Add. Write the answer in descending order of the variable:
(48)

$$5(x^4 - 2x^3 + x^2 - 1) - 2(x^3 + 3x^2 + 1) + (2x^2 - x - 3)$$

21. Multiply. Write the answer in descending order of the variable:
(49)

$$(2x - 3)(2x^2 - 3x + 4)$$

Simplify. Write the answers with all variables in the numerator.

22. $xx(x^2)^{-2}(x^2)(x^{-3}y^0)^5$
(53)

23. $\left(\dfrac{3x^{-2}y^5}{p^{-3}}\right)^{-2}\left(\dfrac{3x^{-2}}{y}\right)^2$
(53)

24. Expand by using the distributive property. Write the answer with all variables in the
(40) denominator.

$$\left(\dfrac{x^2 y^0}{2y^{-1}} - \dfrac{4x^{-2}}{x^0 y}\right)\dfrac{2x^{-2}}{y}$$

25. Simplify by adding like terms. Write the answer with all variables in the numerator.
(41)

$$x^2(p^5)^2 y - \dfrac{3x^2 p^{10}}{y^{-1}} + \dfrac{4x^3 p^8 y}{x^2 p^{-2}} - \dfrac{2p^{10}}{x^{-1}y^{-1}}$$

26. Evaluate: $(x^2 + y^{-2})(x^{-2} - y^2)$ if $2x - 1 = 1$ and $2y + 1 = -1$
(41)

27. Simplify: $\sqrt[3]{8} - \sqrt[4]{16} + \sqrt[5]{32} - \sqrt[6]{64}$
(19)

28. Find the perimeter of this figure in
 (3) centimeters. Corners that look square
      are square.

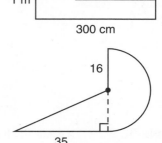

1 m

300 cm

29. Find the area of this figure. Dimen-
 (8) sions are in inches.

16

35

30. A base of the right prism 10 feet high is shown. Find the surface area of the right prism.
 (15) Dimensions are in feet.

15

20   25

30

LESSON 58 *Percent Word Problems*

It is absolutely necessary to be able to visualize percent word problems in order to work them effectively. There is no shortcut that can be used as a substitute for understanding the problem. We will use the statement of the problem to draw "before" and "after" diagrams to help us write the percent equation that will give us the missing parts.

example 58.1 Kathy, John, and Susie have only 20 chickens left. If they began with 80 chickens, what percent of the original flock remains?

solution **A diagram should always be drawn as the first step.**

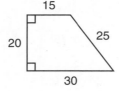

of 80

20 is *WP*

60 is *WP*

Before, 100%   After

The original flock of 80 is on the left. On the right, it is divided into the 20 that remain and the 60 that are missing. We see that we can write two statements that can be used to solve the problem.

(a) 20 is what percent of 80?   or   (b) 60 is what percent of 80?

We will write an equation to solve question (a).

$$\frac{WP}{100} \times 80 = 20 \quad \longrightarrow \quad \frac{100}{80} \cdot \frac{WP}{100} \times 80 = 20 \cdot \frac{100}{80} \quad \longrightarrow \quad WP = \frac{2000}{80}$$

$$\longrightarrow \quad WP = \mathbf{25\%}$$

Thus the other percent is 75 percent. We could also have found 75 percent by solving equation (b). We finish by drawing the diagram with all numbers in place.

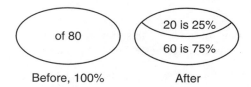

example 58.2   Meme and Jim have 75 thingamabobs. They want to give Hal 20 percent of them. How many thingamabobs do they give Hal?

solution   **A diagram should always be drawn as the first step.**

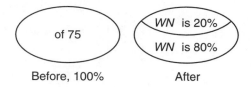

We can use this diagram to help us write two statements that can be used to solve the problem.

(a) What number is 20% of 75?   (b) What number is 80% of 75?

The questions lead to two equations of the form $\frac{P}{100} \times$ of $=$ is.

(a) $\frac{20}{100} \times 75 = WN$ (b) $\frac{80}{100} \times 75 = WN$

We do not have to solve both equations. We will solve equation (a) and subtract this answer from 75 to get the other number.

(a) $\frac{20}{100} \times 75 = WN$ $\longrightarrow$ $\frac{1500}{100} = WN$ $\longrightarrow$ $WN = \mathbf{15}$

Thus, they give Hal 15 and save $75 - 15 = 60$ for themselves. We finish by drawing the diagram with all numbers in place.

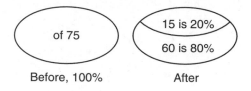

example 58.3   Beau and Christy hide 600 raisins. This is 60 percent more than they hid last month. How many raisins did they hide last month?

solution   **A diagram should always be drawn as the first step.**

We can use this diagram to help us write the statement that can be used to solve the problem. Remember that a 60 percent increase gives us 160 percent.

$$600 \text{ is } 160 \text{ percent of last month}$$

$$\frac{160}{100} \times LM = 600 \quad \longrightarrow \quad \frac{\cancel{100}}{\cancel{160}} \cdot \frac{\cancel{160}}{\cancel{100}} \times LM = 600 \cdot \frac{100}{160} \quad \longrightarrow \quad LM = \frac{60,000}{160}$$

$$\longrightarrow \quad LM = \textbf{375}$$

Thus, last month Beau and Christy hid 375 raisins. We finish by drawing the diagram with all numbers in place.

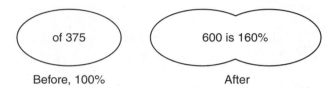

of 375   600 is 160%

Before, 100%   After

practice   In each of the following problems, draw a diagram as an aid in solving the problem:

a.   Jane and Faye have 32 bagatelles left. If they began with 160 bagatelles, what percent of the original number remains?

b.   Caesar's legion had an inventory of 2400 pairs of thongs. If they normally wear out 30 percent of their supply by the end of the fiscal year, how many pairs of thongs remain at the end of the fiscal year?

c.   Christopher and Chad collected 40 items. When they added Cathy's items, their total increased by 150%. What was their new total after Cathy's items were added?

problem set 58

1. (58)   When the votes were counted, it was found that 15 percent of the people in Brenham had voted. If 2100 had voted, how many people lived in Brenham? Draw a diagram as an aid in solving the problem.

2. (58)   T-Willy got 128 pounds of honey from his hive. If this was a 60 percent increase from last year, how much honey did he get last year? Draw a diagram as an aid in solving the problem.

3. (33)   If the product of a number and –5 is increased by 6, the result is 2 less than 3 times the opposite of the number. Find the number.

4. (52)   The average of the first 7 numbers was 21. The average of the next 3 numbers was only 11. What was the overall average of the numbers?

5. (56)   Represent the following numbers as being members of set K:
$$-2, -1, -4, -1, -3, -1, -5, -3$$

6. (46)   Draw a number line and graph the solution of $-6 \leq x \leq -2$.

7. (33)   Write 2310 as a product of prime factors.

8. (28)   If $f(x) = \sqrt{x}$, find $f(4)$.

9. (31)   Solve: $-2[(-3 - 2) - 2(-2 + m)] = -3m - 4^2 - |-2|$

Simplify:

10. (55) $\dfrac{\dfrac{1}{x + y}}{\dfrac{a}{b}}$

11. (55) $\dfrac{m}{\dfrac{a}{mc^2}}$

Use substitution to solve for x and y:

12. (54) $\begin{cases} 2x + 3y = 8 \\ x = y - 1 \end{cases}$

13. (54) $\begin{cases} 3x - y = 3 \\ y = 2x - 1 \end{cases}$

Graph these equations on a rectangular coordinate system:

14. $y = \dfrac{1}{2}x - 2$
(51)

15. $3y + x = -9$
(56)

Add:

16. $-3x + \dfrac{2}{xp^2} - \dfrac{5x}{x^3p}$
(44)

17. $\dfrac{4}{x + y} - \dfrac{3}{y^2}$
(52)

Add. Write the answers with all exponents positive.

18. $ayx^{-1} + bz$
(57)

19. $a^{-2}x^{-1} + bz^{-1}$
(57)

20. Add. Write the answer in descending order of the variable:
(48)

$$2(-x^5 - 3x^3 + x - 2) - 3(x^5 - 2x^3 - x + 1)$$

21. Multiply. Write the answer in descending order of the variable: $(2x - 4)(x - 3)$
(49)

Simplify. Write the answers with all variables in the denominator.

22. $x(x^2)(x^3)^{-3}(y^2y^0)^{-4}$
(53)

23. $\dfrac{(x^2)^{-3}(yx)^2 x^0}{x^2y^{-2}(xy^{-2})^3}$
(53)

24. Expand by using the distributive property. Write the answer with all exponents positive.
(40)

$$\frac{x^{-2}}{4m^2k^{-2}}\left(\frac{4x^2}{m^{-2}k^2} - \frac{8m^{-2}k}{x^{-2}m^0}\right)$$

25. Simplify by adding like terms. Write the answer with all variables in the denominator.
(41)

$$3(xy)^2 m - \frac{2m}{(x^{-1}y^{-1})^2} + \frac{4x^2y^2}{m^{-1}} - \frac{3x^3y^3m^{-1}}{xym^{-2}}$$

26. Evaluate: $(|x| - |y|)(|y| - |x|)$ if $2 - 3x = 5$ and $1 - 2y = 5$
(41)

27. Simplify: $\sqrt[3]{-1} + \sqrt[3]{-8} + \sqrt[3]{-27} + \sqrt[3]{-64} + \sqrt[3]{-125}$
(19)

28. Find the perimeter of this figure in
(3) feet. Corners that look square are square.

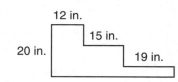

29. Find the area of this trapezoid. Dimen-
(8) sions are in centimeters.

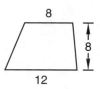

30. A base of the right prism 16 meters high is shown. Find the volume of the right prism.
(20) Dimensions are in meters.

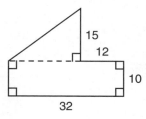

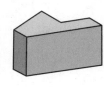

LESSON 59   *Rearranging Before Substitution*

In every substitution problem encountered thus far, one of the equations has expressed x in terms of y, as in the bottom equation in (a), or y in terms of x, as in the top equation in (b).

$$\text{(a)} \quad \begin{cases} 2x + 3y = 5 \\ x = 2y + 3 \end{cases} \qquad \text{(b)} \quad \begin{cases} y = 2x + 4 \\ 2x - y = 7 \end{cases}$$

If neither of the equations is in one of these forms, we begin by rearranging one of the equations.

example 59.1   Use substitution to solve for x and y: (a) $\begin{cases} x - 2y = -1 \\ 2x - 3y = 4 \end{cases}$
(b)

solution   To use substitution to solve this system of equations, it is necessary to rearrange one of the equations. We choose to solve for x in equation (a) because the x term in this equation has a coefficient of 1, and thus we can solve this equation for x in just one step.

$$\begin{array}{ll} x - 2y = -1 & \text{equation (a)} \\ \underline{+\,2y \quad\; +2y} & \text{added } 2y \text{ to both sides} \\ x \qquad = 2y - 1 & \end{array}$$

Now we can substitute the expression $2y - 1$ for x in equation (b) and complete the solution.

$$\begin{array}{ll} 2x - 3y = 4 & \text{equation (b)} \\ 2(2y - 1) - 3y = 4 & \text{substituted } 2y - 1 \text{ for } x \\ 4y - 2 - 3y = 4 & \text{multiplied} \\ y - 2 = 4 & \text{added like terms} \\ y = 6 & \text{added 2 to both sides} \end{array}$$

We can find the value of x by replacing the variable y with the number 6 in either of the original equations. We will use both of the original equations to demonstrate that either one can be used to find x.

Using Equation (a)	Using Equation (b)
$x - 2y = -1$	$2x - 3y = 4$
$x - 2(6) = -1$	$2x - 3(6) = 4$
$x - 12 = -1$	$2x - 18 = 4$
$x = 11$	$x = 11$

Thus the ordered pair of x and y that will satisfy both equations is **(11, 6).**

example 59.2   Use substitution to solve for x and y: (a) $\begin{cases} 2x - y = 10 \\ 4x - 3y = 16 \end{cases}$
(b)

solution   We will first solve equation (a) for y and then substitute the resulting expression for y in equation (b).

$$\begin{array}{ll} 2x - y = 10 & \text{equation (a)} \\ \underline{-2x - 2x} & \text{added } -2x \text{ to both sides} \\ -y = 10 - 2x & \\ y = -10 + 2x & \text{multiplied both sides by } -1 \end{array}$$

Now we substitute $-10 + 2x$ for y in equation (b).

$$4x - 3y = 16 \qquad \text{equation (b)}$$
$$4x - 3(-10 + 2x) = 16 \qquad \text{substituted } -10 + 2x \text{ for } y$$
$$4x + 30 - 6x = 16 \qquad \text{multiplied}$$
$$-2x + 30 = 16 \qquad \text{added like terms}$$
$$-2x = -14 \qquad \text{added } -30 \text{ to both sides}$$
$$x = 7 \qquad \text{divided both sides by } -2$$

To finish the solution, we can use either of the original equations to solve for y.

USING EQUATION (a)	USING EQUATION (b)
$2x - y = 10$	$4x - 3y = 16$
$2(7) - y = 10$	$4(7) - 3y = 16$
$14 - y = 10$	$28 - 3y = 16$
$-y = -4$	$-3y = -12$
$y = 4$	$y = 4$

Thus the solution is the ordered pair **(7, 4)**.

example 59.3   Use substitution to solve for x and y: (a) $\begin{cases} 4x - 2y = 38 \\ 2x + y = 25 \end{cases}$
(b)

solution   We will first solve equation (b) for y and then substitute the resulting expression for y in equation (a).

$$\begin{array}{r} 2x + y = 25 \\ \underline{-2x \qquad\qquad - 2x} \\ y = 25 - 2x \end{array} \qquad \begin{array}{l} \text{equation (b)} \\ \text{added } -2x \text{ to both sides} \end{array}$$

Now we substitute $25 - 2x$ for y in equation (a).

$$4x - 2y = 38 \qquad \text{equation (a)}$$
$$4x - 2(25 - 2x) = 38 \qquad \text{substituted } 25 - 2x \text{ for } y$$
$$4x - 50 + 4x = 38 \qquad \text{multiplied}$$
$$8x = 88 \qquad \text{simplified}$$
$$x = 11 \qquad \text{divided both sides by } 8$$

To finish the solution, we can use either of the original equations to solve for y.

USING EQUATION (a)	USING EQUATION (b)
$4x - 2y = 38$	$2x + y = 25$
$4(11) - 2y = 38$	$2(11) + y = 25$
$44 - 2y = 38$	$22 + y = 25$
$-2y = -6$	$y = 3$
$y = 3$	

Thus the solution is the ordered pair **(11, 3)**.

practice   Use substitution to solve for x and y:

a. $\begin{cases} x - 3y = -7 \\ 2x - 3y = 4 \end{cases}$ b. $\begin{cases} 4x - y = 41 \\ 2x + y = 25 \end{cases}$

problem set 59

1. The store owner gave a 35 percent discount, yet Joe and Carol still had to pay $247 for the camera. What was the original price of the camera? Draw a diagram as an aid in solving the problem.
(58)

2. The weight of the elephant was 1040 percent of the weight of the bear. If the elephant weighed 20,800 pounds, what did the bear weigh? Draw a diagram as an aid in solving the problem.
(58)

3. The gallimaufry contained things large and small in the ratio of 7 to 2. If the total was 1098 items, how many were large?
(39)

4. Given the sets $A = \{-3, -2, -1\}$, $B = \{1, 2, 3\}$, and $C = \{-1, 1, -2, 2, -3, 3\}$, are the following statements true or false?
(56)

(a) $-3 \in A$ (b) $-2 \in B$ (c) $2 \notin C$ (d) $3 \notin C$

5. Write a conjunction that describes this graph.
(46)

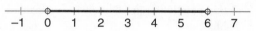

6. 2.625 of what number is 8.00625?   **7.** If $g(x) = -\sqrt{x}$, find $g(9)$.
(30)   *(28)*

8. Solve: $1.591 + 0.003k - 0.002 + 0.002k = -(0.003 - k)$
(31)

Simplify:

9. $\dfrac{\dfrac{1}{x}}{a}$
(55)

10. $\dfrac{x + y}{\dfrac{1}{c}}$
(55)

Use substitution to solve for x and y:

11. $\begin{cases} 2x - 3y = 5 \\ x = -2y - 8 \end{cases}$
(54)

12. $\begin{cases} x + 2y = 5 \\ 3x - y = 1 \end{cases}$
(59)

Graph these equations on a rectangular coordinate system:

13. $y = -3\dfrac{1}{2}$
(51)

14. $4y - 4x = 8$
(56)

Add:

15. $\dfrac{-x}{a^2 b} + \dfrac{a - b}{b}$
(44)

16. $\dfrac{m}{k(k + c)} + \dfrac{m}{k}$
(52)

Add. Write the answers with all exponents positive.

17. $bx + cy^{-1}$
(57)

18. $x^{-1}ay^{-2} - bz^{-1}$
(57)

19. Add. Write the answer in descending order of the variable:
(48)

$$4(x^2 - 3x + 5) - 2(x^3 + 2x^2 - 4) - (2x^4 - 3x^3 + x^2 + 3)$$

20. Multiply. Write the answer in descending order of the variable: $(-5x - 2)(-x + 4)$
(49)

21. Factor the greatest common factor of $12x^4 yp^3 - 4x^3 y^2 pz - 8x^2 p^2 y^2$.
(35)

Simplify. Write the answers with all exponents positive.

22. $\left(4x^0 y^2 m\right)^{-2} \left(2y^{-4} m^0 x\right)^4$
(53)

23. $\dfrac{\left(x^2\right)^{-3} (yx)^2 x^0}{x^2 y^{-2} \left(xy^{-2}\right)^3}$
(53)

24. Expand by using the distributive property. Write the answer with all exponents negative.
(40)

$$\left(\frac{4p^2}{m^2 b^3} - \frac{4m^{-2}}{ab^2 p}\right) \frac{p^{-3} m^2}{4a^{-1} b^{-3}}$$

25. Simplify by adding like terms. Write the answer with all exponents positive.
(41)

$$\frac{4(a^{-1}b^2)^2}{a^0b^2} + \frac{2aab^0}{(a^{-1}b)^{-2}} - \frac{5a^3a^{-1}b^0}{(ab^{-1})^2} - \frac{3(a^0a^3)^{-2}}{a^{-4}b^{-2}}$$

26. Evaluate: $x^{-1}y^{-2} - x^{-2}y^{-3}$ if $1 - 2x = 3$ and $6 + 5y = -4$
(41)

27. Simplify: $2^0|1 - 4| - (-3)^0|1 - 5| - 4^0|1 - 6| + \sqrt[3]{-27}$
(29)

28. Find the area of this figure in square meters. Corners that look square are square.
(8)

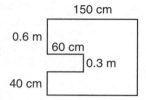
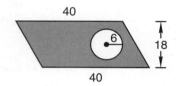

29. Find the area of the shaded portion of this parallelogram. Dimensions are in inches.
(8)

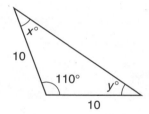

30. Find x and y.
(2)

LESSON 60   *Geometric Solids • Prisms and Cylinders*

60.A

geometric solids

In Lesson 15 we defined a **geometric solid** as a geometric figure that has three dimensions. Some examples of geometric solids are prisms, cylinders, pyramids, cones, and spheres. We show some examples of these types of geometric solids below.

| Right triangular prism | Right circular cylinder | Regular square pyramid | Right circular cone | Sphere |

Although these geometric solids are easy to identify and recognize, they are not necessarily easy to define mathematically. In this book, we will not give the formal definitions of these geometric solids since they are rather complicated. Instead, we will give what mathematicians would consider informal definitions. In this lesson, we will re-examine prisms and cylinders. In later lessons, we will examine pyramids, cones, and spheres.

60.B
prisms and cylinders

A **prism** is a geometric solid where two faces (called **bases**) are identical and parallel polygons and where the other faces are parallelograms (called **lateral faces**). The lateral faces intersect in segments called the **lateral edges** of the prism. The **altitude** of a prism is a perpendicular segment joining the planes of the bases. The length of the altitude is the **height** of the prism. In the figure on the left below, we show a prism with the component parts labeled.

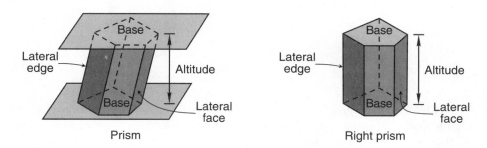

Prism   Right prism

The prism on the right above is a special type of prism. It is called a **right prism.** A right prism is a prism whose lateral edges are at right angles to the bases. Note that in a right prism, the lateral edges are also altitudes. In this book, we will confine our discussion of prisms to right prisms.

Prisms are classified and named according to the shape of their bases. Here we show four examples.

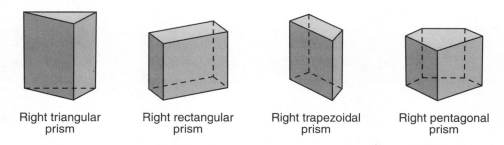

Right triangular   Right rectangular   Right trapezoidal   Right pentagonal
     prism   prism   prism   prism

The right prism on the left is a **right triangular prism** because its bases are triangles. The second right prism is a **right rectangular prism** because its bases are rectangles. The third right prism is a **right trapezoidal prism** because its bases are trapezoids. The fourth right prism is a **right pentagonal prism** because its bases are pentagons.

A **cylinder** is like a prism except that its bases are closed curves instead of polygons. The curved surface between the bases is called the **lateral surface.** The segment joining the centers of the bases is called the **axis** of the cylinder. The **altitude** of a cylinder is a perpendicular segment joining the planes of the bases. The length of the altitude is the **height** of the cylinder. In the figure on the left below, we show a cylinder with the component parts labeled.

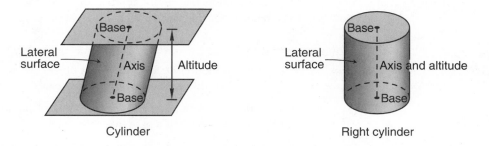

Cylinder   Right cylinder

The cylinder on the right above is a special type of cylinder. It is called a **right cylinder.** A right cylinder is a cylinder whose axis is at right angles to the bases. Note that in a right cylinder, the axis is also its altitude.

Cylinders are classified and named according to the shape of their bases. The right cylinder below is a **right circular cylinder** because its bases are circles. In this book, we will confine our discussion of cylinders to right circular cylinders.

Right circular cylinder

volume of prisms and cylinders
The volume of a prism can be easily computed given the area of a base and the height. We describe in the box below how to compute the volume of a prism. Since a cylinder is like a prism, the volume of a cylinder is computed in the exact same way as the volume of a prism.

> ### VOLUME OF PRISMS AND CYLINDERS
>
> The volume of a prism or a cylinder is equal to the area of a base times the height.

example 60.1
The area of a base of a right pentagonal prism is 28 cm^2 and the length of a lateral edge is 10 cm. Find the volume of the right pentagonal prism.

solution
The volume of a prism is equal to the area of a base times the height. The height of a right prism is the length of a lateral edge. Therefore, we have

$$\text{Volume} = (\text{area of a base})(\text{height})$$

$$= \left(28 \text{ cm}^2\right)(10 \text{ cm})$$

$$= \textbf{280 cm}^3$$

surface area of prisms and cylinders
We define the **lateral surface area** of a prism or a cylinder to be the area of all external surfaces except the bases. Unfortunately, there is no simple way of computing lateral surface areas of prisms or cylinders unless they are right prisms or right cylinders. We describe in the box below how to compute the lateral surface area of a right prism or a right cylinder.

> ### LATERAL SURFACE AREA OF RIGHT PRISMS AND RIGHT CYLINDERS
>
> The lateral surface area of a right prism or a right cylinder is equal to the perimeter of a base times the height.

To find the surface area of a prism or a cylinder, we add the areas of the bases to the lateral surface area.

example 60.2   Find the lateral surface area of this right prism whose bases are regular pentagons. Dimensions are in meters.

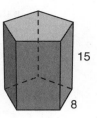

15

8

solution   **The lateral surface area of a right prism is equal to the perimeter of a base times the height.** We can see this if we cut the right prism down a lateral edge (the dotted line) and then press flat. When we do this we get a rectangle.

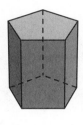

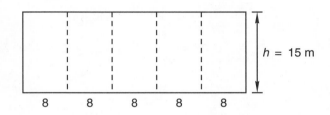

$h = 15\,\text{m}$

8   8   8   8   8

The length of the rectangle is the perimeter of a base of the right prism. Since a base of the right prism is a regular pentagon, the length of each side of a base is 8 meters. Therefore, we have

Perimeter of a base $= 8\,\text{m} + 8\,\text{m} + 8\,\text{m} + 8\,\text{m} + 8\,\text{m} = 40\,\text{m}$

The height of the rectangle is the height of the right prism. The lateral surface area of the right prism is the area of the rectangle which is equal to the perimeter of a base times the height. Therefore, we have

Lateral surface area $= (\text{perimeter of a base})(\text{height})$

$= (40\,\text{m})(15\,\text{m})$

$= \mathbf{600\ m^2}$

practice   **a.**   The area of a base of a right pentagonal prism is 34 in.^{2} and the length of a lateral edge is 12 in. Find the volume of the right pentagonal prism.

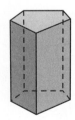

   b.   Find the lateral surface area of this right prism whose bases are regular pentagons. Dimensions are in feet.

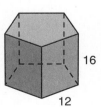

16

12

problem set 60

1.
(58)   Travis peeked around the corner and spied 440 of them lounging in the shade. If this was 60 percent more than Frank spied, how many did Frank spy? Draw a diagram as an aid in solving the problem.

2.
(33)   Lancelot and Guinevere found that the sum of twice a number and 5 is 13 less than the opposite of the number. Find the number.

3. In the first group of 5, the average was 6.5. In the second group of 15, the average was
(52) 4.5. What was the overall average of the two groups?

4. Represent the following numbers as being members of set L:
(56)
$$-12, 0, -8, 4, -4, 4, 0, 8, 8, 12$$

5. The area of a circle is 200 in.^{2}.
(3,8)

    (a) Find the radius of the circle.

    (b) Find the circumference of the circle.

6. Write a conjunction that designates the numbers that are greater than 3 and less than 6.
(46)

7. If $h(x) = |x|$, find $h(-4)$.   **8.** Solve: $2\dfrac{1}{2} + 3\dfrac{1}{16}k + \dfrac{1}{8} = 0$
(28)   (25)

9. If $2x + 5 = -5$ and $3y + 5 = -10$, find the value of $x^3 - y^3$.
(41)

Simplify:

10. $\dfrac{\dfrac{a}{b}}{\dfrac{1}{x}}$ **11.** $\dfrac{x}{\dfrac{1}{a+b}}$
(55)   (55)

Use substitution to solve for x and y:

12. $\begin{cases} x = -19 - 6y \\ 2x + 3y = -11 \end{cases}$ **13.** $\begin{cases} 4x + y = -5 \\ 2x - y = -1 \end{cases}$
(54)   (59)

Graph these equations on a rectangular coordinate system:

14. $y = -2x - 5$ **15.** $3x + 2y = 6$
(51)   (56)

Add:

16. $\dfrac{3ax}{m} + \dfrac{4x}{am^2} + \dfrac{2}{mx}$ **17.** $\dfrac{x}{x+y} + y$
(44)   (52)

Add. Write the answers with all exponents positive.

18. $2x^{-1} + 3y^{-2}$ **19.** $x^{-2}y^{-1} - 4z^{-2}$
(57)   (57)

20. Add. Write the answer in descending order of the variable:
(48)
$$5(-x^5 + 3x^3 - x + 2) + 3(x^5 - 3x^3 - x^2 + x - 3)$$

21. Multiply. Write the answer in descending order of the variable: $(2x - 3)(3x^2 - 2x + 2)$
(49)

Simplify. Write the answers with all exponents negative.

22. $\left(2m^2x^{-3}y^0\right)^{-4}\left(4m^3y^{-1}x^{-5}\right)^2$ **23.** $\left(\dfrac{x^2p^2}{p^0y^{-2}}\right)^{-2}\dfrac{\left(y^{-2}\right)^{-2}}{y^0p^{-3}}$
(53)   (53)

24. Expand by using the distributive property. Write the answer with all variables in the
(40) numerator.
$$\dfrac{x^{-5}y^0}{2p^{-2}y^{-1}}\left(\dfrac{2y^{-2}}{x^{-3}} - \dfrac{4x^5}{p^2}\right)$$

25. Simplify by adding like terms. Write the answer with all exponents negative.
(41)
$$2\left(xy^2\right)^{-1} - \dfrac{9x^{-2}y^{-3}}{\left(x^0y\right)^{-2}} + \dfrac{(3y)^2 x^{-4}}{x^{-2}y^3} - \dfrac{\left(y^{-1}x\right)^2}{x^3}$$

26. Evaluate: $(|x| + |y|)(|x| - |y|)$ if $x = \sqrt[3]{-64}$ and $y = \sqrt[3]{-125}$
(41)

27. Simplify: $\sqrt[4]{16}(1 - |-2|) - \sqrt[4]{81}(2 - |-3|)$
(19)

28. Find the perimeter of this figure in inches. Corners that look square are square.
(3)

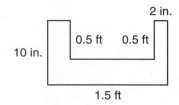

29. Find the area of this figure. Dimensions are in centimeters.
(8)

30. The area of a base of a right pentagonal prism is 30 m² and the length of a lateral edge is 12 m. Find the volume of the right pentagonal prism.
(20,60)

LESSON 61 Subsets • Subsets of the Set of Real Numbers

61.A

subsets **If all the members of one set are also members of a second set, the first set is said to be a** *subset* **of the second set.** If we have the two sets

$$B = \{1, 2\} \qquad A = \{1, 2, 3\}$$

then we can say that set B is a subset of set A because all the members of set B are also members of set A. We use the symbol $\subset$ to mean **is a subset of.** Therefore, we can write

$$B \subset A$$

which is read as "set B is a subset of set A" or as "B is a subset of A." Since there are members of set A which are not members of set B, we say "set B can be properly contained in set A" or simply "set B is a **proper subset** of set A."

The slash can be used to negate the symbol $\subset$. We can write

$$A \not\subset B$$

which is read "set A is not a subset of set B" because all the members of set A are not members of set B.

Suppose set C is defined as

$$C = \{3, 2, 1\}$$

Set C is a subset of set A since all members of C are members of set A. In fact, set C and set A are **equal sets** since they have exactly the same members. We say that "set C is an **improper subset** of A" since equal sets are defined to be improper subsets of each other. Therefore, we can also say "set A is an improper subset of set C."

The **set that has no members** is defined to be a proper subset of every set that has members and to be an improper subset of itself. This set is called the **empty set** or the **null set** and can be designated by using either of the symbols shown here.

$$\{\ \ \} \text{ is the empty set} \qquad \varnothing \text{ is the null set}$$

Thus we can say that $\{\ \ \} \subset A$ or $\varnothing \subset A$, read "the empty set is a subset of set A" and "the null set is a subset of set A," respectively, because **this set is considered to be a subset of every set.**

example 61.1 Given the sets $D = \{0, 1, 2\}$, $E = \{1, 2, 3, \ldots\}$, and $G = \{1, 3, 5\}$, tell which of the following assertions are true and which are false and why.

(a) $E \subset G$ \qquad\qquad (b) $G \subset E$ \qquad\qquad (c) $D \subset E$

solution (a) $E \subset G$ \qquad **False** \qquad All members of set E are not members of set G. For example, 2, which is an element of set E, is not an element of set G.

(b) $G \subset E$ \qquad **True** \qquad All members of set G are members of set E.

(c) $D \subset E$ \qquad **False** \qquad Zero, which is an element of set D, is not a member of set E.

61.B
subsets of the set of real numbers

In Lesson 4, we described those numbers called **real numbers**. Mathematicians use the symbol $\mathbb{R}$ to stand for the set of real numbers. The set of **real numbers** is said to be an **infinite set** because there is an infinite number of members of this set. An infinite set has an infinite number of subsets, but we normally restrict our attention to five subsets of the set of real numbers. These are the sets of **natural numbers, whole numbers, integers, rational numbers,** and **irrational numbers.** We define the set of **natural numbers** (counting numbers) as follows:

$$\text{Natural numbers } N = \{1, 2, 3, \ldots\}$$

If we list the number zero in addition to the set of natural numbers, we have designated the set of **whole numbers.**

$$\text{Whole numbers } W = \{0, 1, 2, 3, \ldots\}$$

We designate the set of **integers** by listing the set of whole numbers and their opposites. The symbol for the set of integers is the symbol $\mathbb{Z}$, which looks like a fancy form of the letter z. The reason for using a form of the letter z to designate the integers is that the German word for "integer" is "zahlen."

$$\text{Integers } \mathbb{Z} = \{\ldots, -3, -2, -1, 0, 1, 2, 3, \ldots\}$$

Every real number is either a rational number or an irrational number. A rational number is a number that **can be** represented as a quotient[†] (fraction) of integers. Thus each of the following numbers is a rational number:

$$\frac{1}{4} \qquad -\frac{3}{17} \qquad -10 \qquad 0.013$$

The numbers $\frac{1}{4}$ and $-\frac{3}{17}$ are already expressed as fractions of integers. The number -10 can be written as a quotient of integers in many ways, such as

$$-\frac{100}{10} \qquad \text{and} \qquad -\frac{3000}{300} \qquad \text{and} \qquad -\frac{270}{27}$$

[†]A fraction of integers whose denominator is not zero.

and the number 0.013 can be written as a fraction of integers in many ways, two of which are

$$\frac{13}{1000} \qquad \text{and} \qquad \frac{39}{3000}$$

Many numbers cannot be written as the ratio of two integers (whose denominator is not zero). Such numbers are called irrational numbers. An example of an irrational number is $\sqrt{2}$. Proving that $\sqrt{2}$ cannot be expressed as the ratio of two integers is beyond the scope of this book. Students interested in the proof should consult a basic text on number theory.

One fact that is useful to know is that if the square root, cube root, or any counting number root of any counting number is not a counting number, then it must be an irrational number. (The justification for such an assertion is too difficult for this text and can be found in more advanced texts.) Therefore, the following numbers are all examples of irrational numbers:

$$\sqrt{2} \quad \sqrt{3} \quad \sqrt{5} \quad \sqrt{6} \quad \sqrt{7} \quad \sqrt{10} \quad \sqrt{11} \quad \sqrt{12} \quad \sqrt{13}$$

Irrational numbers do not necessarily have to be roots of integers. The number π is an example of such an irrational number.

Some useful facts about irrational numbers that can be used by students in the problem sets are as follows:

1. The product of an irrational number and a nonzero rational number is an irrational number.
2. The sum of a rational number and an irrational number is an irrational number.

There are many, many more facts about the real numbers students can learn. Students who choose to study higher mathematics will learn more about the real numbers and their subsets. For our purposes, students need to know that the set of real numbers can be divided into two subsets—the set of rational numbers and the set of irrational numbers. These subsets of the real numbers are said to be **mutually exclusive** because they do not have any members in common.

In the chart below, we summarize what we have learned.

REAL NUMBERS

IRRATIONAL NUMBERS Real numbers that cannot be expressed as the fraction of two integers, such as: $\sqrt[3]{5}, \sqrt{2}, -\sqrt{2}, 2\sqrt{2}, \pi, 3\pi$, etc.	RATIONAL NUMBERS Real numbers that can be expressed as the fraction of two integers, such as: $\frac{1}{2}, 0.3, -\frac{2}{3}$, etc.
	INTEGERS Set of whole numbers and the opposites of the natural numbers: $\dots, -4, -3, -2, -1, 0, 1, 2, 3, 4, \dots$ WHOLE NUMBERS Set of natural numbers and the number 0 $0, 1, 2, 3, 4, \dots$ NATURAL OR COUNTING NUMBERS $1, 2, 3, 4, \dots$

Students are advised to use the chart on the previous page only to get information about which set is a subset of another. The chart should not be used to draw conclusions about how large a set is relative to other sets.

In this book, when we ask to which sets a particular number belongs, we restrict the possible answers to the sets of natural numbers, whole numbers, integers, rational numbers, irrational numbers, and real numbers. Problems such as the following will give practice in distinguishing between these sets.

example 61.2 $\frac{1}{2} \in$ {What subsets of the real numbers}?

solution   This asks that we identify the subsets of the real numbers of which the number $\frac{1}{2}$ is a member. If we restrict our reply to the sets discussed in this lesson, the answer is the sets of **rational** and **real numbers.**

example 61.3 $5 \in$ {What subsets of the real numbers}?

solution   The **naturals, wholes, integers, rationals,** and **reals.**

example 61.4 $3\sqrt{2} \in$ {What subsets of the real numbers}?

solution   Remember the fact stated in the lesson that the square root of a counting number is either a counting number or an irrational number. $\sqrt{2}$ is not a counting number, so it must be an irrational number. Recall also that the product of an irrational number by a rational number is an irrational number. Since 3 is a rational number and $\sqrt{2}$ is an irrational number, $3\sqrt{2}$ is an irrational number. Therefore, $3\sqrt{2}$ is a member of the set of **irrational numbers** and the set of **real numbers.**

example 61.5   Tell whether the following statements are true or false and then explain why:

(a) {Reals} $\subset$ {Integers}   (b) {Irrationals} $\subset$ {Reals}

(c) {Irrationals} $\subset$ {Rationals}   (d) {Wholes} $\subset$ {Naturals}

(e) {Integers} $\subset$ {Reals}

solution   (a) {Reals} $\subset$ {Integers}   **False**   The reals are not a subset of the integers. The integers are a subset of the reals.

(b) {Irrationals} $\subset$ {Reals}   **True**   All irrational numbers are also real numbers.

(c) {Irrationals} $\subset$ {Rationals}   **False**   The irrationals are not a subset of the rationals. In fact, no irrational number is also a rational number and vice versa.

(d) {Wholes} $\subset$ {Naturals}   **False**   The set of whole numbers is the set of natural numbers with the number zero added.

(e) {Integers} $\subset$ {Reals}   **True**   All five sets just discussed are subsets of the real numbers.

practice   **a.** Given the sets $A = \{0, 1, 2, 3, ...\}$, $B = \{0, 2, 4, 6\}$, and $C = \{1, 3, 5, 7\}$, tell which of the following assertions are true and which are false, and why:

(1) $B \subset A$ (2) $B \subset C$ (3) $C \subset A$

For problems b–f, confine your answers to those subsets of the real numbers discussed in this lesson.

b. $\dfrac{11}{6} \in$ {What subsets of the real numbers}?

c. $0.62 \in$ {What subsets of the real numbers}?

d. $4 \in$ {What subsets of the real numbers}?

e. $2\sqrt{2} \in$ {What subsets of the real numbers}?

f. $-4 \in$ {What subsets of the real numbers}?

problem set 61

1.
(39)   The patricians and plutocrats controlled the society. If they were in the ratio of 2 to 13 and a total of 315 belonged, how many were plutocrats?

2.
(52)   There are 10 students in Ms. Cantrell's algebra class. On the first test, six students scored 80%, while the other four students scored 90%. What was the overall average on the test?

3.
(58)   The girls' weightlifting team outlifted the boys' team by 140 percent. If the boys' team lifted 1400 pounds, how many pounds did the girls' team lift? Draw a diagram as an aid in solving the problem.

4.
(58)   Harry and Jack raised roses and petunias in their garden. If 15 percent of the flowers were roses and there were 120 roses, how many flowers were there in all? Draw a diagram as an aid in solving the problem.

5.
(45)   Find the range, median, mode, and mean of the following numbers:

$$6, 7, 8, 8, 16, 13, 12, 8, 7, 10, 11$$

6.
(39)   Draw a number line and graph the solution of $x \not\geq -2$.

7.
(28) $6\frac{4}{5}$ of what number is $1\frac{7}{10}$?

8.
(61)   (a) $-5 \in$ {What subsets of the real numbers}?

(b) $-5\sqrt{3} \in$ {What subsets of the real numbers}?

9.
(61)   (a) $\dfrac{3}{11} \in$ {What subsets of the real numbers}?

(b) $0 \in$ {What subsets of the real numbers}?

10.
(61)   Tell whether the following statements are true or false and explain why:

(a) {Rationals} $\subset$ {Reals}   (b) {Rationals} $\subset$ {Integers}

11.
(61)   Given the sets $A = \{0, 1, 2, 3\}$, $B = \{1, 2, 3, 4, ...\}$, and $C = \{2, 3, 4\}$, are the following statements true or false? Explain.

(a) $A \subset B$ (b) $C \subset B$ (c) $0 \notin A$ (d) $2 \in C$

12.
(31)   Solve: $-[-(-2p)] - 3(-3p + 15) = -(-4)(p - 12)$

13.
(57)   Add. Write the answer with all exponents positive: $x^{-1}y - y^{-1}$

Simplify.

14.
(55)
$$\dfrac{\dfrac{a}{b}}{c + x}$$

15.
(55)
$$\dfrac{a}{\dfrac{b}{c + x}}$$

Use substitution to solve for x and y:

16.
(59)
$$\begin{cases} 4x + y = -5 \\ 2x - y = -1 \end{cases}$$

17.
(59)
$$\begin{cases} x - 3y = -7 \\ 3x + y = -1 \end{cases}$$

Graph these equations on a rectangular coordinate system:

18. $y = -3x$
(51)

19. $y = 3x$
(51)

20. $4 + 3x - y = 0$
(56)

Add:

21.
(44)
$$\dfrac{4xy}{a} + \dfrac{4y}{ab^2} + \dfrac{2}{ab}$$

22. $my + \dfrac{p}{y}$
(44)

Multiply. Write the answers in descending order of the variable.

23. $(4x - 3)(x + 2)$
(49)

24. $(4x + 3)^2$
(49)

Simplify (write the answers with all exponents positive):

25.
(40)
$$\dfrac{a^0 x^2 x^0}{m^2 y^0 m^{-2}}$$

26.
(53)
$$\dfrac{(x^2 y^0)^2 y^0 k^2}{(2x^2 k^5)^{-4} y}$$

27. Factor the greatest common factor of $20x^2 m^5 k^6 - 10x^3 m^4 k^4 + 30x^5 m^4 k^6$.
(35)

28. Simplify: $-2\big[(3 + |-5|) - 6^0(-2 - 1)\big] - (-2)^3 + \sqrt[3]{-8}$
(19)

29. Find the perimeter of this figure.
(3)   Dimensions are in inches.

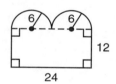

30. Find the lateral surface area of this
(15,60) right prism whose bases are regular
        pentagons. Dimensions are in feet.

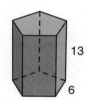

LESSON 62   *Square Roots • Higher Order Roots •*
Evaluating Using Plus or Minus

62.A

square roots   Every positive number has one positive and one negative square root. For example, the number 16 has two square roots: 4 and −4. We can verify that 4 and −4 are square roots of 16 by multiplying each of these numbers by itself to get 16.

$$(4)(4) = 16 \qquad \text{and} \qquad (-4)(-4) = 16$$

We use the square root radical sign, $\sqrt{}$, to designate the positive square root. (*Note*: **It is by convention that the radical sign is used to designate the positive square root and not the negative square root.**) Therefore,

$$\sqrt{4} = 2 \qquad \text{since} \qquad (2)^2 = 4$$

If we wish to indicate the negative square root of 4, we must write

$$-\sqrt{4} = -2$$

We state formally the definition of square root.

DEFINITION OF SQUARE ROOT

If x is greater than zero, then $\sqrt{x}$ is the unique positive real number such that

$$(\sqrt{x})^2 = x$$

Note that the expression or number under the square root sign, which is called the **radicand,** is chosen to be positive. We will defer discussing negative radicands until a future course. In this text, we will always assume that the radicand under a square root sign is positive.

The definition of square root says that the square root of a given positive number is that positive number which multiplied by itself equals the given positive number. Thus the square root of 2 times the square root of 2 is 2. Also, $\sqrt{2.42}$ times $\sqrt{2.42}$ must equal 2.42. If a is a positive number, the square root of a times the square root of a must equal a. Using the definition of square root and assuming that all radicands are positive, we can say that

(a) $\sqrt{2}\sqrt{2} = 2$ (b) $\sqrt{a}\sqrt{a} = a$

(c) $\sqrt{2.42}\sqrt{2.42} = 2.42$ (d) $\sqrt{x-1}\sqrt{x-1} = x - 1$

Recall from Lesson 61 that the square root of a counting number is either a counting number or an irrational number. In Lesson 61, we defined an irrational number as a real number that could not be expressed as the ratio of two integers. An irrational number can also be defined as a number whose decimal representation is a **non-repeating decimal numeral** of infinite length. (An example of a repeating numeral is the decimal representation of $\frac{1}{7} = 0.142857142857\ldots$. The digits 142857 repeat themselves indefinitely.) Therefore, we can never write down an exact decimal representation of an irrational number such as $\sqrt{2}$. We can use a calculator or a computer to give us decimal approximations; however, we will never be able to write an exact decimal representation of an irrational number.

example 62.1   Use a calculator to determine to five decimal places $\sqrt{18}$.

solution   Using a ten-digit calculator, we enter 18 followed by the square root key and get

$$4.242640687$$

We recognize that this number is **not** the exact square root of 18 since $\sqrt{18}$ is an irrational number that cannot be written as a decimal of finite length. Following the instructions given, we determine $\sqrt{18}$ to five decimal places.

4.24264

example 62.2   Use a calculator to determine the two square roots of 10 to six decimal places.

solution   Using a ten-digit calculator, we press 10 followed by the square root key and get

$$3.16227766$$

Rounding to six decimal places, we get

$$3.162278$$

There are two square roots of 10, one positive and one negative, so the two square roots of 10 (rounded to six decimal places) are

     3.162278   and   **−3.162278**

example 62.3   Without using a calculator, write the squares of the counting numbers 1 through 20.

solution

$1^2 = 1$	$2^2 = 4$	$3^2 = 9$	$4^2 = 16$	$5^2 = 25$
$6^2 = 36$	$7^2 = 49$	$8^2 = 64$	$9^2 = 81$	$10^2 = 100$
$11^2 = 121$	$12^2 = 144$	$13^2 = 169$	$14^2 = 196$	$15^2 = 225$
$16^2 = 256$	$17^2 = 289$	$18^2 = 324$	$19^2 = 361$	$20^2 = 400$

We suggest students memorize the squares of the counting numbers from 1 to 15.

example 62.4   Without using a calculator, determine between what two consecutive integers $\sqrt{10}$ lies.

solution   When we speak of where a number lies, we are speaking of where the number lies on the number line. We note that $3^2 = 9$ and $4^2 = 16$. The number whose square is 10 must lie **between 3 and 4.** In fact, since 10 is only slightly greater than 3^2, $\sqrt{10}$ is just a little bit more than 3. Using a calculator, we find that $\sqrt{10} \approx 3.16$. It turns out that if a number is slightly greater than a perfect square n^2, its square root is slightly greater than n. Also, if a number is slightly less than a perfect square n^2, its square root is slightly less than n. For example, $\sqrt{99}$ is slightly less than 10 and $\sqrt{101}$ is slightly greater than 10.

62.B
higher order roots

The notion of square roots can be extended. For example, when we refer to the cube root of a given number, we are referring to the number that when multiplied by itself three times produces the given number. It turns out that every real number only has one real number cube root, which is either negative or positive. For example,

$$\sqrt[3]{8} = 2 \quad \text{since} \quad 2^3 = 8$$

Also, $\sqrt[3]{-8} = -2 \quad \text{since} \quad (-2)^3 = -8$

DEFINITION OF CUBE ROOT

If x is a real number, then $\sqrt[3]{x}$ is the unique positive or negative real number such that

$$\left(\sqrt[3]{x}\right)^3 = x$$

Fourth roots can be defined similarly. However, like square roots, there are two fourth real number roots of a real number—one positive and one negative. When we use the radical sign to refer to a fourth root, we are referring to the positive fourth root.

> DEFINITION OF FOURTH ROOT
>
> If x is a real number, then $\sqrt[4]{x}$ is the unique positive real number such that
> $$\left(\sqrt[4]{x}\right)^4 = x$$

example 62.5   Without using a calculator, determine the following. Note that all answers are integers.

(a) $\sqrt[3]{8}$ (b) $\sqrt[4]{81}$ (c) $\sqrt[3]{-27}$

solution   (a) $\sqrt[3]{8} = \mathbf{2}$ since $2 \cdot 2 \cdot 2 = 8$

(b) $\sqrt[4]{81} = \mathbf{3}$ since $3 \cdot 3 \cdot 3 \cdot 3 = 81$

(c) $\sqrt[3]{-27} = \mathbf{-3}$ since $(-3)(-3)(-3) = -27$

62.C

evaluating using plus or minus

The equation $x^2 = 4$ has two solutions because 2 times 2 equals 4 and (-2) times (-2) also equals 4. The solution to this equation can be written two different ways. The first way is

$$x = 2 \qquad \text{or} \qquad x = -2$$

The second way is

$$x = \pm 2$$

Equations in which the highest power of the variable is 2 are called **quadratic equations.** Sometimes the solution of a quadratic equation is one number plus or minus another number. The solution can look like this

$$7 \pm 2$$

This notation simplifies into two different numbers: 7 plus 2 equals 9, and 7 minus 2 equals 5.

$$7 \pm 2 \qquad \text{means} \qquad 9 \text{ or } 5$$

We customarily write the two answers separated by a comma.

$$9, 5$$

example 62.6   Evaluate: $-2^2 + (-3)^2 \pm \sqrt{4}$

solution   The first term has a value of -4. The second term has a value of $+9$, so we have

$$-4 + 9 \pm \sqrt{4} \qquad \text{simplified}$$
$$= 5 \pm 2 \qquad \text{simplified}$$
$$= \mathbf{7, 3}$$

Thus the expression we are asked to evaluate has two values, 7 and 3.

practice   **a.**   Using a calculator, evaluate $\sqrt{17}$ to four decimal places.

b.   Without using a calculator, determine between what two consecutive integers $\sqrt{27}$ lies.

Evaluate. Do not use a calculator.

c. $\sqrt[3]{-27}$ **d.** $\sqrt{81} - \sqrt{144}$ **e.** $-1^2 + (-2)^2 \pm \sqrt{9}$

**problem set
62**

1. Thor and Igor have 100 and 120 woolly mammoths, respectively. If the average weight
(52) of Thor's woolly mammoths is 1000 lb and the average weight of Igor's woolly
mammoths is 725 lb, then what is the overall average weight of the mammoths?

2. The doctor increased the dosage to 128 percent of the original dosage. If the new dosage
(58) was 3840 units, what was the original dosage? Draw a diagram as an aid in solving the
problem.

3. Odessa could afford the coat because it was sold for 28 percent less than the original
(58) price. If the sale price was $324, what was the original price? Draw a diagram as an aid
in solving the problem.

4. Find the range, median, mode, and mean of the following numbers:
(45)

$$97, 98, 99, 100, 100, 101, 102, 103$$

5. (a) $3 \in$ {What subsets of the real numbers}?
(61)
   (b) $\sqrt{2} \in$ {What subsets of the real numbers}?

6. Evaluate. Do not use a calculator.
(62)
   (a) $\sqrt{9} + \sqrt{16}$ (b) $\sqrt{225} - \sqrt{169}$

7. Without using a calculator, determine between what two consecutive integers $\sqrt{57}$ lies.
(62)

8. Using a calculator, evaluate $\sqrt{19}$ to four decimal places.
(62)

9. Evaluate: $-2^2 + 3^2 \pm \sqrt{4}$
(62)

10. Tell whether the following statements are true or false, and explain why:
(61)
    (a) {Reals} $\subset$ {Rationals}   (b) {Irrationals} $\subset$ {Reals}

11. Solve: $-k(-2 - 3) - (-2)(-k - 5) = -2 - (-2k + 4) + \sqrt[3]{-27}$
(31)

Simplify:

12. $\dfrac{\dfrac{m}{x+y}}{\dfrac{a}{x+y}}$
(55)

13. $\dfrac{\dfrac{m}{x+y}}{\dfrac{m}{x}}$
(55)

14. Add. Write the answer with all exponents positive: $2a^{-1} + 4b^{-2}$
(57)

Use substitution to solve for x and y:

15. $\begin{cases} 5x - 3y = 1 \\ 7x - y = -5 \end{cases}$
(59)

16. $\begin{cases} 5x + 2y = -21 \\ -2x + y = 3 \end{cases}$
(59)

Graph on a rectangular coordinate system:

17. $y = 2$ 18. $y = -3$ 19. $y - x + 1 = 0$
(51) (51) (56)

Add:

20. $\dfrac{a}{x^2 y} + \dfrac{m+c}{y^2} - \dfrac{c}{x^2}$
(44)

21. $1 + \dfrac{y}{x}$
(44)

22. Factor the greatest common factor of $9x^3 y m^5 + 6m^2 y^4 p^4 - 3y^3 m^3$.
(35)

Simplify:

23. $\dfrac{4kp + 4kpx}{4kp}$
(35)

24. $\dfrac{a^{-2} p^2 a (a^0)^2}{(a^{-3})^2 (p^{-2})^{-2}}$
(53)

25. $mx(x^0 y)m^2 x^2(y^2)$
(21)

26. Expand by using the distributive property. Write the answer with all exponents positive.
(40)

$$-\frac{x^{-3}}{y}\left(\frac{x^3}{y^{-1}} - \frac{3x^{-3}}{y^2} + \frac{4x^2}{y^{-3}}\right)$$

27. Simplify by adding like terms: $-2^0 x^2 y^2 x^{-2} + \dfrac{3y^2}{x^2} - \dfrac{4x^{-2}}{y^{-2}} + 5y^2$

(41)

28. Evaluate: $a^{-2}b^{-3} - a^2 b^3$ if $2 - 3a = 8$ and $4b + 4 = 0$

(41)

29. Find the area of the shaded portion of this right triangle. Dimensions are in centimeters.

(8)

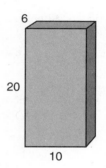

30. Find the volume of this right rectangular prism. Dimensions are in meters.

(20,60)

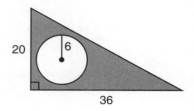

LESSON 63   *Product of Square Roots Rule • Repeating Decimals*

63.A
product of square roots rule

Square roots of many numbers, such as $\sqrt{50}$, $\sqrt{200}$, and $\sqrt{147}$, can be written in simplified form. To write one of these numbers in simplified form, we use the following rule:

> PRODUCT OF SQUARE ROOTS RULE
>
> If m and n are nonnegative real numbers, then
>
> $$\sqrt{m}\,\sqrt{n} = \sqrt{mn} \qquad \text{and} \qquad \sqrt{mn} = \sqrt{m}\,\sqrt{n}$$

This rule can be generalized to the product of any number of factors, and we say that the square root of any product may be written as the product of the square roots of the factors of the product. For example,

$$\sqrt{2 \cdot 5 \cdot 5} \qquad \text{can be written as} \qquad \sqrt{2}\,\sqrt{5}\,\sqrt{5}$$

$$\sqrt{3 \cdot 3 \cdot 3 \cdot 5} \qquad \text{can be written as} \qquad \sqrt{3}\,\sqrt{3}\,\sqrt{3}\,\sqrt{5}$$

We will use this rule in the following problems to help us simplify the expressions $\sqrt{50}$, $\sqrt{200}$, $\sqrt{147}$, and $\sqrt{108}$.

example 63.1   Simplify: $\sqrt{50}$

solution   We will first write 50 as a product of prime factors.

$$\sqrt{5 \cdot 5 \cdot 2}$$

Now we use the product of square roots rule to write the square root of the product as a product of square roots.

$$\sqrt{5}\sqrt{5}\sqrt{2}$$

Now, by definition $\sqrt{5}\sqrt{5} = 5$, so we have

$$\sqrt{5}\sqrt{5}\sqrt{2} = \mathbf{5\sqrt{2}}$$

example 63.2   Simplify: $\sqrt{200}$

solution   First we write 200 as a product of prime factors.

$$\sqrt{200} = \sqrt{2 \cdot 2 \cdot 2 \cdot 5 \cdot 5}$$

Now the square root of the products is written as the product of square roots.

$$\sqrt{2 \cdot 2 \cdot 2 \cdot 5 \cdot 5} = \sqrt{2}\sqrt{2}\sqrt{2}\sqrt{5}\sqrt{5}$$

Since by definition $\sqrt{2}\sqrt{2} = 2$ and $\sqrt{5}\sqrt{5} = 5$, we now have

$$\left(\sqrt{2}\sqrt{2}\right)\sqrt{2}\left(\sqrt{5}\sqrt{5}\right) = (2)\sqrt{2}(5) = \mathbf{10\sqrt{2}}$$

example 63.3   Simplify: $\sqrt{147}$

solution   First we write 147 as a product of prime factors.

(a) $\sqrt{147} = \sqrt{3 \cdot 7 \cdot 7}$ write as product of prime factors

(b) $\sqrt{3 \cdot 7 \cdot 7} = \sqrt{3}\sqrt{7}\sqrt{7}$ root of product equals product of roots

(c) $\sqrt{3}\left(\sqrt{7}\sqrt{7}\right) = \mathbf{7\sqrt{3}}$ definition of square root

example 63.4   Simplify: $\sqrt{108}$

solution   First we write 108 as a product of prime factors.

(a) $\sqrt{108} = \sqrt{2 \cdot 2 \cdot 3 \cdot 3 \cdot 3}$ write as product of prime factors

(b) $\sqrt{2 \cdot 2 \cdot 3 \cdot 3 \cdot 3} = \sqrt{2}\sqrt{2}\sqrt{3}\sqrt{3}\sqrt{3}$ root of product equals product of roots

(c) $\left(\sqrt{2}\sqrt{2}\right)\left(\sqrt{3}\sqrt{3}\right)\sqrt{3} = 2 \cdot 3\sqrt{3} = \mathbf{6\sqrt{3}}$ definition of square root

63.B
repeating decimals

When we write $0.\overline{3}$, we are expressing an abbreviated form of the number 0.333.... The bar over the 3 means that the digit 3 repeats without end. Numbers that contain a repeating decimal are rational numbers. We will show in our *Algebra 2* text how to determine what fraction of integers actually equals a given repeating decimal.

The fractional equivalents of some repeating decimals should be committed to memory. They are

$$\frac{1}{3} = 0.\overline{3} = 0.333... \qquad\qquad \frac{2}{3} = 0.\overline{6} = 0.666...$$

$$\frac{1}{9} = 0.\overline{1} = 0.111... \qquad\qquad \frac{1}{6} = 0.1\overline{6} = 0.1666...$$

practice Simplify:

    a. $\sqrt{75}$ **b.** $\sqrt{200}$ **c.** $\sqrt{189}$

    d. What fraction using counting numbers equals the repeating decimal $0.1\overline{6}$?

problem set 63

1. If the product of –3 and the opposite of a number is decreased by 7, the result is 1 greater
(33) than the number. What is the number?

2. Between Karnak and Edfu, the Pharaoh kept 1020 white goats. If these goats represented
(58) 17 percent of the total flock, how many goats did the Pharaoh have? Draw a diagram as
an aid in solving the problem.

3. After the temple was destroyed, Amenhotep found 1200 precious stones in the ruins. If
(58) 3 percent of these stones were rubies, how many rubies did Amenhotep find? Draw a
diagram as an aid in solving the problem.

4. Seventy sixth-graders had an average weight of 90 pounds. Thirty seventh-graders had an
(52) average weight of 100 pounds. What was the overall average weight of all these students?

5. 1.05 of what number is 4.221?
(30)

6. Use 12 unit multipliers to convert 8 cubic yards to cubic meters.
(53)

Simplify:

7. $\sqrt{300}$ **8.** $\sqrt{50}$
(63)   (63)

9. Indicate whether the following numbers are rational or irrational:
(61)

    (a) 3   (b) $\sqrt{9}$ (c) $-\sqrt{10}$ (d) $0.\overline{3}$

10. (a) $\dfrac{3}{2} \in$ {What subsets of the real numbers}?
(61)

    (b) $\sqrt{169} \in$ {What subsets of the real numbers}?

11. Without using a calculator, determine whether $\sqrt{16.0000001}$ is less than or greater
(62) than 4. Explain your answer.

12. Tell whether the following statements are true or false and explain why:
(61)

    (a) {Irrationals} $\subset$ {Rationals}   (b) {Wholes} $\subset$ {Naturals}

13. Evaluate. Do not use a calculator.
(62)

    (a) $\sqrt{225} - \sqrt{25}$ (b) $\sqrt{49} + \sqrt{81} - \sqrt{36}$

14. Without using a calculator, determine between what two consecutive integers $\sqrt{55}$ lies.
(62)

15. Using a calculator, evaluate $\sqrt{29}$ to four decimal places.
(62)

Use substitution to solve for x and y:

16. $\begin{cases} x - 2y = 8 \\ 2y - 3x = -4 \end{cases}$ **17.** $\begin{cases} 5x - 4y = -6 \\ x - 2y = -6 \end{cases}$
(59)   (59)

18. Write a conjunction that describes this graph.
(46)

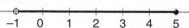

Graph on a rectangular coordinate system:

19. $y = -2x$ **20.** $y - 2x = 2$
(51)   (56)

Simplify:

21. $\dfrac{a}{\dfrac{1}{a+b}}$ **22.** $\dfrac{\dfrac{x}{x+y}}{x}$
(55)   (55)

23. Add. Write the answer in descending order of the variable.
(48)

$$5(x^3 - 2x^2 - 7x) - 3(x^4 + 3x^2 - 4) + 2(x^5 - 3x^2 - 2x + 1)$$

24. Factor the greatest common factor of $15m^2x^5k^4 - 5m^6x^6k^6 + 20m^4xk^5$.
(35)

Simplify. Write the answers with all exponents positive.

25. $\dfrac{3x^2m^5(2x^4m^2)}{3x^2m^5m^{-4}}$
(40)

26. $\left(\dfrac{3x^{-2}}{y^{-3}}\right)^{-2}\left(\dfrac{x^4}{y^6}\right)^2$
(53)

27. Add. Write the answer with all exponents positive: $m^{-2}xy^{-1} + mx^{-1}$
(57)

28. Evaluate: $-x^0 - x^2(x^0)^{-3} - \sqrt[3]{-y}$ if $2x + 5 = 1$ and $y = 64$
(41)

29. Find the area of this figure. Dimen-
(8)   sions are in inches.

30. A base of the right prism 25 feet high is shown. Find the surface area of the right prism.
(15,60)   Dimensions are in feet.

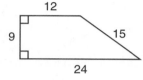 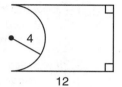

LESSON *64*   Domain • *Additive Property of Inequality*

64.A

domain   In problems in mathematics (and in physics, chemistry, and other mathematically based disciplines), the numbers that may be used as replacements for the variables are often restricted by the nature of the problem or by a restriction stated in the problem. For instance, if a person goes to the store with 25 cents to buy eggs, and eggs cost 10 cents each, the total amount of money that can be spent on eggs can be represented by the equation

$$\text{Total cost} = 10N_E \text{ cents}$$

where N_E represents the number of eggs bought. The customer may buy no eggs or 1 egg or 2 eggs. Thus the total cost of the eggs is as shown in (a), (b), or (c).

    (a)   0 EGGS   (b)   1 EGG   (c)   2 EGGS

         Cost = 10(0)   Cost = 10(1)   Cost = 10(2)

         Cost = 0 cents   Cost = 10 cents   Cost = 20 cents

In (a) we use 0 as the replacement for the variable, and in this case the cost is 0 cents. In (b) we use 1 as the replacement for the variable and find the cost to be 10 cents. In (c) we use 2 as the replacement for the variable and find that the cost is 20 cents. We cannot use 3 as a replacement for the variable because the buyer has only 25 cents to spend. We cannot use $2\frac{1}{2}$ as a replacement for the variable because only whole eggs are sold at the market. Neither could we use −4 as a replacement for the variable because buying −4 eggs makes no sense. We are restricted by the statement of the problem to using only the whole numbers

$$\{0, 1, 2\}$$

as replacements for the variable in the equation.

The set of permissible replacement values for the variables in a particular equation or inequality is called the *domain* for that equation or inequality.

Since **every equation and every inequality has a domain**[†] and since this is an important concept, it is customary in algebra courses to include problems in which the domain is specified. These problems should help with the concept of domain. The domains for the problems in this book were chosen by the author, sometimes with a purpose and sometimes just arbitrarily so that the problems would have specified domains. We will use the capital letter D as the symbol for domain in this book and will indicate the domains as sets by enclosing them within braces. For instance,

(a) $D = \{0, 1, 2\}$ (b) $D = \{\text{Reals}\}$ (c) $D = \{\text{Positive integers}\}$

The domains specified here are (a) the numbers 0, 1, and 2, (b) the set of real numbers, and (c) the set of positive integers. In the problem sets, if a domain is not specified, it should be assumed to be the set of real numbers.

example 64.1   Graph: $x > 2$; $D = \{\text{Real numbers}\}$

solution   We are asked to indicate those real numbers that are greater than 2 on the number line.

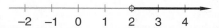

The open circle at 2 indicates that 2 is not to be included in the graph of those values of x that satisfy the conditions of the problem.

example 64.2   Graph: $x \not\geq 3$; $D = \{\text{Integers}\}$

solution   We are asked to indicate the **integers** that are neither greater than nor equal to 3. In other words, we are asked to indicate those integers that are less than 3.

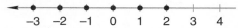

On the number line we have indicated the integers whose values are less than 3. Note that it is not necessary to place an open circle at 3. The arrow on the left indicates an infinite continuation.

example 64.3   Graph: $x \geq -1$; $D = \{\text{Reals}\}$

solution   We are asked to indicate all **real numbers** that are greater than or equal to -1.

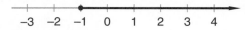

The graph indicates all real numbers that are greater than or equal to -1. The solid circle at -1 indicates that -1 is a member of the domain.

example 64.4   Graph: $x < -1$; $D = \{\text{Positive integers}\}$

solution   The solution is $\varnothing$, the null set, or $\{\ \}$, the empty set, because there are *no* positive integers that are less than -1.

example 64.5   Graph: $x \geq -5$; $D = \{\text{Positive integers}\}$

solution   The graph below indicates the numbers that are greater than or equal to -5 and that are also members of the set of positive integers.

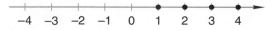

[†]If the domain is not stated, it is implied.

64.B

additive property of inequality

We restate the additive property of equality here.

> ### ADDITIVE PROPERTY OF EQUALITY
> If a, b, and c are any real numbers such that
> $$a = b$$
> then $a + c = b + c$ and $c + a = c + b$

Note that saying $a + c = b + c$ is the same as saying $c + a = c + b$ since the order of addends does not affect the sum. We have learned that we can use the additive property of equality to help us solve some equations. For example, we can solve $x + 4 = 8$ by adding -4 to both sides of the equation.

$$\begin{array}{rcl} x + 4 &=& 8 \\ -4 && -4 \\ \hline x &=& 4 \end{array}$$

The **additive property of inequality** is stated in the same way as the additive property of equality except that we use the > symbol rather than the = sign.

> ### ADDITIVE PROPERTY OF INEQUALITY
> If a, b, and c are any real numbers such that
> $$a > b$$
> then $a + c > b + c$ and $c + a > c + b$

This statement can be used to prove that the same quantity can be added to both sides of an inequality without changing the solution set of the inequality.

example 64.6 Graph: $x + 2 < 0$; $D = \{\text{Reals}\}$

solution We isolate x by adding -2 to both sides of the inequality, as permitted by the additive property of inequality.

$$\begin{array}{rcll} x + 2 &<& 0 & \text{given} \\ -2 && -2 & \text{add } -2 \text{ to both sides} \\ \hline x &<& -2 \end{array}$$

Now we graph the inequality $x < -2$.

The open circle at -2 indicates that -2 is not a member of the solution set.

example 64.7 Graph: $x - 3 \geq -5$; $D = \{\text{Integers}\}$

solution We isolate x by adding $+3$ to both sides of the inequality, as permitted by the additive property of inequality.

$$\begin{array}{rcll} x - 3 &\geq& -5 & \text{given} \\ +3 && +3 & \text{add } +3 \text{ to both sides} \\ \hline x &\geq& -2 \end{array}$$

Now we graph the solution $x \geq -2$ and remember that the domain is the set of integers.

Note that -2 is a solution to the inequality $x \geq -2$.

practice   Graph on a number line:

a. $x \not\leq -2$; $D = \{\text{Positive integers}\}$ **b.** $x \not\leq 4$; $D = \{\text{Reals}\}$

c. $x - 5 \not< 0$; $D = \{\text{Integers}\}$ **d.** $x + 2 < 5$; $D = \{\text{Integers}\}$

problem set   **1.** The number of bacteria increased by 280 percent overnight. If there were 30,000 bacteria
64   (58) yesterday, how many bacteria were present this morning? Draw a diagram as an aid in
solving the problem.

2. When Charles inspected the troops who survived, he found that 3600 were still alive. If
(58) 40 percent died in the fight, how many troops did he begin with? Draw a diagram as an
aid in solving the problem.

3. Edna and Mabel climbed 40 percent of the mountains in the whole country. If they
(58) climbed 184 mountains, how many mountains were in the country? Draw a diagram as
an aid in solving the problem.

4. Six employees at Larry's T-Shirt Palace received $1000 bonuses for their superb work.
(52) Another three employees received $700 bonuses for their great artistry. What was the
overall average bonus that Larry distributed?

5. Find the range, median, mode, and mean of the following numbers:
(45)

$$2, 4, 5, 10, 11, 11, 6, 5, 9, 8$$

6. Graph: $x - 2 \not< -1$; $D = \{\text{Reals}\}$
(64)

7. Write an inequality whose solution is shown in the graph below. Remember to designate
(64) the domain.

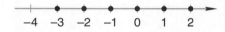

8. Simplify: $\sqrt{72}$
(63)

9. (a) $\sqrt{23}$ is between what two consecutive integers? (Do not use a calculator.)
(62)
(b) Using a calculator, evaluate $\sqrt{23}$ to three decimal places.

10. (a) $0.62 \in \{\text{What subsets of the real numbers}\}$?
(61,63)
(b) $3\sqrt{2} \in \{\text{What subsets of the real numbers}\}$?
(c) $0.\overline{3} \in \{\text{What subsets of the real numbers}\}$?

11. Without using a calculator, evaluate $\sqrt{400} + \sqrt{225} - \sqrt{81} - \sqrt{100}$.
(62)

12. Tell whether the following statements are true or false, and explain why:
(61)
(a) $\{\text{Naturals}\} \subset \{\text{Wholes}\}$ (b) $\{\text{Wholes}\} \subset \{\text{Naturals}\}$

Use substitution to solve for x and y:

13. $\begin{cases} 3x - 2y = 15 \\ 5x + y = 12 \end{cases}$ **14.** $\begin{cases} y + 2x = 12 \\ x + 2y = 12 \end{cases}$
(59)   (59)

Graph the following equations on a rectangular coordinate system:

15. $y = -2x + 5$ **16.** $y = -2x - 5$
(51)   (51)

17. If $g(x) = \left(x^2 - 3x\right)(x - 2)$, find $g(-2)$.
(28)

Multiply:

18. $(4x - 3)(12x + 2)$ **19.** $(3x - 2)(5x - 2)$
(49)   (49)

20. Simplify: $\dfrac{x}{\dfrac{x}{y}}$
(55)

21. Add. Write the answer with all exponents positive: $ax^{-2}y^{-1} + bxy^{-1}$
(57)

22. Factor the greatest common factor of $40x^4ym^7z - 20x^5y^5m^2z + 20xy^2m$.
(35)

Simplify:

23. $\dfrac{4x + 4x^2}{4x}$ **24.** $\dfrac{kp^{-2}k(p^0)^2}{kp(k)(p^{-2})^2}$ **25.** $\left(\dfrac{3m^2}{y^{-4}}\right)^2\left(\dfrac{m}{y}\right)$
(35)   (53)   (53)

26. Simplify by adding like terms. Write the answer with all exponents negative.
(41)

$$-\dfrac{3x^2y^{-2}}{x^{-2}y^{-2}} - 2x^4yy^{-1} + 4x^3xyy^{-1} - \dfrac{2x^2}{x^{-2}}$$

27. Expand by using the distributive property. Write answer with all exponents positive.
(40)

$$-\dfrac{x^{-2}}{y^4}\left(x^2y^4 - \dfrac{3x^{-2}}{y^4} - \dfrac{x^2}{y^{-4}}\right)$$

28. Evaluate: $x - (x^2)^0(x - y) - |x - y|$ if $2x + 6 = -4$ and $4 - 3y = 13$
(41)

29. Find the perimeter of this figure.
(3) Dimensions are in centimeters.

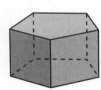

30. The area of a base of a right pentago-
(20,60) nal prism is 40 m^2 and the length of a
lateral edge is 14 m. Find the volume
of the right pentagonal prism.

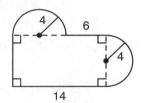

LESSON 65 *Addition of Radical Expressions • Weighted Average*

65.A

addition of radical expressions

In Lesson 18, we found that like terms may be added by adding the numerical coefficients of the terms. Radical expressions that have the same index and the same radicand designate the same number and are like terms. Thus the rule for adding like terms can be used to add like radical expressions. We add like radical expressions by adding the numerical coefficients.

example 65.1 Add: $4\sqrt{2} - 5\sqrt{2} + 12\sqrt{2}$

solution We add these like terms by adding their numerical coefficients.

$$4\sqrt{2} - 5\sqrt{2} + 12\sqrt{2} = (4 - 5 + 12)\sqrt{2} = \mathbf{11\sqrt{2}}$$

example 65.2 Add: $4\sqrt{3} + 3\sqrt{5} - 6\sqrt{3}$

solution Only like radical terms may be added.

$$4\sqrt{3} - 6\sqrt{3} + 3\sqrt{5} = (4 - 6)\sqrt{3} + 3\sqrt{5} = \mathbf{-2\sqrt{3} + 3\sqrt{5}}$$

example 65.3 Add: $-3\sqrt{2} + 5\sqrt{3} - 2\sqrt{2} + 8\sqrt{3}$

solution We omit the intermediate step and write the answer directly by simply adding the coefficients of like radical terms.

$$\mathbf{-5\sqrt{2} + 13\sqrt{3}}$$

example 65.4 Add: $4\sqrt{3} - 2\sqrt{2} + 6\sqrt{5}$

solution No two of these radical terms are like radical terms, so **no further simplification is possible.**

65.B
weighted average

Susan's score improved on each test. Her scores were 60, 71, and 91. The average of her scores is as follows:

$$\text{Average} = \frac{60 + 71 + 91}{3} = \frac{222}{3} = 74$$

The teacher did not think this was a fair grade since every test covered all previous material. The teacher thought that the second test was twice as important as the first test and the third test was four times as important as the first test. In other words, she counted the score on the first test once, the score on the second test twice, and the score on the third test four times. Therefore, she gave Susan one 60, two 71s, and four 91s.

$$\text{Weighted average} = \frac{60 + 71 + 71 + 91 + 91 + 91 + 91}{7} = \frac{566}{7} \approx 80.86$$

The weighted average of 80.86 was a fairer score than the real average of 74. The teacher gave the first test a **weight** of 1 because she counted it once. She gave the second test a weight of 2 because she counted it twice. She gave the third test a weight of 4 because she counted it four times. If we rearrange our numbers, we can use this problem to help define weighted average.

$$\text{Weighted average} = \frac{1(60) + 2(71) + 4(91)}{1 + 2 + 4} = \frac{566}{7} \approx 80.86$$

This shows us that the weighted average is the sum of the products of the scores S and their respective weights W, divided by the sum of the weights.

$$\text{Weighted average} = \frac{W_1(S_1) + W_2(S_2) + W_3(S_3) + \cdots + W_n(S_n)}{W_1 + W_2 + W_3 + \cdots + W_n}$$

example 65.5 Jim's scores were 60, 70, 80, and 90. What is the weighted average of his scores if the tests were weighted 1, 2, 4, and 6, in that order?

solution There were one 60, two 70s, four 80s, and six 90s.

$$\text{Weighted average} = \frac{1(60) + 2(70) + 4(80) + 6(90)}{1 + 2 + 4 + 6} = \frac{1060}{13} \approx \mathbf{81.54}$$

We divided by 13 because there were 13 scores. We note that 13 is the sum of the weights.

example 65.6 In the graduate level course Smith R. was taking, each of the three tests were weighted 20% and the final paper was weighted 40%. Smith's scores on the three tests were 60%, 70%, and 80%. His score on the final paper was 60%. What was Smith's overall score for the course?

solution   Weighting by percentages arises frequently. The first step in such a problem is to convert the percentages cited to their decimal equivalents. The weights for the three tests are 0.2 and the weight for the final paper is 0.4. When we ask for the overall score, we are simply asking for the weighted average. Applying the formula for weighted averages, we get

$$\text{Weighted average} = \frac{(0.2)(0.6) + (0.2)(0.7) + (0.2)(0.8) + (0.4)(0.6)}{0.2 + 0.2 + 0.2 + 0.4}$$

$$= 0.66, \text{ or } \mathbf{66\%}$$

Note that the sum of the weights was simply 1 since the sum of the weights expressed in percents equaled 100%.

practice   Add:

a. $3\sqrt{3} - 2\sqrt{2} + 5\sqrt{3}$ 　　　　　　　　**b.** $12\sqrt{7} + 6\sqrt{7} - 20\sqrt{7}$

c. $\sqrt{2} + 3\sqrt{2} - 4\sqrt{2} + 6\sqrt{3}$

d. The test scores were 70, 80, and 100. What was the weighted average of the test scores if the tests were weighted 1, 5, and 7, in that order?

problem set　**1.** Jaime's scores were 75, 80, 88, and 93. What was the weighted average of his scores if
65　*(65)*　the test scores were weighted 1, 2, 3, and 4, in that order?

2. The troll became incensed when he saw the billy goats prancing across the bridge.
(58)　Finally, he tore the bridge down—but not before 18 percent of the goats had crossed. If 45 goats had crossed, how many goats were there? Draw a diagram as an aid in solving the problem.

3. A 130 percent increase in the doll population resulted in a total of 1610 dolls. How many
(58)　dolls were present before the population increased? Draw a diagram as an aid in solving the problem.

Add:

4. $7\sqrt{5} - \sqrt{5} + 5\sqrt{3} - 3\sqrt{3}$ 　　　　　**5.** $8\sqrt{7} - 4\sqrt{11} - 3\sqrt{7} + 7\sqrt{11}$
(65)　　　　　　　　　　　　　　　　　　　　　　*(65)*

6. Without using a calculator, evaluate the following: $\sqrt{196} - \sqrt{49} - \sqrt{121} + \sqrt{256}$
(62)

7. Graph on a number line: $x + 3 > 5$; $D = \{\text{Positive integers}\}$
(64)

8. Write the inequality that describes this graph. Remember to designate the domain.
(64)

9. Indicate whether the following numbers are rational numbers or irrational numbers:
(61,63)

(a) $0.\overline{37}$ 　　　　　　　(b) $\sqrt{7}$ 　　　　　　　(c) $\sqrt[3]{-64}$

10. (a) $\pi \in \{\text{What subsets of the real numbers}\}$?
(61,63)

(b) $0.\overline{7} \in \{\text{What subsets of the real numbers}\}$?

11. Tell whether the following statements are true or false, and explain why:
(61)

(a) $\{\text{Naturals}\} \subset \{\text{Irrationals}\}$ 　　　　(b) $\{\text{Wholes}\} \subset \{\text{Integers}\}$

Use substitution to solve for x and y:

12. $\begin{cases} x + y = 10 \\ -x + y = 0 \end{cases}$ 　　　　　　　**13.** $\begin{cases} 3x - 3y = 3 \\ x - 5y = -3 \end{cases}$
(59)　　　　　　　　　　　　　　　　　　　　*(59)*

Graph the following equations on a rectangular coordinate system:

14. $y = -\dfrac{1}{2}x$
(51)

15. $\dfrac{1}{2}y = x - 1$
(56)

Add:

16. $\dfrac{a}{x + y} + \dfrac{5}{x^2}$
(52)

17. $1 + \dfrac{a}{b} - \dfrac{a^3}{b^2}$
(44)

18. $x + \dfrac{1}{x} + \dfrac{1}{x^2}$
(44)

19. Add. Write the answer with all exponents positive: $cz^{-1}x^2 + dx^{-1}z$
(57)

20. Simplify: $\dfrac{\dfrac{a}{x}}{\dfrac{1}{a^2}}$
(55)

21. Multiply: $(3p - 4)(2p + 5)$
(49)

22. Expand by using the distributive property. Write the answer with all exponents positive.
(40)

$$-3x^{-2}y^2\left(\dfrac{y^{-2}}{x^{-2}} + 4x^2y - \dfrac{2y^{-2}}{x^{-1}}\right)$$

Simplify:

23. $\dfrac{4kx - 4kx^2}{4kx}$
(35)

24. $\dfrac{x^2x^{-2}x^0y^2}{y^2\left(x^{-4}\right)^2}$
(53)

25. $\left(\dfrac{2x^{-2}y}{p}\right)^2\left(\dfrac{p^2x}{2}\right)^{-2}$
(53)

26. Simplify by adding like terms. Write the answers with all exponents positive.
(41)

$$\dfrac{3a^2x}{m} + \dfrac{5xm^{-1}}{a^{-2}} - \dfrac{4aax^{-1}}{x^{-2}m}$$

27. Evaluate: $-x^{-4} - x^2(x - m)$ if $-10 - 3x = 2x$ and $m + 3 = 6$
(41)

28. Simplify: $-3^0 - 3\left(-2 - 2^0\right)\left(-8^0 - 5\right) - \sqrt[4]{16}$
(19)

29. Find the area of this parallelogram. Dimensions are in inches.
(8)

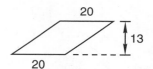

30. Find the lateral surface area of this right prism whose bases are regular pentagons. Dimensions are in feet.
(15,60)

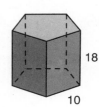

LESSON 66   *Simplification of Radical Expressions • Square Roots of Large Numbers*

66.A

**simplification
of radical
expressions**

In Lesson 63 we learned to simplify expressions such as $\sqrt{50}$ by using the product of square roots rule.

$$\sqrt{50} \;=\; \sqrt{5 \cdot 5 \cdot 2} \;=\; \sqrt{5}\sqrt{5}\sqrt{2} \;=\; 5\sqrt{2}$$

We can use the same procedure to simplify expressions such as

$$\sqrt{8} - \sqrt{50} + \sqrt{98}$$

if we first simplify each expression and then add the like radical terms. We begin by writing each radicand as a product of prime factors.

$$\sqrt{2 \cdot 2 \cdot 2} - \sqrt{5 \cdot 5 \cdot 2} + \sqrt{7 \cdot 7 \cdot 2}$$

Now we write the roots of products as products of roots.

$$\sqrt{2}\sqrt{2}\sqrt{2} - \sqrt{5}\sqrt{5}\sqrt{2} + \sqrt{7}\sqrt{7}\sqrt{2}$$

To finish, we simplify and add like radical terms.

$$2\sqrt{2} - 5\sqrt{2} + 7\sqrt{2} \;=\; 4\sqrt{2}$$

example 66.1   Simplify: $\sqrt{18} + \sqrt{8}$

solution

$\sqrt{18} + \sqrt{8}$	given
$\sqrt{2 \cdot 3 \cdot 3} + \sqrt{2 \cdot 2 \cdot 2}$	write each radicand as a product of prime factors
$\sqrt{2}\sqrt{3}\sqrt{3} + \sqrt{2}\sqrt{2}\sqrt{2}$	write roots of products as products of roots
$3\sqrt{2} + 2\sqrt{2} \;=\; \mathbf{5\sqrt{2}}$	simplify and add like radical terms

example 66.2   Simplify: $8\sqrt{27} - 3\sqrt{75}$

solution   The radicals in this problem have coefficients, so we will use parentheses to help us prevent errors. We can simplify $\sqrt{27}$ and $\sqrt{75}$ as

$$\sqrt{27} \;=\; \sqrt{3 \cdot 3 \cdot 3} \;=\; \sqrt{3}\sqrt{3}\sqrt{3} \;=\; 3\sqrt{3}$$

and

$$\sqrt{75} \;=\; \sqrt{5 \cdot 5 \cdot 3} \;=\; \sqrt{5}\sqrt{5}\sqrt{3} \;=\; 5\sqrt{3}$$

and now we replace $\sqrt{27}$ with $3\sqrt{3}$ and replace $\sqrt{75}$ with $5\sqrt{3}$.

$$8\sqrt{27} - 3\sqrt{75} \;=\; 8\left(3\sqrt{3}\right) - 3\left(5\sqrt{3}\right) \;=\; 24\sqrt{3} - 15\sqrt{3} \;=\; \mathbf{9\sqrt{3}}$$

example 66.3   Simplify: $\sqrt{27} - 3\sqrt{18} - 6\sqrt{45}$

solution

$\sqrt{27} - 3\sqrt{18} - 6\sqrt{45}$	given
$\sqrt{3 \cdot 3 \cdot 3} - 3\sqrt{3 \cdot 3 \cdot 2} - 6\sqrt{3 \cdot 3 \cdot 5}$	radicands written as products of prime factors
$\sqrt{3}\sqrt{3}\sqrt{3} - 3\sqrt{3}\sqrt{3}\sqrt{2} - 6\sqrt{3}\sqrt{3}\sqrt{5}$	write roots of products as products of roots
$3\sqrt{3} - 3 \cdot 3\sqrt{2} - 6 \cdot 3\sqrt{5}$	apply definition of square root
$\mathbf{3\sqrt{3} - 9\sqrt{2} - 18\sqrt{5}}$	simplify

No further simplification is possible since no two of the radical terms are like radical terms.

66.B
square roots of large numbers

We have learned to simplify the square root of a positive integer by first writing the integer as a product of prime numbers and then using the product of square roots rule, as we show here.

$$\sqrt{50} = \sqrt{5 \cdot 5 \cdot 2} = \sqrt{5}\sqrt{5}\sqrt{2} = \mathbf{5\sqrt{2}}$$

A similar but slightly different thought process makes the simplification of some of these expressions somewhat easier. Instead of expressing the integer as a product of prime numbers, we express it as a product of a non-square number and a perfect square. For example, in the problem above, as the first step we would write 50 as the product of 25 and 2

$$\sqrt{50} = \sqrt{25 \cdot 2}$$

and then use the product of square roots theorem to complete the simplification.

$$\sqrt{25 \cdot 2} = \sqrt{25}\sqrt{2} = \mathbf{5\sqrt{2}}$$

This thought process is especially helpful when the radicand has a factor that is the square of 10 or 100 or 1000 or 10,000 or any other power of 10.

$$(10)^2 = 100 \qquad (100)^2 = 10,000 \qquad (1000)^2 = 1,000,000$$
$$\text{and} \qquad (10,000)^2 = 100,000,000$$

We note that all of these products have an even number of zeros: 100 has two; 10,000 has four; 1,000,000 has six; and 100,000,000 has eight. **Thus, when we simplify, we always write the number so that one of its factors is an even power of 10.** An even power of 10 is the number 1 followed by an even number of zeros.

example 66.4   Simplify: $\sqrt{50,000}$

solution   We see four zeros, so we write

$$\sqrt{10,000 \cdot 5} = \sqrt{10,000}\sqrt{5} = \mathbf{100\sqrt{5}}$$

example 66.5   Simplify: $\sqrt{500,000}$

solution   It would not help to write $\sqrt{5 \cdot 100,000}$ because 100,000 has an odd number of zeros, so we write

$$\sqrt{50 \cdot 10,000} = \sqrt{50}\sqrt{10,000} = 100\sqrt{50}$$

Now we simplify $\sqrt{50}$ as $\sqrt{5 \cdot 5 \cdot 2} = \sqrt{5}\sqrt{5}\sqrt{2} = 5\sqrt{2}$. Thus

$$100\sqrt{50} = 100(5\sqrt{2}) = \mathbf{500\sqrt{2}}$$

example 66.6   Simplify: $\sqrt{40,000,000}$

solution   Looking for an even number of zeros, we write

$$\sqrt{1,000,000 \cdot 40} = \sqrt{1,000,000}\sqrt{40} = 1000\sqrt{40}$$

Now we simplify $\sqrt{40}$ as $\sqrt{2 \cdot 2 \cdot 10} = \sqrt{2}\sqrt{2}\sqrt{10} = 2\sqrt{10}$. Thus $1000\sqrt{40}$ can be written as

$$1000(2\sqrt{10}) = \mathbf{2000\sqrt{10}}$$

example 66.7   Simplify: $\sqrt{700,000,000}$

solution   Using eight zeros in one factor, we can write

$$\sqrt{7 \cdot 100,000,000} = \sqrt{7}\sqrt{100,000,000} = \mathbf{10,000\sqrt{7}}$$

practice   Simplify:

     a. $\sqrt{24} + \sqrt{48}$ **b.** $2\sqrt{18} - \sqrt{27}$ **c.** $\sqrt{50,000,000}$

problem set 66

1. ₍₃₃₎ The opposite of a number is tripled and then decreased by 7. The result is 3 greater than twice the number. What is the number?

2. ₍₅₈₎ Rubella found 60 escargots in the dell. This was only 80 percent of her largest find. What was the size of her largest find? Draw a diagram as an aid for solving the problem.

3. ₍₅₈₎ When the moot assembled, the village leader found that only 37 percent of those who attended had oil for their lamps. If 300 people attended the moot, how many had oil for their lamps? Draw a diagram as an aid for solving the problem.

4. ₍₆₅₎ In the Olympics, the athlete received a 90% score on the compulsory exercises, which are weighted 60%. In the optional round, weighted 40%, he received a 100%. What was the athlete's overall score?

5. ₍₄₅₎ In Michael's first quarter algebra class, his test scores were 60, 85, 92, 78, 89, 96, and 92. Find the range, median, mode, and mean of Michael's test scores.

6. ₍₂₈₎ $4\frac{2}{5}$ of what number is $7\frac{7}{10}$?

Solve:

7. ₍₂₅₎ $2\frac{1}{8}x - \frac{1}{5} = (5^2)(2^{-3})$

8. ₍₂₇₎ $0.003k + 0.188 - 0.001k = 0.2k - 0.01$

Simplify:

9. ₍₆₆₎ $5\sqrt{20} - 6\sqrt{32}$ **10.** ₍₆₆₎ $2\sqrt{45} - 3\sqrt{20}$ **11.** ₍₆₆₎ $\sqrt{70,000,000}$

12. ₍₆₄₎ Graph on a number line: $x - 3 \not< -5$; $D = \{\text{Positive integers}\}$

13. ₍₆₁₎ (a) $\sqrt{121} \in \{\text{What subsets of the real numbers}\}$?

     (b) $-17 \in \{\text{What subsets of the real numbers}\}$?

14. ₍₆₁₎ Tell whether the following statements are true or false, and explain why:

     (a) $\{\text{Integers}\} \subset \{\text{Rationals}\}$ (b) $\{\text{Integers}\} \subset \{\text{Wholes}\}$

Use substitution to solve for x and y:

15. ₍₅₉₎ $\begin{cases} x + 2y = 0 \\ 3x + y = -10 \end{cases}$ **16.** ₍₅₉₎ $\begin{cases} 5x + 4y = -28 \\ x - y = -2 \end{cases}$

Add:

17. ₍₅₂₎ $\dfrac{a}{x^2 y} + \dfrac{b}{x + y}$ **18.** ₍₄₄₎ $m + \dfrac{1}{m^2}$

Graph the following equations on a rectangular coordinate system:

19. ₍₅₁₎ $y = 2x + 2$ **20.** ₍₅₁₎ $y = 2x - 2$

Multiply:

21. ₍₄₉₎ $(4x + 5)^2$ **22.** ₍₄₉₎ $(5x - 3)(3x - 1)$

23. ₍₅₇₎ Add. Write the answer with all exponents positive: $px^{-1} + q^{-2}xy$

Simplify:

24. ₍₅₅₎ $\dfrac{x}{\dfrac{1}{xy + b}}$ **25.** ₍₅₅₎ $\dfrac{a}{\dfrac{1}{x}}$

26. ₍₃₅₎ Factor the greatest common factor of $12x^2 y^3 p^4 - 4x^3 y^2 p^6 + 16x^4 y^4 p^4$.

Simplify:

27.
(19) $\left[(-3 - 4^0) - (-3 - 2)\right] - \sqrt{25}$

28.
(53) $\dfrac{(3x^3y^5m^2)^2(x^2y)^{-2}}{x^2y^0y^{-4}}$

29.
(3)   Find the perimeter of this figure. Dimensions are in centimeters.

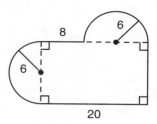

30.
(20,60)   A base of the right prism 2 meters high is shown. Find the volume of the right prism. Dimensions are in meters.

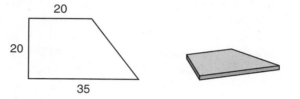

LESSON 67   *Review of Equivalent Equations • Elimination*

67.A

review of equivalent equations

We have said that equivalent equations are equations that have the same solutions. Thus, the solution sets for equivalent equations must be equal sets. The number 2 is a solution to $x + 4 = 6$ and is also a solution to $x^2 - 4 = 0$.

(a)	$x + 4 = 6$		(b)	$x^2 - 4 = 0$	
	$(2) + 4 = 6$			$(2)^2 - 4 = 0$	
	$6 = 6$	True		$4 - 4 = 0$	True

But these equations are not equivalent equations because equation (b) has another solution that is not a solution to equation (a). The other solution of equation (b) is –2.

(a)	$x + 4 = 6$		(b)	$x^2 - 4 = 0$	
	$(-2) + 4 = 6$			$(-2)^2 - 4 = 0$	
	$2 = 6$	False		$4 - 4 = 0$	True

We remember that if every term of a particular equation is multiplied by the same nonzero quantity, the resulting equation is an equivalent equation to the original equation. On the left below, we write the equation $x + y = 6$. On the right, we write the equation $2x + 2y = 12$, which is the original equation with every term multiplied by 2. The ordered pair (4, 2) is a solution to both equations.

$x + y = 6$		$2x + 2y = 12$	
$(4) + (2) = 6$		$2(4) + 2(2) = 12$	
$6 = 6$	True	$8 + 4 = 12$	True

Of course, there is an infinite number of ordered pairs of x and y that will satisfy either of these equations, but it can be shown that any ordered pair that satisfies either one of the equations will satisfy the other equation, and thus we say that these equations are equivalent equations!

67.B
elimination

Thus far, we have been using the substitution method to solve systems of linear equations in two unknowns. Now we will see that these equations can also be solved by using another method. **This new method is called the** *elimination method* **and is sometimes called more meaningfully the** *addition method.* To solve the following system of equations by using elimination,

$$\text{(a)} \quad \begin{cases} x + 2y = 8 \\ 5x - 2y = 4 \end{cases} \text{(b)}$$

we first assume that values of x and y exist that will make both of these equations true equations and that x and y in the equations represent these numbers.[†] Thus $x + 2y$ equals the number 8, and $5x - 2y$ equals the number 4. The additive property of equality permits the addition of equal quantities to both sides of an equation. Thus we can add $5x - 2y$ to the left-hand side of equation (a) and add 4 to the right-hand side of equation (a).

$$
\begin{array}{rl}
\text{(a)} & x + 2y = 8 \\
\text{(b)} & \underline{5x - 2y = 4} \\
& 6x \qquad = 12
\end{array}
$$

By doing this we have eliminated the variable y. Now we can solve the equation $6x = 12$ for x, find that $x = 2$, and use this value for x in *either* of the original equations to find that $y = 3$.

IN EQUATION (a)	IN EQUATION (b)
$x + 2y = 8$	$5x - 2y = 4$
$(2) + 2y = 8$	$5(2) - 2y = 4$
$2y = 6$	$-2y = -6$
$y = 3$	$y = 3$

example 67.1   Solve by using the elimination method:

$$\text{(a)} \quad \begin{cases} 2x - y = 13 \\ 3x + 4y = 3 \end{cases} \text{(b)}$$

If we add the equations in their present form,

$$
\begin{array}{rl}
\text{(a)} & 2x - y = 13 \\
\text{(b)} & \underline{3x + 4y = 3} \\
& 5x + 3y = 16
\end{array}
$$

we find that we have accomplished nothing because we have not eliminated one of the variables. But by proper use of the multiplicative property of equality, we can change the equations into equivalent equations that when added will result in the elimination of one of the variables. We choose to eliminate the variable y, and thus we will multiply every term in

---

[†] If values of x and y do not exist that will simultaneously make both equations true statements, the attempted solution will degenerate into a false equation such as $2 = 4$. The reasons for results like this will be discussed in Lesson 81.

equation (a) by 4 and every term in equation (b) by 1.[†] After the equations are added, we find that we have eliminated the variable y.

$$
\begin{array}{llll}
{}^{\ddagger}\text{(a)} \;\; 2x - \;\; y = 13 & \longrightarrow \; (4) \; \longrightarrow & 8x - 4y = 52 & \text{multiplied by 4} \\
\text{(b)} \;\; 3x + 4y = \;\; 3 & \longrightarrow \; (1) \; \longrightarrow & \underline{3x + 4y = \;\; 3} & \text{multiplied by 1} \\
& & 11x \quad\;\;\; = 55 & \text{added} \\
& & x = \mathbf{5} & \text{divided by 11}
\end{array}
$$

The number 5 can now be used to replace x in either of the original equations or either of the equivalent equations to find the corresponding value of y. We will demonstrate this by replacing x with 5 in both equation (a) and equation (b).

<table>
<tr><td align="center">EQUATION (a)</td><td align="center">EQUATION (b)</td></tr>
<tr><td align="center">$2(5) - y = 13$</td><td align="center">$3(5) + 4y = 3$</td></tr>
<tr><td align="center">$10 - y = 13$</td><td align="center">$15 + 4y = 3$</td></tr>
<tr><td align="center">$-y = 3$</td><td align="center">$4y = -12$</td></tr>
<tr><td align="center">$y = \mathbf{-3}$</td><td align="center">$y = \mathbf{-3}$</td></tr>
</table>

example 67.2   Solve by using the elimination method:

$$
\begin{array}{l}
\text{(a)} \\
\text{(b)}
\end{array}
\left\{
\begin{array}{l}
2x - 3y = 5 \\
3x + 4y = -18
\end{array}
\right.
$$

solution   There are many ways that the multiplicative property of equality can be used to form equivalent equations that when added will result in one of the variables being eliminated. We will show one way here and then repeat the problem and show another way. Look at the x terms in both equations. If we multiply the x term in the top equation by -3, the product will be $-6x$. If we multiply the x term in the bottom equation by 2, the product will be $+6x$. Of course, we must multiply every term in the equations by -3 and by 2, as required by the multiplicative property of equality. Now if we add the equations we can eliminate x since the sum of $+6x$ and $-6x$ is zero.

$$
\begin{array}{llll}
\text{(a)} \;\; 2x - 3y = \;\;\; 5 & \longrightarrow \; (-3) \; \longrightarrow & -6x + 9y = -15 & \text{multiplied by } -3 \\
\text{(b)} \;\; 3x + 4y = -18 & \longrightarrow \; (2) \; \longrightarrow & \underline{6x + 8y = -36} & \text{multiplied by 2} \\
& & 17y = -51 & \\
& & y = -3 &
\end{array}
$$

Now we will use -3 for y in the original equation (a) to find the corresponding value for x.

$$
\begin{array}{ll}
2x - 3y = 5 & \text{original equation (a)} \\
2x - 3(-3) = 5 & \text{substituted } -3 \text{ for } y \\
2x + 9 = 5 & \text{simplified} \\
2x = -4 & \text{added } -9 \text{ to both sides} \\
x = -2 & \text{divided both sides by 2}
\end{array}
$$

The solution is the ordered pair **(–2, –3).**

example 67.3   Solve by using the elimination method, but this time eliminate y.

$$
\begin{array}{l}
\text{(a)} \\
\text{(b)}
\end{array}
\left\{
\begin{array}{l}
2x - 3y = 5 \\
3x + 4y = -18
\end{array}
\right.
$$

[†]This will leave equation (b) unchanged. We say that we multiply by 1 to establish a general procedure for this type of problem.

[‡]The notations $\longrightarrow (4) \longrightarrow$ and $\longrightarrow (1) \longrightarrow$ are just bookkeeping notations and have no mathematical significance. We find them convenient to help us remember the number that we have used as a multiplier.

solution   Look at the *y* terms in both equations. One of them already has a minus sign. If we multiply the *y* term in equation (a) by +4, the product will be −12*y*. If we multiply the *y* term in equation (b) by +3, the product will be +12*y*. Of course, the sum of −12*y* and +12*y* is zero.

$$
\begin{array}{llll}
\text{(a) } 2x - 3y = 5 & \rightarrow \text{ (4) } \rightarrow & 8x - 12y = 20 & \text{multiplied by 4} \\
\text{(b) } 3x + 4y = -18 & \rightarrow \text{ (3) } \rightarrow & \underline{9x + 12y = -54} & \text{multiplied by 3} \\
& & 17x \qquad\quad = -34 \\
& & \quad x = -2
\end{array}
$$

Now we could use $x = -2$ in either of the original equations or either of the equivalent equations to find that the corresponding value of *y* is −3. Again we find that the solution is the ordered pair **(−2, −3).**

example 67.4   Use elimination to solve the system:

$$
\begin{array}{ll}
\text{(a)} & \begin{cases} 2x + 5y = -7 \\ 3x - 4y = 1 \end{cases} \\
\text{(b)} &
\end{array}
$$

solution   Since one of the *y* terms already has a minus sign, we choose to eliminate the *y* terms. We begin by multiplying both equations by the appropriate positive numbers.

$$
\begin{array}{llll}
\text{(a) } 2x + 5y = -7 & \rightarrow \text{ (4) } \rightarrow & 8x + 20y = -28 & \text{multiplied by 4} \\
\text{(b) } 3x - 4y = 1 & \rightarrow \text{ (5) } \rightarrow & \underline{15x - 20y = 5} & \text{multiplied by 5} \\
& & 23x \qquad\quad = -23 \\
& & \quad x = -1
\end{array}
$$

Now we will use −1 for *x* in equation (a) and find the corresponding value of *y*.

$$
\begin{array}{ll}
2x + 5y = -7 & \text{original equation (a)} \\
2(-1) + 5y = -7 & \text{substituted −1 for } x \\
-2 + 5y = -7 & \text{simplified} \\
5y = -5 & \text{added 2 to both sides} \\
y = -1 & \text{divided both sides by 5}
\end{array}
$$

Thus the solution is the ordered pair **(−1, −1).**

practice   Use elimination to solve:

a. $\begin{cases} 3x + 4y = -7 \\ 2x + 3y = -6 \end{cases}$ b. $\begin{cases} 5x + 2y = -3 \\ 2x + 3y = -10 \end{cases}$

problem set 67

1. The postprandial exercises were sit-ups and push-ups. The ratio of sit-ups to push-ups
(39) was 7 to 2. If Hominoid did 9180 exercises, how many were push-ups?

2. We estimate that the giant pyramid of Cheops near Cairo contains 2,300,000 blocks of
(58) stone. If the builders only used 80 percent of the available blocks, how many blocks were available?

3. Harriet was rated at her job with a pretest and a posttest. The posttest score counted
(65) double. If she scored 88 on the pretest and 93 on the posttest, what was the weighted average of her tests?

4. Use six unit multipliers to convert 200 cubic meters to cubic inches.
(53)

5. Solve: $\dfrac{1}{2}x + 0.75 = \dfrac{43}{4}$
(27)

Use elimination to solve for x and y:

6.
(67)
$$\begin{cases} x + y = 4 \\ x - y = 2 \end{cases}$$

7.
(67)
$$\begin{cases} 2x + 3y = 7 \\ 2x - y = 3 \end{cases}$$

8.
(67)
$$\begin{cases} 2x - 4y = -4 \\ 3x + 2y = 18 \end{cases}$$

Simplify:

9.
(66)
$6\sqrt{45} + \sqrt{180,000}$

10.
(66)
$2\sqrt{8} - 3\sqrt{32}$

11.
(66)
$2\sqrt{12} - 3\sqrt{18}$

12.
(64)
Graph on a number line: $x - 3 \not> 1$; $D = \{\text{Reals}\}$

13.
(61,63)
Indicate whether the following numbers are rational numbers or irrational numbers:

(a) -4 　　　　(b) π 　　　　(c) $\dfrac{22}{7}$ 　　　　(d) $8.\overline{3}$

14.
(61)
Tell whether the following statements are true or false, and explain why:

(a) $\{\text{Natural}\} \subset \{\text{Rationals}\}$ 　　　　(b) $\{\text{Integers}\} \subset \{\text{Irrationals}\}$

15.
(62)
(a) Without using a calculator, determine to what integer $\sqrt{145}$ is closest. Explain.

(b) Use a calculator to determine the value of $\sqrt{145}$ to four decimal places.

16.
(59)
Use substitution to solve for x and y: $\begin{cases} 4x + y = 25 \\ x - 3y = -10 \end{cases}$

Graph the following equations on a rectangular coordinate system:

17.
(51)
$x = -2$

18.
(51)
$y = -\dfrac{1}{2}x + 3$

19.
(28)
If $f(x) = x^4 - x^3 + 2x - 5$, find $f(-1)$.

Add:

20.
(52)
$\dfrac{m}{x^2 a} + \dfrac{3}{a(a + x)}$

21.
(44)
$4x + \dfrac{1}{y}$

Simplify:

22.
(55)
$\dfrac{\frac{1}{a}}{a}$

23.
(55)
$\dfrac{a}{\frac{a^2}{a + b}}$

24.
(35)
$\dfrac{12mx + 12mxy}{12mx}$

25.
(53)
$\left(2^2 y^3 p^4\right)^3$

26.
(40)
Expand by using the distributive property. Write the answer with all exponents positive.

$$\left(\frac{y^{-5}}{x^2} - \frac{3y^5 x^{-2}}{p} + \frac{y^5}{x^{-2}}\right)\frac{x^{-2}}{y^5}$$

27.
(41)
Evaluate: $-x^0 - x^2 - a(x - a) - \left|x^2\right|$ 　　if $2x - 8 = 4x$ and $a = \sqrt{16}$

28.
(62)
Simplify: $-2\left\{\left[(-2 - 3) - \left(-2^0 - 2\right) - 2\right] - 2\right\} \pm \sqrt{4}$

29.
(8)
Find the area of the shaded portion of this parallelogram. Dimensions are in inches.

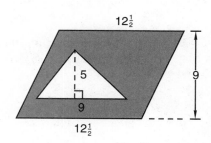

30. Find the surface area of this right trian-
(15,60) gular prism. Dimensions are in feet.

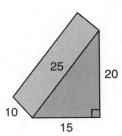

LESSON 68 *More About Complex Fractions*

In Lesson 61 we defined a **rational number** to be a number that **can** be expressed as a fraction of integers. Thus the following are all rational numbers:

$$13 \qquad \frac{4}{7} \qquad -\frac{5}{14} \qquad -\frac{6}{13} \qquad 2\frac{1}{3}$$

The number 13 is a rational number because the number 13 can be expressed as a fraction of integers by writing $\frac{52}{4}$. Of course, the mixed number $2\frac{1}{3}$ can be expressed as a fraction of integers as $\frac{7}{3}$.

An algebraic expression containing variables that is written in fractional form is called a **rational expression** because it has the same form as a rational number that is written as a fraction of integers. Thus all the following are **rational expressions:**

$$\frac{x+y}{4} \qquad \frac{a}{-b+c} \qquad 5 \qquad -\frac{7}{x} \qquad \frac{a+b}{14-x}$$

The number 5 is a rational number and is also considered to be a rational expression because *rational expression* is a general term that describes both rational numbers and rational expressions that include variables and/or numbers. Of course, the denominators of none of these expressions can equal zero. We recognize this fact, and in this section we will omit the restrictive notations that are normally used to emphasize that division by zero is not permissible.

We have learned how to add rational expressions by using the **denominator-numerator same-quantity rule.** We change denominators as required so that rational expressions may be added in three steps, as shown here by adding *a* over *b* to *x* over *y*.

$$\frac{a}{b} + \frac{x}{y} \quad \longrightarrow \quad (1) \;\; \frac{}{by} + \frac{}{by} \qquad \text{LCM used as new denominator}$$

$$(2) \;\; \frac{ay}{by} + \frac{bx}{by} \qquad \text{new numerators determined}$$

$$(3) \;\; \frac{ay+bx}{by} \qquad \text{added}$$

We have also used this same rule to help us simplify fractions of rational expressions (complex fractions).

$$\frac{\dfrac{x}{y}}{\dfrac{b}{c}} = \frac{\dfrac{x}{y} \cdot \dfrac{c}{b}}{\dfrac{b}{c} \cdot \dfrac{c}{b}} = \frac{\dfrac{xc}{yb}}{\dfrac{bc}{bc}} = \frac{\dfrac{xc}{yb}}{1} = \frac{xc}{yb}$$

We will use both of these procedures when we simplify expressions that are fractions of sums of rational expressions. These expressions are also called **complex fractions.**

example 68.1   Simplify: $\dfrac{\dfrac{x}{y} + \dfrac{1}{y}}{\dfrac{x}{y} - \dfrac{1}{y}}$

solution   The simplification is performed in two steps. The first step is to add the two expressions in the numerator and add the two expressions in the denominator.

$$\frac{\dfrac{x}{y} + \dfrac{1}{y}}{\dfrac{x}{y} - \dfrac{1}{y}} = \frac{\dfrac{x+1}{y}}{\dfrac{x-1}{y}}$$

Now use the **denominator-numerator same-quantity rule** by multiplying both the numerator and denominator by $\frac{y}{x-1}$, which is the reciprocal of the denominator $\frac{x-1}{y}$.

$$\frac{\dfrac{x+1}{\cancel{y}} \cdot \dfrac{\cancel{y}}{x-1}}{\dfrac{\cancel{x-1}}{\cancel{y}} \cdot \dfrac{\cancel{y}}{\cancel{x-1}}} = \frac{x+1}{x-1}$$

example 68.2   Simplify: $\dfrac{1 + \dfrac{1}{x}}{7}$

solution   First we add in the numerator.

$$\frac{1 + \dfrac{1}{x}}{7} = \frac{\dfrac{x+1}{x}}{7}$$

Now we finish by multiplying the denominator and the numerator by the reciprocal of 7, which is $\frac{1}{7}$.

$$\frac{\dfrac{x+1}{x} \cdot \dfrac{1}{7}}{\dfrac{\cancel{7}}{1} \cdot \dfrac{1}{\cancel{7}}} = \frac{x+1}{7x}$$

example 68.3   Simplify: $\dfrac{\dfrac{1}{x}}{1 - \dfrac{1}{x}}$

solution   We first add in the denominator.

$$\frac{\dfrac{1}{x}}{1 - \dfrac{1}{x}} = \frac{\dfrac{1}{x}}{\dfrac{x-1}{x}}$$

Now we finish by multiplying the denominator and the numerator by $\frac{x}{x-1}$, which is the reciprocal of $\frac{x-1}{x}$.

$$\frac{\dfrac{1}{\cancel{x}} \cdot \dfrac{\cancel{x}}{x-1}}{\dfrac{\cancel{x-1}}{\cancel{x}} \cdot \dfrac{\cancel{x}}{\cancel{x-1}}} = \frac{1}{x-1}$$

example 68.4   Simplify: $\dfrac{\dfrac{a}{b} + 1}{\dfrac{x}{b} + 4}$

solution   First we add in the numerator and add in the denominator.

$$\frac{\dfrac{a}{b} + 1}{\dfrac{x}{b} + 4} = \frac{\dfrac{a + b}{b}}{\dfrac{x + 4b}{b}}$$

Now we finish by multiplying both the denominator and the numerator by the reciprocal of the denominator.

$$\frac{\dfrac{a + b}{\cancel{b}} \cdot \dfrac{\cancel{b}}{x + 4b}}{\dfrac{\cancel{x + 4b}}{\cancel{b}} \cdot \dfrac{\cancel{b}}{\cancel{x + 4b}}} = \frac{a + b}{x + 4b}$$

example 68.5   Simplify: $\dfrac{a^{-1}x + b^{-1}y}{x^{-1}}$

solution   First we rewrite the expression so that all exponents are positive.

$$\frac{a^{-1}x + b^{-1}y}{x^{-1}} = \frac{\dfrac{x}{a} + \dfrac{y}{b}}{\dfrac{1}{x}}$$

Then we add the two fractions in the numerator.

$$\frac{\dfrac{x}{a} + \dfrac{y}{b}}{\dfrac{1}{x}} = \frac{\dfrac{xb + ya}{ab}}{\dfrac{1}{x}}$$

Now we finish by multiplying both the numerator and the denominator by the reciprocal of $\frac{1}{x}$, which is x.

$$\frac{\dfrac{xb + ya}{ab} \cdot x}{\dfrac{1}{x} \cdot x} = \frac{x(xb + ya)}{ab}$$

practice   Simplify:

a. $\dfrac{\dfrac{1}{w} + \dfrac{c}{w}}{\dfrac{1}{c}}$

b. $\dfrac{\dfrac{1}{m} + 5}{\dfrac{2}{m} - \dfrac{x}{m}}$

c. $\dfrac{ax^{-1} + by^{-1}}{x^{-1}}$

problem set
68

1. If a number is multiplied by 7 and this product is increased by 42, the result is 87 greater
(33)   than twice the opposite of the number. Find the number.

2. When Catman's entourage joined the motorcade, the total number of vehicles increased
(58)   130 percent. If the final count was 345, how many vehicles were present in the
beginning? Draw a diagram as an aid in solving the problem.

3. The new drug saved lives but produced side effects in 37 percent of the people who took
(58)   it. If 1110 people showed side effects, how many took the new drug? Draw a diagram as
an aid in solving the problem.

4. Roland averaged 4 jousts per journey on his first three journeys. He averaged 8 jousts per
(52) journey on his next 27 journeys. What was his overall average number of jousts per journey?

5. Galileo counted the number of falling stars that he observed each night for one week. The
(45) data he collected is shown:

Day	1	2	3	4	5	6	7
# of Falling Stars	122	170	133	134	152	134	119

Find the range, median, mode, and mean of the number of falling stars.

6. Use 12 unit multipliers to convert 12,000 cubic meters to cubic yards.
(53)

7. What fraction of 105 is $5\frac{1}{3}$?
(28)

Simplify. Write the answers with all exponents positive.

8. $\dfrac{3 - \dfrac{a}{b}}{\dfrac{1}{b} + b}$
(68)

9. $\dfrac{x^{-1} + y^{-1}}{x^{-1}}$
(68)

10. $4\sqrt{8} - 3\sqrt{12} + \sqrt{30{,}000}$
(66)

11. $2\sqrt{75} - 4\sqrt{243}$
(66)

Solve:

12. $20\frac{1}{4}x + 5\frac{1}{2} = 7\frac{1}{16}$
(25)

13. $-(-3)^3 - 2^2 = -2(-3k - 4)$
(31)

Use elimination to solve for x and y:

14. $\begin{cases} 5x + 3y = 1 \\ 7x + 3y = 5 \end{cases}$
(67)

15. $\begin{cases} 5x - 2y = 10 \\ 7x - 3y = 13 \end{cases}$
(67)

16. Graph on a number line: $x - 3 < -2$; $D = \{\text{Negative integers}\}$
(64)

17. Tell whether the following statements are true or false, and explain why:
(61)

(a) {Reals} $\subset$ {Irrationals}   (b) {Wholes} $\subset$ {Reals}

18. Use substitution to solve for x and y: $\begin{cases} x + 2y = 15 \\ 3x - y = 10 \end{cases}$
(59)

Graph the following equations on a rectangle coordinate system:

19. $y = -2x + 4$
(51)

20. $y - \frac{1}{3}x = 2$
(56)

Add. Write the answers with all exponents positive.

21. $\dfrac{1}{x^2} + \dfrac{m}{x^3 y} + \dfrac{c}{y}$
(44)

22. $2a^{-1}b - a^{-2}b + 1$
(57)

Simplify:

23. $\left(4x^{-2}y^2 m\right)^{-2} y$
(53)

24. $\left(\dfrac{x^{-1}}{y^{-1}}\right)^{-2} \left(\dfrac{y^2}{x^2}\right)^{-4}$
(53)

25. $\dfrac{x^{-2}y^{-2}\left(p^0\right)^2}{\left(x^2 y^2 p^3\right)^{-2}}$
(53)

26. $-3^2 - \dfrac{1}{(-3)^{-3}} + (-3)^0$
(29)

27. Evaluate $m - \left| -m + n^{-2} \right| + n^2 - \sqrt{m^2}$ if $3m + 7 = 1$ and $n = \sqrt[5]{-1}$
(41)

28. Simplify by adding like terms: $-x^2y + 3yx^2 - \dfrac{4y^3x}{y^2x^{-1}} - \dfrac{7x^{-2}}{x^{-4}y^{-1}}$
(41)

29. Find the perimeter of this figure.
(3) Dimensions are in centimeters.

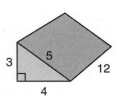

30. Find the volume of this right triangular
(20,60) prism. Dimensions are in meters.

LESSON 69 *Factoring Trinomials*

To begin a quick review of the nomenclature of polynomials in one variable, we say that **a monomial is a single expression of the form ax^n, where a is any real number and n is any whole number.** Thus the following expressions are monomials:

$$4 \qquad 6x^2 \qquad -2x^{15} \qquad 4.163x^4$$

The number 4 can be classified as a monomial because it can be thought of as $4x^0$, and if x is any nonzero real number, then x^0 equals 1, so $4x^0 = 4 \cdot 1 = 4$.

A binomial is the indicated algebraic sum of two monomials and a trinomial is the indicated algebraic sum of three monomials. We use the word *polynomial* as the general descriptive term to describe monomials, binomials, trinomials, and algebraic expressions that are the indicated sum of four or more monomials.

We are familiar with the vertical format for multiplying binomials, as shown here.

(a)
$$\begin{array}{r} x - 6 \\ x + 3 \\ \hline x^2 - 6x \\ + 3x - 18 \\ \hline x^2 - 3x - 18 \end{array}$$

(b)
$$\begin{array}{r} x - 6 \\ x - 3 \\ \hline x^2 - 6x \\ - 3x + 18 \\ \hline x^2 - 9x + 18 \end{array}$$

(c)
$$\begin{array}{r} x + 6 \\ x + 3 \\ \hline x^2 + 6x \\ + 3x + 18 \\ \hline x^2 + 9x + 18 \end{array}$$

In each of these three examples the product is a trinomial. We call these trinomials **quadratic trinomials in x,** or more simply, **quadratic trinomials.** The word *quadratic* tells us that the highest power of the variable is 2.

To reverse the process and factor the trinomials into a product of binomials, we must observe the pattern that developed when we did the multiplications. Note that:

1. The first term of the trinomial is the product of the first terms of the binomials.
2. The last term of the trinomial is the product of the last terms of the binomials.
3. The *coefficient* of the middle term of the trinomial is the *sum* of the last terms of the binomials.
4. If all signs in the trinomial are positive, all signs in both binomials are positive. If a negative sign appears in the trinomial, at least one of the terms of the binomials is negative.

We use these observations to help us factor trinomials. To factor the trinomial

$$x^2 - 3x - 18$$

we first write down two sets of parentheses to form an indicated product.

$$(\qquad)(\qquad)$$

Since the first term in the trinomial is the product of the first terms of the binomials, we enter x as the first term of each binomial.

$$(x\qquad)(x\qquad)$$

Now the product of the last terms of the binomials must equal -18, their sum must equal -3, and at least one of them must be negative. There are six pairs of integral[†] factors of -18:

$$(-18)(1) = -18 \qquad (2)(-9) = -18 \qquad (3)(-6) = -18$$
$$(18)(-1) = -18 \qquad (-2)(9) = -18 \qquad (-3)(6) = -18$$

Their sums are

$$(-18) + (1) = -17 \qquad (2) + (-9) = -7 \qquad (3) + (-6) = -3$$
$$(18) + (-1) = 17 \qquad (-2) + (9) = 7 \qquad (-3) + (6) = 3$$

Note that while all six pairs have a product of -18, only one pair (3 and -6) sums to -3. Therefore, the last terms of the binomials are 3 and -6, and so $(x + 3)$ and $(x - 6)$ are the factors of $x^2 - 3x - 18$ because

$$(x + 3)(x - 6) = x^2 - 3x - 18$$

Thus, the general approach to factoring a quadratic trinomial that has a leading coefficient of 1 is to determine the pair of integral factors of the last term of the trinomial whose sum equals the coefficient of the *middle term*. To factor $x^2 - 8x + 16$, we list the factors of $+16$ and see which pair, if any, sums to -8. If no pair of integral factors has a sum of -8, the trinomial cannot be factored over the integers.

PRODUCT	SUM
$(16)(1) = 16$	$(16) + (1) = 17$
$(-16)(-1) = 16$	$(-16) + (-1) = -17$
$(2)(8) = 16$	$(2) + (8) = 10$
$(-2)(-8) = 16$	$(-2) + (-8) = -10$
$(4)(4) = 16$	$(4) + (4) = 8$
$(-4)(-4) = 16$	$(-4) + (-4) = -8$

Thus we find that the factors of $x^2 - 8x + 16$ are $(x - 4)$ and $(x - 4)$ because the product of the first terms is x^2, the product of the last terms is $+16$, and the sum of the last terms is -8. This may seem to be a complicated procedure, but there is no shortcut until one becomes sufficiently familiar with the process to perform some of the calculations mentally. We will check our solution by multiplying the factors.

$$
\begin{array}{r}
x - 4 \\
x - 4 \\
\hline
x^2 - 4x \\
-4x + 16 \\
\hline
x^2 - 8x + 16 \quad \text{Check}
\end{array}
$$

[†] Since $(2\sqrt{3})(3\sqrt{3}) = 18$, both $2\sqrt{3}$ and $3\sqrt{3}$ are factors of 18. We will not consider nonintegral factors such as these and will concentrate on factors that are integers. The process of factoring a polynomial into expressions all of whose coefficients are integers is defined as factoring over the set of integers.

example 69.1   Factor: $x^2 - 14x - 15$

solution   The last term of the trinomial is –15, so the products of the last terms in the binomial must be –15. Four pairs of integral factors have a product of –15.

$$(3)(-5) = -15 \qquad (-3)(5) = -15 \qquad (-15)(1) = -15 \qquad (15)(-1) = -15$$

Only one pair of integral factors sums to –14.

$$(3) + (-5) = -2 \qquad (-3) + (5) = 2 \qquad \mathbf{(-15) + (1) = -14} \qquad (15) + (-1) = 14$$

Thus the constant terms of the binomials are –15 and 1 because these are the only two factors whose product is –15 and whose sum is –14. So $x^2 - 14x - 15$ in factored form is **$(x - 15)(x + 1)$.** We will check by multiplying the two factors.

$$
\begin{array}{r}
x \ - \ 15 \\
x \ + \ \ 1 \\
\hline
x^2 \ - \ 15x \\
+ \ \ \ x \ - \ 15 \\
\hline
x^2 \ - \ 14x \ - \ 15 \quad \text{Check}
\end{array}
$$

example 69.2   Factor: $x^2 + 3x - 10$

solution   The constant term is –10, which has four pairs of integral factors. They are 1 and –10, 10 and –1, –5 and 2, and 5 and –2. The only pair whose sum is +3 is the pair 5 and –2, so

$$x^2 + 3x - 10 = (x + 5)(x - 2)$$

We note that the trinomial in this problem was written as $x^2 + 3x - 10$ with the powers of the variable x in descending order. **If the trinomial is not in this form, the first step in factoring is to write the trinomial in descending powers of the variable.**

example 69.3   Factor: $-5x + x^2 + 6$

solution   We begin by writing the trinomial in descending powers of the variable as

$$x^2 - 5x + 6$$

The minus sign in the middle term indicates that at least one of the constant terms is a negative number. The last term, +6, is a positive number and is a product of the constant terms, so both of the constants must be negative since their product is positive. Two pairs of negative integers have a product of +6

$$(-3)(-2) = 6 \qquad \text{and} \qquad (-1)(-6) = 6$$

but only the first pair sums to –5.

$$(-3) + (-2) = -5$$

Thus $$x^2 - 5x + 6 = (x - 3)(x - 2)$$

example 69.4   Factor: $x^2 + 5 + 6x$

solution   We begin by writing the trinomial in descending powers of the variable

$$x^2 + 6x + 5$$

There are no minus signs in the trinomial, so all constants in the binomial factors will be positive. The constants therefore are positive integers whose product is +5 and whose sum is +6. The constants are +5 and +1 because

$$(5)(1) = 5 \qquad \text{and} \qquad 5 + 1 = 6$$

Thus $$x^2 + 6x + 5 = (x + 5)(x + 1)$$

practice Factor:

    a. $x^2 - x - 42$ **b.** $x^2 + x - 42$ **c.** $x^2 - 6x - 16$

problem set 69

1. *(58)* When the Huns debouched from the Alpine passes, Attila found that 18 percent of the spearpoints were dull. If 720 spearpoints were dull, how many spears did the Huns bring with them? Draw a diagram as an aid in solving the problem.

2. *(65)* In the graduate level course Diana was taking, each of three tests were weighted 20% and the final paper was weighted 40%. Diana's scores on the tests were 80%, 90%, 100%. Her score on the final paper was 80%. What was Diana's weighted average for the course?

3. *(61,63)* Indicate whether each of the following numbers is a rational number or an irrational number. Explain.

    (a) $0.\overline{142857}$ (b) $\sqrt[3]{27}$ (c) $\sqrt{5}$

Factor. Remember that the product of the constant terms must equal the constant in the trinomial and the sum of the constant terms must equal the coefficient of the middle term.

4. *(69)* $x^2 + 6x - 16$ **5.** *(69)* $x^2 - 6x + 9$ **6.** *(69)* $x^2 - 6x - 27$

7. *(69)* $p^2 - p - 20$ **8.** *(69)* $x^2 - 2x - 15$ **9.** *(69)* $p^2 - 4p - 21$

10. *(69)* $p^2 + p - 20$ **11.** *(69)* $k^2 - 3k - 40$ **12.** *(69)* $m^2 + 9m + 20$

First rearrange in descending order of the variable. Then factor.

13. *(69)* $x^2 + 33 + 14x$ **14.** *(69)* $-13p + p^2 + 36$ **15.** *(69)* $-30 + m^2 - m$

16. *(69)* $11n + n^2 + 18$ **17.** *(69)* $x^2 + 27 + 12x$ **18.** *(69)* $x^2 + 90 - 19x$

Simplify:

19. *(68)* $\dfrac{1 + \dfrac{1}{y}}{\dfrac{1}{y}}$ **20.** *(68)* $\dfrac{\dfrac{a}{b} - 4}{\dfrac{x}{b} - b}$

21. *(66)* $7\sqrt{20} - 5\sqrt{32} - \sqrt{45} - 5\sqrt{8}$ **22.** *(66)* $2\sqrt{18} - 5\sqrt{28} + 4\sqrt{300} - \sqrt{72}$

23. *(28)* If $f(x) = 7\sqrt{x + 18} - 5\sqrt{8x}$, find $f(2)$.

Use elimination to solve for x and y:

24. *(67)* $\begin{cases} 3x + 4y = -7 \\ 3x - 3y = 21 \end{cases}$ **25.** *(67)* $\begin{cases} 2x - 2y = -2 \\ 4x - 5y = -9 \end{cases}$

26. *(59)* Use substitution to solve for x and y: $\begin{cases} 3x + y = 9 \\ x - 4y = -10 \end{cases}$

27. *(41)* Simplify by adding like terms: $ab^2 - \dfrac{3ab}{b^{-1}} + \dfrac{2a^0 b^2}{a^{-1}} - \dfrac{4a^2}{b^2} + 2a^2 b^{-2}$

28. *(41)* Evaluate: $\left(x^2 - 6\right)\left(x^{-3} - x\right)$ if $x - 5 = -8$

29. *(8)* Find the area of this trapezoid. Dimensions are in inches.

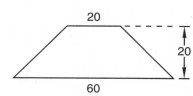

30. A right circular cylinder has a radius
(15,60) of 4 feet and a height of 14 feet, as
shown. Find the surface area of the
right circular cylinder.

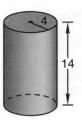

LESSON 70 *Probability • Designated Order*

70.A
probability

The study of probability began when people began studying games of chance such as flipping coins, rolling dice, drawing cards from a deck, or drawing marbles from an urn. Problems from games of chance still provide the best models on which to base a study of elementary probability, and we will concentrate on these problems.

The study of probability is based on the study of outcomes that have an equal chance of occurring. A fair coin should come up heads as often as it comes up tails if we flip it enough times. We will assume that our coins are fair. A die (singular of *dice*) has 6 faces. If we roll it enough times, each face should come up approximately one sixth of the time. We will assume that our dice are fair dice. We will also assume that individual marbles have equal chances of being drawn from an urn.

It is customary to call activities such as flipping coins, rolling dice, blindly selecting cards from a deck, and drawing marbles from an urn **experiments** and to call the individual results **outcomes.** We call the set of equally probable outcomes the **sample space** for the experiment. A toss of a fair coin has two equally probable outcomes. Thus, the sample space for a coin toss is heads or tails, as we show below.

The roll of a single die has six equally probable outcomes. Thus, the figure below shows the sample space for the roll of a single die.

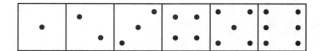

We define the **probability of a particular event** as the number of outcomes that satisfy the requirement divided by the total number of outcomes in the sample space.

$$P(\text{particular event}) = \frac{\text{number of outcomes that satisfy the requirement}}{\text{total number of outcomes in the sample space}}$$

> The probability of any event is a number between 0 and 1 inclusive. If no outcomes satisfy the requirement, the probability is 0, and if every outcome satisfies the requirement, the probability is 1.

Thus we see that a probability of –2 or $7\frac{1}{2}$ is not possible because the probability of any event must be a number between 0 and 1 inclusive.

example 70.1 A fair coin is tossed three times and comes up heads every time. What is the probability that on the next toss it will come up heads?

solution Tossing a coin is an **independent event.** The results of past independent events do not affect future independent events. The probability of a heads on the next toss is $\frac{1}{2}$.

$$P(H) = \frac{\text{number of outcomes that are } H}{\text{total number of outcomes in the sample space}} = \mathbf{\frac{1}{2}}$$

example 70.2 Six green marbles and eight red marbles are placed in an urn. One marble is drawn and then dropped back in the urn. Then a second marble is drawn and dropped back into the urn. Both marbles were red. If another marble is drawn, what is the probability that it will be red?

solution Drawing a marble from an urn is an independent event. Past results have no bearing on future results. There are 8 red marbles and 14 marbles total. Thus, the probability of drawing a red marble is $\frac{8}{14}$, which reduces to $\frac{4}{7}$.

$$P(\text{red marble}) = \frac{\text{number of outcomes that satisfy the requirement}}{\text{total number of outcomes in the sample space}} = \frac{8}{14} = \mathbf{\frac{4}{7}}$$

example 70.3 A single die is rolled three times. The results are   and , in that order. What is the probability that the next roll will produce a number greater than 2?

solution Rolls of a die are independent events. Past results do not count. The sample space for this event is shown here.

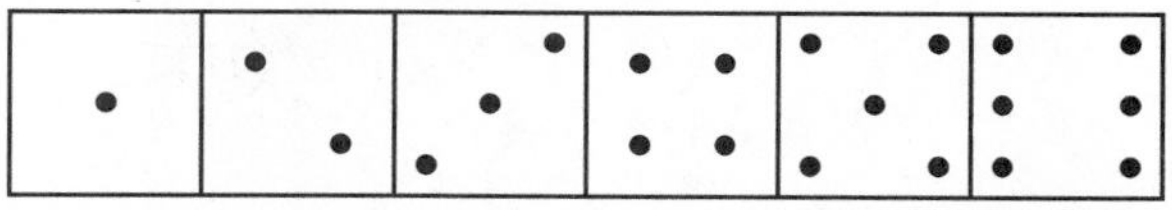

There are six equally possible outcomes in the sample space and four represent a number greater than two.

$$P(>2) = \frac{\text{number of outcomes that are greater than 2}}{\text{total number of outcomes in the sample space}} = \frac{4}{6} = \mathbf{\frac{2}{3}}$$

example 70.4 Two dice are rolled. What is the probability that the sum of the numbers rolled is (a) 7? (b) a number greater than 8?

solution First we draw a diagram of our sample space. The outcomes are the sums of the values on the individual dice, and there are 36 possible outcomes in our sample space.

Outcome of First Die \ Outcome of Second Die	1	2	3	4	5	6
1	2	3	4	5	6	7
2	3	4	5	6	7	8
3	4	5	6	7	8	9
4	5	6	7	8	9	10
5	6	7	8	9	10	11
6	7	8	9	10	11	12

(a)   The event is rolling a 7, and we see that 6 of these outcomes are 7, so

$$P(7) = \frac{\text{number of outcomes that equal 7}}{\text{total number of outcomes in the sample space}} = \frac{6}{36} = \frac{1}{6}$$

Thus, we find that the probability of rolling a 7 is $\frac{1}{6}$.

(b)   The event is rolling a number greater than 8, and we see that 10 of these outcomes are greater than 8, so

$$P(> 8) = \frac{\text{number of outcomes that are greater than 8}}{\text{total number of outcomes in the sample space}} = \frac{10}{36} = \frac{5}{18}$$

Thus, the probability of rolling a number greater than 8 is $\frac{5}{18}$.

70.B
designated order

The probability of future outcomes of independent events happening in a designated order is the product of the probabilities of the individual outcomes. For example, if we toss a coin twice, the probability of getting a heads on the first toss and a tails on the second toss is one fourth.

$$P(H, T) = P(H) \times P(T) = \frac{1}{2} \cdot \frac{1}{2} = \frac{1}{4}$$

We can see why this is true if we draw a **tree diagram** of the problem.

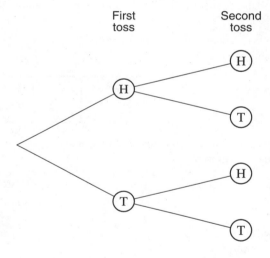

First toss   Second toss

There are two possible outcomes for the first toss, heads or tails, and the same two possible outcomes are possible for the second toss. Therefore, we can get (H, H) or (H, T) if the first toss is H and can get (T, H) or (T, T) if the first toss is T. Thus, there are four possible outcomes but only $\boxed{\text{H} \mid \text{T}}$ satisfies the requirement. So

$$P(H, T) = \frac{\text{number of outcomes that satisfy the requirement}}{\text{total number of possible outcomes}} = \frac{1}{4}$$

example 70.5   A fair coin is tossed four times. What is the probability that the first two times it comes up heads and the last two times it comes up tails?

solution   The probability of independent events happening in a designated order is the product of the probability of the individual events.

$$P(H, H, T, T) = \frac{1}{2} \cdot \frac{1}{2} \cdot \frac{1}{2} \cdot \frac{1}{2} = \frac{1}{16}$$

example 70.6   The spinner shown is spun twice. What is
the probability that the spinner stops on 4
and then on 3?

solution   The probability of getting a 4 and then getting a 3 is the probability of getting a 4 times the
probability of getting a 3. We assume from the drawing that the areas occupied by each of the
numbered regions are equal.

$$P(4, 3) = P(4) \times P(3) = \frac{1}{4} \times \frac{1}{4} = \frac{1}{16}$$

practice   **a.** A fair coin is tossed three times. What is the probability it will come up heads all three
times?

b. A single die is rolled three times. What is the probability that the next roll will produce
a number greater than 3?

c. Two dice are rolled. What is the probability that the sum of the numbers rolled is 6?

d. An urn contains 6 pink marbles and 7 blue marbles. A marble is drawn and dropped back
into the urn. Then a second marble is drawn and dropped back into the urn. Both marbles
were pink. If another marble is drawn, what is the probability that it will be pink?

e. The spinner shown is spun 3 times.
What is the probability that the spinner
stops on 2, then on 4, and then on 3?

problem set   **1.** A single die is rolled three times. What is the probability that the next roll will produce
70   (70) a number greater than 4?

2. Two dice are rolled. What is the probability that the sum of the numbers rolled is
(70)

(a) 4?   (b)   a number greater than 9?

3. A fair coin is tossed 3 times. What is the probability that the first time it comes up heads
(70) and the next two times it comes up tails?

4. The spinner shown is spun twice.
(70) What is the probability that the spinner
stops on 4 and then on 1?

5. An urn contains 5 green marbles and 9 purple marbles. A marble is drawn and dropped
(70) back into the urn. Then a second marble is drawn and dropped back into the urn. Both
marbles are green. If another marble is drawn, what is the probability that it will
be green?

6. Shenandoah's test scores were 70, 80, 80, and 90. What was his weighted average if the
(65) tests were weighted 1, 3, 5, and 4, in that order?

7. (a) Without using a calculator, determine to what integer $\sqrt{99}$ is closest.
(62)

(b) Use a calculator to determine the value of $\sqrt{99}$ to four decimal places.

Factor into the product of two binomials. Remember that the product of the constant terms must equal the constant in the trinomial and the sum of the constant terms must equal the coefficient of the middle term.

8. $m^2 - m - 2$
(69)

9. $y^2 + 2y - 15$
(69)

10. $p^2 + 4p - 5$
(69)

11. $a^2 - 10a + 9$
(69)

12. $b^2 - 2b - 3$
(69)

13. $p^2 - 11p + 10$
(69)

First rearrange in descending order of the variable. Then factor.

14. $a^2 + 32 + 18a$
(69)

15. $12b + b^2 + 27$
(69)

16. $16 + x^2 + 10x$
(69)

17. $15x + 50 + x^2$
(69)

18. $18 + x^2 + 11x$
(69)

19. $3x - 18 + x^2$
(69)

20. $20 - 9x + x^2$
(69)

21. $x^2 + 42 - 13x$
(69)

22. $-3 - 2x + x^2$
(69)

23. Find $f(-3)$ when $f(x) = -2x^2 + 3x - 7$.
(28)

24. Simplify: $2\sqrt{18} - 5\sqrt{8} + 4\sqrt{500} - \sqrt{125}$
(66)

25. Use elimination to solve for x and y:
(67)

$$\begin{cases} 2x + 5y = 7 \\ x + 3y = 4 \end{cases}$$

26. Use substitution to solve for x and y:
(59)

$$\begin{cases} x + y = 10 \\ x + 2y = 15 \end{cases}$$

Simplify. Write the answers with all exponents positive.

27. $\dfrac{\dfrac{m}{y} - y}{\dfrac{1}{y} - 1}$
(68)

28. $\dfrac{x^{-2} + yx^{-1}}{x^{-1}y^2}$
(68)

29. $\dfrac{\dfrac{a}{b} + \dfrac{1}{b}}{\dfrac{a}{b} - \dfrac{1}{b}}$
(68)

30. A right circular cylinder has a radius of 6 centimeters and a height of 24 centimeters, as shown. Find the volume of the right circular cylinder.
(20,60)

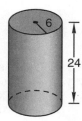

LESSON 71 *Trinomials with Common Factors • Subscripted Variables*

71.A

trinomials with common factors

As the first step in factoring we always check the terms to see if they have a common factor. If they do, we begin by factoring out this common factor. Then we finish by factoring one or both of the resulting expressions.

example 71.1   Factor: $x^3 + 6x^2 + 5x$

solution   If we first factor out the greatest common factor x, we find

$$x^3 + 6x^2 + 5x = x(x^2 + 6x + 5)$$

and now the trinomial can be factored as learned in Lesson 69 to get

$$x(x + 5)(x + 1)$$

example 71.2   Factor: $4bx^3 - 4bx^2 - 80bx$

solution   Here we see that the greatest common factor of all three terms is $4bx$, and if we factor out $4bx$, we find

$$4bx^3 - 4bx^2 - 80bx = 4bx(x^2 - x - 20)$$

Now the trinomial can be factored, and the final result is

$$4bx(x - 5)(x + 4)$$

example 71.3   Factor: $-x^2 + x + 20$

solution   **To factor trinomials in which the coefficient of the second-degree term is negative, it is helpful first to factor out a negative quantity.** Here we will factor out (-1).

$$-x^2 + x + 20 = (-1)(x^2 - x - 20)$$

Now we factor the trinomial to get

$$(-1)(x - 5)(x + 4)$$

which we can simply write as

$$-(x - 5)(x + 4)$$

Note that we could have multiplied the (-1) by either binomial in the factored expression to get

$$(-x + 5)(x + 4) \qquad \text{or} \qquad (x - 5)(-x - 4)$$

either of which is correct. However, it is customary to factor out negative factors so that all binomials in the factored expression have the form $x - c$ where c is a constant.

example 71.4   Factor: $-3x^3 - 6x^2 + 72x$

solution   First we factor out the greatest common factor $-3x$, and then we factor the trinomial.

$$-3x(x^2 + 2x - 24) = -3x(x + 6)(x - 4)$$

Thus we again find that the original trinomial has three factors.

71.B
subscripted variables

We have used the letter N to represent an unknown number but have always used x and y as variables in systems of two equations such as

$$\text{(a)} \quad \begin{cases} 5x + 10y = 125 \\ x + y = 16 \end{cases} \qquad \text{(b)} \quad \begin{cases} 5x + 25y = 290 \\ x = y + 2 \end{cases}$$

We have solved these systems by using either the substitution method or the elimination method. In Lesson 83, we will look at word problems about coins: nickels, dimes, and quarters. In the equations, we will use N_N for the number of nickels, N_D for the number of dimes, and N_Q for the number of quarters. We will solve the equations by using either the substitution method or the elimination method.

example 71.5   Use elimination to solve: $\begin{cases} 5N_N + 10N_D = 125 \\ N_N + N_D = 16 \end{cases}$

solution   We will multiply the bottom equation by −5 and add it to the top equation.

$$5N_N + 10N_D = 125 \quad \rightarrow \quad (1) \quad \rightarrow \quad 5N_N + 10N_D = 125$$
$$N_N + N_D = 16 \quad \rightarrow \quad (-5) \quad \rightarrow \quad \underline{-5N_N - 5N_D = -80}$$
$$5N_D = 45$$
$$N_D = 9$$

Since $N_N + N_D = 16$, $N_N = \mathbf{7}$.

example 71.6   Use substitution to solve: $\begin{cases} 5N_N + 25N_Q = 290 \\ N_Q = N_N + 2 \end{cases}$

solution   We will replace N_Q in the top equation with $N_N + 2$ and then solve.

$$5N_N + 25(N_N + 2) = 290 \qquad \text{replaced } N_Q \text{ with } N_N + 2$$
$$5N_N + 25N_N + 50 = 290 \qquad \text{multiplied}$$
$$30N_N + 50 = 290 \qquad \text{simplified}$$
$$30N_N = 240 \qquad \text{added } -50 \text{ to both sides}$$
$$N_N = \mathbf{8} \qquad \text{divided by 30}$$

Now, since $N_Q = N_N + 2$, $N_Q = \mathbf{10}$.

practice   Factor:

   a. $-4x^3 - 28x^2 - 48x$ **b.** $-x^2 + 24 + 2x$

   c. Use substitution to solve: **d.** Use elimination to solve:

      $\begin{cases} 6N_N + 24N_Q = 360 \\ N_Q = N_N + 5 \end{cases}$ $\begin{cases} 6N_N + 12N_D = 180 \\ N_N + N_D = 12 \end{cases}$

problem set 71

1. *(70)* A fair coin is tossed four times and comes up tails every time. What is the probability it will come up heads if tossed one more time?

2. *(70)* The spinner shown is spun 3 times. What is the probability that the spinner stops on 3, then on 4, and then on 2?

3. *(70)* An urn contains 10 red marbles and 3 black marbles. A marble is drawn and dropped back in the urn. Then a second marble is drawn and dropped back into the urn. The first marble drawn was red and the second was black. If another marble is drawn, what is the probability that it will be black?

4. *(70)* Two dice are rolled. What is the probability that the sum of the numbers rolled is

   (a) 7?   (b) a number greater than 7?

5. *(45)* The rock group the Ladybugs had 7 very successful albums. They sold 2, 4, 6, 5, 6, 8, and 7 million copies, in that order. Determine the range, median, mode, and mean of these numbers.

6. *(65)* On Mohammad's physical, he scored a 90 on the endurance portion and a 72 on the strength portion. If the endurance portion is twice as important as the strength portion, what was Mohammad's weighted score on the physical?

7. Use 10 unit multipliers to convert 10,000 square kilometers to square miles.
(10)

Factor each of the following trinomials. Begin by factoring out the greatest common factor.

8. $2x^2 + 10x + 12$
(71)

9. $5x^2 + 30x + 40$
(71)

10. $x^3 - x^2 - 20x$
(71)

11. $ax^2 + 6ax + 9a$
(71)

12. $-b^3 + 5b^2 + 24b$
(71)

13. $-3m^2 - 30m - 48$
(71)

14. Use elimination to solve:
(71)

$$\begin{cases} 5N_N + 10N_D = 135 \\ N_N + N_D = 17 \end{cases}$$

15. Use substitution to solve:
(71)

$$\begin{cases} 5N_N + 25N_Q = 340 \\ N_Q = N_N + 4 \end{cases}$$

First rearrange in descending order of the variable. Then factor:

16. $x^2 - 10 - 3x$
(69)

17. $x^2 + 12 + 7x$
(69)

18. $4 - 4x + x^2$
(69)

19. $x^2 + 14 + 9x$
(69)

20. $12 + x^2 + 8x$
(69)

21. $-3x - 18 + x^2$
(69)

Simplify:

22. $\dfrac{mx^{-1} + nz^{-3}}{y}$
(68)

23. $\dfrac{\dfrac{a}{x} + x}{\dfrac{1}{x} - 1}$
(68)

24. $5\sqrt{27} - 14\sqrt{12} + 3\sqrt{200} - 4\sqrt{300} + 6\sqrt{72}$
(66)

25. List the perfect squares less than 250.
(62)

26. Indicate whether the following numbers are rational numbers or irrational numbers:
(61,63)

(a) $\dfrac{\pi}{2}$ (b) $3.6\overline{2}$ (c) $\sqrt{81}$ (d) $-3\sqrt{2}$

27. Tell whether the following statements are true or false, and explain why:
(61)

(a) {Wholes} $\subset$ {Rationals}   (b) {Naturals} $\subset$ {Integers}

28. If $x + 24 = 21$, evaluate $x^2 - 9x^{-2} - 4 - |-x| + x^0$.
(41)

29. Find the area of the shaded portion of this trapezoid. Dimensions are in inches.
(8)

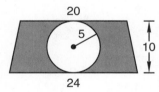

30. Find the surface area of this right triangular prism. Dimensions are in feet.
(15,60)

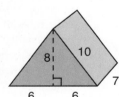

LESSON 72 *Factors That Are Sums • Pyramids and Cones*

72.A
factors that are sums

Sometimes a trinomial has a common factor that is a sum, as we see in the following examples.

example 72.1 Factor: $(a + b)x^2 - (a + b)x - 6(a + b)$

solution Each of the terms has the sum $(a + b)$ as a factor. If we factor out $(a + b)$, we get

$$(a + b)\left(x^2 - x - 6\right)$$

Now we finish by factoring the trinomial.

$$(a + b)(x - 3)(x + 2)$$

example 72.2 Factor: $(x + y)x^2 + 9x(x + y) + 20(x + y)$

solution First we factor out $(x + y)$.

$$(x + y)\left(x^2 + 9x + 20\right)$$

Now we finish by factoring the trinomial.

$$(x + y)(x + 4)(x + 5)$$

example 72.3 Factor: $m(x - 1)x^2 + 7mx(x - 1) + 10m(x - 1)$

solution The greatest common factor of each term of the trinomial is $m(x - 1)$. If we begin by factoring out this term, we get

$$m(x - 1)\left(x^2 + 7x + 10\right)$$

Now we complete the solution by factoring the trinomial $x^2 + 7x + 10$, and the result is

$$m(x - 1)(x + 2)(x + 5)$$

72.B
pyramids and cones

A **pyramid** is a geometric solid with one face a polygon (called the **base**) and the other faces triangles (called **lateral faces**) with a common vertex that is not in the plane of the base. The common vertex is called the **vertex** of the pyramid. The lateral faces intersect in segments called the **lateral edges** of the pyramid. The segment joining the vertex to the center of the base is called the **axis** of the pyramid. The **altitude** of a pyramid is the perpendicular segment from the vertex to the plane of the base. The length of the altitude is the **height** of the pyramid. In the figure on the left below we show a pyramid with the component parts labeled.

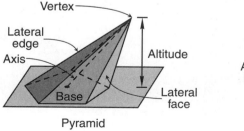
Pyramid

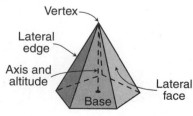
Right pyramid

The pyramid on the right above is a special type of pyramid. It is called a **right pyramid.** A right pyramid is a pyramid whose axis is at a right angle to the base. Note that in a right pyramid, the axis is also its altitude. In this book, we will confine our discussion of pyramids to right pyramids.

There is a certain type of right pyramid that mathematicians consider important. These right pyramids are called **regular pyramids.** A regular pyramid is a right pyramid whose base is a regular polygon (all sides of equal length and all angles of equal measure). The lateral faces of a regular pyramid are identical isosceles triangles. The height of a lateral face is called the **slant height** of the regular pyramid. **Slant height is defined only for regular pyramids.** In a regular pyramid, the altitude and a slant height determine a right triangle. In the figure below, we show a regular pyramid with the component parts labeled.

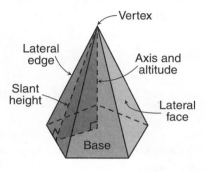

Regular pyramid

A pyramid is classified and named according to the shape of its base. Here we show four examples.

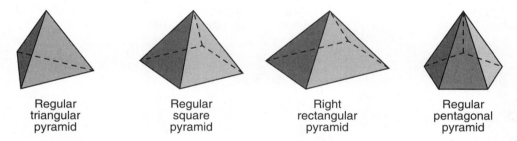

| Regular triangular pyramid | Regular square pyramid | Right rectangular pyramid | Regular pentagonal pyramid |

The right pyramid on the left is a **regular triangular pyramid** because its base is an equilateral triangle. The second right pyramid is a **regular square pyramid** because its base is a square. The third right pyramid is a **right rectangular pyramid** because its base is a rectangle. The fourth right pyramid is a **regular pentagonal pyramid** because its base is a regular pentagon.

A **cone** is like a pyramid except that its base is a closed curve instead of a polygon. The curved surface between the vertex and the base is called the **lateral surface.** The segment joining the vertex to the center of the base is called the **axis** of the cone. The **altitude** of a cone is the perpendicular segment from the vertex to the plane of the base. The length of the altitude is the **height** of the cone. In the figure on the left below, we show a cone with the component parts labeled.

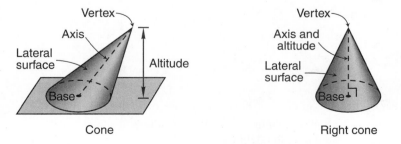

Cone   Right cone

The cone on the right above is a special type of cone. It is called a **right cone.** A right cone is a cone whose axis is at right angles to the base. Note that in a right cone, the axis is also its altitude.

A cone is classified and named according to the shape of its base. The right cone below is a **right circular cone** because its base is a circle. The distance from the vertex to any point of the circle that forms the base is called the **slant height** of the right circular cone. **Slant height is defined only for right circular cones.** In this book, we will confine our discussion of cones to right circular cones.

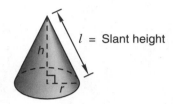

Right circular cone

volume of pyramids and cones   The volume of a pyramid can be easily computed given the area of the base and the height. We describe in the box below how to compute the volume of a pyramid. Since a cone is like a pyramid, the volume of a cone is computed in the exact same way as the volume of a pyramid.

VOLUME OF PYRAMIDS AND CONES

The volume of a pyramid or a cone is equal to one third the area of the base times the height.

---

example 72.4   Find the volume of the right rectangular pyramid.

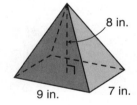

solution   First we find the area of the base of the right rectangular pyramid. Since the base of the right pyramid is a rectangle, the area of the base can be easily computed.

$$\text{Area of base} = (9 \text{ in.})(7 \text{ in.}) = 63 \text{ in.}^2$$

The volume of a pyramid is equal to one third the area of the base times the height. Therefore, we have

$$\text{Volume} = \frac{1}{3}(\text{area of base})(\text{height})$$

$$= \frac{1}{3}(63 \text{ in.}^2)(8 \text{ in.})$$

$$= \mathbf{168 \text{ in.}^3}$$

example 72.5   A right circular cone has a base of radius 6 ft and a height of 8 ft, as shown. Find the volume of the right circular cone.

solution   First we find the area of the base of the right circular cone. Since the base of the right cone is a circle, the area of the base can be easily computed.

$$\text{Area of base} = \pi(6 \text{ ft})^2 = 36\pi \text{ ft}^2$$

The volume of a cone is equal to one third the area of the base times the height. Therefore, we have

$$\text{Volume} = \frac{1}{3}(\text{area of base})(\text{height})$$

$$= \frac{1}{3}(36\pi \text{ ft}^2)(8 \text{ ft})$$

$$= 96\pi \text{ ft}^3$$

$$= 96(3.14) \text{ ft}^3$$

$$= \mathbf{301.44 \text{ ft}^3}$$

surface area   We remember that the lateral faces of a pyramid are the triangular faces between the vertex
of pyramids   and the base. We define the **lateral surface area** of a pyramid to be the sum of the areas of all the lateral faces. To find the surface area of a pyramid, we add the area of the base to the lateral surface area.

example 72.6   Find the surface area of this regular square pyramid. Dimensions are in centimeters.

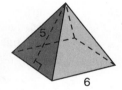

solution   Since the pyramid is a regular square pyramid, the base is a square and the lateral faces are identical isosceles triangles. The area of the base is simply the area of a square with sides of length 6 cm.

$$\text{Area of base} = (6 \text{ cm})^2 = 36 \text{ cm}^2$$

The lateral surface area is four times the area of a lateral face. Each lateral face is an isosceles triangle and looks as follows:

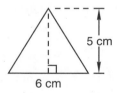

The area of each lateral face is the area of a triangle whose base is of length 6 cm and whose height is of length 5 cm.

$$\text{Area of a lateral face} = \text{area of triangle} = \frac{1}{2}(6 \text{ cm})(5 \text{ cm}) = 15 \text{ cm}^2$$

Thus, the lateral surface area is $4(15 \text{ cm}^2)$, or 60 cm^2. The surface area of the regular square pyramid is the area of the base added to the lateral surface area.

$$\text{Surface area} = \text{area of base} + \text{lateral surface area}$$

$$= 36 \text{ cm}^2 + 60 \text{ cm}^2$$

$$= \mathbf{96 \text{ cm}^2}$$

surface area of cones   We remember that the lateral surface of a cone is the curved surface between the vertex and the base. We define the **lateral surface area** of a cone to be the area of the lateral surface. Unfortunately, there is no simple way of computing the lateral surface area of a cone unless it is a right circular cone. The lateral surface area of a right circular cone is the product of pi, the radius of the circle, and the slant height, or $\pi r l$. To find the surface area of a cone, we add the area of the base to the lateral surface area.

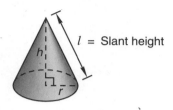

Right circular cone

Lateral surface area = $\pi r l$

example 72.7   A right circular cone has a base of radius 8 m and a slant height of 10 m, as shown. Find the surface area of the right circular cone.

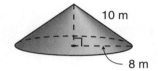

solution   The surface area of a right circular cone is the area of the base added to the lateral surface area. We note that the area of the base is the area of a circle. Also, the formula for the lateral surface area of a right circular cone is $\pi r l$, where r is the radius of the circle and l is the slant height of the right circular cone. Therefore, we have

$$\text{Surface area} = \text{area of base} + \text{lateral surface area}$$

$$= \pi r^2 + \pi r l$$

$$= \pi (8\text{ m})^2 + \pi(8\text{ m})(10\text{ m})$$

$$= 144\pi\text{ m}^2$$

$$= 144(3.14)\text{ m}^2$$

$$= \mathbf{452.16\text{ m}^2}$$

practice   Factor. Begin by factoring out the greatest common factor.

   a. $(a + b)x^2 + 8x(a + b) + 15(a + b)$

   b. $(m - b)x^2c - 2xc(m - b) - 24c(m - b)$

   c. Find the volume of the right rectangular pyramid.

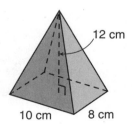

   d. A right circular cone has a base of radius 9 m and a slant height of 15 m, as shown. Find the surface area of the right circular cone.

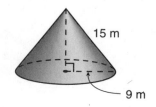

problem set 72

1. ⁽⁷⁰⁾ The spinner shown is spun 3 times. What is the probability that the spinner stops on 2, then 4, and on 2 again?

2. ⁽⁷⁰⁾ An urn contains 7 orange marbles and 8 blue marbles. A marble is drawn and dropped back in the urn. The marble drawn was orange. If another marble is drawn, what is the probability that it will be orange?

3. ⁽⁷⁰⁾ A fair coin is tossed five times and comes up heads three times and tails two times. What is the probability it will come up tails if tossed one more time?

4. ⁽⁷⁰⁾ Two dice are rolled. What is the probability that the sum of the numbers rolled is

(a) 5?   (b) a number greater than 5?

5. ⁽⁶⁵⁾ In an art competition, Spica's ratings were 9 for technique, 8 for style, 9 for originality, and 7 for organization. What was his overall weighted average if the ratings were weighted 5, 4, 5, and 2, in that order?

6. ⁽⁵⁸⁾ For some strange reason, Johnny's new diet caused him to gain weight rather than lose weight. If his weight increased 25 percent to 310 pounds, what did he weigh before he began to diet? Draw a diagram as an aid in solving the problem.

Factor. Begin by factoring out the greatest common factor.

7. ⁽⁷²⁾ $(x - 1)x^2 + 7x(x - 1) + 10(x - 1)$

8. ⁽⁷²⁾ $m(y + 1)x^2 + 4(y + 1)mx + 4(y + 1)m$

9. ⁽⁷²⁾ $(z - 5)x^2 + 5(z - 5)x + 6(z - 5)$

10. ⁽⁷²⁾ $(x + y)m^2 + 12(x + y)m + 35(x + y)$

11. ⁽⁷¹⁾ $2x^3 + 16x^2 + 30x$ 12. ⁽⁷¹⁾ $abx^2 - 5abx - 24ab$

First rearrange in descending order of the variable. Then factor:

13. ⁽⁶⁹⁾ $m^2 + 10m + 16$ 14. ⁽⁶⁹⁾ $-48 - 8n + n^2$ 15. ⁽⁶⁹⁾ $y^2 + 56 - 15y$

16. ⁽⁶⁹⁾ $p^2 - 55 - 6p$ 17. ⁽⁶⁹⁾ $12t + 35 + t^2$ 18. ⁽⁶⁹⁾ $y^2 + 50 + 51y$

19. ⁽²⁷⁾ Solve: $-0.003k - 0.03k - 0.3k - 666 = 0$

20. ⁽⁶⁴⁾ Write a conjunction that describes this graph. Specify the domain.

$$\xleftarrow{\quad} \underset{-5}{\circ} \;\; \underset{-4}{|} \;\; \underset{-3}{|} \;\; \underset{-2}{|} \;\; \underset{-1}{|} \;\; \underset{0}{|} \;\; \underset{1}{|} \;\; \underset{2}{\bullet} \xrightarrow{\quad}$$

Simplify:

21. ⁽⁶⁸⁾ $\dfrac{\dfrac{m}{p} + p}{\dfrac{1}{p} - x}$

22. ⁽⁶⁸⁾ $\dfrac{a + \dfrac{b}{a}}{\dfrac{1}{a} - 4}$

23. ⁽⁶⁸⁾ $\dfrac{x^{-1} + y^{-1}}{(xy)^{-1}}$

24. ⁽²⁸⁾ If $g(x) = \sqrt[3]{x^2 - 1} + 2\sqrt{x + 1}$, find $g(3)$.

25. ⁽⁶⁷⁾ Use elimination to solve:

$$\begin{cases} 5x - 2y = 9 \\ 3x - y = 6 \end{cases}$$

26. ⁽⁷¹⁾ Use substitution to solve:

$$\begin{cases} 10N_D + 25N_Q = 495 \\ N_Q = N_D + 10 \end{cases}$$

27. Tell whether the following numbers are rational numbers or irrational numbers:
(61,63)

(a) $2\sqrt{3}$ (b) $7.\overline{231}$ (c) -14.7 (d) $\sqrt{289}$

28. Simplify: $3\sqrt{18} - 7\sqrt{8} + 3\sqrt{50} + \sqrt{32}$
(66)

29. Find the perimeter of this figure. Dimensions are in centimeters.
(3)

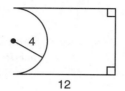

30. Find the volume of the right rectangular pyramid.
(72)

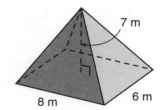

LESSON 73 *Factoring the Difference of Two Squares •*
Probability Without Replacement

73.A

factoring the difference of two squares

Since each of the terms in the following binomials is a perfect square,

$$x^2 - y^2 \qquad 4p^2 - 25 \qquad m^2 - 16$$

these binomials are sometimes called **the difference of two squares.** They can be generated by multiplying the sum and difference of two monomials.

$$
\begin{array}{lll}
x \;+\; y & 2p \;+\; 5 & m \;+\; 4 \\
x \;-\; y & 2p \;-\; 5 & m \;-\; 4 \\
\hline
x^2 + xy & 4p^2 + 10p & m^2 + 4m \\
\; - xy - y^2 & \; - 10p - 25 & \; - 4m - 16 \\
\hline
x^2 \; - y^2 & 4p^2 \; - 25 & m^2 \; - 16
\end{array}
$$

We note in each case that the middle term is eliminated because the numerical coefficients of the addends that would form the middle term have the same absolute value but are opposite in sign.

If we are asked to factor a binomial that is the difference of two squares, such as

$$9m^2 - 49$$

the problem is a problem in recognition. There is no procedure to follow. We recognize that each term of the binomial is a perfect square and that the binomial can be written as

$$(3m)^2 - (7)^2$$

Now from the pattern developed above, we can write

$$9m^2 - 49 = (3m + 7)(3m - 7)$$

In general, the difference of two squares, $F^2 - S^2$, can be factored as follows:

$$F^2 - S^2 = (F - S)(F + S)$$

example 73.1   Factor: $-4 + x^2$

solution   **We recognize that both of the terms are perfect squares.** We begin by reversing the order of the terms and writing the squared terms as

$$x^2 - 4 = (x)^2 - (2)^2$$

and now we can write the factored form as

$$(x + 2)(x - 2)$$

example 73.2   Factor: $49m^2 - a^2$

solution   **We recognize that each of the terms is a perfect square** and that the binomial can be written as

$$(7m)^2 - (a)^2$$

The factored form of this binomial is

$$(7m + a)(7m - a)$$

example 73.3   Factor: $-36a^2 + 25y^2$

solution   **We recognize that both of the terms are perfect squares.** We begin by reversing the order of the terms and writing the squared terms as

$$25y^2 - 36a^2 = (5y)^2 - (6a)^2$$

Now we write the factored form as

$$(5y + 6a)(5y - 6a)$$

example 73.4   Factor: $-36x^6y^4 + 49a^2$

solution   **Again we recognize that both of the terms are perfect squares.** We begin by rearranging the order of the terms and then factoring by inspection.

$$\left(7a + 6x^3y^2\right)\left(7a - 6x^3y^2\right)$$

73.B
probability without replacement

When we make successive random selections of marbles from an urn, the probability of a certain outcome on the second draw is affected by whether or not the marble selected on the first draw is returned before the second draw is made.

example 73.5   An urn contains 3 black marbles and 5 white marbles. A marble is drawn at random and replaced. Then a second marble is randomly drawn. (a) What is the probability that both marbles are black? (b) If the first marble is not replaced before the second marble is drawn, what is the probability that both marbles are black?

solution   (a)   The probability of a black marble on the first draw is $\frac{3}{8}$. Since the first marble is replaced, the probability of a black marble on the second draw is also $\frac{3}{8}$. So

$$P(\text{both black}) = \frac{3}{8} \cdot \frac{3}{8} = \frac{9}{64}$$

(b)   The probability of a black marble on the second draw is not the same because the first marble was not replaced. If the first draw was black, then the probability of a black marble on the second draw is $\frac{2}{7}$ because only 2 black marbles and 7 marbles total remain. Thus, the probability of 2 black marbles when there is no replacement between draws is

$$P(\text{both black}) = \frac{3}{8} \cdot \frac{2}{7} = \frac{6}{56} = \frac{3}{28}$$

example 73.6   An urn contains 4 red marbles and 7 blue marbles. Two marbles are drawn at random. What is the probability that the first is red and the second is blue if the marbles are drawn (a) with replacement? (b) without replacement?

solution   (a)   The probability of a red marble on the first draw is $\frac{4}{11}$. Since the first marble is replaced, the probability of a blue marble on the second draw is $\frac{7}{11}$. So

$$P(\text{red, then blue}) = \frac{4}{11} \cdot \frac{7}{11} = \frac{\mathbf{28}}{\mathbf{121}}$$

(b)   The probability of a blue marble on the second draw is not the same because the first marble was not replaced. If the first draw was red, then the probability of a blue marble on the second draw is $\frac{7}{10}$ because only 10 marbles remain. Thus, the probability of drawing one red marble, then one blue marble when there is no replacement between draws is

$$P(\text{red, then blue}) = \frac{4}{11} \cdot \frac{7}{10} = \frac{28}{110} = \frac{\mathbf{14}}{\mathbf{55}}$$

practice   Factor these binomials:

   a. $64x^2 - 81y^2$ **b.** $-25 + 100m^2$ **c.** $y^4x^2 - 169z^{10}$

   d.   An urn contains 4 purple marbles and 3 pink marbles. Two marbles are drawn at random. What is the probability that both marbles are purple if the marbles are drawn

      (1)   with replacement?   (2)   without replacement?

   e.   An urn contains 5 orange marbles and 6 blue marbles. Two marbles are drawn at random. What is the probability that the first marble is orange and the second marble is blue if the marbles are drawn

      (1)   with replacement?   (2)   without replacement?

problem set   **1.**   An urn contains 6 purple marbles and 4 pink marbles. A marble is drawn at random and
73   *(73)*   not replaced. Then a second marble is drawn. What is the probability that both marbles are purple?

   2.   An urn contains 2 orange marbles and 5 blue marbles. A marble is drawn at random and
   (70)   replaced. Then a second marble is drawn. What is the probability that the first marble is orange and the second marble is blue?

   3.   A fair coin is tossed three times. What is the probability that the first two tosses come up
   (70)   tails and the third toss comes up heads?

   4.   Two dice are rolled. What is the probability that the sum of the numbers rolled is
   (70)
      (a)   3?   (b)   a number less than 3?

   5.   Rosemary saw 900 of them in all. If this number was 150 percent greater than the number
   (58)   she expected to see, how many did she expect to see? Draw a diagram as an aid in solving the problem.

   6.   Hannibal noted that the average weight of the first 4 animals was 2000 pounds. The
   (52)   average weight of the next 96 animals was only 100 pounds. What was the average weight of all the animals?

Factor these binomials.

   7. $4p^2x^2 - k^2$ **8.** $-4m^2 + 25p^2x^2$ **9.** $-9x^2 + 4y^2$
   (73)   *(73)*   *(73)*

   10. $9k^2a^2 - 49$ **11.** $p^2 - 4k^2$ **12.** $36a^2x^2 - k^2$
   (73)   *(73)*   *(73)*

Factor the trinomials. Always begin by writing the trinomials in descending order of the variables and by factoring out the greatest common factor.

13. $x^2 - x - 20$ **14.** $4x^2 - 4x - 80$ **15.** $2b^2 - 48 - 10b$
(69)   (71)   (71)

16. $-90 - 39x + 3x^2$ **17.** $(a + b)x^2 + 7(a + b)x + 10(a + b)$
(71)   (72)

18. $pm^2 + 9pm + 20p$ **19.** $5k^2 + 30 + 25k$ **20.** $-x^2 - 8x - 7$
(71)   (71)   (71)

21. Graph on a number line: $-6 \leq x \leq 3$; $D = \{\text{Integers}\}$
(64)

22. Indicate whether each of the following numbers is a rational number or an irrational
(61,63) number:

(a) $\dfrac{\pi}{2}$ (b) $32.\overline{76}$ (c) $-3\sqrt{3}$ (d) $-\sqrt{121}$

23. Use 10 unit multipliers to convert 25,000 square miles to square kilometers.
(10)

24. Use elimination to solve: **25.** Use substitution to solve:
(67)   (71)

$$\begin{cases} 5x - 2y = 3 \\ 2x - 3y = -1 \end{cases}$$ $$\begin{cases} N_P + N_N = 175 \\ N_P + 5N_N = 475 \end{cases}$$

26. Add: $\dfrac{x}{x(x + y)} + \dfrac{1}{x} - \dfrac{y}{x + y}$
(52)

Simplify:

27. $3\sqrt{125} + 2\sqrt{45} - \sqrt{50,000}$ **28.** $\dfrac{x^{-1} + 1}{yx^{-1} + x}$
(66)   (68)

29. Solve: $-[2(-3 - k)] = -4(-3) - |-3|k$
(31)

30. A right circular cone has a base of
(72) radius 3 in. and a height of 4 in., as
shown. Find the volume of the right
circular cone.

LESSON 74 *Scientific Notation*

In science courses, it is sometimes necessary to use extremely large numbers and extremely small numbers. For example, to calculate the number of molecules in 1000 liters of gas, it would be necessary to multiply 1000 times 1000 times a very large number such as 26,890,000,000,000,000,000, which represents the number of molecules in a cubic centimeter of gas. Besides requiring a lot of paper, multiplying these numbers in their present form is cumbersome and often leads to errors since it is easy to miscount the number of zeros. If we use a type of mathematical shorthand called **scientific notation,** however, computations such as the above can be performed easily and accurately.

To write a number in scientific notation, the numerator and the denominator are multiplied by the required power of 10 that will place the decimal point immediately to the right of the first nonzero digit in the number (*Note*: We are simply applying the denominator-numerator same-quantity rule). For example, if we wish to write the number

0.0000416

in scientific notation, we would like to place the decimal point between the 4 and the 1.

$$4.16$$

To accomplish this, we multiply the number by 10^5, and we must also divide by 10^5 to keep from changing the value of the expression

$$0.0000416 = \frac{0.0000416}{1} \frac{10^5}{10^5} = \frac{4.16}{10^5}$$

Now, if we remember that $\frac{1}{10^5}$ can be written as 10^{-5}, we can write

$$0.0000416 = \frac{4.16}{10^5} = 4.16 \times 10^{-5}$$

We have described the algebraically correct procedure, but since scientific notation is used so often, we prefer to use another thought process which is much easier to use but not quite so rigorous.

When we look at numbers written in scientific notation, such as

$$4.16 \times 10^{+b} \qquad \text{and}^\dagger \qquad 4.16 \times 10^{-b}$$

we think of 10^{+b} as a decimal point indicator that tells us that the true location of the decimal point is really b places to the right of where it is written and 10^{-b} as a decimal point indicator that tells us that the true location of the decimal point is really b places to the left of where it is written. If we use this thought process, the 10^{-7} in the notation

$$4.165 \times 10^{-7}$$

tells us that the **true location** of the decimal point **is really** seven places **to the left** of where it is written, giving

$$0.0000004165$$

as the number being designated. In a like manner, the exponential expression 10^7 in the notation

$$4.165 \times 10^7$$

tells us that the **true location** of the decimal point **is really** seven places **to the right** of where it is written, giving

$$41,650,000$$

which is the number being designated.

It is helpful to use a two-step procedure to write a number in scientific notation. The first step is to place the decimal point immediately to the right of the first nonzero digit in the number. Then we follow this notation with the power of 10 that designates the true location of the decimal point. If we use this procedure to write

$$714,600,000$$

in scientific notation, we begin by placing the decimal point immediately to the right of the first nonzero digit (which is 7) and dropping the terminal zeros.

$$7.146$$

Now we follow this with $\times 10^8$ to indicate that the **true location of the decimal point is really eight places to the right of where we have written it.**

$$7.146 \times 10^8$$

---

†The replacements for b are restricted to positive integers.

example 74.1   Write 0.000316 in scientific notation.

solution   **We always begin by writing the decimal point immediately after the first nonzero digit.**

$$3.16 \times 10^?$$

Now we must choose an exponent for 10 that tells us what the true location of the decimal point **really is.** Since it **really is** four places to the left of where we have written it, the proper exponent is −4. Thus

$$0.000316 \qquad \text{equals} \qquad \mathbf{3.16 \times 10^{-4}}$$

example 74.2   Write 0.000316×10^{-7} in scientific notation.

solution   We begin by writing 0.000316 in scientific notation.

$$0.000316 = 3.16 \times 10^{-4}$$

Thus we can rewrite the original expression as

$$3.16 \times 10^{-4} \times 10^{-7}$$

and this simplifies to

$$\mathbf{3.16 \times 10^{-11}}$$

example 74.3   Write 0.000316×10^{7} in scientific notation.

solution   We write 0.000316 as 3.16×10^{-4} and simplify.

$$0.000316 \times 10^7 = \left(3.16 \times 10^{-4}\right) \times 10^7 = 3.16 \times 10^{-4} \times 10^7 = \mathbf{3.16 \times 10^3}$$

example 74.4   Write the following numbers in scientific notation:

(a) 47,800   (b) $47,800 \times 10^{-7}$ (c) $47,800 \times 10^{7}$

solution

(a) 47,800   equals $\mathbf{4.78 \times 10^4}$

(b) $47,800 \times 10^{-7}$ equals $4.78 \times 10^4 \times 10^{-7} = \mathbf{4.78 \times 10^{-3}}$

(c) $47,800 \times 10^{7}$ equals $4.78 \times 10^4 \times 10^7 = \mathbf{4.78 \times 10^{11}}$

practice   Write in scientific notation:

a.   49,900   **b.** $49,900 \times 10^{-11}$ **c.** 0.000499×10^3

problem set 74

1. (73)   An urn contains 6 green marbles and 6 yellow marbles. Two marbles are drawn at random. What is the probability that the first one is green and the second is yellow if the marbles are drawn

(a)   with replacement?   (b)   without replacement?

2. (73)   An urn contains 7 gold coins and 6 silver coins. Two coins are drawn at random. What is the probability that both coins are gold if the coins are drawn without replacement?

3. (70)   What is the probability that when a fair coin is tossed four times that it comes up heads all four times?

4. (39)   The ratio of withs to withouts was 3 to 11. If 5600 were huddled in the forest, how many were withs?

5. (58)   The cost of building a house increased 20 percent every year. If it costs $74,000 to build a house one year, what would it cost to build the same house the next year?

6. (52)   The average score of the first 6 games was 7.80 points per game. The average score of the next 4 games was 11.2 points per game. What was the overall average score for all the games?

7. Graph on a number line: $x - 3 \not> 4$; $D = \{\text{Integers}\}$
(64)

Write in scientific notation:

8. 0.000478
(74)

9. 0.000478×10^6
(74)

10. 0.000478×10^{-8}
(74)

Factor these binomials. Always factor the common factor first.

11. $5x^2 - 5y^2$
(73)

12. $45x^2 - 20m^2$
(73)

13. $4a^2 - 9b^2$
(73)

14. $49a^2p^2 - a^2$
(73)

Factor the trinomials. Always begin by writing the trinomials in descending order of the variables and by factoring out the greatest common factor.

15. $x^2 + 9x + 20$
(69)

16. $-20 + x^2 + x$
(69)

17. $x^2(a + b) + 28(a + b) + 11x(a + b)$
(72)

18. $(x - a)y^2 - 28(x - a) + 3y(x - a)$
(72)

19. $x^3 + 10x^2 + 24x$
(71)

20. $ax^2 - 2ax - 15a$
(71)

21. Add: $\dfrac{1}{xc} + \dfrac{b}{x(c + x)} + \dfrac{5}{c + x} - \dfrac{2}{c}$
(52)

22. Use substitution to solve:
(59)
$$\begin{cases} 7x + y = -18 \\ 4x - 2y = 0 \end{cases}$$

23. Use elimination to solve:
(71)
$$\begin{cases} N_D + N_Q = 40 \\ 10N_D + 25N_Q = 475 \end{cases}$$

24. Graph the following equation on a rectangular coordinate system: $y = -2x - 1$
(51)

Simplify:

25. $4\sqrt{80} + 8\sqrt{45} - 4\sqrt{48} + \sqrt{30{,}000}$
(66)

26. $\dfrac{x^{-3}xy^2(y)^{-2}x^{-4}}{(x^0yy^{-2})^2(x^2y^{-3})^{-2}}$
(53)

27. Expand by using the distributive property. Write the answer with all exponents positive.
(40)
$$\frac{2x^2}{y^2}\left(\frac{-x^2}{2y^{-3}} + \frac{x^2a^4}{a^{-2}y^{-2}}\right)$$

28. If $f(x) = 2x^2 - 3x - 4$, find $f(-2)$.
(28)

29. Find the area of this trapezoid. Dimensions are in centimeters.
(8)

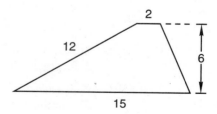

30. Find the surface area of this regular square pyramid. Dimensions are in meters.
(72)

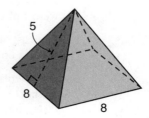

LESSON 75 *Writing the Equation of a Line • Slope-Intercept Method of Graphing*

75.A

writing the equation of a line

We remember that the graph of a vertical line is everywhere equidistant from the y axis. In the figure on the left, every point on the line A is 3 units to the left of the y axis, and the equation of this vertical line is

$$x = -3$$

Every point on line A satisfies the equation $x = -3$ as every point on line A has -3 as its x coordinate. The y coordinate can be any real number since there are no restrictions on it. Every point on line B has 5 as its x coordinate, so the equation of line B is

$$x = 5$$

The graph of every vertical line on the coordinate plane has the form

$$x = k$$

where k is the value of the x coordinate of any point on the vertical line. Note that k can be either positive or negative.

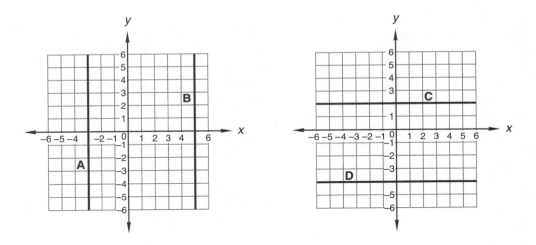

The graph of a horizontal line is everywhere equidistant from the x axis. Every point on line C is 2 units above the x axis, and the equation of this line is

$$y = 2$$

Every point on line C has a y coordinate of 2, and so the equation of line C is

$$y = 2$$

Note that there are no restrictions on the value of the x coordinate, so the points on the graph of the line $y = 2$ are those points whose x coordinates can be any real number and whose y coordinates must be 2. Applying similar reasoning, note that every point on line D has -4 as its y coordinate, so its equation is

$$y = -4$$

If we use k to represent the value of the y coordinate of any point on a horizontal line, we can say that the equation of a horizontal line is

$$y = k$$

Thus, we see that the equations of vertical and horizontal lines can be determined by inspection. These equations contain an x and one number or a y and one number.

$$x = +5 \qquad x = -3 \qquad y = +2 \qquad y = -4$$

The equation of a line that is neither vertical nor horizontal cannot be so simply written. However, the equations of these lines can be written in what we call the **slope-intercept form.** The following equations are equations of three different lines written in slope-intercept form.

(a) $y = -6x + 2$ \qquad (b) $y = \dfrac{2}{3}x - 5$ \qquad (c) $y = 0.007x + 3$

We note that each equation contains an equals sign, a y, an x, and two numbers. **The only difference in the equations is that the numbers are different.**

We use the letters m and b when we write this equation without specifying the two numbers.

$$y = mx + b$$

Since the equation of any line that is not a vertical line or a horizontal line can be written in this form, the problem of finding the equation of a given line is reduced to the problem of finding the two numbers that will be the values of m and b in the equation.

intercept In the slope-intercept form of the equation $y = mx + b$, we will call the constant b the **intercept** of the equation because b is the y coordinate of the line at the point where the line intercepts the y axis. Note that b is the value of y when x has a value of 0. The figure shows the graphs of two lines. Line E intercepts the y axis at $+4$, so the intercept b in the equation of this line has a value of 4. Line F intercepts the y axis at -3, so the intercept b in the equation of this line has a value of -3.

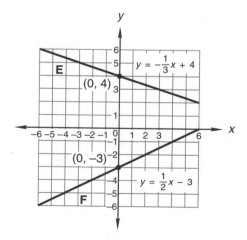

example 75.1 Find the y intercept of the line whose equation is $y = 3x - 5$.

solution The equation of the line $y = 3x - 5$ is written in the form $y = mx + b$. The constant b is the y intercept, so in this case, the y intercept is **–5.**

Another way to solve this problem is to remember that the y intercept is the y coordinate of the point of intersection of the line and the y axis. In other words, the y intercept is the value of y which satisfies the equation of the line when x is set equal to 0. Setting $x = 0$ in the equation of the line, we get

$$y = 3(0) - 5$$

$$= -5$$

Therefore, the line intersects the y axis at -5 and the y intercept is -5.

example 75.2   Find the y intercept of the line shown.

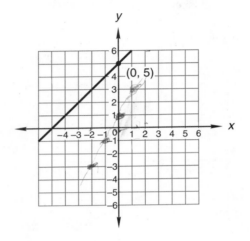

solution   The line shown intersects the y axis at $y = 5$, so the y intercept is **5.**

slope   **In the slope-intercept form, $y = mx + b$, we call the constant m the slope of the line.** Thus, in the equation $y = -2x + 6$, we say that the slope of this line is -2 because the coefficient of x is -2. **We note that the slope has both a sign and a magnitude** (absolute value). A line represented by a line segment that points toward the upper right-hand part of the coordinate plane has a positive slope. A line represented by a line segment that points toward the lower right-hand part of the coordinate plane has a negative slope. As a mnemonic to help us remember this, we will use the little man and his car. **He always comes from the left-hand side, as shown here.**

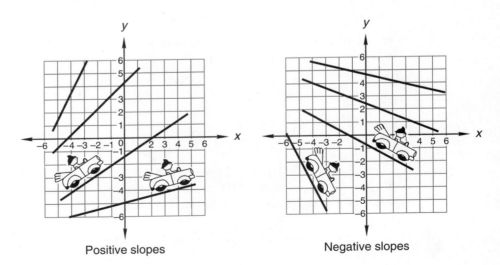

Positive slopes   Negative slopes

The little man sees the first set of lines as uphill with positive slopes and the second set of lines as downhill with negative slopes.

The magnitude, or absolute value, of the slope is defined to be the ratio of the absolute value of the change in the y coordinate to the absolute value of the change in the x coordinate as we move from one point on the line to another point on the line.

$$|m| = \frac{|\text{change in } y|}{|\text{change in } x|}$$

The figure on the left shows the graph of a line that has a negative slope. To find the magnitude of the slope of this line, we arbitrarily choose two points on the line, draw a right triangle, and label the lengths of the triangle. This has been done in the figure on the right.

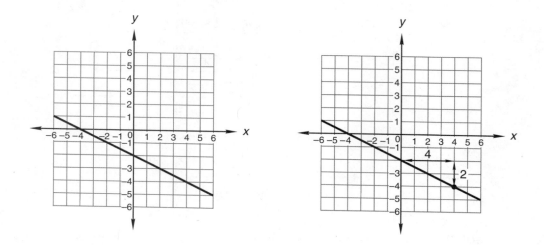

The length of the horizontal leg of the triangle is 4 and is the difference of the x coordinates of the two points. The length of the vertical leg of the triangle is 2 and is the difference of the y coordinates of the two points. Since the magnitude of the slope is the ratio of the absolute value of the change in the y coordinate to the absolute value of the change in the x coordinate, we see that the magnitude, or absolute value, of the slope of this line is $\frac{1}{2}$.

$$|m| = \frac{|\text{change in } y|}{|\text{change in } x|} \quad \rightarrow \quad |m| = \frac{2}{4} \quad \rightarrow \quad |m| = \frac{1}{2}$$

We call the change in x the **run** and the change in y the **rise.** Using these words, the magnitude of the slope can be defined as the **absolute value of the rise over the absolute value of the run.**

$$|\text{Slope}| = \frac{|\text{rise}|}{|\text{run}|} \quad \text{or} \quad |m| = \frac{|\text{rise}|}{|\text{run}|}$$

The general form of the equation of a line is $y = mx + b$, and to write the equation of this line, we need to know (1) the value of the intercept b, (2) the sign of the slope, and (3) the magnitude, or absolute value, of the slope. We see that

1. The y coordinate of the point where the line intercepts the y axis is -2, so $b = -2$.

2. The line points to the lower right and thus the *sign* of the slope is negative.

3. The magnitude of the slope is $\frac{2}{4}$, which is equivalent to $\frac{1}{2}$.

So the equation of this line is

$$y = -\frac{1}{2}x - 2$$

example 75.3   Find the equations of the lines graphed in the accompanying figures.

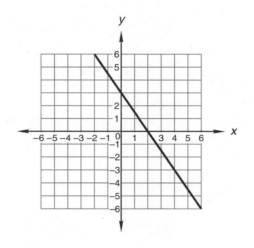
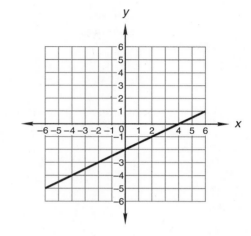

solution   The desired equation is $y = mx + b$, and we need to find m and b.

By inspection, $b = +3$.
By inspection, the sign of m is $-$.

The desired equation is $y = mx + b$, and we need to find m and b.

By inspection, $b = -2$.
By inspection, the sign of m is $+$.

Now we need to find the magnitudes, or absolute values, of the slopes. We will arbitrarily choose two points on each of the lines, draw the right triangles, and compute the slopes.

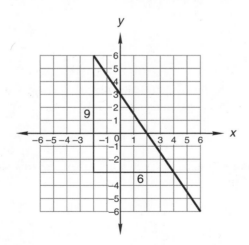
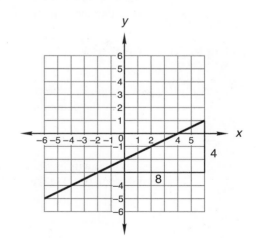

$$|m| = \frac{9}{6} = \frac{3}{2}$$

So $b = +3$ and $m = -\frac{3}{2}$.

Using these values in $y = mx + b$ yields

$$y = -\frac{3}{2}x + 3$$

$$|m| = \frac{4}{8} = \frac{1}{2}$$

So $b = -2$ and $m = +\frac{1}{2}$.

Using these values in $y = mx + b$ yields

$$y = \frac{1}{2}x - 2$$

75.B

slope-intercept method of graphing

Thus far, we have graphed a line by finding ordered pairs of x and y that lie on the line. To graph $y = -\frac{3}{5}x + 2$, we choose values for x and write them in a table.

x	0	5	–5
y			

Then we use each of these numbers one at a time in the equation and find the corresponding values of y.

x	0	5	–5
y	2	–1	5

We finish by graphing the ordered pairs on the coordinate system below and drawing the line.

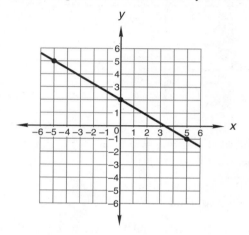

This method is dependable, but it is time-consuming. We can use the slope and the intercept of the line to get an accurate graph in less time. We will demonstrate this method by graphing the same line again.

example 75.4   Graph $y = -\dfrac{3}{5}x + 2$.

solution   We begin by writing the slope in the form of a fraction that has a positive denominator. If we do this, the denominator will be +5 and the numerator will be –3.

$$y = \frac{-3}{+5}x + 2$$

Now we will graph the line in three steps, as shown below. As the first step, we graph the intercept (0, 2) in the left-hand figure.

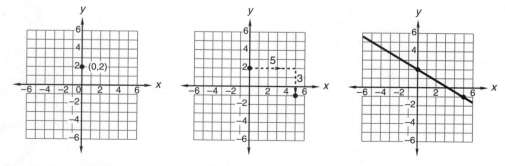

Now in the center figure, from the intercept we move to the right (the positive x direction) a distance of 5 (the denominator of the slope representing the "run"). Then we move up or down the distance indicated by the numerator of the slope. We move down 3 since our numerator is −3 and the numerator represents the "rise." We graph this new point, and in the figure on the right we draw the line through the two points.

example 75.5   Use the slope-intercept method to graph the equation $x - 2y = 4$.

solution   As the first step, we write the equation in slope-intercept form by solving for y.

$$x - 2y = 4 \quad \longrightarrow \quad -2y = -x + 4 \quad \longrightarrow \quad 2y = x - 4 \quad \longrightarrow \quad y = \frac{1}{2}x - 2$$

Now we write the slope as a fraction with a positive denominator.

$$y = \frac{+1}{+2}x - 2$$

In the figure on the left we graph the intercept $(0, -2)$. In the figure in the middle we move from the intercept a horizontal distance of $+2$ (to the right) and a vertical distance of $+1$ (up). In the figure on the right we draw the line through the two points.

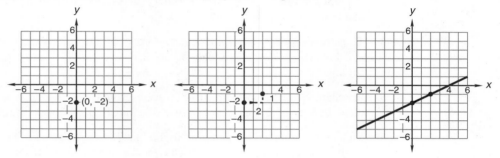

When the points are close together, as in this case, it is difficult to draw the line accurately. To get another point, we multiply the denominator and the numerator of the slope by a convenient integer and use the new form of the slope to get the second point. For the line under discussion, we will multiply the slope by 2 and get

$$\frac{+1}{+2} \cdot \frac{(2)}{(2)} \quad \longrightarrow \quad \frac{+2}{+4}$$

In the figures below, we use the same intercept but move an x distance of $+4$ and a y distance of $+2$ to find the new point.

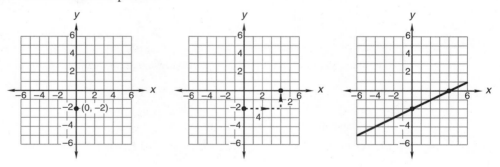

practice   Find the equations of these lines:

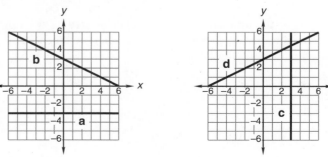

Use the slope-intercept method to graph the equations:

e. $y = -\dfrac{2}{3}x + 2$ **f.** $5 + 3y = x$

problem set 75

1.
(70) Richardson has a bag with 5 white marbles and 7 red marbles. A marble is drawn at random and replaced. Then another marble is randomly drawn. What is the probability that the first marble will be red and the second marble will be white?

2.
(70) The spinner shown is spun 4 times. What is the probability that the spinner stops on 4, 2, 3, and 1, in that order?

3.
(73) David has a bucket with 5 yellow golf balls and 9 white golf balls. A ball is drawn at random and not replaced. Then another ball is randomly drawn. What is the probability that both are white golf balls?

4.
(58) Three percent of the caterpillars metamorphosed into butterflies. If Ramona could count 120 butterflies, how many caterpillars had there been? Draw a diagram as an aid in solving the problem.

5.
(58) Sakahara socked it to them. If 4800 were present and Sakahara socked 34 percent of them, how many did he sock? Draw a diagram as an aid in solving the problem.

6.
(58) Muhammad counted the tents and found that 784 were patched. If there were 1400 tents in all, what percent was patched? Draw a diagram as an aid in solving the problem.

Find the equations of these lines:

7.
(75)

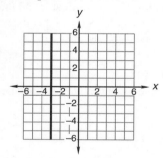

8.
(75)

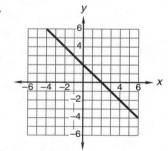

Use the slope-intercept method to graph these equations on a rectangular coordinate system:

9.
(75) $y = -\dfrac{3}{2}x + 3$ **10.**
(75) $2y = -x + 2$

Write these numbers in scientific notation:

11.
(74) 0.00123×10^{-5} **12.**
(74) 0.00123×10^{8}

Factor these binomials. Always factor the common factor first.

13.
(73) $b^3x^2 - 4b^3$ **14.**
(73) $16x^2 - a^2$ **15.**
(73) $-m^2 + 9p^2$

Factor the trinomials. Always begin by writing the trinomials in descending order of the variables and by factoring out the greatest common factor.

16.
(69) $x^2 + 3x - 10$ **17.**
(69) $4x + x^2 - 21$

18.
(71) $5x^2 - 15x - 50$ **19.**
(71) $x^3 - 3x^2 + 2x$

20.
(72) $18(x + y) + 9z(x + y) + z^2(x + y)$

21.
(72) $(m + a)x^2 + 3(m + a)x - 18(m + a)$

22. Use elimination to solve:
₍₆₇₎

$$\begin{cases} 4x - 5y = -1 \\ 2x + 3y = 5 \end{cases}$$

23. Use substitution to solve:
₍₇₁₎

$$\begin{cases} N_Q + N_D = 25 \\ N_Q = N_D + 3 \end{cases}$$

Simplify:

24. $15\sqrt{12} - 30\sqrt{18} + 2\sqrt{300}$
₍₆₆₎

25. $\dfrac{5}{-3^{-2}} - \sqrt[5]{-32}$
₍₂₉₎

26. $\dfrac{x^{-2} y^0 \left(x^{-2}\right)^{-2} y^2}{\left(y^2 x^{-4}\right)^2 \left(y^3 x^2\right)^{-1}}$
₍₅₃₎

27. $\dfrac{a^{-1} + b^{-1}}{a^{-1} b^{-1}}$
₍₆₈₎

28. Solve: $2.2x - 0.1x + 0.02x = -2 - 0.12$
₍₂₇₎

29. Find the area of this figure. All angles
₍₈₎ are right angles. The dimensions are in
inches.

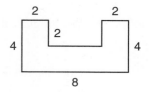

30. A right circular cone has a base of
₍₇₂₎ radius 4 ft and a slant height of 5 ft, as
shown. Find the surface area of the
right circular cone.

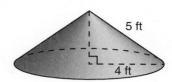

LESSON 76   *Consecutive Integers*

If we use the letter N to designate an unspecified integer and then look at the number line,

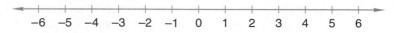

we see that the integer to the right of any given integer is one greater than the given integer. Thus we may use

$$N + 1$$

to designate the next greater integer, $N + 2$ to designate the next greater integer, etc. Integers that are 1 unit apart are called **consecutive integers.**

example 76.1   Find three consecutive integers such that the sum of the first and third is 146.

solution   We will designate the consecutive integers as

$$N \qquad N + 1 \qquad \text{and} \qquad N + 2$$

The sum of the first integer and the third integer is 146, so we write

$$N + N + 2 = 146$$

and now we solve for N.

$$2N + 2 = 146 \qquad \text{added}$$
$$2N = 144 \qquad \text{simplified}$$
$$N = 72 \qquad \text{divided}$$

Thus $N + 1 = 73$, and $N + 2 = 74$. The desired integers are **72, 73,** and **74.**

Check:
$$72 + 74 = 146$$
$$146 = 146 \qquad \text{Check}$$

example 76.2 Find three consecutive integers such that twice the sum of the first two is 2 less than 3 times the third.

solution We designate the integers as

$$N \qquad N + 1 \qquad \text{and} \qquad N + 2$$

Note that twice the sum of the first two consecutive integers, $2(N + N + 1)$, is two less than 3 times the third consecutive integer, $3(N + 2)$. To create an equality, we must add 2 to $2(N + N + 1)$ so that we can write the following equation:

$$2(N + N + 1) + 2 = 3(N + 2)$$
$$2(2N + 1) + 2 = 3(N + 2) \qquad \text{simplified}$$
$$4N + 2 + 2 = 3N + 6 \qquad \text{multiplied}$$
$$4N + 4 = 3N + 6 \qquad \text{simplified}$$
$$N = 2 \qquad \text{solved}$$

Thus, the integers are **2, 3,** and **4.**

Check:
$$2(2 + 3) + 2 = 3(4) \quad \longrightarrow \quad 12 = 12 \qquad \text{Check}$$

example 76.3 Find four consecutive integers such that 6 times the sum of the first and fourth is 26 less than 10 times the third.

solution We will use N, $N + 1$, $N + 2$, and $N + 3$ to designate the four consecutive integers. When we write the equation below, we add 26 to the left-hand side because 6 times the sum is 26 less than the right-hand side. We want the left-hand side to be equal to the right-hand side.

$$6(N + N + 3) + 26 = 10(N + 2) \qquad \text{equation}$$
$$6(2N + 3) + 26 = 10(N + 2) \qquad \text{simplified}$$
$$12N + 18 + 26 = 10N + 20 \qquad \text{multiplied}$$
$$12N + 44 = 10N + 20 \qquad \text{simplified}$$
$$2N = -24 \qquad \text{simplified}$$
$$N = -12 \qquad \text{divided}$$

Thus the integers are **−12, −11, −10,** and **−9.**

Check:
$$6(-12 - 9) + 26 = 10(-10) \quad \longrightarrow \quad -100 = -100 \qquad \text{Check}$$

practice **a.** Find three consecutive integers such that the sum of the first and third is 142.

b. Find four consecutive integers such that 8 times the sum of the first and the third is 40 greater than 10 times the fourth.

problem set 76

1. Find four consecutive integers such that twice the sum of the first and third is 11 greater than 3 times the second.
(76)

2. Seventy-eight percent of the more successful students tended to be serendipitous. If there were 18,400 more successful students in the district, how many tended to be serendipitous? Draw a diagram as an aid in solving the problem.
(58)

3. An urn contains 8 gold coins and 7 silver coins. A coin is drawn at random and not replaced. Then another coin is randomly drawn. What is the probability that the first coin will be gold and the second coin will be silver?
(73)

4. Two dice are rolled. What is the probability that the sum of the numbers rolled is
(70)

(a)   greater than 6?   (b)   less than 6?

5. Find the equations of lines (a) and (b).
(75)

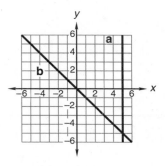

Use the slope-intercept method to graph these equations on a rectangular coordinate system:

6. $y = -\dfrac{1}{3}x + 2$
(75)

7. $y - 2x = 1$
(75)

Write the following numbers in scientific notation:

8. $430{,}000 \times 10^{-2}$
(74)

9. 4300×10^{7}
(74)

Factor the binomials. If there is a common factor, factor it as the first step.

10. $-9x^2 + m^2$
(73)

11. $4x^2 - 9m^2$
(73)

12. $125m^2 - 5x^2$
(73)

13. $-72k^2 + 2x^2$
(73)

Factor the trinomials. Always begin by writing the trinomials in descending order of the variables and by factoring out the greatest common factor.

14. $x^2 - 5x - 14$
(69)

15. $-x^3 + 4x^2 + 12x$
(71)

16. $ax^2 + 7xa + 10a$
(71)

17. $24x + 2x^2 + 70$
(71)

18. $24 + 27x + 3x^2$
(71)

19. $-px + px^2 - 2p$
(71)

20. Use substitution to solve:
(71)
$$\begin{cases} N_N = N_Q + 15 \\ 5N_N + 25N_Q = 525 \end{cases}$$

21. Use elimination to solve:
(67)
$$\begin{cases} 2x + 2y = 14 \\ 3x - 2y = -4 \end{cases}$$

22. Tell whether the following statements are true or false, and explain why:
(61)

(a)   {Rationals} $\subset$ {Integers}   (b)   {Integers} $\subset$ {Irrationals}

23. Add: $\dfrac{a}{x^2} + \dfrac{2}{ax^2} + \dfrac{b}{x^3} - \dfrac{1}{a^2}$
(44)

24. If $f(x) = x^{-5} + x^{-4} + x^{-3} + x^{-2} + x^{-1}$, find $f(1)$.
(28)

Simplify:

25. $3\sqrt{20} - 2\sqrt{80} + 2\sqrt{125} - \sqrt{500}$
(66)

26. $\dfrac{1}{(-3)^{-2}} + 3^0 - \sqrt[3]{-8} - \dfrac{1}{-3^{-2}}$
(29)

27. Simplify by adding like terms: $\dfrac{a^2x^5}{y} - 3aax^6x^{-1}y^{-1} + \dfrac{4a^2y^{-1}}{x^{-5}} - \dfrac{3aax^3y^{-2}}{y}$
₍₄₁₎

28. Expand by using the distributive property. Write the answer with all exponents positive.
₍₄₀₎

$$\dfrac{3x^2y^{-2}}{ax^{-1}}\left(\dfrac{x^3}{y^2} - \dfrac{2x^{-2}a}{y^{-2}} + \dfrac{4x^{-2}y^2}{a^{-1}x}\right)$$

29. Solve: $-x + 4 - (-2)(-x - 5) = -(-2x - |4|)$
₍₃₁₎

30. Find the volume of this right triangular
_(20,60) prism. Dimensions are in centimeters.

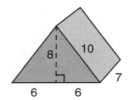

LESSON 77 *Consecutive Odd and Consecutive Even Integers • Fraction and Decimal Word Problems*

77.A

consecutive odd and consecutive even integers

In Lesson 76, we noted that if we use N to represent some unknown integer, then the next larger integer is $N + 1$, the next is $N + 2$, etc. This is because consecutive integers are 1 unit apart on the number line. **Consecutive even integers are different because consecutive integers are 2 units apart.** If we look at the number line,

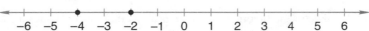

we see that -4 and -2 are consecutive even integers and that they are 2 units apart. **Consecutive odd integers are also 2 units apart.** The numbers -3 and -1 are consecutive odd integers, and on the number line we see that they are 2 units apart.

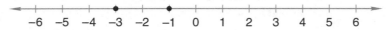

Thus, if we use N to designate an unspecified odd/even integer, the next greater odd/even integer is $N + 2$, the next is $N + 4$, etc.

example 77.1 Find three consecutive even integers such that the sum of the first and second equals the sum of the third and -10.

solution We will represent the unknown even integers as N, $N + 2$, and $N + 4$.

Thus, $\qquad\qquad N + (N + 2) = (N + 4) + (-10)$

Now we solve and get

$$2N + 2 = N - 6$$

$$N = -8$$

so the integers are **-8, -6,** and **-4.**

Check: $\qquad\qquad (-8) + (-6) = (-4) + (-10)$

$$-14 = -14$$

example 77.2   Find three consecutive odd integers such that the sum of the first and third is 7 greater than the second decreased by 18.

solution   We use N, $N + 2$, $N + 4$, etc., to represent consecutive odd integers. Thus, we can write the problem as

$$N + (N + 4) - 7 = (N + 2) - 18$$

and solve: $$2N - 3 = N - 16$$

$$N = -13$$

So $N + 2 = -11$ and $N + 4 = -9$.

Check: $$(-13) + (-9) - 7 = (-11) - 18$$

$$-29 = -29 \qquad \text{Check}$$

example 77.3   Find four consecutive odd integers such that the sum of the first and fourth is 25 greater than the opposite of the third.

solution   We will use N, $N + 2$, $N + 4$, and $N + 6$ to represent the four consecutive odd integers. From the information given in the problem we can write

$$N + (N + 6) - 25 = -(N + 4)$$

and solve: $$2N - 19 = -N - 4$$

$$3N = 15$$

$$N = 5$$

So $N + 2 = 7$, and $N + 4 = 9$, and $N + 6 = 11$.

Check: $$(5) + (11) - 25 = -(9)$$

$$-9 = -9 \qquad \text{Check}$$

77.B
fraction and decimal word problems

We have drawn diagrams to help us visualize percent word problems. Since problems involving fractional and decimal parts are essentially the same as percent problems, similar diagrams can be used to help with these. The "before" diagrams for these problems will represent 1 instead of 100 percent. The equations shown are the equations for fractional and decimal parts of a number.

$$F \times \text{of} = \text{is} \qquad \text{or} \qquad D \times \text{of} = \text{is}$$

example 77.4   Lopez used a 5-iron, but the ball covered only $\frac{4}{5}$ of the required distance. If she hit the ball 112 yards, what was the required distance?

solution   The "before" diagram represents 1 instead of 100 percent.

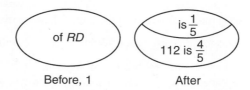

Before, 1   After

From this, we see that $\frac{4}{5}$ of the required distance (referred to as RD) is 112.

$$F \times \text{of} = \text{is} \quad \longrightarrow \quad \frac{4}{5}RD = 112 \quad \longrightarrow \quad RD = \textbf{140 yards}$$

example 77.5   McAbee guessed that the total was 30.24, but this was 7.2 times the total. What was the total?

solution   The following diagram shows that 30.24 is 7.2 of the total:

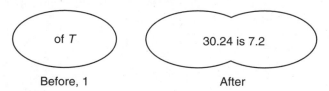

Before, 1   After

We solve the problem using the appropriate equation.

$$D \times \text{of} = \text{is} \quad \longrightarrow \quad 7.2T = 30.24 \quad \longrightarrow \quad T = \frac{30.24}{7.2} \quad \longrightarrow \quad T = \mathbf{4.2}$$

example 77.6   Three fourths of the tickets had been sold, and there were 420 tickets left. How many tickets were printed?

solution   We draw a diagram of the problem noting that the tickets left represent one fourth of the total number of tickets.

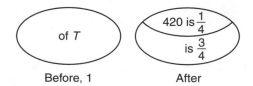

Before, 1   After

We solve the problem using the appropriate equation.

$$F \times \text{of} = \text{is}$$

$$\frac{1}{4}T = 420$$

$$T = \mathbf{1680}$$

practice   **a.**   Find three consecutive even integers such that the sum of the first and third equals the sum of the second and −14.

b.   The golfer used a 6-iron, but the ball traveled only $\frac{5}{6}$ of the required distance. If the golfer hit the ball 180 yards, what was the required distance?

c.   Seven eighths of the tickets had been sold, and there were 560 tickets left. How many tickets were printed?

problem set 77   **1.** Find four consecutive odd integers such that the sum of the second and third is 19 greater than the fourth.
(77)

2. Nolan guessed that the total was 46.08, but this was 6.4 times the total. What was the total?
(77)

3. Seven eighths of the football fans were wearing red. If 42,000 fans were wearing red, how many fans were at the game? Draw a diagram as an aid in solving the problem.
(77)

4. Two fair dice are rolled. What is the probability that the sum of the numbers rolled is 7?
(70)

5. An urn contains 4 black marbles and 7 grey marbles. A marble is drawn at random and replaced. Then a second marble is drawn. What is the probability that both marbles are black?
(70)

6. A fair coin is tossed 5 times. What is the probability that it will come up tails all five times?
(70)

7.
(45)
If the sum of three numbers is 495 and the first two numbers are 101.7 and 173.8, what is the average of the three numbers?

8.
(75)
Find the equations of lines (a) and (b).

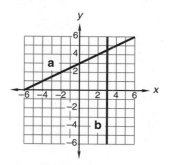

Graph the following equations on a rectangular coordinate system:

9.
(75)
$2x + y + 2 = 0$

10.
(75)
$y = -4$

Write the following numbers in scientific notation:

11.
(74)
7000×10^{-7}

12.
(74)
0.000007×10^{-3}

Factor the binomials. Always factor the common factor first.

13.
(73)
$4x^2 - 49$

14.
(73)
$x^2 - 9x^2y^2$

15.
(73)
$3p^2 - 12k^2$

16.
(73)
$-4m^2 + k^2$

Factor the trinomials. Always begin by writing the trinomials in descending order of the variables and by factoring out the greatest common factor.

17.
(69)
$x^2 - 6x + 9$

18.
(71)
$2x^2 - 8x + 8$

19.
(71)
$2x^2 + 8x + 8$

20.
(71)
$2x^2 + 20x + 50$

21.
(71)
$3x^2 - 30x + 75$

22.
(71)
$ax^2 - 12ax + 36a$

23.
(59)
Use substitution to solve:

$$\begin{cases} x + 3y = 16 \\ 2x - y = 4 \end{cases}$$

24.
(71)
Use elimination to solve:

$$\begin{cases} N_N + N_D = 500 \\ 5N_N + 10N_D = 3000 \end{cases}$$

25.
(61,63)
(a) $-3 \in$ {What subsets of the real numbers}?

(b) $-0.\overline{777} \in$ {What subsets of the real numbers}?

26.
(64)
Graph on a number line: $4 \le x < 10$; $D =$ {Integers}

Simplify:

27.
(68)
$\dfrac{x + y^{-1}}{x^2y^{-1} - 5}$

28.
(66)
$2\sqrt{75} - 6\sqrt{27} + \sqrt{30,000}$

29.
(31)
Solve: $-2|-2| - 2^2 - 3(-2 - x) = -2(x - 3 - 2)$

30.
(15,60)
A right circular cylinder has a radius of 8 inches and a length of 40 inches, as shown. Find the surface area of the right circular cylinder.

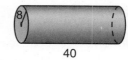

40

LESSON 78 *Rational Equations*

Often we need to solve an equation in which some of the terms of the equations have denominators that are numbers other than the number 1. The equations

$$\frac{y}{2} + \frac{1}{4} = \frac{y}{6} \qquad \text{and} \qquad \frac{3y}{2} + \frac{8 - 4y}{7} = 3$$

are equations of this type. Because the terms of the equations are all rational expressions, we call these equations **rational equations. There are many ways that these equations can be solved, but the most straightforward method of attack is to eliminate the denominators first by a judicious application of the multiplicative property of equality.** Since Lesson 44, we have been adding rational expressions by using the least common multiple of the original denominators as the new denominators. To eliminate the denominators in these equations, we will again use the least common multiple, but we will use it in a different way. As permitted by the multiplicative property of equality, we will **multiply the numerator of every term in the equation by the least common multiple of all the denominators of the terms of the equation.** Since every denominator is guaranteed to be a factor of the least common multiple, we are able to eliminate the denominators in one step. The remainder of the solution is straightforward.

example 78.1   Solve: $\dfrac{y}{2} + \dfrac{1}{4} = \dfrac{y}{6}$

solution   **The least common multiple of the denominators is 12. We will multiply the numerator of every term by 12 and cancel the denominators.**

$$12 \cdot \frac{y}{2} + 12 \cdot \frac{1}{4} = 12 \cdot \frac{y}{6}$$

Now divide each of the denominators into 12 to get

$$6y + 3 = 2y$$
$$4y = -3$$
$$y = -\frac{3}{4}$$

example 78.2   Solve: $\dfrac{2x}{7} - \dfrac{3x}{2} = \dfrac{1}{3}$

solution   We begin by multiplying each numerator by 42, which is the **least common multiple of the denominators.**

$$(42)\frac{2x}{7} - (42)\frac{3x}{2} = (42)\frac{1}{3}$$

Now we cancel the denominators and solve.

$$\frac{\overset{6}{(\cancel{42})}2x}{\cancel{7}} - \frac{\overset{21}{(\cancel{42})}3x}{\cancel{2}} = \frac{\overset{14}{(\cancel{42})}1}{\cancel{3}} \quad \longrightarrow \quad 12x - 63x = 14$$

$$\longrightarrow \quad -51x = 14 \quad \longrightarrow \quad x = -\frac{14}{51}$$

example 78.3   Solve: $\dfrac{3y}{2} + \dfrac{8 - 4y}{7} = 3$

solution   The beginner often makes mistakes when trying to eliminate denominators when one or more of the terms has a binomial expression as the numerator. A simple ploy that will prevent this common mistake is to enclose the binomial in the numerator in parentheses first.

$$\frac{3y}{2} + \frac{(8 - 4y)}{7} = 3$$

Now we multiply every numerator by the **least common multiple of the denominator,** which is 14.

$$14 \cdot \frac{3y}{2} + 14 \cdot \frac{(8 - 4y)}{7} = 14 \cdot 3$$

Now divide, simplify, and complete the solution.

$$21y + 2(8 - 4y) = 42 \longrightarrow 21y + 16 - 8y = 42$$

$$\longrightarrow 13y = 26 \longrightarrow y = 2$$

example 78.4   Solve: $\dfrac{x + 1}{4} - \dfrac{3}{2} = \dfrac{2x - 9}{10}$

solution   First we enclose the binomials in parentheses.

$$\frac{(x + 1)}{4} - \frac{3}{2} = \frac{(2x - 9)}{10}$$

Now we multiply every numerator by the **least common multiple of the denominators,** which is 20.

$$20 \frac{(x + 1)}{4} - 20 \cdot \frac{3}{2} = 20 \frac{(2x - 9)}{10}$$

Now we divide, simplify, and complete the solution.

$$5(x + 1) - 30 = 2(2x - 9) \longrightarrow 5x + 5 - 30 = 4x - 18$$

$$\longrightarrow 5x - 25 = 4x - 18 \longrightarrow x = 7$$

practice   Solve:

a. $\dfrac{z}{4} - \dfrac{1}{3} = \dfrac{z}{2}$ **b.** $\dfrac{y + 2}{3} - \dfrac{5}{2} = \dfrac{2y - 4}{8}$

problem set 78

1. Find three consecutive even integers such that 3 times the sum of the first two is 48 less than the third.
(77)

2. Find four consecutive odd integers such that 4 times the sum of the first and third is 4 larger than 4 times the fourth.
(77)

3. Lee has an urn with 8 white marbles and 10 black marbles. A marble is drawn at random and not replaced. Then a second marble is drawn randomly. What is the probability that the first is white and the second is black?
(73)

4. A single die is rolled 4 times and comes up 3, 4, 5, and 6. What is the probability that the next roll will produce a number greater than 2?
(70)

5. The average of five numbers is 790.6. If the first four numbers are 80.2, 91.6, 123, and 204.7, what is the sum of the five numbers?
(45)

6. When the pilgrims counted noses, they got a count that was 128 percent too high. If they
(58) counted 9120 noses, what was the correct count? Draw a diagram as an aid in solving the
problem.

7. Four thousand two hundred carnations were reserved for use on the float. If this was only
(77) $\frac{7}{10}$ of the flowers needed, how many flowers are needed for the float? Draw a diagram as
an aid in solving the problem.

Solve:

8. $\frac{y}{7} + \frac{y+1}{4} = 6$
(78)

9. $\frac{x}{2} - \frac{1}{3} = \frac{x}{4}$
(78)

10. Write the equations of lines (a) and (b):
(75)

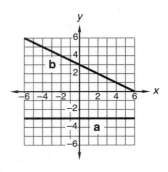

11. Graph the following equation on a rectangular coordinate system: $y = 3x + 4$
(75)

Write the following numbers in scientific notation:

12. 0.0003×10^{-3}
(74)

13. 4000×10^4
(74)

Factor completely:

14. $x^2 - 9x + 20$
(69)

15. $2ax^2 - 20ax + 42a$
(71)

16. $13mx + 42m + mx^2$
(71)

17. $32x^2 - 18a^2$
(73)

18. $25m^2a^2 - 4a^2$
(73)

19. $-36k^2 + 9m^2y^2$
(73)

20. Use substitution to solve:
(71)

$$\begin{cases} N_Q = N_D + 300 \\ 10N_D + 25N_Q = 8200 \end{cases}$$

21. Use elimination to solve:
(67)

$$\begin{cases} 4x - 3y = -3 \\ 2x + 4y = -18 \end{cases}$$

22. (a) $-2\sqrt{3} \in$ {What subsets of the real numbers}?
(61,63)

(b) $0.\overline{49} \in$ {What subsets of the real numbers}?

23. Add: $\dfrac{a}{x^2y} + \dfrac{b}{x^2y^2} + \dfrac{c}{x^2y^3} - \dfrac{d}{x^3y^3}$
(44)

Simplify:

24. $2\sqrt{54} - 3\sqrt{24} + 8\sqrt{600} - \sqrt{96}$
(66)

25. $\dfrac{x^0 x^2 y^{-2} \left(x^0\right)^{-2}}{\left(x^2\right)^{-3} \left(y^{-2}\right)^3 y^0}$
(53)

26. Evaluate: $\left(\dfrac{\sqrt[3]{x}}{4}\right)^{-2} \left(x^{-1}x\right)\left(\dfrac{\sqrt{y}}{\sqrt[4]{y}}\right)$ if $x = 8$ and $y = 16$
(29)

27. Expand by using the distributive property. Write the answer with all exponents positive.
(40)

$$\left(\frac{ax^2}{y^2} - \frac{3x}{xy^2} + \frac{2y^2}{x^{-2}}\right) \frac{2x^{-2}}{y^2}$$

28. Graph on a number line: $x + 5 \not< 2$; $D = $ {Reals}
(64)

29. Find the perimeter of this figure. All
(3) angles are right angles. Dimensions
    are in centimeters.

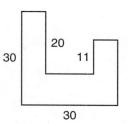

30. A right circular cylinder has a radius
(20,60) of 6 meters and a length of 18 meters,
    as shown. Find the volume of the right
    circular cylinder.

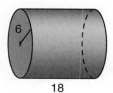

LESSON 79   *Systems of Equations with Subscripted Variables*

In Lesson 92 we will introduce uniform motion word problems. These problems will require
the use of variables that represent rate or speed and time. Rather than use the usual variables
x, y, and z, we will use variables that are easy to associate with the words in the problem. If we
need a variable to represent the rate of Mike, we will use R_M, which can be read as "the rate
of Mike" or "R sub M." If we need a variable to represent Joanie's rate, we will use R_J, which
can be read as "the rate of Joanie" or "R sub J." In the same way, Bud's time and Sadie's time
will be represented by the variables T_B and T_S, respectively, which can be read as "the time of
Bud" and "the time of Sadie" or as "T sub B" and "T sub S." The first problem we will solve
involves the rates and times of Anne and Pat and uses the variables R_A, T_A, R_P, and T_P.

example 79.1   Solve the following system of equations for R_A:

$$R_A T_A + R_P T_P = 320 \qquad R_P = 50 \qquad T_P = 4 \qquad T_A = 3$$

solution   In the equation on the left, we will substitute 50, 4, and 3 for R_P, T_P, and T_A, respectively,

$$R_A(3) + 50(4) = 320$$

and solve.

$$3R_A + 200 = 320 \quad \longrightarrow \quad 3R_A = 120 \quad \longrightarrow \quad R_A = \mathbf{40}$$

The equations for the next example come from a story problem about a turtle and a rabbit.
Thus, R_R and T_R stand for the rate of the rabbit and the time of the rabbit, and R_T and T_T stand
for the rate of the turtle and the time of the turtle.

example 79.2   Solve the following system of equations for T_R and T_T:

$$R_T T_T + 120 = R_R T_R \qquad R_T = 2 \qquad R_R = 10 \qquad T_T = T_R$$

solution   We begin by substituting 2 and 10 for R_T and R_R, respectively, in the first equation.

$$\text{(a)} \quad 2T_T + 120 = 10T_R$$

We have used the first three given equations thus far. The remaining given equation is $T_T = T_R$. We can use this equation to change T_T to T_R or to change T_R to T_T in equation (a). We choose to change T_T to T_R. We do this and then complete the solution.

$$2T_R + 120 = 10T_R \qquad \text{substituted } T_R \text{ for } T_T$$
$$\underline{-2T_R \qquad\qquad -2T_R} \qquad \text{added } -2T_R \text{ to both sides}$$
$$120 = 8T_R$$

$$\frac{120}{8} = \frac{8T_R}{8} \qquad \text{divided both sides by 8}$$

$$T_R = \mathbf{15}$$

And since $T_T = T_R$, $\qquad\qquad\qquad\qquad T_T = \mathbf{15}$

Now we will solve the equations for a problem in which Little Brother and Sis take a trip. We will use R_L and T_L for the rate and time of Little Brother, and R_S and T_S for the rate and time of Sis.

example 79.3 Solve the following system of equations for T_L and T_S:

$$R_L T_L = R_S T_S \qquad R_L = 40 \qquad R_S = 80 \qquad T_S = T_L - 5$$

solution We begin with the first equation by replacing R_L with 40 and R_S with 80.

$$40T_L = 80T_S$$

Now we will replace T_S with $T_L - 5$ and multiply using the distributive property.

$$40T_L = 80(T_L - 5) \quad \longrightarrow \quad 40T_L = 80T_L - 400$$

Now we complete the solution.

$$40T_L = 80T_L - 400$$
$$\underline{-80T_L \quad -80T_L} \qquad\qquad \text{added } -80T_L \text{ to both sides}$$
$$-40T_L = \qquad\quad -400$$

$$\frac{-40T_L}{-40} = \frac{-400}{-40} \qquad \text{divided both sides by } -40$$

So $T_L = \mathbf{10}$, and since $T_S = T_L - 5$

$$T_S = 10 - 5 \quad \longrightarrow \quad T_S = \mathbf{5}$$

The following equations are from a problem about a freight train and an express train. We symbolize the rate and time of the freight train by R_F and T_F and those for the express train by R_E and T_E.

example 79.4 Solve the following system of equations for R_F and R_E:

$$R_F T_F = R_E T_E \qquad T_F = 16 \qquad T_E = 12 \qquad R_E = R_F + 15$$

solution In the equation on the left, we will substitute 16, 12, and $R_F + 15$ for T_F, T_E, and R_E, respectively.

$$R_F T_F = R_E T_E \quad \longrightarrow \quad R_F(16) = (R_F + 15)(12) \quad \longrightarrow \quad 16R_F = 12R_F + 180$$
$$\longrightarrow \quad 4R_F = 180 \quad \longrightarrow \quad R_F = \mathbf{45}$$

And since $R_E = R_F + 15$,

$$R_E = 45 + 15 \quad \longrightarrow \quad R_E = \mathbf{60}$$

practice **a.** Given: $R_A T_A + R_P T_P = 460$, $R_P = 50$, $T_P = 4$, $T_A = 2$. Find R_A.

b. Given: $R_T T_T + 200 = R_R T_R$, $R_T = 10$, $R_R = 15$, $T_R = T_T + 10$. Find T_R and T_T.

problem set
79

1. Find four consecutive even integers such that 4 times the sum of the first and fourth is 8
(77) greater than 12 times the third.

2. John has a mug that contains 7 Greek coins and 5 Roman coins. A coin is drawn at
(73) random and not replaced. Then another coin is randomly drawn. What is the probability that the first coin was Greek and the second coin was Roman?

3. Two dice are rolled. What is the probability that the sum of the numbers rolled is
(70)

(a) 9? (b) a number less than 9?

4. Seven eighths of the workers of London's fish market used scurrilous language. If 400
(77) did not use scurrilous language, how many worked in the fish market?

5. Hannah's test grades were 80, 85, 75, and 92. What is her weighted average if the test
(65) grades were weighted 2, 4, 3, and 2, in that order?

6. With the new tractor, Martha could plow 67 percent of the farm in 2 weeks. If she could
(58) plow 268 acres in two weeks, how large was the farm? Draw a diagram as an aid in solving the problem.

7. Given: $R_A T_A + R_P T_P = 500$, $R_P = 25$, $T_P = 9$, $T_A = 5$. Find R_A.
(79)

8. Given: $R_H T_H = R_X T_X$, $R_H = 3$, $R_X = 6$, $T_X = T_H - 3$. Find T_X and T_H.
(79)

Solve:

9. $\dfrac{x}{4} - \dfrac{x + 2}{3} = 12$ **10.** $\dfrac{2y}{4} - \dfrac{y}{7} = \dfrac{y - 3}{2}$ **11.** $\dfrac{p}{6} - \dfrac{2p}{5} = \dfrac{4p - 5}{15}$
(78)   (78)   (78)

12. Graph on a rectangular coordinate system: $y = -\dfrac{1}{2}x + 2$
(75)

Write the following numbers in scientific notation:

13. 0.000135×10^{-17} **14.** $135{,}000 \times 10^{-17}$
(74)   (74)

Factor the trinomials. Always begin by writing the trinomials in descending order of the variables and by factoring out the greatest common factor.

15. $-30 - 13x + x^2$ **16.** $2m^2 - 24m + 70$
(69)   (71)

17. $-x^3 + 14x^2 - 40x$ **18.** $4m^2 n^2 - 49x^2 n^2 p^2$
(71)   (73)

19. $x^2(r + 2) + 10(r + 2) + 7x(r + 2)$ **20.** $4z^2(x + y) - 21z(x + y) + (x + y)z^3$
(72)   (72)

21. Use substitution to solve: **22.** Use elimination to solve:
(59)   (71)

$$\begin{cases} x + 3y = 16 \\ 2x - 3y = -4 \end{cases}$$ $$\begin{cases} N_N + N_D = 22 \\ 5N_N + 10N_D = 135 \end{cases}$$

23. Indicate whether the following numbers are rational numbers or irrational numbers:
(61)

(a) $\dfrac{\pi}{100}$ (b) $-\dfrac{0.031}{10}$ (c) $\sqrt{256}$ (d) -4.75

24. Add: $\dfrac{a}{xy} + \dfrac{4}{x(x + y)} - \dfrac{1}{y}$ **25.** Simplify: $5\sqrt{45} - 3\sqrt{180} + 2\sqrt{20}$
(52)   (66)

26. Evaluate: $\dfrac{\sqrt{x}}{11} - y^0 + \dfrac{\sqrt[4]{7}}{3} + \sqrt[3]{-1}$ if $\dfrac{x-21}{5} = 20$ and $\dfrac{y+27}{27} = 4$
(41)

27. Use nine unit multipliers to convert 23,000 cubic meters to cubic feet.
(53)

28. Solve: $-[-2(x-4) - |-3|] = -2x - 8$
(31)

29. Find the area of the shaded portion of
(8)   this rectangle. The figure in the center
of the rectangle is a trapezoid with a
height of 2 inches. Dimensions are in
inches.

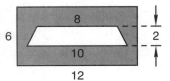

30. A base of the right solid 25 feet high is shown. Find the surface area of the right solid.
(15)   Dimensions are in feet.

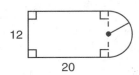

LESSON 80   *Operations with Scientific Notation*

In Lesson 74 we introduced the topic of scientific notation and discussed the method of writing a number in scientific notation. Scientific notation is particularly useful in problems that require the multiplication and division of very large or very small numbers. We will discuss multiplication first.

multiplication   We begin by multiplying the numbers 4,000,000 and 20,000,000 by using scientific notation. As the first step we write both numbers in scientific notation.

$$4{,}000{,}000 = 4 \times 10^6 \qquad 20{,}000{,}000 = 2 \times 10^7$$

Then we note that the numbers are to be multiplied by writing

$$(4 \times 10^6)(2 \times 10^7)$$

Since the order of multiplication of real numbers does not affect the value of the product, we may rearrange the order of the multiplication and place the powers of 10 last.

$$(4 \cdot 2)(10^6 \cdot 10^7)$$

Now we multiply 4 by 2 and get 8 and multiply the powers of 10 by using the product rule for exponents to get 10^{13}. Thus our answer is the number

$$8 \times 10^{13}$$

example 80.1   Write the numbers 0.003×10^{-4} and 2×10^{20} in scientific notation and then multiply.

solution   First we write the numbers in scientific notation.

$$(0.003 \times 10^{-4})(2 \times 10^{20}) = (3 \times 10^{-7})(2 \times 10^{20})$$

Next, we rearrange the order of the factors and then we multiply.

$$(3 \cdot 2)(10^{-7} \cdot 10^{20}) = \mathbf{6 \times 10^{13}}$$

example 80.2 Multiply: $(0.00004 \times 10^{-5})(700,000)$

solution We write the numbers in scientific notation, rearrange the order of factors, and then multiply.

$$(4 \times 10^{-10})(7 \times 10^5) = (4 \cdot 7)(10^{-10} \cdot 10^5) = 28 \times 10^{-5}$$
$$= \mathbf{2.8 \times 10^{-4}}$$

division A similar procedure is used to divide numbers written in scientific notation. The powers of 10 are handled separately from the other numbers. To divide 20,000,000 by 4,000,000, we first write both numbers in scientific notation.

$$\frac{20,000,000}{4,000,000} = \frac{2 \times 10^7}{4 \times 10^6}$$

We can think of this expression as a product of fractions, which we simplify as follows:

$$\left(\frac{2}{4}\right)\left(\frac{10^7}{10^6}\right) = 0.5 \times 10^1 = 5$$

example 80.3 Divide 0.0016 by 400,000.

solution We write both numbers in scientific notation as the numerator and denominator of a fraction,

$$\frac{1.6 \times 10^{-3}}{4 \times 10^5}$$

which we then express of as a product of fractions. We then simplify both fractions and multiply them.

$$\left(\frac{1.6}{4}\right)\left(\frac{10^{-3}}{10^5}\right) = 0.4 \times 10^{-8}$$

Now to finish we write 0.4×10^{-8} in scientific notation as

$$\mathbf{4 \times 10^{-9}}$$

multiplication and division The procedure for simplifying a problem such as

$$\frac{(0.06 \times 10^5)(300,000)}{(1000)(0.00009)}$$

is first to simplify both the numerator and denominator by using scientific notation. Next, we rearrange the expression into a product of fractions and then simplify each fraction.

$$\frac{(6 \times 10^3)(3 \times 10^5)}{(1 \times 10^3)(9 \times 10^{-5})} = \frac{6 \cdot 3}{1 \cdot 9} \times \frac{10^3 \cdot 10^5}{10^3 \cdot 10^{-5}} = \frac{18}{9} \times \frac{10^8}{10^{-2}} = 2 \times 10^{10}$$

example 80.4 Simplify: $\dfrac{(0.0007 \times 10^{-23})(4000 \times 10^6)}{(0.00004)(7,000,000)}$

solution We will begin by writing every number in scientific notation. Next, we rearrange the expression into a product of two fractions and then simplify each fraction.

$$\frac{(7 \times 10^{-27})(4 \times 10^9)}{(4 \times 10^{-5})(7 \times 10^6)} = \frac{7 \cdot 4}{4 \cdot 7} \times \frac{10^{-27} \cdot 10^9}{10^{-5} \cdot 10^6} = \frac{28}{28} \times \frac{10^{-18}}{10^1} = \mathbf{1 \times 10^{-19}}$$

example 80.5   Simplify: $\dfrac{\left(20 \times 10^{-45}\right)\left(400 \times 10^{20}\right)}{(100{,}000)\left(0.0008 \times 10^{-15}\right)}$

solution   First we write all numbers in scientific notation.

$$\frac{\left(2 \times 10^{-44}\right)\left(4 \times 10^{22}\right)}{\left(1 \times 10^{5}\right)\left(8 \times 10^{-19}\right)}$$

Now we group the exponentials and the other numbers and simplify.

$$\frac{2 \cdot 4}{1 \cdot 8} \times \frac{10^{-44} \cdot 10^{22}}{10^{5} \cdot 10^{-19}} = \frac{8}{8} \times \frac{10^{-22}}{10^{-14}} = \mathbf{1 \times 10^{-8}}$$

practice   Simplify:

   a. $\dfrac{\left(0.07 \times 10^{2}\right)(800{,}000)}{(10{,}000)(0.0000004)}$
          b. $\dfrac{\left(0.04 \times 10^{-9}\right)\left(50 \times 10^{16}\right)}{(0.000004)(50{,}000)}$

problem set 80

1. (76) Cindy had three consecutive even integers. She found that the product of their sum and 3 was 20 greater than 8 times the third integer. What were Cindy's integers?

2. (70) Binro has an urn with 5 purple marbles, 6 red marbles, and 4 green marbles. She randomly draws one marble. What is the probability that

   (a)   the marble is red?   (b)   the marble is purple?   (c)   the marble is green?

3. (70) A fair coin is tossed 5 times. What is the probability that the first three times it comes up tails and the next two times it comes up heads?

4. (58) The fairies outnumbered the hamadryads by 130 percent. If there were 460 fairies in the clearing, how many hamadryads were present?

5. (77) Querulous was not satisfied because the sinecure did not pay enough. It paid 4125 pounds, but this was only five thirteenths of what he expected. How much did Querulous expect?

Simplify:

6. (80) $\dfrac{\left(0.08 \times 10^{7}\right)(900{,}000)}{(20{,}000)(0.000003)}$
       7. (80) $\dfrac{\left(0.0006 \times 10^{-31}\right)\left(8000 \times 10^{9}\right)}{(0.0000002)(400{,}000)}$

Solve:

8. (79) Given: $R_F T_F = R_S T_S$, $T_S = 6$, $T_F = 5$, $R_F - 16 = R_S$. Find R_S and R_F.

9. (79) Given: $R_M T_M = R_R T_R$, $R_M = 8$, $R_R = 2$, $T_R = 5 - T_M$. Find T_M and T_R.

10. (79) Given: $R_G T_G + R_B T_B = 100$, $R_G = 4$, $R_B = 10$, $T_B = T_G + 3$. Find T_G and T_B.

Solve:

11. (78) $\dfrac{3x}{2} - \dfrac{5 - x}{3} = 7$
    12. (78) $\dfrac{2x - 3}{5} - \dfrac{2x}{10} = \dfrac{1}{2}$
    13. (25) $3\dfrac{1}{8}x - 4\dfrac{2}{5} = 7\dfrac{1}{2}$

14. (75) Graph on a rectangular coordinate system: $y = \dfrac{3}{5}x - 1$

15. (64) Graph on a number line: $x \nleq 2$; $D = \{\text{Positive integers}\}$

Factor completely:

16. (71) $x^3 + 9x^2 + 8x$
         17. (71) $-ax^2 + 48a - 13xa$

18. (73) $bcx^2 - a^2cb$
           19. (73) $(x - a)y^2 - 16(x - a)$

20. Use substitution to solve:
(71)

$$\begin{cases} N_N = N_D + 12 \\ 5N_N + 10N_D = 510 \end{cases}$$

21. Use elimination to solve:
(67)

$$\begin{cases} 7x - 4y = 29 \\ 3x + 5y = -1 \end{cases}$$

22. (a) $42\sqrt{7} \in$ {What subsets of the real numbers}?
(61)

(b) $\sqrt[3]{-64} \in$ {What subsets of the real numbers}?

23. Add: $\dfrac{3}{a} + \dfrac{4}{a^2} + \dfrac{7}{a^2(a + x)} - \dfrac{1}{a(a + x)}$
(52)

Simplify:

24. $\dfrac{a^{-1}b^{-1} + ab}{(ab)^{-1}}$
(68)

25. $\dfrac{\left[x^2\left(y^5\right)^{-2}\right]^{-3}}{\left(x^0 y^2\right)y^{-2}}$
(53)

26. $\dfrac{4 + \dfrac{1}{y^2}}{\dfrac{x}{y} + \dfrac{m}{y^2}}$
(68)

27. Expand by using the distributive property. Write the answer with all exponents positive:
(40)

$$\frac{x^{-2}}{y^2 a}\left(\frac{y^2 a^{-3}}{x^{-2}} + \frac{3x^{-4}}{y^{-2}a^{-4}} - \frac{x^2}{a^{-1}y^{-2}}\right)$$

28. Evaluate: $\sqrt[4]{x + 9} + \left(\dfrac{\sqrt{x - 8}}{2}\right) - \sqrt[3]{\dfrac{x}{9}}$ if $\dfrac{x - 9}{3} = 21$
(41)

29. Find the perimeter of this figure. Dimensions are in centimeters.
(3)

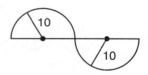

30. The area of a base of the right pentag-
(20,60) onal prism is 38 m² and the length of a lateral edge is 15 m. Find the volume of the right pentagonal prism.

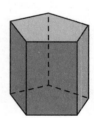

LESSON 81 *Graphical Solutions • Inconsistent Equations • Dependent Equations*

81.A

graphical solutions

In Lesson 48, we noted that the degree of a term of a polynomial is the sum of the exponents of the variables in the term. Thus $2xy^5$ is a sixth-degree term, $4x$ is a first-degree term, and xy is a second-degree term.

Also, we remember that the degree of a polynomial is the same as the degree of its highest-degree term and that the degree of a polynomial equation is the same as the degree of the highest-degree term in the equation. Thus

$$x^4y + 4y \qquad\qquad \text{is a fifth-degree polynomial}$$

$$x^4y + 4y = x \qquad\qquad \text{is a fifth-degree polynomial equation}$$

$$x + 2y = 4 \qquad\qquad \text{is a first-degree polynomial equation}$$

In Lesson 88 we will learn to solve second-degree polynomials equations by factoring, but until then, we will continue to concentrate on first-degree equations. We have learned that the graph of a first-degree polynomial equation in two unknowns is a straight line and that we call this kind of equation a linear equation. We have learned to find the solution to a system of two linear equations by using the **substitution method** and the **elimination method.** Here we will see that we can find the solution to a system of two linear equations by **graphing** each of the equations and visually estimating the coordinates of the point where the two lines cross. The shortcoming of this method is that it is inexact because the coordinates of the crossing point must be estimated. We can check to see whether the coordinates of the crossing point are really the solutions of both equations by checking to see if the coordinates satisfy both equations.

example 81.1   Solve by graphing: $\begin{cases} y = x + 1 \\ y = -2x + 4 \end{cases}$

solution   We can use two different methods for graphing the lines: the method of plotting points discussed in Lesson 51 or the slope-intercept method discussed in Lesson 75. We will use the slope-intercept method. The slope of the first line is 1 and the intercept is 1; the graph of this line is labeled *A*. The slope of the second line is –2 and its intercept is 4; the graph of this line is labeled *B*.

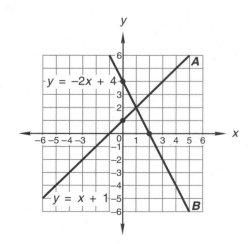

It appears that the lines cross at $x = 1$ and $y = 2$; we can check algebraically whether or not this is indeed a solution by substituting these values into the original equations.

$$2 = 1 + 1 \qquad\qquad \text{True}$$

$$2 = -2(1) + 4 \qquad\qquad \text{True}$$

Therefore, the solution to the two linear equations is **(1, 2)**.

example 81.2   Solve by graphing: $\begin{cases} y = 2 \\ y = x \end{cases}$

solution   We graph the lines as the first step.

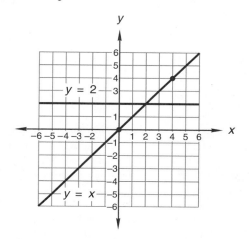

It appears that the lines cross at $x = 2$, $y = 2$, so we surmise our graphical solution is $(2, 2)$. After substituting the values $x = 2$ and $y = 2$ into the original equations and finding that these values for x and y do indeed satisfy both equations, we find that the solution to the linear equations is **(2, 2)**.

example 81.3   Solve by graphing: $\begin{cases} y = x + 2 \\ y = x - 1 \end{cases}$

solution

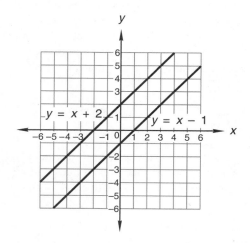

It appears from the graph that the lines are parallel and thus never intersect. If this is so, no point lies on both of the lines and no ordered pair will satisfy both equations. An attempt at solving this system by substitution or elimination will degenerate into a false numerical statement. The equations given in this problem are called **inconsistent equations.** We will look into inconsistent equations in detail in the next section.

81.B

inconsistent equations

Inconsistent equations are equations that have no common solution. On the left is a system of two linear equations, and the figure shows the graphs of the two equations.

$$\begin{cases} x + y = 2 \\ x + y = -3 \end{cases}$$

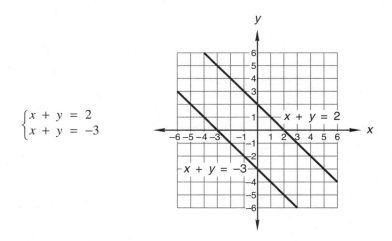

From the figure we see that the lines appear to be parallel and do not appear to intersect. If they do not intersect, there is no one point that lies on both of the lines, and hence no ordered pair of x and y will satisfy both equations. If we try to use either the substitution method or the elimination method, we will end up with a false numerical statement. To demonstrate this result, we will attempt to solve the given system by both methods.

SUBSTITUTION	ELIMINATION
$(-3 - y) + y = 2$	$-x - y = -2$
$-3 - y + y = 2$	$\dfrac{x + y = -3}{0 = -5}$ False
$-3 = 2$ False	

In both cases the final result is a false numerical statement.

In Lessons 54 and 67, we discussed the substitution and elimination methods in some detail. We saw that before either method was used, an assumption was necessary. We assumed that a value of x and y existed that would simultaneously satisfy both equations and that the symbols x and y in the equations represented these numbers. From the graph of the parallel lines shown previously, we see that our assumption was invalid. There is no point that is common to both lines and whose coordinates satisfy both equations. Since our assumption was invalid, the substitution and elimination methods do not produce a solution.

example 81.4   Determine whether the following set of equations have a common solution: $\begin{cases} y = x + 2 \\ y = x - 1 \end{cases}$

solution   The equations given are the same as in example 81.3. The graphs of the two equations appear parallel and it appears that the two lines will never intersect, meaning that the two equations do not share a solution. We will confirm this algebraically by attempting to solve the two equations.

We substitute the expression for y in the second equation into the first equation to get

$$x - 1 = x + 2 \qquad \text{substitution}$$

$$-1 = 2 \quad \text{False} \qquad \text{subtracted } x \text{ from both sides}$$

Note that we end up with a false statement. This means that our **original equations do not share a common solution.**

81.C

dependent equations

We have defined equivalent equations to be equations that have the same solution set. If we multiply every term on both sides of an equation by the same nonzero quantity, the resulting equation is an equivalent equation to the original equation. In the figure on the left, we have graphed the equation

$$y - x = 2$$

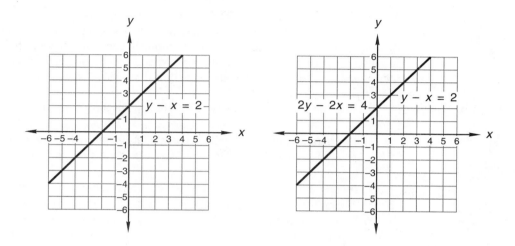

There is an infinite number of ordered pairs of x and y whose coordinates satisfy the equation, and the graph of these points (x, y) is the line in the figure. If we multiply every term in the given equation by some quantity, say the number 2,

$$y - x = 2 \qquad \text{multiplied by (2) yields} \qquad 2y - 2x = 4$$

we get the equation $2y - 2x = 4$, which is an equivalent equation to the original equation. Thus all ordered pairs of x and y that satisfy the original equation also satisfy the new equation, and the graph of the new equation is the same as the graph of the original equation. If we are asked to find a graphical solution to a system that consists of a pair of equivalent equations such as the pair being discussed,

$$\text{(a)} \quad \begin{cases} y - x = 2 \\ \text{(b)} \quad 2y - 2x = 4 \end{cases}$$

we find that the graph of both equations is the single line of either figure above. Thus any ordered pair that is a solution to one of the equations is also a solution to the other equation. **Equivalent linear equations are called *dependent equations*.** If we try to find the solution to our pair of dependent equations, we find that the result will always be a true numerical statement. We will attempt to solve the system above by using both substitution and elimination.

example 81.5   Determine whether the following set of equations is dependent: $\begin{cases} y - x = 2 \\ 2y - 2x = 4 \end{cases}$

solution   We have seen that the graph of these two equations are identical. Therefore, the two equations have the same solution set.

Let us assume we do not know how the graphs of these equations look. We will algebraically try to determine the solution to these equations. We will attempt to solve the system above by using both substitution and elimination.

| SUBSTITUTION | ELIMINATION |
| | |

SUBSTITUTION

(a) $y - x = 2$

(b) $2y - 2x = 4$

$2(x + 2) - 2x = 4$

$2x + 4 - 2x = 4$

$4 = 4$ True

ELIMINATION

(a) $y - x = 2$

(b) $2y - 2x = 4$

$-2y + 2x = -4$

$\underline{2y - 2x = 4}$

$0 = 0$ True

On the left we solved equation (a) for y and substituted this expression for y in equation (b). The result reduced to the true statement that 4 equals 4. On the right we multiplied each term in equation (a) by -2 and then added the resulting equation to equation (b). The result was the true statement that 0 equals 0. This indicates that any ordered pair of x and y that satisfies one of the equations will satisfy the other equation. Thus the equations are **dependent.**

summary Two linear equations in two unknowns fall into one of three categories:

1. **Consistent equations,** which are equations that have a single ordered pair as a common solution. The graphs of consistent equations intersect, as shown in figure (a).
2. **Inconsistent equations,** which are equations that have no common solution. The graphs of inconsistent equations are parallel lines, as shown in figure (b).
3. **Dependent equations,** which are equivalent equations, are the same equation in two different forms. The graph of two dependent equations is a single line, as shown in figure (c).

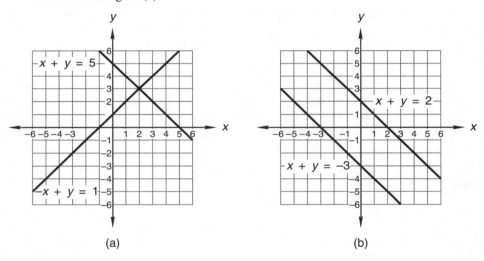

(a)   (b)

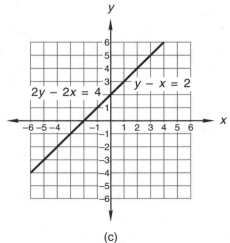

(c)

example 81.6 Consider the equations $y = 2x + 5$ and $y = x$. Is this pair of equations consistent, inconsistent, or dependent?

solution Let's see if these equations have one point in common. Since $y = x$, we substitute x for y in the first equation:

$$x = 2x + 5 \qquad \text{substituted}$$

$$x = -5 \qquad \text{solved}$$

Since $y = x$, y is also equal to -5. The graphs of these two equations have only one point in common, $(-5, -5)$, so the equations are **consistent.**

practice Solve by graphing. Confirm that the solutions obtained by graphing are correct by substituting them back into the original equations.

a. $\begin{cases} y = x - 1 \\ y = -2x + 5 \end{cases}$
b. $\begin{cases} y = x \\ y = 4 \end{cases}$

c. Consider the equations $x + y = 7$ and $x + y = 9$. Are these equations consistent, inconsistent, or dependent?

problem set 81

1. (77) Find three consecutive even integers such that 4 times the sum of the first and third is 16 greater than 7 times the second.

2. (76) Find four consecutive integers such that if the sum of the first and third is increased by 10, the result is 6 greater than 4 times the fourth.

3. (70) Two dice are rolled. What is the probability that the sum of the numbers rolled is

(a) 2?
(b) a number greater than 10?

4. (58) Thomas won first place at a local tennis tournament. He achieved a first serve 33 times out of 55 times. What was Thomas' first serve percentage?

5. (77) The new hog food supplement increased the weight gain by $\frac{2}{5}$. If the weight gain used to be 300 pounds, what was the new weight gain?

6. (58) After some of the leprechans ran into the forest, the number of little people remaining decreased by 35%. If 105 ran into the forest, how many were originally present?

7. (77) What fraction of $7\frac{2}{5}$ is $49\frac{1}{3}$?

Solve the following sets of equations by graphing them on a rectangular coordinate system. Check your answers by substituting them back into the original equations.

8. (81) $\begin{cases} y = x - 6 \\ y = -x \end{cases}$
9. (81) $\begin{cases} y = x + 1 \\ y = -x - 1 \end{cases}$

10. (81) Consider the equations $y = x + 5$ and $y = x$. Is this pair of equations consistent, inconsistent, or dependent? Check your answer by graphing the equation on a rectangular coordinate system.

Simplify:

11. (80) $\dfrac{(0.003 \times 10^7)(700,000)}{(5000)(0.0021 \times 10^{-6})}$
12. (80) $\dfrac{(0.0007 \times 10^{-10})(4000 \times 10^5)}{(0.0004)(7000)}$

13. Given: $R_G T_G + R_B T_B = 120$, $R_G = 4$, $R_B = 10$, $T_G = T_B + 2$. Find T_G and T_B.
(79)

14. Given: $R_K T_K = R_N T_N$, $R_K = 6$, $R_N = 3$, $T_K = T_N - 8$. Find T_K and T_N.
(79)

Solve:

15. $\dfrac{x}{3} + \dfrac{5x + 3}{2} = 5$
(78)

16. $\dfrac{y + 3}{2} - \dfrac{4y}{3} = \dfrac{1}{6}$
(78)

Factor completely:

17. $ax^2 + 6a - 7ax$
(71)

18. $-mx^2 - 8m - 6mx$
(71)

19. $mx^2 - 9ma^2$
(73)

20. $b^2(x + a) + 2b(x + a) - 24(x + a)$
(72)

21. Use substitution to solve:
(59)
$$\begin{cases} x + 5y = 17 \\ 2x - 4y = -8 \end{cases}$$

22. Use elimination to solve:
(71)
$$\begin{cases} N_N + N_D = 30 \\ 5N_N + 10N_D = 250 \end{cases}$$

23. Simplify: $4\sqrt{28} - 3\sqrt{63} + \sqrt{175} - 9\sqrt{7}$
(66)

24. Evaluate: (a) $3 \pm \sqrt{169}$ (b) $9 \pm \sqrt{144}$ (c) $2 \pm \sqrt{361}$
(62)

Simplify:

25. $\dfrac{\dfrac{x}{y} - 1}{\dfrac{x}{y} + m}$
(68)

26. $\dfrac{x^2\left(2y^{-2}\right)^{-3}}{\left(4x^2\right)^{-2}}$
(53)

27. $\dfrac{1}{-3^{-2}} - 3 - (-3)^2$
(29)

28. Evaluate: $\dfrac{\sqrt[3]{x + 2} + 11}{3} + \sqrt{y^3}$ if $\dfrac{x - 22}{5} = (2)^3$ and $2y = 8$
(41)

29. Expand by using the distributive property. Write the answer with all exponents positive.
(40)
$$\dfrac{x^{-2}}{a^2 y^{-2}}\left(\dfrac{x^4 a^5}{y^4} - \dfrac{3x^{-4}}{a^{-4} y^2} + \dfrac{x^2}{a^{-2} y^2}\right)$$

30. A base of the right prism is the isosceles triangle shown. The height of the right prism is
(20,60) 20 inches. Find the volume of the right prism.

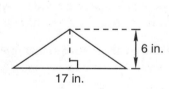

6 in.

17 in.

LESSON 82   *Evaluating Functions • Domain and Range*

82.A
evaluating functions

In Lesson 28, we were introduced to the concept of a function and to the use of functional notation. We learned in Lesson 28 that an expression in an independent variable x can be considered a **function of x** if the expression has just one value for every value of x. For example, suppose we define the function

$$f(x) = x^2 + 5$$

We find that for every value of x we choose, the function f applied to that value of x yields exactly one answer. For example,

$$f(1) = (1)^2 + 5 = 6$$

$$f(-1) = (-1)^2 + 5 = 6$$

$$f(2) = (2)^2 + 5 = 9$$

$$f(\sqrt{2}) = (\sqrt{2})^2 + 5 = 2 + 5 = 7$$

Note that f applied to each value of x produces just one value. Note that a function f applied to two different values of x can produce the same answer. For instance, in the example above, f applied to 1 and -1 yields the same answer, 6.

We expand upon what we learned earlier through some examples.

example 82.1   If $f(x) = x^2 + x - 10$, find $f(5)$.

solution   To find $f(5)$, we replace x everywhere with 5.

$f(x) = x^2 + x - 10$	function
$f(5) = (5)^2 + (5) - 10$	replaced x with 5
$f(5) = \mathbf{20}$	simplified

example 82.2   If $h(x) = x^2 + x + 1$, find $h(a^2)$.

solution   Note that in this example, we are not evaluating the function for some numerical value of x but applying the function to some expression, as shown. In later courses in mathematics, the skill of applying a function to expressions will be very important.

To find $h(a^2)$, replace x with a^2, as shown.

$h(x) = x^2 + x + 1$	function
$h(a^2) = (a^2)^2 + a^2 + 1$	replaced x with a^2
$h(a^2) = \mathbf{a^4 + a^2 + 1}$	simplified

example 82.3   If $f(x) = x^2 + 1$, find $f(x + 2)$.

solution   To find $f(x + 2)$, we replace x everywhere with $x + 2$.

$f(x) = x^2 + 1$	function
$f(x + 2) = (x + 2)^2 + 1$	replaced x with $x + 2$
$f(x + 2) = \mathbf{x^2 + 4x + 5}$	simplified

82.B
domain and range

In this text, we will use only the real numbers as replacements for x, and we accept only values of $f(x)$ that are real numbers. Therefore, **we cannot use numbers as replacements for x that result in division by zero or that require us to take square roots of negative numbers.** If a number is an acceptable replacement for x, we say that the number is a member of the **domain** of the function. We call the set of all possible outputs of a function the **range.** Below, we state formally the definition of a function.

DEFINITION OF A FUNCTION

A **function** is a mapping from one set called the **domain** to another set called the **range** such that

1. Each element of the domain is mapped to precisely one element of the range, and
2. Each element of the range corresponds to at least one member of the domain.

Another way to define the domain and range of a function is as follows:

Domain of f = set of acceptable x values or set of inputs

Range of f = set of resulting y values or set of outputs

It is much easier to determine the domain of many functions than it is to determine their ranges. In the examples as well as the problem sets, we will usually ask students to determine the domains of functions. We will only ask for the range of a function if it is immediately apparent.

example 82.4   If $f(x) = 2x$, find the domain and range of the function f.

solution   We see that the function f can be applied to any real value of x so the domain of f is the set of real numbers. We can write this as:

Domain of f = **{set of all real numbers}**

The range of f is all those values that $f(x)$ can assume. It turns out that the range of f is also the set of real numbers, as is apparent from the graph of f.

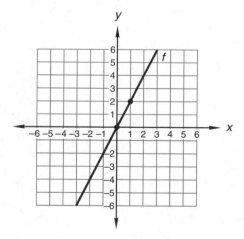

We see from the graph that the set of all possible y values of points on the graph of f is the set of real numbers.

Range of f = **{set of all real numbers}**

example 82.5   If $f(x) = 3$, find the domain and range of the function f.

solution   We see that the function f can be applied to any real number, so

$$\text{Domain of } f = \{\textbf{set of all real numbers}\}$$

The only value the function f ever attains is 3. Whether $x = 0$ or $x = 1{,}000{,}000$, $f(x) = 3$. Therefore,

$$\text{Range of } f = \{\textbf{3}\}$$

example 82.6   If the graph of a function f is as shown, determine the domain and range of f.

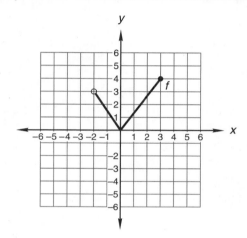

solution   The open circle at $(-2, 3)$ indicates that the point $(-2, 3)$ is *not* on the graph of f. The domain of f is the set of numbers for which f "makes sense" or is defined. We use mathematical shorthand to describe the domain of f.

$$\text{Domain of } f = \big\{x \in \mathbb{R} \mid \textbf{–2} < x \leq \textbf{3}\big\}$$

The symbol $\mid$ means "such that." We recall from Lessons 56 and 61 that the symbol $\in$ means "an element of" and $\mathbb{R}$ is shorthand for the set of real numbers. The range of f is the set of resulting y values for those x values in the domain of f. We see in this case that the y values of the points on the graph of f can vary from 0 to 4, inclusive. So

$$\text{Range of } f = \big\{y \in \mathbb{R} \mid \textbf{0} \leq y \leq \textbf{4}\big\}$$

example 82.7   Find the domain of the function $f(x) = \sqrt{5 - x}$.

solution   We want to find the set of all acceptable x values. The radicand, $5 - x$, cannot be negative since the square root of a negative number is not a real number. (Note that $5 - x$ can be zero since we can determine the square root of zero.) Therefore, we must describe all x such that

$$5 - x \geq 0$$

Solving for x, we find that

$$5 \geq x$$

Therefore,

$$\text{Domain of } f = \big\{x \in \mathbb{R} \mid x \leq \textbf{5}\big\}$$

example 82.8   Find the domain of the function $g(x) = \dfrac{1}{x}$.

solution   We want to find the set of all acceptable x values. Note that $g(x) = \frac{1}{x}$ has value whenever x does not equal zero. Therefore,

$$\text{Domain of } g = \{x \in \mathbb{R} \mid x \neq 0\}$$

practice   **a.**   If $f(x) = 2x^2 + 3x - 5$, find $f(m^2)$.

   b.   If $g(x) = x^2 - 4$, find $g(m + 2)$.

   c.   If $f(x) = 3x$, find the domain and range of function f.

   d.   If $g(x) = 2$, find the domain and range of function g.

   e.   If the graph of a function f is as shown, determine the domain and range of f.

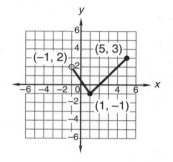

   f.   Find the domain of the function $g(x) = \sqrt{3 - x}$.

problem set   **1.**   Find four consecutive odd integers such that 6 times the sum of the first and the third is
82   (77)   3 more than 5 times the opposite of the fourth.

   2.   The fountain contains 20 pennies and 9 dimes. A coin is randomly taken and not replaced.
   (73)   A second coin is randomly taken. What is the probability that both coins are pennies?

   3.   Two dice are rolled. What is the probability that the sum of the numbers rolled is
   (70)
   (a)   8?   (b)   a number less than 8?

   4.   Mr. Pollack's biology class observed the growth of pea plants. If 5 pea plants grew to
   (52)   30 cm and 15 pea plants grew to 50 cm, what was the overall average height of the pea
   plants?

   5.   Diana jogged every day for a week. On that week she jogged 3, 5, 4, 5, 6, 2, and 5 miles,
   (45)   respectively. What is the range, median, mode, and mean of these distances?

   6.   Only $\frac{2}{17}$ of the teachers were sciolists. If 3000 were not sciolists, how many teachers were
   (77)   there in all?

   7.   If $f(x) = x^2 + 1$, find $f(x + 1)$.   **8.**   Find the domain of $g(x) = \sqrt{4 - x}$.
   (82)   (82)

   9.   If $f(x) = -1$, find the domain and range of function f.
   (82)

   10.   If the graph of function f is as shown,
   (82)   determine the domain and range of f.

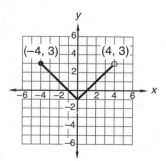

11. Given: $R_M T_M + R_S T_S = 170$, $R_M = 20$, $R_S = 30$, $T_M = T_S + 1$. Find T_M and T_S.
(79)

Solve the following sets of equations by graphing them on a rectangular coordinate system. Check your answers by substituting them back into the original equations.

12. $\begin{cases} y = x + 4 \\ y = -x + 2 \end{cases}$
(81)

13. $\begin{cases} y = 2 \\ x = -3 \end{cases}$
(81)

14. Consider the equations $y = x + 2$ and $y = -x - 1$. Is this pair of equations
(81) consistent, inconsistent, or dependent? Check your answer by graphing the equations on a rectangular coordinate system.

15. Simplify: $\dfrac{(0.0056 \times 10^{-5})(100{,}000 \times 10^{-14})}{8000 \times 10^{15}}$
(80)

Solve:

16. $\dfrac{x + 2}{5} - \dfrac{x}{10} = \dfrac{3}{20}$
(78)

17. $\dfrac{3x - 4}{2} + \dfrac{1}{5} = \dfrac{x}{10}$
(78)

Factor completely:

18. $4a^2 - 160 + 12a$
(71)

19. $-m^3 + k^2 m$
(73)

20. $x^4(y + 1) + 2(y + 1)x^3 + x^2(y + 1)$
(72)

21. Use substitution to solve:
(71)

$\begin{cases} 5N_N + 10N_D = 450 \\ N_D = N_N + 30 \end{cases}$

22. Use elimination to solve:
(67)

$\begin{cases} 5x - 2y = 7 \\ 4x + y = 3 \end{cases}$

23. Indicate whether the following numbers are rational numbers or irrational numbers:
(61)

    (a) $3\pi - (7\pi - 4\pi)$ (b) $2(\sqrt{2} + 1) - 2\sqrt{2}$ (c) $\sqrt{101.2 - \dfrac{6}{5}}$

Add:

24. $\dfrac{1}{xc^2} + \dfrac{b}{x(c + x)} + \dfrac{5}{x^2 c^2}$
(52)

25. $\dfrac{4}{x + y} + \dfrac{6}{x} - \dfrac{4}{ax}$
(52)

26. Simplify: $7\sqrt{20} - 5\sqrt{32} + 2\sqrt{45} - 2\sqrt{180}$
(66)

27. Expand: $\dfrac{x^{-2}a}{y^2}\left(\dfrac{a^4 y^{-2}}{x} - \dfrac{3x^2 a}{y^2}\right)$
(40)

28. Simplify: $\dfrac{x^2 y^{-1} + y}{a - xy^{-1}}$
(68)

29. Find the area of this figure. Dimen-
(8) sions are in centimeters.

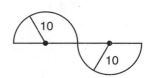

30. Find the lateral surface area of this
(15,60) right prism whose bases are regular pentagons. Dimensions are in meters.

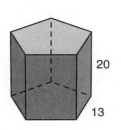

LESSON 83 Coin Problems

When we solve a problem, we read the problem and search for statements about quantities that are equal. Each time we find a statement of equality, we write it as an algebraic equation. When we have the same number of independent equations as we have variables, we solve the equations by using substitution, elimination, or by graphing.

The word problems that we have been working thus far have contained only one statement about quantities that are equal. We have worked these problems by using one equation and one variable. Now we will begin solving word problems that contain two statements about quantities that are equal. We will turn each of the statements into an equation that has two variables. Then we will solve the equations by using either substitution or elimination. The first problems of this kind are called **coin problems.**

In coin problems one statement will be about the number of coins. This statement will be like one of the following:

(a)   The number of nickels plus the number of dimes equals 40.

$$N_N + N_D = 40$$

(b)   There were six more nickels than dimes.

$$N_N = N_D + 6$$

The other statement will be about the value of the coins. Two examples are:

(c)   The value of the nickels plus the value of the dimes equals $4.65.

$$5N_N + 10N_D = 465$$

(d)   The value of the dimes and quarters equaled $25.10.

$$10N_D + 25N_Q = 2510$$

To avoid decimal numbers, we will often write all values in cents, as in (c) and (d).

example 83.1   Jack and Betty have 28 coins that are nickels and dimes. If the value of the coins is $1.95, how many coins of each type do they have?

solution   This is a typical problem about coins. It says that the number of nickels plus the number of dimes equals 28 and that the value of the nickels plus the value of the dimes equals 195 cents.

$$\text{(a) } N_N + N_D = 28$$

$$\text{(b) } 5N_N + 10N_D = 195$$

The values of N_N and N_D that will simultaneously satisfy both equations may be found using either the substitution method or the elimination method.

SUBSTITUTION

$$5(28 - N_D) + 10N_D = 195$$

$$140 - 5N_D + 10N_D = 195$$

$$140 + 5N_D = 195$$

$$5N_D = 55$$

$$N_D = \mathbf{11}$$

And since $N_N + N_D = 28$

$$N_N = \mathbf{17}$$

ELIMINATION

$$\begin{array}{r} -5N_N - 5N_D = -140 \\ 5N_N + 10N_D = 195 \\ \hline 5N_D = 55 \end{array}$$

$$N_D = \mathbf{11}$$

And since $N_N + N_D = 28$

$$N_N = \mathbf{17}$$

example 83.2   Ming has \$4.45 in quarters and dimes. She has 8 more quarters than dimes. How many coins of each type does she have?

solution   This problem has two statements about things that are equal. The first is that the value of the quarters plus the value of the dimes equals 445 pennies. We write this as

$$\text{(a) } 25N_Q + 10N_D = 445$$

Since she has 8 more quarters, we add 8 to the number of dimes so the two sides of the equation will be equal.

$$\text{(b) } N_D + 8 = N_Q$$

To solve, we will substitute equation (b) into equation (a).

$$25(N_D + 8) + 10N_D = 445 \qquad \text{substituted}$$

$$25N_D + 200 + 10N_D = 445 \qquad \text{multiplied}$$

$$35N_D + 200 = 445 \qquad \text{simplified}$$

$$35N_D = 245 \qquad \text{added } -200 \text{ to both sides}$$

$$N_D = \mathbf{7}$$

Thus, $N_Q = (7) + 8 = \mathbf{15}$

example 83.3   Orlando had a hoard of 22 nickels and dimes whose value was \$1.35. How many coins of each type did he have?

solution   The two statements of equality are:

(a) The number of nickels plus the number of dimes equaled 22.

$$\text{(a) } N_N + N_D = 22$$

(b) The value of the nickels plus the value of the dimes equaled 135 pennies.

$$\text{(b) } 5N_N + 10N_D = 135$$

This time we will use elimination. We multiply each term in (a) by -5 to get (a′), which we add to (b).

$$
\begin{array}{ll}
\text{(a′)} & -5N_N - 5N_D = -110 \\
\text{(b)} & \underline{5N_N + 10N_D = 135} \\
& 5N_D = 25 \\
& N_D = \mathbf{5} \\
\end{array}
$$

Since $N_N + N_D = 22$, $N_N = \mathbf{17}$

practice   Solve:

a.   Ahmad and Regina have 36 coins that are nickels and dimes. If the value of the coins is \$2.90, how many coins of each type do they have?

b.   Emil has \$6.45 in quarters and dimes. He has 9 more quarters than dimes. How many coins of each type does he have?

problem set
83

1. Heidi and Micah have 51 dimes and nickels. If the value of the coins is $4.10, how many
   (83) coins of each type were there?

2. There were 40 dimes and quarters in the drawer. Peggy counted them and found that their
   (83) total value was $4.75. How many coins of each type were there?

3. For 10 days the business averaged $650.50 in transactions per day. For the following
   (52) 20 days, the average was $874.75. What was the overall average for all 30 days?

4. A paroxysm of laughter escaped a few. If the ratio of the laughers to the stolid was 2 to
   (39) 17, and 7600 were in the throng, how many did not laugh?

5. Frank's cookie jar has 10 chocolate chip cookies and 5 peanut butter cookies. Frank
   (73) randomly picks and eats one cookie, then randomly picks and eats another cookie. What
   is the probability that he ate a chocolate chip cookie the first time and a peanut butter
   cookie the second time?

6. The spinner shown is spun 4 times.
   (70) What is the probability that the spinner
   stops on 2, 3, and 2, in that order?

7. If $f(x) = x^3 + 2$, find $f(3)$.   8. If $g(x) = x^2 - 7x$, find $g(a + b)$.
   (82)   (82)

9. Find the domain of the function $f(x) = \sqrt{9 - x}$.
   (82)

10. Find the domain and range of $f(x) = -5$.
    (82)

11. Find the domain and range of the func-   12. Find the equations of lines (a) and (b).
    (82) tion g whose graph is shown.   (75)

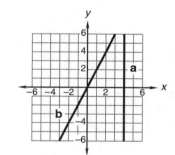

13. Solve by graphing the following set of equations on a rectangular coordinate system.
    (81) Check your answers by substituting them back into the original equations.

$$\begin{cases} y = x + 2 \\ y = -x \end{cases}$$

14. Consider the equations $y = 2x + 1$ and $y = -2x + 1$. Is this pair of equations
    (81) consistent, inconsistent, or dependent? Check your answer by graphing the equations on
    a rectangular coordinate system.

Simplify:

15. $\dfrac{(0.0016 \times 10^{-7})(3000 \times 10^5)}{1,200,000}$ 16. $\dfrac{(0.003 \times 10^{-5})(700 \times 10^{14})}{21,000,000}$
    (80)   (80)

17. Given: $R_P T_P = R_M T_M$, $R_P = 45$, $R_M = 15$, $T_P = T_M - 8$. Find T_P and T_M.
    (79)

18. Given: $R_G T_G + 10 = R_P T_P$, $T_G = 4$, $T_P = 2$, $R_P = R_G + 45$. Find R_P and R_G.
    (79)

Solve:

19.
(78)
$\dfrac{x}{3} - 2 = \dfrac{4 - x}{5}$

20.
(78)
$\dfrac{x}{4} - \dfrac{1}{2} = \dfrac{2 - x}{8}$

Factor:

21.
(71)
$28x + 11x^2 + x^3$

22.
(73)
$-xy^2 + 4a^2x$

23.
(73)
$x^2(z + 1) - (z + 1)y^2$

24.
(67)
Use elimination to solve: $\begin{cases} 3x + 2y = 11 \\ 2x - 3y = 16 \end{cases}$

25.
(64)
Graph on a number line: $-3 \le x < 2$; $D = \{\text{Reals}\}$

26.
(61)
Tell whether or not the following statements are true or false, and explain why:

   (a) $\{\text{Wholes}\} \subset \{\text{Naturals}\}$

   (b) $\{\text{Integers}\} \subset \{\text{Rationals}\}$

27.
(44)
Add: $\dfrac{1}{a^2} + \dfrac{2b}{a^3} - \dfrac{3b}{4a^3}$

28.
(68)
Simplify: $\dfrac{abc^{-1} - c^{-2}}{4 - ac^2}$

29.
(41)
Evaluate: $x\left(x^{-5} - y\right) - x^2$ if $x = -2$ and $y + 3 = \sqrt{81} - 3$

30.
(20)
A base of the right solid 23 inches high is shown. Find the volume of the right solid. Dimensions are in inches.

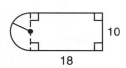

LESSON 84   *Multiplication of Radicals • Functions*

84.A

multiplication of radicals

We have used the product of square roots rule to help us simplify radical expressions such as the square root of 50.

$$\sqrt{50} = \sqrt{5 \cdot 5 \cdot 2} = \sqrt{5}\sqrt{5}\sqrt{2} = 5\sqrt{2}$$

The rule is restated here.

THE PRODUCT OF SQUARE ROOTS RULE

If m and n are nonnegative real numbers, then

$$\sqrt{m}\,\sqrt{n} = \sqrt{mn} \qquad \text{and} \qquad \sqrt{mn} = \sqrt{m}\,\sqrt{n}$$

We can use this rule to multiply radical expressions whose radicands are different.

$$\sqrt{2}\sqrt{3} = \sqrt{6}$$

example 84.1   Simplify: $4\sqrt{3} \cdot 3\sqrt{2}$

solution   Since the order of the factors does not affect the product in the multiplication of real numbers, we will rearrange the factors as

$$4 \cdot 3\sqrt{3}\sqrt{2}$$

and 4 is multiplied by 3 and $\sqrt{3}$ is multiplied by $\sqrt{2}$ to yield

$$\mathbf{12\sqrt{6}}$$

example 84.2   Simplify: $4\sqrt{3} \cdot 6\sqrt{6}$

solution   Again we will rearrange the order of the indicated multiplications to get

$$4 \cdot 6\sqrt{3}\sqrt{6}$$

and multiply 4 by 6 and $\sqrt{3}$ by $\sqrt{6}$ to get

$$24\sqrt{18}$$

Since $\sqrt{18}$ can be written as $3\sqrt{2}$, we can write

$$24\sqrt{18} = 24(3\sqrt{2}) = \mathbf{72\sqrt{2}}$$

example 84.3   Simplify: $4\sqrt{3}(5\sqrt{2} + 6\sqrt{3})$

solution   The notation indicates that $4\sqrt{3}$ is to be multiplied by both terms within the parentheses.

$$4\sqrt{3}(5\sqrt{2} + 6\sqrt{3}) = 4\sqrt{3} \cdot 5\sqrt{2} + 4\sqrt{3} \cdot 6\sqrt{3}$$

Now we rearrange the order of the factors in each term to get

$$4 \cdot 5\sqrt{3}\sqrt{2} + 4 \cdot 6\sqrt{3}\sqrt{3}$$

Lastly, we perform the indicated multiplications.

$$\mathbf{20\sqrt{6} + 72}$$

example 84.4   Simplify: $4\sqrt{2}(3\sqrt{2} + 5)$

solution   First we multiply as indicated

$$4\sqrt{2} \cdot 3\sqrt{2} + 4\sqrt{2} \cdot 5$$

and now simplify.

$$\mathbf{24 + 20\sqrt{2}}$$

84.B
functions   We can think of an algebraic function as a **function machine,** as we show here. The function machine below will accept any real number as the input, will square it, and will add 5 to get the output.

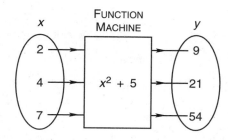

Two squared plus 5 is 9. Thus the function machine takes in a 2 and puts out a 9. We say that the **image** of 2 is 9. Four squared plus 5 is 21, so the output y value is 21 when the x input is 4.

Seven squared plus 5 is 54, so the output of this function machine is a *y* value of 54 when the *x* value of the input is 7. In other words, the image of 4 is 21, and the image of 7 is 54. **We do not need an algebraic expression to define a function because the function can be described as a** *mapping* **or a** *correspondence***, as we show below.**

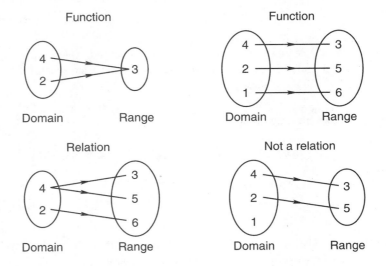

The rule for a function may also be stated by a list of ordered pairs such that every first member is paired with exactly one second member. Thus, the following set of ordered pairs defines a **relation** but does not define a function

$$(4, 3), \quad (5, 7), \quad (9, 3), \quad (4, -5), \quad (8, 14), \quad (6, -3)$$

because the first and the fourth pairs have different answers (images) for 4. **A** *relation* **is defined as a pairing that matches each element of the domain with one or more images in the range.** The following set of ordered pairs *does* define a function:

$$(4, 3), \quad (5, 7), \quad (9, 3), \quad (4, 3), \quad (8, 14), \quad (6, -3)$$

We restate our earlier definition of *function* to include different ways of defining a function.

We use the word *function* **to describe a mapping from each member of the input set, which is called the** *domain***, to exactly one member of the output set, which is called the** *range***. Each member of the domain maps to an** *image* **in the range.** Thus, the word *function* brings to mind the following:

1. The numbers that are acceptable as inputs and the algebraic rule (if one exists) that can be used to find the unique output that is paired with each input.
2. A table of ordered pairs of inputs and outputs where each input member is paired with exactly one output and all equal inputs have the same outputs.
3. A set of ordered pairs such that no two ordered pairs have the same first element and different second elements.
4. The graph of the geometric points whose coordinates are the ordered pairs just described.

example 84.5   Does the diagram designate a function?

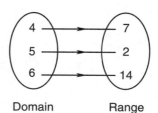

solution   **Yes.** The elements of the domain are specified. There is one image and only one image for each member of the domain. We do not have an equation, but we can find the images by looking at the diagram.

example 84.6   Does the diagram designate a function?

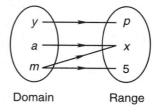

solution   **No.** The members of the domain are specified, but *m* has two images. For the diagram to designate a function, *m* may only have one image.

example 84.7   Does the diagram designate a function?

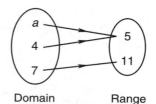

solution   **Yes.** The domain is specified, and each member of the domain has exactly one image. True, 5 is the image of both *a* and 4, but this is permissible.

example 84.8   Does the diagram designate a function?

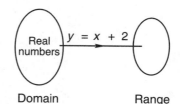

solution   **Yes.** The diagram says that we can use any real number for *x*, so the domain is specified. The members of the range are not specified, but the equation will allow us to find the value of *y* that is paired with any real number we use for *x*. Since there is only one value of *y* for each value of *x*, the diagram designates a function.

example 84.9   Does either of the sets of ordered pairs shown below designate a function?

(a) $\{(4, 6), (7, 2), (4, 5)\}$ (b) $\{(4, 8), (15, 6), (11, 7)\}$

solution   **Set (a) does not designate a function** because 4 has two different images. In other words, there are two ordered pairs where the first coordinates are the same, yet the second coordinates are different. **Set (b) does designate a function.** The domain is specified, and there is exactly one image for every member of the domain. In other words, there are no two ordered pairs where the first coordinates are the same and the second coordinates are different.

example 84.10   Which of the following sets of ordered pairs are functions?

(a) $\{(1, 2), (2, 3), (3, 4), (4, 5)\}$ (b) $\{(1, 2), (2, 3), (1, 3), (4, 5)\}$

(c) $\{(4, 3), (2, 2), (4, 3), (3, 3)\}$ (d) $\{(1, -1), (4, -1), (-1, -1), (3, -2)\}$

solution   A set of ordered pairs in which every first number is paired with a unique second number is a function. So we look for first numbers that are the same. In set (a), all the first numbers are different and each first number has a second number, so **set (a) describes a function.** Set (b) is not a function because two ordered pairs have 1 as a first number, but the second numbers are different. **Set (c) is a function** because this set does not have any two ordered pairs where the values of *x* are the same and the values of *y* are different. There are two ordered pairs in which 4 is the value of *x*, but both of these ordered pairs have 3 as the value of *y*. In set (d) three of the values of *y* are −1, but **set (d) is a function** because all the values of *x* are different.

example 84.11   Does the diagram designate a function?

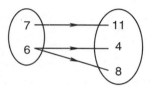

solution   **No.** The number 6 has two images. The diagram designates a relation since a relation is a pairing that matches each element of one set with one or more members of another set.

example 84.12   Does the diagram designate a function or a relation?

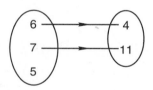

solution   **Neither.** For a correspondence to be called a relation, there must be one or more images for each element of the domain. In order to be called a function, there must be exactly one image for each element of the domain. In the diagram the number 5 does not have even one image, and thus the diagram does not designate either a function or a relation.

practice   Multiply and simplify:

a. $5\sqrt{12} \cdot 4\sqrt{3}$ **b.** $3\sqrt{2}(4\sqrt{3} + 5\sqrt{6})$

Which of the following diagrams depict functions?

c.   **d.**

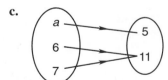   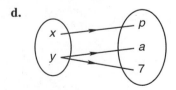

e.   What is the domain of the diagram shown in Problem c?

f.   What is the range of the diagram shown in Problem d?

g.   Which of the following sets of ordered pairs can represent a function?

(1) $\{(2, 1), (1, 2), (2, 2)\}$ (2) $\{(1, 2), (1, 2), (2, 2)\}$

(3) $\{(1, 2), (1, 3), (1, 4)\}$ (4) $\{(2, 1), (3, 1), (4, 1)\}$

problem set
84

1. When the piggy bank was opened, it yielded $4.75 in nickels and pennies. If there were
   (83) 175 coins in all, how many were nickels and how many were pennies?

2. The nickels and dimes all fell on the floor. There were 12 more nickels than dimes, and
   (83) the total value of the coins was $5.10. How many nickels and how many dimes were on
   the floor?

3. The room was a mess. In 1 hour Gretchen picked up 80 percent of the toys on the floor.
   (58) If she picked up 128 toys, how many toys were on the floor to begin with?

4. Ramses cogitated. He thought of three consecutive even integers and found that 3 times
   (77) the sum of the first two was 58 less than 14 times the opposite of the third. What were
   his integers?

5. Leona found three consecutive integers such that the product of 5 and the sum of the first
   (76) two was 7 greater than the opposite of the third. What were her integers?

6. Two dice are rolled. What is the probability that the sum of the numbers rolled is
   (70)

   (a) 11?   (b) a number greater than or equal to 5?

7. Indicate which of the following diagrams designates a function.
   (84)

   (a) 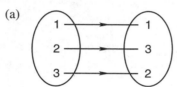   (b)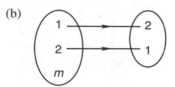

   (c) 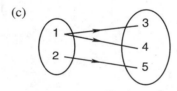   (d)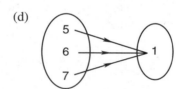

8. Which of the following sets of ordered pairs designates a function?
   (84)

   (a) $\{(1, 0), (1, 1), (1, 3), (1, 4)\}$ (b) $\{(0, 1), (1, 2), (0, 1), (2, 3)\}$

   (c) $\{(-1, 1), (-2, 1), (1, -1)\}$ (d) $\{(1, 0), (0, 1)\}$

9. If $f(x) = 2x^2 - 3x + 2$, find $f(a + 1)$.
   (82)

10. Find the domain of the function $g(x) = \sqrt{11 - x}$.
    (82)

11. Find the domain and range of the   12. Find the equations of lines (a) and (b).
    (82) graphed function.   (75)

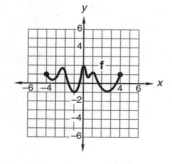   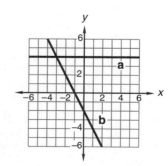

13. Solve by graphing and check.   14. Solve by elimination:
    (81)   (67)

   $$\begin{cases} y = -2x - 2 \\ y = -4 \end{cases}$$ $$\begin{cases} 4x + 3y = -14 \\ 3x + 2y = -10 \end{cases}$$

15. Consider the equations $x + y + 2 = 0$ and $2x + 2y + 4 = 0$. Are these equations
(81) consistent, inconsistent, or dependent? Check your answer by graphing the equations on
a rectangular coordinate system.

Simplify:

16. $\dfrac{(0.00032 \times 10^{-5})(4000 \times 10^{7})}{(160,000)(0.00002)}$ **17.** $\dfrac{(a^{-3})^{0}(a^{2})^{0}(a^{-2})^{-2}}{a^{4}(x^{-5})^{-2}xx^{2}}$
(80)   (53)

18. Write an inequality whose solution set is described by the graph shown below.
(64)

$$-4 \quad -3 \quad -2 \quad -1 \quad 0 \quad 1 \quad 2 \quad 3 \quad 4$$

19. Given: $R_{M}T_{M} = R_{K}T_{K}$, $R_{M} = 30$, $R_{K} = 10$, $T_{M} = 16 - T_{K}$. Find T_{M} and T_{K}.
(79)

Solve:

20. $\dfrac{3 + x}{4} - \dfrac{x}{3} = 5$ **21.** $-0.2 - 0.02 - 0.02x = 0.4(1 - x) - 0.012$
(78)   (31)

Factor the trinomials. Always begin by writing the trinomials in descending order of the
variables and by factoring out the greatest common factor.

22. $x^{3} + 20x + 9x^{2}$ **23.** $abx^{2} - 6ab + abx$
(71)   (71)

24. Add: $\dfrac{1}{x^{2}} - \dfrac{3a}{x - a} - \dfrac{2}{x}$ **25.** Multiply: $(4 + x)(x^{2} + 2x + 3)$
(52)   (49)

26. Without using a calculator, determine whether $\sqrt[3]{26.981}$ is greater than or less than 3.
(62) Explain.

27. Evaluate: $-x^{2}(x^{-2} - y) - |x - y^{4}|$ if $x = -3$ and $y = -2$
(19)

28. What fraction of $3\frac{1}{8}$ is $1\frac{1}{8}$?
(28)

29. Find the area of this parallelogram.
(8) Dimensions are in centimeters.

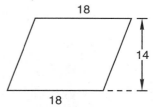

30. Find the surface area of this right trian-
(15,60) gular prism. Dimensions are in inches.

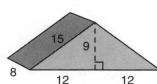

LESSON 85   *Stem-and-Leaf Plots • Histograms*

85.A

stem-and-leaf plots

When we gather data, we often need a way to display the data so that it can be analyzed.
Suppose the following test scores were made by a class of 30 students:

92, 75, 69, 56, 88, 62, 75, 82, 90, 74,

65, 70, 80, 96, 81, 87, 95, 58, 96, 89,

91, 81, 83, 94, 86, 88, 95, 74, 87, 85

We can find the mean (average) of the scores by adding the scores on a calculator and dividing by 30. If we do this we find that the mean score is 81.47.

$$\text{Mean} = \frac{\text{sum of the 30 scores}}{30} = \frac{2444}{30} = 81.47$$

To find the range, mode, and median (middle score) of the scores, we need to arrange the numbers in order from least to greatest. A graphing calculator will do this for us in one step. If a graphing calculator is not available, a **stem-and-leaf plot** can be used to organize the data quickly. We note that all the scores begin with 5, 6, 7, 8, and 9, so we list these numbers vertically as our stem, as shown in the leftmost column.

STEM		STEM	LEAF
5		5	6
6		6	9
7		7	5
8		8	8
9		9	2

We call the second part of each number a **leaf.** The first five numbers in our list are 92, 75, 69, 56, and 88. So we use 2 as the first leaf on the 9 stem, 5 as the first leaf on the 7 stem, 9 as the first leaf on the 6 stem, 6 as the first leaf on the 5 stem, and 8 as the first leaf on the 8 stem, as we show in the figure on the right above. Now we place the rest of the leaves on the proper stem in the order that they appear, as shown.

STEM	LEAF
5	6, 8
6	9, 2, 5
7	5, 5, 4, 0, 4
8	8, 2, 0, 1, 7, 9, 1, 3, 6, 8, 7, 5
9	2, 0, 6, 5, 6, 1, 4, 5

This method of displaying data is called a **stem-and-leaf plot** since the first number can be thought of as a branch on a tree and the numbers to the right represent leaves on the branch. Now, if we arrange the leaves on each stem in order from least to greatest, we get the figure below.

STEM	LEAF
5	6, 8
6	2, 5, 9
7	0, 4, 4, 5, 5
8	0, 1, 1, 2, 3, 5, 6, 7, 7, 8, 8, 9
9	0, 1, 2, 4, 5, 5, 6, 6

This stem-and-leaf plot has the same shape as the one above, but we can use this plot to arrange the scores in order from least to greatest.

56, 58, 62, 65, 69, 70, 74, 74, 75, 75,

80, 81, 81, 82, 83, 85, 86, 87, 87, 88,

88, 89, 90, 91, 92, 94, 95, 95, 96, 96

We know that it is possible to compute the mean (average) of the scores without arranging the scores in order from least to greatest. But now that the scores are in order from least to greatest, we can find the range, mode, and median. The scores range from 56 to 96 and the range of the scores is the difference between these numbers, which is 40.

$$\text{Range} = 96 - 56 = 40$$

From our list of scores we can see that seven scores appear twice. But no score appears more than twice, so there are seven modes. They are 74, 75, 81, 87, 88, 95, and 96. There are 30 scores and so there are an even number of scores. Thus, the median score will be halfway between the fifteenth and sixteenth score. The fifteenth score is 83 and the sixteenth score is 85, so the median score is 84.

$$\text{Median} = \frac{83 + 85}{2} = 84$$

example 85.1   Mark went to the driving range to test out the new golf club his brother Frank bought him for Christmas. He hit twenty balls in a row and the distances the balls traveled were (measured in yards) as follows:

150, 165, 176, 148, 181, 173, 162, 175, 174, 167,

168, 169, 170, 172, 173, 182, 184, 147, 180, 141

Create a stem-and-leaf plot of the distances listed by using the first two digits of each number listed as the stem and the last digit as the leaf. Find in which ten-yard stem the most golf balls landed.

solution   Note that the digits forming the leaves do not have to be in any particular order. We chose to list digits forming the leaves in the order they appeared. From the table, it is obvious that the ten-yard stem where the most golf balls landed was the interval **170–179** yards.

STEM	LEAF
14	8, 7, 1
15	0
16	5, 2, 7, 8, 9
17	6, 3, 5, 4, 0, 2, 3
18	1, 2, 4, 0

example 85.2   Find the (a) range, (b) median, (c) mode, and (d) mean of the data shown in this stem-and-leaf plot.

STEM	LEAF
84	8, 9, 6, 8
85	4, 2, 3, 3
86	2, 3, 7, 5, 2
87	6, 6, 3, 3

solution   We begin by listing the data points in order from least to greatest.

846, 848, 848, 849, 852, 853,

853, 854, 862, 862, 863, 865,

867, 873, 873, 876, 876

(a)   The scores range from 846 to 876. The range is the difference of these two numbers, or **30.**

(b)   This set of numbers has an odd number of members (17), so it has a middle number, or median, of **862.**

(c)   There are five modes: **848, 853, 862, 873,** and **876.**

(d)   To find the mean, we divide the sum of the numbers by the number of numbers.

$$\text{Mean} = \frac{\text{sum of the 17 numbers}}{17} = \frac{14620}{17} = \mathbf{860}$$

85.B

histograms

The data from our stem-and-leaf plot of the test scores in the previous section show us that there were two scores in the 50s, three scores in the 60s, five scores in the 70s, twelve scores in the 80s, and eight scores in the 90s. If we turn the stem-and-leaf plot on its side, we get the figure on the left below.

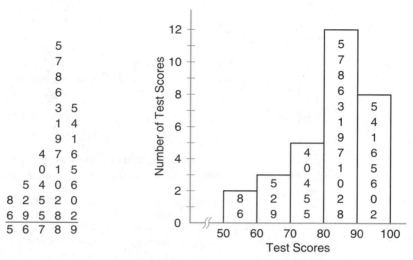

On the right above we show the same data displayed in a figure called a **histogram,** which is a bar graph of a **frequency distribution.** This graph shows us that there were two scores in the 50s, three scores in the 60s, five scores in the 70s, twelve scores in the 80s, and eight scores in the 90s. As we see, histograms do not give us precise information but do give us at a glance a good idea of how data is distributed.

example 85.3

The speeds of 40 cars as they passed a checkpoint are shown in the frequency distribution table below. (a) How many cars had a speed greater than or equal to 25 miles per hour and less than 30 miles per hour? (b) What was the mode interval? (c) What percent of the cars drove at a speed less than 40 miles per hour?

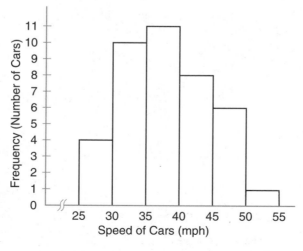

solution

Histograms are frequency distributions that give you a good idea about how the data is spread out, but it is difficult to get exact information from many of them. Note that each bar in the bar graph represents data greater than or equal to the leftmost number in the interval and less than the rightmost number in the interval. For example, the bar over the interval from 25 to 30 mph represents the number of cars whose speeds are greater than or equal to 25 mph, yet less than 30 mph.

(a) The 25–30 interval has a height of 4, so **4** cars had a speed greater than or equal to 25 mph and less than 30 mph.

(b) The mode interval is the interval that includes the most cars. This is the **35–40 interval,** which includes 11 cars.

(c) The number of cars with speeds less than 40 mph is the number of cars in the first three intervals. So 4 + 10 + 11 equals 25 cars. There were 40 cars in all, so

$$\text{the fraction of cars with speeds less than 40 mph} = \frac{25}{40} = 0.625$$

Thus, **62.5%** of the cars drove at a speed less than 40 miles per hour.

practice

a. Cindy carefully counted the protozoa in 20 slides. The numbers she counted in the 20 slides were as follows:

132, 128, 136, 130, 142, 151, 111, 123, 135, 145,

127, 129, 148, 149, 150, 118, 139, 142, 150, 149

Make a stem-and-leaf plot of the number of protozoa counted.

b. Find the range of numbers counted.   **c.** Find the median of the data.

d. Find the mode of the data.   **e.** Find the mean of the data.

f. Using the stem-and-leaf plot, create a frequency distribution table of the data.

g. Using the frequency distribution table, determine how many slides contained between 120 and 149 (inclusive) protozoa.

h. What percentage of the slides contained strictly fewer than 130 protozoa?

problem set 85

1.
(83) The total value of the pennies and nickels was $14.50. Emet and Callaway counted the coins and found that the total was 450 coins. How many coins of each type did they have?

2.
(58) The salesperson reduced the price 14 percent to be able to sell the car for $3440. What was the original price of the car? How much was the price reduced?

3.
(77) Robin and Andrea found four consecutive even integers such that the product of 3 and the sum of the first and second was 18 greater than 5 times the third. What were the integers?

4.
(39) The ratio of eloquent to inarticulate was 3 to 14. If there were 102 involved in the dialogue, how many were eloquent?

5.
(70) A fair coin is tossed four times. What is the probability that the first toss will be heads, the next two tosses will be tails, and the last toss will be heads?

6.
(45,85) The entire twenty-person squad kicked the ball in the air. The distances the ball was kicked were (measured in yards) as follows:

41, 52, 63, 35, 43, 51, 54, 48, 65, 38,

31, 45, 47, 54, 53, 62, 59, 42, 40, 39

(a) Graph the distances listed on a stem-and-leaf plot.

(b) Determine the range of the numbers listed.

(c) Determine the median of the numbers listed.

(d) Determine the mode(s) of the numbers listed.

(e) Determine the mean of the numbers listed.

7. (a) Create a frequency distribution using the data given in problem 6.
_(85)_

    (b) Determine the mode interval.

    (c) Determine what percentage of the distances were 49 yards or less.

8. LeAnn has a blue velvet bag that contains 10 diamonds and 8 sapphires. She draws one
_(73)_ gem at random and does not replace it. Then she draws a second gem at random. What
is the probability that she draws a diamond first and a sapphire second?

9. Which of the following diagrams depict functions?
_(84)_

(a)
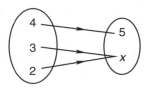

(b)
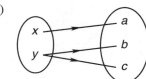

(c)
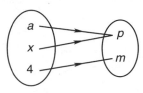

(d)
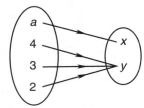

Simplify:

10. $3\sqrt{2} \cdot 4\sqrt{12} - 6\sqrt{54}$
_(84)_

11. $3\sqrt{2}\left(5\sqrt{12} - 8\sqrt{8}\right)$
_(84)_

12. What is the domain and range of the
_(82)_ graphed function?

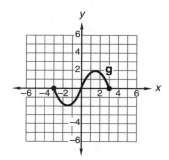

13. Solve the following set of equations by graphing it on a rectangular coordinate system.
_(81)_ Check your answer by substituting it back into the original equations.

$$\begin{cases} y = x \\ y = -\dfrac{1}{2}x + 3 \end{cases}$$

14. Use elimination to solve:
_(67)_

$$\begin{cases} 3x + 4y = 32 \\ 5x - 4y = 0 \end{cases}$$

15. Use substitution to solve:
_(71)_

$$\begin{cases} 10N_D + 25N_Q = 495 \\ N_Q = N_D + 10 \end{cases}$$

16. Consider the equations $3x + 4y = 7$ and $6x + 8y = 13$. Is this pair of equations
_(81)_ consistent, inconsistent, or dependent? Explain your answer.

17. Simplify: $\dfrac{\left(4000 \times 10^{-23}\right)\left(0.00035 \times 10^{15}\right)}{5000 \times 10^5}$
_(80)_

18. Given: $R_K T_K + 60 = R_M T_M,\ T_K = 3,\ T_M = 2,\ R_K + R_M = 125.$ Find R_K and R_M.
_(79)_

Factor completely:

19. $-2p^2 + 110 + 12p$
_(71)_

20. $-49 + t^2$
_(73)_

21. $30a^2b^3c^4 - 15ab^4c^5 + 45ab^4c^4$
(35)

Solve:

22. $-\dfrac{x+2}{3} - \dfrac{2x+8}{7} = 4$
(78)

23. $4\dfrac{2}{3}x - \dfrac{1}{5} = 3\dfrac{2}{3}$
(25)

24. (a) $\dfrac{2\sqrt{9}}{3} \in$ {What subsets of the real numbers}?
(61)

   (b) $\sqrt[3]{-1} \in$ {What subsets of the real numbers}?

25. Simplify: (a) $\dfrac{1}{-3^{-3}}$ (b) -3^{-3} (c) $-(-3)^{-3}$
(36)

26. Expand by using the distributive property. Write the answer with all exponents positive.
(40)

$$x^{-2}y^{-1}\left(\frac{x^{-1}}{y^{-1}} - \frac{4x^2y^0}{(y^{-3})^2} + \frac{1}{x^{-2}y^{-1}}\right)$$

27. Graph on a number line: $x \not> 4$; $D =$ {Integers}
(64)

28. Evaluate: $-x^0 - x(x - y^2)$ if $x = -3$ and $y = -4$
(19)

29. Simplify by adding like terms: $\dfrac{ax^{-4}}{(x^{-2})^2} + \dfrac{3a^{-2}a^3}{a^0} - \dfrac{6a^5}{(a^{-2})^{-2}} + 3a$
(41)

30. Find the volume of the right rectangu-
(72)   lar pyramid.

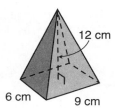

12 cm

6 cm   9 cm

LESSON 86   *Division of Polynomials*

In the problem sets since Lesson 49 we have been finding the product of two polynomials. Now we investigate the inverse process, the division of polynomials.

The simplest type of polynomial division is the division of a polynomial by a monomial. The desired result can be obtained by dividing each term of the polynomial by the monomial, as shown in the following examples.

example 86.1   Divide $3x^3 + 7x^2 - x$ by x.

solution   We will divide each of the three terms by x.

$$\frac{3x^3}{x} + \frac{7x^2}{x} - \frac{x}{x} = 3x^2 + 7x - 1$$

example 86.2 Divide $12x^{12} - 8x^8 + 4x^6$ by $4x^4$.

solution We will divide every term by $4x^4$.

$$\frac{12x^{12}}{4x^4} - \frac{8x^8}{4x^4} + \frac{4x^6}{4x^4} = \mathbf{3x^8 - 2x^4 + x^2}$$

Before considering the method of dividing a polynomial by a binomial, we will complete a long division problem involving the natural numbers, an algorithm with which we are familiar. The method of dividing a polynomial by a binomial is very similar.

$$12\overline{\smash{\big)}49} \quad \begin{array}{c} 4 \\ \hline \end{array} \quad \text{so} \quad 49 \div 12 = 4\frac{1}{12}$$
$$\underline{48}$$
$$1$$

We multiplied 4 by 12 and recorded the product of 48 below the 49. Next we **mentally changed the sign** of the $+48$ to -48 and then just added algebraically to find the remainder of 1.

example 86.3 Divide $-2x^2 + 3x^3 + 5x + 50$ by $-3 + x$.

solution The first step is to write both polynomials in descending powers of the variable and use the same format for division as we used above.

$$x - 3 \,\overline{\smash{\big)}\, 3x^3 - 2x^2 + 5x + 50}$$

To determine the first term of the quotient, divide the first term of the divisor into the first term of the dividend; in this case, divide x into $3x^3$ and get $3x^2$. Record as indicated.

$$\begin{array}{r} 3x^2 \\ x - 3 \,\overline{\smash{\big)}\, 3x^3 - 2x^2 + 5x + 50} \end{array}$$

Now multiply the term $3x^2$ by $x - 3$ and record as shown below.

$$\begin{array}{r} 3x^2 \\ x - 3 \,\overline{\smash{\big)}\, 3x^3 - 2x^2 + 5x + 50} \\ \underline{3x^3 - 9x^2} \end{array}$$

Now **mentally change the sign** of both $3x^3$ and $-9x^2$ and add algebraically.

$$\begin{array}{r} 3x^2 \\ x - 3 \,\overline{\smash{\big)}\, 3x^3 - 2x^2 + 5x + 50} \\ \underline{3x^3 - 9x^2} \\ 7x^2 \end{array}$$

Now bring down the $+5x$.

$$\begin{array}{r} 3x^2 \\ x - 3 \,\overline{\smash{\big)}\, 3x^3 - 2x^2 + 5x + 50} \\ \underline{3x^3 - 9x^2} \\ 7x^2 + 5x \end{array}$$

Now divide the x of $x - 3$ into $7x^2$, get $7x$, and record as shown.

$$\begin{array}{r} 3x^2 + 7x \\ x - 3 \,\overline{\smash{\big)}\, 3x^3 - 2x^2 + 5x + 50} \\ \underline{3x^3 - 9x^2} \\ 7x^2 + 5x \end{array}$$

Multiply $7x$ by $x - 3$ and record.

$$
\begin{array}{r}
3x^2 + 7x \\
x - 3 \overline{\smash{)}\, 3x^3 - 2x^2 + 5x + 50} \\
\underline{3x^3 - 9x^2} \\
7x^2 + 5x \\
\underline{7x^2 - 21x}
\end{array}
$$

Now **mentally change the sign** of both $7x^2$ and $-21x$ and add algebraically. Repeat the procedure until the remainder of 128 is obtained.

$$
\begin{array}{r}
3x^2 + 7x + 26 \\
x - 3 \overline{\smash{)}\, 3x^3 - 2x^2 + 5x + 50} \\
\underline{3x^3 - 9x^2} \\
7x^2 + 5x \\
\underline{7x^2 - 21x} \\
26x + 50 \\
\underline{26x - 78} \\
128
\end{array}
$$

Thus we find that

$$
\frac{3x^3 - 2x^2 + 5x + 50}{x - 3} = \mathbf{3x^2 + 7x + 26 + \frac{128}{x - 3}}
$$

example 86.4   Divide $2x^3 - x - x^2 + 4$ by $-2 + x$.

solution   As the first step, we rearrange both expressions in descending powers of the variable and write

$$
x - 2 \overline{\smash{)}\, 2x^3 - x^2 - x + 4}
$$

Now we divide using the same procedure we used in the last example.

$$
\begin{array}{r}
2x^2 + 3x + 5 \\
x - 2 \overline{\smash{)}\, 2x^3 - x^2 - x + 4} \\
\underline{2x^3 - 4x^2} \\
3x^2 - x \\
\underline{3x^2 - 6x} \\
5x + 4 \\
\underline{5x - 10} \\
14
\end{array}
$$

Thus,

$$
(2x^3 - x - x^2 + 4) \div (-2 + x) = \mathbf{2x^2 + 3x + 5 + \frac{14}{x - 2}}
$$

In all the examples we have shown, all the terms beginning with the highest degree term have nonzero coefficients. We show how to divide polynomials where some of these lower degree terms are "missing."

example 86.5   Divide $-2x + 5 + 3x^3$ by $-3 + x$.

solution   We begin by writing both polynomials in descending order of the variable and using the format for long division.

$$
x - 3 \overline{\smash{)}\, 3x^3 - 2x + 5}
$$

We note that the dividend has an x^3 term and an x term but no x^2 term. A good ploy to avoid confusion is to insert an x^2 term with zero as its coefficient, as shown below. Of course, zero multiplied by x^2 equals zero, so the polynomial is really unchanged. Now we perform the division using the same procedure we learned earlier in this lesson.

$$
\require{enclose}
\begin{array}{r}
3x^2 + 9x + 25 \\
x - 3 \enclose{longdiv}{3x^3 + 0x^2 - 2x + 5} \\
\underline{3x^3 - 9x^2 } \\
9x^2 - 2x \\
\underline{9x^2 - 27x } \\
25x + 5 \\
\underline{25x - 75} \\
80
\end{array}
$$

Thus,

$$\frac{3x^3 - 2x + 5}{x - 3} = 3x^2 + 9x + 25 + \frac{80}{x - 3}$$

example 86.6 Divide $-4 + x^3$ by $-3 + x$.

solution Again we begin by rearranging each polynomial and using the long division format.

$$x - 3 \enclose{longdiv}{x^3 - 4}$$

This time, we see that the dividend does not have an x^2 term or an x term. We will insert these terms and give each of them a coefficient of zero. Then we will divide.

$$
\begin{array}{r}
x^2 + 3x + 9 \\
x - 3 \enclose{longdiv}{x^3 + 0x^2 + 0x - 4} \\
\underline{x^3 - 3x^2 } \\
3x^2 + 0x \\
\underline{3x^2 - 9x } \\
9x - 4 \\
\underline{9x - 27} \\
23
\end{array}
$$

Thus,

$$\left(-4 + x^3\right) \div (-3 + x) = x^2 + 3x + 9 + \frac{23}{x - 3}$$

practice Divide:

a. $\left(5x^3 - 9x^2 + x\right) \div x$

b. $\left(-3x^2 + 6x^3 + x - 40\right) \div (-2 + x)$

c. $\dfrac{x^3 - 5}{x - 2}$

d. $\left(3x^3 - 5x + 4\right) \div (x - 4)$

problem set 86

1. (83) There were 143 more Susan B. Anthony dollars than there were quarters. If the total value of the coins was $153, how many Susan B. Anthony dollars were there?

2. (83) The collection had 60 coins that were nickels and dimes. If the total value of the coins was $5, how many nickels were in the collection?

3. (76) Find three consecutive integers such that -4 times the sum of the first and third is 13 less than 7 times the opposite of the second.

4. (58) Forty percent of the crop was destroyed by the thunderstorm. If the farm consisted of 570 acres, how many acres were affected by the thunderstorm?

5. (33) If eight less than seven times a number is twelve more than two times the number, then what is the number?

6. The scores on the test were as follows:
(45,85)

$$85, 93, 68, 79, 85, 87, 95, 75,$$

$$82, 91, 65, 73, 81, 98, 46$$

   (a) Determine the range, median, mode, and mean of this set of numbers.

   (b) Create a stem-and-leaf plot of the data.

   (c) Create a frequency distribution table of the data.

   (d) Identify the mode interval in the graph of (c).

Divide:

7. $(20x^4 + 5x^3 - 10x^2 + 30x) \div 5x$ **8.** $(x^3 - 3x^2 + 2x + 5) \div (x + 2)$
(86)   (86)

9. $(x^3 - 1) \div (x + 3)$ **10.** $(-5x^3 + 14x^2 - x + 10) \div (x + 2)$
(86)   (86)

11. Which of the following sets of ordered pairs designate functions?
(84)

   (a) (4, –3), (5, –3), (6, –3)   (b) (4, –3), (–3, 4), (–2, 4)

   (c) (4, –3), (4, 3), (–4, 6)   (d) (4, –3), (–2, –4), (8, 3)

Simplify:

12. $4\sqrt{3} \cdot 6\sqrt{6} \cdot 3\sqrt{3} \cdot 2\sqrt{2}$ **13.** $3\sqrt{2}(7\sqrt{2} - \sqrt{6})$
(84)   (84)

14. Find the domain of the function $f(x) = \sqrt{11 - x}$
(82)

15. If $f(x) = x^2 - 2x + 3$, find $f(x + 4)$.
(82)

16. Find the equations of lines (a) and (b).
(75)

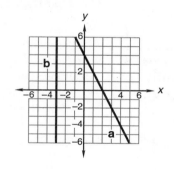

17. Solve by graphing and check: **18.** Solve by substitution:
(81)   (59)

$$\begin{cases} y = 3x - 2 \\ y = -x + 2 \end{cases}$$ $$\begin{cases} 4x - 5y = -26 \\ x - y = -6 \end{cases}$$

19. Consider the equations $3x + 4y = 9$ and $3x - 4y = 9$. Is this pair of equations
(81) consistent, inconsistent, or dependent? Explain your answer.

20. Simplify: $\dfrac{(0.0003 \times 10^{-8})(8000 \times 10^6)}{0.004 \times 10^5}$
(80)

21. Given: $R_M T_M + 6 = R_D T_D$, $R_M = 3$, $R_D = 12$, $T_M = 4 + T_D$. Find T_M and T_D.
(79)

Factor completely:

22. $ax^2 + 4ax + 4a$ **23.** $-10 - 3x + x^2$
(71)   (69)

24. $-4ax^2 + 9a$ **25.** $20x + 12x^2 + x^3$
(73)   (71)

26. Solve: $\dfrac{x}{2} - \dfrac{3 + x}{4} = \dfrac{1}{6}$ **27.** Add: $\dfrac{5}{x^2 + y} + \dfrac{3}{x^2} - \dfrac{2}{y}$
(78)   (52)

28. Evaluate: $\dfrac{\sqrt[3]{x - a}}{2}$ if $x = -100$ and $a = -127$
(62)

29. Find the area of this trapezoid. Dimen-
(8) sions are in centimeters.

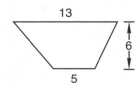

30. A base of the right solid 6 meters high is shown. Find the surface area of the right solid.
(15) Dimensions are in meters.

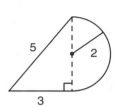 

LESSON 87 *More on Systems of Equations • Tests for Functions*

87.A

more on systems of equations

When we solve systems of equations using the substitution method, sometimes it is necessary to rearrange one of the equations before the necessary substitutions can be accomplished. In the examples shown here, we will have to rearrange the equation that relates the time variables before we can substitute.

example 87.1 Given: $R_E T_E = R_W T_W$, $R_E = 200$, $R_W = 250$, $T_E + T_W = 9$. Find T_E and T_W.

solution We begin by replacing R_E with 200 and R_W with 250 to find

$$200T_E = 250T_W$$

Now we must use the equation $T_E + T_W = 9$ to substitute for T_E or for T_W. The equation cannot be used in its present form and must be solved for T_E by adding $-T_W$ to both sides or be solved for T_W by adding $-T_E$ to both sides. We will work the problem both ways to show that the final results will be the same.

$$
\begin{array}{ll}
T_E + T_W = 9 \\
\underline{ - T_W \quad\quad - T_W} \\
T_E \quad\quad = 9 - T_W
\end{array}
\qquad\qquad
\begin{array}{ll}
T_E + T_W = 9 \\
\underline{-T_E \quad\quad\quad - T_E} \\
\quad\quad T_W = 9 - T_E
\end{array}
$$

Now we will substitute $9 - T_W$ for T_E and solve the resulting equation for T_W.

Now we will substitute $9 - T_E$ for T_W and solve the resulting equation for T_E.

$$
\begin{array}{rl}
200(9 - T_W) &= 250T_W \\
1800 - 200T_W &= 250T_W \\
\underline{+\,200T_W \quad\quad +200T_W} \\
1800 &= 450T_W
\end{array}
\qquad
\begin{array}{rl}
200T_E &= 250(9 - T_W) \\
200T_E &= 2250 - 250T_E \\
\underline{250T_E \quad\quad\quad + 250T_E} \\
450T_E &= 2250
\end{array}
$$

$$T_W = \frac{1800}{450} \quad\longrightarrow\quad T_W = 4 \qquad\qquad T_E = \frac{2250}{450} \quad\longrightarrow\quad T_E = 5$$

Since $T_E + T_W = 9$, we can solve for T_E by replacing T_W with 4.

$$
\begin{array}{r}
T_E + 4 = 9 \\
-4 \quad -4 \\
\hline
T_E \quad\;\; = 5
\end{array}
$$

Since $T_E + T_W = 9$, we can solve for T_W by replacing T_E with 5.

$$
\begin{array}{r}
5 + T_W = 9 \\
-5 \qquad -5 \\
\hline
T_W = 4
\end{array}
$$

Thus we see that while one procedure leads to our solving for T_E first and the other leads to our solving for T_W first, both procedures yield the same answer.

example 87.2   Given: $R_1 T_1 + R_2 T_2 = 360$, $R_1 = 30$, $R_2 = 40$, $T_1 + T_2 = 10$. Find T_1 and T_2.

solution   The time equation cannot be used in its present form. We decide to solve the time equation for T_1.

$$
\begin{array}{r}
T_1 + T_2 = 10 \\
- T_2 \qquad - T_2 \\
\hline
T_1 \qquad = 10 - T_2
\end{array}
$$

Now we replace R_1 with 30, R_2 with 40, and T_1 with $10 - T_2$ and then solve.

$30(10 - T_2) + 40T_2 = 360$	substituted
$300 - 30T_2 + 40T_2 = 360$	multiplied
$300 + 10T_2 = 360$	simplified
$10T_2 = 60$	added −300 to both sides
$T_2 = 6$	divided both sides by 10

Thus, $T_1 = 4$

87.B

tests for functions

We remember that a function has only one value of y for each value of x. Given a graph, we can determine whether the graph could be that of a function by applying the **vertical line test,** stated below:

> VERTICAL LINE TEST
>
> A graph on the coordinate plane represents the graph of a function provided that any vertical line intersects the graph in at most one point.

Therefore, the graph on the left below represents the graph of a function since any vertical line intersects the graph in at most one point. The graph on the right below, however, is not the graph of a function since there are vertical lines that intersect the graph at more than one point.

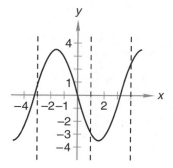

Graph of a function

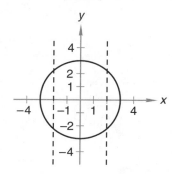

Graph of a relation but not a function

example 87.3   Determine if each graph shown represents the graph of a function:

(a)   (b)   (c)

solution   (a) This graph **is not the graph of a function** because it does not pass the vertical line test. That is, a vertical line can be drawn so that it intersects the graph at more than one point. The y axis is one such line.

(b) This graph **is the graph of a function** since every vertical line drawn intersects the graph in at most one point.

(c) This graph **is not the graph of a function** because it does not pass the vertical line test. A vertical line drawn to the right of the y axis will intersect the graph at more than one point.

practice   Find the values of all the unknowns:

    a. $R_1T_1 = R_2T_2$, $T_1 + T_2 = 60$, $R_1 = 3$, $R_2 = 6$

    b. $R_OT_O = R_ST_S + 16$, $R_O + R_S = -1$, $T_O = 8$, $T_S = 4$

Determine whether each graph represents the graph of a function:

c. 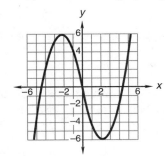   **d.**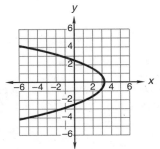

e.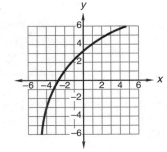

problem set   **1.** The big sack contained $30 in nickels and dimes. If there were 500 coins in the sack, how
87   *(83)*   many were nickels and how many were dimes?

    2. Juan had $5.25 in nickels and quarters. If he had 15 more nickels than quarters, how
    (83)   many coins of each type did he have?

    3. Find four consecutive integers such that 3 times the sum of the first and third is 84 greater
    (76)   than the opposite of the second.

    4. Of the people who voted, ninety percent voted for Sammy. If 1930 people voted, how
    (58)   many voted for Sammy?

5.
(73) An urn has 7 white marbles and 10 red marbles. Philip chooses one marble randomly and then another marble randomly. What is the probability that he picks two red marbles if

(a) he replaces the first marble?   (b) he does not replace the first marble?

6.
(45,85) The ages of the first 15 presidents at the time of their first inaugurations are listed below:

$$57, 61, 57, 57, 58, 57, 61, 54,$$

$$68, 51, 49, 64, 50, 48, 65$$

(a) Make a stem-and-leaf plot of the data provided.

(b) Using the graph in (a), make a frequency distribution table.

(c) Determine the range, median, mode, and mean of the data given.

7.
(87) Given: $R_T T_T + R_J T_J = 180$, $R_J + R_T = 20$, $T_T = 8$, $T_J = 10$. Find R_J and R_T.

8.
(87) Indicate whether each graph shown represents the graph of a function:

(a)
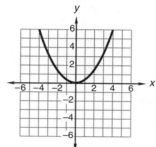

(b)
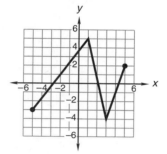

(c)
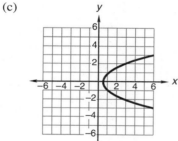

(d)
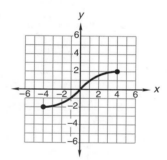

Divide:

9.
(86) $(x^3 - 2x^2 + 4) \div (x + 2)$

10.
(86) $(2x^3 - 3x^2 + 2x - 4) \div (x - 3)$

11.
(86) $(32x^4 + 16x^3 - 4x^2 + 8x) \div (4x)$

12.
(84) Which of the following diagrams depict functions?

(a)
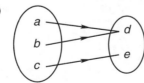

(b)
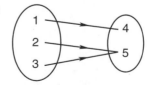

(c)
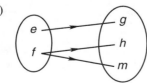

(d)
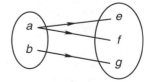

13.
(84) Simplify: $3\sqrt{2}(4\sqrt{2} + 6\sqrt{6})$

14.
(82) If $f(x) = 9 - 2x - x^2$, find $f(y + 1)$.

15. Find the domain and range of the graphed function.
(82)

16. Find the equations of lines (a) and (b).
(75)

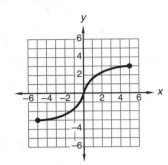

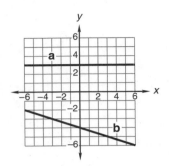

17. Solve by graphing and check:
(81)

$$\begin{cases} y = -2 \\ y = 2x - 2 \end{cases}$$

18. Solve by elimination:
(67)

$$\begin{cases} 3x - y = 8 \\ x + 2y = 12 \end{cases}$$

19. Consider the equations $y = x$ and $y = 3x$. Is this pair of equations consistent,
(81) inconsistent, or dependent? Explain your answer.

20. Simplify: $\dfrac{(0.0072 \times 10^{-4})(100{,}000)}{6000 \times 10^{-24}}$
(80)

Factor the trinomials. Always begin by writing the trinomials in descending order of the variables and by factoring out the greatest common factor.

21. $max^2 + 9xma + 14ma$
(71)

22. $-x^3 - 35x - 12x^2$
(71)

23. Solve: $(3x)^0(-2 - 3x) - x = -3(-2 - 3)$
(31)

24. Evaluate: $-b \pm \sqrt{b}$ if $b - 40 = \sqrt{81}$
(62)

25. Use a calculator to determine the following square roots to five decimal places:
(62)

   (a) $\sqrt{11}$ (b) $\sqrt{17}$ (c) $\sqrt{54}$ (d) $\sqrt{30}$

Simplify:

26. $\dfrac{\dfrac{x}{y} - 1}{\dfrac{a}{y} + b}$
(68)

27. $\dfrac{(x^2)^{-2}(y^0)^2 yy^3}{(y^{-2})^3 yy^4 y^{-1} x}$
(53)

28. Expand by using the distributive property. Write the answer with all exponents positive.
(40)

$$\left(\frac{x^{-2}}{y} + x^2 y - \frac{3x^{-4}a}{y} \right) \frac{x^{-2}}{y}$$

29. Find the perimeter of this figure. Dimensions are in inches.
(3)

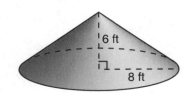

30. A right circular cone has a base of radius 8 ft and a height of 6 ft, as shown. Find the volume of the right circular cone.
(72)

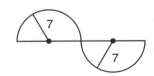

LESSON 88   *Quadratic Equations • Solution of Quadratic Equations by Factoring*

88.A

quadratic equations

Quadratic equations are second-degree polynomial equations. *Second-degree* in x means that the greatest exponent of x in any term is 2. Both of these equations are quadratic equations in x because the greatest exponent of x is 2.

$$4 - 3x = 2x^2 \qquad 3x^2 - 2x + 4 = 0$$

The equation on the right is in **standard form** because all nonzero terms are on the left of the equals sign and the terms are written in descending order of the variable. The coefficient of x^2 cannot be zero, but either of the other two numbers can be zero. Thus, each of the following equations is also a quadratic equation in x:

$$4x^2 = 0 \qquad 4x^2 + 2x = 0 \qquad 4x^2 - 3 = 0$$

To designate a general quadratic equation, we use the letter a to represent the coefficient of x^2, the letter b to represent the coefficient of x, and the letter c to represent the constant term. Using these letters to represent the constants in the equation, we can write a general quadratic equation in standard form as

$$ax^2 + bx + c = 0$$

If we let $a = 1$, $b = -3$, and $c = -10$, we have the equation

$$x^2 - 3x - 10 = 0$$

If we substitute either 5 or –2 for the variable x in the quadratic equation $x^2 - 3x - 10 = 0$, the equation will be transformed into a true equation, as shown here.

IF $x = 5$	IF $x = -2$
$(5)^2 - 3(5) - 10 = 0$	$(-2)^2 - 3(-2) - 10 = 0$
$25 - 15 - 10 = 0$	$4 + 6 - 10 = 0$
$0 = 0$	$0 = 0$

The numbers 5 and –2 are the only numbers that will satisfy the equation above. **Every quadratic equation has at most two distinct numbers that will make the equation a true statement.**[†] For that matter, every third-degree polynomial equation in one variable has at most three distinct numbers that will satisfy the equation; every fourth-degree polynomial equation in one variable has at most four distinct numbers that will satisfy the equation, etc. To generalize, we can say that every nth-degree polynomial equation in one variable (n is a natural number) has at most n distinct roots.

88.B

solution of quadratic equations by factoring

Some quadratic equations can be solved by using the zero factor theorem.

> ZERO FACTOR THEOREM
>
> If p and q are any real numbers and if $p \cdot q = 0$, then either $p = 0$ or $q = 0$, or both p and q equal 0.

[†]We say *at most* because some quadratic equations have only one distinct root. For instance, the only root of the equation $x^2 - 4x + 4 = 0$ is the number +2.

This says that **if the product of two real numbers is zero, one or both of the numbers are zero.** Thus if we indicate the product of 4 and an unspecified number by writing

$$4(\ \ ) = 0$$

the only number that we can place in the parentheses that will make the equation a true equation is the number zero.

In the same way, if we indicate the product of two unspecified numbers by writing

$$(\ \ )(\ \ ) = 0$$

the quantity in the first parentheses or the quantity in the second parentheses or both quantities must equal zero or else the product will not equal zero.

Now let's look at the equation

$$(x - 3)(x + 5) = 0$$

Here we have two quantities multiplied and the product is equal to zero. From the **zero factor theorem,** we know that at least one of the quantities must equal zero if the product is to equal zero, so either

$$x - 3 = 0 \qquad\qquad \text{or} \qquad\qquad x + 5 = 0$$

$$x - 3 = 0 \ \longrightarrow \ x = 3 \qquad\qquad x + 5 = 0 \ \longrightarrow \ x = -5$$

Thus the two values of x that satisfy the condition stated are 3 and –5.

We can use the zero factor theorem to help us solve quadratic equations that can be factored. We do this by first writing the equation in standard form and factoring the polynomial; then we set each of the factors equal to zero and solve for the values of the variable.

example 88.1   Use the factor method to find the roots of $x^2 - 18 = 3x$.

solution   First we write the equation in standard form, and then we factor.

$$x^2 - 3x - 18 = 0 \ \longrightarrow \ (x + 3)(x - 6) = 0$$

Since the product $(x + 3)(x - 6)$ equals zero, we know that one or both of these factors must equal zero by the zero factor theorem.

$$\text{If } x + 3 = 0 \qquad\qquad \text{If } x - 6 = 0$$
$$x = \mathbf{-3} \qquad \text{or} \qquad\qquad x = \mathbf{+6}$$

To check, we will use –3 and +6 as values for x in the original equation.

If $x = -3$	If $x = 6$
$(-3)^2 - 18 = 3(-3)$	$(6)^2 - 18 = 3(6)$
$9 - 18 = -9$	$36 - 18 = 18$
$-9 = -9$ Check	$18 = 18$ Check

example 88.2   Find the roots of $-25 = -4x^2$.

solution   First we write the equation in standard form, $4x^2 - 25 = 0$, and then we factor to get $(2x - 5)(2x + 5) = 0$. For this to be true, either $2x - 5$ equals zero or $2x + 5$ equals zero.

$$\text{If } 2x - 5 = 0 \qquad\qquad \text{If } 2x + 5 = 0$$
$$2x = 5 \qquad\qquad\qquad 2x = -5$$
$$x = \frac{5}{2} \qquad\qquad\qquad x = -\frac{5}{2}$$

To check, we will use $\frac{5}{2}$ and $-\frac{5}{2}$ as values for x in the original equation.

$$\text{IF } x = \frac{5}{2} \qquad\qquad\qquad \text{IF } x = -\frac{5}{2}$$

$$-25 = -4\left(\frac{5}{2}\right)^2 \qquad\qquad -25 = -4\left(-\frac{5}{2}\right)^2$$

$$-25 = -4\left(\frac{25}{4}\right) \qquad\qquad -25 = -4\left(\frac{25}{4}\right)$$

$$-25 = -25 \qquad \text{Check} \qquad\qquad -25 = -25 \qquad \text{Check}$$

example 88.3   Find the values of x that satisfy $x - 56 = -x^2$.

solution   First we rewrite the equation in standard form.

$$x^2 + x - 56 = 0$$

Now we factor.

$$(x + 8)(x - 7) = 0$$

For this to be true, either $x + 8$ equals zero or $x - 7$ equals zero.

$$\text{IF } x + 8 = 0 \qquad\qquad \text{IF } x - 7 = 0$$

$$x = \mathbf{-8} \qquad \text{or} \qquad x = \mathbf{7}$$

To check, we will use -8 and $+7$ as replacements for x in the original equation.

$$\text{IF } x = -8 \qquad\qquad\qquad \text{IF } x = 7$$

$$(-8) - 56 = -(-8)^2 \qquad\qquad (7) - 56 = -(7)^2$$

$$-8 - 56 = -64 \qquad\qquad\qquad 7 - 56 = -49$$

$$-64 = -64 \qquad \text{Check} \qquad\qquad -49 = -49 \qquad \text{Check}$$

example 88.4   Solve $3x^2 - 6x = 9$.

solution   We begin by writing the equation in standard form.

$$3x^2 - 6x - 9 = 0$$

We now factor the trinomial. We begin by factoring out the greatest common factor of all three terms.

$$3x^2 - 6x - 9 = 0$$

$$3\left(x^2 - 2x - 3\right) = 0 \qquad\qquad \text{factored GCF}$$

$$3(x - 3)(x + 1) = 0 \qquad\qquad \text{factored trinomial}$$

At this point, we can divide both sides by 3 to get

$$(x - 3)(x + 1) = 0$$

By the zero factor theorem, we know that at least one factor must be equal to zero.

$$\text{IF } x - 3 = 0 \qquad\qquad \text{IF } x + 1 = 0$$

$$x = \mathbf{3} \qquad \text{or} \qquad x = \mathbf{-1}$$

Finally, we check our answers.

$$3(3)^2 - 6(3) = 9 \qquad\qquad 3(-1)^2 - 6(-1) = 9$$

$$3(9) - 18 = 9 \qquad\qquad\qquad 3(1) + 6 = 9$$

$$9 = 9 \qquad \text{Check} \qquad\qquad 9 = 9 \qquad \text{Check}$$

practice   Solve by factoring:

    a. $x^2 = -5x + 24$ **b.** $-48 + x^2 = -8x$

class project   Have each student write his or her birthday as a three- or four-digit number. For example, a birthday of November 4 would be written as 1104, and a birthday of September 6 would be written as 906. Put this list on the chalkboard for the students to copy and use in problem 7.

problem set 88

1. (83) The bowl contained 150 coins. If they were all pennies and nickels and their total value was $2.70, how many coins of each type were there?

2. (83) The second bowl also contained $2.70 in pennies and nickels. If there were 54 more pennies than nickels in this bowl, how many were pennies and how many were nickels?

3. (58) When the home team scored, 78 percent of the crowd stood and cheered, and the rest were dejected. If 8800 were dejected, how many stood and cheered?

4. (77) Find four consecutive odd integers such that 4 times the sum of the first and fourth is 3 greater than 7 times the third.

5. (70) A candy dish contains seven peppermints and four chocolates. Fred picks one candy randomly. What is the probability that it will not be a peppermint?

6. (45) The sum of four numbers is 396.80. The first two numbers are 96.8 and 100.1. Find the average of the four numbers.

7. (85) Use the data gathered in class to solve the following:

    (a) Create a stem-and-leaf plot with the two digits representing the months as stems and the two digits representing the days as the leaves.

    (b) Use the graph drawn for (a) to draw a frequency distribution table.

    (c) Using the graph in (b), determine which month is the mode month.

Solve by factoring:

8. (88) $28 = x^2 - 3x$ **9.** (88) $x^2 = 25$

10. (88) $x^2 - 6 = x$ **11.** (88) $-x^2 - 8x = 16$

12. (79) Given: $R_P T_P + R_K T_K = 170$, $T_P = 2$, $T_K = 3$, $R_P = R_K + 10$. Find R_K and R_P.

13. (84,87) Which of the following diagrams depict functions?

    (a) 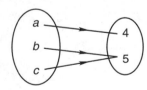   (b)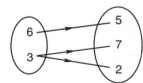

    (c) 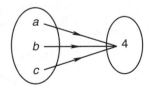   (d)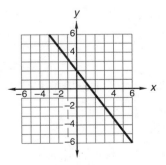

Divide:

14. (86) $(2x^3 - 5x + 4) \div (x + 2)$ **15.** (86) $(3x^3 - 4) \div (x - 5)$

16. (86) $(2x^4 - 3x^3 + 2x^2 - x) \div (x)$

17. Find the domain of the function $f(x) = \sqrt{x+1}$.
(82)

18. Find the equations of lines (a) and (b).
(75)

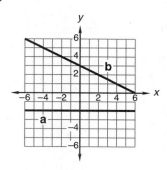

Simplify:

19. $5\sqrt{5}\left(2\sqrt{10} - 3\sqrt{3}\right)$ **20.** $4\sqrt{7}\left(2\sqrt{7} - 3\sqrt{14}\right)$
(84)   (84)

21. If $g(x) = 7 - 3x^2 + 2x$, find $g(x+1)$.
(82)

22. Solve by graphing and check: **23.** Use elimination to solve:
(81)   (67)

$$\begin{cases} y = 2x + 3 \\ x = -3 \end{cases}$$ $$\begin{cases} 3x + 5y = 16 \\ 4x - 3y = 2 \end{cases}$$

24. Simplify: $\dfrac{(0.016 \times 10^{-5})(300 \times 10^{6})}{(20{,}000 \times 10^{4})(400 \times 10^{-8})}$
(80)

25. Graph on a number line: $x + 2 \nleq 4$; $D = \{\text{Positive integers}\}$
(64)

26. Solve: $1\dfrac{3}{5}x - 2^{-2} = \dfrac{1}{10}$ **27.** Add: $\dfrac{1}{a} + \dfrac{2}{a^2} + \dfrac{3}{a+x}$
(25)   (52)

28. Evaluate: $\dfrac{-b \pm \sqrt{b^2}}{2a}$ if $b - 5 = 17$ and $a = \dfrac{b}{2}$
(62)

29. Simplify: $-\left(-4 - 2^{0}\right) - |-2| + \dfrac{1}{-2^{-3}}$
(36)

30. Find the surface area of this regular
(72) square pyramid. Dimensions are
in yards.

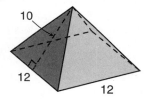

LESSON 89   *Value Problems*

We remember that when we read word problems, we look for word statements about
quantities that are equal. Then we transform each of these word statements into an
algebraic equation which makes the same statement of equality. We use as many
variables as are necessary. When we have written as many independent equations as we
have variables, we solve the equations by using the substitution method or the
elimination method. When we write the equations, instead of x and y, we use meaningful
variables so that we can remember what these variables represent. We have used two equations
in two variables to solve coin problems. These problems are of a genre called **value problems.**
We will look at other types of value problems in this lesson. They are very similar to coin
problems.

example 89.1   Airline fares for flights from Tifton to Adel are $30 for first class and $25 for tourist class. If a flight had 52 passengers who paid a total of $1360, how many first-class passengers were on the trip?

solution   There are two statements of equality here. The number of first-class passengers plus the number of tourist-class passengers equals 52.

$$\text{(a) } N_F + N_T = 52$$

The cost of the first-class tickets plus the cost of the tourist tickets equals 1360.

$$\text{(b) } 30N_F + 25N_T = 1360$$

We will solve these equations by using elimination. We will multiply (a) by –30 to get (a′), which we then add to (b):

(a′) $-30N_F - 30N_T = -1560$

(b) $\underline{30N_F + 25N_T = 1360}$

$-5N_T = -200 \quad \rightarrow \quad \dfrac{-5N_T}{-5} = \dfrac{-200}{-5} \quad \rightarrow \quad N_T = 40$

Therefore, $N_F = \mathbf{12}$ because there were 52 in all.

example 89.2   Wataksha's dress shop sold less expensive dresses for $20 each and more expensive ones for $45 each. The shop took in $1375 and sold 20 more of the less expensive dresses than the more expensive dresses. How many of each kind did they sell?

solution   Again we have statements of equality. The first is that the value of the less expensive dresses plus the value of the expensive dresses equals $1375. $\big(N_L$ stands for the number of less expensive dresses and N_M stands for the number of more expensive dresses.$\big)$

$$\text{(a) } 20N_L + 45N_M = 1375$$

The other statement of equality is that the shop sold 20 more of the less expensive dresses. Thus, we add 20 to the number of expensive dresses to get a statement of equality.

$$\text{(b) } N_L = N_M + 20$$

We will use substitution to solve.

$$
\begin{array}{ll}
20(N_M + 20) + 45N_M = 1375 & \text{substituted} \\
20N_M + 400 + 45N_M = 1375 & \text{multiplied} \\
65N_M + 400 = 1375 & \text{simplified} \\
65N_M = 975 & \text{added } -400 \text{ to both sides} \\
N_M = \mathbf{15} & \text{divided} \\
N_L = \mathbf{35} & \text{since } N_L \text{ is 20 more than } N_M
\end{array}
$$

practice   **a.**   Tickets for good seats cost $8, and tickets for the other seats cost $3. If 18 tickets were sold for a total of $119, how many tickets for good seats were sold?

b.   At a basketball game, adult tickets sold for 5 dollars and children's tickets sold for 2 dollars. If 175 tickets were sold for a total of 686 dollars, how many of each type were sold?

**problem set
89**

1.
(89)   Oatmeal cookies cost 45 cents each and fig bars cost 30 cents each. If the group spent $7.35, how many oatmeal cookies were purchased if they numbered 7 less than the number of fig bars purchased?

2.
(83)   When the box broke open, $82 in quarters and dimes fell out. If there were 300 more quarters than dimes, how many dimes and how many quarters were there?

3.
(77)   Find three consecutive odd integers such that 4 times the sum of the first two is 62 less than the product of –30 and the third.

4. When the mob stormed the Bastille, only 23 percent had a weapon of any kind. If 1610
(58) had a weapon, how many were in the mob?

5. Some of the sounds were susurrant, but $\frac{3}{17}$ of the sounds were plangent. If 2800 sounds
(77) were susurrant, how many sounds were there in all?

6. Two dice are rolled. What is the probability that the sum of the numbers rolled is
(70)
    (a)   not less than 7?   (b)   not more than 7?

7. Luke tried the golf club that his wife Clara gave him and hit golf balls the following
(85) distances (measured in yards):

$$100, 110, 95, 90, 85, 97, 105, 125,$$
$$128, 135, 125, 129, 108, 109, 137$$

Draw a histogram that shows the frequency distribution of the distances.

8. (a)   For the set of distances given in problem 7, find the range, median, mode, and mean.
(45)
    (b)   Determine the percentage of the distances that were less than 99 yards.

Solve by factoring:

9. $x^2 - 12x + 35 = 0$ **10.** $4x^2 - 9 = 0$ **11.** $-49 = -9p^2$
(88)   (88)   (88)

12. $17x = -x^2 - 60$ **13.** $x^2 = 12x - 32$ **14.** $-9x^2 + 4 = 0$
(88)   (88)   (88)

15. Given: $R_M T_M + 10 = R_T T_T$, $R_M = 20$, $R_T = 55$, $T_M + T_T = 7$. Find T_M and T_T.
(87)

16. Which of the following diagrams, graphs, or sets of ordered pairs represent functions?
(84,87)
    (a)   (b)

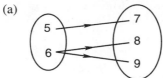   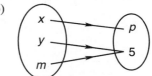

    (c)   (d)

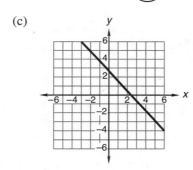   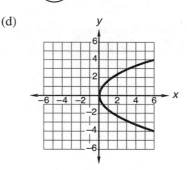

    (e)   (4, –2), (4, –5), (3, 4)   (f)   (1, –2), (3, –2), (6, –2)

17. What is the domain and range for (b) and (f) in problem 16?
(84)

Divide:

18. $\left(x^2 - x - 6\right) \div (x + 2)$ **19.** $\left(3x^3 - 1\right) \div (x + 4)$
(86)   (86)

20. If $f(x) = 3x^2 - 6x + 20$, find $f(2 - a)$.
(82)

21. Find the equations of lines (a) and (b).
(75)

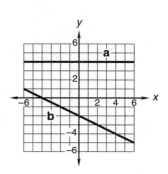

22. Solve by graphing and check:
(81)

$$\begin{cases} y = 2x - 2 \\ y = -x + 4 \end{cases}$$

23. Use elimination to solve:
(67)

$$\begin{cases} 3x + 4y = 28 \\ 2x - 3y = -4 \end{cases}$$

24. Simplify: $3\sqrt{5}(5\sqrt{10} - 2\sqrt{5})$
(84)

25. Indicate whether or not the following numbers are rational numbers or irrational numbers:
(61,63)

(a) $5\sqrt{3}$ (b) 0.03   (c) $\pi + 1 - \pi$ (d) 4.777...

Simplify:

26. $\dfrac{(0.0006 \times 10^{-23})(300 \times 10^{14})}{90,000 \times 10^{25}}$
(80)

27. $\dfrac{xya^{-1} + y^{-1}}{xy^{-1} - a^{-1}}$
(68)

28. Evaluate: $-\left|-x^2\right| + (-x)(-y) + \sqrt[4]{y^2}$ if $x = -3$ and $y = 4$
(62)

29. Simplify: (a) $\dfrac{1}{-3^{-2}}$ (b) $\dfrac{1}{(-3)^{-2}}$ (c) $-(-3)^{-2}$
(36)

30. A base of the right prism 19 centimeters high is shown. Find the volume of the right
(20,60) prism. Dimensions are in centimeters.

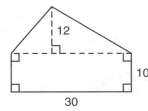
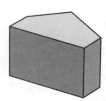

LESSON 90 *Word Problems with Two Statements of Equality*

The coin problems and the general value problems we have studied thus far have contained two statements about quantities that are equal. We have solved these problems by using two equations in two unknowns (variables). Many other problems contain two statements of equality and are solved the same way. We will look at some of these in this lesson. We will write the equations and give the answers. Use substitution or elimination to see if you get the same answers.

example 90.1 Together Charles and Nelle picked 92 quarts of berries. If Charles picked 6 more quarts than Nelle picked, how many quarts did each of them pick?

solution (a) The number Charles picked plus the number Nelle picked equaled 92.

$$N_C + N_N = 92$$

(b) Charles picked 6 more quarts than Nelle picked. **To avoid adding 6 to the wrong side, we begin with an equation that we know is incorrect.**

$$N_N = N_C \qquad \text{incorrect}$$

Charles picked 6 more than Nelle picked, so we add 6 to the number that Nelle picked to get the correct statement of equality.

$$N_N + 6 = N_C \qquad \text{correct}$$

$$\text{ANSWER} \qquad N_C = 49 \qquad N_N = 43$$

example 90.2   The number of boys in Sarah's class exceeded the number of girls by 7. If there were a total of 29 pupils in the class, how many were boys and how many were girls?

solution   (a) The number of boys exceeded the number of girls by 7. Thus we add 7 to the number of girls.

$$N_B = N_G \qquad \text{incorrect}$$

$$N_B = N_G + 7 \qquad \text{correct}$$

(b) The number of boys plus the number of girls equaled 29.

$$N_B + N_G = 29$$

$$\text{ANSWER} \qquad N_B = \mathbf{18} \qquad N_G = \mathbf{11}$$

example 90.3   Phillip cut a 38-meter rope into two pieces. The long piece was 9 meters longer than the short piece. What were the two lengths?

solution   (a) The length of the long piece plus the length of the short piece equaled 38 meters.

$$L + S = 38$$

(b) The long piece was 9 meters longer than the short piece, so we add 9 to S.

$$L = S \qquad \text{incorrect}$$

$$L = S + 9 \qquad \text{correct}$$

$$\text{ANSWER} \qquad L = \mathbf{23.5} \qquad S = \mathbf{14.5}$$

example 90.4   The sum of two numbers is 72. The difference of the numbers is 26. What are the numbers?

solution   (a) The large number plus the small number equals 72.

$$L + S = 72$$

(b) The large number minus the small number equals 26.

$$L - S = 26$$

$$\text{ANSWER} \qquad L = \mathbf{49} \qquad S = \mathbf{23}$$

example 90.5   The greater of two numbers is 16 greater than the smaller. When added together, their sum is 4 less than 3 times the smaller. What are the numbers?

solution   (a) The greater number is 16 greater than the smaller.

$$G = S \qquad \text{incorrect}$$

$$G - 16 = S \qquad \text{correct}$$

(b) The sum is 4 less than 3 times the smaller.

$$G + S = 3S \qquad \text{incorrect}$$

$$G + S + 4 = 3S \qquad \text{correct}$$

$$\text{ANSWER} \qquad G = \mathbf{36} \qquad S = \mathbf{20}$$

example 90.6   The ratio of two numbers is 5 to 4 and the sum of the numbers is 63. What are the numbers?

solution   (a) The ratio of the numbers is 5 to 4.

$$\frac{N_1}{N_2} = \frac{5}{4} \quad \longrightarrow \quad 4N_1 = 5N_2$$

(b) The sum of the numbers is 63.

$$N_1 + N_2 = 63$$

ANSWER $N_1 = 35$ $N_2 = 28$

practice   **a.**   The sum of two numbers is 98. The difference of the same two numbers is 40. What are the numbers?

b.   The number of girls in Marvin's class exceeded the number of boys by 11. If there were 37 pupils in the class, how many were girls and how many were boys?

class project   You will need a meter stick measurement on the wall. Have each student measure his or her height to the nearest centimeter. Put this list on the chalkboard for the students to copy and use in problem 6.

problem set 90

1.
(90)   The sum of two numbers is 48. The difference of the same two numbers is 24. What are the numbers?

2.
(90)   The number of girls in Stephen's class exceeded the number of boys by 8. If there were 36 pupils in the class, how many were girls and how many were boys?

3.
(90)   Gertrude cut a 76-meter rope into two pieces. The long piece was 12 meters longer than the short piece. How long was each piece?

4.
(89)   Shields and Jim sold tickets to the basketball game. Good seats were $5 each, and poor seats were only $2 each. If 210 people attended and paid $660, how many people bought good seats?

5.
(65)   Student grades were based on weighted averages. The final test was weighted at 4 times the weight of a weekly test. If Marion had an average of 92.4 on the 10 regular weekly tests and scored 84 on the final, what was her weighted average?

6.
(45,85)   Use the data gathered in class to solve the following:

(a)   Create a stem-and-leaf plot of the data gathered.

(b)   Create a histogram of the data gathered.

(c)   Determine the range, median, mode, and mean of the data gathered.

7.
(53)   Use 12 unit multipliers to convert 1000 cubic yards to cubic meters.

Solve by factoring:

8. $2x^2 + 20x + 50 = 0$
(88)

9. $3x^2 = -33x - 90$
(88)

10. $2x^2 - 18 = 0$
(88)

11. $27 - 3p^2 = 0$
(88)

12. Given: $R_M T_M = R_B T_B$, $R_B = 5$, $R_M = 4$, $T_M + T_B = 18$. Find T_M and T_B.
(87)

13. Which of the following diagrams, graphs, or sets of ordered pairs represent functions?
(84,87)

(a)

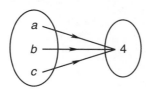

(b)

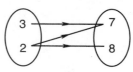

(c)

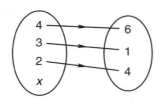

(d)

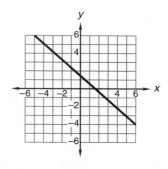

    (e)   (4, 3), (3, 2), (3, –2)   (f)   (4, 2), (3, –2), (7, –8)

Divide:

14. $\left(3x^3 - 2x - 4\right) \div (x + 1)$ **15.** $\left(2x^3 - 2x^2 - 4\right) \div (x + 1)$
(86)   (86)

16. If $f(x) = 3x^3 - 4x^2 + 7x - 9$, find $f(4)$.
(82)

Simplify:

17. $3\sqrt{27} - 2\sqrt{3}\left(4\sqrt{3} - 5\sqrt{12}\right)$ **18.** $2\sqrt{2} \cdot 3\sqrt{3} \cdot 5\sqrt{12}$
(84)   (84)

19. Find the equations of lines (a) and (b).
(75)

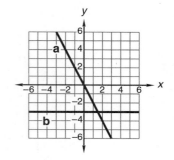

20. Solve by graphing and check: **21.** Use substitution to solve:
(81)   (54)

$$\begin{cases} y = \dfrac{2}{3}x - 3 \\ y = -x + 2 \end{cases}$$

$$\begin{cases} y = -3x + 10 \\ 2x + 2y = 8 \end{cases}$$

22. Simplify: $\dfrac{\left(3000 \times 10^{-5}\right)\left(0.004 \times 10^{10}\right)}{\left(200 \times 10^{14}\right)(0.000002)}$
(80)

23. (a) $\sqrt{49} \in$ {What subsets of the real numbers}?
(61)
     (b) $-\sqrt{144} \in$ {What subsets of the real numbers}?

24. Graph on a number line: $x + 4 \not> 2$; $D = $ {Reals}
(64)

Solve:

25. $\dfrac{3x + 2}{5} - \dfrac{x}{2} = 5$ **26.** $-3x^0(-2 - 3)4x = -2(x + 2)$
(78)   (31)

27. Evaluate: $|-x| - x^0 - x^2(x - y)$ if $x = -2$ and $y = \sqrt[3]{64} - 8$
(41)

28. Add: $\dfrac{x}{x+1} + \dfrac{x^2}{x(x+1)} - \dfrac{2}{x}$
(52)

29. Simplify: (a) -3^{-2} (b) $(-3)^{-2}$ (c) $-(-3)^{-2}$
(36)

30. A right circular cone has a base of
(72) radius 12 in. and a slant height of
20 in., as shown. Find the surface area
of the right circular cone.

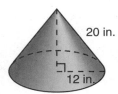

20 in.

12 in.

LESSON 91 *Multiplicative Property of Inequality • Spheres*

91.A
multiplicative property of inequality

With one glaring exception, the rules for solving inequalities are the same as the rules for solving equations. The following two rules apply to both equalities and inequalities:

> ADDITION RULE
>
> The same quantity can be added to both sides of an equation or inequality without changing the solution set of the equation or inequality.

> MULTIPLICATION RULE (POSITIVE)
>
> Every term on both sides of an equation or inequality can be multiplied by the same positive number without changing the solution set of the equation or inequality.

The glaring exception occurs when we multiply by a negative number! The truth of a statement of equality is not altered by multiplying by a negative number.

$$5 = 2 + 3 \qquad \text{True}$$

Now multiply every term by -2 and get

$$5(-2) = 2(-2) + 3(-2) \;\longrightarrow\; -10 = -4 - 6 \qquad \text{Still true!}$$

But the truth of a statement of inequality is altered!

$$8 > 5 \qquad \text{True}$$

Now we multiply every term by -2 and get

$$-16 > -10 \qquad \text{Now false!}$$

Thus, when every term on both sides of an inequality is multiplied by a negative number, the inequality symbol must be reversed so that the solution set of the inequality will not be changed. To show this, we will repeat the problem.

$$8 > 5 \qquad \text{True}$$

Now we multiply every term by -2 and get

$$-16 < -10 \qquad \text{Still true!}$$

example 91.1   Graph the solution: $-x \geq 2$; $D = \{\text{Reals}\}$

solution   We solve the given inequality for $+x$ by multiplying both sides by (-1) and **reversing the inequality symbol.**

$$-x \geq 2 \qquad\qquad \text{original inequality}$$

$$(-1)(-x) \leq (-1)(2) \qquad \text{multiplied by } -1 \text{ and reversed inequality symbol}$$

$$x \leq -2 \qquad\qquad \text{simplified}$$

Thus we want to graph the solution of $x \leq -2$.

The graph indicates that the number -2 and all real numbers less than -2 satisfy the stated inequality.

example 91.2   Graph the solution: $4 - x \leq 6$; $D = \{\text{Integers}\}$

solution   We first isolate $-x$ by adding -4 to both sides. **Note that we do not reverse the inequality symbol when we *add* a negative quantity to both sides of an inequality.**

$$\begin{array}{rr} 4 - x \leq & 6 \\ -4 \qquad\quad & -4 \\ \hline -x \leq & 2 \end{array}$$

Now we **multiply** both sides by -1 and **reverse the inequality symbol** to get

$$x \geq -2$$

And if we graph $x \geq -2$ for integer x, we get

example 91.3   Graph the solution: $-3x + 4 \leq 13$; $D = \{\text{Reals}\}$

solution   We add -4 to both sides to get $-3x \leq 9$ and then multiply both sides by $-\frac{1}{3}$ **and reverse the inequality symbol** to get

$$x \geq -3$$

Note that multiplying by $-\frac{1}{3}$ is the same as dividing by -3. **Therefore, we see that in general when we divide both sides of an inequality by a negative number, we need to reverse the inequality sign.** We graph the solution to the inequality to indicate all real numbers that are greater than or equal to -3.

91.B

spheres   A **sphere** is a perfectly round, three-dimensional shape. All points on the surface of a sphere are the same distance from the center. This distance is the radius of the sphere.

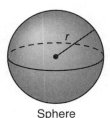

Sphere

The volume of a sphere is equal to $\frac{4}{3}\pi r^3$, and the surface area of a sphere is equal to $4\pi r^2$. Proofs of these formulas are beyond the scope of this book.

volume   **The volume of a sphere is exactly two thirds the volume of the smallest right circular**
of spheres   **cylinder into which the sphere fits.** The radius of the right circular cylinder equals the radius of the sphere, and the height of the right circular cylinder is twice the radius of the sphere.

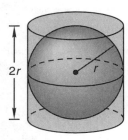

$$\text{Area of a base } = \pi r^2$$

$$\text{Volume of cylinder } = (2r)\pi r^2$$

$$= 2\pi r^3$$

$$\text{Volume of sphere } = \frac{2}{3}(2\pi r^3)$$

$$= \frac{4}{3}\pi r^3$$

Volume of the sphere equals $\frac{2}{3}$ the volume of the cylinder

Close your eyes and try to remember this diagram. It will help you remember the formula for the volume of a sphere. The first proof of this method of finding the volume of a sphere is attributed to the Greek philosopher Archimedes (287–212 B.C.).

$$\textbf{Volume of a sphere } = \ \frac{4}{3}\pi r^3$$

example 91.4   Find the volume of a sphere whose radius is 3 cm.

solution   The formula for the volume of a sphere of radius r is given by

$$\text{Volume } = \ \frac{4}{3}\pi r^3$$

Substituting 3 cm for r, we get

$$\text{Volume } = \ \frac{4}{3}\pi(3 \text{ cm})^3$$

$$= 36\pi \text{ cm}^3$$

$$= 36(3.14) \text{ cm}^3$$

$$= \textbf{113.04 cm}^3$$

surface area of spheres

There is an easy way to remember how to find the surface area of a sphere. The surface area of a sphere equals the sum of the areas of four circles, each with a radius whose length equals the length of the radius of the sphere. A picture to aid your memory shows a sphere and four circles, each of which has a radius the same as the radius of the sphere.

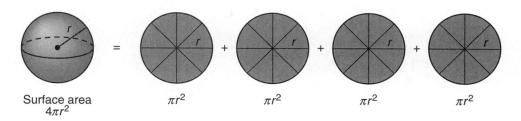

Surface area
$4\pi r^2$ πr^2 πr^2 πr^2 πr^2

Close your eyes and try to place the diagram above in your memory. If you do, it will be easier to remember that the surface area of a sphere equals the sum of the areas of four circles, each with a radius whose length equals the length of the radius of the sphere.

$$\text{Surface area of a sphere} = 4\pi r^2$$

example 91.5   Find the surface area of a sphere whose radius is 4 m.

solution   The formula for the surface area of a sphere of radius r is given by

$$\text{Surface area} = 4\pi r^2$$

Substituting 4 m for r, we get

$$\text{Surface area} = 4\pi(4 \text{ m})^2$$
$$= 64\pi \text{ m}^2$$
$$= 64(3.14) \text{ m}^2$$
$$= \mathbf{200.96 \text{ m}^2}$$

practice   Graph on a number line:

a. $-x \geq 5$; $D = \{\text{Reals}\}$ **b.** $2 - x \nleq 1$; $D = \{\text{Integers}\}$

c. $-3x + 5 > 1$; $D = \{\text{Integers}\}$

d. Find the volume of a sphere whose radius is 4 in.

e. Find the surface area of a sphere whose radius is 5 ft.

problem set 91

1.
(90)
There were 90 more orchids on the first float than there were on the second float. If there were 630 orchids altogether, how many were on each float?

2.
(89)
Seed corn was $5 per bag, whereas dog food cost only $3 per bag. Wewoka bought 50 bags and spent $190. How many bags of dog food did she buy?

3.
(83)
Wetumka had $6.50 in dimes and quarters. If he had 5 more quarters than dimes, how many coins of each type did he have?

4.
(58)
When the first frost came, the number of people wearing shoes jumped 180 percent. If 5600 people now wear shoes, how many people wore shoes before the frost?

5. Edward was bird watching and each day he recorded the number of stellar jays that he
(45) saw. The numbers he recorded for one week are 52, 49, 48, 54, 50, 47, and 50. What is
the range, median, mode, and mean of his recorded data?

Graph on a number line:

6. $-x \geq 3$; $D = \{$Reals$\}$ **7.** $4 \leq x < 7$; $D = \{$Integers$\}$
(91)   (64)

8. $3 - x \not\leq 1$; $D = \{$Reals$\}$
(91)

Solve by factoring:

9. $21 = 10x - x^2$ **10.** $-49 = -4x^2$ **11.** $32 = -x^2 - 12x$
(88)   (88)   (88)

12. Given: $R_H T_H - 125 = R_O T_O$, $T_H = 2$, $T_O = 3$, $R_H + R_O = 85$. Find R_H and R_O.
(87)

13. Which of the following diagrams, graphs, or sets of ordered pairs depict functions?
(84,87)

(a) 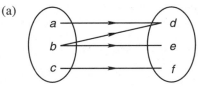   (b)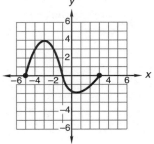

(c) (4, 7), (3, 7), (9, 2)

(d) (4, 7), (3, 7), (4, 2)

(e) 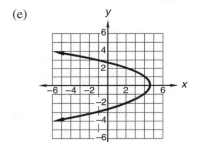   (f)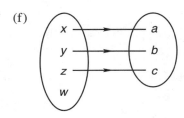

14. What is the domain and range for (b) and (c) in problem 13?
(82,84)

15. Divide: $\left(x^4 - 2x^2 - 4\right) \div (x + 2)$
(86)

16. Find the equations of lines (a) and (b).
(75)

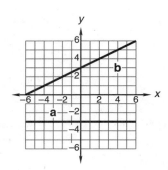

Simplify:

17. $5\sqrt{75} - 2\sqrt{108} + 5\sqrt{12}$ **18.** $2\sqrt{6}\left(3\sqrt{6} - 2\sqrt{12}\right)$
(66)   (84)

19. Solve by graphing and check: **20.** Use elimination to solve:
(81)   (67)

$$\begin{cases} y = -x + 1 \\ y = 2x + 4 \end{cases} \qquad \begin{cases} 4x - 3y = 14 \\ 5x - 4y = 18 \end{cases}$$

21. Simplify: $\dfrac{(0.00004 \times 10^{15})(700 \times 10^{-5})}{14{,}000 \times 10^{-21}}$
₍₈₀₎

22. (a) $-3\dfrac{1}{3} \in$ {What subsets of real numbers}?
_(61,63)

     (b) $2.\overline{23} \in$ {What subsets of real numbers}?

Solve:

23. $\dfrac{4x}{3} - \dfrac{x+1}{5} = 10$ **24.** $3x^0 - 2x^0 - 3(x^0 - 2x) = -2x(4 - 3)$
₍₇₈₎   ₍₃₁₎

25. Evaluate: $-b \pm \sqrt{b^2 - 4ac}$ if $a = -3$, $c = 4$, and $b + 5 = \sqrt{16}$
₍₆₂₎

Simplify:

26. $\dfrac{\dfrac{3x}{y} - 2}{a - \dfrac{4}{y}}$
₍₆₈₎

27. $\dfrac{ab^{-1} + a^{-1}}{a^{-1}b}$
₍₆₈₎

28. Evaluate: (a) $-x^{-3}$ (b) $\dfrac{1}{-(-x)^{-3}}$ if $x = \sqrt{16} - \sqrt[4]{16} - \sqrt{4} - \sqrt[3]{8}$
_(36,41)

29. Find the volume of the sphere shown
₍₉₁₎ whose radius is 1 cm.

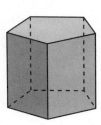

30. The area of a base of a right pentago-
_(20,60) nal prism is 60 m² and the length of a
lateral edge is 13 m. Find the volume
of the right pentagonal prism.

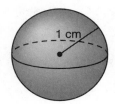

LESSON 92   *Uniform Motion Problems About Equal Distances*

Since Lesson 79 we have been using substitution to solve systems of four simultaneous equations involving four unknowns such as

$$R_F T_F = R_E T_E \qquad T_F = 16 \qquad T_E = 12 \qquad R_E = R_F + 15$$

These equations are typical of the equations that we will learn to write in this lesson to help us solve uniform motion word problems. Uniform motion problems are so named because the statement of the problem tells about objects or things that move at a uniform rate or at an average rate.

The statements of equality made in uniform motion problems are statements of equality that concern **distance,** statements of equality that concern **rate,** and statements of equality that concern **time,** and that use the relationship

$$\text{Distance} = \text{rate} \times \text{time} \qquad \text{or} \qquad D = RT$$

The statements about rate and time are not difficult to locate in the wording of the problem, but the beginner often has trouble identifying the statement that defines the relationship that concerns distance. **Since the distance equation is the troublesome one, we will consider this equation to be the key equation for this type of problem, and we will always write this equation first.** Then we will write the equations that concern time and the equations that concern rate. **When we have as many independent equations as we have variables, we will use the substitution method and/or the elimination method to solve for the variables.**

The statements of the distances discussed in the problems can be represented graphically by drawing diagrams in which arrows represent the distances. The problems in this book will usually describe two distances. In this lesson, we will investigate problems that describe two equal distances.

One of these diagrams will result when the problem states that two distances are equal. In (a) the objects traveled in the same direction, and in (b) they traveled in opposite directions. Both diagrams give us the same equation.

example 92.1 On Tuesday the express train made the trip in 12 hours. On Wednesday the freight train made the same trip in 16 hours. Find the rate of each train if the rate of the freight train was 15 kilometers per hour less than the rate of the express train.

solution We read the problem and disregard statements about time and rate and look for the statement about distance. This information allows us to draw the diagram and from the diagram get the following equation:

$$\text{Distance express} = \text{Distance freight}$$
$$\text{(a) } D_E = D_F$$

This is the distance equation, which is the key equation for this uniform motion problem. Now the distance the express traveled equals the rate of the express times the time the express traveled, or

$$D_E = R_E T_E$$

and the distance the freight traveled equals the rate of the freight times the time the freight traveled, or

$$D_F = R_F T_F$$

Now, if we substitute $R_E T_E$ for D_E and $R_F T_F$ for D_F in equation (a), we get

$$R_E T_E = R_F T_F$$

which is the distance equation for this problem in final form.

The statement of the problem gives the time of the express as 12 hours and the time of the freight as 16 hours, so

$$T_E = 12 \qquad T_F = 16$$

Now we have three equations but four unknowns, R_E, T_E, R_F, and T_F. **Thus, we need one more equation so that the number of equations will equal the number of unknowns.** We get the final equation from the statement in the problem concerning rates, which says that the rate of the express is 15 kilometers per hour greater than the rate of the freight. **Writing this equation is tricky.** In an effort to avoid the common error of adding 15 to the wrong side, we first write

$$R_F = R_E \qquad \text{incorrect}$$

which we know is incorrect because the rate of the express is greater than the rate of the freight. We add 15 to R_F so that the equation will have equal quantities on both sides.

$$R_E = R_F + 15$$

We have found four equations in four unknowns

$$R_E T_E = R_F T_F \qquad T_E = 12 \qquad T_F = 16 \qquad R_E = R_F + 15$$

and we use the substitution method to solve for R_F and R_E.

$$
\begin{array}{ll}
R_E T_E = R_F T_F & \text{equation} \\
(R_F + 15)12 = R_F(16) & \text{substituted} \\
12R_F + 180 = 16R_F & \text{multiplied} \\
-4R_F = -180 & \text{simplified} \\
4R_F = 180 & \text{multiplied by } -1 \\
R_F = 45 \, \dfrac{\text{km}}{\text{hr}} & \text{divided}
\end{array}
$$

Since $R_E = R_F + 15$,

$$R_E = 60 \, \frac{\text{km}}{\text{hr}}$$

example 92.2   The members of the girls club hiked to Lake Tenkiller at 2 miles per hour. Mr. Ali gave them a ride back home at 12 miles per hour. Find their hiking time if it was 5 hours longer than their riding time. How far was it to Lake Tenkiller?

solution   We begin by drawing a diagram of the distances traveled and writing the distance equation.

$$D_H = D_R \qquad \text{so} \qquad R_H T_H = R_R T_R$$

Next we reread the problem and write the other three equations.

$$R_H = 2 \qquad R_R = 12 \qquad T_H = T_R + 5$$

Now we substitute these equations into the distance equation and solve.

$$
\begin{array}{ll}
2(T_R + 5) = 12T_R & \text{substituted} \\
2T_R + 10 = 12T_R & \text{multiplied} \\
10 = 10T_R & \text{added } -2T_R \text{ to both sides} \\
T_R = 1 & \text{divided both sides by 10}
\end{array}
$$

Since $T_H = T_R + 5$,

$$T_H = 6 \, \text{hr}$$

Thus the distance is either 2 times 6 or 12 times 1, both of which equal **12 miles.**

example 92.3 Durant drove to the oasis in 2 hours and Madill walked to the oasis in 10 hours. How far is it to the oasis if Durant drove 16 miles per hour faster than Madill walked?

solution We begin by drawing a diagram of the distances traveled and writing the distance equation.

$$D_D = D_W \qquad \text{so} \qquad R_D T_D = R_W T_W$$

Now we reread the problem to get the time and rate equations.

$$T_D = 2 \qquad T_W = 10 \qquad R_D = R_W + 16$$

Now we solve.

$$(R_W + 16)2 = R_W(10) \qquad \text{substituted}$$
$$2R_W + 32 = 10R_W \qquad \text{multiplied}$$
$$32 = 8R_W \qquad \text{added } -2R_W \text{ to both sides}$$
$$4 = R_W \qquad \text{divided}$$

Thus $R_D = 20$, and since $T_D = 2$, the distance equals 2 times 20, or **40 miles.**

practice **a.** Candide and Pangloss walked to the site of the disaster in 9 hours. The next morning they jogged back home in 3 hours. How far did they jog if they jogged 4 miles per hour faster than they walked?

b. On Monday, Voltaire drove to town at 60 miles per hour. On Tuesday, he drove to town at 40 miles per hour. If the total traveling time for both trips was 15 hours, how far was it to town?

problem set 92

1. In the morning the passenger train made the trip in 3 hours. In the afternoon the freight
(92) train made the same trip in 7 hours. Find the rate of each if the rate of the freight train was 40 miles per hour less than the rate of the passenger train. Begin by drawing a diagram of distances traveled and writing the distance equation.

2. Vanessa rode her bike to the conclave at 10 kilometers per hour and then walked back to
(92) school at 4 kilometers per hour. If the round trip took her 14 hours, how far was it to the site of the conclave? Begin by drawing a diagram of distances traveled and writing the distance equation.

3. The sum of four numbers is 12,000.16. The first three numbers are 4200, 1700, and 3400.
(45) Find the average of the four numbers.

4. Ice cream bars cost 30 cents and whifferdils cost 50 cents. Gary and Cavender treated all
(89) the kids, and they spent $13.50. How many kids had whifferdils if they numbered 5 less than those who had ice cream bars?

5. Fustian phrases obscured 0.62 of the points the speaker tried to make. If he tried to make
(77) 50 points, how many points was the audience able to comprehend?

6. The tank contains 9 volleyballs and 7 soccer balls. The coach draws one ball at random
(73) and does not replace it. Then he randomly draws another ball. What is the probability that both are soccer balls?

Graph the solutions of these inequalities on number lines:

7. $-4x + 4 \geq 8$; $D = \{\text{Reals}\}$ **8.** $4 - x \ngeq 3$; $D = \{\text{Integers}\}$
(91)   (91)

Solve by factoring:

9. $x^2 = -6x - 8$ **10.** $9 = 4x^2$ **11.** $x^2 = -12x - 32$
(88)   (88)   (88)

12. Find the domain and range of the
(82)   graphed function.

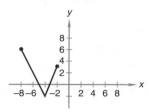

13. Find the equations of lines (a) and (b).
(75)

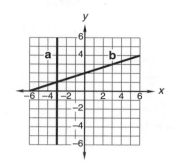

14. Divide: $(x^3 - 4) \div (x - 5)$
(86)

Simplify:

15. $3\sqrt{45} - 2\sqrt{180} + 2\sqrt{80{,}000}$
(66)

16. $3\sqrt{2}\left(4\sqrt{20} - 3\sqrt{2}\right)$
(84)

17. Solve by graphing and check:
(81)

$$\begin{cases} y = -2x + 4 \\ y = -2 \end{cases}$$

18. Use elimination to solve:
(67)

$$\begin{cases} 3x + y = 20 \\ 2x - 3y = -5 \end{cases}$$

19. Simplify: $\dfrac{0.000030 \times 10^{-18}}{\left(5000 \times 10^{-14}\right)\left(300 \times 10^{5}\right)}$
(80)

20. Tell whether the following statements are true or false, and explain why:
(61)

(a)   {Reals} $\subset$ {Rationals}   (b)   {Wholes} $\subset$ {Naturals}

21. Use 12 unit multipliers to convert 10,000 cubic yards to cubic meters.
(53)

Solve:

22. $\dfrac{x}{5} - \dfrac{4 + x}{7} = 5$
(78)

23. $2\dfrac{1}{8}x - 3\dfrac{1}{4} = 2\dfrac{1}{16}$
(25)

24. $p - (-p) - 5(p - 3) - (2p - 5) = 3(p + 2p)$
(31)

25. Evaluate: $\left|-x^2\right| - |x| + x\left(x - y^0\right)$ if $x = -\sqrt{9}$ and $5y = 20$
(41)

Simplify:

26. $-3^0 - \left[(-3 + 5) - (-2 - 5)\right]$
(29)

27. (a) -2^{-2} (b) $\dfrac{1}{-2^{-3}}$ (c) $-(-2)^{-2}$ (d) $\sqrt[7]{-128}$
(36,62)

28. Expand by using the distributive property. Write the answer with all exponents positive.
(40)

$$\left(\frac{x^{-1}y}{a^{-2}} + \frac{x^4 y}{a^2} - \frac{x^{-3}y^2}{ya^{-4}}\right)\frac{x^{-4}y}{a^{-2}}$$

29. Find the surface area of the sphere
(91)   shown whose radius is 2 in.

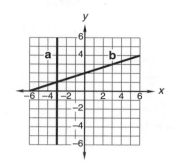

30. Find the lateral surface area of this
(15,60) right prism whose bases are regular
        pentagons. Dimensions are in feet.

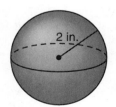
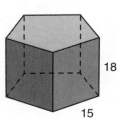

LESSON 93 *Products of Rational Expressions • Quotients of Rational Expressions*

93.A
products of rational expressions

Fractions are multiplied by multiplying the numerators to form the numerator of the product and by multiplying the denominators to form the denominator of the product. Thus to multiply

$$\frac{4x}{5} \cdot \frac{3xa}{y}$$

we multiply the numerators to get $12x^2a$ and multiply the denominators to get $5y$.

$$\frac{4x}{5} \cdot \frac{3xa}{y} = \frac{12x^2a}{5y}$$

Sometimes we encounter indicated products of rational expressions whose simplification is facilitated if the terms are first factored and all canceling that is possible is performed before any multiplication is done.

example 93.1   Simplify: $\dfrac{x^2 - 25}{x^2 - 7x} \cdot \dfrac{x^2 + 3x}{x^2 - 2x - 15}$

solution   If we multiply the expressions in their present form, we get a very complicated expression for the product.

$$\frac{(x^2 - 25)(x^2 + 3x)}{(x^2 - 7x)(x^2 - 2x - 15)} = \frac{x^4 - 25x^2 + 3x^3 - 75x}{x^4 - 9x^3 - x^2 + 105x}$$

This expression has x raised to the fourth power in both the numerator and the denominator and is very difficult to simplify. If we factor and cancel before we multiply, however, the simplified form can be obtained quickly and easily.

$$\frac{(x - 5)(x + 5)}{x(x - 7)} \cdot \frac{x(x + 3)}{(x + 3)(x - 5)} = \frac{x + 5}{x - 7}$$

example 93.2   Simplify: $\dfrac{x^2 + x - 6}{x^2 - 4x - 21} \cdot \dfrac{x^2 - 8x + 7}{x^2 - x - 2}$

solution   Problems like this one are encountered only in algebra books. **These problems are carefully contrived to give the students practice in factoring and canceling.** Thus we factor and cancel like factors that appear in both the numerator and denominator.

$$\frac{(x + 3)(x - 2)}{(x - 7)(x + 3)} \cdot \frac{(x - 7)(x - 1)}{(x - 2)(x + 1)} = \frac{x - 1}{x + 1}$$

93.B
quotients of rational expressions

In Lesson 55 we learned to simplify expressions such as

$$\frac{\dfrac{a}{b}}{\dfrac{c}{d}}$$

by using the **denominator-numerator same-quantity rule** to justify multiplying both the denominator and the numerator by $\frac{d}{c}$, which is the reciprocal of the denominator.

$$\frac{\dfrac{a}{b}}{\dfrac{c}{d}} = \frac{\dfrac{a}{b} \cdot \dfrac{d}{c}}{\dfrac{c}{d} \cdot \dfrac{d}{c}} = \frac{\dfrac{ad}{bc}}{1} = \frac{ad}{bc}$$

If the same division problem had been stated by writing

$$\frac{a}{b} \div \frac{c}{d}$$

we see that the same result can be obtained by inverting the divisor and multiplying.

$$\frac{a}{b} \div \frac{c}{d} = \frac{a}{b} \cdot \frac{d}{c} = \frac{ad}{bc}$$

We can use this procedure to simplify quotients of more complicated rational expressions.

example 93.3   Simplify: $\dfrac{x^2 - 2x}{x^2 + 2x - 8} \div \dfrac{x^2 + 5x}{x^2 + 7x + 12}$

solution   As the first step we invert the divisor and change the division symbol to a multiplication dot. Then we factor and cancel as in the two previous examples.

$$\frac{x^2 - 2x}{x^2 + 2x - 8} \cdot \frac{x^2 + 7x + 12}{x^2 + 5x} = \frac{x(x - 2)}{(x + 4)(x - 2)} \cdot \frac{(x + 4)(x + 3)}{x(x + 5)} = \frac{x + 3}{x + 5}$$

example 93.4   Simplify: $\dfrac{x^2 - x - 6}{x^2 - 3x - 10} \div \dfrac{x^2 + 5x + 4}{x^2 - x - 20}$

solution   Again as the first step we invert the divisor and indicate multiplication rather than division. Then we factor and cancel.

$$\frac{x^2 - x - 6}{x^2 - 3x - 10} \cdot \frac{x^2 - x - 20}{x^2 + 5x + 4} = \frac{(x - 3)(x + 2)}{(x - 5)(x + 2)} \cdot \frac{(x - 5)(x + 4)}{(x + 4)(x + 1)} = \frac{x - 3}{x + 1}$$

practice   Simplify:

a. $\dfrac{x^2 - x - 6}{x^2 - 6x - 16} \div \dfrac{x^2 - 3x}{x^2 - 3x - 40}$

b. $\dfrac{x^2 + 12x + 36}{x^2 + 13x + 42} \cdot \dfrac{x^2 + 4x - 21}{x^2 + 2x - 24}$

problem set 93

1.
(92)
Norma and David crawled to the barn and then hopped back to the house. They crawled at 300 centimeters per minute and hopped at 400 centimeters per minute. If the round trip took 7 minutes, how long did they crawl? How far was it to the barn? Begin by drawing a diagram of distances traveled and writing the distance equation.

2.
(92)
Annette drove to Shawnee in 4 hours and drove back in 3 hours. What were her speeds if her speed coming back was 11 miles per hour greater than her speed going? Begin by drawing a diagram of distances traveled and writing the distance equation.

3.
(89)
Tickets to the carnival were $3 for adults and $2 for kids. Tommy was a big spender, as he took 77 people to the carnival and spent $209 for their tickets. How many kids did he pay for?

4. Hobert and Higgs counted the boys and girls at the assembly. There were 179 students
(90) and 13 more boys than girls. How many boys and how many girls were present?

5. When the time came to stand up and be counted, only 92 people stood up. If 460 people
(58) were present, what percent stood up and were counted?

6. Five thirteenths of the citizens believed that the cause of their difficulty was
(77) procrastination. If 400 did not agree with this analysis, how many citizens lived in the
community?

7. Owen flipped a fair coin 5 times. What is the probability that it came up heads, then tails,
(70) then heads, then tails, and finally heads?

Simplify:

8. $\dfrac{x^2 - 16}{x^2 + x - 12} \cdot \dfrac{x^2 + 5x + 6}{x^2 - 2x - 8}$
(93)

9. $\dfrac{x^3 - 4x}{x^2 + 7x + 10} \div \dfrac{x^2 - 2x}{x^2 - 25}$
(93)

Graph the solutions of these inequalities on number lines:

10. $-x - 3 \not> 2$; $D = \{\text{Reals}\}$
(91)

11. $-3 < x < 2$; $D = \{\text{Reals}\}$
(64)

Solve by factoring:

12. $40 = -x^2 - 14x$
(88)

13. $4x^2 - 16 = 0$
(88)

14. Which of the following diagrams, graphs, or sets of ordered pairs depict functions?
(84,87)

(a) $(-3, 2), (3, 2), (5, 2)$

(b) $(-3, -2), (5, -2), (7, -2)$

(c)
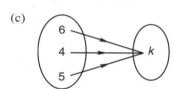
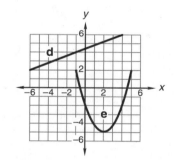

15. Divide: $\left(3x^3 - 4\right) \div (x + 3)$
(86)

Simplify:

16. $3\sqrt{6} \cdot 2\sqrt{5} - \sqrt{120}$
(84)

17. $4\sqrt{12}\left(3\sqrt{2} - 4\sqrt{3}\right)$
(84)

18. Find the domain and range of the
(82) graphed function.

19. Find the equations of lines (a) and (b).
(75)

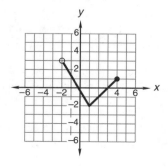

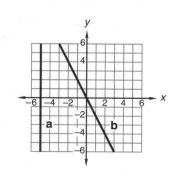

20. Solve by graphing and check:
(81)

$$\begin{cases} y = 2x - 4 \\ y = -x + 2 \end{cases}$$

21. Use substitution to solve:
(59)

$$\begin{cases} 3x + 5y = -14 \\ -2x + y = 5 \end{cases}$$

22. Simplify: $\dfrac{(0.000004)(0.003 \times 10^{21})}{(20{,}000 \times 10^8)(0.002 \times 10^{15})}$
(80)

Solve:

23. $\dfrac{x-5}{7} + \dfrac{x}{4} = \dfrac{1}{2}$
(78)

24. $-2(3x - 4^0) + 3x - 2^0 = -(x - 3^2)$
(31)

25. Evaluate: $-y^0(-y^2 - 4y) - ay$ if $y = -\sqrt[4]{16}$ and $a = \sqrt[3]{-125}$
(62)

26. Expand: $(3x + 3y)^2$
(49)

27. Add: $\dfrac{x}{ya^2} + \dfrac{xa}{a^2 y^2} - \dfrac{3}{ay} - \dfrac{a}{ay^2}$
(44)

28. Simplify: (a) $\dfrac{1}{-3^{-3}}$ (b) $\dfrac{1}{(-3)^{-3}}$ (c) $-(-3)^{-3}$ (d) $\sqrt[3]{-64}$
(36,62)

29. Find the perimeter of this figure. Dimensions are in centimeters.
(3)

30. A base of the right prism 14 meters high is shown. Find the volume of the right prism. Dimensions are in meters.
(20,60)

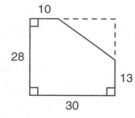
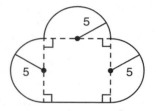

LESSON 94   *Uniform Motion Problems of the Form*
$D_1 + D_2 = N$

In the uniform motion problems we have worked up to now, two people or things have traveled equal distances. The distance diagrams have looked like one of the following:

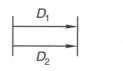

These diagrams have indicated that our distance equation should be of the form $R_1T_1 = R_2T_2$. Now we will consider problems that state the sum of two distances equals a given number. The diagrams and equations of these problems will have the following forms:

$$D_1 + D_2 = 352 \qquad \text{so} \qquad R_1T_1 + R_2T_2 = 352$$

example 94.1   A southbound bus left Fort Walton Beach at 9 a.m. Two hours later a northbound bus left the same station. If the buses traveled at the same rate and were 352 kilometers apart at 2 p.m., find the rate of the buses.

solution   The statement of the problem leads to the following distance diagram:

The distance equation is $D_N + D_S = 352$ or $R_NT_N + R_ST_S = 352$. The southbound bus traveled for 5 hours and the northbound bus traveled for 3 hours.

$$T_N = 3 \qquad T_S = 5$$

The rates were the same, so $R_N = R_S$.

Now we have four equations in four unknowns.

$$R_NT_N + R_ST_S = 352 \qquad T_N = 3 \qquad T_S = 5 \qquad R_N = R_S$$

We use substitution to solve.

$$R_N(3) + R_N(5) = 352 \quad \longrightarrow \quad 8R_N = 352 \quad \longrightarrow \quad R_N = \mathbf{44 \ \frac{km}{hr}}$$

Therefore,

$$R_S = \mathbf{44 \ \frac{km}{hr}}$$

example 94.2   A train starts from Toledo at 11 a.m. and heads for Mackinaw, 332 kilometers away. At the same time, a train leaves Mackinaw and heads for Toledo at 65 kilometers per hour. If the trains meet at 1 p.m., what is the rate of the first train?

solution   First we draw the diagram and write the distance equation.

$$D_1 + D_2 = 332 \qquad \text{so} \qquad R_1T_1 + R_2T_2 = 332$$

Then we reread the problem and write the other three equations.

$$T_1 = 2 \qquad T_2 = 2 \qquad R_2 = 65$$

Now we substitute and solve:

$R_1(2) + 65(2) = 332$	substituted
$2R_1 + 130 = 332$	multiplied
$2R_1 = 202$	added −130 to both sides
$R_1 = \mathbf{101 \ \frac{km}{hr}}$	divided by 2

example 94.3 The ships were 400 miles apart at midnight and were headed directly toward each other. If they collided at 8 a.m., find the speed of both ships if one was 20 miles per hour faster than the other.

solution First we draw the diagram and write the distance equation. We use the subscript F to designate quantities associated with the faster ship and the subscript S to designate quantities associated with the slower ship.

$$D_F + D_S = 400 \qquad \text{so} \qquad R_F T_F + R_S T_S = 400$$

The other three equations are

$$T_F = 8 \qquad T_S = 8 \qquad R_F = R_S + 20$$

Now we substitute and solve.

$$
\begin{aligned}
(R_S + 20)(8) + R_S(8) &= 400 & \text{substituted} \\
8R_S + 160 + 8R_S &= 400 & \text{multiplied} \\
16R_S + 160 &= 400 & \text{simplified} \\
16R_S &= 240 & \text{added } -160 \text{ to both sides} \\
R_S &= \textbf{15 mph} & \text{divided by 16}
\end{aligned}
$$

Thus, $$R_F = \textbf{35 mph}$$

practice **a.** An eastbound bus left Ukiah at noon. Two hours later a westbound bus left the same station. If the buses traveled at the same rate and were 500 kilometers apart at 6 p.m., find the rate of each bus.

b. A train starts from Peoria at 2 p.m. and heads for Reedley, 750 kilometers away. At the same time, a train leaves Reedley and heads for Peoria at 85 kilometers per hour. If the trains meet at 5 p.m., what is the rate of the first train?

problem set 94

1. *(94)* Two ships were 700 miles apart at midnight and were headed directly toward each other. If they collided at 10 a.m., find the speeds of both ships if one was traveling 30 miles per hour faster than the other. Begin by drawing a diagram of distances traveled and writing the distance equation.

2. *(92)* At noon Joyce drove to the lake at 30 miles per hour, but she made the long walk back home at 4 miles per hour. How long did she walk if she was gone for 17 hours? How far did she walk? Begin by drawing a diagram of distances traveled and writing the distance equation.

3. *(89)* Pitts bought pots for $5 each, and Joe bought buckets for $7 each. If they spent $1140 for 192 utensils, how many of each type did they buy?

4. *(77)* Nine sixteenths of the girls believed that saltation was salubrious. If the other 700 girls were undecided, how many girls had made up their minds concerning this topic?

5. *(65)* Arcelia's final exam was given 3 times the weight of a weekly test. Her scores on the five weekly tests were 70, 75, 80, 85, and 90. Her score on the final was 80. What was Arcelia's overall weighted average on all the tests?

6. When the stranger came into the forest, 37 percent of the little people ran to hide. If 2520
$^{(58)}$ refused to hide, how many little people lived in the forest?

7. Margaret rolls two fair dice. What is the probability that the sum of the numbers rolled is
$^{(70)}$

(a) not less than 8?   (b) not more than 8?

8. If the reciprocal of a number is $-\frac{1}{9}$, what is the additive inverse of the same number?
$^{(9,11)}$

Simplify:

9. $\dfrac{4x + 12}{x^2 + 11x + 30} \cdot \dfrac{4x^2 + 20x}{x^3 - 4x^2 - 21x}$ **10.** $\dfrac{x^2 + 11x + 24}{x^2 + 3x} \div \dfrac{x^2 + 13x + 40}{4x^2 + 20x}$
$^{(93)}$ $^{(93)}$

11. Find the domain and range of the   **12.** Find the equations of lines (a) and (b).
$^{(82)}$ graphed function. $^{(75)}$

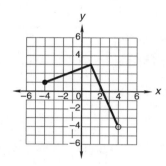 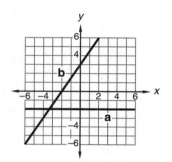

13. Graph on a number line: $-4 \le x < 1$; $D = \{\text{Integers}\}$
$^{(64)}$

Solve by factoring:

14. $x^2 = 7x + 30$ **15.** $100 = 9p^2$
$^{(88)}$ $^{(88)}$

16. What is the domain of the function $f(x) = \sqrt{17 - 2x}$?
$^{(82)}$

17. If $f(x) = 10x^2 - 7x + 3$, find $f(x - 2)$.
$^{(82)}$

18. Divide: $(2x^3 + 5x^2 - 1) \div (2x + 1)$
$^{(86)}$

Simplify:

19. $4\sqrt{3} \cdot 5\sqrt{6} + \sqrt{5} \cdot 2$ **20.** $4\sqrt{12}(3\sqrt{2} - 3\sqrt{12})$
$^{(84)}$ $^{(84)}$

21. Solve by graphing and check: **22.** Use substitution to solve:
$^{(81)}$ $^{(54)}$

$$\begin{cases} y = x \\ x = -3 \end{cases} \qquad\qquad \begin{cases} y = 2x + 4 \\ 2y - x = -1 \end{cases}$$

23. Simplify: $\dfrac{(0.00035 \times 10^{15})(200,000)}{(1000 \times 10^{-45})(0.00007)}$
$^{(80)}$

24. (a) $0.037 \in \{\text{What subsets of the real numbers}\}$?
$^{(61)}$

     (b) $\sqrt[3]{-8} + \sqrt[4]{16} \in \{\text{What subsets of the real numbers}\}$?

Solve:

25. $\dfrac{x - 7}{4} - \dfrac{x}{2} = \dfrac{1}{8}$ **26.** $-p^0(p - 4) - (-p^0)p + 3^0(p - 2) = -p - 6^0$
$^{(78)}$ $^{(31)}$

27. Simplify: $-3\left[(-2^0 - 5^0) - 2 - (4 - 6)(-2)\right] - |-(-6 + 2)|$
$^{(29)}$

28. Expand by using the distributive property. Write the answer with all exponents positive.
(40)

$$4x^2y^{-1}\left(\frac{p^0y}{x^2} - 3x^{-2}y^4 - \frac{2}{x^{-2}y^{-1}}\right)$$

29. Find the volume of the sphere shown
(91)   whose radius is 3 in.

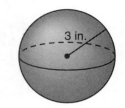

30. A right circular cylinder has a radius of
(15,60) 18 feet and a height of 9 feet, as shown.
Find the surface area of the right circular cylinder.

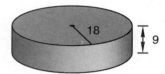

LESSON 95 *Graphs of Non-Linear Functions • Recognizing Shapes of Various Non-Linear Functions*

95.A

graphs of non-linear functions

A function of the form

$$f(x) = mx + b \qquad \text{where } m \neq 0$$

is called a *linear function*. Some examples of linear functions are

$$f(x) = x + 1 \qquad g(x) = 2x - 1 \qquad h(x) = \frac{1}{2}x - \frac{1}{4}$$

The graph of a linear function is a line. This fact is the reason that linear functions are so named. (Mathematics dictionaries define *linear* as an adjective meaning "in a straight line.")

In this lesson, we will examine the shapes of functions that are not linear functions. We call these functions **non-linear functions.** These arise frequently in business, science, computer science, and engineering, as well as in higher-level mathematics courses.

We show throughout this lesson the graphs of some types of non-linear functions. Students may confirm that these graphs are accurate by tediously plotting points on the graphs. We will show examples of quadratic functions, cubic functions, square root functions, and absolute value functions. In this lesson, our goal is to recognize the shapes of these functions.

quadratic functions

A quadratic function is a function of the form

$$f(x) = ax^2 + bx + c \qquad \text{where } a \neq 0$$

The graphs of quadratic functions are called *parabolas*. The simplest, most basic quadratic function is $f(x) = x^2$. We show the graph of $f(x) = x^2$. We then show the graphs of $f(x) = (x - 3)^2$, $f(x) = x^2 - 3$, and $f(x) = -x^2$. Note that the graphs of these functions are simply the graph of $f(x) = x^2$ translated horizontally or vertically, or "flipped."

x	-2	-1	0	1	2
x^2	4	1	0	1	4

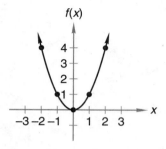

$f(x) = x^2$

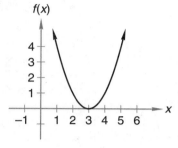

$f(x) = (x - 3)^2$

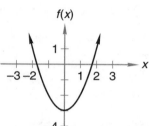

$f(x) = x^2 - 3$

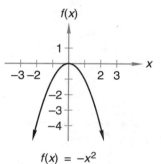

$f(x) = -x^2$

cubic functions

A cubic function is a function of the form

$$f(x) = ax^3 + bx^2 + cx + d \qquad \text{where } a \neq 0$$

Cubic functions are much more difficult to graph, so students may want to use a graphing calculator or computer to graph cubic functions. We first graph the most basic cubic function $f(x) = x^3$, and then graph other more complicated cubic functions, such as $f(x) = (x - 2)^3$, $f(x) = x^3 - 2$, and $f(x) = -x^3$. Note that the graphs of these functions are simply the graph of $f(x) = x^3$ translated horizontally or vertically, or flipped.

x	-2	-1	0	1	2
x^3	-8	-1	0	1	8

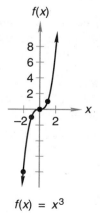

$f(x) = x^3$

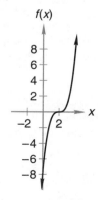

$f(x) = (x - 2)^3$

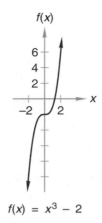

$$f(x) = x^3 - 2$$

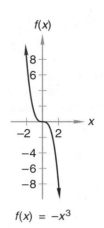

$$f(x) = -x^3$$

square root functions   The function

$$f(x) = \sqrt{x}$$

is called the *square root function*. Below we graph the function $f(x) = \sqrt{x}$ as precisely as we can by laboriously plotting points. We also show examples of variants of the square root function and their graphs. The graphs of these functions are simply the graph of $f(x) = \sqrt{x}$ translated (horizontally or vertically) or flipped. To the best of the author's knowledge, there is no name that is commonly used to describe this class of functions. For all these functions examined, the function is defined only when the radicand is greater than or equal to zero. (*Note*: In the table below, values of $\sqrt{x}$ are rounded to one decimal place.)

x	0	1	2	3	4	5	6	7	8	9
$\sqrt{x}$	0	1.0	1.4	1.7	2.0	2.2	2.4	2.6	2.8	3.0

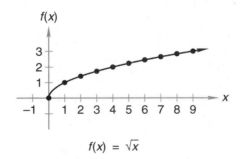

$$f(x) = \sqrt{x}$$

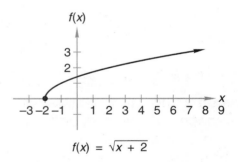

$$f(x) = \sqrt{x + 2}$$

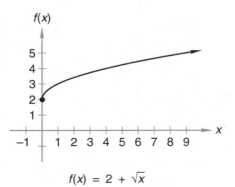

$$f(x) = 2 + \sqrt{x}$$

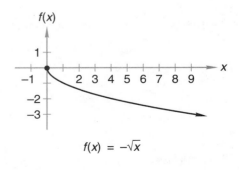

$$f(x) = -\sqrt{x}$$

absolute value functions

The function

$$f(x) = |x|$$

is called the *absolute value function*. Below we graph the absolute value function as well as variants of the absolute value function. The graphs of the variants of the absolute value function are the graph of $f(x) = |x|$ translated (horizontally or vertically) or flipped.

x	-3	-2	-1	0	1	2	3
$|x|$	3	2	1	0	1	2	3

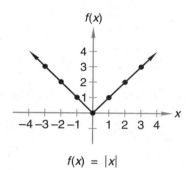

$f(x) = |x|$

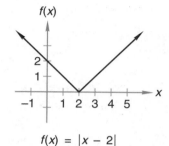

$f(x) = |x - 2|$

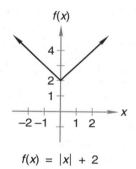

$f(x) = |x| + 2$

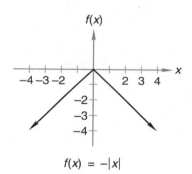

$f(x) = -|x|$

95.B

recognizing shapes of various non-linear functions

In the examples below, we shall practice the skill of recognizing and sketching the basic shapes of various types of elementary functions.

example 95.1   The graph of a quadratic function could resemble which of the following graphs?

(a) 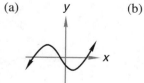   (b) 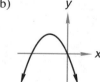   (c) 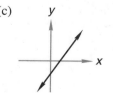   (d)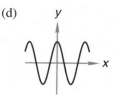

solution   Only the graph depicted in (**b**) looks like the one of the graphs shown as an example of a graph of a quadratic function.

example 95.2   Given the equations of the following functions:

$$f(x) = x^3 + 1 \qquad g(x) = |x - 2| \qquad h(x) = -\sqrt{x} \qquad L(x) = x^2 + x + 1$$

Identify the function whose graph most resembles the specified shape shown:

(a)   (b)   (c)    (d)

solution   From the graphs of the various types of functions examined, we identify the function whose graph has the shape depicted.

(a) $L(x) = x^2 + x + 1$ (b) $f(x) = x^3 + 1$

(c) $g(x) = |x - 2|$ (d) $h(x) = -\sqrt{x}$

example 95.3   Shown below are the shapes of the graphs of various functions:

(a)   (b)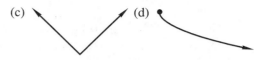

Match each of the following functions to one of the graphs shown above:

$$f(x) = -x^3 + 3 \qquad g(x) = -x^2 + 5 \qquad h(x) = 1 + \sqrt{x} \qquad k(x) = |x - 3|$$

solution   From our study of the various types of functions and their corresponding graphs, we are able to match each given equation to a graph.

(a) $g(x) = -x^2 + 5$ (b) $f(x) = -x^3 + 3$

(c) $k(x) = |x - 3|$ (d) $h(x) = 1 + \sqrt{x}$

practice   **a.**   Given are equations of four functions:

$$f(x) = x^2 + 2 \qquad g(x) = -|x| - 1 \qquad h(x) = x^3 + 1 \qquad k(x) = \sqrt{x}$$

Shown below are four shapes. For each shape, identify which function has a graph that most resembles the shape.

(1)    (2)

(3)    (4)

b.   Shown below are four shapes:

(1)    (2)

(3)    (4)

Match to each shape the function defined below whose graph most closely resembles the specified shape.

$$f(x) = |x| \qquad g(x) = -x^3 + 1 \qquad h(x) = \sqrt{x} \qquad k(x) = -(x + 1)^2$$

problem set
95

1. Gaskin and Sloan raced to the cotton patch. Gaskin's speed was 12 kilometers per hour,
$_{(92)}$ while Sloan's was only 8 kilometers per hour. What was the time of each if Gaskin's time
was 5 hours less than Sloan's time? Begin by drawing a diagram of distances traveled and
writing the distance equation.

2. The cars were 300 miles apart at noon and were headed directly toward each other. If they
$_{(94)}$ collided at 3 p.m., find the speeds of both cars if one was traveling 10 miles per hour
faster than the other. Begin by drawing a diagram of distances traveled and writing the
distance equation.

3. The sum of two numbers is 30 and the difference of the numbers is 12. What are the two
$_{(90)}$ numbers?

4. Find four consecutive odd integers such that the product of -3 and the sum of the first
$_{(77)}$ and fourth is 30 less than 10 times the opposite of the third.

5. Eighty percent of the children preferred the wild goose ride to the ferris wheel. If
$_{(58)}$ 300 children preferred the ferris wheel, how many preferred the wild goose ride?

6. Only 13 percent of the tribe did not want Sleeping Bear to be chief. If there were
$_{(58)}$ 3000 members of the tribe, how many wanted Sleeping Bear to be chief?

7. A bag contains 10 purple marbles and 9 pink marbles. Two marbles are drawn at random.
$_{(73)}$ What is the probability that the first marble is purple and the second marble is pink if the
marbles are drawn

    (a) with replacement?   (b) without replacement?

8. Smith, while editing his latest book, counted the number of editing errors in the first ten
$_{(45,85)}$ chapters as follows:

$$24, 32, 17, 25, 27, 25, 18, 31, 29, 26$$

    (a) Make a stem-and-leaf plot of the data provided.

    (b) Using the graph in (a), make a frequency distribution table.

    (c) Determine the range, median, mode, and mean of the data.

9. Given are equations of four functions:
$_{(95)}$

$$f(x) = -x^2 + 5 \qquad g(x) = |x| + 5 \qquad h(x) = \sqrt{x} \qquad k(x) = x^3$$

Shown below are four shapes. For each shape, identify which function has a graph that
most resembles the shape.

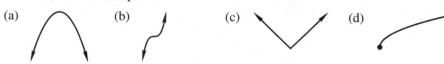

    (a)   (b)   (c)   (d)

10. Shown below are four shapes:
$_{(95)}$

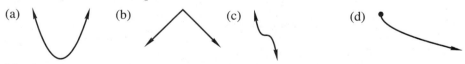

    (a)   (b)   (c)   (d)

Match to each shape the function defined below whose graph most closely resembles the
specified shape.

$$f(x) = -|x| \qquad g(x) = -\sqrt{x} \qquad h(x) = -x^3 \qquad k(x) = (x - 5)^2$$

Simplify:

11. $\dfrac{x^2 + 5x + 6}{-x^2 - 3x} \div \dfrac{x^2 + 7x + 10}{x^3 + 8x^2 + 15x}$ **12.** $\dfrac{4x^2 + 8x}{x^2 + 8x + 12} \div \dfrac{4x^2 - 16}{x^2 + 3x - 18}$
$_{(93)}$ $_{(93)}$

13. Graph: $-x + 4 \le 2$; $D = \{\text{Integers}\}$
$_{(91)}$

Solve by factoring:

14. $24 = -x^2 - 10x$
(88)

15. $-4 + 9x^2 = 0$
(88)

16. If $f(x) = 12x - x^2 + 6$, find $f(x - 5)$.
(82)

17. Divide: $(x^4 - x - 4) \div (x - 1)$
(86)

18. Find the domain and range of the graphed function.
(82)

19. Find the equations of lines (a) and (b).
(75)

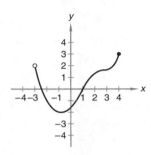

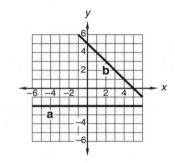

Simplify:

20. $3\sqrt{2} \cdot 4\sqrt{3} \cdot 4\sqrt{6} - 3\sqrt{2}$
(84)

21. $3\sqrt{2}(5\sqrt{12} - 6\sqrt{36})$
(84)

22. Solve by graphing and check:
(81)

$$\begin{cases} y = x + 2 \\ y = -x \end{cases}$$

23. Use elimination to solve:
(67)

$$\begin{cases} 5x - 2y = 18 \\ 3x + y = 24 \end{cases}$$

24. Simplify: $\dfrac{(0.00042 \times 10^{-15})(300,000)}{(180,000 \times 10^{-14})(7000 \times 10^{-23})}$
(80)

25. (a) $\dfrac{5\sqrt{2}}{7} \in$ {What subsets of the real numbers}?
(61)

    (b) $\sqrt{289} \in$ {What subsets of the real numbers}?

Simplify:

26. $\dfrac{xy - y^{-1}}{xy^{-1} - 4}$
(68)

27. (a) $\dfrac{1}{-3^{-2}}$ (b) $\dfrac{1}{(-3)^{-2}}$ (c) $-(-2)^{-2}$
(36)

28. Solve: $\dfrac{3x}{2} - \dfrac{x - 5}{6} = 3$
(78)

29. Find the surface area of the sphere shown whose radius is 3 cm.
(91)

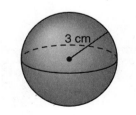

30. Find the volume of this right triangular prism. Dimensions are in meters.
(20,60)

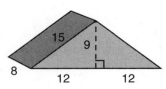

LESSON 96 *Difference of Two Squares Theorem*

In Lesson 62 we introduced the topic of square roots and noted that every positive real number has both a positive square root and a negative square root. Because 2 times 2 equals 4 and –2 times –2 also equals 4,

$$(2)(2) = 4 \qquad \text{and} \qquad (-2)(-2) = 4$$

we say that the two square roots of 4 are +2 and –2. **But when we use the radical, $\sqrt{}$, to indicate the square root of a positive number, we are designating the principal or positive square root.** For example,

$$\sqrt{4} = 2$$

If we wish to indicate the negative square root, we must use a minus sign in front of the radical. For example, to designate the negative square root of 4, we must write

$$-\sqrt{4}$$

which equals –2.

If we are asked to find the numbers that satisfy the equation

$$x^2 = 4$$

we know that the numbers are +2 and –2 because

$$(+2)^2 = 4 \qquad \text{and also} \qquad (-2)^2 = 4$$

The general form of the equation $x^2 = 4$ is

$$p^2 = q^2$$

If we add $-q^2$ to both sides, we can factor

$$p^2 = q^2 \quad \longrightarrow \quad p^2 - q^2 = 0 \quad \longrightarrow \quad (p + q)(p - q) = 0$$

Applying the zero factor theorem to solve for p, we find that if $p + q = 0$, then $p = -q$, and if $p - q = 0$, then $p = q$. We show this calculation below.

$$\begin{array}{ll}
\text{IF} \quad p + q = 0 & \qquad \text{IF} \quad p - q = 0 \\
\phantom{\text{IF} \quad p} \underline{- q \quad -q} & \qquad \phantom{\text{IF} \quad p} \underline{+ q \quad +q} \\
\phantom{\text{IF} \quad} p = -q & \qquad \phantom{\text{IF} \quad} p = q
\end{array}$$

The theorem that describes the solution to an equation of the form $p^2 = q^2$ is called the **difference of two squares theorem.**

DIFFERENCE OF TWO SQUARES THEOREM

If p and q are real numbers and if $p^2 = q^2$, then

$$p = q \qquad \text{or} \qquad p = -q$$

A quadratic equation in x has an x^2 term as the highest power of the variable. A quadratic equation in p has a p^2 term as the highest power of the variable. **It is very important to realize that in a beginning algebra book the $\pm$ sign arises only in the solution of a quadratic equation.** For example,

$$\text{If} \qquad m^2 = 3 \qquad \text{then} \qquad m = \pm\sqrt{3}$$

There are two solutions to this equation because $(\sqrt{3})^2$ equals 3 and $(-\sqrt{3})^2$ equals 3. A common mistake of beginners is to use the $\pm$ sign whenever the square root symbol is encountered.

$$\sqrt{9} = \pm 3 \qquad \textbf{NO! NO! NO!}$$

The square root sign is used to designate *only* the positive square root of a number.

$$\sqrt{9} = 3 \qquad \text{correct}$$

In this case there is no equation to be solved. The equals sign is written by us to show that $\sqrt{9}$ has the value of +3. If we wish to designate the negative square root of 9, we write

$$-\sqrt{9} = -3$$

example 96.1   Solve: $p^2 = 16$

solution   We know that the general equation $p^2 = q^2$ has two solutions, which are $p = q$ and $p = -q$. In the same way the given equation has two solutions, which are

$$p = +4 \qquad \text{and} \qquad p = -4$$

We usually combine these notations and write

$$p = \pm \mathbf{4}$$

example 96.2   Solve: $p^2 = 41$

solution   To use the form $p^2 = q^2$, it is helpful to write the given equation as

$$p^2 = (\sqrt{41})^2$$

If we do this, we can write the answer as

$$p = \pm\sqrt{\mathbf{41}}$$

example 96.3   Solve: $k^2 = 13$

solution   We omit the intermediate step and write the solution by inspection.

$$k = \pm\sqrt{\mathbf{13}}$$

practice   Use the difference of two squares theorem to write the answers to the following equations:

a. $p^2 = 169$ **b.** $q^2 = 23$ **c.** $w^2 = 14$

problem set 96

1. At 3 p.m., Brunhilde headed north at 30 kilometers per hour. Two hours later Ludwig
(94)   headed south at 40 kilometers per hour. At what time will they be 340 kilometers apart? Begin by drawing a diagram of distances traveled and writing the distance equation.

2. Alphasia headed for the rodeo at 9 a.m. at 30 miles per hour. At 11 a.m. Bubba headed
(92)   after her at 60 miles per hour. What time was it when Bubba caught Alphasia? Begin by drawing a diagram of distances traveled and writing the distance equation.

3. Billye ran to town at 8 kilometers per hour and then walked back home at 3 kilometers
(92)   per hour. How far was it to town if the round trip took 11 hours? Begin by drawing a diagram of distances traveled and writing the distance equation.

4. Marfugge had $72.50 in quarters and half-dollars. If he had 190 coins in all, how many
(83)   of each type did he have?

5. Fifteen percent of the seniors voted for Gina. If 289 seniors voted for the other
(58)   candidates, how many seniors voted in the election?

6. The 3000 hawks and eagles filled the sky. The number of hawks was 1800 greater than
(90) 3 times the number of eagles. How many of each kind were there?

7. Lorijayne rolls two fair dice. Find the probability that the sum of the numbers rolled is
(70)

　(a) 4　　　　　　　　　　　　　　　　(b)　a number greater than 4

8. Use the difference of two squares theorem to write the answers to the following
(96) equations:

　(a) $p^2 = 49$　　　　　　(b) $p^2 = 39$　　　　　　(c) $k^2 = 11$

9. Given are the equations of five functions:
(95)

　　$a(x) = 3x + 2$　　　$b(x) = x^2 + 5$　　　$c(x) = \sqrt{x}$　　　$d(x) = |x| + 4$　　　$e(x) = -x^3$

　Shown below are five shapes. For each shape identify which function has a graph that
　most resembles the shape.

10. Simplify: $\dfrac{x^3 + 2x^2 - 15x}{x^2 + 5x} \div \dfrac{x^3 - 6x^2 + 9x}{x^2 - 3x}$
(93)

11. Graph on a number line: $-4 - x \not> -2$; $D = \{\text{Negative integers}\}$
(91)

Solve by factoring:

12. $-56 = 15x + x^2$　　　　　　　　　　　　**13.** $-81 + 4x^2 = 0$
(88)　　　　　　　　　　　　　　　　　　　　　　(88)

14. What is the domain of the function $f(x) = \sqrt{2x - 3}$?
(82)

15. Find the equations of lines (a) and (b).
(75)

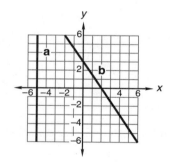

16. Divide: $\left(x^3 - x^2 - 2\right) \div (x + 1)$
(86)

Simplify:

17. $4\sqrt{2} \cdot 3\sqrt{3} \cdot 5\sqrt{6}$　　　　　　　　　　**18.** $3\sqrt{2}\left(2\sqrt{2} - 3\sqrt{8}\right)$
(84)　　　　　　　　　　　　　　　　　　　　　　(84)

19. Solve by graphing and check:　　　　　　**20.** Use elimination to solve:
(81)　　　　　　　　　　　　　　　　　　　　　　(67)

$$\begin{cases} y = 2x \\ x = -1 \end{cases}$$　　　　　　　　　　　　$$\begin{cases} 3x + 5y = -13 \\ 2x - 3y = 23 \end{cases}$$

21. Simplify: $\dfrac{(42,000,000)\left(0.0001 \times 10^{-5}\right)}{\left(7000 \times 10^{14}\right)\left(200,000 \times 10^{-8}\right)}$
(80)

22. Indicate whether each of the following numbers is rational or irrational:
(61,63)

　(a) $\pi + 2$　　　　(b) $\sqrt{2} + 3$　　　　(c) $\sqrt{\dfrac{36}{4}}$　　　　(d) $7.4\overline{333}$

Solve:

23. $\dfrac{k-4}{2} - \dfrac{k+6}{3} = 5$ **24.** $3\dfrac{1}{3}x - \dfrac{1}{6} = \dfrac{5}{12}$
(78) (25)

25. $m - m^0(m-4) - (-2)m + (-2)(m - 4^0) = m - 6$
(31)

Simplify:

26. (a) $\dfrac{ax + a^2x^2}{ax}$ (b) $-(-3)^{-2}$
(35,36)

27. $-3^0\left[(-3^2 + 4)(-2^2 - 2) - (-2) + 4\right] - \sqrt[3]{-8}$
(62)

28. Evaluate: $-p^0 - p^2(p - a^0) - ap + |-ap|$ if $a = -3$ and $p = -4$
(29)

29. Find the area of the shaded portion of this parallelogram. Dimensions are in inches.
(8)

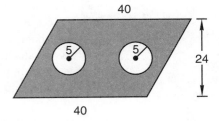

30. A base of the right solid 24 feet high is shown. Find the surface area of the right solid. Dimensions are in feet.
(15)

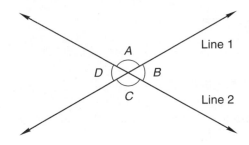

LESSON 97 *Angles and Triangles • Pythagorean Theorem • Pythagorean Triples*

97.A

angles and triangles

It is interesting to note that mathematicians often disagree on definitions and on terminology. Most authors use similar definitions, but not all do. The definition of an angle is a good example. Most agree that two intersecting lines form four angles. Here are shown two intersecting lines and the four angles formed.

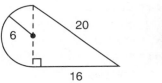

If we look only at angle *B*, we see that it is formed by part of lines 1 and 2. We call these parts **half lines** or **rays.**

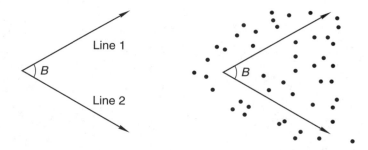

European authors generally define an angle to be the opening between the rays. Thus, to them the angle is the set of points bounded by the rays. American authors tend to define the angle to be the rays themselves. To them the angle is the set of points that make up the rays. Others say that the rays are the sides of the angle but do not say what the angle is. Some do not speak of the opening at all, but define an angle to be a rotation of a ray about its endpoint. A precise definition is not required in this book, so we will just say

> **An angle is formed by two half lines or rays that are in the same plane and that have a common endpoint.**

To begin a quick review of angle measures, we remember that if two straight lines intersect and are perpendicular to one another, we define the measure of each of the four angles created to be 90 degrees. We also remember that instead of writing the word *degrees*, it is customary to place a small elevated circle after the number that designates the number of degrees. Thus 90 degrees can be written as 90°, and 47 degrees and 135 degrees can be written as 47° and 135°, respectively. We see here two intersecting perpendicular lines with the resulting 90° angles.

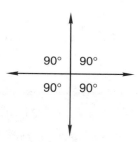

With this definition of a 90° angle and two axioms, it can be proved, by using geometry, that **the sum of the interior angles of any triangle is 180°.** We show three triangles and note that the sum of the three interior angles in each triangle is 180°.

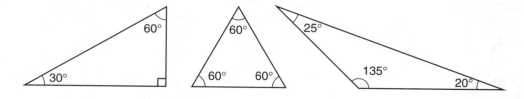

The triangle on the left has one angle that has a measure of 90°. Any triangle that contains a right angle is called a **right triangle,** and the side of the triangle that is opposite the right angle is always the longest side. We call this side of a right triangle the **hypotenuse.** The other two sides are called **legs,** or simply, **sides.** Right triangles have a special property (described in the next section) that makes them very useful in mathematics, engineering, and physics.

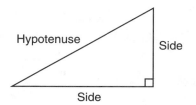

97.B
Pythagorean theorem

It can be shown that **the square drawn on the hypotenuse of a right triangle has the same area as the sum of the areas of the squares drawn on the other two sides.** While this theorem was known to the Egyptians as early as the Middle Kingdom (circa 2000 B.C.), the geometric proof of the theorem is normally attributed to a Greek philosopher and mathematician named **Pythagoras.** Pythagoras was born on the Aegean island of Samos and was later associated with a school or brotherhood in the town Crotona on the Italian peninsula in the sixth century B.C. We call the theorem for which he supposedly developed the proof the **Pythagorean theorem.**

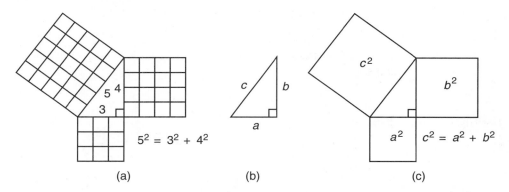

(a)   (b)   (c)

In (a) we show a right triangle whose sides have lengths of 3 and 4 units, respectively, and whose hypotenuse has a length of 5 units. A square has been drawn on each of the three sides, and since the area of a square whose sides have a length of L is L^2, we see that the areas of the two squares on the sides are 4^2 and 3^2, respectively, and that the sum of these two areas equals 25 square units. This is the same as the area of the square drawn on the hypotenuse, which equals 5^2, or 25, square units. Figure (b) shows another triangle whose sides have lengths of a and b and whose hypotenuse has a length of c. The area of a square drawn on the hypotenuse would be c^2, and the areas of the squares drawn on sides a and b would be a^2 and b^2, respectively, as shown in (c). We normally label the hypotenuse as c and the other two sides as a and b. Thus the general algebraic expression of the **Pythagorean theorem is**

$$a^2 + b^2 = c^2$$

where c is the length of the hypotenuse and a and b represent the lengths of the other two sides (legs).

This theorem can be used to find the length of a side of a right triangle if the lengths of the other two sides are known.

example 97.1   Given the triangle with the lengths of the sides as shown, use the Pythagorean theorem to find a.

solution   The square of the length of the hypotenuse equals the sum of the squares of the lengths of the other two sides. Thus,

$$5^2 = 4^2 + a^2 \;\longrightarrow\; 25 = 16 + a^2 \;\longrightarrow\; 9 = a^2$$

We use the difference of two squares theorem to finish the solution.

$$a^2 = 9 \qquad \text{which leads to} \qquad a = +3 \qquad \text{or} \qquad a = -3$$

While –3 is the solution to the equation $a^2 = 9$, it is not a solution to the problem at hand because physical lengths are designated by positive numbers. Thus we reject this solution and say that

$$a = \mathbf{3}$$

example 97.2   Find side p.

solution   We apply the Pythagorean theorem to this triangle to write

$$p^2 = 5^2 + 4^2$$

Now we simplify and use the difference of two squares theorem.

$$p^2 = 41 \;\longrightarrow\; p^2 = \left(\sqrt{41}\right)^2 \;\longrightarrow\; p = \sqrt{41} \qquad \text{or} \qquad p = -\sqrt{41}$$

Since sides of the triangles do not have negative lengths, we discard the negative result and say

$$p = \sqrt{\mathbf{41}}$$

example 97.3   Find k.

solution   We use the Pythagorean theorem to write

$$\left(\sqrt{61}\right)^2 = k^2 + 5^2$$

and now we simplify.

$$61 = k^2 + 25$$

Now we finish the solution by using the difference of two squares theorem.

$$36 = k^2 \;\longrightarrow\; (6)^2 = k^2$$

so $6 = k$ or $-6 = k$

Since –6 has no meaning as the length of a side of a triangle, we say

$$k = \mathbf{6}$$

example 97.4   Find side m.[†]

solution   By using the Pythagorean theorem we can write

$$m^2 = 12^2 + 8^2$$

[†]The Greeks must have drawn some of their right triangles as this one is drawn because the word *hypotenuse* comes from the Greek words *hypo*, meaning "under," and *teinein*, meaning "to stretch," so *hypotenuse* means "stretched under."

and now we simplify and solve.

$$m^2 = 208 \quad \rightarrow \quad m^2 = (\sqrt{208})^2 \quad \rightarrow \quad m = \sqrt{208} \quad \rightarrow \quad m = \mathbf{4\sqrt{13}}$$

Note that when solving for m, we do not consider negative values for m since it represents a length.

97.C
Pythagorean triples

It is useful to commit to memory the lengths of the sides of certain right triangles. We show some of these right triangles below.

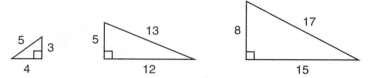

Note that all the sides of the right triangles shown are integers. The triplets of numbers describing the lengths of the three sides of right triangles whose sides are integer lengths are called **Pythagorean triples.** (*Note*: These triples are usually written in ascending order. For example, we would refer to the 3-4-5 right triangle when referring to the triangle on the left above.)

It is useful to know that any multiple of a Pythagorean triple is also a Pythagorean triple. For example, the following right triangles have sides whose lengths are a multiple of the 3-4-5 Pythagorean triple.

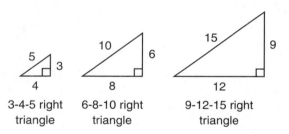

3-4-5 right triangle   6-8-10 right triangle   9-12-15 right triangle

example 97.5   Recall the appropriate Pythagorean triple to find the unknown length in each of the following right triangles.

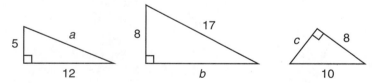

solution   Instead of applying the Pythagorean theorem, we will recall those Pythagorean triples we earlier committed to memory. We note that the triangle on the far right has sides whose lengths are a multiple of the 3-4-5 Pythagorean triple.

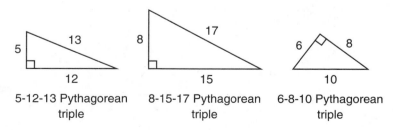

5-12-13 Pythagorean   8-15-17 Pythagorean   6-8-10 Pythagorean
triple   triple   triple

Therefore,

$$a = \mathbf{13} \qquad b = \mathbf{15} \qquad c = \mathbf{6}$$

practice   Use the Pythagorean theorem to find the unknown lengths.

a.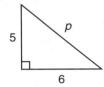

b.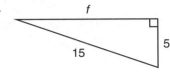

Recall the appropriate Pythagorean triple to find the unknown length in each of the following right triangles:

c.

d.

problem set   **1.** Wendy drove at 60 miles per hour. Thus, she made the trip in 1 hour less than it took
97   (92)   Deborah because Deborah only drove at 50 miles per hour. How long did each of them drive and how long was the trip? Begin by drawing a diagram of distances traveled and writing the distance equation.

2. It took Theseus 60 hours to get there with black sails and 100 hours to come back with
(92)   white sails. How far was it if his speed with black sails was 2 miles per hour greater than his speed with white sails? Begin by drawing a diagram of distances traveled and writing the distance equation.

3. Spann found a sack that contained $9000 in $5 bills and $10 bills. Margaret helped count
(89)   the money and found that there were 1250 bills in all. How many were $5 bills and how many were $10 bills?

4. If the sum of −4 and the opposite of a number is multiplied by −3, the result is 6 less than
(33)   the product of the number and 2. What is the number?

5. Find four consecutive integers such that 4 times the sum of the first and fourth is 1 less
(76)   than 9 times the third.

6. Louwon was elated! Her overall average rating was 120. If her first rating was 96 and her
(65)   second rating was weighted at double value, what was her second rating?

7. Calvin could see 32. This was only 20 percent of the number that Tooley could see. How
(58)   many could Tooley see?

8. Recall the appropriate Pythagorean triple to find the unknown length in each of the
(97)   following right triangles:

(a)   (b)   (c) 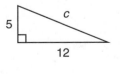   (d)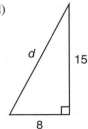

9. Use the Pythagorean theorem to find k.
(97)

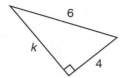

10. Find the equations of lines (a) and (b).
(75)

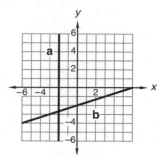

11. Use the difference of two squares theorem to write the answers to the following
(96) equations:

(a) $x^2 = 36$ (b) $x^2 = 24$ (c) $x^2 = 17$

12. Given below are five shapes:
(95)

(a)   (b)   (c)   (d)   (e)

Match to each shape the function defined below whose graph most closely resembles the specified shape.

$f(x) = -x^2 + 5$ $g(x) = x^3$ $h(x) = -|x|$ $L(x) = -2x + 3$ $p(x) = \sqrt{x}$

13. Simplify: $\dfrac{x^2 + x - 20}{x^2 + 6x - 16} \div \dfrac{x^2 - 2x - 8}{x^2 + 10x + 16}$
(93)

14. Solve by factoring: $100 = 25x - x^2$ **15.** If $f(x) = 9 - 4x^2$, find $f(x + h)$.
(88)   (82)

16. Which of the following diagrams, graphs, or sets of ordered pairs depict functions?
(84,87)

(a) $(-2, 1), (2, -1), (7, -1)$ (b) $(1, 3), (-1, -3), (-3, 1)$

(c) 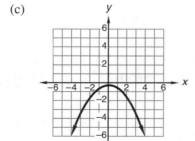   (d)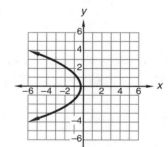

(e)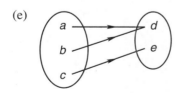

17. Divide: $(x^3 - x) \div (x + 2)$
(86)

Simplify:

18. $3\sqrt{2} \cdot 5\sqrt{3} + 5\sqrt{54}$ **19.** $5\sqrt{2}(3\sqrt{6} - 2\sqrt{36})$
(84)   (84)

20. Solve by graphing and check: $\begin{cases} y = x + 2 \\ y = -x + 4 \end{cases}$
(81)

21. Simplify: $\dfrac{(36,000 \times 10^{-5})(400,000)}{(0.0006 \times 10^{-4})(600 \times 10^5)}$
(80)

Solve:

22. $\dfrac{x}{4} - \dfrac{x-2}{7} = 1$ **23.** $-(-3)k^0 - 3^0k + (-2)(2-k) - (-3)(k+2) = 0$
(78)   (31)

24. Expand: (a) $(2m + 2p)^2$ (b) $(2m - 2p)^2$
(49)

25. Evaluate: $\dfrac{-b \pm \sqrt{b^2 - 4ac}}{2a}$ if $a = 2$, $b = 5$, and $c = 2$
(62)

26. Expand by using the distributive property. Write the answer with all exponents positive.
(40)

$$\frac{x^{-2}}{a^2}\left(x^2 a^2 y^0 - \frac{4x^4 y^2}{a^2} - \frac{x^{-2}}{a^2 x^2}\right)$$

Simplify:

27. $\dfrac{pk^{-1} - 4}{k - k^{-1}}$ **28.** (a) $\dfrac{-3 - 3x}{3}$ (b) $\dfrac{-2^2}{-2^{-2}}$
(68)   (35,36)

29. Find the perimeter of this figure. Dimensions are in centimeters.
(3)

30. A right circular cylinder has a radius of 12 meters and a height of 20 meters, as shown. Find the volume of the right circular cylinder.
(20,60)

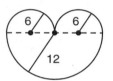

LESSON 98   *Distance Between Two Points • Slope Formula*

98.A

distance between two points

In Lesson 97, we discussed the use of the Pythagorean theorem in algebraic form to find the missing side of a triangle. To find length c of the triangle shown below, we write

$$c^2 = 4^2 + 7^2$$

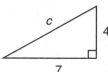

and solve to find that $c = \sqrt{65}$.

$$c^2 = 16 + 49$$
$$c^2 = 65$$
$$c = \sqrt{65}$$

Note that we just took the positive square root when solving for c since c represents a length. In the examples below, we will only solve for the positive square root when solving for a length since lengths must be positive. The distance between two points is defined to be the length of the straight line segment joining the two given points. Therefore, if we are given the coordinates of two points, we can find the distance between the points by graphing the points, drawing the triangle, and then solving the triangle to find the length of the hypotenuse.

example 98.1   Find the distance between the points whose coordinates are (4, 2) and (–3, –2).

solution   The first step is to graph the points, as done in the figure on the left.

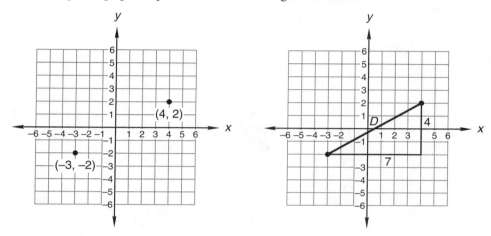

Then we connect the points with a straight line segment, as shown in the figure on the right. We then draw a right triangle whose legs are parallel to the x and y axes and indicate the lengths of the legs. Next we use the Pythagorean theorem to find the length of the hypotenuse.

$$D^2 = 7^2 + 4^2 \quad \rightarrow \quad D^2 = 65 \quad \rightarrow \quad D = \sqrt{65}$$

example 98.2   Find the distance between the points (3, –4) and (–5, 2).

solution   We graph the points and draw the required triangle, as shown in the figure.

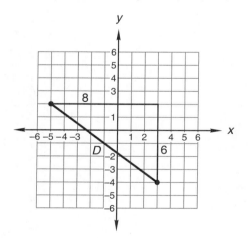

The distance between the points is found by using the Pythagorean theorem.

$$D^2 = 8^2 + 6^2$$

$$D^2 = 64 + 36$$

$$D^2 = 100$$

$$D = \mathbf{10}$$

98.B

slope formula   In Lesson 75 the slope of a straight line was defined to be the ratio of the change in the y coordinate to the change in the x coordinate as we move from one point on the line to another point on the line. To demonstrate, we will find the slope of the line through the points $(4, 3)$ and $(-2, -2)$ by first graphing the points and drawing the line, as shown in the figure on the left. The sign of the slope of this line is positive because the graphed line segment points toward the upper right. On the right we draw the triangle to determine the magnitude (absolute value) of the slope. From the triangle we see that the difference in the x coordinates of the two points is 6 and the difference in the y coordinates is 5. Thus the slope of this line is $+\frac{5}{6}$.

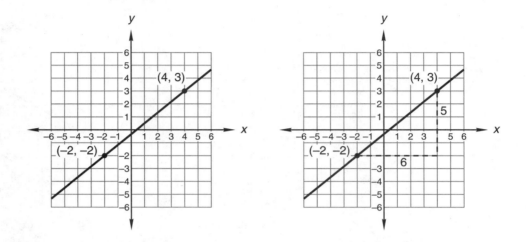

It is not necessary to graph the points to find the slope of the line. If we call the two points point 1 and point 2 and give them the coordinates (x_1, y_1) and (x_2, y_2), respectively, we can derive a relationship from which the slope for the line through these two points can be determined algebraically.

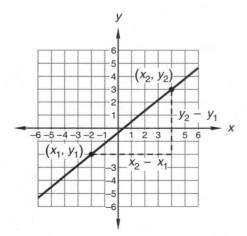

We label the legs of the right triangle formed $y_2 - y_1$ and $x_2 - x_1$. It is important to note that these quantities may be negative as well as positive. The absolute values of these quantities are the lengths of the legs of the right triangle formed. The quantities $y_2 - y_1$ and $x_2 - x_1$ represent the change in the y and x coordinates, respectively. The ratio of the change in y coordinates, $y_2 - y_1$, to the change in x coordinates, $x_2 - x_1$, is defined to be the slope of the line passing through the points (x_1, y_1) and (x_2, y_2).

We summarize what we have discussed in the box below.

SLOPE OF A LINE THROUGH TWO POINTS

Given points $P_1 = (x_1, y_1)$ and $P_2 = (x_2, y_2)$, the line that passes through points P_1 and P_2 has the slope

$$m = \frac{y_2 - y_1}{x_2 - x_1}$$

Note: Which point is considered P_1 and which point is considered P_2 does not matter.

---

example 98.3   Find the slope of the line that passes through the points $(-3, 4)$ and $(5, -2)$.

solution   Either point can be designated as point 1. We will use $(-3, 4)$ as point 1 and $(5, -2)$ as point 2.

$$m = \frac{y_2 - y_1}{x_2 - x_1} \quad \rightarrow \quad m = \frac{-2 - (4)}{5 - (-3)} \quad \rightarrow \quad m = \frac{-6}{8} \quad \rightarrow \quad m = -\frac{3}{4}$$

example 98.4   Work example 98.3 again, but this time use $(5, -2)$ as point 1 and $(-3, 4)$ as point 2.

solution

$$m = \frac{y_2 - y_1}{x_2 - x_1} \quad \rightarrow \quad m = \frac{4 - (-2)}{-3 - (5)} \quad \rightarrow \quad m = \frac{6}{-8} \quad \rightarrow \quad m = -\frac{3}{4}$$

The slope of the line was found to be $-\frac{3}{4}$ no matter which point was designated as point 1. **We see from these two examples that the slope can be determined by using this formula, and we also see that care must be exercised to prevent mistakes in handling the positive and negative signs of the numbers.** In the figure below, we use the familiar graphical method. We see from this figure that the sign of the slope is negative and the magnitude is $\frac{6}{8}$, so the slope is $-\frac{6}{8}$, or $-\frac{3}{4}$, the same slope found by using the slope formula.

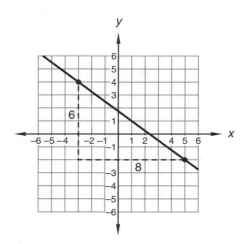

practice   **a.**   Find the distance between $(4, -2)$ and $(-4, -4)$.

Use the slope formula to find the slope of the line that passes through:

   b. $(-4, -7)$ and $(-8, -3)$ **c.** $(4, 7)$ and $(-14, -12)$

problem set 98

1. At noon, Sarah headed from Elk City to Idabel at 60 miles per hour. Two hours later, Joan
   (94) headed from Idabel to Elk City at 46 miles per hour. If it is 332 miles from Elk City to
   Idabel, what time did they meet? Begin by drawing a diagram of distances traveled and
   writing the distance equation.

2. Willy drove to Castle Rock at 40 miles per hour and returned walking 4 miles per hour.
   (92) Find his walking time if it was 9 hours longer than his driving time. How far was it to
   Castle Rock? Begin by drawing a diagram of distances traveled and writing the distance
   equation.

3. David added 7 to twice the opposite of a number and then multiplied this sum by 3. Wade
   (90) got the same result by adding 42 to 3 times the opposite of the number. What was the
   number?

4. Find four consecutive even integers such that if the sum of the first and the third is
   (77) multiplied by 3, the result is 10 greater than 5 times the fourth.

5. The blue light special caused the shoppers to increase by 250 percent. If 180 shoppers
   (58) were there before the special, how many were there after the special was announced?

6. The length of time that the girls ran was 20 percent greater than the length of time the
   (58) boys ran. If the girls ran for 48 hours, how long did the boys run?

7. Roger rolls two fair dice. Find the probability that the sum of the numbers rolled is
   (70)
   (a)   12   (b)   less than 12

8. Recall the appropriate Pythagorean triple to find the unknown length in each of the
   (97) following right triangles:

   (a)   (b)   (c) 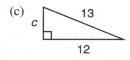   (d)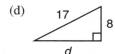

9. Use the Pythagorean theorem to find g.
   (97)

   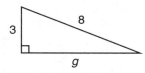

10. Given the points $(-4, 5)$ and $(2, 3)$:
    (98)
    (a)   Find the slope of the line that passes through these two points.
    (b)   Find the distance between these two points.

11. Given the points $(-4, -2)$ and $(4, -6)$:
    (98)
    (a)   Find the slope of the line that passes through these two points.
    (b)   Find the distance between these two points.

12. Use the difference of two squares theorem to find all the solutions to the following
    (96) equations:
    (a) $x^2 = 49$ (b) $x^2 = 12$ (c) $x^2 = 3$

13. Given the following five functions:
    (95)
    $$f(x) = 3x + 1 \quad g(x) = \sqrt{x} \quad h(x) = |x| \quad k(x) = x^3 + 1 \quad p(x) = x^2 - 5$$
    Identify the function whose graph most resembles the shape shown.

    (a)   (b)   (c)   (d)    (e)

Simplify:

14.
(93)
$\dfrac{x^2 + 2x}{4x + 12} \div \dfrac{x^2 - 2x - 8}{x^2 - x - 12}$

15.
(84)
$3\sqrt{2}\left(6\sqrt{6} - 4\sqrt{12}\right) + 2\sqrt{3}\sqrt{6}$

16. Solve by factoring: $-14 = -x^2 - 5x$
(88)

17. What is the domain and range of the graphed function?
(82)

18. Find the equations of lines (a) and (b).
(75)

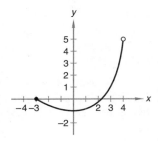

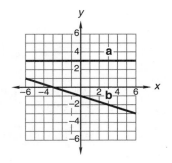

19. Divide: $\left(x^3 + 6x^2 + 6x + 5\right) \div (x + 5)$
(86)

20. Solve by graphing: $\begin{cases} y = -x \\ y = -4 \end{cases}$
(81)

21. Simplify: $\dfrac{(0.00042 \times 10^8)(15,000)}{(500 \times 10^7)(0.02 \times 10^8)}$
(80)

22. Graph on a number line: $-x + 2 \not< 3$; $D = \{\text{Integers}\}$
(91)

Solve:

23. $\dfrac{y}{3} - \dfrac{y - 2}{5} = 3$
(78)

24. $-2k^0 - 4k + 6\left(-k - 2^0\right) - (-5k) = -(2 - 5)k - 4k$
(31)

25. Find x if $x = \sqrt{b^2 - 4ac}$ and if $b = 11$, $a = 5$, and $\dfrac{c + 10}{2} = 6$.
(41)

Simplify:

26. $-2 - 2^0(-3 - 2) - (-4 + 6)\left(-5^0 + 2\right) - 2^2 - \sqrt[5]{-243}$
(62)

27. (a) $\dfrac{5x^2 - 5x}{5x}$ (b) $\dfrac{-3^0}{-3^{-2}}$
(35,36)

28. $\dfrac{3x - y^{-1}}{2xy^{-1} - 4}$
(68)

29. Find the volume of the sphere shown whose radius is 2 in.
(91)

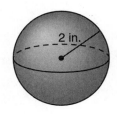

30. A base of the right prism 16 feet high is shown. Find the surface area of the right prism. Dimensions are in feet.
(15,60)

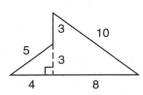

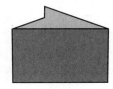

LESSON 99 Uniform Motion—Unequal Distances

Some uniform motion problems tell us that one person or object traveled a distance that is greater by a specified amount than the distance traveled by another person or object. The distance diagram for these problems usually takes one of the following forms:

In the picture on the left, both started from the same place and *P* went 50 farther than *A*. In the picture on the right, *A* started out 50 in front of *P*, and they both ended at the same place. In either case the distance that *A* traveled plus 50 equals the distance that *P* traveled. The distance equation for both diagrams is the same.

$$D_A + 50 = D_P \qquad \text{so} \qquad R_A T_A + 50 = R_P T_P$$

example 99.1   At 8 p.m. Achilles left camp and headed south at 20 kilometers per hour. At 10 p.m. Patroclos headed south from the same camp. If Patroclos was 50 kilometers ahead by 3 a.m., what was his speed?

solution   Since they had the same starting point, both arrows begin at the same point. Patroclos went farther, so his arrow is longer.

Patroclos went 50 kilometers farther, so we write the distance equation as

$$D_A + 50 = D_P$$

and we substitute $R_A T_A$ for D_A and $R_P T_P$ for D_P to get

$$R_A T_A + 50 = R_P T_P$$

We reread the problem to get the rate and time equations.

$$R_A = 20 \qquad T_A = 7 \qquad T_P = 5$$

Now we solve.

$$(20)(7) + 50 = R_P(5) \qquad \text{substituted}$$
$$140 + 50 = 5R_P \qquad \text{simplified}$$
$$190 = 5R_P \qquad \text{simplified}$$
$$R_P = 38 \ \frac{\text{km}}{\text{hr}} \qquad \text{divided}$$

example 99.2   Rachel has a 15-kilometer head start on Charlene. How long will it take Charlene to catch Rachel if Rachel travels at 70 kilometers per hour and Charlene travels at 100 kilometers per hour?

solution   Rachel began 15 kilometers ahead and they ended up in the same place, so the distance diagram is

We get the distance equation from the diagram as

$$15 + D_R = D_C$$

and we replace D_R with $R_R T_R$ and D_C with $R_C T_C$ to get

$$15 + R_R T_R = R_C T_C$$

Then we reread the problem to get the other three equations.

$$R_R = 70 \qquad R_C = 100 \qquad T_R = T_C$$

Now we solve.

$$15 + 70T_R = 100T_C \qquad \text{substituted}$$
$$15 + 70T_C = 100T_C \qquad \text{used fact } T_R = T_C$$
$$15 = 30T_C \qquad \text{simplified}$$
$$\frac{1}{2} = T_C \qquad \text{divided}$$

So Charlene will catch Rachel in $\frac{1}{2}$ **hour.**

example 99.3   Harry and Jennet jog around a circular track that is 210 meters long. Jennet's rate is 230 meters per minute, while Harry's rate is only 200 meters per minute. In how many minutes will Jennet be a full lap ahead?

solution   This problem is simpler if we straighten it out and get the following distance diagram.

We get the distance equation from this diagram as

$$D_H + 210 = D_J \qquad \text{so} \qquad R_H T_H + 210 = R_J T_J$$

The time equation is $T_H = T_J$, and the rate equations are $R_J = 230$, $R_H = 200$. Thus the four equations are

$$R_H T_H + 210 = R_J T_J \qquad T_H = T_J \qquad R_J = 230 \qquad R_H = 200$$

We use substitution to solve.

$$200T_H + 210 = 230T_H \qquad \text{substituted}$$
$$210 = 30T_H \qquad \text{simplified}$$
$$7 \text{ minutes} = T_H \qquad \text{divided}$$

Thus $T_J = 7$ minutes because $T_J = T_H$. Therefore, Jennet will be a full lap ahead of Harry in **7 minutes.**

practice   **a.** At 5 a.m. Napoleon headed south from Waterloo at 4 kilometers per hour. At 7 a.m. Wellington headed south from Waterloo. If Wellington passed Napoleon and was 20 kilometers ahead of Napoleon at 2 p.m., how fast was Wellington traveling?

b. Helen has a 4-kilometer head start on Paris. How long will it take Paris to catch Helen if Helen travels at 6 kilometers per hour and Paris travels at 8 kilometers per hour?

problem set   **1.** Ferris and Julia jog around a circular track that is 500 meters long. Julia's rate is **99**   (99)   250 meters per minute, while Ferris's rate is only 230 meters per minute. In how many minutes will Julia be a full lap ahead? Begin by drawing a diagram of distances traveled and writing the distance equation.

2. Eleanor started out at 60 miles per hour at 9 a.m., two hours before Alexi started out to (99)   catch her. If she was still 60 miles ahead at 3 p.m., how fast was Alexi driving? Begin by drawing a diagram of distances traveled and writing the distance equation.

3. The product of 5 and the sum of a number and –8 is 9 greater than the product of 2 and (33)   the opposite of the number. Find the number.

4. When the car overturned, the jar broke and spilled 450 nickels and quarters all over the (83)   freeway. If their value was $62.50, how many coins of each type were there?

5. When the nurse gave the shots, she noticed that 34 percent of the people winced and the (58)   rest were stolid. If 3300 people were stolid, how many shots did she give?

6. Bobby and Joan found four consecutive integers such that 5 times the sum of the second (76)   and third was 6 less than 7 times the first. What were their integers?

Use the Pythagorean theorem to find the unknown lengths in the following right triangles:

7.   **8.**   **9.**
(97)   (97)   (97)

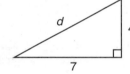   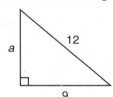   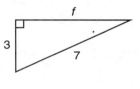

10. Given the points (4, 3) and (7, –2):
(98)
   (a) Find the slope of the line that passes through these two points.
   (b) Find the distance between these two points.

11. Given the points (4, –2) and (–2, 3):
(98)
   (a) Find the slope of the line that passes through these two points.
   (b) Find the distance between these two points.

12. Given the following five functions:
(95)
$$f(x) = x^3 \quad g(x) = x^2 \quad h(x) = x \quad k(x) = -x^2 \quad p(x) = -x^3$$

Identify the function whose graph most resembles the shape shown.

(a)   (b)   (c)   (d)   (e)

13. Use the difference of two squares theorem to find all the solutions to the following (96)   equations:

   (a) $x^2 = 64$ (b) $x^2 = 32$ (c) $x^2 = 11$

14. Simplify: $\dfrac{x^2 + 11x + 28}{-x^2 + 5x} \div \dfrac{x^2 + x - 12}{x^3 - 3x^2 - 10x}$
(93)

15. Solve by factoring: $81 = 4x^2$
(88)

16. Indicate whether the following numbers are rational numbers or irrational numbers:
(61,63)

    (a) $0.\overline{3}$ (b) $\sqrt{12 + 4}$ (c) $\sqrt{9 - 4}$ (d) $\dfrac{25}{7}$

17. What is the domain of $f(x) = \sqrt{3x - 4}$?
(82)

18. Find the equations of lines (a) and (b).
(75)

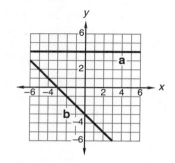

19. Divide: $(x^3 - 4) \div (x - 4)$
(86)

Simplify:

20. $3\sqrt{2} \cdot 4\sqrt{3} \cdot 5\sqrt{12} + 2\sqrt{8}$ **21.** $3\sqrt{2}(5\sqrt{2} - 4\sqrt{42})$
(84)   (84)

22. Solve by graphing and check: $\begin{cases} y = x - 4 \\ y = -x + 2 \end{cases}$
(81)

23. Graph on a number line: $-x - 3 < 2$; $D = \{\text{Reals}\}$
(91)

24. Simplify: $\dfrac{(22{,}000 \times 10^{-7})(500)}{(0.0011)(0.002 \times 10^{14})}$
(80)

25. Add: $\dfrac{x}{x + 4} + \dfrac{3}{x} - \dfrac{x + 2}{x^2}$ **26.** Solve: $\dfrac{p}{6} - \dfrac{p + 2}{4} = \dfrac{1}{3}$
(52)   (78)

27. Evaluate: $-x^0 y(y - x^0) - x^2 y^{-1}$ if $2x = -4$ and $y = \sqrt[3]{-64}$
(41,62)

28. Simplify: (a) $\dfrac{-2p^2 a^2 - p^2 a}{-p^2 a}$ (b) $\dfrac{-3^2}{-(-3)^{-2}}$
(35,36)

29. Find the surface area of the sphere
(91) shown whose radius is 4 cm.

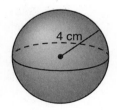

30. A base of the right prism 10 meters high is shown. Find the volume of the right prism.
(20,60) All angles are right angles. Dimensions are in meters.

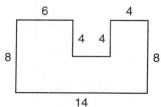 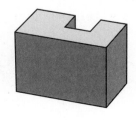

LESSON *100* *Place Value • Rounding Numbers*

100.A
place value

In this book we have rounded most answers to a few decimal places and have not extensively practiced the skill of rounding numbers. In this lesson we will review the process of rounding to any designated number of digits. Future problem sets will provide problems that allow us to practice rounding.

We use the 10 digits

$$0, \ 1, \ 2, \ 3, \ 4, \ 5, \ 6, \ 7, \ 8, \ 9$$

to write the decimal numerals that we use to represent numbers. The value of a digit in a numeral depends on the position of the digit with respect to the decimal point. For instance, in the numeral

$$40{,}632{,}903.195034$$

the first 9 has a value of 900 because it is in the hundreds' place, three places to the left of the decimal point. The second 9 has a value of only $\frac{9}{100}$ because it is written in the hundredths' place, which is two places to the right of the decimal point.

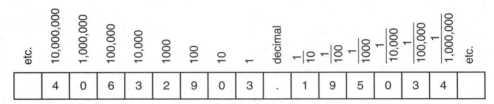

It is important to note that the first place to the right of the decimal point is the tenths' place, whereas the tens' place is not one place but two places to the left of the decimal point. The first place to the left of the decimal point is the units' (or ones') place.

100.B
rounding numbers

Often we use numbers that are approximations of other numbers. For instance, the circumference of the earth at the equator is 24,874 miles. This measurement is to the nearest mile and is a difficult number to remember. So we say that the circumference is 25,000 miles and say that we have rounded 24,874 to the nearest thousand. This is because 24,874 is closer to 25,000 than it is to 24,000. Thus, when we round, we change the digits at the end of a number to zeros.

Rounding requires three steps, and mistakes can be avoided if a circle and an arrow are used as aids. To demonstrate, we will round 24,874 to the nearest thousand.

1. Circle the digit in the place to which we are rounding and mark the digit to its right with an arrow.

$$2\,④\,8\,7\,4$$

2. Change the arrow-marked digit and all digits to its right to zero

$$2\,④\,0\,0\,0$$

3. Leave the circled digits unchanged or increase 1 unit as determined by the following rules:

   (a) If the arrow-marked digit was originally less than 5, do not change the circled digit.

(b) If the arrow-marked digit was originally greater than 5 or is a 5 followed somewhere by a nonzero digit, increase the circled digit by 1 unit. This rule applies to the problem we are working, so we finish by writing.

$$2\,\overset{\downarrow}{\textcircled{5}}\,0\;0\;0$$

(c) If the arrow-marked digit was originally a terminal 5 or a 5 followed only by zeros, the number is halfway between the two possible numbers for the rounded answer; the circled digit can be left unchanged or can be increased by 1 as you wish. The procedure to be used in this case is really not important, and we will try to avoid this case in the problem sets. Concentrate on remembering rules (a) and (b).

example 100.1   Round 47,258,312.065 to the nearest ten thousand.

solution   We circle the ten-thousands' digit and mark the digit to its right with an arrow.

$$47{,}2\textcircled{5}\overset{\downarrow}{8}{,}312.065$$

Next we change the arrow-marked digit and all digits to its right to zero.

$$47{,}2\textcircled{5}\overset{\downarrow}{0}{,}000.000$$

Since the arrow-marked digit was originally greater than 5, we increase the circled digit 1 unit, and our answer is

$$47{,}2\textcircled{6}\overset{\downarrow}{0}{,}000.000\quad\text{which is}\quad\mathbf{47{,}260{,}000}$$

example 100.2   Round 104.06245327 to the nearest thousandth.

solution   We circle the thousandths' digit and mark the digit to its right with an arrow.

$$104.06\textcircled{2}\overset{\downarrow}{4}5327$$

Then we change the arrow-marked digit and all digits to its right to zero.

$$104.06\textcircled{2}\overset{\downarrow}{0}0000$$

Since the arrow-marked digit was originally less than 5, we do not change the circled digit. Thus our answer is as follows because the terminal zeros have no value.

104.062

example 100.3   Round 0.00041378546 to the nearest one-hundred-millionth.

solution   We circle the one-hundred-millionths' place and mark the digit to its right with an arrow.

$$0.0004137\textcircled{8}\overset{\downarrow}{5}46$$

Now we change to zero the arrow-marked digit and all digits to the right of the arrow-marked digit.

$$0.0004137\textcircled{8}\overset{\downarrow}{0}00$$

The arrow-marked digit was originally 5, and it was followed by the nonzero digits 4 and 6. Thus we increase the circled digit from 8 to 9 and get

0.00041379

example 100.4 Round 2.0031664567 to five decimal places.

solution The fifth decimal place is the hundred-thousandths' place, which we circle. Then we mark the next digit with an arrow.

$$2.0031 \; ⑥ \; \overset{\downarrow}{6}4567$$

Since the arrow-marked digit is greater than 5, when we change it and the following digits to zero we increase the circled digit 1 unit from 6 to 7, and our answer is

2.00317

example 100.5 Round $314.0\overline{364}$ to (a) five decimal places, (b) nine decimal places, (c) the nearest one-hundredth, and (d) the nearest ten.

solution The line over the 364 tells us that these digits repeat, so the number is

$$314.0364364364364\ldots$$

We round this number as specified:

(a) Five decimal places   **314.03644**

(b) Nine decimal places   **314.036436436**

(c) Nearest hundredth   **314.04**

(d) Nearest ten   **310**

practice Round:

  a. 59,742,004.012 to the nearest ten thousand

  b. 513.129347 to the nearest ten-thousandth

  c. $63.0\overline{149}$ to six decimal places

problem set 100

1. Boesch had a 40-meter head start. How long did it take Louis to catch up if Louis traveled
(99) at 10 meters per second while Boesch traveled at only 6 meters per second? Begin by drawing a diagram of distances traveled and writing the distance equation.

2. Robert ran to the redoubt while Wilbur walked to the parapet. Both distances were the
(92) same, but Robert's speed was 6 miles per hour while Wilbur's was 8 miles per hour. What was the time of each if Robert's time was 2 hours longer than Wilbur's? Begin by drawing a diagram of distances traveled and writing the distance equation.

3. The 60-foot rope was cut into two pieces. One of the pieces was 10 feet longer than 4
(90) times the length of the other piece. How long were the two pieces?

4. Penelope and Miranda found four consecutive odd integers such that 5 times the sum of
(77) the first two was 5 less than 19 times the fourth. What were the integers?

5. Night came and the mangroves and palmettos closed in on their victim. If 27 percent
(58) were mangroves and 511 were palmettos, how many total shrubs were on the attack?

6. Angela rolls a fair die nine times and each time she rolls a three. What is the probability
(70) that on her next roll, she will roll another three?

7. Use a calculator when necessary.
(100)

    (a) Round 104.06253527 to the nearest ten-thousandth.

    (b) Round 413.0527 to the nearest hundred.

    (c) Round $\frac{2}{7}$ to the nearest hundredth.

8. Recall the appropriate Pythagorean triple to find the unknown length in each of the
(97) following right triangles:

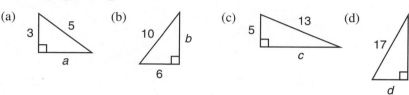

  (a)   (b)   (c)   (d)

9. Use the Pythagorean theorem to find s.   **10.** Find the equations of lines (a) and (b).
(97)   (75)

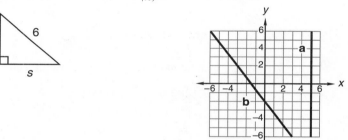

11. Given the points (4, 3) and (7, –2):
(98)

    (a) Find the slope of the line that passes through these two points.

    (b) Find the distance between these two points.

12. Given the following five functions:
(95)

    $f(x) = -x^3 + 1$ $g(x) = -(x + 1)^2$ $h(x) = x^2$ $k(x) = 1 + x^3$ $p(x) = 2x$

    Identify the function whose graph most resembles each shape shown.

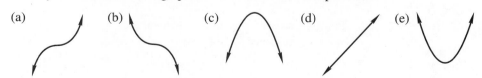

  (a)   (b)   (c)   (d)   (e)

13. Use the difference of two squares theorem to find all the solutions to the following
(96) equations:

    (a) $x^2 = 169$ (b) $x^2 = 48$ (c) $x^2 = 2$

14. Simplify: $\dfrac{x^2 + 8x + 15}{x^2 + 3x} \div \dfrac{x^2 + 3x - 10}{x^3 - 6x^2 + 8x}$
(93)

15. Solve by factoring: $35 = -12x - x^2$
(88)

16. Which of the following diagrams, graphs, or sets of ordered pairs depict functions?
(84,87)

(a)   (3, –1), (–1, 3), (1, 3)   (b)   (2, 3), (–2, 3), (3, –2), (–3, 2)

(c)

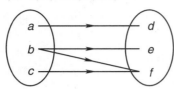

(d)   (e)

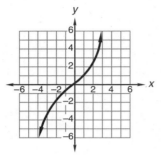   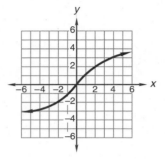

17. Divide: $\left(x^3 + 12x + 5\right) \div (x + 2)$
(86)

Simplify:

18. $3\sqrt{30{,}000} - 9\sqrt{300} + 3\sqrt{2} \cdot 5\sqrt{6}$ **19.** $3\sqrt{2}\left(4\sqrt{8} - 3\sqrt{12}\right)$
(84)   (84)

20. Solve by graphing and check: $\begin{cases} y = 2x \\ y = -x + 6 \end{cases}$
(81)

21. Graph on a number line: $-2 \geq -2x + 2$; $D = \{$Integers$\}$
(91)

22. Simplify: $\dfrac{\left(400 \times 10^5\right)\left(0.0008 \times 10^{14}\right)}{\left(20{,}000 \times 10^{-30}\right)(0.00002)}$
(80)

23. (a) $\dfrac{3 + 4\sqrt{2}}{5} \in \{$What subsets of the real numbers$\}$?
(61)

   (b) $\sqrt{2} \cdot \sqrt{8} \in \{$What subsets of the real numbers$\}$?

24. Add: $\dfrac{4}{x^2} - \dfrac{x + 3}{4x} - \dfrac{2x}{x + 1}$ **25.** Solve: $\dfrac{x}{4} - \dfrac{x + 2}{6} = 4$
(52)   (78)

26. Find x if $x = \sqrt{b^2 - 4ac}$ and $a = 2$, $b = 12$, and $4(c + 2) = 48$.
(41)

Simplify:

27. $\dfrac{x^2 - ax^2 - 3x^3}{x^2}$ **28.** $-2^2 - 2\left[(-3 - 2)(-5 - 4)\right]\left[-3^0(-2 - 5)\right]$
(35)   (29)

29. Find the area of this figure. Dimen-
(8) sions are in inches.

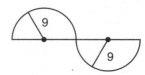

30. A base of the right prism 15 feet high is shown. Find the surface area of the right prism.
(15,60) All angles are right angles. Dimensions are in feet.

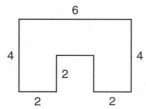   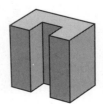

LESSON *101* *Factorable Denominators*

Algebra books tend to emphasize the factoring of trinomials and binomials because the ability to factor is important and also because doing these exercises provides experience in manipulating expressions that contain variables. Thus, all algebra books contain problems such as this one:

$$\text{Simplify: } \frac{x^2 + x - 20}{x^2 - x - 12} \div \frac{x^2 + 7x + 10}{x^2 + 9x + 14}$$

For the same reasons, algebra books present problems requiring the addition of rational expressions whose denominators are factorable. These problems are designed so that the addition is facilitated if one or more of the denominators are factored before the addition is attempted. The key to these problems is recognizing that they are contrived problems designed to give practice in factoring.

example 101.1   Add: $\dfrac{6x}{x^2 - x - 12} - \dfrac{p}{x - 4}$

solution   We recognize this problem as a problem designed to give practice in factoring. We begin by factoring the first denominator.

$$\frac{6x}{(x - 4)(x + 3)} - \frac{p}{x - 4}$$

And now we can see that the least common multiple of the denominators is

$$(x - 4)(x + 3)$$

We use this as our new denominator and add.

$$\frac{}{(x - 4)(x + 3)} - \frac{}{(x - 4)(x + 3)} \quad \rightarrow \quad \frac{6x}{(x - 4)(x + 3)} - \frac{p(x + 3)}{(x - 4)(x + 3)}$$

$$= \frac{6x - px - 3p}{x^2 - x - 12}$$

Note that the answer could also have been expressed with the denominator in factored form.

example 101.2   Add: $\dfrac{7}{x^2 - 5x - 6} - \dfrac{5}{x^2 - 6x}$

solution   As the first step we factor both denominators.

$$\frac{7}{(x - 6)(x + 1)} - \frac{5}{x(x - 6)}$$

and we see that the least common multiple of the denominators is $x(x - 6)(x + 1)$. We use this as our new denominator.

$$\frac{7x}{x(x - 6)(x + 1)} - \frac{5(x + 1)}{x(x - 6)(x + 1)} = \frac{2x - 5}{x(x - 6)(x + 1)}$$

example 101.3   Add: $\dfrac{4x + 2}{x^2 + x - 6} - \dfrac{4}{x^2 + 3x}$

solution   We begin by factoring both denominators.

$$\frac{4x + 2}{(x + 3)(x - 2)} - \frac{4}{x(x + 3)}$$

We see that the LCM of the denominators is $x(x + 3)(x - 2)$, so we rewrite the expression above as

$$\frac{x(4x + 2)}{x(x + 3)(x - 2)} - \frac{4(x - 2)}{x(x + 3)(x - 2)}$$

Since the denominators are now equal, we can combine the two terms into one.

$$\frac{4x^2 + 2x - 4x + 8}{x(x + 3)(x - 2)} = \frac{4x^2 - 2x + 8}{x(x + 3)(x - 2)}$$

practice   Add:

a. $\dfrac{9x}{x^2 - 4x - 21} - \dfrac{7}{x - 7}$ b. $\dfrac{4}{x^2 - 10x + 9} - \dfrac{5}{x^2 - x}$

problem set 101

1. *(99)* At the pole My Bequest was only 40 feet behind Flying Lady. How long did it take My Bequest running at 54 feet per second to catch Flying Lady running at 46 feet per second? Begin by drawing a diagram of distances traveled and writing the distance equation.

2. *(94)* Ed and Alice walked to the dock at 5 miles per hour, jumped into the boat, and motored to Destin at 15 miles per hour. If the total distance was 20 miles and the trip took 2 hours in all, how far did they go by boat? Begin by drawing a diagram of distances traveled and writing the distance equation.

3. *(90)* Charles opened the old trunk and found $6750 in $1 bills and $10 bills. If there were 150 more ones than tens, how many of each kind were there?

4. *(77)* Find three consecutive even integers such that 4 times the first equals 16 times the sum of the third and the number 2.

5. *(77)* On the first day of the sale, the girls sold $\frac{1}{5}$ of their cookies. If they still had 384 cookies left at the end of the first day of the sale, how many cookies did they bring to the sale?

6. *(73)* Cindy has a jar that contains 3 green marbles and 9 purple marbles. She randomly draws one marble and then draws another marble. What is the probability of drawing two purple marbles

   (a)   without replacement?   (b)   with replacement?

7. *(45)* Rebekah counted the different species of flowers that bloomed in her garden over a ten-week period. The number of different species each week was

   $$147,\ 168,\ 172,\ 203,\ 181,\ 172,\ 190,\ 186,\ 178,\ 183$$

   Determine the range, median, mode, and mean of the data given.

Add:

8. *(101)* $\dfrac{p}{x^2 - 9} + \dfrac{2x}{x^2 - 3x}$ 9. *(101)* $\dfrac{8x}{x^2 - 6x + 8} + \dfrac{7}{(x - 2)^2}$

10. *(100)* Round. Use a calculator when necessary.

   (a) $\sqrt{2}$ to the nearest ten-thousandth.

   (b) $0.\overline{6}$ to the nearest hundredth.

   (c)   3500.63210 to the nearest thousand.

11. Use the Pythagorean theorem to find a.
(97)

12. Find the equations of lines (a) and (b).
(75)

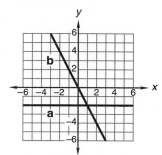

13. Given the points $(4, -3)$ and $(-4, 2)$:
(98)

(a) Find the slope of the line that passes through these two points.

(b) Find the distance between these two points.

14. Identify which of the following graphs could be the graph of a quadratic function:
(95)

(a) 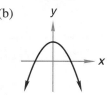 (b) (c) 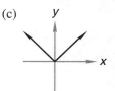 (d)

15. Use the difference of two squares theorem to find all the solutions to the following equations:
(96)

(a) $x^2 = 225$ (b) $x^2 = 72$ (c) $x^2 = 29$

16. Simplify: $\dfrac{x^3 + 11x^2 + 24x}{x^2 + 10x + 21} \div \dfrac{4x^2 + 32x}{4x + 40}$
(93)

17. Solve $-81 + 4x^2 = 0$ by factoring.
(88)

18. Indicate whether the following numbers are rational numbers or irrational numbers:
(61,63)

(a) $\dfrac{\sqrt{2}}{2}$ (b) $\dfrac{\pi}{100}$ (c) $0.\overline{8}$ (d) $5\dfrac{1}{3}$

Simplify:

19. $2\sqrt{60,000} + 3\sqrt{2400}$
(66)

20. $4\sqrt{5} \cdot 2\sqrt{3} + 5\sqrt{3}(\sqrt{3} + 2\sqrt{5})$
(84)

21. Solve by graphing: $\begin{cases} y = -2x \\ y = -2 \end{cases}$
(81)

22. Graph: $-4 - x \not< 2$; $D = \{\text{Reals}\}$
(91)

Solve:

23. $\dfrac{5x}{3} - \dfrac{x-5}{2} = 14$
(78)

24. $-2x(4 - 3^0) - (2x - 5) + 3x - 2 = -2^0x$
(31)

Simplify:

25. (a) $\dfrac{-4x^2 - 8x^2a}{-4x^2}$ (b) $\dfrac{-3^{-2}}{(-3)^2}$
(35,36)

26. $\dfrac{\dfrac{5p}{x} - 4}{\dfrac{3}{x} - x}$
(68)

27. Evaluate: $-x - xk(x - k)$ if $x = -4$ and $k = 5$
(16)

28. Simplify. Write the answer with all exponents positive: $\dfrac{x^2a(x^2a)(x^{-2})^2 x^0xa^2}{(a^{-3})^2 ax^{-2}x^4x}$
(53)

29. Find the perimeter of this figure.
₍₃₎ Dimensions are in centimeters.

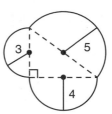

30. The area of a base of a right hexagonal
_(20,60) prism is 36 m² and the length of a lat-
eral edge is 8 m. Find the volume of
the right hexagonal prism.

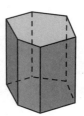

LESSON 102 *Absolute Value Inequalities*

We review the concept of absolute value by saying that every real number except zero can be thought of as having two qualities or parts. One of the parts is designated by the plus or minus sign, and the other part is the numerical part. We can think of the numerical part as designating the quality of "bigness" of the number, and we call this quality the **absolute value** of the number. Thus we say that the two numbers

$$3 \qquad \text{and} \qquad -3$$

both have an absolute value of 3 although one of them is a positive number and one of them is a negative number.

We designate the absolute value of a number by enclosing the number within vertical lines. Thus we designate the absolute value of 3 by writing $|3|$, and we designate the absolute value of -3 by writing $|-3|$. Of course, the absolute value of both of these numbers is 3.

$$|3| = 3 \qquad |-3| = 3$$

It is difficult to describe the absolute value of a number by using words. Most authors do not like to speak of the "bigness" of a number as we have done, for they feel that bigness can be confused with the concept of *greater than* that is used to compare numbers. For this reason, many prefer the formal definition of absolute value used in more advanced courses. This definition uses symbols and does not use words.

The definition is in three parts and we have avoided using the definition thus far because the third part is confusing to some people.

(a) If $x > 0$, $|x| = x$

(b) If $x = 0$, $|x| = 0$

(c) If $x < 0$, $|x| = -x$

Part (a) speaks of the absolute value of positive numbers, which are numbers that are greater than zero. Part (b) describes the absolute value of zero. Part (c) can be confusing because of the minus sign. Part (c) describes the absolute value of negative numbers, which are numbers that are less than zero. Using the definition of absolute value stated on the previous page, we see that the absolute value of –3 is 3.

$$|-3| = -(-3) = 3$$

Thus when we write

$$\text{If } x < 0, \qquad |x| = -x$$

we are not saying that the absolute value is a negative number but that the absolute value of a negative number is the opposite of the negative number, which is a positive number.

> The absolute value of a nonzero real number is a positive number. The absolute value of zero is zero.

$$|3| = +3 \qquad |-3| = +3 \qquad |0| = 0$$

In an attempt to describe the absolute value of a number by using words, many authors define the absolute value of a number to be the number that describes the distance on the number line from the origin to the graph of the number being considered. If we use this definition, we will find that +3 and –3 have the same absolute value, for they are both 3 units from the origin, and thus both numbers have an absolute value of 3.

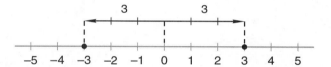

Other authors note that every nonzero real number has an opposite. They say that the absolute value of either member of a pair of opposites is the positive member of the pair. Thus, the absolute value of either

$$3 \qquad \text{or} \qquad -3$$

is 3, the positive member of the pair. If we remember this, we can see that there are two answers to the following question:

$$|\text{What numbers?}| = 4$$

Here we ask what numbers have an absolute value of 4. Of course, the answers are +4 and –4 because both of these numbers have an absolute value of 4. It is customary to use a single-letter variable as the unknown, so we will restate the question by writing

$$|x| = 4$$

and as we have said, the two values of x that satisfy this condition are +4 and –4.

Often it is desirable to display the solution of an absolute value equation or inequality in graphical form. The graph of the solution to the equation $|x| = 4$ is the graph of the numbers +4 and –4, as shown here.

In the examples in this lesson, as well as in the problem sets, we will graph all real numbers that satisfy the inequalities. That is, we will assume unless specified otherwise that the domain D equals the set of real numbers.

example 102.1   Graph: $|x| > 2$

solution   We are asked to indicate on the number line every real number whose absolute value is greater than 2.

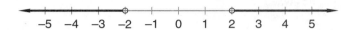

We note that the solution set to this inequality contains both positive and negative numbers. Those positive numbers greater than 2 and those negative numbers less than –2 satisfy the given inequality.

example 102.2   Graph: $|x| \leq 3$

solution   We are asked to indicate on the number line the location of all real numbers whose absolute value is equal to or less than 3.

We note that all integers that are greater than or equal to –3 and that are also less than or equal to 3 have an absolute value that is equal to or less than 3.

example 102.3   Graph: $|x| < -4$

solution

We have not graphed a solution for the given condition because there are no real numbers that satisfy the given condition. The statement $|x| < -4$ asks for the real number replacements for x whose absolute values are less than –4. There are no real numbers that satisfy this condition since the absolute value of any nonzero real number is greater than zero. If we use the formal language of sets we say that the solution set is the empty set { }, or the null set $\emptyset$, and we say that the bare number line shown is the graph of this set because no members have been designated.

example 102.4   Graph: $|x| > -4$

solution

This one is also tricky. The absolute value of every number is zero or a number greater than zero. Certainly, then, if the absolute value of every real number is equal to or greater than zero, the absolute value of every real number is also greater than –4. Thus the solution to the stated condition is the set of real numbers, which is graphed by indicating the entire number line.

example 102.5   Graph: $-|x| \geq -3$

solution   We begin by multiplying both sides of the inequality by –1 and also **reversing the inequality symbol,** and we find

$$|x| \leq 3$$

which is graphed below.

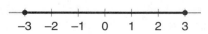

example 102.6   Graph: $-|x| - 2 > -5$

solution   First we must solve the inequality for $+|x|$ by isolating $|x|$ on one side of the inequality.

$$-|x| - 2 > -5 \qquad \text{given}$$
$$-|x| > -3 \qquad \text{added } +2 \text{ to both sides}$$
$$|x| < 3 \qquad \text{multiplied both sides by } -1$$
$$\qquad \qquad \text{and \textbf{reversed the inequality symbol}}$$

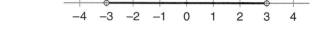

practice   Graph on a number line those real values of x that satisfy the following inequalities:

a. $-|x| - 9 > -11$ **b.** $|x| > 0$

problem set 102

1.
(94) At noon the armadillo left the wild kingdom and headed north at 3 kilometers per hour. Two hours later the raccoon left the same kingdom and headed south at 5 kilometers per hour. At what time will the animals be 38 kilometers apart? Begin by drawing a diagram of distances traveled and writing the distance equation.

2.
(90) When the debris was cleared away, there were 52 bricks left. Some were red and the rest were white. The red bricks numbered 16 more than twice the number of white bricks. How many bricks of each color were there?

3.
(83) Stephanie threw her pennies into the sandbox and then Shannon added her nickels. If they threw in 10 more pennies than nickels and threw in $29.50 total, how many nickels were in the sandbox?

4.
(76) Find four consecutive integers such that 5 times the opposite of the first is 5 greater than the product of −3 and the sum of the third and fourth.

5.
(58) Twelve percent of the inhabitants had white hair. If 4224 inhabitants had colored hair, how many inhabitants were there in all?

6.
(70) Courtney flips a fair coin four times. What is the probability that the coin will come up heads four times in a row?

Graph on a number line those real values of x that satisfy the following inequalities:

7. $|x| > 2$ **8.** $|x| - 2 \le 0$ **9.** $-|x| + 5 > 2$
(102)   (102)   (102)

Add:

10. $\dfrac{4}{x - 4} + \dfrac{5}{x^2 - 16}$ **11.** $\dfrac{4}{x^2 + 2x + 1} - \dfrac{3}{x + 1}$
(101)   (101)

12. Use a calculator when necessary.
(100)
(a) Round $\sqrt{5}$ to the nearest thousandth.

(b) Round 2654 to the nearest thousand.

(c) Round $572.0\overline{562}$ to the nearest hundredth.

13. Recall the appropriate Pythagorean triple to find the unknown length in each of the
(97) following right triangles:

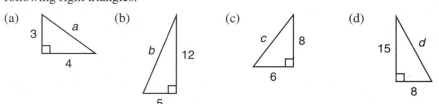

14. Use the Pythagorean theorem to find p.
(97)

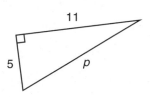

15. Given the points $(5, -3)$ and $(7, -2)$:
(98)

    (a) Find the slope of the line that passes through these two points.

    (b) Find the distance between these two points.

16. Given the following five functions:
(95)

$$f(x) = x^2 \quad g(x) = -|x| + 1 \quad h(x) = 2x - 1 \quad k(x) = |x| \quad p(x) = -\frac{1}{2}x + 1$$

Identify the function whose graph most resembles the shape shown.

17. Use the difference of two squares theorem to find all the solutions to the following
(96) equations:

    (a) $x^2 = 5$ (b) $x^2 = 8$ (c) $x^2 = 19$

18. Simplify: $\dfrac{x^3 + x^2 - 12x}{x^2 + 4x} \div \dfrac{x^2 - 11x + 24}{x^2 + 2x - 80}$
(93)

19. Solve by factoring: $-80 = x^2 + 18x$
(88)

20. What is the domain and range of the
(82) graphed function?

21. Find the equations of lines (a) and (b).
(75)

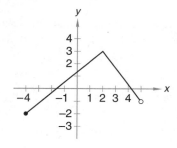

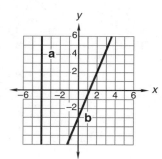

22. Divide: $(2x^3 + x^2 - 3x) \div (2x + 3)$
(86)

23. Simplify: $3\sqrt{6,000,000} - 5\sqrt{60,000} + 2\sqrt{3}(3\sqrt{2} - 5\sqrt{3})$
(84)

24. Solve by graphing: $\begin{cases} x = 2 \\ y = -\dfrac{1}{2}x + 6 \end{cases}$
(81)

25. Solve: $\dfrac{5x}{2} - \dfrac{x - 3}{5} = 7$
(78)

Simplify:

26. $\dfrac{(0.0004 \times 10^{15})(0.06 \times 10^{41})}{(30,000,000)(400 \times 10^{-21})}$
(80)

27. (a) $\dfrac{-3x - 9x^2}{-3x}$ (b) $\dfrac{-2^{-2}}{(-2)^2}$
(35,36)

28. Find x if $x = \dfrac{\sqrt{b^2 - 4ac}}{2a}$ and if $a = 10$, $b = 13$, and $8c = 5$.
₍₄₁₎

29. Find the area of this figure. Dimensions are in inches.
₍₈₎

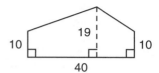

30. Find the surface area of this right triangular prism. Dimensions are in feet.
_(15,60)

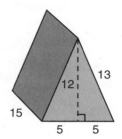

LESSON *103 More on Rational Equations*

In Lesson 78 we discussed the solution of rational equations in which all denominators are integers. In these problems we found that the recommended first step is to multiply the numerator of every term in the equation by the least common multiple of the denominators. Since every denominator is a factor of the least common multiple, this procedure permits us to cancel every denominator, as we see in the following example.

example 103.1   Solve: $\dfrac{y}{2} + \dfrac{1}{4} = \dfrac{y}{6}$

solution   As the first step we will multiply every numerator by 12, the least common multiple of the denominators.

$$12\left(\frac{y}{2}\right) + 12\left(\frac{1}{4}\right) = 12\left(\frac{y}{6}\right) \quad \longrightarrow \quad 6y + 3 = 2y \quad \longrightarrow \quad 4y = -3 \quad \longrightarrow \quad y = -\frac{3}{4}$$

The denominators of the equation in example 103.1 are all real numbers. In this lesson we will discuss equations whose denominators contain variables. If there are variables in the denominator, the replacement values of the variables are restricted. For instance, if the given equation is

$$\frac{t - 2}{t} = \frac{14}{3t} - \frac{1}{3}$$

the number zero would not be a permissible value for t, for if we substitute the number zero for t, we find

$$\frac{0 - 2}{0} = \frac{14}{3(0)} - \frac{1}{3} \quad \longrightarrow \quad -\frac{2}{\mathbf{0}} = \frac{14}{\mathbf{0}} - \frac{1}{\mathbf{3}} \qquad \text{incorrect}$$

which is meaningless, for division by zero is not defined.

If our equation is

$$\frac{n}{n+2} = \frac{3}{5}$$

we cannot accept –2 as a value for n, for if we try to substitute –2 for n, we obtain

$$\frac{(-2)}{(-2)+2} = \frac{3}{5} \quad \longrightarrow \quad -\frac{2}{0} = \frac{3}{5} \qquad \text{incorrect}$$

which contains an expression in which zero is the denominator of a fraction, and division of a nonzero real number by zero is not defined.

Thus, as our first step in the solution of rational equations whose terms have variables in one or more denominators, we will list the unacceptable values of the variable, which, of course, are those values of the variable that would cause any denominator to equal zero.

example 103.2   Solve: $\dfrac{t-2}{t} = \dfrac{14}{3t} - \dfrac{1}{3}$

solution   ($t \neq 0$). As the next step we multiply every term by $3t$, the least common multiple of the denominators. This will allow us to cancel the denominators, and then we will solve the resulting equation.

$$3t\left(\frac{t-2}{t}\right) = 3t\left(\frac{14}{3t}\right) - 3t\left(\frac{1}{3}\right) \quad \longrightarrow \quad 3t - 6 = 14 - t$$

$$\longrightarrow \quad 4t = 20 \quad \longrightarrow \quad t = \mathbf{5}$$

example 103.3   Solve: $\dfrac{n}{n+2} - \dfrac{3}{5} = 0$

solution   ($n \neq -2$). Now we multiply every term by $(5)(n+2)$, the least common multiple of the denominators, cancel the denominators, and solve.

$$(5)(n+2)\frac{(n)}{(n+2)} - \frac{3}{5}(5)(n+2) = 0 \quad \longrightarrow \quad 5n - 3(n+2) = 0$$

$$\longrightarrow \quad 5n - 3n - 6 = 0 \quad \longrightarrow \quad 2n = 6 \quad \longrightarrow \quad n = \mathbf{3}$$

example 103.4   Solve: $\dfrac{2}{3n} - \dfrac{2}{n+4} = 0$

solution   ($n \neq 0, -4$). Now we multiply every term by $(3n)(n+4)$, cancel the denominators, and solve.

$$(3n)(n+4)\frac{(2)}{(3n)} - \frac{(2)}{(n+4)}(3n)(n+4) = 0 \quad \longrightarrow \quad 2(n+4) - 6n = 0$$

$$\longrightarrow \quad 2n + 8 - 6n = 0 \quad \longrightarrow \quad 8 = 4n \quad \longrightarrow \quad n = \mathbf{2}$$

example 103.5   Solve: $\dfrac{4}{x} - \dfrac{7}{x-2} = 0$

solution   ($x \neq 0, 2$). Now multiply each term by $x(x-2)$, cancel the denominators, and solve.

$$x(x-2)\frac{4}{x} - \frac{x(x-2)}{1} \cdot \frac{7}{x-2} = 0 \quad \longrightarrow \quad 4x - 8 - 7x = 0$$

$$\longrightarrow \quad -3x = 8 \quad \longrightarrow \quad x = -\frac{8}{3}$$

example 103.6 Solve: $\dfrac{4}{p} - \dfrac{3}{p-4} = 0$

solution $(p \neq 0, 4)$. We multiply each term by $p(p-4)$, which is the least common multiple of the denominators, cancel the denominators, and solve.

$$p(p-4)\dfrac{4}{p} - p(p-4)\dfrac{3}{p-4} = 0 \;\longrightarrow\; 4p - 16 - 3p = 0$$

$$\longrightarrow\; p - 16 = 0 \;\longrightarrow\; p = \mathbf{16}$$

practice Solve:

a. $\dfrac{5}{t} - \dfrac{2}{t-3} = 0$

b. $\dfrac{8}{y} + \dfrac{5}{y-3} = 0$

problem set 103

1. (94) Frederick headed for Lutzen at 3 kilometers per hour. Later he increased his speed to 4 kilometers per hour. If it was 52 kilometers to Lutzen and the total time of travel was 15 hours, how long did he travel at 3 kilometers per hour? Begin by drawing a diagram of distances traveled and writing the distance equation.

2. (92) Josephine walked to Brundig and then trotted back home. She walked at 2 miles per hour and trotted at 4 miles per hour. How far was it to Brundig if her walking time was 2 hours longer than her trotting time? Begin by drawing a diagram of distances traveled and writing the distance equation.

3. (33) If the sum of a number and 10 is multiplied by 5, the result is 2 greater than 7 times the opposite of the number. What is the number?

4. (89) Cookies sold for 10 cents and doughnuts for 20 cents. Pericles bought 25 items for $3.50. How many doughnuts and how many cookies did he buy?

5. (90) Parking fees were based on a weighted value. The first hour was weighted at 5 times the cost of each of the other hours. What was the charge for 6 hours of parking if the second hour cost $1?

6. (58) When the battle began, there were 30 percent more brigantines than men-of-war. If there were 260 brigantines, how many total soldiers took part in the battle?

7. (70) Two fair dice are rolled. Find the probability that the sum of the numbers rolled is

(a) less than 6

(b) greater than 6

Solve:

8. (103) $\dfrac{p-4}{p} = \dfrac{16}{5p} - \dfrac{1}{5}$

9. (103) $\dfrac{3}{4n} = \dfrac{3}{n+3}$

Graph on a number line those real values of x that satisfy the following inequalities:

10. (102) $-|x| + 4 \geq -2$

11. (102) $|x| - 4 > -1$

Add:

12. (101) $\dfrac{4}{a-2} + \dfrac{6a}{a^2-4}$

13. (101) $\dfrac{5}{x+4} - \dfrac{3}{x^2+2x-8}$

14. (100) Use a calculator when necessary.

(a) Round $\sqrt{3}$ to the nearest ten-thousandth.

(b) Round $\frac{1}{6}$ to the nearest thousandth.

(c) Round 1053.7625 to the nearest hundred.

15. Use the Pythagorean theorem to find p.
(97)

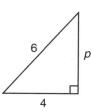

16. Find the equations of lines (a) and (b).
(75)

17. Given the points $(-2, -3)$ and $(-5, 6)$:
(98)

(a) Find the slope of the line that passes through these points.

(b) Find the distance between these points.

18. The graph of which of the following
(95) functions most resembles the shape to
the right?

(a) $f(x) = x^2$

(b) $g(x) = \sqrt{x}$

(c) $h(x) = -\sqrt{x}$

(d) $k(x) = x^3$

19. Simplify: $\dfrac{x^2 + 10x + 25}{x^2 + 5x} \div \dfrac{x^2 + 8x + 15}{x^3 + x^2 - 6x}$
(93)

20. Solve by factoring: $4x^2 - 81 = 0$
(88)

21. Which of the following diagrams, graphs, or sets of ordered pairs depict functions?
(84,87)

(a) $(-5, -3), (5, -3), (-3, 5), (-5, 3)$

(b) $(4, -2), (-4, 2), (-2, -4), (2, 4)$

(c)

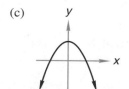

(d)

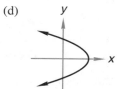

(e)

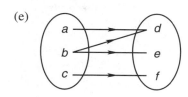

22. Divide: $\left(x^3 - 4\right) \div (x + 7)$
(86)

23. Simplify: $3\sqrt{2} \cdot 4\sqrt{3} - 4\sqrt{60,000} + 2\sqrt{3}\left(3\sqrt{2} - \sqrt{3}\right)$
(84)

24. Solve by graphing and check: $\begin{cases} y = x - 2 \\ y = -\dfrac{1}{2}x + 1 \end{cases}$
(81)

25. (a) $\dfrac{4\sqrt{9}}{5} \in$ {What subsets of the real numbers}?
(61)

(b) $\sqrt{169} - \sqrt{225} \in$ {What subsets of the real numbers}?

Simplify:

26. (a) $\dfrac{3x - 3x^2}{3x}$ (b) $\dfrac{-4^{-2}}{-(-2)^{-2}}$ **27.** $\dfrac{a^2 + \dfrac{1}{a}}{ax + \dfrac{b}{a}}$
(35,36)   (68)

28. Evaluate: $-x - x^2 + (-x)^3(x - y)$ if $x = -3$ and $y = -5$
(19)

29. Find the perimeter of this figure.
(3)   Dimensions are in centimeters.

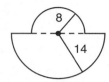

30. A base of the right prism 13 meters high is shown. Find the volume of the right prism.
(20,60)   Dimensions are in meters.

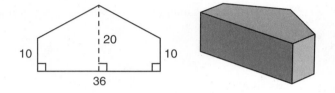

LESSON *104*   *Abstract Rational Equations*

In the preceding lesson we discussed the fact that when we have equations with variables in the denominator, such as

$$\frac{4}{x} - \frac{3}{x - 2} = \frac{7}{2x}$$

the values we may use to replace x are restricted because a denominator can never equal zero. Thus, in the equation above, we cannot use 0 or +2 for x, for either of these will cause at least one denominator to equal zero. We often note the impermissible values of the variable for a problem by listing them using a notation such as $(x \neq 0)$, $(x \neq 2)$, $(x, m \neq 0)$, etc., as we do in the following examples. We will omit these notations in the problem sets and assume that values of unknown quantities are chosen such that no denominator of any term equals zero.

example 104.1   Find m: $\dfrac{1}{x} + \dfrac{b}{m} = c$ $(x, m \neq 0)$

solution   The least common multiple of the denominators is xm. Thus we begin by multiplying[†] every term by xm, the least common multiple of the denominators, and then we cancel the denominators.

$$(xm)\frac{1}{x} + (xm)\frac{b}{m} = cxm$$

This leaves us with the following equation:

$$m + xb = cxm$$

[†]Permitted by the multiplicative property of equality.

Now we use the additive property of equality to place all terms with m's on one side and all other terms on the other side.

$$m + xb = cxm$$
$$\underline{-m \qquad\qquad\qquad - m}$$
$$xb = cxm - m$$

Then we factor out the m on the right-hand side and finish by dividing both sides by $(cx - 1)$.

$$xb = m(cx - 1) \quad\longrightarrow\quad \frac{xb}{cx - 1} = \frac{m(cx - 1)}{(cx - 1)} \quad\longrightarrow\quad m = \frac{xb}{cx - 1} \qquad (cx - 1 \neq 0)$$

example 104.2   Find b: $\dfrac{a}{b} + \dfrac{c}{d} = x \qquad (b, d \neq 0)$

solution   As the first step we multiply each term by bd, the least common multiple of the denominators,

$$(bd)\frac{a}{b} + (bd)\frac{c}{d} = bdx$$

and cancel the denominators.

$$da + bc = bdx$$

Now we use the additive property of equality as necessary to position all terms that contain b on one side of the equation (either side) and all terms that do not contain b on the other side. We decide to position all terms that contain b on the right-hand side of the equation by adding $-bc$ to both sides.

$$da + bc = bdx$$
$$\underline{- bc \qquad\qquad - bc}$$
$$da \qquad = bdx - bc$$

Now factor out the b on the right-hand side,

$$da = b(dx - c)$$

and as a last step divide both sides of the equation by $dx - c$.

$$\frac{da}{(dx - c)} = b\frac{(dx - c)}{(dx - c)} \quad\longrightarrow\quad b = \frac{da}{dx - c} \qquad (dx - c \neq 0)$$

example 104.3   Find x: $\dfrac{a}{b} - c = \dfrac{d}{x} \qquad (b, x \neq 0)$

solution   First we eliminate the denominators by multiplying both sides of the equation by bx.

$$(bx)\frac{a}{b} - (bx)c = (bx)\frac{d}{x} \quad\longrightarrow\quad xa - bxc = bd$$

Now, since all x terms are already on one side and all other terms are on the other side, we factor out the x and divide both sides by the coefficient of x.

$$x(a - bc) = bd \quad\longrightarrow\quad \frac{x(a - bc)}{(a - bc)} = \frac{bd}{(a - bc)} \quad\longrightarrow\quad x = \frac{bd}{a - bc} \qquad (a - bc \neq 0)$$

example 104.4   Find x: $\dfrac{a}{x} - y + \dfrac{m}{n} = k \qquad (x, n \neq 0)$

solution First we eliminate the denominators by multiplying both sides of the equation by xn.

$$(\cancel{x}n)\frac{a}{\cancel{x}} - xny + (x\cancel{n})\frac{m}{\cancel{n}} = xnk \longrightarrow na - xny + xm = xnk$$

Now we move all terms that contain x to the right-hand side, factor out the x, and divide by the coefficient of x.

$$\begin{array}{l} na - xny + xm = xnk \\ \underline{\quad + xny - xm \qquad\qquad + xny - xm \quad} \\ na \qquad\qquad\qquad = xnk + xny - xm \end{array} \longrightarrow na = x(nk + ny - m)$$

$$\longrightarrow \frac{na}{(nk + ny - m)} = \frac{x(\cancel{nk + ny - m})}{(\cancel{nk + ny - m})}$$

$$\longrightarrow \frac{na}{nk + ny - m} = x \quad (nk + ny - m \neq 0)$$

practice **a.** Find b: $\dfrac{3z}{m} + \dfrac{n}{b} = f$ \qquad\qquad **b.** Find m: $\dfrac{3a}{y} - s + \dfrac{k}{m} = x$

problem set 104

1. (92) Milton ran north at 8 kilometers per hour. Four hours later Harriet set out in pursuit at 16 kilometers per hour. How long did it take Harriet to catch Milton? Begin by drawing a diagram of distances traveled and writing the distance equation.

2. (92) The train made the trip in 4 hours. The girls walked it in 48 hours. How far was it if the speed of the train was 55 miles per hour faster than the girls walked? Begin by drawing a diagram of distances traveled and writing the distance equation.

3. (77) Find three consecutive odd integers such that 4 times the first is 14 less than twice the sum of 2 and the third.

4. (89) Gold was worth 422 marks a gram and copper was worth 4 marks a gram. If Brother Gregory had an 8-gram mixture of gold and copper that was worth 2122 marks, how many grams of gold did he have?

5. (58) Thirty percent of the people did not like the king. If 81,150 people did not like the king, how many people lived in the kingdom?

6. (73) Debby has a bag that contains 13 green marbles and 7 gray marbles. She randomly draws 3 marbles without replacement. What is the probability of drawing 3 green marbles?

7. (104) Find n: $\dfrac{a}{n} - m + \dfrac{5k}{x} = y$ \qquad **8.** (104) Find d: $\dfrac{2c}{a} - x = \dfrac{b}{d}$

Solve:

9. (103) $\dfrac{1 + m}{m} - \dfrac{3}{m} = 0$ \qquad\qquad **10.** (103) $\dfrac{3}{4x} = \dfrac{2}{x + 5}$

11. (78) $\dfrac{x}{5} - \dfrac{3 + x}{7} = 0$ \qquad\qquad **12.** (103) $\dfrac{2}{x} - \dfrac{3}{x - 1} = 0$

Graph on a number line those real values of x that satisfy the following inequalities:

13. (102) $-|x| - 2 < -4$ \qquad\qquad **14.** (102) $-|x| + 2 \geq 1$

Add:

15. (101) $\dfrac{4}{x^2 - 4} + \dfrac{3x}{x - 2}$ \qquad\qquad **16.** (101) $-\dfrac{x}{x + 5} - \dfrac{3x}{x^2 + 3x - 10}$

17. (100) Use a calculator when necessary.

(a) Round $\sqrt{26}$ to the nearest hundredth.

(b) Round π to the nearest millionth.

(c) Round 5247.6732 to the nearest ten.

18. Use the Pythagorean theorem to find k.
(97)

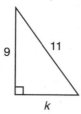

19. Find the equations of lines (a) and (b).
(75)

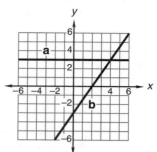

20. Given the points $(-4, 2)$ and $(-10, 6)$:
(98)

(a) Find the slope of the line that passes through these points.

(b) Find the distance between these points.

21. The graph of which of the following
(95) functions most resembles the shape to the right?

(a) $f(x) = x^2$
(b) $g(x) = -x^3$

(c) $h(x) = -\sqrt{x}$
(d) $k(x) = x^3$

22. Solve by factoring: $63 = -x^2 - 16x$
(88)

23. What is the domain of the function $f(x) = \sqrt{1 - 4x}$?
(82)

24. Simplify: $4\sqrt{20{,}000} - 15\sqrt{8} + 3\sqrt{2}\left(4\sqrt{2} - 5\right)$
(84)

25. Find x if $x = \dfrac{-b \pm \sqrt{b^2 - 4ac}}{2a}$ and $a = 2$, $b - 1 = 2$, and $c + 1 = -1$.
(62)

26. Solve: $2x^0(x - 2) - 3x - 4 - [-(-2)] - 7^0 = -2x - 4$
(31)

27. Evaluate: $-x^2 - x\left(xy - xy^2\right)$ if $x = -2$ and $y = -3$
(19)

28. Simplify: (a) $\dfrac{4x^2ay - 4xay}{4xay}$ (b) $\dfrac{-2^{-2}}{-\left(-2^0\right)^{-3}}$
(35,36)

29. Find the area of the shaded portion of
(8) this parallelogram. Dimensions are in inches.

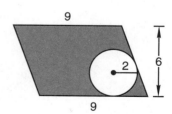

30. Find the lateral surface area of this
(15,60) right prism whose bases are regular hexagons. Dimensions are in feet.

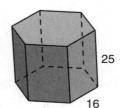

LESSON 105   *Factoring by Grouping*

Some expressions can be simplified if we note that two terms have common factors. If we consider the expression

$$xy + 3ay + bx + 3ba$$

we note that the first two terms have y as a factor. If we factor y out of the first two terms, we get

$$y(x + 3a) + bx + 3ba$$

Now we note that the last two terms have b as a factor. If we factor b out of the last two terms, we get

$$y(x + 3a) + b(x + 3a)$$

Now we can factor out $(x + 3a)$ and get

$$(x + 3a)(y + b)$$

Many books call this type of factoring **factoring by grouping** because we grouped the terms that had y as a factor and those that had b as a factor.

example 105.1   Factor: $xya - 4a + xyb - 4b$

solution   We note that the first two terms have a as a factor and that the last two terms have b as a factor. We begin by using parentheses to **group** these terms.

$$(xya - 4a) + (xyb - 4b)$$

Now we factor a from the first group and b from the second.

$$a(xy - 4) + b(xy - 4)$$

Lastly, we recognize that both of these terms have $xy - 4$ as a factor, so we factor out this expression.

$$\mathbf{(xy - 4)(a + b)}$$

We can get the same result via a different route. We note that the first and third terms have xy as a factor and the second and fourth terms have 4 as a factor. We group these terms and get

$$(xya + xyb) + (-4a - 4b)$$

We factor xy from the first group and -4 from the second group and get

$$xy(a + b) + (-4)(a + b)$$

Now we factor $(a + b)$ from both terms and get

$$(a + b)(xy - 4)$$

example 105.2   Factor: $ac + 2ad + 2bc + 4bd$

solution   We recognize the form and note that the first and third terms have a common factor of c. We note that the second and fourth terms have a common factor of $2d$, so we rearrange the terms and use parentheses as follows:

$$(ac + 2bc) + (2ad + 4bd)$$

Now we factor these terms as

$$c(a + 2b) + 2d(a + 2b)$$

and complete the problem by factoring out $a + 2b$. The final result is

$$(a + 2b)(c + 2d)$$

Now we try another way. We group the terms that have a as a factor and the terms that have b as a factor.

$$(ac + 2ad) + (2bc + 4bd)$$

From the first group we factor out a, and from the second group we factor out $2b$.

$$a(c + 2d) + 2b(c + 2d)$$

Now we note the common factor of $c + 2d$. So we factor one more time.

$$(c + 2d)(a + 2b)$$

We always begin the factoring process by searching for common monomial factors. We recognize that these problems are contrived problems in which two terms have one common factor and two other terms have another common factor. Further, once each pair of terms is factored, more factoring is possible if the resulting factored terms share a common binomial factor.

practice   Factor:

  a. $mba - 7a + mbn - 7n$ **b.** $ns + 3nx + 2cs + 6cx$

**problem set
105**

1.
(92)
Louis ran to Versailles and then walked back to town. His running rate was 6 kilometers per hour and his walking rate was 3 kilometers per hour. How far was it to Versailles if the round trip took 6 hours? Begin by drawing a diagram of distances traveled and writing the distance equation.

2.
(99)
Roger Goose had a 500-yard head start on Willa. If Willa's speed was 40 yards per second and Roger's speed was only 20 yards per second, how long did it take Willa to catch up? Begin by drawing a diagram of distances traveled and writing the distance equation.

3.
(89)
Prince Valiant bought some replacement armor for 540 florins. He bought helmets for 4 florins each and cuirasses for 6 florins each. If he bought 100 pieces of armor, how many helmets did he buy?

4.
(77)
Find four consecutive even integers such that -6 times the sum of the second and fourth is 8 less than 11 times the opposite of the third.

5.
(58)
Demosthenes had white pebbles and black pebbles. If 27 percent of his pebbles were white and he had 438 black pebbles, how many pebbles did he have in all?

6.
(70)
Martha flips a fair coin 9 times. What is the probability that on the next toss it will come up heads?

Factor by grouping:

7.
(105)
$ac - ad + bc - bd$

8.
(105)
$ab + 4a + 2b + 8$

9.
(105)
$ab + ac + xb + xc$

10.
(105)
$2mx - 3m + 2pcx - 3pc$

11.
(105)
$4k - kxy + 4pc - pcxy$

12.
(105)
$ac - axy + dc - dxy$

Find b in the following equations:

13.
(104)
$\dfrac{a}{b} + \dfrac{1}{c} = d$

14.
(104)
$\dfrac{a}{x} - \dfrac{1}{c} = \dfrac{b}{d}$

Solve:

15.
(103)
$\dfrac{4}{x} - \dfrac{2}{x - 4} = 0$

16.
(78)
$\dfrac{x}{4} - \dfrac{x + 6}{5} = 1$

Graph on a number line those real values of x that satisfy the following inequalities:

17. $|x| + 5 < 2$
(102)

18. $-|x| - 1 \geq 1$
(102)

Add:

19. $\dfrac{4}{x^2 - 9} - \dfrac{3}{x + 3}$
(101)

20. $\dfrac{5}{x + 2} - \dfrac{3x}{x^2 + 5x + 6}$
(101)

21. Use a calculator when necessary.
(100)

    (a) Round $\sqrt{13}$ to the nearest hundredth.

    (b) Round 2π to the nearest hundred thousandth.

    (c) Round 57,634.679 to the nearest thousand.

22. Use the Pythagorean theorem to find k.
(97)

23. Solve by graphing and check:
(81)

$$\begin{cases} y = x - 3 \\ y = -x + 3 \end{cases}$$

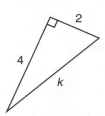

24. Given the following four functions:
(95)

$$f(x) = |x + 3| \quad g(x) = x^2 + 2 \quad h(x) = -|x| \quad p(x) = -(x + 2)^2$$

Identify the function whose graph most resembles the shape shown.

(a)   (b)   (c)   (d)

25. Given the points $(0, 0)$ and $(6, 8)$:
(98)

    (a) Find the slope of the line that passes through the points.

    (b) Find the distance between these points.

Simplify:

26. $\sqrt{50,000} - 25\sqrt{125} + 5\sqrt{5}(5\sqrt{5} - 5)$
(84)

27. $\dfrac{x^2 + 6x + 9}{x^2 + 3x} \div \dfrac{x^3 + 5x^2 + 6x}{x^2 + 2x}$
(93)

28. Find x if $x = \dfrac{-b \pm \sqrt{b^2 - 4ac}}{2a}$ and $a = 3$, $b = -2$, and $c = -1$.
(62)

29. Find the perimeter of this figure.
(3)   Dimensions are in centimeters.

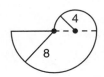

30. Find the volume of the right rectangu-
(72) lar pyramid.

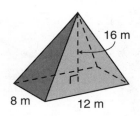

LESSON *106* *Linear Equations • Equation of a Line Through Two Points*

106.A
linear equations

The graph of a first-degree equation in two unknowns is a straight line. This is the reason we call these equations linear equations.

The standard form of the equation of a straight line is

$$ax + by + c = 0$$

where a, b, and c are constants (and where a and b are not both zero). The following are equations of straight lines in standard form:

$$4x + y + 1 = 0 \qquad -2x - y - 11 = 0$$

We remember that if the equation of a line is written so that y is expressed as a function of x, such as

$$y = mx + b$$

we say that we have written the equation in **slope-intercept form.** In this equation m represents the slope of the line and b represents the y intercept of the line, which is the y coordinate of the point where the line in question crosses the y axis.

106.B
equation of a line through two points

Thus far, we have learned how to draw the graph of a given linear equation and have learned how to find a good approximation of the equation of a given line. Both of these exercises have helped us to understand the relationship between the equation of a line and the graph of a line.

Algebra books usually contain three other types of straight line problems that are helpful in exploring this relationship. In the first type we are given the coordinates of two points and asked to find the equation of the line that passes through the two points.

example 106.1   Find the equation of the line that passes through the points (4, 2) and (–5, –3).

solution   The slope-intercept form of the desired equation is $y = mx + b$, and **we need to find the values of m and b.** First we graph the two points and draw the line in the figure on the left. If we draw the slope triangle so that the sides of the triangle terminate on these points, as we have done in the figure on the right,

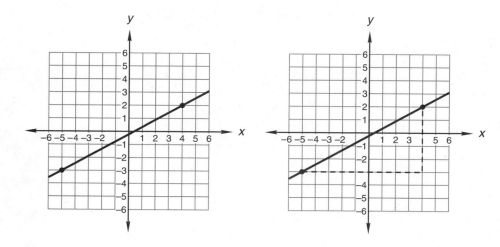

we can determine the **exact value of the slope** to be $+\frac{5}{9}$. We say the exact value because we were given the exact coordinates of two points on the line and were able to determine precisely the lengths of the sides of the slope triangle.

We could have also determined the slope by applying the slope formula that we learned in Lesson 98. We use the slope formula to find the slope of the line passing through points $P_1 = (4, 2)$ and $P_2 = (-5, -3)$.

$$m = \frac{y_2 - y_1}{x_2 - x_1} = \frac{(-3) - (2)}{(-5) - (4)} = \frac{-5}{-9} = \frac{5}{9}$$

Remember that which point we choose as P_1 and which we choose as P_2 does not affect the calculation of m.

We can see from the graph that the value of the intercept is approximately -0.3. **This estimated value of the intercept is not acceptable when the exact coordinates of two points on the graph are known, for we can find the exact value for the intercept.** We know the exact value of the slope, so we can write the desired equation as

$$y = \frac{5}{9}x + b$$

We know the exact values of the coordinates of two points that lie on the line. We can use the coordinates of either of these points for x and y in the equation above and find the exact value of b algebraically.

USING (4, 2)	USING (−5, −3)
$y = \dfrac{5}{9}x + b$	$y = \dfrac{5}{9}x + b$
$(2) = \dfrac{5}{9}(4) + b$	$(-3) = \dfrac{5}{9}(-5) + b$
$\dfrac{18}{9} = \dfrac{20}{9} + b$	$-\dfrac{27}{9} = -\dfrac{25}{9} + b$
$-\dfrac{2}{9} = b$	$-\dfrac{2}{9} = b$

Now that we have the exact values of m and b, we can write the exact equation of the line that passes through the two points as

$$y = \frac{5}{9}x - \frac{2}{9}$$

example 106.2   Find the equation of the line that passes through the points $(4, -2)$ and $(-3, 4)$.

solution   The general form of the desired equation is $y = mx + b$. We choose to solve the problem without graphing the line. First we determine the slope m by applying the slope formula to the points $P_1 = (4, -2)$ and $P_2 = (-3, 4)$.

$$m = \frac{y_2 - y_1}{x_2 - x_1} = \frac{(4) - (-2)}{(-3) - (4)} = \frac{6}{-7} = -\frac{6}{7}$$

Now we have

$$y = -\frac{6}{7}x + b$$

and we can find the exact value of b by substituting either $(4, -2)$ or $(-3, 4)$ for x and y and solving algebraically for b. We will use the point $(4, -2)$.

$$-2 = -\frac{6}{7}(4) + b$$

$$-\frac{14}{7} = -\frac{24}{7} + b$$

$$\frac{10}{7} = b$$

So the desired equation is

$$y = -\frac{6}{7}x + \frac{10}{7}$$

and the values that we have found for the slope and the intercept are exact.

We see from these two examples that when we are given the coordinates of two points that lie on the line, the exact equation of the line can be determined. Estimated values of the slope and intercept are not acceptable for this type of problem.

example 106.3 Find the equation of the line that passes through the points $(4, 3)$ and $(4, -3)$.

solution When we graph the points and draw the line, we find that the line is a vertical line. Vertical and horizontal lines can be thought of as special cases. By inspection, the equation of this line is $x = 4$.

The change in y is 6 and the change in x is zero. If we try to find the slope of this line by applying the slope formula, we get $\frac{6}{0}$ or $-\frac{6}{0}$, which has no value. Thus we say that the slope of this line is **undefined**.

Whenever someone says that the slope of a line is undefined, they are discussing a vertical line. Every line except a vertical line has a defined slope.

practice Find the equations of the lines that pass through the following pairs of points:

a. $(3, -5)$ and $(2, -1)$ **b.** $(-3, -3)$ and $(6, 5)$

problem set 106

1.
(94)
The passenger train headed north at 70 miles per hour at 6 a.m. At 8 a.m. the freight train headed south from the same station at 30 miles per hour. At what time will the trains be 440 miles apart? Begin by drawing a diagram of distances traveled and writing the distance equation.

2.
(92)
The sciolist headed for town at 30 miles per hour. Two hours later, the charlatan began his pursuit at 50 miles per hour. How long did it take the charlatan to catch the sciolist? Begin by drawing a diagram of distances traveled and writing the distance equation.

3.
(83)
There were quarters and dimes in profusion. Their value was $9.55, and there were 64 coins in all. How many were quarters and how many were dimes?

4.
(77)
Find three consecutive even integers such that if the sum of 5 and the second is multiplied by -7, the result is 11 greater than 5 times the opposite of the third.

5.
(58)
Seventeen percent of the mob had a propensity for jogging and the rest just wanted to walk. If 3825 wanted to jog, how many were in the mob?

6. Letha rolls two fair dice. Find the probability that the sum of the numbers rolled is
(70)

(a) 2   (b) greater than 2

Find the equation of the line that passes through the following pairs of points:

7. (2, 5) and (−4, −3)   **8.** (−2, −2) and (5, 5)
(106)   *(106)*

Factor by grouping:

9. $ab + 15 + 5a + 3b$ **10.** $ay + xy + ac + xc$
(105)   *(105)*

11. $3mx - 2p + 3px - 2m$ **12.** $kx - 15 - 5k + 3x$
(105)   *(105)*

13. $xpc + pc^2 + 4x + 4c$ **14.** $acb - ack + 2b - 2k$
(105)   *(105)*

15. Find y: $\dfrac{x}{y} + \dfrac{1}{m} = p$ **16.** Find c: $\dfrac{k}{m} + \dfrac{1}{c} = x$
(104)   *(104)*

17. Find b: $\dfrac{1}{b} + \dfrac{k}{x} = y$ **18.** Find m: $\dfrac{1}{m} + \dfrac{b}{c} = \dfrac{x}{y}$
(104)   *(104)*

19. Graph on a number line those real values of x that satisfy the inequality $-|x| + 4 > 2$.
(102)

Solve:

20. $\dfrac{12}{x} + \dfrac{1}{4x} = 7$ **21.** $\dfrac{9}{4x} = \dfrac{5}{x + 11}$
(103)   *(103)*

Add:

22. $\dfrac{4}{x^2 - 25} - \dfrac{x}{x - 5}$ **23.** $\dfrac{3x}{x^2 - x - 6} - \dfrac{3}{x - 3}$
(101)   *(101)*

24. Use a calculator when necessary.
(100)

(a) Round $\sqrt{11}$ to the nearest thousandth.

(b) Round $45{,}732.\overline{654}$ to the nearest ten thousand.

(c) Round $\frac{5}{9}$ to the nearest tenth.

Simplify:

25. $3\sqrt{30{,}000} - 5\sqrt{27} + 5\sqrt{3}(2\sqrt{3} - 2)$ **26.** (a) $\dfrac{6x + 6}{6}$ (b) $\dfrac{-3^{-2}}{(-2)^2}$
(84)   *(35,36)*

27. Use the Pythagorean theorem to find k.
(97)

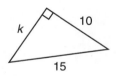

28. Find the distance between (−5, 3) and (4, −2).
(98)

29. Find x if $x = \dfrac{-b \pm \sqrt{b^2 - 4ac}}{2a}$ and $a = 1$, $b = -3$, and $c = 2$.
(62)

30. A base of the right prism 17 inches high is shown. Find the surface area of the right prism.
(15,60) All angles are right angles. Dimensions are in inches.

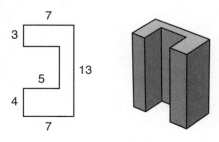

LESSON *107* *Line Parallel to a Given Line • Equation of a Line with a Given Slope*

107.A

line parallel to a given line

To find the slope of a line that is to be parallel to a given line, all that we need to do is realize that two parallel lines have the same slope.

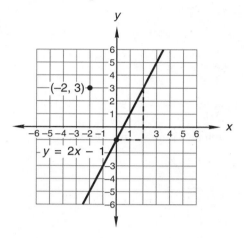

In the figure we have graphed the line whose equation is $y = 2x - 1$. We see from the equation and from the triangle drawn in the graph that the slope of this line is 2. **Any line that is parallel to this line must have the same slope of 2.** Thus if we are asked to find the equation of the line that is parallel to this line and that passes through $(-2, 3)$, we are already halfway home, for the slope of the new line has to be 2.

$$y = 2x + b$$

Now we can use the coordinates $(-2, 3)$ for x and y and find b algebraically.

$3 = 2(-2) + b$	replaced x and y with -2 and 3
$3 = -4 + b$	multiplied
$7 = b$	added 4 to both sides

So the equation of the line is

$$y = 2x + 7$$

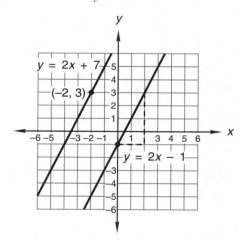

We have found the exact slope and the exact intercept. Estimated values for the slope and intercept will not be acceptable for this kind of problem.

example 107.1   Find the equation of the line through $(-1, -3)$ that is parallel to $4x + 3y = 7$.

solution   The equation of the new line is

$$y = mx + b$$

and we have to find m and b. **If the new line is to be parallel to the line $4x + 3y = 7$, the new line must have the same slope as the line $4x + 3y = 7$.** If we write $4x + 3y = 7$ in slope-intercept form, we find

$$y = -\frac{4}{3}x + \frac{7}{3}$$

and the slope of this line is $-\frac{4}{3}$. So the slope of the new line must be $-\frac{4}{3}$.

$$y = -\frac{4}{3}x + b$$

We find the value of b by using the coordinates $(-1, -3)$ for x and y and solving algebraically for b.

$$-3 = -\frac{4}{3}(-1) + b \qquad \text{substituted}$$

$$-\frac{9}{3} = \frac{4}{3} + b \qquad \text{multiplied}$$

$$-\frac{13}{3} = b \qquad \text{added } -\frac{4}{3} \text{ to both sides}$$

Thus the desired equation is

$$y = -\frac{4}{3}x - \frac{13}{3}$$

and again we have found the exact value of the slope and the exact value of the intercept.

107.B

equation of a line with a given slope

Finding the equation of a line with a given slope that passes through a given point is the easiest problem type of all. The slope of the desired equation is *given* in the statement of the problem. All we have to do is find the value of the intercept.

example 107.2   Find the equation of the line that passes through the point $(3, 4)$ and has a slope of $-\frac{3}{4}$.

solution   The equation of the line in question is $y = mx + b$, and we need to determine the proper values for m and b. The statement of the problem tells us that the slope is $-\frac{3}{4}$, and if we use this value for m in the equation, we find

$$y = -\frac{3}{4}x + b$$

If we use $(3, 4)$ for x and y in this equation, we can solve algebraically for b.

$$4 = -\frac{3}{4}(3) + b$$

$$4 = -\frac{9}{4} + b \quad \longrightarrow \quad \frac{16}{4} = -\frac{9}{4} + b \quad \longrightarrow \quad b = \frac{25}{4}$$

So the equation is

$$y = -\frac{3}{4}x + \frac{25}{4}$$

and the numbers $-\frac{3}{4}$ and $\frac{25}{4}$ are the exact values of the slope and the intercept.

example 107.3   Find the equation of the line that passes through the point (–5, 11) and has a slope of $\frac{1}{7}$.

solution   The statement of the problem gives us the slope, so we can write

$$y = \frac{1}{7}x + b$$

Now we use the values –5 and 11 for x and y and solve for b.

$$11 = \frac{1}{7}(-5) + b \quad \longrightarrow \quad \frac{77}{7} = -\frac{5}{7} + b \quad \longrightarrow \quad b = \frac{82}{7}$$

So the equation is

$$y = \frac{1}{7}x + \frac{82}{7}$$

and the numbers $\frac{1}{7}$ and $\frac{82}{7}$ are the exact values of the slope and the intercept.

example 107.4   Find the equation of the line that passes through the point (–50, 40) and has a slope of $-\frac{1}{2}$.

solution   Again we have been given the slope, so we can write

$$y = -\frac{1}{2}x + b$$

Now to find b, we replace y with 40 and x with –50 and solve.

$$40 = -\frac{1}{2}(-50) + b$$

$$40 = 25 + b$$

$$15 = b$$

Thus the desired equation is

$$y = -\frac{1}{2}x + 15$$

practice   Find the equation of the line that passes through:

   a.   The point (–1, 2) and is parallel to $y = -3x + 1$.

   b.   The point (–2, –3) and is parallel to $3x + 2y = 5$.

   c.   The point (2, 3) and has a slope of $-\frac{2}{5}$.

   d.   The point (–3, 7) and has a slope of $\frac{1}{4}$.

problem set 107

   1. *(92)*   Birthe rode to town in the bus at 20 miles per hour. Then she trotted back home at 8 miles per hour. If her total traveling time was 14 hours, how far was it to town? Begin by drawing a diagram of distances traveled and writing the distance equation.

   2. *(99)*   Soren had a 36-mile head start. If Erik caught him in 3 hours, how fast was Erik traveling if his speed was twice that of Soren's? Begin by drawing a diagram of distances traveled and writing the distance equation.

   3. *(58)*   Flexner marked the bench down $20 and sold it for 60 percent of the original price. What was the original price of the bench?

   4. *(83)*   Weir and Max put $75 in quarters and dimes in the box. There were 400 more dimes than quarters. How many coins of each type were there?

   5. *(77)*   Find three consecutive odd integers such that the product of –7 and the sum of the first and third is 27 greater than the product of 11 and the opposite of the second.

6. Find the equation of the line that passes through the point (–2, 3) and is parallel to the
(107) line whose equation is $y = 2x + 1$.

7. Find the equation of the line that passes through the point (0, 1) and is parallel to the line
(107) whose equation is $y = -\frac{1}{2}x - 3$.

8. Find the equation of the line that passes through the points (–3, –2) and (5, –3).
(106)

9. Find the equation of the line that passes through the points (5, –1) and (0, 0).
(106)

10. Find the distance between (–2, 3) and (4, 5).
(98)

Factor by grouping:

11. $km^2 + 2c - 2m^2 - kc$
(105)

12. $6a - xya - xyb + 6b$
(105)

13. $abx - 2yc + xc - 2yab$
(105)

14. $4xn + abn - abm - 4xm$
(105)

15. Find c: $\dfrac{a}{c} - \dfrac{1}{x} = b$
(104)

16. Find m: $\dfrac{k}{m} + \dfrac{x}{y} = p$
(104)

17. Graph on a number line those real values of x that satisfy the inequality $-4 - |x| \leq -4$.
(102)

Solve:

18. $\dfrac{7}{y} + \dfrac{3}{y - 2} = 0$
(103)

19. $\dfrac{x - 2}{3x} = \dfrac{4}{x} - \dfrac{1}{5}$
(103)

20. Use a calculator when necessary.
(100)

(a) Round $\sqrt{30}$ to the nearest hundredth.

(b) Round 4349.3766 to the nearest hundred.

(c) Round $\frac{3}{7}$ to the nearest ten-thousandth.

21. The graph of which of the following
(105) functions most resembles the shape to
the right?

(a) $f(x) = -|x|$

(b) $g(x) = |x|$

(c) $h(x) = \sqrt{x}$

(d) $k(x) = x^3$

22. Add: $\dfrac{9}{x^2 - 81} - \dfrac{x}{x - 9}$
(101)

23. Solve by factoring: $120 = -22x - x^2$
(88)

Simplify:

24. $\dfrac{(21{,}000 \times 10^{-42})(7{,}000{,}000)}{(0.0003 \times 10^{-21})(700 \times 10^{15})}$
(80)

25. $\sqrt{15} + 2\sqrt{3} \cdot 5\sqrt{5} + 2\sqrt{15}(\sqrt{15} - 3)$
(84)

26. Solve: $x^0 - 3x(2 - 4^0) - (-3) - 2(x - 3) = 3x - (-4)$
(31)

27. Find x if $x = \dfrac{-b \pm \sqrt{b^2 - 4ac}}{2a}$ and $\dfrac{a}{3} - 3 = 9$, $b = 7$, and $4c + 11 = 9$.
(62)

28. Simplify: (a) $\dfrac{-3^{-2}}{-(-3)^{-3}}$ (b) $\dfrac{6xy + 6xy^2}{6xy}$
(35,36)

29. Find the volume of the sphere shown
(91) whose radius is 5 cm.

30.
(72) A right circular cone has a base of radius 5 m and a height of 11 m, as shown. Find the volume of the right circular cone.

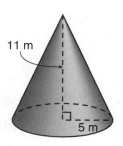

LESSON 108   *Square Roots Revisited • Radical Equations*

108.A

square roots revisited

Both –2 and +2 are square roots of 4 because

$$(-2)^2 = 4 \qquad \text{and} \qquad (+2)^2 = 4$$

But when we write $\sqrt{4}$, we are indicating the positive or principal square root of 4, which, of course, is the number 2.

> **DEFINITION OF SQUARE ROOT**
>
> If x is greater than zero, then $\sqrt{x}$ is the unique positive real number such that
>
> $$(\sqrt{x})^2 = x$$

We can state this definition in words by saying that the principal square root of a given positive number is that positive number which, multiplied by itself, yields the given number. Thus

$$\sqrt{2}\sqrt{2} = 2 \qquad \sqrt{7}\sqrt{7} = 7 \qquad \text{and} \qquad \sqrt{3.14}\sqrt{3.14} = 3.14$$

and also

$$(\sqrt{2})^2 = 2 \qquad (\sqrt{7})^2 = 7 \qquad \text{and} \qquad (\sqrt{3.14})^2 = 3.14$$

It is necessary to remember that algebraic expressions represent particular real numbers that are determined by the values assigned to the variables. Thus, if a particular algebraic expression represents a positive real number, the definition of the square root given in the box above applies to the expression. For example,

$$\left(\sqrt{x^2 + 4}\right)^2 = x^2 + 4 \qquad \left(\sqrt{\frac{amx^2}{p}}\right)^2 = \frac{amx^2}{p} \qquad (\sqrt{x + 6})^2 = x + 6$$

$$\left(\sqrt{x^4 + 3x^2 + 5}\right)^2 = x^4 + 3x^2 + 5$$

108.B

radical equations

There is only one number that will satisfy the equation $x = 2$, and that number is 2. If we replace x with 2 in this equation, we find

$$2 = 2$$

which is a true statement. If we square both sides of the original equation,

$$(x)^2 = (2)^2 \longrightarrow x^2 = 4$$

the result is the equation $x^2 = 4$. While the equation $x = 2$ had only one solution, the equation $x^2 = 4$ has two numbers that satisfy it, the numbers +2 and –2.

REPLACING x WITH +2   REPLACING x WITH –2

$$(+2)^2 = 4 \qquad\qquad (–2)^2 = 4$$

$$4 = 4 \qquad \text{True} \qquad 4 = 4 \qquad \text{True}$$

We began with the equation $x = 2$, whose only solution is 2. We squared both sides and got the equation $x^2 = 4$, which also has the number 2 as a solution but has another solution, which is the number –2. **It can be shown that if both sides of an equation are squared, all of the solutions to the original equation (if any exist) are also solutions to the resulting equation, but the reverse is not true, for all of the solutions of the resulting equation are not necessarily solutions of the original equation.**

example 108.1 Solve: $\sqrt{x - 2} + 3 = 0$

solution We wish to **isolate the radical** on one side of the equation so that we may square both sides of the equation. We begin by adding –3 to both sides of the equation and get

$$\sqrt{x - 2} = -3$$

Now we square both sides and get

$$(\sqrt{x - 2})^2 = (-3)^2 \longrightarrow x - 2 = 9 \longrightarrow x = 11$$

Now we must check our solution in the original equation.

$$\sqrt{11 - 2} + 3 = 0 \longrightarrow \sqrt{9} + 3 = 0 \longrightarrow 3 + 3 = 0 \longrightarrow 6 = 0 \quad \text{False}$$

We see that while 11 is a solution of the second equation, $x - 2 = 9$, it is not a solution to the original equation $\sqrt{x - 2} + 3 = 0$. Thus we see that there is no real number replacement for x that will satisfy the first equation, and we say that **the solution set of this equation is the empty set.**

example 108.2 Solve: $\sqrt{x - 2} - 6 = 0$

solution We first **isolate the radical** on one side by adding +6 to both sides of the equation.

$$\sqrt{x - 2} = 6$$

Now we square both sides to eliminate the radical and then solve the resulting equation.

$$(\sqrt{x - 2})^2 = (6)^2 \longrightarrow x - 2 = 36 \longrightarrow x = 38$$

Now we will check this solution in the original equation.

$$\sqrt{(38) - 2} - 6 = 0 \longrightarrow \sqrt{36} - 6 = 0 \longrightarrow 6 - 6 = 0 \longrightarrow 0 = 0 \quad \text{Check}$$

Thus $x = \mathbf{38}$ is a solution to the original equation.

example 108.3 Solve: $\sqrt{x^2 + 9} - 5 = 0$

solution First we **isolate the radical** and get

$$\sqrt{x^2 + 9} = 5$$

Now we eliminate the radical by squaring both sides of the equation.

$$\left(\sqrt{x^2 + 9}\right)^2 = (5)^2 \longrightarrow x^2 + 9 = 25$$

Now we will simplify, factor, and use the zero factor theorem to solve.

$$x^2 - 16 = 0 \quad \longrightarrow \quad (x + 4)(x - 4) = 0$$

$$\longrightarrow \quad x = 4 \qquad \text{or} \qquad x = -4$$

Since neither of these solutions to the second equation is guaranteed to be a solution of the original equation, both solutions must be checked in the original equation.

CHECK $x = +4$ CHECK $x = -4$

$$\sqrt{(4)^2 + 9} = 5 \qquad\qquad \sqrt{(-4)^2 + 9} = 5$$

$$\sqrt{25} = 5 \qquad\qquad\qquad \sqrt{25} = 5$$

$$5 = 5 \quad \text{Check} \qquad\qquad 5 = 5 \quad \text{Check}$$

Thus both $x = \mathbf{4}$ and $x = \mathbf{-4}$ are solutions.

example 108.4   Solve: $\sqrt{x - 1} - 3 + x = 0$

solution   We begin by adding $+3 - x$ to both sides of the equation to **isolate the radical** and get

$$\sqrt{x - 1} = 3 - x$$

Now we square both sides to eliminate the radical.

$$(\sqrt{x - 1})^2 = (3 - x)^2 \quad \longrightarrow \quad x - 1 = 9 - 6x + x^2$$

Next we simplify, factor, and use the zero factor theorem to solve.

$$x^2 - 7x + 10 = 0 \quad \longrightarrow \quad (x - 2)(x - 5) = 0$$

$$\longrightarrow \quad x = 2 \qquad \text{or} \qquad x = 5$$

Now we must check both 2 and 5 in the original equation.

CHECK $x = 2$ CHECK $x = 5$

$$\sqrt{x - 1} - 3 + x = 0 \qquad\qquad \sqrt{x - 1} - 3 + x = 0$$

$$\sqrt{2 - 1} - 3 + 2 = 0 \qquad\qquad \sqrt{5 - 1} - 3 + 5 = 0$$

$$1 - 3 + 2 = 0 \qquad\qquad\qquad 2 - 3 + 5 = 0$$

$$0 = 0 \quad \text{Check} \qquad\qquad 4 \neq 0 \quad \text{Does not check}$$

Thus $x = \mathbf{2}$ is a solution of the original equation, but $x = 5$ is not a solution of the original equation.

example 108.5   Solve: $\sqrt{2x - 3} = \sqrt{x + 2}$

solution   One radical expression is isolated on each side of the equation, so we begin by squaring both sides of the equation.

$$(\sqrt{2x - 3})^2 = (\sqrt{x + 2})^2 \quad \longrightarrow \quad 2x - 3 = x + 2 \quad \longrightarrow \quad x = 5$$

Now we will check $x = 5$ in the original equation.

$$\sqrt{2(5) - 3} = \sqrt{5 + 2} \quad \longrightarrow \quad \sqrt{7} = \sqrt{7} \qquad \text{Check}$$

Therefore, $x = \mathbf{5}$ is a solution to the original equation.

practice   Solve:

     a. $\sqrt{x - 6} - 3 = 0$ **b.** $\sqrt{x - 6} - 6 + x = 0$

problem set 108

     1. The doyenne walked to the meeting at 2 miles per hour and caught a ride home in an old
     (92) truck at 10 miles per hour. How far was it to the meeting place if her total traveling time
     was 18 hours? Begin by drawing a diagram of distances traveled and writing the distance
     equation.

2. The gun sounded, and 3 hours later Bill was 6 miles ahead of Rose. How fast did Rose
(99) run if Bill's speed was 10 miles per hour? Begin by drawing a diagram of distances
traveled and writing the distance equation.

3. Gold bricks sold for $400 each, while pyrite bricks were only $3 each. To stock his booth,
(89) Grimsby bought 123 bricks for $21,013. How many of each kind did he buy?

4. Roger and Gwenn picked 178 quarts of berries. If Roger picked 8 more quarts than
(90) Gwenn picked, how many quarts did Gwenn pick?

5. Carolyn has a purse that contains 6 silver coins and 3 gold coins. She draws one coin at
(73) random and then draws a second coin. What is the probability that the first coin is silver
and the second coin is gold

    (a) with replacement?   (b) without replacement?

6. The final exam grade of 94 was given the weight of 10 weekly grades. If the average of
(65) the 10 weekly grades was 76, what was the weighted average grade for the entire course?

Solve and check your answers.

7. $\sqrt{x^2 + 11} - 9 = 0$ **8.** $\sqrt{x - 3} - 4 = 0$
(108)   (108)

9. $\sqrt{4x - 5} = \sqrt{x + 4}$ **10.** $\sqrt{x + 1} + x - 11 = 0$
(108)   (108)

11. Find the equation of the line that passes through the point $(-1, 2)$ and is parallel to
(107) $y = -3x + 1$.

12. Find the equation of the line that passes through $(4, 2)$ and $(-5, -7)$.
(106)

Factor by grouping:

13. $rt^2 + 3m + 3r + t^2m$ **14.** $6c - xyc - xyd + 6d$
(105)   (105)

15. Find y: $\dfrac{x}{y} - \dfrac{1}{c} - d = k$ **16.** Find x: $\dfrac{x}{3} - \dfrac{2 + x}{5} = -3$
(104)   (103)

17. Use a calculator when necessary.
(100)

    (a) Round $\frac{\pi}{6}$ to the nearest thousandth.

    (b) Round $0.0\overline{374}$ to the nearest ten-thousandth.

    (c) Round $\sqrt{169}$ to the nearest ten.

18. Use the Pythagorean theorem to find c.   **19.** Find the equations of lines (a) and (b).
(97)   (75)

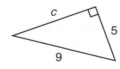
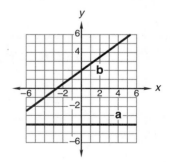

Add:

20. $\dfrac{y^{-1}}{x} + \dfrac{3}{yx} - \dfrac{2}{x + y}$ **21.** $\dfrac{3x + 2}{x - 4} - \dfrac{2x}{x^2 - 16}$
(68)   (101)

22. Solve by graphing and check: $\begin{cases} y = 3x \\ y = -x + 4 \end{cases}$
(81)

23. Simplify: $\dfrac{x^2 - 25}{x^2 - 12x + 35} \div \dfrac{x^2 + x - 6}{x^2 - 4x - 21}$
(93)

24. Divide: $\left(2x^3 + 3x^2 + 5x + 4\right) \div (x - 1)$
(86)

25. Find the domain and range of the func-
(82) tion shown.

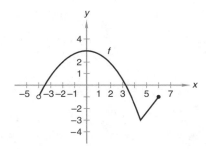

Simplify:

26. $\dfrac{xz^{-1} - z^{-2}}{az^{-1} - 3xz^{-2}}$
(68)

27. $-\left[\left(-2^0\right)\left(-3^2\right) - (-2) - \sqrt[5]{-32}\right] - [-3(-5 + 7)]$
(62)

28. Find x if $x = \dfrac{-b \pm \sqrt{b^2 - 4ac}}{2a}$ and $\dfrac{a}{7} - 3 = 0$, $b = -9$, and $8c + 13 = 7$.
(62)

29. Find the area of this figure. Corners
(8)   that look square are square. Dimen-
      sions are in inches.

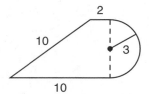

30. Find the surface area of this regular
(72) square pyramid. Dimensions are
      in feet.

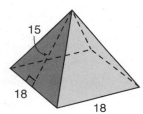

LESSON *109* *Advanced Trinomial Factoring*

Thus far, we have restricted our trinomial factoring to trinomials such as

$$x^2 - x - 6$$

in which the coefficient of the x^2 term is 1, and to trinomials that can be reduced to this form by factoring a common factor. Trinomials whose leading coefficient is not 1 can be formed by multiplying binomials, as we see here.

$$
\begin{array}{r}
3x + 2 \\
2x - 3 \\
\hline
6x^2 + 4x \\
-9x - 6 \\
\hline
6x^2 - 5x - 6
\end{array}
$$

We note that the first term of the trinomial is the product of the first two terms of the binomials and that the last term of the trinomial is the product of the last terms of the binomials, **but, alas, the coefficient of the middle term of the trinomial is not the sum of the last two terms of the binomials.** The middle term is the sum of the product of the first term of the first binomial and the last term of the second binomial and the product of the last term of the first binomial and the first term of the second binomial. It is easier to see this if we write the original indicated multiplication in horizontal form and note that the middle term is the sum of the products of the means and the extremes.[†]

$$\overbrace{(3x + 2)(2x - 3)}^{\text{extremes}} = 6x^2 - 5x - 6$$
$$\underbrace{}_{\text{means}}$$

example 109.1   Factor: $-7x - 15 + 2x^2$

solution   We begin by writing the trinomial in descending power of the variable.

$$2x^2 - 7x - 15$$

Now to factor $2x^2 - 7x - 15$, we remember that the product of the first terms of the binomials is $2x^2$, the product of the last terms of the binomials is -15, and the middle term is the sum of the products of the means and extremes. Since the term $2x^2$ is the product of the first terms of the binomial, we write

$$(2x \quad)(x \quad)$$

Now the four pairs of integral factors of -15 are (a) $+15$ and -1, (b) -15 and $+1$, (c) $+5$ and -3, and (d) -5 and $+3$. Now we must try each pair **twice** and see what middle term will result in each case.

For (15, −1) $(2x + 15)(x - 1)$ middle term is $13x$
                        $(2x - 1)(x + 15)$ middle term is $29x$

For (5, −3) $(2x + 5)(x - 3)$ middle term is $-x$
                        $(2x - 3)(x + 5)$ middle term is $7x$

For (−15, 1) $(2x - 15)(x + 1)$ middle term is $-13x$
                        $(2x + 1)(x - 15)$ middle term is $-29x$

For (−5, 3) $(2x - 5)(x + 3)$ middle term is x
                        $(2x + 3)(x - 5)$ middle term is $-7x$

We will use the last entry because the sum of the products of the means and the extremes is $-7x$. Thus we see that $2x^2 - 7x - 15$ can be factored over the integers as **$(2x + 3)(x - 5)$.**

We say that a polynomial can be "factored over the integers" if it can be factored into the product of linear terms where all the coefficients and constants are integers. All the problems in the problem sets will be contrived so that the polynomials can be factored over the integers.

[†]Mathematicians sometimes use the word *mean* to mean "middle" and the word *extreme* to mean "end." Thus the mean terms in the multiplication shown are the middle terms, and the extreme terms are the end terms.

example 109.2   Factor: $3x^2 - x - 2$

solution   We begin by writing as follows:

$$(3x \quad)(x \quad)$$

The second terms of the binomials must have a product of –2. The two pairs of possible integral factors of –2 are (a) –2 and +1, and (b) +2 and –1. We will try each pair **twice** and check to see what middle term results.

$$(3x + 1)(x - 2) \qquad \text{middle term is } -5x$$
$$(3x - 2)(x + 1) \qquad \text{middle term is } +x$$
$$(3x - 1)(x + 2) \qquad \text{middle term is } +5x$$
$$(3x + 2)(x - 1) \qquad \text{middle term is } -x$$

The sum of the products of the means and extremes of the last multiplication gives us a middle term of –x. Thus, these are the desired factors.

$$3x^2 - x - 2 = (3x + 2)(x - 1)$$

example 109.3   Factor: $5x^2 - 13x - 6$

solution   To begin we write as follows:

$$(5x \quad)(x \quad)$$

The pairs of integral factors of –6 are (a) +1 and –6, (b) –1 and +6, (c) +3 and –2, and (d) +2 and –3. We try each pair twice until we find that the pair we need is +2 and –3 because

$$5x^2 - 13x - 6 = (5x + 2)(x - 3)$$

practice   Factor:

a. $-11x - 21 + 2x^2$ **b.** $3x^2 + 5x - 2$

problem set 109

1. (92) The track team ran to the cemetery at 8 miles per hour and trotted back home at 6 miles per hour. If the total trip took 7 hours, how far was it to the cemetery? Begin by drawing a diagram of distances traveled and writing the distance equation.

2. (94) At 4 a.m. the northbound train left at 40 miles per hour. At 6 a.m. the southbound train left the same station at 60 miles per hour. At what time will the trains be 880 miles apart? Begin by drawing a diagram of distances traveled and writing the distance equation.

3. (89) Small pizzas were $3 and large pizzas were $5. To feed the throng, it was necessary to spend $475 for 125 pizzas. How many pizzas of each type were purchased?

4. (77) Mark thought of three consecutive odd integers. He added the first to twice the third and multiplied this sum by –3. The result was 3 less than the product of 8 and the opposite of the second. What were the numbers?

5. (39) The ratio of bees to moths was 13 to 5. If there were a total of 2610 bees and moths in the bar, how many were moths and how many were bees?

6. (58) Only 300 of the larvae metamorphosed into butterflies. If there were 2500 larvae at the outset, what percent became butterflies?

Factor the trinomials. Always begin by writing the trinomials in descending order of the variables and by factoring out the greatest common factor.

7. (109) $3x^2 - 14x - 5$ **8.** (71) $2x^2 + 8 + 10x$ **9.** (109) $18 - 15x + 2x^2$

10. (109) $-15 + 7x + 2x^2$ **11.** (71) $8x - 24 + 2x^2$ **12.** (71) $2x^2 - 24 - 8x$

13. (71) $2x^2 - 6x + 4$ **14.** (109) $2x^2 - 18 + 9x$ **15.** (71) $2x^2 + 4 + 6x$

Solve and check your answers.

16.
(108) $\sqrt{x + 3} = x - 3$ **17.**
(108) $\sqrt{3x - 3} = \sqrt{x + 7}$

18.
(107)   Find the equation of the line through $(4, -3)$ that is parallel to $y = -2x + 2$.

19.
(106)   Find the equation of the line that passes through the points $(2, 5)$ and $(-4, -3)$.

20.
(104)   Find x: $\dfrac{a}{c} + \dfrac{1}{x} = k$

Factor by grouping:

21.
(105) $y^2 t - 12m + 3mt - 4y^2$ **22.**
(105) $xm + 4m + xy + 4y$

23.
(97)   Use the Pythagorean theorem to find f.   **24.**
(75)   Find the equations of lines (a) and (b).

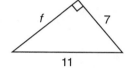

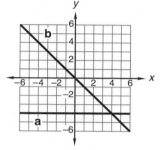

25.
(102)   Graph on a number line those real values of x that satisfy the inequality $3 - |x| \geq 1$.

26.
(81)   Solve by graphing: $\begin{cases} y = 2x + 2 \\ y = -x - 1 \end{cases}$ **27.**
(103)   Solve: $\dfrac{4}{p} - \dfrac{3}{p - 4} = 0$

28.
(93)   Simplify: $\dfrac{x^2 + 5x + 6}{x^3 + 7x^2 + 10x} \div \dfrac{x^3 + 11x^2 + 24x}{x^2 + 2x - 15}$

29.
(62)   Find x if $x = \dfrac{-b \pm \sqrt{b^2 - 4ac}}{2a}$ and $\dfrac{a}{3} = \dfrac{16}{12}$, $b = -6$, and $c - 9 = -13$.

30.
(20)   A base of the right solid 18 centimeters high is shown. Find the volume of the right solid. Dimensions are in centimeters.

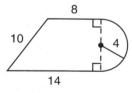

LESSON *110* *Vertical Shifts • Horizontal Shifts • Reflection About the x Axis • Combinations of Shifts and Reflections*

110.A
vertical shifts

In Lesson 95, we studied the shapes of some non-linear functions. We begin this lesson by recalling the graphs of the functions $f(x) = x^2$, $g(x) = x^3$, $h(x) = \sqrt{x}$, and $p(x) = |x|$. Some people refer to these functions as **parent functions.** Parent functions are the simplest form of a particular type of function. For example, $y = x^2$ is the parent function for quadratic functions.

Parent functions:

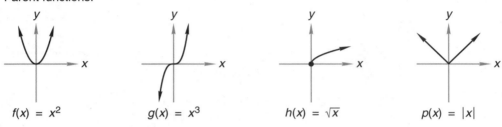

$f(x) = x^2$ $g(x) = x^3$ $h(x) = \sqrt{x}$ $p(x) = |x|$

In this section and the next section, we will show how modifying the equation of a parent function gives us the equation of a new function whose graph is the graph of the parent function translated vertically or horizontally. Suppose, for example, we create a new function (designated by capital letters) where we take the parent function and add one. We show below the graphs of these new functions.

New functions:

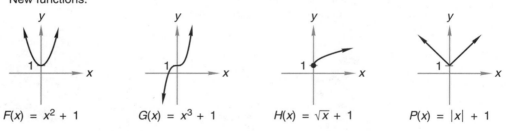

$F(x) = x^2 + 1$ $G(x) = x^3 + 1$ $H(x) = \sqrt{x} + 1$ $P(x) = |x| + 1$

Note that the graphs of the parent functions were all shifted vertically up by one unit when 1 was added to the equation of the function. Suppose we added –1 to each of the parent equations and defined the new functions to be the parent functions added to –1. We would see that the graphs of the parent functions would be shifted –1 unit vertically. In other words, the graphs of the parent functions would be shifted down one unit.

New functions:

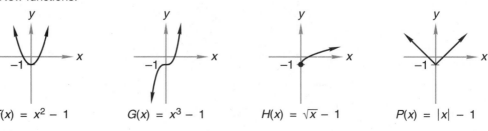

$F(x) = x^2 - 1$ $G(x) = x^3 - 1$ $H(x) = \sqrt{x} - 1$ $P(x) = |x| - 1$

In general, we find that if we add k to the equation of a function, the graph of the new function is the graph of the original function shifted vertically k units. We summarize this fact in the box below.

VERTICAL SHIFTS OF THE GRAPH OF A FUNCTION

The graph of the function of F where

$$F(x) = f(x) + k$$

is the graph of f shifted vertically k units.

The statement of the fact above may seem intimidating. When reading the statement, think of f as the original function and F as the new function. The statement simply says that the graph of the function F, which is the equation of $f(x)$ added to k, is the graph of f shifted k units vertically.

example 110.1   Sketch the graph of $F(x) = |x| + 3$.

solution   The graph of $F(x) = |x| + 3$ is the graph of $f(x) = |x|$ shifted vertically 3 units.

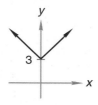

110.B

horizontal shifts   Let us return to our examination of the original functions f, g, h, and p shown at the beginning of the lesson. Suppose in every one of the equations we replace x with $x - 1$. We use capital letters to designate the new functions.

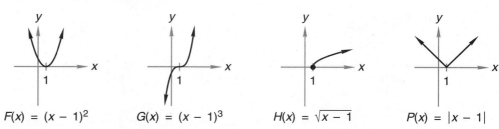

$F(x) = (x - 1)^2$ $G(x) = (x - 1)^3$ $H(x) = \sqrt{x - 1}$ $P(x) = |x - 1|$

We see that the graphs of F, G, H, and P are the graphs of f, g, h, and p shifted one unit to the right. We show below what happens when we replace x with $x + 1$ in the equations of f, g, h, and p.

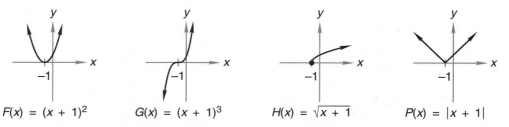

$F(x) = (x + 1)^2$ $G(x) = (x + 1)^3$ $H(x) = \sqrt{x + 1}$ $P(x) = |x + 1|$

We see from these examples that if we replace x with $x - k$ in the equations of functions f, g, h, and p that the graphs of the resulting functions F, G, H, and P will be the graphs of f, g, h, and p shifted horizontally by k units.

We summarize what we have learned in the box below.

HORIZONTAL SHIFTS OF THE GRAPH OF A FUNCTION

The graph of the function of F where

$$F(x) = f(x - k)$$

is the graph of f shifted horizontally k units.

Note that $x + 1$ is the same as $x - (-1)$. Thus, replacing x with $x + 1$ in the equation of f will cause the graph of the resulting equation F to be the graph of f shifted -1 unit horizontally. In other words, the graph of F is the graph of f shifted to the left one unit.

example 110.2   Sketch the graph of $F(x) = \sqrt{x - 3}$.

solution   The graph of F is the graph of $f(x) = \sqrt{x}$ shifted 3 units to the right.

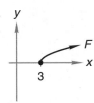

110.C
reflection about the *x* axis

Let us begin with the functions f, g, h, and p defined at the beginning of the lesson. Suppose we created new functions F, G, H, and P by multiplying f, g, h, and p by -1. The graphs of F, G, H, and P would be as shown.

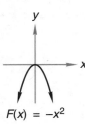
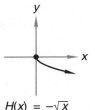
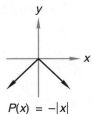

$F(x) = -x^2$ $G(x) = -x^3$ $H(x) = -\sqrt{x}$ $P(x) = -|x|$

We see that the graphs of f, g, h, and p have all been "flipped" to form the graphs of F, G, H, and P. We say that, for example, f and F are reflections of each other about the x axis.

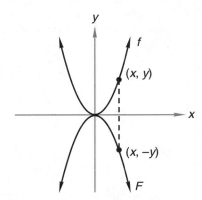

If we choose a point (x, y) on the graph of f, then the point $(x, -y)$ is on the graph of F, as shown above.

We summarize what we have learned in the box below.

REFLECTIONS ABOUT THE x AXIS

The graph of the function of F where

$$F(x) = -f(x)$$

is the graph of f reflected about the x axis.

We can think of "reflecting about the x axis" informally as "flipping upside-down."

example 110.3   Sketch the graph of $F(x) = -x^3$.

solution   We remember that the graph of $F(x) = -x^3$ is the reflection of the graph of $f(x) = x^3$ about the x axis.

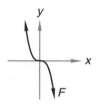

110.D

combinations of shifts and reflections

We shall examine some examples involving a combination of shifts and reflections.

example 110.4   Sketch the graph of $F(x) = -|x| + 3$.

solution   The graph of F is a combination of a reflection and a vertical shift. It is the reflection of the absolute value function about the x axis shifted up vertically 3 units.

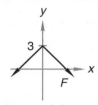

$$F(x) = -|x| + 3$$

We can show the process step-by-step below.

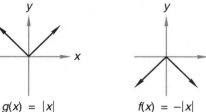

$g(x) = |x|$	$f(x) = -|x|$	$F(x) = -|x| + 3$
	Graph of g reflected about the x axis	Graph of f shifted up 3 units.

practice   Sketch the graphs of the following functions:

    a. $f(x) = x^2 + 3$ **b.** $g(x) = (x + 3)^2$ **c.** $h(x) = -x^2$

d. Suppose $f(x) = |x|$ and $F(x) = |x + 3|$. Which of the following statements is true?

   (1) The graph of F is the graph of f shifted vertically 3 units up.

   (2) The graph of F is the graph of f shifted horizontally 3 units to the right.

   (3) The graph of F is the graph of f shifted horizontally 3 units to the left.

   (4) The graph of F is the graph of f shifted vertically 3 units down.

**problem set
110**

1.
(99) The brigantine was sailing at full speed and was 30 miles at sea when Lord Nelson began to give chase at twice the speed of the brigantine. If Nelson caught up in 6 hours, how fast was the brigantine traveling? Begin by drawing a diagram of distances traveled and writing the distance equation.

2.
(99) The freight train headed north at 9 a.m. at 40 miles per hour. Two hours later, the express train headed north at 60 miles per hour. What time was it when the express was 20 miles further from the town than the freight? Begin by drawing a diagram of distances traveled and writing the distance equation.

3.
(76) Find three consecutive integers such that –7 times the sum of the first and the third is 12 greater than the product of 10 and the opposite of the second.

4.
(77) Find four consecutive odd integers such that the opposite of the sum of the first two is 4 greater than the product of the fourth and –4.

5.
(58) The sable was marked down 23 percent for the sale, yet its sale price was still $15,400. What was the original price of the sable?

6.
(58) When the announcer asked the question in the shopping mall, 60 percent of the responses were fatuous. If 3000 answers were not fatuous, how many answers were fatuous? How many people answered the question?

7.
(110) Sketch the graphs of the following functions:

   (a) $f(x) = x^2 - 1$ (b) $g(x) = (x - 1)^2$ (c) $h(x) = -x^2$

8.
(110) Suppose $f(x) = x^3$ and $F(x) = (x + 3)^3$. Which of the following statements is true?

   (a) The graph of F is the graph of f shifted vertically 3 units up.

   (b) The graph of F is the graph of f shifted horizontally 3 units to the right.

   (c) The graph of F is the graph of f shifted vertically 3 units down.

   (d) The graph of F is the graph of f shifted horizontally 3 units to the left.

Factor the trinomials. Always begin by writing the trinomials in descending order of the variables and by factoring out the greatest common factor.

9.
(109) $6y^2 - 15y - 36$ **10.**
(109) $3 + 2z^2 - 7z$ **11.**
(109) $2y^2 - 5y - 3$

Solve and check your answers:

12.
(108) $\sqrt{x + 2} - 4 = 1$ **13.**
(108) $\sqrt{x - 3} - 5 = 3$

14.
(107) Find the equation of the line through $(-2, 5)$ that is parallel to $y = \frac{2}{5}x - 3$.

15.
(107) Find the equation of the line that passes through $(-2, -3)$ and has a slope of $-\frac{1}{5}$.

Factor by grouping:

16.
(105) $a^2b - 2c^3m + mb - 2a^2c^3$ **17.**
(105) $6ax + 7am^3 + 12d^3x + 14m^3d^3$

18.
(104) Find c: $\dfrac{a}{b} + \dfrac{c}{d} = x$ **19.**
(103) Find x: $\dfrac{4}{x} - \dfrac{3}{x - 3} = 0$

20. Use a calculator whenever necessary.
(100)

(a) Round 9π to the nearest tenth.

(b) Round 0.50013642 to the nearest one.

(c) Round $\frac{12}{13}$ to the nearest hundred-thousandth.

21. Recall the appropriate Pythagorean triple to find the unknown length in each of the
(97) following right triangles:

(a) 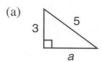 (b) 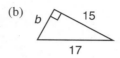 (c)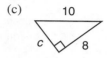

22. Graph on a number line those real values of x that satisfy the inequality $-2 - |x| > -5$.
(102)

23. Solve: $\dfrac{x}{4} - \dfrac{x-2}{3} = 7$ **24.** Add: $\dfrac{3x}{\left(x^2 + 7x + 10\right)} - \dfrac{3}{(x+5)^2}$
(78)   (101)

25. Which of the following diagrams, graphs, or sets of ordered pairs depict functions?
(84,87)

(a) $(5, 6), (6, 5), (7, 5), (-5, 6)$

(b) 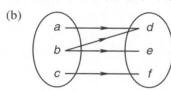   (c)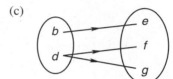

(d) 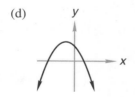   (e)

Simplify:

26. $p - 3p^0 - 2\left(p - 4^0\right) - (-3) - 2 = -3^0(2 - p)$ **27.** $\dfrac{x\left(x^{-2}y\right)^{-2}\left(x^{-2}y\right)x^{-2}}{\left(xy^{-2}\right)^{-2}x^{-2}y^{-4}yy^3x^2}$
(31)   (53)

28. Find x if $x = \dfrac{-b \pm \sqrt{b^2 - 4ac}}{2a}$ and if $a = 5$, $b = 7$, and $4c = 9$.
(62)

29. Find the surface area of the sphere
(91) shown whose radius is 6 in.

30. A right circular cone has a base of
(72) radius 7 ft and a slant height of 19 ft, as
shown. Find the surface area of the
right circular cone.

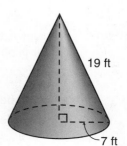

LESSON *111* *More on Conjunctions • Disjunctions*

111.A

more on conjunctions

We remember that a conjunction is a statement of two conditions, both of which must be met. The conjunction

$$4 < x < 14$$

tells us that x must be greater than 4 **and** that x must also be less than 14. Another way to state these conditions is to write

$$x > 4 \qquad \text{and} \qquad x < 14$$

The statement

$$4 < x + 3 < 10$$

is also a conjunction. It says that $x + 3$ is greater than 4 and that $x + 3$ is also less than 10. A good way to read these is to cover up the end numbers and the signs of inequality one at a time and read

$$4 < x + 3 \qquad \text{and} \qquad x + 3 < 10$$

We solve the inequality on the left and then solve the inequality on the right.

$$
\begin{array}{ll}
4 < x + 3 & x + 3 < 10 \\
\underline{-3 \qquad -3} & \underline{\quad -3 \quad -3} \\
1 < x & x < 7
\end{array}
\qquad \text{subtracted 3 from both sides}
$$

We could have simplified the conjunction in one step by adding -3 to all three parts of the inequality at the same time.

$$
\begin{array}{c}
4 < x + 3 < 10 \\
\underline{-3 \qquad -3 \quad -3} \\
1 < x < 7
\end{array}
$$

example 111.1 Graph: $-5 \le x - 4 < 2$; $D = \{\text{Integers}\}$

solution We will begin by simplifying the conjunction by adding $+4$ in three places.

$$
\begin{array}{c}
-5 \le x - 4 < 2 \\
\underline{+4 \qquad +4 \quad +4} \\
-1 \le x \qquad < 6
\end{array}
\qquad D = \{\text{Integers}\}
$$

The following graph shows all integers that are greater than or equal to -1 and are also less than 6.

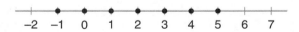

111.B

disjunctions

The conjunction is a statement of two conditions, both of which must be met. The conjunction uses or implies the use of the word **and**.

$$x > -2 \qquad \textbf{and} \qquad x \le 4 \qquad \text{can be written} \qquad -2 < x \le 4$$

A **disjunction** is also a statement of two conditions. A disjunction is satisfied if either of the conditions is met. A disjunction uses the word **or**.

$$x \le -2 \qquad \textbf{or} \qquad x > 1; \; D = \{\text{Reals}\}$$

This disjunction is satisfied by any real number that is less than or equal to –2. It is also satisfied by any real number that is greater than 1. This is a graph of the disjunction.

example 111.2   Graph $x \geq 3$ or $x \leq -2$; $D = \{\text{Integers}\}$.

solution   This disjunction is satisfied by any integer that is greater than or equal to 3. It is also satisfied by any integer that is less than or equal to –2.

example 111.3   Graph $x > 15$ or $x \leq 10$; $D = \{\text{Reals}\}$

solution   The word *or* tells us that there are two sets of numbers that satisfy this dual condition.

We have indicated all real numbers that are less than or equal to 10 *or* are greater than 15.

practice   Graph:

   a. $6 \leq x - 2 < 7$; $D = \{\text{Reals}\}$ **b.** $-x > -3$ or $x \geq 7$; $D = \{\text{Integers}\}$

problem set 111

1.
(99) Homer drove as fast as he could to get 60 miles ahead of Mae. If Homer drove at 17 miles per hour and accomplished his goal 20 hours after they both began, how fast did Mae drive? Begin by drawing a diagram of distances traveled and writing the distance equation.

2.
(92) Wanatobe walked to the moot at 4 miles per hour and then rode back home in a bus at 24 miles per hour. If her total traveling time was 14 hours, how far was it to the moot? Begin by drawing a diagram of distances traveled and writing the distance equation.

3.
(89) Peaches were $7 a bushel and apples were $6 a bushel. Harry sold $346 worth and sold 29 more bushels of peaches than apples. How many bushels of each did he sell?

4.
(33) The sum of 13 and the opposite of a number was multiplied by 3. This result was 11 less than twice the number. What was the number?

5.
(58) The dress was marked down 20 percent of its original price for the sale, and it still sold for $120. What would it sell for if the markdown of the original price was only 10 percent? (*Hint*: Find the original price and take 10 percent off that price.)

6.
(70) Stephen flips a fair coin 7 times and each time it comes up heads. What is the probability that on his next toss, it will come up tails?

7.
(110) Sketch the graph of the following functions:

   (a) $f(x) = \sqrt{x}$ (b) $g(x) = -\sqrt{x}$ (c) $h(x) = \sqrt{x-1}$ (d) $k(x) = 1 + \sqrt{x}$

8.
(110) Suppose $f(x) = x^2$ and $F(x) = x^2 + 1$. Which of the following statements is true?

   (a) The graph of F is the graph of f shifted vertically one unit up.

   (b) The graph of F is the graph of f shifted horizontally one unit to the right.

   (c) The graph of F is the graph of f shifted vertically one unit down.

   (d) The graph of F is the graph of f shifted horizontally one unit to the left.

9. Find the equation of the line that passes through (2, 5) and (−3, −4).
(106)

Graph the following conjunctions and disjunctions on a number line:

10. $0 \le x + 6 < 11$; $D = \{\text{Integers}\}$ **11.** $x < -1$ or $x \ge 5$; $D = \{\text{Reals}\}$
(111)   (111)

Factor the trinomials. Always begin by writing the trinomials in descending order of the variables and by factoring out the greatest common factor.

12. $3x^2 - 5 + 14x$ **13.** $-27 + 24x + 3x^2$
(109)   (71)

14. $9x - 5 + 2x^2$ **15.** $3x^2 - 7 - 20x$
(109)   (109)

Solve and check your answer:

16. $4\sqrt{y} = 20$ **17.** $\sqrt{x - 4} - 8 = 0$
(108)   (108)

18. Factor by grouping: $a^2c + bc + 3a^2 + 3b$
(105)

19. Find x: $\dfrac{a}{x} - \dfrac{1}{c} = \dfrac{1}{d}$ **20.** Solve by factoring: $45 = x^2 + 4x$
(104)   (88)

21. Graph on a number line those values of x that satisfy the inequality $-4 - |x| \le -4$.
(102)

22. Find the distance between (−5, 2) and (3, −7).
(98)

23. Find the domain of the function $f(x) = \sqrt{6 - x}$.
(82)

24. Indicate whether the following numbers are rational numbers or irrational numbers:
(61)

   (a) $\sqrt{3} + 5$ (b) 0.653214   (c) $\sqrt{\dfrac{225}{169}}$ (d) $\dfrac{\pi}{7}$

Simplify:

25. $4\sqrt{2}\left(5\sqrt{2} - 2\sqrt{12}\right)$ **26.** $\dfrac{-3^{-3}(-3)^{-2}}{3^{-2}}$
(84)   (36)

27. Expand by using the distributive property. Write the answer with all exponents positive.
(40)

$$\frac{x^{-2}a^2}{y}\left(\frac{ya^{-2}}{x^{-2}} - \frac{3x^{-2}a^2}{y} - \frac{x^2a^{-2}}{y^{-1}}\right)$$

28. Find x if $x = \dfrac{-b \pm \sqrt{b^2 - 4ac}}{2a}$ and if $a = -\dfrac{1}{2}$, $b = -1$, and $4c + 7 = 37$.
(62)

29. Find the perimeter of this figure.
(3)   Dimensions are in centimeters.

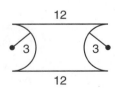

30. Find the volume of this right triangular
(20,60)   prism. Dimensions are in meters.

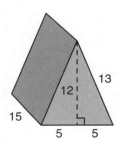

LESSON 112 *More on Multiplication of Radical Expressions*

Thus far, our most advanced radical multiplication problem has been of the form

$$\sqrt{3}(5 + \sqrt{12})$$

This notation indicates that $\sqrt{3}$ is to be multiplied by both of the terms inside the parentheses and that the products are to be added.

$$\sqrt{3}(5 + \sqrt{12}) = 5\sqrt{3} + \sqrt{36} = 5\sqrt{3} + 6$$

In this lesson, we will consider problems of the same form as

$$(4 + \sqrt{3})(5 + \sqrt{12})$$

We have four multiplications indicated. Both 4 and $\sqrt{3}$ must be multiplied by each term in the second parentheses and the four products can be simplified as shown here.

$$(4 + \sqrt{3})(5 + \sqrt{12}) = 4 \cdot 5 + 4\sqrt{12} + 5\sqrt{3} + \sqrt{3} \cdot \sqrt{12}$$
$$= 20 + 8\sqrt{3} + 5\sqrt{3} + 6$$
$$= 26 + 13\sqrt{3}$$

example 112.1 Multiply: $(2 + \sqrt{2})(3 + \sqrt{8})$

solution We will multiply 2 and $\sqrt{2}$ by both numbers in the second parentheses and simplify the result.

$$2 \cdot 3 + 2\sqrt{8} + 3\sqrt{2} + \sqrt{2} \cdot \sqrt{8} = 6 + 4\sqrt{2} + 3\sqrt{2} + 4$$
$$= \mathbf{10 + 7\sqrt{2}}$$

example 112.2 Multiply: $(4 + \sqrt{5})(2 - 2\sqrt{5})$

solution We have four multiplications to perform, which are

$$4(2) + 4(-2\sqrt{5}) + \sqrt{5}(2) + \sqrt{5}(-2\sqrt{5})$$

Now we multiply and simplify the results.

$$8 - 8\sqrt{5} + 2\sqrt{5} - 10 = \mathbf{-2 - 6\sqrt{5}}$$

example 112.3 Multiply: $(2 + \sqrt{2})(3 + 2\sqrt{2})$

solution We perform the multiplication and then simplify by adding like terms.

$$6 + 4\sqrt{2} + 3\sqrt{2} + 4 = \mathbf{10 + 7\sqrt{2}}$$

example 112.4 Expand: $(\sqrt{2}x + \sqrt{3}y)^2$

solution We rewrite the problem as $(\sqrt{2}x + \sqrt{3}y)(\sqrt{2}x + \sqrt{3}y)$. Now we perform the four multiplications and get

$$2x^2 + \sqrt{6}xy + \sqrt{6}xy + 3y^2$$

Now we add like terms and get

$$\mathbf{2x^2 + 2\sqrt{6}xy + 3y^2}$$

practice Multiply:

a. $(5 + \sqrt{2})(3 + \sqrt{8})$ **b.** $(2 + \sqrt{5})(4 - 3\sqrt{5})$

c. $(\sqrt{2} + \sqrt{5})^2$ **d.** $(\sqrt{2}x + \sqrt{7}y)^2$

problem set
112

1. The northbound bus had been on the road at 50 miles per hour for 4 hours before the
(94) southbound bus left the same station at 45 miles per hour. How long was the southbound
bus on the road before the buses were 580 miles apart? Begin by drawing a diagram of
distances traveled and writing the distance equation.

2. Judy walked into the city at 5 kilometers per hour and then rode a bus back home at
(92) 30 kilometers per hour. It was a long trip—she spent 21 hours traveling. How far did she
walk? Begin by drawing a diagram of distances traveled and writing the distance
equation.

3. Maxine bought 176 stamps for $10.75. She bought some 5-cent stamps and some 20-cent
(89) stamps. How many of each kind did she buy?

4. Of the 1200 displays at the flower show, 300 had at least 1 rose. What fraction of the
(77) displays did not contain any roses?

5. The ruler heard requests from all 195 subjects. If the ratio of haves to have-nots in the
(39) kingdom was 11 to 2, how many of these subjects were haves?

6. Nancy has a box that contains 5 red marbles and 4 blue marbles. She randomly draws
(73) 2 marbles, one after the other without replacement. What is the probability that the first
marble drawn is red and the second marble drawn is blue?

7. Sketch the graphs of the following functions:
(110)

   (a) $f(x) = x^3$ (b) $g(x) = -x^3$ (c) $h(x) = x^3 - 1$ (d) $k(x) = (x + 1)^3$

8. Suppose $f(x) = |x|$ and $F(x) = |x - 2|$. Which of the following statements is true?
(110)

   (a) The graph of F is the graph of f shifted vertically two units up.

   (b) The graph of F is the graph of f shifted horizontally two units to the right.

   (c) The graph of F is the graph of f shifted vertically two units down.

   (d) The graph of F is the graph of f shifted horizontally two units to the left.

9. Multiply: (a) $\left(2 - 3\sqrt{12}\right)\left(3 + 2\sqrt{12}\right)$ (b) $\left(\sqrt{2a} - \sqrt{3p}\right)^2$
(112)

10. Find the equation of the line that passes through (3, 1) and (–2, –4).
(106)

11. Find the equation of the line that passes through the point (–2, –3) and is parallel to the
(107) line $y = -\frac{2}{3}x + 5$.

Graph the following conjunctions and disjunctions on number lines:

12. $4 \leq x - 3 < 6$; $D = \{$Integers$\}$
(111)

13. $x + 2 < 5$ or $x + 2 \geq 6$; $D = \{$Reals$\}$
(111)

Factor the trinomials. Always begin by writing the trinomials in descending order of the
variables and by factoring out the greatest common factor.

14. $2x^2 - 6 - 4x$ 15. $3x^2 - 4 - x$ 16. $3x^2 + 28x - 20$
(71)   (109)   (109)

Solve and check your answers:

17. $2\sqrt{x} - 4 = 3$ 18. $\sqrt{x + 5} - 3 = 2$
(108)   (108)

Factor by grouping:

19. $xr + ax - br - ab$ 20. $xy + 3y - x^2 - 3x$
(105)   (105)

Graph on a number line those real values of x that satisfy the following inequalities:

21. $-|x| + 2 \geq -1$ 22. $-2 < x + 1 \leq 2$
(102)   (111)

23. Find m: $\dfrac{a}{b} + \dfrac{x}{m} - \dfrac{1}{c} = p$
(104)

24. Solve by graphing: $\begin{cases} y = -x + 3 \\ y = -2 \end{cases}$
(81)

25. Find the domain and range of the function f whose graph is shown.
(82)

26. Find the equations of lines (a) and (b).
(75)

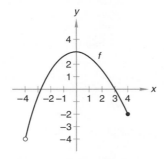

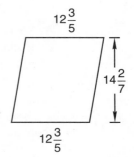

27. Divide: $(x^3 - 2x - 4) \div (x + 2)$
(86)

28. Add: $\dfrac{5x + 2}{x - 3} - \dfrac{2x + 2}{x^2 - 9}$
(101)

29. Find the area of this parallelogram. Dimensions are in inches.
(8)

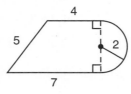

$12\dfrac{3}{5}$

$14\dfrac{2}{7}$

$12\dfrac{3}{5}$

30. A base of the right solid 9 feet high is shown. Find the surface area of the right solid. Dimensions are in feet.
(15)

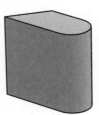

LESSON *113*   *Direct Variation • Inverse Variation*

113.A

direct variation

Suppose that in every classroom of a particular school, there are twice as many boys as there are girls. We can express this relationship mathematically by writing the equation

$$B = 2G$$

where B stands for the number of boys and G stands for the number of girls. Then we can use the equation to find the number of boys in any classroom if we are told the number of girls in that room, or to find the number of girls in a room if we are told the number of boys in that room.

In another school there are three times as many boys in each room as there are girls. For this school, the relationship can be expressed mathematically by writing

$$B = 3G$$

In the equation for the first school, we had the variables B and G and the constant was the number 2. In the equation for the other school, the equation is the same equation except that the constant is the number 3. The general form of the relationship is

$$B = kG$$

where k represents the constant for any particular school.

We call a relationship such as this, where one variable is expressed as a constant times another variable, a *direct variation* or a *direct proportion*, and the constant in the equation is called the *constant of proportionality*.

If we consider a third school and are told

1. That the number of boys in any room **varies directly** as the number of girls in the room, or
2. That the number of boys in any room **is directly proportional to** the number of girls in the room,

we have been told that the relationship between the number of boys and girls in any room in the school may be stated mathematically as

$$B = kG$$

Before we can solve any problem, we need to know the constant of proportionality for this school. If we are told the number of boys and girls in any room in the school, we can use these values in the equation to solve for k. If there are 30 boys and 5 girls in one room and we use these values for B and G in the equation, we find

$$30 = k(5) \qquad \text{and thus} \qquad k = 6$$

Since we have found the constant for this school, we may write the relationship for this school as

$$B = 6G$$

Now, if we are given the number of girls in any room in this school, we can solve for the number of boys; conversely, we can find the number of girls if we are given the number of boys.

The key to this type of problem is recognizing that the verbal statement denotes a direct variation or a direct proportion and realizing the equation that is implied by this statement. We will give some examples here. On the left is the key verbal statement, and on the right is the equation that is implied by the statement.

STATEMENT	EQUATION
The weight of a substance **varies directly** as the volume of the substance.	$W = kV$
Force **varies directly** as the current.	$F = kC$
The distance traveled **varies directly** as the time.	$D = kT$

The words **directly proportional** imply the same equation as do the words **varies directly.**

STATEMENT	EQUATION
The circumference of a circle is **directly proportional** to the length of the radius.	$C = kR$
The volume of a right circular cylinder of fixed radius is **directly proportional** to its height.	$V = kH$

In each of the relationships just discussed, the equation contained an unknown **constant of proportionality k. We begin the solution of any direct variation problem by finding the constant of proportionality for that problem.** Then we can solve for the value of one unknown if we are given the value of the other unknown.

example 113.1   The mass of a substance varies directly as the volume of the substance. If the mass of 2 liters of the substance is 10 kilograms, what will be the volume of 35 kilograms of the substance?

solution   We will solve the problem in *four steps*.

Step 1: Recognize that the words **varies directly** imply the relationship

$$M = kV$$

Step 2: Reread the problem to find the values of M and V that can be used to find the value of k. Use these values to solve for k.

$$(10) = k(2) \longrightarrow k = 5$$

Step 3: Replace k in the equation with the value we have found.

$$M = 5V$$

Step 4: Reread the problem to find that we are asked to find the value of V if M is 35. We replace M in the equation with 35 and solve for V by dividing by 5.

$$35 = 5V \longrightarrow \frac{35}{5} = \frac{\cancel{5}V}{\cancel{5}} \longrightarrow V = \textbf{7 liters}$$

example 113.2   The distance traversed by a car traveling at a constant speed is directly proportional to the time spent traveling. If the car goes 75 kilometers in 5 hours, how far will it go in 7 hours?

solution   We will use the same four steps.

Step 1: $D = kT$ write the equation

Step 2: $75 = k(5) \longrightarrow k = 15$ solve for k

Step 3: $D = 15T$ put k in the equation

Step 4: $D = (15)(7) \longrightarrow D = \textbf{105 km}$ solve for D

example 113.3   Under certain conditions the pressure of a gas varies directly as the temperature. When the pressure is 800 pascals, the temperature is 400 K. What is the temperature when the pressure is 400 pascals?

solution   Again we will use four steps in our solution.

Step 1: $P = kT$ write the equation

Step 2: $800 = k(400) \longrightarrow k = 2$ solve for k

Step 3: $P = 2T$ put k in the equation

Step 4: $400 = 2T \longrightarrow T = \textbf{200 K}$ substitute 400 for p and solve for T

113.B

inverse variation

When a problem states that one variable **varies inversely** as the other variable or that the value of one variable is **inversely proportional** to the value of the other variable, an equation of the form

$$V = \frac{k}{W}$$

is implied, where k is the constant of proportionality and V and W are the two variables. If we look at the equations for direct variation and inverse variation

DIRECT VARIATION EQUATION   INVERSE VARIATION EQUATION

$$V = kW \qquad\qquad\qquad V = \frac{k}{W}$$

we see that each equation contains two variables and one constant of proportionality k. In both equations, the constant k is the numerator! **In a direct variation equation, both variables are in the numerator; in an inverse variation equation, one variable is in the numerator and the other variable is in the denominator!**

STATEMENT	EQUATION
The pressure of a perfect gas **varies inversely** as the volume.	$P = \dfrac{k}{V}$
The current **varies inversely** as the resistance.	$C = \dfrac{k}{R}$
The velocity is **inversely proportional** to the time.	$V = \dfrac{k}{T}$

Inverse variation problems are solved in the same way as the direct variation problems. First we recognize the equation implied by the statement of inverse variation. Then we find the constant of proportionality for the problem and use this constant in the equation to find the final solution.

example 113.4   Under certain conditions, the pressure of a perfect gas varies inversely as the volume. When the pressure of a quantity of gas is 7 pascals, the volume is 75 liters. What would be the volume if the pressure is increased to 15 pascals?

solution   We will use the same four steps that we used for direct variation problems.

Step 1: $P = \dfrac{k}{V}$ write the equation

Step 2: $7 = \dfrac{k}{75} \quad\longrightarrow\quad k = 525$ solve for k

Step 3: $P = \dfrac{525}{V}$ substitute 525 for k

Step 4: $15 = \dfrac{525}{V} \quad\longrightarrow\quad V = \dfrac{525}{15}$ substitute 15 for P and solve for V

$\longrightarrow\quad V = \textbf{35 liters}$

example 113.5   To travel a fixed distance, the rate is inversely proportional to the time required. When the rate is 60 kilometers per hour, the time required is 4 hours. What would be the time required for the same distance if the rate were increased to 80 kilometers per hour?

solution   We will use the same four steps.

Step 1: $R = \dfrac{k}{T}$ write the equation

Step 2: $60 = \dfrac{k}{4}$ $\longrightarrow$ $k = 240$ solve for k

Step 3: $R = \dfrac{240}{T}$ substitute 240 for k

Step 4: $80 = \dfrac{240}{T}$ $\longrightarrow$ $T = \dfrac{240}{80}$ substitute 80 for R and solve for T

$\longrightarrow$ $T = 3\,\text{hr}$

practice   **a.**   The mass of a substance varies directly as the volume of the substance. If a mass of 30 kg of a substance has a volume of 6 liters, what is the volume of 65 kg of the substance?

b.   Under certain conditions the pressure of a gas varies directly as the temperature. When the pressure is 1200 pascals, the temperature is 300 K. What is the temperature when the pressure is 300 pascals?

c.   Under certain conditions, the pressure of an ideal gas varies inversely as the volume. When the pressure of a quantity of gas is 9 pascals, the volume is 100 liters. What would be the volume if the pressure is increased to 20 pascals?

problem set 113

1.
(113)   To travel a given distance, the rate is inversely proportional to the time required. Tom noted that if he drove home at 100 kilometers per hour, the trip would take 5 hours. How long would it take him to drive home if he drove at 125 kilometers per hour?

2.
(113)   The mass of a substance varies directly as the volume of the substance. If the mass of 7 liters of the substance is 42 kilograms, what will be the volume of 63 kilograms of the substance?

3.
(92)   Wormley ran to the store at 8 kilometers per hour and rode a bus home at 20 kilometers per hour. If his round trip traveling time was 7 hours, how far was it to the store? Begin by drawing a diagram of distances traveled and writing the distance equation.

4.
(113)   The distance traversed by a car traveling at a constant speed is directly proportional to the time spent traveling. If the car goes 90 kilometers in 9 hours, how far will it go in 5 hours?

5.
(89)   The red carnations sold for 50 cents a bunch and the white carnations sold for 40 cents a bunch. Mike bought 27 bunches for $12.30. How many of each kind did he get?

6.
(113)   Peaches varied directly as apples. When there were 40 peaches, there were 120 apples. How many apples went with 500 peaches?

7.
(110)   Sketch the graphs of the following functions:

(a) $f(x) = |x|$ (b) $g(x) = -|x|$ (c) $h(x) = 1 + |x|$ (d) $k(x) = |x + 1|$

8.
(110)   Suppose $f(x) = \sqrt{x}$ and $F(x) = \sqrt{x} - 1$. Which of the following statements is true?

(a)   The graph of F is the graph of f shifted vertically 1 unit up.

(b)   The graph of F is the graph of f shifted horizontally 1 unit to the right.

(c)   The graph of F is the graph of f shifted vertically 1 unit down.

(d)   The graph of F is the graph of f shifted horizontally 1 unit to the left.

Multiply:

9.
(112) $(2 + \sqrt{3})(4 - 5\sqrt{12})$ **10.**
(112) $(2 + \sqrt{2})(4 - 3\sqrt{8})$ **11.**
(112) $(5 + \sqrt{6})(2 - 3\sqrt{24})$

Graph the following conjunctions and disjunctions on number lines:

12. $-2 \leq x + 5 < 3$; $D = \{\text{Reals}\}$
(111)

13. $x + 2 \geq 5$ or $x + 3 \leq 0$; $D = \{\text{Reals}\}$
(111)

Factor the trinomials. Always begin by writing the trinomials in descending order of the variables and by factoring out the greatest common factor.

14. $12x^2 + 60x + 72$ **15.** $40 + 5x^2 - 30x$ **16.** $3r^2 - 9r - 390$
(71)   (71)   (71)

Solve and check your answers:

17. $2\sqrt{x} + 2 = 5$ **18.** $\sqrt{x - 4} - 2 = 6$
(108)   (108)

19. Find y: $\dfrac{x}{y} - m + \dfrac{1}{c} = k$ **20.** Find m: $\dfrac{m + 5}{m} = \dfrac{3}{2m} - \dfrac{2}{5}$
(104)   (103)

21. Find the distance between $(-5, -2)$ and $(3, 7)$.
(106)

22. Factor by grouping: $xy - 3y - 2x + 6$
(105)

23. Solve by factoring: $-8 = -x^2 + 7x$
(88)

24. Find the equation of the line that passes through $(-2, -5)$ and is parallel to $y = 2x + 4$.
(107)

25. Find k.
(97)

Simplify:

26. $\dfrac{(35{,}000 \times 10^{-41})(700 \times 10^{14})}{(7000 \times 10^{21})(0.00005 \times 10^{15})}$ **27.** $\dfrac{(x^{-2})^{-3}(x^{-2}y^2)}{x^2yy^0(x^0y)^{-2}}$
(80)   (53)

28. Find x if $x = \dfrac{-b \pm \sqrt{b^2 - 4ac}}{2a}$ and if $a = 3$, $b = 3$, and $4c = 1$.
(62)

29. Find the area of this trapezoid. Dimen-
(8)   sions are in centimeters.

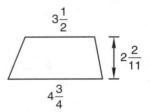

30. A base of the right solid 3 meters high is shown. Find the surface area and the volume of
(15,20) the right solid. Dimensions are in meters.

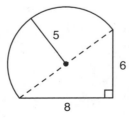   

LESSON 114   *Exponential Key • Exponential Growth • Using the Graphing Calculator to Graph Exponential Functions*

114.A
exponential key

The calculator provides a convenient and powerful means of performing calculations. One function that calculators can perform is exponentiation. That is, the calculator can be used to raise one number to the power of another number. For example, a calculator can help us evaluate the following expressions:

$$3^7 \qquad (5.5)^4 \qquad (3.14)^3 \qquad 3^{2.5}$$

Which key(s) on the calculator to use to perform these calculations depends on the calculator. On most scientific calculators, the y^x key is the one to use to perform exponentiation. On some graphing calculators, the key to use for exponentiation is the $\wedge$ key.

We use either a scientific calculator or a graphing calculator to compute 2^5, which we know to be 32.

	SCIENTIFIC CALCULATOR			GRAPHING CALCULATOR	
	Key	Display		Key	Display
Step 1: press	2	2	press	2	2
Step 2: press	y^x	2	press	$\wedge$	2^
Step 3: press	5	5	press	5	2^5
Step 4: press	=	32	press	ENTER	32

The actual keystrokes required on the various calculators may differ a little; however, the answer to a particular problem will be the same for all calculators.

example 114.1   Evaluate $(1.06)^8$ using a calculator.

solution   We show the keystrokes required by the most commonly used calculators.

	SCIENTIFIC CALCULATOR			GRAPHING CALCULATOR	
	Key(s)	Display		Key(s)	Display
Step 1: press	1 . 0 6	1.06	press	1 . 0 6	1.06
Step 2: press	y^x	1.06	press	$\wedge$	1.06^
Step 3: press	8	8	press	8	1.06^8
Step 4: press	=	**1.593848075**	press	ENTER	**1.593848075**

114.B
exponential growth

Jimmy had 150 rabbits. If the number of rabbits doubled every year, he would have 300 rabbits at the end of 1 year, 600 at the end of 2 years, and so forth. We use R_0 to indicate the number of rabbits in the beginning, we use R_1 to indicate the number of rabbits at the end of the first year, etc.

$$\text{In the beginning: } R_0 = 150 \qquad\qquad = 150 \cdot 2^0$$
$$\text{At the end of 1 year: } R_1 = 150 \cdot 2 \qquad = 150 \cdot 2$$
$$\text{At the end of 2 years: } R_2 = 150 \cdot 2 \cdot 2 \qquad = 150 \cdot 2^2$$
$$\text{At the end of 3 years: } R_3 = 150 \cdot 2 \cdot 2 \cdot 2 = 150 \cdot 2^3$$
$$\text{At the end of } t \text{ years: } R_t = 150 \cdot 2^t$$

The graph of the number of rabbits as time goes on looks like this:

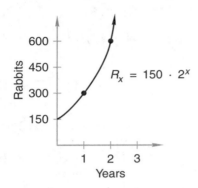

This type of growth is called **exponential growth.** The general form of the equation describing the number of rabbits at the end of t years has the equation

$$R_t = R_0 y^t \qquad \text{or in function notation} \qquad R(t) = R_0 y^t$$

where R_0 is the number of rabbits initially (or in other words, when $t = 0$). The number y is called the **growth multiplier.**

Equations such as the one discussed describing the growth of the number of rabbits are called **exponential equations.** One area in which exponential equations arise is in banking, as we show below.

A bank will pay you to let the bank use your money. Each year the bank will pay you a percentage of the amount you deposit. The amount you deposit is called the **principal.** The amount the bank pays you is called the **interest.** If you deposit $100 at 4 percent annual interest, at the end of 1 year the bank will give you back your $100 plus 4 percent of $100, which is $4. This equals 1.04 times your original deposit.

Principal: $100

At the end of 1st year, you have: ($100)(1.04)

Continuing this process, we see that at the end of the nth year, the amount you would have would be

$$\$100(1.04)^n$$

In the case discussed, the interest rate of 4% is **compounded annually.** This means that the interest payment is made once a year at the end of each year, and that the interest calculation is applied to the total amount accumulated and not just to the principal. In general, if a bank pays an interest rate of r (which is a percent expressed as decimal) compounded annually and if A_0 is the starting amount of money, then the amount of money that would be in the bank after t years would be

$$A_t = A_0(1 + r)^t \qquad \text{or in function notation} \qquad A(t) = A_0(1 + r)^t$$

We see that the equation has the form

$$A_t = A_0 y^t$$

and so is an exponential equation.

example 114.2   The number of bacteria in the dish tripled every month. If there were 2500 bacteria at first, how many bacteria were there in 10 months?

solution   The form of the equation is

$$A_t = A_0 y^t$$

where y is the growth multiplier (3), t is the number of months (10), and A_0 is the starting number of bacteria (2500). Now we substitute.

$$A_{10} = 2500(3)^{10}$$

We use the $\boxed{y^x}$ key to evaluate 3^{10}.

ENTER	DISPLAY
$\boxed{3}$	3
$\boxed{y^x}$	3
$\boxed{1}\ \boxed{0}$	10
$\boxed{=}$	59049

Thus our answer is

$$2500(59{,}049) = \mathbf{1.4762 \times 10^8}$$

example 114.3   James deposited \$500 at 7 percent interest compounded annually. How much money did he have after 14 years? How much interest did he earn?

solution   We show the equation describing how much money is in a bank account, where A_0 is the opening amount in the account, r is the interest rate expressed as a decimal, and A_t is the amount in the account at the end of t years. The formula assumes the interest rate is compounded annually.

$$A_t = A_0(1 + r)^t$$

Now we substitute and get

$$A_{14} = \$500(1 + 0.07)^{14}$$

First we evaluate $(1.07)^{14}$.

ENTER	DISPLAY
$\boxed{1}\ \boxed{.}\ \boxed{0}\ \boxed{7}$	1.07
$\boxed{y^x}$	1.07
$\boxed{1}\ \boxed{4}$	14
$\boxed{=}$	2.57853415

We multiply this by \$500, round to the nearest cent, and get

\$1289.27

In 14 years the amount on deposit went from \$500 to \$1289.27! Since James began with \$500 and ended with \$1289.27, the interest he earned was

$$\$1289.27 - \$500 = \mathbf{\$789.27}$$

114.C
using the graphing calculator to graph exponential functions

There are a plethora of graphing calculators on the market, each with its own particular instructions for use. Instead of focusing on any particular graphing calculator, we will speak about general features that are common to most all of the graphing calculators.

We will use the graphing calculator as a tool for graphing exponential functions. For example, let us graph the function

$$y = 2^x$$

We first enter the function into the calculator. The equation may look as follows, depending on the type of calculator:

$$Y_1 = 2^{\wedge}x$$

$$F1(x) = 2^{\wedge}x$$

The next step is to define the range of values of the x coordinate and y coordinate we want displayed on the screen. Suppose we let x vary from –5 to 5. We now must select y values that will allow us to see as much of the graph of the function as possible. We note first that y is always greater than 0. A quick calculation shows that $2^5 = 32$ and $2^{-5} = \frac{1}{32}$. Therefore, it would be advantageous to graph the function $y = 2^x$ for x values ranging from –5 to 5 and y values from 0 to 32. On the graphing calculator, these parameters may be shown as follows:

$$X \min = -5$$

$$X \max = 5$$

$$X \text{ scl} = 1$$

$$Y \min = 0$$

$$Y \max = 32$$

$$Y \text{ scl} = 1$$

X scl and Y scl refer to scale used on the x and y axes. We arbitrarily decided for the scales for both axes to be one unit for every tick mark or division point shown.

The graph we get should look something like the following:

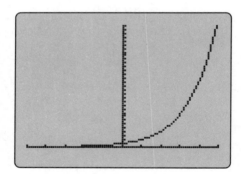

example 114.4   Use the graphing calculator to graph the function $y = \left(\dfrac{1}{2}\right)^x$.

solution   We enter the equation of the function into the graphing calculator. The equation displayed on the screen of the calculator is likely to look something like:

$$Y_1 = 0.5^{\wedge}x$$

$$F1(x) = 0.5^{\wedge}x$$

We arbitrarily choose the range of values for x to be from –5 to 5. We could have chosen other ranges for values of x, but figure that the general shape of the function should be evident over this range. Since Y must always be positive, we chose Y values to range from 0 to 32, since $\left(\frac{1}{2}\right)^{-5} = 32$ and $\left(\frac{1}{2}\right)^5 = \frac{1}{32}$.

The graph we get should look something like the following:

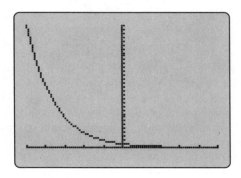

On this graph, each tick mark designates one unit.

practice   **a.**   Use either a scientific or a graphing calculator to compute the following expressions to four decimal places:

   (1) $(2.5)^3$ (2) $(0.5)^{0.5}$ (3) $(3.14)^{1/3}$

   b.   Sketch the graphs of the following functions. Then use a graphing calculator to graph the functions and confirm the sketches.

   (1) $y = 3^x$ (2) $y = \left(\frac{1}{3}\right)^x$

   c.   Harriet deposited $900 at 8% interest compounded annually. Write an equation that tells how much money is in the account after n years. Apply this equation to find the amount in the account after 12 years. How much total interest was earned in the 12 years?

problem set   **1.**   The number of bacteria in the petri dish quadrupled every hour. There were 1000 bacteria
114   *(114)*   at $t = 0$.

   (a)   Write an exponential equation that expresses the number of bacteria as a function of time.

   (b)   Using the equation in (a), find how many bacteria there were at $t = 24$ hours.

   2.   Allegra deposited $700 at 9 percent interest compounded annually.
   (114)

   (a)   Write an equation that expresses the amount of money in the account as a function of n, where n equals the number of years since the original deposit was made.

   (b)   Using the equation in (a), determine how much money is in the account at $n = 11$ years.

   (c)   What was the total interest earned at $n = 11$ years?

   3.   Use either a scientific or a graphing calculator to compute the following expressions to
   (114)   four decimal places:

   (a) $(3.14)^4$ (b) $(3.14)^{2.5}$ (c) $(0.25)^{0.5}$

   4.   Sketch the graph of $y = 2^x$. Then use a graphing calculator to confirm your sketch.
   (114)

   5.   The number of girls in each class varied directly as the number of boys. One class had 3
   (113)   boys and 21 girls. If another class had 5 boys, how many girls were in this class?

   6.   Productivity varied inversely as the number of distractions. When there were 6
   (113)   distractions, 500 items were produced. What would be the number of items produced if there were 10 distractions?

   7.   Howell hopped to the hostel at 5 miles per hour and hobbled back to the helicopter at 2
   (92)   miles per hour. How far was it to the hostel if the round trip took 28 hours? Begin by drawing a diagram of distances traveled and writing the distance equation.

8. Sketch the graphs of the following functions:
(110)

   (a) $f(x) = -x^2$ (b) $g(x) = x^2 + 3$ (c) $h(x) = (x + 3)^2$ (d) $k(x) = (x - 3)^2$

9. Find the equation of the line that passes through $(4, -1)$ and is parallel to $y = -\frac{1}{4}x - 2$.
(107)

10. Find the equation of the line that passes through $(4, -1)$ and $(-1, 4)$.
(106)

11. Find the equation of the line whose slope is -3 and that passes through the point $(-1, -1)$.
(107)

12. Use six unit multipliers to convert 160,000 cubic meters to cubic inches.
(53)

13. Graph on a number line: $x + 4 > 7$ or $x - 2 \le 0$; $D = \{\text{Reals}\}$
(111)

Multiply:

14. $\left(4 + 3\sqrt{5}\right)\left(1 - \sqrt{5}\right)$ **15.** $\left(3 + 2\sqrt{2}\right)\left(3 - \sqrt{2}\right)$
(112)   (112)

Solve:

16. $\dfrac{p + 8}{3p} = \dfrac{5}{2p} + \dfrac{1}{4}$ **17.** $4\dfrac{1}{2}x + \dfrac{3}{5} = \dfrac{1}{4}$
(103)   (25)

18. Divide: $\left(7x^3 - 2x - 2\right) \div (x + 2)$
(86)

Factor:

19. $5x^2 + 17x + 6$ **20.** $4x^2 + 4x + 1$ **21.** $2x^2 l + 6x^2 - 5l - 15$
(109)   (109)   (105)

22. Find z: $\dfrac{p}{m} - \dfrac{x}{z} + a = k$ **23.** Solve: $\sqrt{x - 7} + 4 = 9$
(104)   (108)

24. Solve by graphing: $\begin{cases} y = \dfrac{1}{2}x - 2 \\ x = -4 \end{cases}$ **25.** Simplify: $\dfrac{\dfrac{mp^2}{x} - \dfrac{z}{x^2}}{\dfrac{y}{x^2} - \dfrac{5a}{x}}$
(81)   (68)

26. Find the distance between $(0, 2)$ and $(-5, 0)$.
(98)

27. Evaluate: $-xy - y^x - x\left(\dfrac{y}{x}\right)$ if $y = -3$ and $x = -2$
(36)

28. Simplify: $-3\left[\left(-3^0 - 3\right)^2\left(-3^3 - 3\right) - (-3)\right] - \sqrt[3]{-27}$
(62)

29. Find the area of this figure. Dimen-
(8)   sions are in inches.

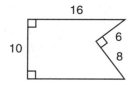

30. A base of the right solid 5 feet high is shown. Find the surface area and the volume of the
(15,20)   right solid. Dimensions are in feet.

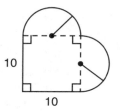 

LESSON *115   Linear Inequalities*

Below we have graphed the line whose equation is $y = \frac{1}{2}x + 1$. We see that this line divides the set of all the points of the plane into three mutually exclusive subsets:

1. The set of points that lie on the line.

2. The set of points that lie above the line (region A).

3. The set of points that lie below the line (region B).

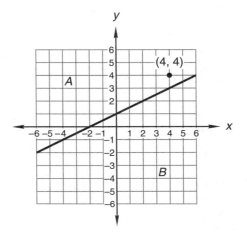

It can be shown that the coordinates of any point in the plane either will satisfy the equation of a given line or will satisfy one of the two linear inequalities that define the regions on either side of the line. For this particular line, we can say that the coordinates of any point in the plane will satisfy one and only one of the following:

$$y > \frac{1}{2}x + 1 \qquad y = \frac{1}{2}x + 1 \qquad y < \frac{1}{2}x + 1$$

The points in the regions denoted by A and B above do not lie on the line, and the coordinates of any point in region A or region B will satisfy one and only one of the inequalities. To see which of these inequalities defines the region above the line, we will choose a test point that clearly lies on one side of the line and test the coordinates of this point in both inequalities. We choose the point (4, 4).

$$y > \frac{1}{2}x + 1 \qquad\qquad y < \frac{1}{2}x + 1$$

$$4 > \frac{1}{2}(4) + 1 \qquad\qquad 4 < \frac{1}{2}(4) + 1$$

$$4 > 2 + 1 \qquad\qquad 4 < 2 + 1$$

$$4 > 3 \quad\text{True} \qquad\qquad 4 < 3 \qquad\text{False}$$

Thus the coordinates of all points above the line satisfy the inequality $y > \frac{1}{2}x + 1$. If we choose any point below the line in region B, we can show that its coordinates satisfy the other inequality, $y < \frac{1}{2}x + 1$. We choose the point (0, 0).

$$y < \frac{1}{2}x + 1 \quad\longrightarrow\quad 0 < \frac{1}{2}(0) + 1 \quad\longrightarrow\quad 0 < 1 \quad\text{True}$$

We indicate in the next figure that the coordinates of all points above the line satisfy the inequality $y > \frac{1}{2}x + 1$ and that the coordinates of all points below the line satisfy the inequality $y < \frac{1}{2}x + 1$.

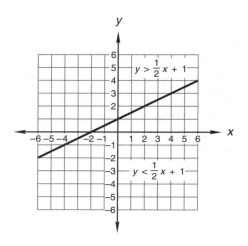

example 115.1   Graph the inequality: $y > -x + 2$

solution   We first graph the line $y = -x + 2$ in the figure on the left below. We show the line as a dashed line to indicate that the points on the line do not satisfy the stated inequality, which uses a *greater than* and not a *greater than or equal to* symbol. Had the inequality used a *greater than or equal to* symbol, the line would have been drawn as a solid line. We choose the point $(0, 0)$ as a test point because it clearly lies on one side of the line and also because it is the easiest test point to use.

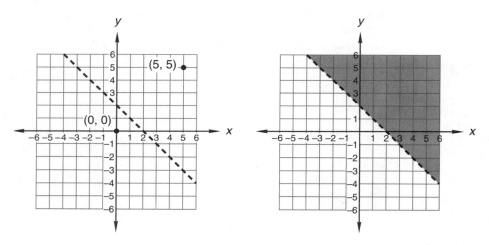

$$(0) > (-0) + 2$$

$$0 > 2 \qquad \text{False}$$

The coordinates of this point do not satisfy the inequality, so the coordinates of any point above the line must satisfy the inequality. We confirm this by testing the coordinates of the point $(5, 5)$.

$$(5) > (-5) + 2$$

$$5 > -3 \qquad \text{True}$$

We indicate that the coordinates of all points above the line satisfy the given condition by shading the region above the line in the figure on the right.

example 115.2   Graph: $y \leq 2x - 1$

solution   In the figure on the left below, we have graphed the line $y = 2x - 1$. We show the line as a solid line because we wish to indicate that the points on the line satisfy the stated inequality.

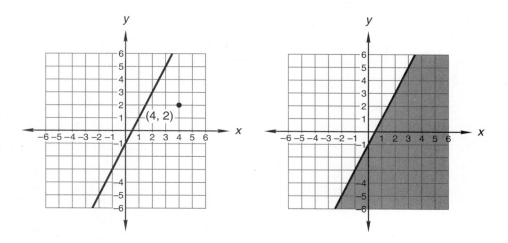

We could use the test point $(1, 0)$, but this is rather close to the line. To be sure we have a point that is well on one side of the line, we choose the point $(4, 2)$.

$$2 < 2(4) - 1$$

$$2 < 7 \qquad \text{True}$$

Thus the coordinates of the points on the line or in the region to the right of the line satisfy the stated inequality. We indicate the solution by shading this region in the figure on the right above.

example 115.3   Graph: $y > -2$

solution   In the figure on the left below, we have graphed the line $y = -2$. We show the line as a dashed line because the points on the line do not satisfy the inequality $y > -2$. We choose $(0, 0)$ as the test point.

$$0 > -2 \qquad \text{True}$$

We shade the region above the line in the figure on the right to indicate that the coordinates of any point above the line will satisfy the stated inequality.

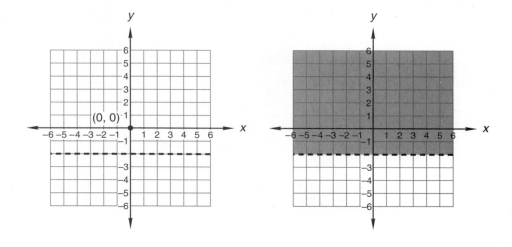

example 115.4   Graph the following inequality on a rectangular coordinate system: $x < 3$

solution   In the figure on the left below, we graph the equation $x = 3$. We draw the line as a dashed line because points on the line do not satisfy $x < 3$, the given inequality. We will use the point (0, 0) as our test point.

$$0 < 3 \qquad \text{True}$$

We shade the region to the left of the dashed line in the figure on the right to indicate that all points in this region will satisfy the inequality $x < 3$.

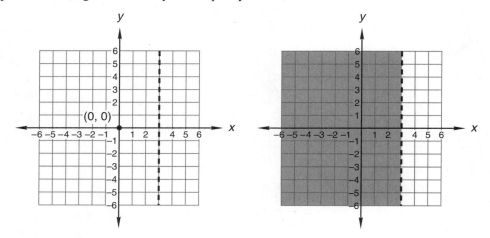

practice   Graph:

a. $x < -2$ **b.** $y \le 3x - 2$ **c.** $y \ge \dfrac{1}{2}x + 1$

problem set
115

1. At first there were 17 boring beetles. The number of boring beetles doubled every day.
(114)
  (a) Write an equation that describes the number of beetles there would be after n days.

  (b) Using the equation in (a), determine the number of beetles there would be after 30 days.

2. Pressure varies inversely as the volume. When the pressure is 10 pascals, the volume is
(113) 150 liters. What would the volume be if the pressure is reduced to 3 pascals?

3. Attractiveness varies inversely with the wiggles. At 300 wiggles the attractiveness is 10.
(113) What would the attractiveness be at 150 wiggles?

4. Rosie ran to the park at 7 miles per hour and walked back home at 3 miles per hour. How
(92) far was it to the park if the round trip took 20 hours? Begin by drawing a diagram of distances traveled and writing the distance equation.

5. Mickey and Yarberry saved nickels and dimes. They had a total of 34 coins whose value
(83) was $2.70. How many of each kind of coin did they have?

6. Brenda has a jar that contains 5 blue tacks and 7 red tacks. She draws 3 tacks at random
(73) without replacement. What is the probability that all 3 are red?

Graph the following inequalities on the rectangular coordinate system:

7. $y > x$ **8.** $y \le x + 1$ **9.** $x < -5$
(115)   (115)   (115)

10. Sketch the graph of $G(x) = \sqrt{x + 1}$.   **11.** Sketch the graph of $F(x) = -x^2 - 1$.
(110)   (110)

12. Sketch the graph of the function $y = \left(\dfrac{1}{2}\right)^x$. Then use a graphing calculator to confirm
(114) your sketch.

13. Find the equation of the line that passes through (-2, 5) and (3, -2).
(106)

14. Find the equation of the line that passes through (-2, 5) and is parallel to $y = -\frac{1}{3}x + 2$.
(107)

Graph those values of x that satisfy the following inequalities on number lines:

15. $4 \geq |x|$; $D = \{\text{Integers}\}$ **16.** $4 \leq x + 3 < 7$; $D = \{\text{Reals}\}$
(102)   *(111)*

Multiply:

17. $(3 + 2\sqrt{2})(5 - 3\sqrt{2})$ **18.** $(4 + \sqrt{3})(2 - 4\sqrt{3})$
(112)   *(112)*

Factor:

19. $9x^2 + 6x + 1$ **20.** $25x^2 - y^2$ **21.** $5z^2 + 2z - 7$
(109)   *(73)*   *(109)*

Solve:

22. $-2\sqrt{x} + 4 = -1$ **23.** $\dfrac{k - 3}{2k} = \dfrac{3}{6k} - \dfrac{1}{4}$
(108)   *(103)*

24. Find m: $\dfrac{x}{m} - \dfrac{c}{d} = d$
(104)

25. Which of the following diagrams, graphs, or sets of ordered pairs depict functions?
(84,87)

(a)
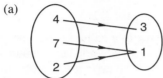

(b)
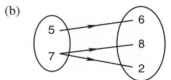

(e) $(4, -2), (3, 5), (7, 6)$

(f) $(4, -2), (5, -2), (3, 5)$

(g) $(4, -2), (4, 7), (3, 5)$

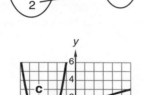

26. Evaluate: $xy - a - ya(y - a)$ if $x = -2$, $y = \sqrt[3]{-125}$, and $a = -1$
(62)

Simplify:

27. $\dfrac{4x^2 y^{-2} (x^2)^{-2} y^2 xy}{(2x^0)^2 x^2 y^{-2} (xy)}$ **28.** $\dfrac{(21{,}000 \times 10^{-40})(5000 \times 10^{-20})}{(0.0003 \times 10^{14})(0.0007 \times 10^{28})}$
(53)   *(80)*

29. Find the volume of the sphere shown whose radius is 6 cm.
(91)

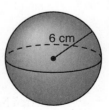

30. The area of a base of a right hexagonal prism is 60 m^2 and the length of a lateral edge is 7.5 m. Find the volume of the right hexagonal prism.
(20,60)

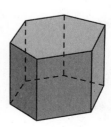

LESSON *116*   *Quotient Rule for Square Roots*

The product rule for square roots tells us that the square root of a product equals the product of the square roots.

$$\sqrt{3 \cdot 2} = \sqrt{3}\sqrt{2}$$

In a similar fashion, the quotient rule for square roots tells us that the square root of a quotient (fraction) equals the quotient of the square roots.

$$\sqrt{\frac{3}{2}} = \frac{\sqrt{3}}{\sqrt{2}}$$

The expression on the right has the irrational number $\sqrt{2}$ in the denominator. We can change the denominator to the rational number 2 by multiplying both the numerator and the denominator by $\sqrt{2}$.

$$\frac{\sqrt{3}}{\sqrt{2}} = \frac{\sqrt{3}}{\sqrt{2}} \cdot \frac{\sqrt{2}}{\sqrt{2}} = \frac{\sqrt{6}}{2}$$

This process of changing a denominator to a rational number is called *rationalizing the* **denominator.** Many people prefer fractions with rational denominators. If we go along with their preference, we can say the following: **An expression containing square roots is in the simplified form when no square roots are in the denominator and no radicand has a factor that is a perfect square.**

example 116.1   Write $\sqrt{\dfrac{5}{3}}$ in simplified form.

solution   We begin by writing the radical as a fraction of radicals.

$$\sqrt{\frac{5}{3}} = \frac{\sqrt{5}}{\sqrt{3}}$$

We finish by multiplying both top and bottom by $\sqrt{3}$.

$$\frac{\sqrt{5}}{\sqrt{3}} = \frac{\sqrt{5}}{\sqrt{3}} \cdot \frac{\sqrt{3}}{\sqrt{3}} = \frac{\sqrt{15}}{3}$$

example 116.2   Simplify: $\dfrac{4 + \sqrt{3}}{\sqrt{2}}$

solution   To simplify, we must change the denominator to a rational number. Thus, we multiply by $\sqrt{2}$ over $\sqrt{2}$.

$$\frac{4 + \sqrt{3}}{\sqrt{2}} \cdot \frac{\sqrt{2}}{\sqrt{2}} = \frac{4\sqrt{2} + \sqrt{6}}{2}$$

This may appear to some as more complicated than the original expression, but this form is preferred by many people because no radical appears in the denominator.

example 116.3   Simplify: $\dfrac{2 + \sqrt{15}}{\sqrt{5}}$

solution   We will multiply top and bottom by $\sqrt{5}$.

$$\frac{2 + \sqrt{15}}{\sqrt{5}} \cdot \frac{\sqrt{5}}{\sqrt{5}} = \frac{2\sqrt{5} + \sqrt{75}}{5} = \frac{2\sqrt{5} + 5\sqrt{3}}{5}$$

practice   Simplify:

a. $\sqrt{\dfrac{6}{23}}$ b. $\dfrac{4 + \sqrt{5}}{\sqrt{3}}$

problem set   **1.**   Diana deposited $10,000 in an account that pays an 8 percent interest rate compounded
116   (114)   annually.

(a)   Write an equation that expresses the amount of money in the account as a function
of n, where n equals the number of years since the original deposit was made.

(b)   Use the equation in (a) to determine how much money is in the account at
$n = 5$ years.

(c)   What was the total interest earned at $n = 5$ years?

2.   Anastasia deposited $1100 in the bank and received 6 percent interest compounded
(114)   annually.

(a)   Write an equation that expresses the amount of money in the account as a function
of n, where n equals the number of years since the original deposit was made.

(b)   Use the equation in (a) to determine how much money is in the account at
$n = 20$ years.

(c)   What was the total interest earned at $n = 20$ years?

3.   For a meshed gear of a fixed radius, the number of revolutions per minute varies
(113)   inversely as the number of gear teeth. If a particular gear had 100 teeth, it would revolve
at 10 revolutions per minute (rpm). What rpm would result if the number of teeth were
reduced to 25?

4.   Hannibal rode the elephant to the outskirts of Rome at 2 kilometers per hour and then
(92)   took a chariot back to camp at 10 kilometers per hour. If the total trip took 18 hours, how
far was it from camp to the outskirts of Rome? Begin by drawing a diagram of distances
traveled and writing the distance equation.

5.   Bustles just were not selling, so Julie marked them down 40 percent so that the sale price
(58)   would be $3.60 each. What was the price before the sale?

6.   The cheap dresses were $15 and the more expensive ones were $50. On Saturday the
(89)   store took in $550 and sold 15 more cheap dresses than expensive dresses. How many
dresses of each type did the store sell?

Simplify:

7. $\dfrac{2 + 3\sqrt{6}}{\sqrt{2}}$ **8.** $\sqrt{\dfrac{2}{5}}$ **9.** $\dfrac{4 + 2\sqrt{10}}{\sqrt{5}}$
(116)   (116)   (116)

Graph the following inequalities on the rectangular coordinate system:

10. $y \le x - 3$ **11.** $y > \dfrac{1}{2}x + 1$
(115)   (115)

12.   Sketch the graph of $F(x) = |x + 2|$.
(95)

13.   Sketch the graph of $G(x) = (x + 1)^2 + 2$.
(110)

Sketch the graphs of the following exponential functions. Then use a graphing calculator to
confirm your sketch.

14. $y = 3^x$ **15.** $y = \left(\dfrac{1}{3}\right)^x$
(114)   (114)

16. Find the equation of the line that passes through $(5, -2)$ and is parallel to $y = -3x + 2$.
(107)

17. Find the equation of the line whose slope is -5 and that passes through the point $(-4, -3)$.
(107)

18. Graph on a number line: $x + 2 > 6$ or $x - 3 \leq -6$; $D = \{\text{Reals}\}$
(111)

Multiply:

19. $(3 + 2\sqrt{2})(2 - 4\sqrt{2})$ **20.** $(2 + 3\sqrt{3})(2 - \sqrt{3})$
(112)   (112)

21. Solve and check your answer: $\sqrt{x - 3} - 2 = 5$
(108)

Factor the trinomials. Always begin by writing the trinomials in descending order of the variables and by factoring out the greatest common factor.

22. $3x^2 + 25x - 18$ **23.** $3x^2 - 4 - x$
(109)   (109)

Factor by grouping:

24. $ab + 15 + 5a + 3b$ **25.** $ay + xy + ac + xc$
(105)   (105)

26. Find c: $\dfrac{a}{x} - \dfrac{m}{c} + b = k$
(104)

27. Use a calculator to evaluate the following expressions to four decimal places:
(114)

   (a) $(2.718)^2$ (b) $(1.414)^2$ (c) $(2.718)^{3.14}$

28. Simplify: $-2\left[\left(-2^0 - 2^2\right)\left(-2^3 - 2\right) + (-2)\right]\left[-(-3)(-2)^2\right]$
(19)

29. Find the surface area of the sphere
(91)   shown whose radius is 8 in.

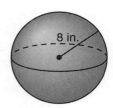

30. A base of the right prism 15 feet high is shown. Find the surface area and the volume of
(15,20,60)   the right prism. Dimensions are in feet.

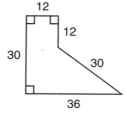

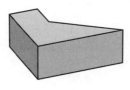

LESSON 117 *Direct and Inverse Variation Squared*

Direct and inverse variation statements are not always simple statements of direct variation or inverse variation. Often one variable will vary as the other variable squared or the other variable cubed.

STATEMENT	IMPLIED EQUATION
The weight of a body varies inversely with the square of the distance to the center of the earth.	$W = \dfrac{k}{D^2}$
The distance required to stop is directly proportional to the square of the velocity.	$D = kV^2$
The price of a diamond varies directly as the square of its weight.	$P = kW^2$
The strength of the field is inversely proportional to the cube of the radius.	$S = \dfrac{k}{R^3}$

These problems are solved in the same way that simple variation problems are solved. First we recognize the statement of the implied variation and write down the indicated equation. Then we find k, insert its value in the equation, and solve for the required unknown.

example 117.1 The distance required for an automobile to stop is directly proportional to the square of its velocity. If a car can stop in 200 meters at 20 kilometers per hour, what will be the required stopping distance at 28 kilometers per hour?

solution Step 1: $D = kV^2$ write equation

Step 2: $200 = k(20)^2 \longrightarrow k = 0.5$ find k

Step 3: $D = 0.5V^2$ put k in equation

Step 4: $D = 0.5(28)^2 \longrightarrow D = \mathbf{392\ m}$ solve for D

example 117.2 The distance a body falls varies directly as the square of the time that it falls. If it falls 144 feet in 3 seconds, how far will it fall in 10 seconds?

solution Step 1: $D = kt^2$ write equation

Step 2: $144 = k(3)^2 \longrightarrow k = 16$ find k

Step 3: $D = 16t^2$ put k in equation

Step 4: $D = 16(10)^2 \longrightarrow D = \mathbf{1600\ ft}$ solve for D

example 117.3 The weight of a body on or above the surface of the earth varies inversely with the square of the distance from the body to the center of the earth. If a body weighs 10,000 pounds at a distance of 5000 miles from the center of the earth, how much would it weigh 50,000 miles from the center of the earth?

solution   Step 1: $W = \dfrac{k}{D^2}$ write equation

Step 2: $10{,}000 = \dfrac{k}{(5000)^2}$ $\longrightarrow$ $10{,}000(5000)^2 = k$ find k

$\longrightarrow$ $25 \times 10^{10} = k$

Step 3: $W = \dfrac{25 \times 10^{10}}{D^2}$ put k in equation

Step 4: $W = \dfrac{25 \times 10^{10}}{(50{,}000)^2}$ $\longrightarrow$ $W = \dfrac{25 \times 10^{10}}{25 \times 10^8}$ solve for W

$\longrightarrow$ $W = \textbf{100 pounds}$

practice   **a.**   The weight of a body on or above the surface of the earth varies inversely with the square of the distance from the body to the center of the earth. If a body weighs 50,000 pounds at a distance of 6000 miles from the center of the earth, how much would it weigh 25,000 miles from the center of the earth?

problem set   **1.**   The distance required for an automobile to stop is directly proportional to the square of
117   *(117)*   its velocity. If a car can stop in 1800 meters from a velocity of 30 kilometers per hour, what will be the required distance at 28 kilometers per hour?

2.   The distance a body falls varies directly as the square of the time that it falls. If it falls
(117)   256 feet in 4 seconds, how far will it fall in 13 seconds?

3.   Greens vary directly as purples squared. When there were 4 greens, there were 2 purples.
(113)   How many greens would be present if there were 6 purples?

4.   The number of red marbles varied inversely as the square of the number of blue marbles.
(117)   When there were 4 reds, there were 20 blues. How many reds would there be if there were only 4 blues?

5.   The number of gremlins increased exponentially. At the beginning there was just one.
(114)   After one day there were two, and after two days, there were four. In fact, every day the number of gremlins doubled.

(a)   Write an equation that expresses how many gremlins there were after n days.

(b)   Use a graphing calculator to graph the equation found in (a).

(c)   How many gremlins would there be after 9 days?

6.   The ratio of rabbits to squirrels in the forest was 7 to 5. If there were 16,800 of them total,
(39)   how many were rabbits and how many were squirrels?

Simplify:

7. $\sqrt{\dfrac{7}{3}}$ **8.** $\dfrac{2\sqrt{2} + \sqrt{2}}{\sqrt{2}}$
(116)   *(116)*

9.   Graph the inequality $y < 2x + 1$ on the rectangular coordinate system.
(115)

10.   Sketch the graph of $F(x) = -|x| - 3$.
(110)

11.   Sketch the graph of $G(x) = \sqrt{x - 1} + 1$.
(110)

Sketch the graphs of the following exponential functions. Then use a graphing calculator to confirm your sketch.

12. $y = 4^x$
(114)

13. $y = \left(\dfrac{1}{4}\right)^x$
(114)

14. Find the equation of the line that passes through $(-2, 5)$ and $(3, -2)$.
(106)

15. Find the equation of the line that passes through $(-2, 5)$ and has a slope of $-\frac{1}{4}$.
(107)

16. Find the equation of the line that passes through $(-2, 5)$ and is parallel to $y = -\frac{1}{3}x + 2$.
(107)

Graph on number lines those values of x that satisfy the following inequalities:

17. $-2 - |x| > -4$; $D = \{\text{Reals}\}$
(102)

18. $4 \leq x + 2 < 7$; $D = \{\text{Integers}\}$
(111)

19. $x - 1 \leq 2$ or $x + 1 > 5$; $D = \{\text{Reals}\}$
(111)

20. Solve and check your answer: $\sqrt{x + 2} - 4 = 1$
(108)

Factor the trinomials. Always begin by writing the trinomials in descending order of the variables and by factoring out the greatest common factor.

21. $2x^2 + 25 + 15x$
(109)

22. $6x^2 - 40 + 56x$
(109)

Factor by grouping:

23. $kx - 15 - 5k + 3x$
(105)

24. $3mx - 2p + 3px - 2m$
(105)

25. Find a: $\dfrac{x}{a} - \dfrac{1}{k} = \dfrac{m}{c}$
(104)

26. Solve: $\dfrac{p - 5}{p} = \dfrac{5}{3p} - \dfrac{1}{5}$
(103)

27. Simplify: $-3\left[(-2^0 - 3) - (-5 + 7)(-2^2 + 3)\right] - \left[(-6^0 - 2) + \sqrt[3]{-64}\right]$
(62)

28. Find x if $x = \dfrac{-b \pm \sqrt{b^2 - 4ac}}{2a}$ and if $a = -2$, $b + 4 = 1$, and $c - 7 = -5$.
(62)

29. Find the area of this figure. Dimensions are in centimeters.
(8)

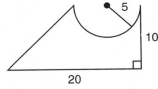

30. Find the lateral surface area of this right prism whose bases are regular hexagons. Dimensions are in meters.
(15,60)

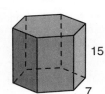

LESSON *118* *Completing the Square*

We remember from Lesson 96 that if

$$x^2 = 3$$

then

$$x = +\sqrt{3} \qquad \text{or} \qquad x = -\sqrt{3}$$

We can express this compactly as

$$x = \pm\sqrt{3}$$

since $\pm$ is the symbol for "plus or minus." Here we simply apply what we call the difference of two squares theorem, which we recall below. $\big[$To apply the theorem to the equation above, rewrite the equation as $x^2 = (\sqrt{3})^2.\big]$

DIFFERENCE OF TWO SQUARES THEOREM
If p and q are real numbers and if $p^2 = q^2$, then
$$p = q \qquad \text{or} \qquad p = -q$$
In other words,
$$p = \pm q$$

If the variable x were replaced by a sum, the procedure would be the same.

$$(x + 2)^2 = 3 \qquad\qquad \text{equation}$$
$$(x + 2)^2 = (\sqrt{3})^2 \qquad \text{rewrote equation}$$
$$x + 2 = \pm\sqrt{3} \qquad\quad \text{applied difference of two squares theorem}$$
$$x = -2 \pm \sqrt{3} \qquad \text{solved}$$

Every quadratic equation can be written in the same form that these two equations have. For example,

$$x^2 + 4x - 5 = 0 \qquad \text{can be written as} \qquad (x + 2)^2 = 9$$

We can solve this equation by applying the difference of two squares theorem.

$$(x + 2)^2 = 9 \;\rightarrow\; (x + 2)^2 = 3^2 \;\rightarrow\; x + 2 = \pm 3 \;\rightarrow\; x = \pm 3 - 2 = -5, 1$$

The process of writing the equation in the form

$$(x + a)^2 = b$$

is called **completing the square.** In this lesson we will consider quadratic equations in which the coefficient of the x term is 1. In the next lesson and in *Algebra 2*, we will consider coefficients of x that are not 1. We can complete the square by using five steps. We will use parentheses to help us with the concept.

1. Write the equation in descending powers of the variable on the left-hand side of the equals sign. The right-hand side of the equation is the number zero.
2. Use the additive property of equality to move the constant term to the right-hand side of the equals sign.
3. Divide the coefficient of the x term by 2. Square the result and add this number to both sides of the equation.

4. The trinomial on the left-hand side is now a perfect square. Write the left-hand side as a perfect square. Simplify the right-hand side.

5. Complete the solution by applying the difference of two squares theorem and simplifying.

example 118.1   Solve $x^2 + 6 = -10x$ by completing the square.

solution   1. The first step is to put all three terms on the left-hand side of the equals sign and write the terms in descending powers of x.

$$x^2 + 10x + 6 = 0$$

2. Now we move the constant term 6 to the other side of the equation by adding -6 to both sides of the equation.

$$x^2 + 10x = -6$$

3. The coefficient of x is 10. We divide 10 by 2 and square the result.

$$\left(\frac{10}{2}\right)^2 = 25$$

We add this quantity to both sides of the equation.

$$x^2 + 10x + 25 = -6 + 25$$

4. The expression on the left is a perfect square. Next, we simplify both sides of the equation.

$$x^2 + 10x + 25 = 19$$

Now we rewrite the equation.

$$(x + 5)^2 = \left(\sqrt{19}\right)^2$$

5. Now we apply the difference of two squares theorem and solve for x.

$$x + 5 = \pm\sqrt{19} \qquad \text{applied difference of two squares theorem}$$

$$\mathbf{x = -5 \pm \sqrt{19}} \qquad \text{solved}$$

Many people have difficulty recognizing

$$(x^2 + 10x + 25) \qquad \text{as} \qquad (x + 5)^2$$

There is an easy way we can remember how to write a trinomial that we know to be a perfect square as a binomial squared. We remember that the constant in the binomial is half the coefficient of x in the trinomial.

$$\left(x^2 + \textcircled{10}x + 25\right) = (x + 5)^2$$

For example, if given the following trinomial, which we know to be a perfect square,

$$\left(x^2 + 9x + \frac{81}{4}\right)$$

we would write this as $\left(x + \frac{9}{2}\right)^2$. Note that the constant term $\frac{9}{2}$ is half of 9 and is also the square root of $\frac{81}{4}$.

example 118.2   Complete the square to solve $x^2 + 3 = -5x$.

solution   First we rewrite the equation in standard form.

$$x^2 + 5x + 3 = 0$$

To complete the square, we will have to do three things that may cause difficulty. Let us look at these three things first. Then we will complete the square.

1. First we will have to find the square of one half the coefficient of x.

$$\left(\frac{5}{2}\right)^2 = \frac{25}{4}$$

2. After we add $\frac{25}{4}$ to both sides, we will have to combine $\frac{25}{4}$ and -3, as we see below. To combine these numbers, we will write -3 so that it has a denominator of 4.

$$\frac{25}{4} - 3 \qquad \text{expression}$$

$$\frac{25}{4} - \frac{12}{4} \qquad 3 \text{ equals } \frac{12}{4}$$

$$\frac{13}{4} \qquad \text{added}$$

3. Finally, we will have to write $\left(x^2 + 5x + \frac{25}{4}\right)$, which we know to be a perfect square, as a binomial squared. The constant term of the binomial will be $\frac{5}{2}$ because this is half of 5.

$$\left(x^2 + 5x + \frac{25}{4}\right) = \left(x + \frac{5}{2}\right)^2$$

Now we apply the steps in completing the square.

Step 1: $x^2 + 5x + 3 = 0$ rearranged

Step 2: $(x^2 + 5x \quad) = -3$ moved constant term by adding -3 to both sides

Step 3: $x^2 + 5x + \frac{25}{4} = -3 + \frac{25}{4}$ added $\frac{25}{4}$ to both sides

Step 4: $\left(x + \frac{5}{2}\right)^2 = \frac{13}{4}$ simplified

This equation can be written as

$$\left(x + \frac{5}{2}\right)^2 = \left(\sqrt{\frac{13}{4}}\right)^2$$

We now apply the difference of two squares theorem:

Step 5: $x + \frac{5}{2} = \pm\sqrt{\frac{13}{4}}$ applied difference of two squares theorem

$$x = -\frac{5}{2} \pm \frac{\sqrt{13}}{2} \qquad \text{solved}$$

example 118.3 Complete the square to solve $x^2 + 1 = 3x$.

solution We will use the same five steps.

Step 1: $x^2 - 3x + 1 = 0$ rearranged

Step 2: $x^2 - 3x = -1$ moved constant

Now we will take one half of -3, square it, and add it to both sides.

Step 3: $x^2 - 3x + \dfrac{9}{4} = -1 + \dfrac{9}{4}$ added $\dfrac{9}{4}$ to both sides

Step 4: $\left(x - \dfrac{3}{2} \right)^2 = \dfrac{5}{4}$ simplified

$\left(x - \dfrac{3}{2} \right)^2 = \left(\sqrt{\dfrac{5}{4}} \right)^2$ rewrote equation

Step 5: $x - \dfrac{3}{2} = \pm\sqrt{\dfrac{5}{4}}$ applied difference of two squares theorem

$x = \dfrac{3}{2} \pm \dfrac{\sqrt{5}}{2}$ added $\dfrac{3}{2}$ to both sides

practice Solve by completing the square.

a. $x^2 - 9 = -7x$ **b.** $x^2 - 5x = 6$

problem set 118

1. Reds varied inversely as yellows squared. When there were 10 reds, there were
(117) 100 yellows. How many reds were present when the yellows were reduced to 5?

2. The seriousness of the situation grew exponentially. In fact, the seriousness S at time t is
(114) given by the equation $S(t) = 3(2.71)^t$ where t is measured in minutes.

(a) What is the seriousness at the beginning (that is, at $t = 0$)?

(b) What is the seriousness, rounded to the nearest hundredth, at $t = 10$ minutes?

3. The freight train headed south at 9 a.m., and the express train headed north from the same
(94) station at noon. At 3 p.m., the trains were 420 miles apart. What was the speed of each if
the speed of the express train was 20 miles per hour greater than the speed of the freight
train? Begin by drawing a diagram of distances traveled and writing the distance
equation.

4. There was $2900 in the pot. If there were 293 more $1 bills than $10 bills, how many bills
(89) of each kind were there?

5. Find four consecutive even integers such that the product of -12 and the sum of the first
(77) and fourth is 6 less than the product of 19 and the opposite of the third.

6. A fair coin is flipped two times. What is the probability that the coin comes up heads first
(70) and then tails second?

7. Hannah received an estate of $50,000 from her grandmother. She invested it and received
(114) 12 percent interest compounded annually.

(a) Write an equation that expresses the amount of money in the account as a function
of n, where n equals the number of years since the original deposit was made.

(b) Use the equation in (a) to determine how much money is in the account at the end
of $n = 10$ years.

(c) What was the total interest earned at $n = 10$ years?

Solve the following quadratic equations by completing the square:

8. $x^2 + 2x - 4 = 0$
(118)

9. $x^2 + 3x - 8 = 0$
(118)

10. $x^2 + 2x - 5 = 0$
(118)

11. $x^2 + 4x - 7 = 0$
(118)

Simplify:

12. $\sqrt{\dfrac{2}{7}}$
(116)

13. $\sqrt{\dfrac{5}{12}}$
(116)

14. $\dfrac{4 + \sqrt{3}}{\sqrt{6}}$
(116)

15. Graph the following set of inequalities on the rectangular coordinate system:
(115)

$$\begin{cases} y \le -x + 2 \\ y \ge x \end{cases}$$

16. Sketch the graph of $G(x) = x^3 + 1$.
(110)

17. Sketch the graph of $F(x) = -\sqrt{x} - 2$.
(110)

18. Sketch the graphs of the following exponential functions. Then use a graphing calculator
(114) to confirm your sketches.

(a) $y = 5^x$

(b) $y = \left(\dfrac{1}{5}\right)^x$

19. Find the equation of the line that passes through $(2, 4)$ and is parallel to $y = \frac{1}{5}x - 6$.
(107)

20. Find the equation of the line that passes through $(-3, 2)$ and $(5, -3)$.
(106)

Graph the solutions to the following inequalities on number lines:

21. $4 \le x - 2 \le 8$; $D = \{\text{Integers}\}$
(111)

22. $3 - |x| > 2$; $D = \{\text{Reals}\}$
(102)

23. $x + 1 < -2$ or $x - 1 \ge 2$; $D = \{\text{Reals}\}$
(111)

Factor the trinomials. Always begin by writing the trinomials in descending order of the variables and by factoring out the greatest common factor.

24. $3x^2 - 35 - 16x$
(109)

25. $-2x + 3x^2 - 5$
(109)

26. $2x^2 - 5x - 12$
(109)

Factor by grouping:

27. $p^2c - ab + p^2b - ac$
(105)

28. $2y + mx^3 + my + 2x^3$
(105)

29. Solve and check your answer: $\sqrt{4x + 1} - 1 = 2$
(108)

30. Find the volume and the surface area
(72) of this regular square pyramid.

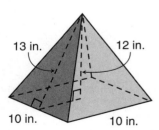

13 in.   12 in.

10 in.   10 in.

LESSON 119   *The Quadratic Formula • Use of the Quadratic Formula*

119.A

the quadratic formula

In the preceding lesson we learned how to complete the square to solve a quadratic equation. This method requires several steps and is time-consuming. **If we write a quadratic equation in standard form, using *a*, *b*, and *c* to represent the constants, and complete the square, we can develop a formula that can be used to find the values of *x* that will satisfy any quadratic equation.**

$$ax^2 + bx + c = 0$$ general form of a quadratic equation

$$x^2 + \frac{b}{a}x + \frac{c}{a} = 0$$ divided both sides by *a*

$$x^2 + \frac{b}{a}x = -\frac{c}{a}$$ added $-\frac{c}{a}$ to both sides
(additive property of equality)

$$x^2 + \frac{b}{a}x + \frac{b^2}{4a^2} = \frac{b^2}{4a^2} - \frac{c}{a}$$ added $\left(\frac{b}{2a}\right)^2 = \frac{b^2}{4a^2}$ to both sides

$$\left(x + \frac{b}{2a}\right)^2 = \frac{b^2 - 4ac}{4a^2}$$ simplified both sides

$$\left(x + \frac{b}{2a}\right)^2 = \left(\sqrt{\frac{b^2 - 4ac}{4a^2}}\right)^2$$ rewrote equation

$$x + \frac{b}{2a} = \pm\sqrt{\frac{b^2 - 4ac}{4a^2}}$$ applied difference of two squares theorem

$$x + \frac{b}{2a} = \pm\frac{\sqrt{b^2 - 4ac}}{\sqrt{4a^2}}$$ applied quotient of square roots rule

$$x = -\frac{b}{2a} \pm \frac{\sqrt{b^2 - 4ac}}{2a}$$ added $-\frac{b}{2a}$ to both sides and simplified

$$x = \frac{-b \pm \sqrt{b^2 - 4ac}}{2a}$$ added rational expressions

119.B

use of the quadratic formula

By completing the square on $ax^2 + bx + c = 0$, we have derived the **quadratic formula.**

$$x = \frac{-b \pm \sqrt{b^2 - 4ac}}{2a} \qquad (a \neq 0)$$

This formula expresses *x* in terms of the constants *a*, *b*, and *c* of the original quadratic equation. If we wish to use this formula to find the values of *x* that satisfy a particular quadratic equation, it is necessary to compare the particular quadratic equation with the equation $ax^2 + bx + c = 0$ to determine the values of *a*, *b*, and *c*.

example 119.1   Use the quadratic formula to determine the roots of the equation $3x^2 + 2x - 7 = 0$.

solution   The general form of the quadratic equation is $ax^2 + bx + c = 0$. If we write our equation and the general equation one over the other

$$ax^2 + bx + c = 0 \qquad \text{general equation}$$

$$3x^2 + 2x + (-7) = 0 \qquad \text{our equation}$$

we see that 3 corresponds to a, 2 corresponds to b, and -7 corresponds to c. If we use these numbers as replacements for a, b, and c in the quadratic formula, we can find the roots of the equation.

$$x = \frac{-b \pm \sqrt{b^2 - 4ac}}{2a} \qquad \text{quadratic formula}$$

$$x = \frac{-(2) \pm \sqrt{(2)^2 - 4(3)(-7)}}{2(3)} \qquad \text{substituted}$$

$$x = \frac{-2 \pm \sqrt{4 + 84}}{6} \qquad \text{simplified under the radical}$$

$$x = \frac{-2 \pm \sqrt{88}}{6} \qquad \text{added 4 and 84}$$

$$x = \frac{-2 \pm 2\sqrt{22}}{6} \qquad \sqrt{88} \text{ equals } 2\sqrt{22}$$

$$x = \frac{-1 \pm \sqrt{22}}{3} \qquad \text{simplified}$$

Thus the two real numbers that will satisfy the given equation are

$$x = \frac{\mathbf{-1 + \sqrt{22}}}{\mathbf{3}} \qquad \text{and} \qquad x = \frac{\mathbf{-1 - \sqrt{22}}}{\mathbf{3}}$$

example 119.2   Use the quadratic formula to determine the roots of $-6 = -x^2 + x$.

solution   We begin by writing the given equation in standard form as

$$x^2 - x - 6 = 0$$

Now we compare this equation to the equation $ax^2 + bx + c = 0$ to determine the numbers that correspond to a, b, and c.

$$ax^2 + bx + c = 0 \qquad \text{general equation}$$

$$x^2 + (-1)x + (-6) = 0 \qquad \text{our equation}$$

We see that $a = 1$, $b = -1$, and $c = -6$.

$$x = \frac{-b \pm \sqrt{b^2 - 4ac}}{2a} \qquad \text{quadratic formula}$$

$$x = \frac{-(-1) \pm \sqrt{(-1)^2 - 4(1)(-6)}}{2(1)} \qquad \text{substituted}$$

$$x = \frac{1 \pm \sqrt{25}}{2} \qquad \text{simplified}$$

$$x = \frac{1 \pm 5}{2} \qquad \sqrt{25} \text{ equals 5}$$

$$x = \mathbf{3, -2} \qquad \text{solved}$$

example 119.3 Use the quadratic formula to find the values of x that satisfy the equation $-x = 7 - x^2$.

solution We begin by writing the given equation in standard form and comparing it to the equation $ax^2 + bx + c = 0$.

$$ax^2 + \quad bx + \quad c \quad = 0 \qquad \text{general equation}$$

$$x^2 + (-1)x + (-7) = 0 \qquad \text{our equation}$$

We see that $a = 1$, $b = -1$, and $c = -7$.

$$x = \frac{-b \pm \sqrt{b^2 - 4ac}}{2a} \quad \longrightarrow \quad x = \frac{-(-1) \pm \sqrt{(-1)^2 - 4(1)(-7)}}{2(1)}$$

$$\longrightarrow \quad x = \frac{1 \pm \sqrt{1 + 28}}{2} \quad \longrightarrow \quad x = \frac{1 \pm \sqrt{29}}{2}$$

practice Use the quadratic equation to find the roots of the following equations:

a. $2x^2 - 3x - 7 = 0$

b. $3x - 1 = -2x^2$

problem set 119

1.
(117)
The weight of a body on or above the surface of the earth varies inversely with the square of the distance from the body to the center of the earth. If a body weighs 6000 pounds at a distance of 10,000 miles from the center of the earth, how much would it weigh 5000 miles from the center of the earth?

2.
(114)
Maureen deposited $19,000 at 11 percent interest compounded annually.

(a) Write an equation that expresses the amount of money in the account as a function of n, where n equals the number of years since the original deposit was made.

(b) Use the equation in (a) to determine how much money is in the account at the end of $n = 8$ years.

(c) What was the total interest earned at $n = 8$ years?

3.
(117)
Greens varied inversely as blues squared. When there were 5 greens, there were 50 blues. How many greens were there when there were only 10 blues?

4.
(92)
The express train made the trip in 20 hours. The freight train took 25 hours because it was 10 miles per hour slower than the express train. What was the speed of each train? Begin by drawing a diagram of distances traveled and writing the distance equation.

5.
(58)
Inflation took its toll, and the merchant had to mark the suit up 30 percent so it would sell for $156. What was the original price of the suit?

6.
(89)
Good ones were $7 each and sorry ones were only $3 each. If Fiona spent $414 and bought 2 more good ones than sorry ones, how many of each kind did she buy?

7.
(77)
Find three consecutive odd integers such that -3 times the sum of the first and third is 50 greater than 8 times the opposite of the second.

Use the quadratic formula to solve the following quadratic equations. Begin by writing each equation in standard form so that it can be compared to $ax^2 + bx + c = 0$ in order to determine the values of a, b, and c.

8. $-3x = -2x^2 + 10$
(119)

9. $-2x = 5 - x^2$
(119)

10. $x^2 + 2x - 11 = 0$
(119)

11. $5x^2 - 6x - 4 = 0$
(119)

Solve the following quadratic equations by completing the square:

12. $-3x = -x^2 + 10$ **13.** $-2x = 5 - x^2$ **14.** $x^2 + 2x - 11 = 0$
(118)   (118)   (118)

Simplify:

15. $\left(4 + 2\sqrt{2}\right)\left(\sqrt{2} + 2\right)$ **16.** $\sqrt{\dfrac{3}{8}}$ **17.** $\dfrac{\sqrt{2} + 1}{\sqrt{2}}$
(112)   (116)   (116)

18. Graph the following inequalities on the rectangular coordinate system: $\begin{cases} y \geq x \\ y \geq -x + 2 \end{cases}$
(115)

19. Sketch the graph of $F(x) = -x^3 - 3$.
(110)

20. Sketch the graph of $G(x) = (x - 3)^2 + 1$.
(110)

21. Sketch the graphs of the following exponential functions. Then use a graphing calculator
(114)   to confirm your sketches.

     (a) $y = 2^x$ (b) $y = 3^x$ (c) $y = 4^x$

     (d)   What point do all three graphs have in common?

22. Find the equation of the line that passes through the points $(-2, 3)$ and $(4, 5)$.
(106)

23. Find the equation of the line that passes through the point $(1, 3)$ and is parallel to
(107) $y = -x + 8$.

24. Graph on a number line: $-3 + |x| \geq -2$; $D = \{\text{Reals}\}$
(102)

Factor:

25. $2x^2 - 5x - 25$ **26.** $acb - ack + 2b - 2k$
(109)   (105)

Solve:

27. $-56 = 15x + x^2$ **28.** $\sqrt{x - 3} + 4 = 5$
(88)   (108)

29. Simplify: $\dfrac{x + \dfrac{4x}{3y}}{\dfrac{2ax}{y} + 4}$
(68)

30. Find the volume and the surface area
(72)   of this right circular cone.

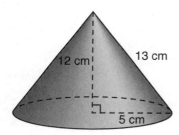

12 cm   13 cm

5 cm

LESSON 120 *Box-and-Whisker Plots*

Another graphical method used to display data is called the **box-and-whisker plot.** It uses five dots, two rectangles called *boxes*, and lines on the end of the boxes called *whiskers* to divide a set of data into four equal or approximately equal groups. We will show how to construct a box-and-whisker plot for a set of data. We shall use the same data as presented in Lesson 85. In that lesson, we were given test scores for a class of 30 students. We begin by rewriting the test scores in order from least to greatest.

56, 58, 62, 65, 69, 70, 74, 74, 75, 75, 80, 81, 81, 82, 83,
85, 86, 87, 87, 88, 88, 89, 90, 91, 92, 94, 95, 95, 96, 96

Now we draw a number line that covers the full range of our data.

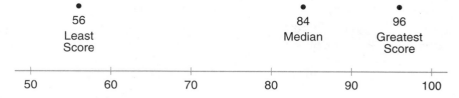

The three dots above the number line represent the location of the least score 56, the median score 84, and the greatest score 96. Now we find the median score of those scores less than 84 and the median score of those scores greater than 84. There are fifteen scores less than 84. Fifteen is an odd number, so the median score of these numbers, called the **first quartile,** is the eighth score on the ordered list. Therefore,

First quartile = 74

There are fifteen scores greater than 84. Fifteen is an odd number, so the median score between these numbers, called the **third quartile,** is the eighth score after the median of the ordered list. Therefore,

Third quartile = 90

Now we have five dots above the number line that represent the location of the least score 56, the first quartile score 74, the median score 84, the third quartile score 90, and the greatest score 96, as shown below.

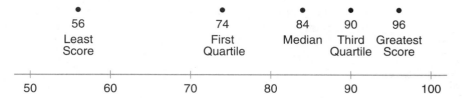

Next, we make a box with the first quartile score and the third quartile score on the outer sides. Then we draw a line inside the box, through the median score. Finally, we draw two lines called **whiskers** from the sides of the box to the dots that mark the location of the least score and the greatest score, as shown below.

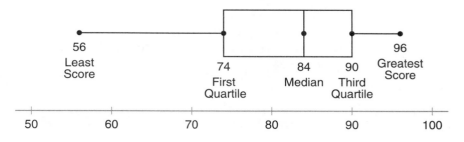

The box-and-whisker plot shown on the previous page separates the scores into four approximately equal groups. This allows us to see how the scores are spread out. Approximately one fourth of the scores lie in the region denoted by the leftmost whisker, which extends from the least score to the first quartile. The left half of the box, which extends from the first quartile to the median, shows where the next approximate one fourth of the scores lie. The right half of the box, which extends from the median to the third quartile, shows where the next approximate one fourth of the scores lie. The next approximate one fourth of the scores lie in the region denoted by the rightmost whisker, which extends from the third quartile to the greatest score. Thus, the box contains approximately one half of the data points, while each whisker contains approximately one fourth of the data points.

example 120.1　Shown are the salaries of twelve mathematics textbook editors (in thousands of dollars):

$$25, 23, 35, 33, 29, 31, 18, 21, 27, 19, 24, 28$$

Construct a box-and-whisker plot of this data.

solution　We begin by arranging the data from least to greatest.

$$18, 19, 21, 23, 24, 25, 27, 28, 29, 31, 33, 35$$

We note that the range of the data is from 18 to 35. The median is halfway between the sixth and seventh numbers, 25 and 27. Thus the median is 26. Below, we show a number line that covers the range and indicates the least number, median, and greatest number.

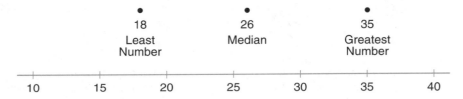

Now to determine the sides of the box, we need to find the value of the first quartile number and the third quartile number. The first quartile number is the median of the set of the first six numbers in the ordered list. This is the number between the third and fourth numbers, 21 and 23. Thus the first quartile is 22. Similarly, the third quartile number is the median of the last six numbers in the ordered list. Thus, the third quartile is halfway between the ninth and tenth numbers, 29 and 31. Thus the third quartile is 30. We now have all the information to draw our box-and-whisker plot. Note that the box-and-whisker plot for this example divides the data into four equal groups.

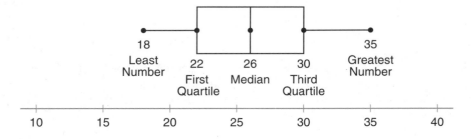

example 120.2　The box-and-whisker plot shows the scores made on the final exam by 150 students. (a) Find the range, median, mode, and mean of the scores. (b) Describe the distribution of the scores.

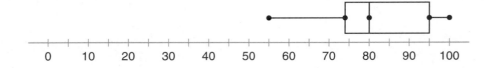

solution (a) It appears that the scores range from about 55 to 100, so the range is **45.** The median (middle score) is marked by the middle dot at about **80.** The mode and the mean **cannot be determined** from a box-and-whisker plot.

(b) The box-and-whisker plot provides some information for a given set of data. It identifies the lowest and the highest scores and the middle score. Approximately one fourth of the scores fall in each interval between any pair of consecutive dots.

practice   **a.** The box-and-whisker plot shows the scores made on the weekly math test by 100 students.

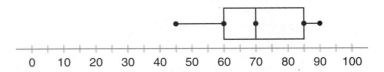

(1) Find the range, median, mode, and mean of the scores.

(2) Describe the distribution of the scores.

b. The number of points scored in the last twelve tournaments by the winning basketball team were as follows:

$$82, 100, 98, 80, 84, 86, 93, 98, 95, 93, 110, 120$$

Construct a box-and-whisker plot of these scores.

problem set   **1.** The box-and-whisker plot shows the starting salaries (in thousands of dollars) of new
120 *(45,120)* math Ph.D.'s.

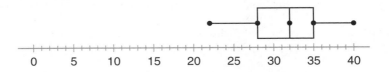

(a) Find the range, median, mode, and mean of the salaries.

(b) Describe the distribution of the salaries.

2. The winning scores in the last twelve championship football games were as follows:
(120)

$$37, 45, 7, 10, 19, 13, 23, 21, 27, 25, 33, 35$$

Construct a box-and-whisker plot of these scores.

3. The number of birds tripled every hour. If there were 100 birds at first, how many were
(114) there in 10 hours? (*Hint*: Use the formula $A_t = A_0 y^t$.)

4. The weight of a body on or above the surface of the earth varies inversely with the square
(117) of the distance from the body to the center of the earth. If a body weighs 25,000 pounds at a distance of 100,000 miles from the center of the earth, how much would it weigh 5000 miles from the center of the earth?

5. Paula ran to Hugo in 6 hours, while Busking walked the same distance in 72 hours. How
(92) fast did Paula run if her speed was 11 kilometers per hour faster than Busking's? How far was it to Hugo? Begin by drawing a diagram of distances traveled and writing the distance equation.

6. Horses sold for $400 each and ponies for only $100. Weir spent $4500 and bought 5 more
(89) horses than ponies. How many horses did she buy?

7. Judy deposited $500 she received from Frank at 5 percent interest compounded annually.
(114)

(a) Write an equation that expresses the amount of money in the account as a function of n, where n equals the number of years since the original deposit was made.

(b) Use the equation in (a) to determine how much money is in the account at $n = 3$ years.

(c) What was the total interest earned at $n = 3$ years?

8. The ratio of dullards to scholars was 2 to 17. If there were 38,000 people at the university,
(39)   how many were scholars?

9. Four times the sum of twice the number and 7 exceeds the value of the number by 70.
(33)   What is the number?

Use the quadratic formula to solve the following quadratic equations:

10. $-2 = x^2 + 6x$ **11.** $-7x = 4 - 2x^2$
(119)   (119)

Solve the following quadratic equations by completing the square:

12. $-5 = x^2 - 7x$ **13.** $-3x = 4 - x^2$
(118)   (118)

Solve by factoring:

14. $-4 + 9x^2 = 0$ **15.** $5 = -x^2 - 6x$
(88)   (88)

16. Sketch the graph of $F(x) = |x + 1| - 1$.
(110)

17. Sketch the graph of $G(x) = -(x - 3)^3$.
(110)

18. Graph on a number line: $0 \not\leq -x - 3 \not\leq 2$; $D = \{Reals\}$
(111)

19. Find the equations of lines (a) and (b).
(75)

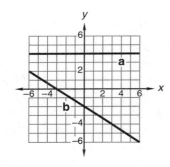

20. Graph the following inequalities on the rectangular coordinate system:
(115)

(a) $y \geq -3x + 2$ (b) $y < x$

21. Find the equation of a line that passes through the points $(8, 6)$ and $(-1, 3)$.
(106)

Simplify:

22. (a) $\sqrt{\dfrac{5}{8}}$ (b) $\dfrac{\sqrt{5} + 3}{\sqrt{5}}$ **23.** $-3\sqrt{12}\left(2\sqrt{6} - 5\sqrt{8}\right)$
(116)   (84)

Factor:

24. $-33 + 30x + 3x^2$ **25.** $ax^2 + 5a - 4x^2 - 20$
(71)   (105)

26. Are the following numbers rational numbers or irrational numbers?
(61)

(a) $\sqrt{8}$ (b) $\sqrt{3^2 + 4^2}$ (c) $\dfrac{\pi}{2\pi}$

27. Which of the following diagrams, graphs, or sets of ordered pairs depict functions?
(84,87)

(a)
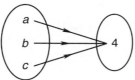

(b)
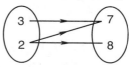

(c)
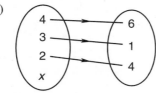

(d)
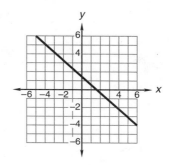

    (e)   (4, 3), (3, 2), (3, −2)   (f)   (4, 2), (4, 3), (4, 3)   (g)   (4, 2), (3, −2), (7, −8)

28. If $f(x) = x^2 - 2x + 3$, find $f(x + 2)$.
(82)

29. Simplify by adding like terms. Write your answer with all variables in the denominator.
(41)

$$x^2 y^{-2} - \frac{3x^2}{y^2} + \frac{12x^4 xy^{-2}}{x^3} - \frac{3x^2 y^2}{x^{-4}}$$

30. A base of the right solid 8 inches high is shown. Find the surface area and the volume of
(15,20) the right solid. Dimensions are in inches.

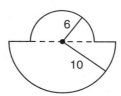
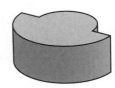

Properties of the Set of Real Numbers

A.A
big words with small meanings

Every discipline has big words with small meanings. These words are not intimidating to people who have used them for a long time. When talking to another doctor, a doctor will use words such as mandible, clavicle, and scapula. The doctor will use the words jawbone, collar bone, and shoulder blade to convey the same meanings when talking to a patient. In mathematics, we use the words **identity, inverse, associative, commutative,** and **distributive** to describe five properties of the set of real numbers. These words have very simple meanings.

A.B
identity and inverse

Think of a number. Then add 0 to the number. The result is **identically** the number you thought of. Then multiply your number by 1. The result is **identically** the number you thought of. We give big names with small meanings to the number 0 and the number 1. We say that the number 0 is the **identity for addition** and the number 1 is the **identity for multiplication.** That's all there is to it.

The identity for addition (the additive identity) is the number 0 because

$$4 + 0 = 4 \qquad \text{and} \qquad -13 + 0 = -13$$

The identity for multiplication (the multiplicative identity) is the number 1 because

$$4 \cdot 1 = 4 \qquad \text{and} \qquad (-13) \cdot (1) = -13$$

Pick any number. What number do you add to your number so that the sum is the number 0? The opposite of the number, of course. If the number you picked was +4, you would add −4 to get a sum of 0. If the number you picked was −13, you would add 13 to get a sum of 0 because +13 is the opposite of −13.

We say that −4 is the **additive inverse** of +4 and that +13 is the additive inverse of −13. **Every number has its own special additive inverse.** If you add a number and its additive inverse, the result is zero, which is the additive identity.

> The additive inverse of +37 is −37.
>
> The additive inverse of −163 is +163.
>
> The additive inverse of −1485.6 is +1485.6.
>
> The additive inverse of −p is +p.

If your number was +4, what number would you multiply by to get a product of +1? You would multiply by 1 over +4, of course. If your number was −13, you would multiply by 1 over −13.

$$4 \cdot \frac{1}{4} = 1 \qquad (-13) \times \left(\frac{1}{-13} \right) = 1$$

We say that the **multiplicative inverse** of 4 is 1 over 4, and the multiplicative inverse of –13 is 1 over –13. We see that the multiplicative inverse of a number is just one over that number. **Thus, the multiplicative inverse of a number is the same thing as the reciprocal of the number. Every number has its own special multiplicative inverse.** The product of a number and its multiplicative inverse **is always the multiplicative identity.**

The multiplicative inverse of -5 is $-\dfrac{1}{5}$.

The multiplicative inverse of $-\dfrac{1}{5}$ is -5.

The multiplicative inverse of 42 is $\dfrac{1}{42}$.

The multiplicative inverse of $\dfrac{1}{42}$ is 42.

The multiplicative inverse of $-p$ is $-\dfrac{1}{p}$.

A.C
commutative property

The sum of 2 and 3 equals the sum of 3 and 2. The sum of a and b equals the sum of b and a.

$$2 + 3 = 3 + 2 \qquad a + b = b + a$$

The product of 2 and 3 equals the product of 3 and 2. The product of a and b equals the product of b and a.

$$2 \cdot 3 = 3 \cdot 2 \qquad a \cdot b = b \cdot a$$

If we exchange the order of the numbers when we add two numbers, the sum is the same. If we exchange the order of the numbers when we multiply two numbers, the product is the same. We would call these properties (peculiarities) of the set of real numbers the **exchange property for addition** and the **exchange property for multiplication** except for a historical occurrence.

The first modern universities (so called because "universal" truths were studied) were the universities of Paris and Bologna. These schools began as a collection of scholars and teachers in the 1100s. The teachers and the students came from many countries, and they all spoke Latin because all the books they used were written in Latin. All classes were taught in Latin. The Latin word meaning "to exchange" was *commutare*. Thus, at these universities, they used a form of this word to describe the exchange properties. Today we call these properties the **commutative property of addition** and the **commutative property of multiplication.** What do these big words tell us? They just tell us that

$$4 + 2 = 2 + 4 \qquad \text{and that} \qquad 4 \cdot 2 = 2 \cdot 4$$

If we use letters instead of numbers, we can write

$$a + b = b + a \qquad \text{and} \qquad ab = ba$$

A.D
associative property

We remember that addition is a binary operation because only two numbers can be added in one step. If we want to find the sum of three numbers, we must add twice.

$$(4 + 2) + 3 \qquad 4 + (2 + 3)$$
$$= 6 + 3 \qquad\quad = 4 + 5$$
$$= 9 \qquad\qquad\; = 9$$

On the left, we "associated" 4 and 2 and found that their sum was 6. Then we added 6 to 3 to get 9. On the right, we "associated" 2 and 3 and found their sum was 5. Then we added 4 to 5 to get 9. Because we can "associate" the first two numbers or the last two numbers of a three-number addition problem, we say that **real numbers are associative under the operation of addition,** and we call this fact the **associative property of addition.** Do not complain. Remember that doctors talk about mandibles, clavicles, and scapulae. Every discipline has its own jargon.

Now guess what? We can do the same thing for multiplication. Multiplication is also a binary operation because only two numbers can be multiplied in one step. If we want to find the product of three numbers, we must multiply twice.

$$(4 \cdot 2)3 \qquad 4(2 \cdot 3)$$

$$= 8 \cdot 3 \qquad = 4 \cdot 6$$

$$= 24 \qquad\quad = 24$$

On the left we associated the first two numbers for the first multiplication, and on the right we associated the last two numbers. Because we will get the same answer both ways with any three real numbers, we say that the **real numbers are associative under the operation of multiplication,** and we call this fact the **associative property of multiplication.**

A.E
distributive property

The product of a number and a sum can be found two different ways. If we consider

$$4(3 + 2)$$

we find that we get the same answer if we begin by adding $3 + 2$ and then multiplying by 4 or if we multiply 4 by 3 and multiply 4 by 2 and then add.

Adding first	Multiplying first
$4(3 + 2)$	$4(3 + 2)$
$= 4(5)$	$= (4)(3) + (4)(2)$
$= 20$	$= 20$

When we multiply first, mathematicians say that we have **distributed** the multiplication over addition, and they call this property the **distributive property.** When we are faced with an expression that has variables inside the parentheses, such as

$$4(b + c)$$

we cannot add first because we do not know what numbers b and c represent. But we can multiply and get

$$4(b + c) = 4b + 4c$$

Before 1965, teachers would tell students to "multiply out." Now many teachers say "use the distributive property to expand." This phrase just means to "multiply out."

A.F
field properties

The set of real numbers is **closed** under the operations of addition and multiplication. This means that the sum of any two real numbers and the product of any two real numbers is a real number. The set of real numbers has nine other properties. We say that any set of numbers that is closed under the operations of multiplication and addition and has these nine properties constitutes a **field.** There is no special significance attached to the word field. We have to use some name, and field is possibly as good a name as any other. It is the word that we use to describe a set that, when used in the operations of addition and multiplication, has these nine properties. The chart below gives the names of the properties and both a numerical and an abstract example of each property.

Properties of a Field		
Addition	Name	Multiplication
$4 + 0 = 4$ $a + 0 = a$	IDENTITY	$4 \cdot 1 = 4$ $a \cdot 1 = a$
$4 + (-4) = 0$ $a + (-a) = 0$	INVERSE	$4 \cdot \dfrac{1}{4} = 1$ $a \cdot \dfrac{1}{a} = 1$
$4 + (3 + 2) = (4 + 3) + 2$ $a + (b + c) = (a + b) + c$	ASSOCIATIVE PROPERTY	$(4 \cdot 3) \cdot 2 = 4 \cdot (3 \cdot 2)$ $(a \cdot b) \cdot c = a \cdot (b \cdot c)$
$4 + 2 = 2 + 4$ $a + b = b + a$	COMMUTATIVE PROPERTY	$4 \cdot 2 = 2 \cdot 4$ $ab = ba$
DISTRIBUTIVE PROPERTY $4(3 + 2) = 4 \cdot 3 + 4 \cdot 2$ $a(b + c) = ab + ac$		

We note that there are four properties listed under addition and that the same four properties are listed under multiplication. These are the **identity,** the **inverse,** the **associative property,** and the **commutative property.** At the bottom of the chart we state the **distributive property** in the middle of the page since the **distributive property includes both addition and multiplication.**

Before the late 1960s, the study of the properties of the set of real numbers was reserved for college-level abstract algebra and advanced math courses. In such courses students study the properties of the set of real numbers and identify other systems that have similar properties.

In Algebra 1 students are often confused by the study of properties of real numbers because they cannot see why these properties are given so much attention. Why do we need to have an identity for addition? Why is it helpful for every number to have an additive inverse? These are questions that will be answered in more advanced mathematics courses. At this point we will content ourselves with the knowledge that the concepts described by the big words are easily understood, and we will learn not to be intimidated by them.

APPENDIX B Glossary

abscissa   The *x* coordinate of a point in a rectangular coordinate system.

absolute value   In reference to a number, the positive number that describes the distance on a number line of the graph of the number from the origin. The absolute value of zero is zero.

acute angle   An angle whose measure is between 0° and 90°.

acute triangle   A triangle in which all the angles are acute.

addend   Any one of a set of numbers to be added.

addition   The operation of combining two numbers or quantities to form a sum.

additive inverse   For any nonzero real number, the opposite of the number. The sum of any real number and its additive inverse is zero.

additive property of inequality   A property of real numbers such that, for any real numbers a, b, and c, if $a > b$, then $a + c > b + c$ and also $c + a > c + b$.

algebraic expression   An expression obtained by combining constants and/or variables using the arithmetic operators $+$, $-$, $\times$, or $\div$.

algebraic phrase   A meaningful arrangement of numbers and variables.

algebraic proof   Use of definitions, axioms, and deductive reasoning to prove algebraic assertions.

altitude   In reference to a triangle, the perpendicular distance from either the base of the triangle or an extension of the base to the opposite vertex. Any one of the three sides can be designated as the base.

angle   The figure formed by two rays that have a common endpoint. Also, the measure of the rotation of a ray about its endpoint from an initial position to a final position.

area   The number that tells how many square units are contained in a closed figure.

associative property   A property of real numbers that notes that, for any real numbers a, b, and c, $(a + b) + c = a + (b + c)$ and $(a \cdot b) \cdot c = a \cdot (b \cdot c)$.

average   In statistics, the sum of a set of numbers divided by the number of numbers in the set. Also called the *mean*.

axiom   A statement that is assumed to be true without proof. Also called *postulate*.

basic arithmetic operations   Addition, subtraction, multiplication, and division.

binomial   A polynomial of two terms.

box-and-whisker plot   In statistics, a method of displaying data using two rectangles called "boxes" and lines on the ends of the boxes called "whiskers" to divide a set of data into four equal or approximately equal groups.

Cartesian coordinate system   A standard method of locating points in the plane that uses pairs of numbers denoting distances along two fixed intersecting number lines, called the *axes*. The axes are perpendicular to each other and intersect at the origin of both axes. The system is named for the French mathematician René Descartes. Also called a *rectangular coordinate system*.

centimeter   Metric unit of measurement: 1 centimeter = 10 millimeters; 100 centimeters = 1 meter.

chord   In reference to a circle, a line segment whose endpoints are on the circle.

circle   A planar geometric figure in which every point on the figure is the same distance from a point called the *center* of the circle.

circumference   The distance around a circle. Also called the *perimeter* of the circle.

coefficient   Any factor or any product of factors of a product.

commutative property   A property of real numbers that notes that, for any real numbers a and b, $a + b = b + a$ and $a \cdot b = b \cdot a$.

complex fraction   A fraction whose numerator or denominator (or both) contains a fraction.

concave polygon   A polygon in which one or more interior angles have a measure greater than $180°$.

conditional equation   An equation whose truth or falsity depends on the numbers used to replace the variables in the equation.

conjunction   A statement of two conditions which must both be true in order for the statement to be true.

consecutive integers   Integers that are 1 unit apart.

consistent equations   Simultaneous equations that have a single solution. The graphs of consistent equations are lines that intersect at a single point.

constant   A quantity whose value does not change.

constant of proportionality   A constant in an equation that defines the relationship of two or more variables. For example, in the equation $y = 4m^2x$, the number 4 is the constant of proportionality.

convex polygon   A polygon in which all interior angles have a measure less than or equal to $180°$.

coordinate   A number that is associated with a point on a graph.

coordinate plane   A plane with a coordinate system that can be used to designate the position of any point in the plane.

cube   A geometric solid that has six identical square faces.

cubic unit   A cube having edges that measure one unit in length.

curve   The path traced by a moving point.

data   In statistics, numerical information.

decagon   A polygon with ten sides.

decimal number   A number designated by a linear arrangement of one or more of the 10 digits and that uses a decimal point to define the place value of the digits.

decimal system   The system of numeration that uses decimal numbers.

deductive reasoning   The process of reasoning logically from clearly stated premises to a conclusion.

degree   A unit of measure for angles. A right angle is a $90°$ angle and a straight angle is a $180°$ angle.

degree of a polynomial   The degree of the highest-degree term in the polynomial, calculated as follows: The degree of a term in a polynomial is the sum of the exponents in the term. For example, the terms x^5, x^3y^2, and xy^2mp are all fifth-degree terms.

denominator   The number or quantity under the fraction bar in a fraction; i.e. the divisor in a fraction. For example, in the fraction $\frac{a}{b}$, the number b is the *denominator*.

dependent equations   Simultaneous equations whose solution sets are equal. The graphs of dependent equations are single lines.

dependent variable   When considering a function, the variable whose value depends on the value assigned to another variable, called the *independent variable*. For example, in the function $y = 2x + 3$, y is regarded as the dependent variable.

diameter   In reference to a circle, the length of a chord of a circle that passes through the center of the circle.

difference   The result of subtracting one number or quantity from another number or quantity.

digit   Any of the 10 symbols of the decimal system: 0, 1, 2, 3, 4, 5, 6, 7, 8, 9.

dimension   A measure of spatial extent, especially length, width, and height.

direct variation   A relationship between two variables such that their ratio is constant. For example, the equation $y = kx$ defines a direct variation between x and y where k is the *constant of proportionality*.

disjunction   A statement of two conditions of which only one condition must be true in order for the statement to be true.

distributive property   A property of real numbers that notes that, for any real numbers a, b, and c, $a(b + c) = ab + ac$ and $(b + c)a = ba + ca$.

dividend   A number or quantity that is divided by another number or quantity. For example, in the expression $a \div b$, the number a is the *dividend*.

division   The inverse operation of multiplication. If one number or quantity is divided by another number or quantity, the result is called the *quotient*.

divisor   A number or quantity that divides another number or quantity. For example, in the expression $a \div b$, the number b is the *divisor*.

dodecagon   A polygon with twelve sides.

domain of a function   The set of numbers which are permissible replacement values for the independent variable of a function.

element of a set   Any one of the individual objects or members belonging to a set.

empty set   The set that has no members, denoted by the symbol $\varnothing$ or the notation { }. Also called the *null set*.

equality   The property of two things being equal and symbolized by the equals sign.

equals sign   Symbol of equality (=).

equation   An algebraic statement consisting of two algebraic expressions connected by an equals sign.

equiangular polygon   A polygon whose angles all have equal measure.

equiangular triangle   A triangle whose three angles all have equal measure. Each angle in an equiangular triangle has a measure of 60°.

equilateral polygon   A polygon whose sides all have equal length.

equilateral triangle   A triangle whose three sides all have equal length. Each angle in an equilateral triangle has a measure of 60°.

equivalent equations   Equations that have the same solution set.

even integer   Any member of the set $\{\ldots, -6, -4, -2, 0, 2, 4, 6, \ldots\}$.

event   In statistics, an outcome of an experiment.

exponent   The number that indicates that number of times the base of a power is to be used as a factor.

exponential function   A function of the form $y = kb^x$, where k and b are constants and $b \neq 0$ or $b \neq 1$.

factor   One of two or more numbers or quantities that are multiplied to form a product. For example, 1, 2, 3, and 6 are all factors of 6; $x + 1$ and $x - 2$ are factors of $x^2 - x - 2$.

fraction   A quotient indicated by writing two numbers vertically and separating them with a short line segment called the *fraction bar*.

function   A mapping that pairs each member of a set called the *domain* with exactly one member of another set called the *range*.

functional notation   The use of letters and parentheses to indicate a functional relationship. For example, $f(x) = x^2 + 2x + 2$.

geometric figure   A figure made up of straight lines or curved lines or both.

geometric solid   A geometric figure that has three dimensions.

graph   The mark(s) made on a coordinate system that indicates the location of a point or a set of points.

greatest common factor   Of two or more items, the product of all prime factors common to every term, each to the highest power that it occurs in any of the terms.

heptagon   A polygon with seven sides.

hexagon   A polygon with six sides.

histogram   In statistics, a method of displaying data using a bar graph that represents the frequency of occurrence of data values.

hypotenuse   The side opposite the right angle in a right triangle.

image   In a function, the element of the range that is paired with a particular element of the domain.

improper fraction   A fraction whose numerator is greater than the denominator. An improper fraction can always be written as a *mixed number*.

inconsistent equations   Simultaneous equations that have no common solution. The graphs of inconsistent equations are parallel lines.

independent events   In statistics, events such that the outcome of one event does not affect the probability of the occurrence of another event.

independent variable   When considering a function, the variable whose value can be chosen. For example, in the function $y = 2x + 3$, x is regarded as the independent variable.

index   In a radical expression, the number that indicates what root is to be taken.

inequality   A mathematical statement comparing quantities that are not equal.

integer   Any member of the set $\{ \ldots, -4, -3, -2, -1, 0, 1, 2, 3, 4, \ldots \}$.

intercept   In reference to a graph on a rectangular coordinate system, the x intercept is the point where the graph crosses the x axis and the y intercept is the point where the graph crosses the y axis.

inverse operation   An operation which "undoes" another operation. For example, addition and subtraction are inverse operations. Also, multiplication and division are inverse operations.

inverse variation   A relationship between two variables such that their product is constant. For example, the equation $xy = k$ or $y = \frac{k}{x}$ defines an inverse variation between x and y where k is the *constant of proportionality*.

irrational number   Any number that cannot be written as a quotient of integers. For example, the numbers $\sqrt{2}$, $\sqrt[4]{17}$, π, and e are irrational numbers.

isosceles triangle   A triangle that has at least two sides of equal length.

kilometer   Metric unit of measurement: 1 kilometer = 1000 meters.

lateral surface area   The total area of the "sides" of a geometric solid.

lead coefficient   Of a polynomial, the coefficient of the term with the greatest exponent. For example, in the polynomial $5x^2 - 3x + 2$ the lead coefficient is 5.

least common multiple   The smallest number that can be divided evenly by each of a given set of numbers. For example, 6, 12, and 27 have a least common multiple of 108.

length   The distance between two designated points in a geometric figure.

like terms   Terms that have the same variables in the same form or in equivalent forms so that the terms (excluding numerical coefficients) represent the same number regardless of the nonzero values assigned the variables.

line   In mathematics, a straight curve that has no width and no end.

line segment   A part of a line that consists of two endpoints and all points between the endpoints.

linear equation   A first-degree polynomial equation in one or more variables.

literal coefficient   A coefficient containing only letters.

literal factor   A factor that is a letter.

mean   In statistics, the sum of a set of numbers divided by the number of numbers in the set. Also called the *average*.

measure of central tendency   In statistics, a value that tells what number is at the center of a set of data. Different measures of central tendency include the median, mode, and mean.

median   In statistics, the middle number in a set of numbers when they are arranged in order from the least to the greatest. If there is an odd number of numbers in the set, the median is the middle number. If there is an even number of numbers in the set, the median is the average of the two middle numbers.

members of a set   Elements of a set.

meter   Metric unit of measurement: 1 meter = 100 centimeters; 1000 meters = 1 kilometer.

millimeter   Metric unit of measurement: 10 millimeters = 1 centimeter.

minuend   The number from which another number is to be subtracted. For example, in the expression $a - b$, the number a is the minuend.

mixed number   A number of the form of an integer plus a proper fraction, written without a plus sign $\left(\text{e.g., } 2\frac{1}{3}\right)$.

mode   In statistics, the number in a set of numbers that appears more than any other number.

monomial   A polynomial that has only one term.

multiplication   The operation of combining two numbers or quantities to form a product.

multiplicative inverse   For any nonzero real number, the reciprocal of the number. The product of any nonzero real number and its multiplicative inverse is 1.

multivariable equation   An equation that contains more than one variable.

natural numbers   The set of numbers that we use to count objects or things. Also called the *positive integers*, i.e., any member of the set $\{1, 2, 3, \dots\}$.

negative exponent   An exponent preceded by a minus sign, defined as follows: If n is any real number and x is any real number that is not zero, then $1/x^n = x^{-n}$.

nonagon   A polygon with nine sides.

null set   The set that has no members, denoted by the symbol $\varnothing$ or the notation { }. Also called the *empty set*.

number   An idea that is designated by a numeral.

number line   A line divided into units of equal length with one point chosen as the origin, or zero point. The numbers to the right of zero are the positive real numbers, and the numbers to the left of zero are the negative real numbers.

numeral   A single symbol or a collection of symbols that is used to express the idea of a particular number.

numerator   The number or quantity above the fraction bar in a fraction; i.e. the dividend in a fraction. For example, in the fraction $\frac{a}{b}$, the number a is the numerator.

numerical coefficient   A coefficient that is a number.

numerical expression   A meaningful arrangement of numerals that has a single value.

numerical factor   A factor that is a number.

obtuse angle   An angle whose measure is between 90° and 180°.

obtuse triangle   A triangle which contains an obtuse angle.

octagon   A polygon with eight sides.

odd integer   Any member of the set $\{\ldots, -5, -3, -1, 1, 3, 5, \ldots\}$.

operation   The process of carrying out a rule or procedure such as adding, subtracting, multiplying, dividing, or taking a root of.

opposites   Two numbers with the same absolute value but with different signs.

order of operations   The order in which operations are performed on an algebraic expression.

ordered pair   A pair of numbers in a designated order that are enclosed in parentheses. For example, if the notation (5, 4) is an ordered pair of x and y, the value of x is 5 and the value of y is 4.

ordinate   The y coordinate of a point in a rectangular coordinate system.

origin   A beginning point. On a number line or coordinate plane, the number zero is associated with the origin.

outcome   A possible result in a probability problem.

overall average   In statistics, the sum of all the numbers divided by the number of numbers.

parallel lines   Lines in the same plane that do not intersect.

parallelogram   A quadrilateral that has two pairs of parallel sides.

pentagon   A polygon with five sides.

percent   One part in 100. For example, 60 percent means sixty-hundredths.

perimeter   The distance around the outside of a closed, planar geometric figure.

perpendicular lines   Two lines which intersect at right angles.

pi (π)   The ratio of the circumference of a circle to the diameter of that circle; $\pi \approx 3.14$.

planar geometric figure   Any figure that is drawn on a flat surface (i.e., any figure that has two dimensions).

polygon   Any simple, closed, planar geometric figure whose sides are line segments.

polynomial   An algebraic expression with one or more variables having only terms with real number coefficients and whole number powers of the variables.

positive real number   Any number that can be used to describe a physical distance greater than zero.

postulate   A statement that is assumed to be true without proof. Also called *axiom*.

power rule for exponents   A rule for exponents: If m, n, and x are real numbers and $x \neq 0$, then $\left(x^m \right)^n = x^{mn}$.

prime factor   A factor that is a prime number.

prime number   A natural number greater than 1 whose only whole number factors are 1 and the number itself.

primitive term   A basic mathematical term that cannot be defined exactly. The term is defined as best as is possible and then used to define other terms.

product   The result of multiplying two or more numbers or quantities.

product of square roots rule   A rule for evaluating products of radical expressions: If m and n are nonnegative real numbers, then $\sqrt{m}\sqrt{n} = \sqrt{mn}$ and $\sqrt{mn} = \sqrt{m}\sqrt{n}$.

product rule for exponents   A rule for exponents: If m, n, and x are real numbers and $x \neq 0$, then $x^m \cdot x^n = x^{m+n}$.

proper fraction   A fraction whose numerator is less than the denominator.

proportion   An equation or other statement which indicates that two ratios are equal.

quadrilateral   A polygon with four sides.

quotient   The result of dividing one number or quantity by another number or quantity.

quotient rule for exponents   A rule for exponents: If m, n, and x are real numbers and $x \neq 0$, then $x^m/x^n = x^{m-n} = 1/x^{n-m}$.

quotient rule for square roots   A rule for square roots: The square root of a quotient (fraction) equals the quotient of the square roots. For example, $\sqrt{3/2} = \sqrt{3}/\sqrt{2}$.

range   In statistics, the difference between the largest number and the smallest number in a set of numbers.

range of a function   The set of all images of the elements of the domain of a function.

rational expression   An algebraic expression that is written in fractional form.

rational equation   An equation in which at least one term is a rational expression.

rational number   Any number that can be written as a quotient of integers (division by zero excluded).

real numbers   The set of numbers that includes all members of the set of rational numbers and all members of the set of irrational numbers.

reciprocal   For any nonzero real number, the number in inverted form. For example, the reciprocal of 3 is $\frac{1}{3}$ and the reciprocal of $\frac{3}{4}$ is $\frac{4}{3}$.

rectangle   A parallelogram with four right angles.

regular polygon   A polygon in which all sides have the same length and all angles have the same measure.

relation   A pairing that matches each element of the domain with one or more images in the range.

rhombus   An equilateral parallelogram.

right angle   An angle whose measure is 90°.

right triangle   A triangle that has one right angle.

scalene triangle   A triangle that has no sides of equal length.

scientific notation   A method of writing a number as the product of a number between 1 and 10 with a power of 10. For example, 3241.5 in scientific notation is 3.2415×10^3, and 0.00063 in scientific notation is 6.3×10^{-4}.

set   A collection of objects. The individual objects that make up a set are called its *elements* or *members*.

set notation   The method of designating a set by enclosing the numbers of the set within braces.

simplify   To break down into the simplest, most easily understood form.

simultaneous equations   Two or more equations that together specify conditions for two or more variables. The solution of simultaneous equations involves finding values of the variables that satisfy both equations.

square   A rhombus with four right angles.

square root   A number that when multiplied by itself gives a given number.

square unit   A square having sides that measure one unit in length.

standard form   In reference to a polynomial equation, one in which the terms are in descending powers of the variable with all nonzero terms to the left of the equals sign.

statistics   The study of the collection, organization, and interpretation of numerical data.

stem-and-leaf plot   In statistics, a method of displaying data using certain digits as "stems" and the remaining digit or digits as "leaves."

straight angle   An angle whose measure is 180°.

subscripted variable   A variable with a subscript, i.e., a little letter, set slightly below and to the right of the variable $\left(\text{e.g., } N_D\right)$.

subtraction   The inverse operation of addition. If one number or quantity is subtracted from another number or quantity, the result is called the *difference*.

subtrahend   The number that is to be subtracted from another number. For example, in the expression $a - b$, the number b is the *subtrahend*.

sum   The result of adding two or more numbers or quantities.

surface area   The total area of all the exposed surfaces of a geometric solid.

trapezoid   A quadrilateral that has exactly two parallel sides.

triangle   A polygon with three sides.

trinomial   A polynomial of three terms.

undecagon   A polygon with eleven sides.

unit multiplier   A fraction that has units and has a value of 1. Unit multipliers are used to change the units of a number.

variable   A letter used to represent a number.

vertex   In reference to a polygon, a "corner" of the polygon.

volume   The number that tells how many cubic units are contained in a geometric solid.

weighted average   In statistics, the sum of the products of values and their weights, divided by the sum of the weights.

whole number   Any member of the set $\{0, 1, 2, 3, \ldots\}$.

zero exponent   An exponent of zero, which is evaluated as follows: If x is any real number that is not zero, then $x^0 = 1$.

Answers

1. $\frac{3}{5}$ 2. $\frac{1}{8}$ 3. $1\frac{2}{3}$ 4. $\frac{8}{15}$ 5. $\frac{7}{40}$ 6. $\frac{13}{24}$ 7. $\frac{18}{65}$ 8. $\frac{4}{15}$

9. $\frac{43}{45}$ 10. $\frac{11}{17}$ 11. $\frac{11}{26}$ 12. $\frac{6}{35}$ 13. $1\frac{11}{56}$ 14. $\frac{17}{20}$ 15. $\frac{21}{22}$

16. $5\frac{7}{10}$ 17. $13\frac{17}{24}$ 18. $8\frac{21}{40}$ 19. $7\frac{8}{15}$ 20. $20\frac{5}{8}$ 21. $8\frac{14}{15}$

22. $23\frac{14}{33}$ 23. $63\frac{7}{10}$ 24. $36\frac{47}{104}$ 25. $5\frac{43}{65}$ 26. $13\frac{77}{190}$ 27. $21\frac{47}{170}$

28. $12\frac{23}{56}$ units   29. $17\frac{74}{77}$ units   30. $9\frac{1}{16}$ units

practice

a. 70   b. $x = 40$; $y = 100$ c. $x = 34$; $y = 34$

1. Right angles   2. Straight angle

3. An acute angle is an angle that is smaller than a right angle.

4. An obtuse angle is an angle that is larger than a right angle, but smaller than a straight angle.

5. (a) 90°   (b) 180°   (c) 360°   6. Equilateral polygons   7. Equiangular polygons

8. Regular polygons

9. (a) A right triangle is a triangle that contains one right angle.

   (b) An acute triangle is a triangle that contains three acute angles.

   (c) An obtuse triangle is a triangle that contains one obtuse angle.

   (d) An equiangular triangle is a triangle that contains three angles of equal measure.

10. (a) An isosceles triangle is a triangle that has at least two sides of equal length.

   (b) An equilateral triangle is a triangle that contains three sides of equal length.

   (c) A scalene triangle is a triangle that contains three sides of unequal length.

11. 50   12. 40   13. $\frac{7}{9}$ 14. $\frac{31}{35}$ 15. $\frac{1}{3}$ 16. $\frac{11}{15}$ 17. $\frac{4}{7}$ 18. $6\frac{1}{2}$

19. $7\frac{5}{8}$ 20. $13\frac{1}{10}$ 21. $12\frac{14}{15}$ 22. $15\frac{4}{15}$ 23. $9\frac{3}{10}$ 24. $8\frac{2}{15}$ 25. $3\frac{1}{15}$

26. $2\frac{5}{6}$ 27. $1\frac{5}{6}$ 28. $7\frac{5}{9}$ cm   29. $6\frac{7}{8}$ m   30. $5\frac{8}{15}$ units

practice

a. 30 cm   b. 3 m   c. 38 km   d. 10π in. = 31.4 in.   e. $(18 + 3\pi)$ ft = 27.42 ft

1. 180°   2. (a) 60°   (b) 60°

3. The angles opposite the sides of equal length have equal measures.

4. The sides opposite the angles of equal measure have equal lengths.

5. Parallelogram   **6.** Trapezoid   **7.** 40 in.   **8.** 4 ft   **9.** 12π cm = 37.68 cm

10. 8π m = 25.12 m   **11.** 90 in.   **12.** 80 in.   **13.** $(12 + 2\pi)$ in. = 18.28 in.

14. $(26 + 3\pi)$ in. = 35.42 in.   **15.** 60   **16.** 35   **17.** $\dfrac{7}{9}$ **18.** $\dfrac{1}{6}$ **19.** 1   **20.** $7\dfrac{1}{4}$

21. $11\dfrac{8}{9}$ **22.** $21\dfrac{1}{2}$ **23.** $8\dfrac{1}{16}$ **24.** $13\dfrac{31}{56}$ **25.** $1\dfrac{1}{3}$ **26.** $11\dfrac{7}{33}$ **27.** $\dfrac{11}{12}$

28. $25\dfrac{15}{16}$ **29.** $26\dfrac{11}{15}$ ft   **30.** $3\dfrac{1}{6}$ yd

practice   **a.** $12\dfrac{3}{5}$ **b.** $2\dfrac{4}{11}$ **c.** 760.939   **d.** 724.74   **e.** 302.061   **f.** 100.7

g. 75(12)(2.54) cm   **h.** $\dfrac{450}{(12)(5280)}$ mi

problem set 4

1. A number is an idea. A numeral is a symbol used to express the idea of a number.

2. (a) Decimal system   (b) The Hindus of India   (c) 0, 1, 2, 3, 4, 5, 6, 7, 8, 9

3. (a) 1, 2, 3, 4, 5, …   (b) 1, 2, 3, 4, 5, …

4. A positive real number is any number that can be used to describe a physical distance greater than zero.

5. (a) A rectangle is a parallelogram with four right angles.

(b) A rhombus is an equilateral parallelogram.

(c) A square is a rhombus with four right angles.

(d) Yes

6. 20(2.54) cm   **7.** 25(12)(2.54) cm   **8.** 50 cm   **9.** 6 m   **10.** 16π in. = 50.24 in.

11. 10π ft = 31.4 ft   **12.** 54 cm   **13.** 110 cm   **14.** $(24 + 4\pi)$ cm = 36.56 cm

15. $(24 + 5\pi)$ cm = 39.7 cm   **16.** 55   **17.** $\dfrac{1}{3}$ **18.** $13\dfrac{5}{8}$ **19.** $2\dfrac{7}{8}$ **20.** $90\dfrac{5}{16}$

21. $8\dfrac{2}{5}$ **22.** 30   **23.** $\dfrac{27}{40}$ **24.** $4\dfrac{20}{39}$ **25.** 6.03301   **26.** 7.98209   **27.** 55.4984

28. 44   **29.** $13\dfrac{7}{8}$ m   **30.** $5\dfrac{1}{2}$ km

practice   **a.** 4   **b.** 4.2   **c.** −4   **d.** −8   **e.** 5

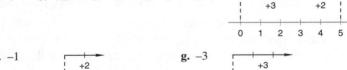

f. −1   **g.** −3

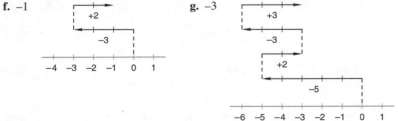

problem set 5

1. (a) {1, 2, 3, 4, …}   (b) {0, 1, 2, 3, 4, …}   (c) {…, −3, −2, −1, 0, 1, 2, 3, …}   **2.** Origin

3. (a) A dot on the number line that represents the location of the number

(b) The number that the point represents

(c) The greater number is further to the right-hand side on the number line.

4. 8   **5.** 8   **6.** 12   **7.** −10   **8.** −10   **9.** 18

10. –5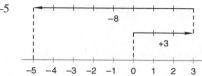

11. 1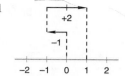

12. 7

13. 2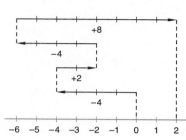

14. $\dfrac{28}{2.54}$ in.   **15.** $\dfrac{42}{(2.54)(12)}$ ft   **16.** 70 in.   **17.** 20π ft = 62.8 ft   **18.** 66 yd

19. $(36 + 6\pi)$ yd = 54.84 yd   **20.** 30   **21.** $14\dfrac{1}{9}$ **22.** $90\dfrac{5}{16}$ **23.** 12   **24.** $\dfrac{36}{59}$

25. $1\dfrac{109}{176}$ **26.** 23.12   **27.** 34.86   **28.** 0.9696   **29.** 4.003   **30.** $12\dfrac{1}{3}$ mi

practice   **a.** –6   **b.** –17   **c.** –17   **d.** –14

problem set 6

1. Add the absolute values of the numbers and give the result the same sign as that of the numbers.

2. Take the difference of the absolute values of the numbers and give it the sign of the number whose absolute value is greater.

3. Commutative property   **4.** (a) Sum (b) Difference (c) Product (d) Quotient

5. 5   **6.** –3   **7.** 3   **8.** –1   **9.** 0

10. 34(100) cm

11. 6(5280)(12) in.

12. 9 cm

13. 14π m = 43.96 m   **14.** –11   **15.** –17   **16.** 4

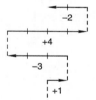

17. –1   **18.** 0   **19.** –5   **20.** –20   **21.** –3   **22.** –12

23. –11   **24.** 7   **25.** –7   **26.** 54 km

27. $(50 + 5\pi)$ km = 65.7 km   **28.** 65   **29.** 4   **30.** $5\dfrac{7}{10}$ in.

practice   **a.** 7   **b.** 1   **c.** 7   **d.** 5

problem set 7

1. (a) –2 (b) 2 (c) 0   **2.** Additive inverse

3. (a) {1, 2, 3, 4, …} (b) {0, 1, 2, 3, 4, …} (c) {…, –3, –2, –1, 0, 1, 2, 3, …}

4. –4   **5.** 4   **6.** –4   **7.** 4   **8.** $\dfrac{2200}{100}$ m   **9.** $\dfrac{3000}{(12)(5280)}$ mi   **10.** 96 in.

11. 24π ft = 75.36 ft   **12.** 8   **13.** –2   **14.** 4   **15.** 5   **16.** 0   **17.** 0   **18.** 3

19. –3   **20.** –9   **21.** 18   **22.** 224 yd   **23.** $(26 + 8\pi)$ yd = 51.12 yd   **24.** 30

25. $11\dfrac{5}{8}$ **26.** 20   **27.** $1\dfrac{1}{4}$ **28.** 443.61413   **29.** 0.1465712   **30.** $22\dfrac{1}{2}$ cm

practice   **a.** 57 in.^{2} **b.** 34 ft^2 **c.** 25π cm^2 = 78.5 cm^2 **d.** (22 + 2π) m^2 = 28.28 m^2

problem set 8

1. (a) $-\frac{1}{2}$ (b) $\frac{1}{2}$ (c) 0   2. Additive inverse   3. Right angles   4. Straight angle

5. 36(12)(2.54) cm   6. $\frac{44(2.54)}{(100)}$ m   7. 5 cm   8. 20 m^2 9. 6π in. = 18.84 in.

10. 16π ft^2 = 50.24 ft^2 11. 5   12. –14   13. –17   14. 1   15. 0   16. 2

17. 6   18. 15   19. 7   20. –10   21. 130 yd   22. (28 + 7π) yd = 49.98 yd

23. 30 cm^2 24. 24 cm^2 25. 45   26. $1\frac{5}{9}$ 27. 15

28. 5   29. 0.02   30. $27\frac{1}{2}$ m

practice   **a.** –8   **b.** –6   **c.** –12   **d.** 15   **e.** 2   **f.** –2   **g.** –2   **h.** 8

problem set 9

1. (a) Positive number   (b) Negative number   2. (a) –3 (b) 3 (c) 0   3. Opposite

4. 10   5. –10   6. –10   7. 15   8. 6   9. 2   10. –6   11. –2   12. 8

13. $\frac{320}{(2.54)(12)}$ ft   14. $\frac{65(100)}{(2.54)}$ in.   15. 12 in.   16. 3 ft   17. 25π yd^2 = 78.5 yd^2

18. –7   19. –4   20. –3   21. –5   22. –8   23. –2   24. 110 cm

25. (60 + 10π) cm = 91.4 cm   26. 54 m^2 27. 15 m^2 28. 37.04

29. 0.8866   30. $14\frac{1}{6}$ km

practice   **a.** Undefined   **b.** Indeterminate   **c.** 16   **d.** 240   **e.** 44(5280)^2 ft^2 **f.** $\frac{3500}{(100)^2}$ m^2

problem set 10

1. Commutative property   2. (a) Subtraction (b) Addition (c) Division (d) Multiplication

3. (a) $-\frac{1}{3}$ (b) $\frac{1}{3}$ (c) 0   4. Opposite   5. –24   6. 24   7. 48   8. $\frac{1}{2}$ 9. $\frac{5}{6}$

10. Undefined   11. 50(2.54) cm   12. 48(2.54)^2 cm^2 13. 5 cm   14. 120 m^2

15. 16π in. = 50.24 in.   16. 36π ft^2 = 113.04 ft^2 17. –4   18. –3   19. 8   20. 1

21. –10   22. –4   23. –5   24. 150 yd   25. 140 cm^2 26. 20 cm^2

27. (16 + 2π) cm^2 = 22.28 cm^2 28. $1\frac{1}{3}$ 29. 3.03   30. $6\frac{2}{3}$ m

practice   **a.** –102   **b.** 9   **c.** 5   **d.** 3

problem set 11

1. (a) $\frac{1}{2}$ (b) $-\frac{1}{2}$ (c) 1   2. Multiplicative inverse   3. Zero. Division by 0 is undefined.

4. Yes   5. An acute angle is an angle that is smaller than a right angle.

6. An obtuse angle is an angle that is larger than a right angle and smaller than a straight angle.

7. 25(100) cm   8. 40(100)^2 cm^2 9. $12\frac{1}{4}$ in.   10. 4 ft   11. 49π yd^2 = 153.86 yd^2

12. 4   13. –20   14. 1   15. –20   16. 22   17. 6   18. 0   19. 0   20. –16

21. –12   22. 7   23. 14   24. $\frac{2}{3}$ 25. 0   26. (38 + 4π) cm = 50.56 cm

27. 180 m^2 28. 35 m^2 29. 63 in.^{2} 30. $18\frac{1}{5}$ ft

practice   **a.** 25   **b.** 6   **c.** 26   **d.** Undefined

problem set 12

1. (a) 2 (b) –2 (c) 1   **2.** Multiplicative inverse   **3.** Zero. Division by 0 is undefined.
4. No   **5.** (a) 90° (b) 180° (c) 360°   **6.** 80(12)(2.54) cm   **7.** $12(12)^2$ in.^{2}
8. 3 cm   **9.** 3 m   **10.** –2   **11.** –1   **12.** 28   **13.** 62   **14.** 79   **15.** 33
16. 42   **17.** –40   **18.** –27   **19.** –4   **20.** –31   **21.** 35   **22.** 8   **23.** –12
24. 10   **25.** $-\dfrac{1}{3}$ **26.** $(26 + 5\pi)$ km = 41.7 km   **27.** 144 in.^{2} **28.** 30 in.^{2}
29. 70 ft^2 **30.** 60

practice   **a.** 396   **b.** –10   **c.** 36   **d.** 2
e. There are seven negative signs; therefore, the product must be negative.

problem set 13

1. Negative number   **2.** (a) $\dfrac{1}{3}$ (b) $-\dfrac{1}{3}$ (c) 1   **3.** Reciprocal
4. Zero. Division by 0 is undefined.   **5.** Equilateral polygons   **6.** 60(5280)(12) in.
7. $125(5280)^2$ ft^2 **8.** 7 cm   **9.** 9π m^2 = 28.26 m^2 **10.** –2   **11.** 3   **12.** –12
13. –2   **14.** 18   **15.** 16   **16.** –13   **17.** 30   **18.** –16   **19.** –4   **20.** $24\dfrac{3}{5}$
21. –17   **22.** –20   **23.** $-1\dfrac{1}{4}$ **24.** Indeterminate   **25.** 140 in.   **26.** 230 ft^2
27. 64 ft^2 **28.** $\left(48 + \dfrac{9\pi}{2}\right)$ ft^2 = 62.13 ft^2 **29.** 70 yd^2 **30.** $11\dfrac{2}{3}$ mi

practice   **a.** 4   **b.** –16   **c.** –19   **d.** 44

problem set 14

1. A numerical expression contains only numbers; an algebraic expression may contain numbers and may contain letters.
2. The value of an expression is the number it represents.
3. (a) A variable of an algebraic expression is a letter that represents an unspecified number.
   (b) A variable
4. Positive number   **5.** Equiangular polygons   **6.** $\dfrac{300(2.54)}{(100)}$ m   **7.** $100(3)^2$ ft^2
8. 4 in.   **9.** 4 ft   **10.** 12   **11.** 14   **12.** –30   **13.** 32   **14.** 13   **15.** –31
16. –70   **17.** –12   **18.** –11   **19.** –7   **20.** –3   **21.** 6   **22.** –126   **23.** –3
24. 12   **25.** $(50 + 9\pi)$ yd = 78.26 yd   **26.** 600 cm^2
27. $(20 + 2\pi)$ cm^2 = 26.28 cm^2 **28.** 60 m^2 **29.** 25   **30.** 0.06

practice   **a.** 52 in.^{2} **b.** 336 ft^2 **c.** 8800π cm^2 = 27,632 cm^2 **d.** $(228 + 39\pi)$ m^2 = 350.46 m^2

problem set 15

1. (a) Surface area (b) Multiply the perimeter of a base by the height of the right solid.
2. (a) 3 (b) –3 (c) 1   **3.** Reciprocal   **4.** Zero. Division by 0 is undefined.
5. 112(12)(2.54) cm   **6.** $60(1000)^2$ m^2 **7.** 12 cm   **8.** 54 m^2 **9.** 64π km^2 = 200.96 km^2
10. 8   **11.** –4   **12.** 14   **13.** 8   **14.** –9   **15.** –25   **16.** 1   **17.** 5   **18.** –11
19. 13   **20.** –17   **21.** 36   **22.** –21   **23.** Indeterminate   **24.** $1\dfrac{1}{4}$ **25.** 150 in.
26. $\left(70 + \dfrac{25\pi}{2}\right)$ ft^2 = 109.25 ft^2 **27.** $-\dfrac{1}{15}$ **28.** $-1\dfrac{1}{2}$ **29.** $13\dfrac{3}{4}$ yd   **30.** 208 cm^2

practice   **a.** –24   **b.** 64   **c.** 18

problem set 16

1. Negative number   2. (a) Sum   (b) Difference   (c) Product   (d) Quotient

3. Regular polygons   4. $\dfrac{100}{2.54}$ in.   5. $\dfrac{152}{(2.54)^2}$ in.^{2} 6. 84 in.   7. 221 ft^2

8. 81π yd^2 = 254.34 yd^2 9. –8   10. –2   11. –25   12. 0   13. 48   14. 18

15. 30   16. 20   17. –30   18. –3   19. –14   20. 0   21. 14   22. $-1\dfrac{5}{6}$

23. $9\dfrac{2}{3}$ 24. $(34 + 10\pi)$ mi = 65.4 mi   25. 96 cm^2 26. $(240 - 36\pi)$ m^2 = 126.96 m^2

27. 100   28. $2\dfrac{3}{4}$ 29. 28   30. 108 km^2

practice   **a.** 8   **b.** 8   **c.** $a(b + c) = ab + ac$ **d.** 8   **e.** $2mxy - 6mp$ **f.** $axy + bxy - 2cxy$

problem set 17

1. The coefficient of an expression is any one factor of the expression, or any product of factors of the expression.

2. (a) A numerical coefficient of an expression is a coefficient that consists of numerals only.
   (b) A literal coefficient of an expression is a coefficient that consists of variables or letters only.

3. Commutative property for addition   4. Commutative property for multiplication

5. $\dfrac{250}{100}$ m   6. $\dfrac{5000}{(100)^2}$ m^2 7. 16 cm   8. 5 m   9. 24 in.^{2} 10. 35   11. –45

12. $mxab - mxb$ 13. $-4yd - 4ycx$ 14. $2xa + 2xbc$ 15. $3ax + 6ay$ 16. 10

17. 4   18. 22   19. –60   20. 0   21. –20   22. –2   23. –2   24. –48

25. $1\dfrac{3}{8}$ 26. Undefined   27. 150 ft   28. $(40 + 8\pi)$ yd^2 = 65.12 yd^2

29. 12 mi   30. 24π cm^2 = 75.36 cm^2

practice   **a.** $-6xy + x + 4$ **b.** $-3xyz + 3xy$ **c.** $9acy - 2ac$ **d.** $4 + 2x - 9xy$

problem set 18

1. A term of an algebraic expression is a single symbol, a product, or a quotient.

2. Terms of an algebraic expression can be called like terms when they have the same variables in the same or equivalent forms.

3. (a), (c), (d)   4. $a(b + c) = ab + ac$ 5. $\dfrac{1500}{(2.54)(12)}$ ft   6. $\dfrac{1250}{(12)^2}$ ft^2 7. 16 in.

8. 81π ft^2 = 254.34 ft^2 9. $-2xyz + 2xy$ 10. $-x - 4 + 2xy$ 11. $4x + 2xy$

12. $3xy - 6mx$ 13. $2pxy - 6pk$ 14. 27   15. 26   16. 0   17. 0   18. –162

19. –7   20. –7   21. –7   22. –21   23. $-1\dfrac{1}{3}$ 24. $-\dfrac{2}{3}$

25. $(36 + 12\pi)$ yd = 73.68 yd   26. 54 cm^2 27. $(64 - 9\pi)$ m^2 = 35.74 m^2 28. 3.8

29. 2.03   30. 1660 in.^{2}

practice   **a.** 4   **b.** –4   **c.** –35   **d.** –4   **e.** –30   **f.** –11   **g.** 144   **h.** –44

problem set 19

1. Like terms   2. Positive number

3. (a) A right triangle is a triangle that contains one right angle.
   (b) An acute triangle is a triangle that contains three acute angles.
   (c) An obtuse triangle is a triangle that contains one obtuse angle.
   (d) An equiangular triangle is a triangle in which all angles have equal measure.

4. $\dfrac{10,000}{(12)(5280)}$ mi   **5.** $\dfrac{15,000}{(5280)^2}$ mi^2 **6.** 4 cm   **7.** 63 m^2 **8.** 16   **9.** –16   **10.** 0

11. –18   **12.** 2   **13.** –2   **14.** –288   **15.** –1   **16.** $-6mxy - my$ **17.** $-4a - 8 - 2ax$

18.
$4x - xap$ **19.** $20pxy - 8cxy$ **20.** $8kc - 4ka + 12km$ **21.** 40   **22.** 64   **23.** 3
6

24. –9   **25.** Undefined   **26.** 142 km   **27.** $(96 + 8\pi)$ in.^{2} = 121.12 in.^{2} **28.** $2\dfrac{3}{5}$

29. 4.002   **30.** 408 ft^2

practice   **a.** $(400 + 20\pi)$ in.^{3} = 462.8 in.^{3} **b.** 720π ft^3 = 2260.8 ft^3 **c.** 600 cm^3

problem set 20

1. (a), (d)   **2.** No   **3.** (a) $\{1, 2, 3, \ldots\}$ (b) $\{0, 1, 2, 3, \ldots\}$ (c) $\{\ldots, -3, -2, -1, 0, 1, 2, 3, \ldots\}$

4. $\dfrac{50(100)}{(2.54)}$ in.   **5.** $\dfrac{600}{(3)^2}$ yd^2 **6.** 41 in.   **7.** 5 ft   **8.** 18   **9.** 12   **10.** –16

11. –1   **12.** –3   **13.** –24   **14.** –144   **15.** 22   **16.** $3 + x - 2xy$

17. $-5kpx - kp - 3kx$ **18.** $3x + 12$ **19.** $16x - 8px$ **20.** $2ax - 6px + 4x$ **21.** –27

22. 39   **23.** 5   **24.** 36   **25.** –8   **26.** $(20 + 8\pi)$ cm = 45.12 cm   **27.** 60 m^2

28. 60 km^2 **29.** $21\dfrac{1}{5}$ in.   **30.** 450 ft^3

practice   **a.** x^8y^6 **b.** $x^{11}y^7m^2$ **c.** $-6x^2y^3 - 4xy$ **d.** $2x^6y + 3xy - 5xy^6$

problem set 21

1. Negative number   **2.** $a(b + c) = ab + ac$

3. (a) An isosceles triangle is a triangle that has at least two sides of equal length.

(b) An equilateral triangle is a triangle that contains three sides of equal length.

(c) A scalene triangle is a triangle that contains three sides of unequal length.

4. $\dfrac{366}{(2.54)(12)}$ ft   **5.** $\dfrac{5000}{(1000)^2}$ km^2 **6.** 19 cm   **7.** 100π m^2 = 314 m^2 **8.** x^6y^4

9. m^6x^5 **10.** k^6y^7 **11.** a^5b^8 **12.** $5xyz - 3yz$ **13.** $15 - 5k + kx$

14. $8ab^2 - 3ab$ **15.** $x^2 - 4xy + 2x^2y$ **16.** $10 - 20p$ **17.** $3px - 2xy$

18. $3a - 2ab$ **19.** –49   **20.** –1   **21.** 5   **22.** –35   **23.** 16   **24.** 0   **25.** 4

26. 190 in.   **27.** 75 ft^2 **28.** $-\dfrac{3}{4}$ **29.** 0.000048   **30.** 78π yd^2 = 244.92 yd^2

practice   **a.** 2 satisfies the equation.   **b.** –2 and –5 are roots of the equation.

problem set 22

1. (a) An equation is an algebraic statement consisting of two algebraic expressions connected by an equals sign.

(b) A conditional equation is an equation whose truth or falsity depends on the replacement values of the variables within it.

2. Roots   **3.** (a), (b), (d)   **4.** 72(2.54) cm   **5.** 55(100)^2 cm^2 **6.** 17 cm   **7.** 2 m

8. 1 satisfies the equation.   **9.** –3 is a root of the equation.   **10.** x^5y^5 **11.** $a^{11}b^3$

12. $p^6m^6y^3$ **13.** $4p^3k^4x^5$ **14.** $-4 + py - y$ **15.** $2m - 2 - 3mc$ **16.** $-3xy + 2xy^2$

17. $-8mx^2y + 23x$ **18.** $3ax - 2a$ **19.** $20xy - 8axy$ **20.** $8ax + 2bx - 6mx$

21. –18   **22.** 13   **23.** –5   **24.** –37   **25.** –16   **26.** $(12 + 2\pi)$ km = 18.28 km

27. 24 in.^{2} **28.** $(150 - 25\pi)$ ft^2 = 71.5 ft^2 **29.** 20   **30.** 270 in.^{3}

practice   **a.** 12   **b.** –11   **c.** $\dfrac{7}{8}$ **d.** $-\dfrac{41}{42}$

problem set 23

1. To solve an equation means to find the value(s) of the unknown that makes the equation true.
2. Two equations are said to be equivalent if *every* solution of either one of the equations is also a solution of the other equation.
3. 180°   **4.** 150(100) cm   **5.** $116(2.54)^2$ cm^2 **6.** 11 in.   **7.** 3 ft   **8.** 14
9. $-\dfrac{3}{10}$ **10.** $-\dfrac{15}{8}$ **11.** –2 satisfies the equation.   **12.** 3 is a root of the equation.
13. $m^5x^4y^5$ **14.** $m^2x^4y^3$ **15.** x^5y^6 **16.** $-9 + 2x$ **17.** –5   **18.** $4ax + 8bx$
19. $6x + 12$ **20.** $4mypx - 12abpx$ **21.** 7   **22.** –30   **23.** –8   **24.** –16   **25.** $-\dfrac{5}{6}$
26. $(26 + 12\pi)$ yd $= 63.68$ yd   **27.** 325 cm^2 **28.** $10\dfrac{1}{2}$ **29.** $-1\dfrac{1}{2}$ **30.** 24 m^2

practice   **a.** 45   **b.** 10   **c.** 5   **d.** $\dfrac{45}{4}$

problem set 24

1. Positive number   **2.** (b), (c)   **3.** (a) 60°   (b) 60°   **4.** 280(5280)(12) in.
5. $45(12)^2$ in.^{2} **6.** 216 cm^2 **7.** 6 m   **8.** 2   **9.** 5   **10.** $\dfrac{9}{8}$ **11.** –2   **12.** $\dfrac{17}{10}$
13. 10   **14.** $\dfrac{3}{2}$ **15.** 15   **16.** 2   **17.** 5 satisfies the equation.   **18.** $m^2p^2x^4y^6$
19. $3p^6x^3y^3$ **20.** $-7a + 8$ **21.** $2mx^2y - 2mxy^2$ **22.** $3axy - 5pxy$ **23.** 4
24. 2   **25.** 24   **26.** –21   **27.** 40 km   **28.** 76 in.^{2} **29.** $(104 - 16\pi)$ ft$^2 = 53.76$ ft^2
30. 1520 cm^3

practice   **a.** 2   **b.** $-\dfrac{2}{63}$ **c.** 0.13   **d.** 0.8

problem set 25

1. (a), (d)   **2.** (a) Subtraction   (b) Addition   (c) Division   (d) Multiplication
3. $\dfrac{508}{2.54}$ in.   **4.** $\dfrac{15,000}{(100)^2}$ m^2 **5.** 12 cm   **6.** 8   **7.** $\dfrac{1}{6}$ **8.** $\dfrac{5}{3}$ **9.** $\dfrac{2}{3}$ **10.** 4
11. $\dfrac{14}{3}$ **12.** –6   **13.** 8   **14.** 0.7   **15.** (a) 1   (b) 1   (c) Yes   (d) Yes
16. –2 and 4 are roots of the equation.   **17.** k^4x^7y **18.** $a^8b^5x^5$ **19.** $c - 4$
20. $-a^2x^2$ **21.** $8xy - 12x + 8ax$ **22.** –3   **23.** 19   **24.** –43   **25.** $-\dfrac{4}{5}$
26. $\left(15 + \dfrac{5\pi}{2}\right)$ m $= 22.85$ m   **27.** 264 km^2 **28.** 22   **29.** 0.02   **30.** 468 in.^{2}

practice   **a.** $\dfrac{1}{2}$ **b.** $\dfrac{3}{5}$ **c.** 2   **d.** –6

problem set 26

1. Negative number   **2.** (a) $\{1, 2, 3, \ldots\}$ (b) $\{0, 1, 2, 3, \ldots\}$ (c) $\{\ldots, -3, -2, -1, 0, 1, 2, 3, \ldots\}$
3. $\dfrac{1000}{100}$ m   **4.** $\dfrac{525}{(2.54)^2}$ in.^{2} **5.** 90 in.^{2} **6.** 4 ft   **7.** 4   **8.** 7   **9.** $\dfrac{6}{35}$
10. $\dfrac{11}{3}$ **11.** $-\dfrac{1}{14}$ **12.** 0.4   **13.** –2   **14.** –3   **15.** $\dfrac{9}{5}$
16. (a) 10   (b) 10   (c) Yes   (d) Yes   **17.** –7 satisfies the equation.   **18.** m^6y^9
19. $a^3k^{10}m^6$ **20.** $-2a + ax - 3$ **21.** $5a^2bc - bc$ **22.** $28 - 12x^2$ **23.** –14

24. –6   **25.** 4   **26.** 21   **27.** 2240 mi   **28.** 54 cm^2 **29.** 19 m

30. 24π km^3 = 75.36 km^3

practice   **a.** $xy^4p - xy^2p$ **b.** $2x^2y^2 - 2x^2y$ **c.** $3xp^8 - 3x^3p^{11}$ **d.** $2x^2m^4 - 8x^2m^3$

e. 210   **f.** $2\frac{8}{13}$

problem set 27

1. (a), (c), (d)   **2.** The angles opposite the sides of equal length have equal measures.

3. $\frac{63,400}{(12)(5280)}$ mi   **4.** $\frac{5800}{(12)^2}$ ft^2 **5.** 9 cm^2 **6.** $\frac{7}{8}$ **7.** $\frac{9}{2}$ **8.** 14   **9.** $-\frac{9}{4}$

10. 60   **11.** 0.2   **12.** 3   **13.** $-\frac{1}{5}$ **14.** 1   **15.** (a) –1 (b) –1 (c) Yes (d) Yes

16. –3 and 1 are roots of the equation.   **17.** $p^2x^6y^4$ **18.** $3p^7x^6y^4$ **19.** $-7x + 8x^2 - 5$

20. $-5p^2xy$ **21.** $4ax^3 - 8x^2$ **22.** 0   **23.** –11   **24.** –31   **25.** Indeterminate

26. 48 m   **27.** 150 km^2 **28.** 63 in.^{2} **29.** $x = 50;\ y = 80$ **30.** 88π ft^2 = 276.32 ft^2

practice   **a.** 48   **b.** 15   **c.** $\frac{4}{5}$ **d.** 990   **e.** –2   **f.** 2

problem set 28

1. Negative number   **2.** The sides opposite the angles of equal measure have equal lengths.

3. $\frac{3938(2.54)}{(100)}$ m   **4.** $200(1000)^2$ m^2 **5.** 10 in.   **6.** 100   **7.** $\frac{5}{6}$ **8.** 3

9. –1   **10.** 6   **11.** –3   **12.** 8   **13.** 42   **14.** $-\frac{5}{4}$ **15.** $\frac{17}{6}$

16. (a) 6 (b) 6 (c) Yes (d) Yes   **17.** 10 satisfies the equation.   **18.** x^3y^{11} **19.** m^7y^4

20. $4cp - 6c - p$ **21.** $-3m^2xy + 8mxy^2$ **22.** $x^5y - x^3y^2z^3$ **23.** –30   **24.** 108

25. –23   **26.** –20   **27.** $(16 + 3\pi)$ ft = 25.42 ft   **28.** 456 mi^2 **29.** 5   **30.** 624 cm^3

practice   **a.** 8   **b.** $\frac{1}{16}$ **c.** 9   **d.** 1   **e.** –1   **f.** 1   **g.** 1

h. $x^3y^{-3}z^6$ **i.** x^8 **j.** $2y^4 - 6x^{-3}$

problem set 29

1. (a), (b)   **2.** Parallelogram   **3.** $500(12)(2.54)$ cm   **4.** $180(3)^2$ ft^2 **5.** 16 in.   **6.** $\frac{1}{4}$

7. 16   **8.** 1   **9.** 32   **10.** 225   **11.** 5   **12.** –4   **13.** –3   **14.** 14   **15.** $\frac{3}{2}$

16. 1000   **17.** 0   **18.** –5   **19.** $m^{-2}x^2$ **20.** b^2 **21.** –4   **22.** $3x^3y^4 - 5x^2y^4$

23. $y^2 + 2xy$ **24.** 36   **25.** –5   **26.** $-\frac{7}{3}$ **27.** 172 ft   **28.** 120 mi^2

29. $(64 - 9\pi)$ cm^2 = 35.74 cm^2 **30.** 66 m^2

practice   **a.** $5(3N - 5)$ **b.** $3(N - 50)$ **c.** $5N - 13$ **d.** $3(-N - 7)$

e. 64   **f.** 0.75   **g.** 3.84

problem set 30

1. Positive number   **2.** Trapezoid   **3.** $10,000(12)(2.54)$ cm   **4.** $135(5280)^2$ ft^2

5. 12 cm   **6.** $5N - 8$ **7.** $3(-N - 7)$ **8.** 26   **9.** 0.75   **10.** $\frac{1}{9}$ **11.** –27

12. –1   **13.** 28   **14.** 98   **15.** –11   **16.** 10   **17.** $\frac{49}{3}$ **18.** $\frac{13}{2}$ **19.** $\frac{17}{5}$

20. 100   **21.** 5   **22.** $a^{-2}x^{-4}y^8$ **23.** p^2 **24.** $3m^2x^2y + 8m^2xy^2$ **25.** $1 - 3xy^2$

26. 36   **27.** –37   **28.** $(60 + 12\pi)$ m $= 97.68$ m   **29.** 150 km^2

30. 160π in.$^3 = 502.4$ in.^{3}

practice   **a.** 2   **b.** 1   **c.** 8

problem set 31

1. (a), (c)

2. (a) A rectangle is a parallelogram with four angles of equal measure.

(b) A rhombus is a parallelogram with four sides of equal length.

(c) A square is a rhombus with four angles of equal measure.

(d) Yes

3. $\dfrac{20(100)}{(2.54)}$ in.   **4.** $\dfrac{1800}{(1000)^2}$ km^2 **5.** 25 in.^{2} **6.** $7(N - 5)$ **7.** $2(-N) - 7$

8. $7N - 51$ **9.** $4N - 15$ **10.** 38   **11.** 19.84   **12.** $\dfrac{1}{16}$ **13.** 9   **14.** 1

15. $\dfrac{7}{10}$ **16.** 640   **17.** –3   **18.** $-\dfrac{26}{5}$ **19.** $\dfrac{33}{20}$ **20.** 1020   **21.** $\dfrac{13}{2}$

22. –12   **23.** –1 is a root of the equation.   **24.** $3mp^{-2}x - 5mx$ **25.** $1 - 2x^{-1}$

26. $1 - 5y^4$ **27.** –10   **28.** 52   **29.** $(26 + 3\pi)$ ft $= 35.42$ ft   **30.** 870 cm^3

practice   **a.** 25   **b.** 2

problem set 32

1. (a) Surface area   (b) Multiply the perimeter of a base by the height of the right solid.

2. (a) Natural numbers (or counting numbers)   (b) Whole numbers   (c) Integers

3. $\dfrac{1828}{(2.54)(12)}$ ft   **4.** $\dfrac{57}{(3)^2}$ yd^2 **5.** 14 cm   **6.** 19   **7.** 50   **8.** 0.05   **9.** $\dfrac{1}{25}$

10. –64   **11.** –1   **12.** 36   **13.** 21   **14.** 8   **15.** $-\dfrac{1}{18}$ **16.** 40   **17.** 4

18. $\dfrac{4}{3}$ **19.** (a) 4   (b) –4   (c) No   (d) No   **20.** $-7k^2p^{-4}y$ **21.** $2 - 8x^{-8}y^4$

22. $3 - 12x^3y^{-5}$ **23.** –24   **24.** 132   **25.** –43   **26.** $-\dfrac{27}{7}$ **27.** 100 m^2

28. –2.03   **29.** $6\dfrac{3}{5}$ km   **30.** 478 in.^{2}

practice   **a.** 4   **b.** –2   **c.** $2 \cdot 2 \cdot 3 \cdot 3 \cdot 3$ **d.** $2 \cdot 2 \cdot 2 \cdot 2 \cdot 5 \cdot 5$

problem set 33

1. Negative number   **2.** The angles opposite the sides of equal length have equal measures.

3. $\dfrac{9140}{(2.54)(12)}$ ft   **4.** $\dfrac{28,000}{(5280)^2}$ mi^2 **5.** 22 cm   **6.** 3   **7.** –70   **8.** $2 \cdot 2 \cdot 3 \cdot 5$

9. $3 \cdot 5 \cdot 7$ **10.** 51.25   **11.** $\dfrac{1}{8}$ **12.** $-\dfrac{1}{27}$ **13.** 1   **14.** 84   **15.** –30

16. $\dfrac{28}{5}$ **17.** 34   **18.** –279   **19.** $-\dfrac{4}{7}$ **20.** $\dfrac{9}{2}$ **21.** $5x^2y^3$ **22.** $2x^{-4} + 2y^5$

23. $4 - 3p^7x^{-3}$ **24.** 2   **25.** 46   **26.** 27   **27.** –21   **28.** 40 m^2

29. 156π in.$^2 = 489.84$ in.^{2} **30.** $x = 70; y = 40$

practice   **a.** $2xy^3m$ **b.** $5a^2b^2c^2$ **c.** $4xyp$

problem set 34

1. (a), (c) 2. π 3. $\dfrac{85,000(2.54)}{(100)(1000)}$ km 4. $\dfrac{3200(2.54)^2}{(100)^2}$ m^2

5. (a) 24π in. = 75.36 in. (b) 144π in.^{2} = 452.16 in.^{2} 6. 6 7. 8 8. $2 \cdot 3 \cdot 3 \cdot 5$

9. $2 \cdot 2 \cdot 2 \cdot 3 \cdot 3 \cdot 3$ 10. 42 11. $-\dfrac{1}{125}$ 12. 25 13. –1 14. $\dfrac{1}{3}$

15. 3 16. –1 17. 110 18. 2 19. 2 20. $2ab^2c$ 21. $5xy^2m^2$ 22. $11xy$

23. $4 - 8x$ 24. $1 - 2x^5y^{12}$ 25. 32 26. –4 27. –43 28. –35

29. 44 ft 30. 240 cm^3

practice a. $5az^5(3az^3 - 7)$ b. $2a^2b^2(1 + a + ab^4)$ c. $1 - x$ d. $1 - 7x$

problem set 35

1. (a) Surface area (b) Multiply the perimeter of a base by the height of the right solid.

2. $\dfrac{6(12)(2.54)}{(100)}$ m 3. $20(12)^2(2.54)^2$ cm^2 4. 60 cm^2 5. –3 6. 7

7. $2 \cdot 2 \cdot 2 \cdot 2 \cdot 2 \cdot 5$ 8. $2 \cdot 3 \cdot 7 \cdot 7$ 9. 0.58 10. $\dfrac{1}{16}$ 11. 27 12. 10

13. –15 14. $\dfrac{1}{3}$ 15. 4 16. $-\dfrac{13}{4}$ 17. $\dfrac{13}{7}$ 18. 3 is a root of the equation.

19. $3x^2y^2p(x^2 - 2y^3p^3)$ 20. $2a^2x^2m(3am^4 + a^2x^3m^4 + 2)$ 21. $x + 1$ 22. $1 - 4x$

23. $x^3y^3 + 7x^2$ 24. $x^5 - 3x^7y^{-1}$ 25. $p^5y^{10} - 1$ 26. 1 27. –12

28. $(6 + 2\pi)$ m^2 = 12.28 m^2 29. –5 30. 664 in.^{2}

practice a. $\dfrac{x^4}{y^2} - \dfrac{3x^2y}{m}$ b. $\dfrac{m^2x}{b^3} - \dfrac{3a^2m}{b} + \dfrac{6am^2}{b^4}$ c. $-\dfrac{1}{16}$ d. –16 e. $\dfrac{1}{64}$ f. 64

problem set 36

1. (b), (d) 2. The sides opposite the angles of equal measure have equal lengths.
3. $80(3)(12)(2.54)$ cm 4. $36(3)^2(12)^2$ in.^{2}

5. (a) 18π cm = 56.52 cm (b) 81π cm^2 = 254.34 cm^2 6. 7 7. –2 8. $2 \cdot 5 \cdot 5 \cdot 5$

9. $-\dfrac{1}{4}$ 10. –4 11. $5\dfrac{1}{3}$ 12. 17 13. $\dfrac{85}{16}$ 14. 7 15. $\dfrac{3}{4}$ 16. $-\dfrac{9}{5}$

17. $2a^2x(2y^4p - 3x^3)$ 18. $3ax^2y^4(ax^2y^2 + 3 - 2ax^2yz)$ 19. $1 - 3x$ 20. $3x - 1$

21. $-x^4y^{-3} + 7x^4y^{-4}$ 22. $3x^5y^{-2} - 9y^7$ 23. $\dfrac{15y}{z} - \dfrac{4x^2}{yz}$ 24. –15 25. –34

26. –129 27. 5 28. 120 m 29. $(16\pi - 16)$ in.^{2} = 34.24 in.^{2} 30. 8

practice a. b. $x > 4$

problem set 37

1. –40 2. 8 3. $17(5280)(12)(2.54)$ cm 4. $200(5280)^2(12)^2$ in.^{2} 5. 30 in.

6. 7. $x \ge 2$ 8. $2 \cdot 2 \cdot 2 \cdot 3 \cdot 3 \cdot 5$ 9. $-\dfrac{1}{4}$

10. –4 11. 0.012 12. 10 13. $\dfrac{4}{3}$ 14. 10 15. $\dfrac{1}{2}$ 16. $\dfrac{11}{7}$

17. (a) 5 (b) –5 (c) No (d) No 18. $3ax^2y^2(4ax^3y^5 - 1)$

19. $3a^2x^3y(5a^3xy^5 + a^2y^6 - 3x^3)$ 20. $x + 3$ 21. $x - 1$ 22. $6y^2 - 10x^2$

23. $1 - x^{-1}y^4$ 24. $\dfrac{ab^4}{c^2k} - \dfrac{2axb^2}{c^2}$ 25. –3 26. 24 27. –10 28. $-\dfrac{3}{4}$

29. $(40 + 16\pi)$ cm = 90.24 cm 30. 736 m^3

practice   **a.** 204   **b.** 10,000

problem set 38

1. 1560   **2.** –10   **3.** 5   **4.** Negative number   **5.** $\dfrac{49(100)}{(2.54)(12)}$ ft

6. (a) 6 cm   (b) 12π cm = 37.68 cm   **7.**   **8.** $x \le -2$

9. $\dfrac{1}{36}$ **10.** $-\dfrac{1}{25}$ **11.** 6   **12.** 2   **13.** $-\dfrac{13}{28}$ **14.** 4   **15.** 4   **16.** 7

17. $4a^2x^2y^4(xy - 2a^2)$ **18.** $6a^2xm^5(m - 3a^3x^2)$ **19.** $x - 3$ **20.** $x - 5$ **21.** $3xy$

22. $12z - 21x^2y^{-3}$ **23.** $\dfrac{a^2x^3}{c^3} - \dfrac{3a^2}{x^2}$ **24.** –72   **25.** 10   **26.** –49   **27.** $\dfrac{8}{3}$

28. $(96 + 50\pi)$ m^2 = 253 m^2 **29.** $2\dfrac{11}{12}$ in.   **30.** 912 ft^2

practice   **a.** 39   **b.** 217   **c.**   **d.** $x \ge -1;\; x \nleq -1$

problem set 39

1. 49   **2.** 56   **3.** –5   **4.** –1   **5.** $\dfrac{300(1000)(100)}{(2.54)}$ in.   **6.** 180 cm^2

7.   **8.**   **9.** $2 \cdot 3 \cdot 3 \cdot 5 \cdot 5$

10. (b), (c)   **11.** 1   **12.** –9   **13.** –14   **14.** $\dfrac{1}{2}$ **15.** 66   **16.** $\dfrac{10}{3}$ **17.** $\dfrac{28}{3}$

18. $3xy^3z^5(x - 3y^3z)$ **19.** $4xy(x - 3y + 6x^2y^2)$ **20.** $x + 1$ **21.** $3 - x$ **22.** $-3x$

23. $1 + 3x^5y^7$ **24.** $4ax - \dfrac{8x^3}{a^2}$ **25.** 3   **26.** –3   **27.** –18   **28.** 3

29. $(80 + 10\pi)$ m = 111.4 m   **30.** 630 in.^{3}

practice   **a.** $y^{-1}z^3$ **b.** $m^6p^{-1}z^{16}d^3$ **c.** $z^{-3}x^4m^{-3} - 3z^{-2}m^{-2}$ **d.** $\dfrac{m^{-8}w^{-4}x^{-1}c^{-1}}{3} - \dfrac{w^2x^{-3}m^{-4}}{3}$

problem set 40

1. 36   **2.** 980   **3.** 11   **4.** –1   **5.** $\dfrac{30(100)^2}{(2.54)^2}$ in.^{2} **6.** $x \le 1;\; x \ngtr 1$

7. (b), (d)   **8.** $\dfrac{1}{27}$ **9.** 27   **10.** 0.04515   **11.** –20   **12.** $-\dfrac{11}{2}$ **13.** 2

14. $\dfrac{5}{4}$ **15.** 0   **16.** $2a^2x(2y^4p - 3x^3)$ **17.** $3ax^2y^4(ax^2y^2 + 3 - 2ax^2yz)$

18. $1 - 6x$ **19.** $1 + 4y$ **20.** x^2y^{-2} **21.** $xy^{-4}z^{-4}$ **22.** $bm^{-5} - 4ab^{-5}$

23. $a^{-6}x^{-5} - x^{-2}$ **24.** $-x^3y^2 + 5x^{-3}y^{-2}$ **25.** 48   **26.** 13   **27.** –101   **28.** $-\dfrac{34}{7}$

29. $(936 - 144\pi)$ cm^2 = 483.84 cm^2 **30.** $x = 55;\; y = 70$

practice   **a.** $4x^{-2}y - 5xy$ **b.** $-3a^{-8}b^{11} + 6a^{-8}b^6$ **c.** –2   **d.** 5

problem set 41

1. 45   **2.** 20

3. (a) Natural numbers (or counting numbers)   (b) Whole numbers   (c) Integers

4. $\dfrac{40(100)}{(2.54)(12)}$ ft   **5.** (a) 2.82 in.   (b) 17.71 in.   **6.**

7.   **8.** $2 \cdot 3 \cdot 3 \cdot 3 \cdot 5$ **9.** –26   **10.** $\dfrac{3}{4}$ **11.** 92

12. –5   **13.** –5   **14.** –5   **15.** $3x^2yp^3(y^4p^3 - 3y^3 + 4p)$ **16.** $2xy^2(x - 3x^3 - 6y^3)$

17. $1 + 4y$ **18.** $1 - k$ **19.** $\dfrac{1}{x^2 y^{-8}}$ **20.** $\dfrac{1}{x^{-1} y^4 p^2}$ **21.** $\dfrac{1}{xy^2 z^{-1}} - \dfrac{1}{x^2 y^{-3}}$

22. $\dfrac{1}{ab^{-1}} - \dfrac{2}{a^3 b^{-3}}$ **23.** $-6x^2 p$ **24.** $-2m^2 y^{-2}$ **25.** 7   **26.** 17   **27.** 19

28. -1 **29.** $\left(24 + \dfrac{9\pi}{2}\right) \text{ft}^2 = 38.13 \text{ ft}^2$ **30.** $56\pi \text{ cm}^2 = 175.84 \text{ cm}^2$

practice   **a.** $\dfrac{13}{8}x + \dfrac{3}{2}$ **b.** $-\dfrac{1}{5}w - \dfrac{3}{2}$

problem set 42

1. 918   **2.** 5   **3.** Negative number   **4.** $\dfrac{58}{(2.54)^2 (12)^2} \text{ ft}^2$ **5.** 20 cm

6. $x > 1; \; x \not\le 1$ **7.** $\dfrac{5}{3}$ **8.** -15 **9.** 6   **10.** 5.05   **11.** $\dfrac{1}{3}$ **12.** 2   **13.** 11

14. $-x + \dfrac{5}{3}$ **15.** $\dfrac{1}{4}x + 1$ **16.** $2x^2 m^3 y\left(2m^2 - x^2 y^2\right)$ **17.** $2m^2 x^2\left(2x^3 - 1 + 3m^3\right)$

18. $1 - 3xy$ **19.** $x + 1$ **20.** $\dfrac{xy^8}{m^5}$ **21.** $x^3 y^5 p^2$ **22.** $\dfrac{x^5}{z^6} - 3$ **23.** $3p^2 xy$

24. $\dfrac{1}{x^{-1} y^{-5}}$ **25.** 18   **26.** -2 **27.** -11 **28.** $\dfrac{5}{9}$ **29.** $(40 + 20\pi) \text{ m} = 102.8 \text{ m}$

30. $2000\pi \text{ in.}^3 = 6280 \text{ in.}^3$

practice   **a.** 420   **b.** 12,600   **c.** $12a^{10} b^4$ **d.** $60x^6 y^2 m^3$

problem set 43

1. 48   **2.** 4   **3.** $\dfrac{500}{(2.54)(12)(3)} \text{ yd}$ **4.**

5.
  6. -20 **7.** 40   **8.** -30 **9.** $\dfrac{8}{5}$ **10.** 0

11. 7   **12.** $-\dfrac{1}{3}x + \dfrac{4}{3}$ **13.** $-x + 2$ **14.** 1200   **15.** $8a^3 b^2$

16. $mk\left(6mk^4 - 2k^2 - 1\right)$ **17.** $x^3 y^2 m\left(x - ym + 5x^3 m\right)$ **18.** $4x - 8$ **19.** $\dfrac{x - 1}{m}$

20. $x^{-9} y^{-1}$ **21.** $\dfrac{x^{-7} y^{-11}}{m^{-5}}$ **22.** $1 - \dfrac{3}{m^{-4} z^{-1}}$ **23.** $5m^2 y + 6m^2 x^2 y$

24. $3my^2 - \dfrac{4m^2 y^2}{x^2}$ **25.** 13   **26.** 18   **27.** 66   **28.** $\dfrac{10}{3}$ **29.** 120 in.^{2}

30. $(152 + 24\pi) \text{ ft}^2 = 227.36 \text{ ft}^2$

practice   **a.** $\dfrac{10m - 6}{3m + 2}$ **b.** $\dfrac{9 - 7ap}{xy^3 + m}$ **c.** $\dfrac{xmc^3 + m^4 + ac^3}{m^4 c^3}$ **d.** $\dfrac{mp + 3 - 4p^3}{p^3}$

problem set 44

1. 1848   **2.** 7   **3.** $\dfrac{170}{(12)^2 (3)^2} \text{ yd}^2$ **4.** 169 in.^{2} **5.** $x < -2; \; x \not\ge -2$

6. $2 \cdot 2 \cdot 2 \cdot 3 \cdot 7$ **7.** 12   **8.** $\dfrac{5}{2}$ **9.** -2 **10.** $\dfrac{3}{8}$ **11.** $-\dfrac{4}{3}$ **12.** -7

13. $\dfrac{2}{3}x + \dfrac{7}{3}$ **14.** $\dfrac{3}{4}x + 2$ **15.** 600   **16.** $12w^2 y^3$ **17.** $\dfrac{3x + 4m}{3x^2 m}$

18. $\dfrac{9b + 3a + ab}{3ab}$ **19.** $xyz\left(8x^4 y - 16xyz - 1\right)$ **20.** $5 - 25xy$ **21.** $p^{-2} z^6$

22. $a^{-1}k^{-3}p$ **23.** $y^2 + 4m^3y^7$ **24.** $\dfrac{y^{-3}}{a^{-2}x^{-2}}$ **25.** 2 **26.** $-\dfrac{10}{3}$ **27.** -68

28. Undefined **29.** $(48 - 4\pi)$ ft^2 = 35.44 ft^2 **30.** $3\dfrac{5}{6}$ mi

practice

a. Range = 9; median = 8.5; mode = 9; mean = 7.75

b. Range = 30; median = 81; mode = 81; mean = 81.56 **c.** 19

problem set 45

1. 450 **2.** Range = 7; median = 7; mode = 6; mean = 7.57 **3.** $\dfrac{80,500}{(2.54)(12)(5280)}$ mi

4. (a) 3.39 cm (b) 21.29 cm **5.**  **6.**

7. -25 **8.** 20 **9.** 667 **10.** 8 **11.** $-\dfrac{10}{3}$ **12.** 13 **13.** $-\dfrac{3}{2}x + \dfrac{5}{2}$

14. $\dfrac{2}{5}x + \dfrac{4}{5}$ **15.** 270 **16.** $24a^4m^3x$ **17.** $\dfrac{x+1}{a^2m}$ **18.** $\dfrac{20y + 4x + xy}{4xy}$

19. $3a^2b^4c^5(1 - 2b^2c)$ **20.** $1 - 2kp$ **21.** $\dfrac{1}{k^2m^{-7}}$ **22.** $\dfrac{1}{a^2b^{-4}}$

23. $\dfrac{1}{p^4y^4} - \dfrac{1}{x^{-2}p^{-6}y^4}$ **24.** $-2x^2y^{-2}$ **25.** 6 **26.** $\dfrac{1}{9}$ **27.** 30 **28.** 5

29. 15 m **30.** $(192 + 16\pi)$ in.^{3} = 242.24 in.^{3}

practice

a. 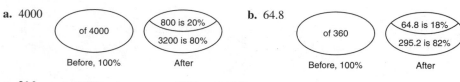 **b.**

c. $-3 < x \le 2$ **d.** $-2 \le x < 5$

problem set 46

1. 5 **2.** Range = 34; median = 83; mode = 83; mean = 83.67 **3.** $\dfrac{42,000}{(12)^2(5280)^2}$ mi^2

4. 60 in. **5.** $x \ge -3$; $x \not< -3$ **6.** **7.** 0.06

8. -55 **9.** $-\dfrac{5}{2}$ **10.** -1.7 **11.** $\dfrac{3}{2}$ **12.** 6 **13.** $\dfrac{5}{3}x + \dfrac{4}{3}$ **14.** $\dfrac{1}{2}x + \dfrac{5}{2}$

15. 1125 **16.** $30x^5y^4z^2$ **17.** $\dfrac{6}{x^2 + y}$ **18.** $\dfrac{ad + 20d^2 + 4b}{4d^3}$ **19.** $xyz(-x + 2z)$

20. $a - 2b$ **21.** $\dfrac{p^8}{m^2}$ **22.** x^8y^8 **23.** $1 - 4a^4x^3$ **24.** $\dfrac{1}{m^{-2}y^2} + \dfrac{1}{m^{-2}xy^2}$ **25.** 0

26. $-\dfrac{9}{4}$ **27.** $-\dfrac{95}{8}$ **28.** -1 **29.** 92 ft^2 **30.** $(1368 + 216\pi)$ cm^2 = 2046.24 cm^2

practice

a. 4000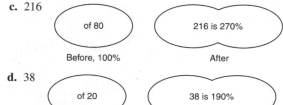

of 4000 | 800 is 20% / 3200 is 80%

Before, 100% | After

b. 64.8

of 360 | 64.8 is 18% / 295.2 is 82%

Before, 100% | After

c. 216

of 80 | 216 is 270%

Before, 100% | After

d. 38

of 20 | 38 is 190%

Before, 100% | After

problem set 47

1. 8000 farthings   2. 19   3. $\dfrac{42(12)(2.54)}{(100)}$ m   4. (a) 8 cm   (b) 64π cm^2 = 200.96 cm^2

5. 90

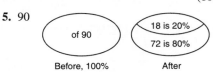

Before, 100%   After

6. 98

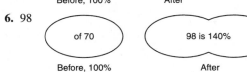

Before, 100%   After

7.
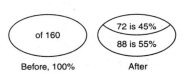

8. 90   9. 9   10. −460

11. 38   12. 0   13. $-\dfrac{1}{2}x + \dfrac{3}{2}$

14. $x + 2$ 15. 2520   16. $2c^3$ 17. $\dfrac{c^2 + 4}{b}$ 18. $\dfrac{16 + c + 20a}{4a}$

19. $5x^2y^2m^2\left(y^3 - 2x^2m\right)$ 20. $4a - xy$ 21. $\dfrac{x^{-1}}{y^{-2}}$ 22. $\dfrac{y^{-7}}{m^{-8}p^{-6}}$

23. $1 - \dfrac{1}{a^{-1}x^{-1}y^{-7}}$ 24. k^5m^2 25. −22   26. $-\dfrac{161}{243}$ 27. −26   28. 20

29. 30 m   30. $(560 + 56\pi)$ in.^{3} = 735.84 in.^{3}

practice   a. $-2x^5 - 7x^4 + 7x^3 + 3x^2 - 2x - 3$ b. $-14x^4 - 2x^3 + 9x^2 - 11x + 5$

problem set 48

1. −20   2. Range = 10; median = 7.5; mode = 11; mean = 7.5

3. $\dfrac{28{,}000(2.54)^2}{(100)^2(1000)^2}$ km^2 4. 242 in.^{2} 5. 55%

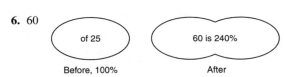

of 160   72 is 45%   88 is 55%

Before, 100%   After

6. 60

of 25   60 is 240%

Before, 100%   After

7. $-2 \le x < 3$ 8. $3 \cdot 3 \cdot 5 \cdot 7$

9. $\dfrac{1}{4}$ 10. 5   11. 0.9

12. −3   13. −18

14. $-3x + 3$ 15. 1800   16. $\dfrac{31}{30}$ 17. $\dfrac{ac^2x + b + dc^2x^2}{c^2x^2}$ 18. $5x^3 + 3x^2 + 4$

19. $x^2y^4p^2\left(4y - 3x^3\right)$ 20. $xy - 1$ 21. $x^{-5}y^6$ 22. k^3p^{-8} 23. $p^3y^{-5} - p^3y^{-3}$

24. $\dfrac{y^{-1}}{m^{-1}}$ 25. 16   26. $-\dfrac{64}{9}$ 27. −13   28. 0   29. 78 ft^2 30. $x = 20$; $y = 20$

practice   a. $10x^2 - 14x - 12$ b. $25x^2 - 60x + 36$ c. $3x^3 - 7x^2 + 11x - 3$

problem set 49

1. 600   2. Range = 35; median = 74.5; mode = 71; mean = 78.5

3. $\dfrac{10{,}000(12)(2.54)}{(100)(1000)}$ km   4. (a) 22π in. = 69.08 in.   (b) 121π in.^{2} = 379.94 in.^{2}

5. 50

of 200   50 is 25%   150 is 75%

Before, 100%   After

6. 260%

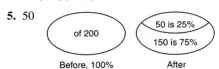

of 80   208 is 260%

Before, 100%   After

7. $-3 < x \le 6$ 8. $\dfrac{2}{5}$

9. $-\dfrac{1}{5}$ 10. 45   11. −0.5

12. $-\dfrac{13}{11}$ **13.** -10 **14.** b^3c^2 **15.** 1 **16.** $\dfrac{ad^2 + 32d^3 + 4mx}{4d^4}$

17. $x^4 + x^3 - 3x^2 + 5$ **18.** $2x^2 - x - 6$ **19.** $4x^2 + 4x + 1$ **20.** $4m^3px\left(2xy^4 - 1\right)$

21. $\dfrac{1}{m^{-8}x^6y^{-4}}$ **22.** $\dfrac{1}{m^5x^{-3}y^{-1}}$ **23.** $\dfrac{1}{x^2} - \dfrac{3}{p^6y^6}$ **24.** $-8p^3x^2y - 2p^{-1}xy$

25. $-\dfrac{9}{2}$ **26.** $\dfrac{9}{4}$ **27.** -5 **28.** 23 **29.** $(22 + 2\pi)\ \text{ft}^2 = 28.28\ \text{ft}^2$

30. $320\pi\ \text{yd}^2 = 1004.8\ \text{yd}^2$

practice   **a.** 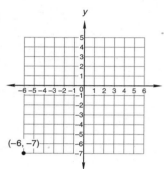   **b.**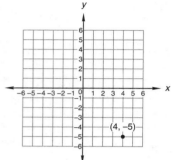

problem set 50

1. -6 **2.** 10 **3.** $\dfrac{15(1000)^2(100)^2}{(2.54)^2}\ \text{in.}^2$ **4.** 1400

5. 68

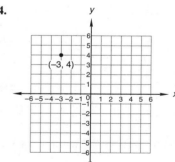

6. 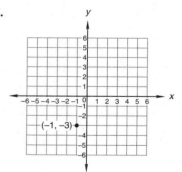   **7.** $3 \cdot 5 \cdot 7 \cdot 11$ **8.** $\dfrac{1}{6}$

9. -11 **10.** 3.5 **11.** -7 **12.** $-\dfrac{1}{5}w - \dfrac{6}{5}$ **13.** c^2x^2d

14.   **15.**

16. $\dfrac{62}{63}$ **17.** $\dfrac{16x^2 + 12x - 3}{4x^4}$ **18.** $x^5 - x^3 + 5x - 3$ **19.** $4x^2 - 4x + 1$

20. $x^3 - x^2 + x + 3$ **21.** $x^2 - 1$ **22.** $\dfrac{x^5}{y^7}$ **23.** $1 + \dfrac{4x^8}{a^2y^4}$ **24.** $-\dfrac{1}{m^{-2}x^{-1}y^{-1}}$

25. -8 **26.** $\dfrac{3}{4}$ **27.** -15 **28.** $(20 + 10\pi)\ \text{cm} = 51.4\ \text{cm}$ **29.** $384\ \text{in.}^2$

30. $(288 + 96\pi)\ \text{m}^3 = 589.44\ \text{m}^3$

practice

a.

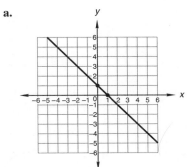

b.

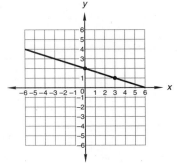

c.

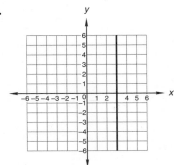

d.

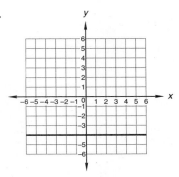

problem set 51

1. 450   **2.** Range = 24; median = 15; mode = 15; mean = 14.56

3. $\dfrac{10(1000)(100)}{(2.54)(12)}$ ft   **4.** (a) 3.18 cm (b) 31.75 cm^2

5. 12%

6. 165.6

7.

8. −2   **9.** $\dfrac{40}{99}$ **10.** −2.1

11. $\dfrac{1}{7}$ **12.** −32

13. $8m^3x^2y$ **14.**

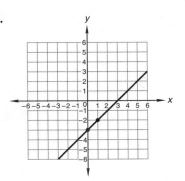

15.

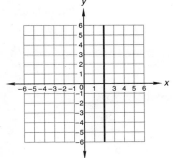

16. $\dfrac{16x + c + 4mx^3}{4x^3}$ **17.** $\dfrac{4b^2 + 6a^2 + ac}{8a^3b^2}$ **18.** $4x^4 - x^3 - 5x + 3$

19. $10x^2 + 14x - 12$ **20.** $x^2 + 6x + 9$ **21.** $2kp(2kz - 3k^2pz^5 - kpz^2 - 2)$

22. $\dfrac{y^{-2}p^{-2}}{x^{-5}}$ **23.** $x^{-8}y^{-8} - a^{-1}x^{-2}y^{-6}$ **24.** $-8p^3x^2y - 2p^3xy$ **25.** 12

26. $-\dfrac{3}{4}$ **27.** –21   **28.** 2400 in.^{2} **29.** $(24 - 2\pi)$ in.^{2} = 17.72 in.^{2}

30. 2112π ft^2 = 6631.68 ft^2

practice   **a.** $\dfrac{xm - bmy + y(c + d)}{my}$ **b.** $\dfrac{b(5b + c) - x(a + b) + cb(a + b)}{b(a + b)}$ **c.** 20 lb

problem set 52   **1.** –1   **2.** 25.5 lb   **3.** $\dfrac{70(12)^2 (2.54)^2}{(100)^2}$ m^2 **4.** 672

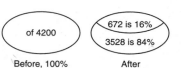

5. 1400%

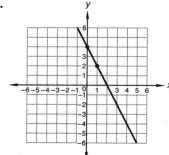

6.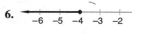

7. 2.02   **8.** $\dfrac{3}{2}$ **9.** $-\dfrac{20}{3}$ **10.** 3.15   **11.** $-\dfrac{3}{4}$ **12.** $-\dfrac{3}{2}a + \dfrac{5}{2}$ **13.** 840

14.

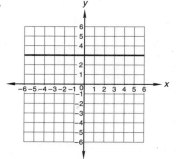

15.

16. $\dfrac{4ad - ca^2b^2 - mbd}{a^3b^2d}$ **17.** $\dfrac{x(2x + a) + d(a + b)}{x(a + b)}$ **18.** $x^3 - 5x^2 + 4x + 11$

19. $25x^2 - 30x + 9$ **20.** $5x^3 + 17x^2 + 19x + 7$ **21.** $1 - 4y$ **22.** $p^{14}x^{-2}$ **23.** $-2x^2$

24. $-\dfrac{m^{-5}y^{-2}}{x^{-2}} + \dfrac{3m^{-5}}{x^{-2}y^{-2}}$ **25.** 1   **26.** $\dfrac{3}{4}$ **27.** Indeterminate   **28.** 110 cm

29. 480 in.^{2} **30.** $(6000 + 1500\pi)$ m^3 = 10,710 m^3

practice   **a.** $x^9y^6z^{-15}$ **b.** $9m^{10}x^{-10}$ **c.** $75(2.54)^3$ cm^3 **d.** $\dfrac{28(100)^3}{(2.54)^3}$ in.^{3}

problem set 53   **1.** 1278   **2.** 162.16 lb   **3.** $50(2.54)^3$ cm^3 **4.** 400

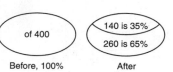

5. 57

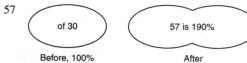

6. $x < 5; \; x \not\geq 5$

7. $2 \cdot 3 \cdot 3 \cdot 5 \cdot 11$ **8.** $-\dfrac{5}{3}$ **9.** $-\dfrac{2}{3}$ **10.** –9   **11.** –16   **12.** $12c^4$

13.
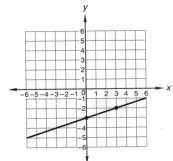

14.
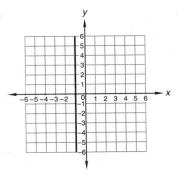

15. $\dfrac{15km - 20apk + 18p}{15p^2k^2}$ **16.** $\dfrac{ab^2 - 4x(b + c)}{b^2(b + c)}$ **17.** $7x^5 - 6x^4 - 4x + 8$

18. $3x^2 + 5x - 12$ **19.** $4x^2 - 49$ **20.** $3kbm^2(3km^2 - b^3 + 4b^2m)$

21. $x^4y^{-6}z^{-2}$ **22.** $x^{-2}y^6m^8$ **23.** $1 - \dfrac{15}{x^{-3}m^{-2}}$ **24.** $-2xy^{-1} - 2xy^{-2}$

25. $\dfrac{1}{8}$ **26.** 5   **27.** 3   **28.** 1.5 m   **29.** $(150 + 72\pi)$ in.^{2} = 376.08 in.^{2} **30.** 1350 ft^2

practice   **a.** $(6, 4)$ **b.** $(-10, -3)$

problem set 54

1. 7   **2.** 94   **3.** $\dfrac{140}{(2.54)^3}$ in.^{3} **4.** 5%

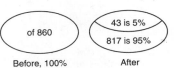

5. 182.4

6.

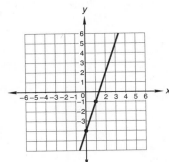 **7.** $-\dfrac{5}{2}$

8. 1.45   **9.** $-\dfrac{8}{9}$ **10.** $(2, 3)$ **11.** $(-1, 2)$ **12.** 1575

13.
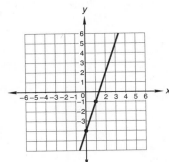

14.
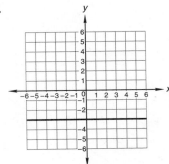

15. $\dfrac{xkc + bkcm - 2m}{kc^2m}$ **16.** $\dfrac{7y - 3x}{y(x - y)}$ **17.** $-2x^3 + 3x^2 + 5x + 4$

18. $16x^2 - 16x + 4$ **19.** $x^3 - x^2 + 3x + 5$ **20.** $1 - 2m$ **21.** $\dfrac{1}{a^{-12}b^{16}z^8}$

22. $\dfrac{1}{x^{25}y^{-10}z^{10}}$ **23.** $\dfrac{x^2m^4}{p^2k} - p^2m^4$ **24.** $-\dfrac{1}{a^{-2}k^{-2}y} - \dfrac{6}{k^6y}$ **25.** $\dfrac{95}{8}$ **26.** $\dfrac{77}{9}$

27. 87   **28.** $(14 + 3\pi)$ cm = 23.42 cm   **29.** 4 m^2 **30.** 6720 m^3

practice   **a.** $\dfrac{x}{md}$ **b.** $\dfrac{z}{r}$ **c.** $\dfrac{nd}{ab}$ **d.** $w(w + c)$

problem set 55

1. 252   **2.** 360   **3.** $\dfrac{24{,}000}{(12)^3(3)^3}\ \text{yd}^3$ **4.** 266

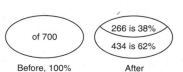

of 700   266 is 38%

434 is 62%

Before, 100%   After

5. 150%

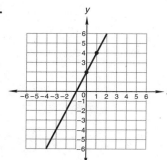

of 18   · 27 is 150%

Before, 100%   After

6.
```
    -1   0   1   2   3   4   5
```

7. $\dfrac{1}{4}$ **8.** $-\dfrac{2}{3}$ **9.** $\dfrac{1}{6}$

10. $\dfrac{m}{nz}$ **11.** $\dfrac{d(m + 1)}{n}$ **12.** $(1, 2)$ **13.** $(-2, -2)$ **14.** $8x^3py$

15.

16.

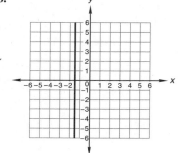

17. $\dfrac{6x - ab - 4x^3yc}{4x^3y}$ **18.** $\dfrac{a(x + y) - mx^2}{x^2(x + y)}$ **19.** $-3x^5 - 3x^3 + 2x + 1$

20. $12x^2 + 14x - 10$ **21.** $x^2ym(1 - 4m^2 + 2x^2y^2m^5)$ **22.** $\dfrac{y^8}{4z^2}$ **23.** $\dfrac{x^9p^{15}}{27y^{12}z^9}$

24. $\dfrac{p^{-2}k^{-1}}{x^{-2}} - \dfrac{1}{p^{-2}}$ **25.** $3mx + \dfrac{4}{mx}$ **26.** $\dfrac{14}{9}$ **27.** -5 **28.** 9.6 m

29. 135 in.^{2} **30.** 204 ft^2

practice   **a.** $K = \{0, 1, 3, 5, 9\}$ **b.** (a) True   (b) True   (c) True   (d) False

c.

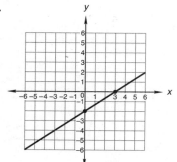

problem set 56

1. -5 **2.** $30(3)^3(12)^3$ in.^{3} **3.** $K = \{0, 2, 4, 6, 8, 10\}$

4. (a) False   (b) True   (c) True   (d) False   **5.** (a) 5.64 cm   (b) 35.42 cm

6. 55

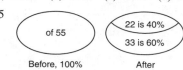

of 55   22 is 40%

33 is 60%

Before, 100%   After

7. 99

of 55

Before, 100%

99 is 180%

After

8. $-5 < x \le -1$ **9.** 9 **10.** 8

11. 4 **12.** $\dfrac{amdc}{nx}$ **13.** $\dfrac{x}{c(x+y)}$

14. $(8, -1)$ **15.** $(2, 2)$

16.

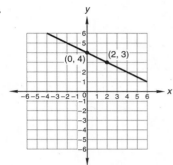

17.

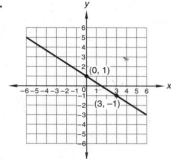

18. $\dfrac{8xp - 3x + a}{4x^3 p}$ **19.** $\dfrac{m - k(b + c)}{b(b + c)}$, **20.** $x^2 - 5x + 25$ **21.** $x^2 - 6x + 9$

22. $25x^{-6}$ **23.** $\dfrac{y^{-3}m^{-9}}{8x^{-6}p^{-12}}$ **24.** $p^{-2}x^{-8} + 2x^{-8}p^{-4}y^2$ **25.** $\dfrac{z^{-1}}{x^{-1}y^{-1}}$ **26.** 6

27. 26 **28.** 740 cm^2 **29.** $x = 65$; $y = 50$ **30.** 4224 m^3

practice **a.** $\dfrac{ay^2 - bx}{xy^2}$ **b.** $\dfrac{x^3 - a^3by}{a^3x^2y}$

problem set 57

1. 560 **2.** Range = 92 kg; median = 775 kg; mode = 745 kg; mean = 777.5 kg

3. $\dfrac{8400}{(12)^3}$ ft^3 **4.** $L = \{-7, -5, -3, -1, 1, 3, 5, 7\}$

5. (a) True (b) True (c) False (d) False **6.** 20%

7. $-4 \le x \le 2$ **8.** $-\dfrac{1}{2}$ **9.** -9.2 **10.** $\dfrac{1}{ax}$

of 180

Before, 100%

36 is 20%

144 is 80%

After

11. $\dfrac{b(a + b)}{c}$ **12.** $(3, 3)$ **13.** $(-15, -27)$

14.

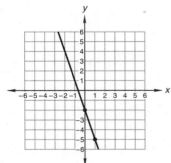

15.

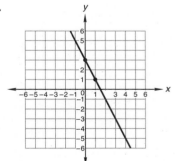

16. $\dfrac{4a^2 - 6a + b}{a^2}$ **17.** $\dfrac{a(x + y) + 4ax^2y(x + y) - mx^2y}{x^2y(x + y)}$ **18.** $\dfrac{x + azy}{y}$

19. $\dfrac{y + ax}{xy}$ **20.** $5x^4 - 12x^3 + x^2 - x - 10$ **21.** $4x^3 - 12x^2 + 17x - 12$ **22.** x^{-15}

23. $y^{-12}p^{-6}$ **24.** $1 - \dfrac{8}{x^4y^2}$ **25.** $-2x^2p^{10}y + 2xp^{10}y$ **26.** 0 **27.** 0 **28.** 800 cm

29. $(280 + 128\pi)$ in.^{2} = 681.92 in.^{2} **30.** 1800 ft^2

practice   **a.** 20%

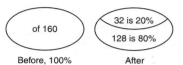

b. 1680

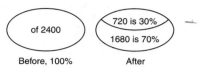

c. 100

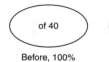

problem set 58

1. 14,000

2. 80 lb

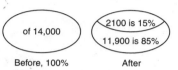

3. 4   **4.** 18

5. $K = \{-5, -4, -3, -2, -1\}$

6.

7. $2 \cdot 3 \cdot 5 \cdot 7 \cdot 11$ **8.** 2   **9.** $-\dfrac{20}{7}$ **10.** $\dfrac{b}{a(x + y)}$ **11.** $\dfrac{m^2 c^2}{a}$ **12.** $(1, 2)$

13. $(2, 3)$ **14.**

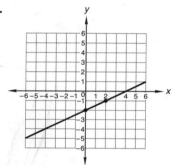

15.

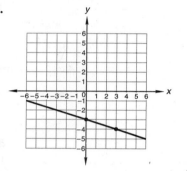

16. $\dfrac{-3x^3 p^2 + 2x - 5p}{x^2 p^2}$ **17.** $\dfrac{4y^2 - 3(x + y)}{y^2 (x + y)}$ **18.** $\dfrac{ay + bzx}{x}$ **19.** $\dfrac{z + ba^2 x}{a^2 xz}$

20. $-5x^5 + 5x - 7$ **21.** $2x^2 - 10x + 12$ **22.** $\dfrac{1}{x^6 y^8}$ **23.** $\dfrac{1}{x^9 y^{-10}}$ **24.** $1 - \dfrac{2k^3}{m^4}$

25. $\dfrac{2}{x^{-2} y^{-2} m^{-1}}$ **26.** -1 **27.** -15 **28.** 11 ft   **29.** 80 cm^2 **30.** 7520 m^3

practice   **a.** $(11, 6)$ **b.** $(11, 3)$

problem set 59

1. $380

2. 2000 lb

3. 854

4. (a) True   (b) False   (c) False   (d) False   **5.** $0 < x < 6$ **6.** 3.05

7. -3 **8.** 1.6   **9.** $\dfrac{1}{xa}$ **10.** $c(x + y)$ **11.** $(-2, -3)$ **12.** $(1, 2)$

13.
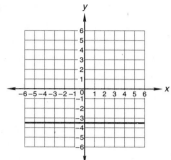

14.
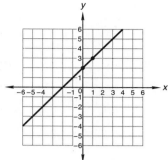

15. $\dfrac{-x + a^2(a - b)}{a^2 b}$ **16.** $\dfrac{m + m(k + c)}{k(k + c)}$ **17.** $\dfrac{bxy + c}{y}$ **18.** $\dfrac{az - bxy^2}{xy^2 z}$

19. $-2x^4 + x^3 - x^2 - 12x + 25$ **20.** $5x^2 - 18x - 8$ **21.** $4x^2 py\left(3x^2 p^2 - xyz - 2py\right)$

22. $\dfrac{x^4}{y^{20} m^2}$ **23.** $\dfrac{y^{10}}{x^9}$ **24.** $\dfrac{p^{-1}}{a^{-1}} - \dfrac{p^{-4}}{b^{-1}}$ **25.** $\dfrac{b^2}{a^2} - 3b^2$ **26.** $-\dfrac{1}{8}$ **27.** -9

28. 1.77 m^2 **29.** $(720 - 36\pi) \text{ in.}^2 = 606.96 \text{ in.}^2$ **30.** $x = 35; \ y = 35$

practice   **a.** 408 in.^3 **b.** 960 ft^2

problem set 60   **1.** 275

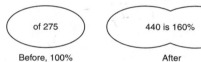

2. -6 **3.** 5

4. $L = \{-12, -8, -4, 0, 4, 8, 12\}$

5. (a) 7.98 in. (b) 50.11 in.

6. $3 < x < 6$ **7.** 4

8. $-\dfrac{6}{7}$ **9.** 0 **10.** $\dfrac{ax}{b}$ **11.** $x(a + b)$ **12.** $(-1, -3)$ **13.** $(-1, -1)$

14.
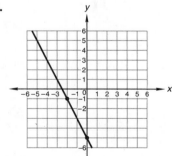

15.
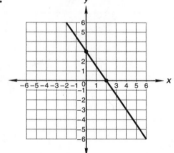

16. $\dfrac{3a^2 x^2 m + 4x^2 + 2am}{am^2 x}$ **17.** $\dfrac{x + y(x + y)}{x + y}$ **18.** $\dfrac{2y^2 + 3x}{xy^2}$ **19.** $\dfrac{z^2 - 4x^2 y}{x^2 yz^2}$

20. $-2x^5 + 6x^3 - 3x^2 - 2x + 1$ **21.** $6x^3 - 13x^2 + 10x - 6$ **22.** $\dfrac{m^{-2} y^{-2}}{x^{-2}}$

23. $x^{-4} p^{-1}$ **24.** $x^{-2} p^2 y^{-1} - 2y$ **25.** $x^{-1} y^{-2}$ **26.** -9 **27.** 1 **28.** 68 in.

29. $(288 + 36\pi) \text{ cm}^2 = 401.04 \text{ cm}^2$ **30.** 360 m^3

practice   **a.** (1) True. All of set B is contained in set A.

(2) False. None of set B is contained in set C.

(3) True. All of set C is contained in set A.

b. Rationals, reals   **c.** Rationals, reals   **d.** Naturals, wholes, integers, rationals, reals

e. Irrationals, reals   **f.** Integers, rationals, reals

problem set 61

1. 273   **2.** 84%   **3.** 3360 lb

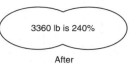

of 1400 lb

Before, 100%

3360 lb is 240%

After

4. 800

of 800

Before, 100%

120 is 15%

680 is 85%

After

5. Range = 10; median = 8; mode = 8; mean = 9.64   **6.**

$-4 \quad -3 \quad -2 \quad -1 \quad 0$

7. $\dfrac{1}{4}$ **8.** (a) Integers, rationals, reals   (b) Irrationals, reals

9. (a) Rationals, reals   (b) Wholes, integers, rationals, reals

10. (a) True. The set of rational numbers is a subset of the set of real numbers.

(b) False. The set of rational numbers contains numbers that are not in the set of integers.

11. (a) False. Zero, a member of set A, is not a member of set B.

(b) True. All members of set C are members of set B.

(c) False. Zero is a member of set A.

(d) True. Two is a member of set C.

12. -1 **13.** $\dfrac{y^2 - x}{xy}$ **14.** $\dfrac{a}{b(c + x)}$ **15.** $\dfrac{a(c + x)}{b}$ **16.** $(-1, -1)$ **17.** $(-1, 2)$

18.

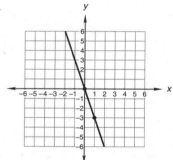

19.

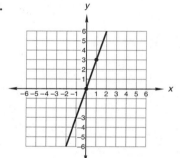

20.

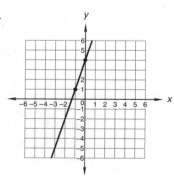

21. $\dfrac{4xyb^2 + 4y + 2b}{ab^2}$ **22.** $\dfrac{my^2 + p}{y}$

23. $4x^2 + 5x - 6$ **24.** $16x^2 + 24x + 9$

25. x^2 **26.** $\dfrac{16x^{12}k^{22}}{y}$

27. $10x^2m^4k^4\left(2mk^2 - x + 3x^3k^2\right)$ **28.** -16

29. $(48 + 12\pi)$ in. = 85.68 in.   **30.** 390 ft^2

practice   **a.** 4.1231   **b.** 5 and 6   **c.** -3 **d.** -3 **e.** 0, 6

problem set 62   **1.** 850 lb   **2.** 3000 units

of 3000 units

Before, 100%

3840 units is 128%

After

3. $450

Before, 100%   After

4. Range = 6; median = 100; mode = 100; mean = 100

5. (a) Naturals, wholes, integers, rationals, reals   (b) Irrationals, reals

6. (a) 7   (b) 2   **7.** 7 and 8   **8.** 4.3589   **9.** 3, 7

10. (a) False. Some real numbers are not rational numbers.

   (b) True. The set of irrational numbers is a subset of the set of real numbers.

11. 1   **12.** $\dfrac{m}{a}$ **13.** $\dfrac{x}{x+y}$ **14.** $\dfrac{2b^2+4a}{ab^2}$ **15.** $(-1,-2)$ **16.** $(-3,-3)$

17.

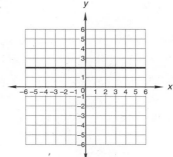

18.

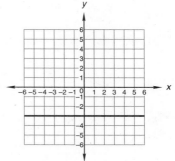

19.

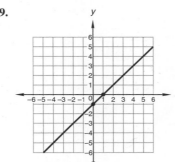

20. $\dfrac{ay+x^2(m+c)-cy^2}{x^2y^2}$ **21.** $\dfrac{x+y}{x}$

22. $3ym^2\left(3x^3m^3+2y^3p^4-y^2m\right)$

23. $1+x$ **24.** $\dfrac{a^5}{p^2}$ **25.** $m^3x^3y^3$

26. $-1+\dfrac{3}{x^6y^3}-\dfrac{4y^2}{x}$ **27.** $4y^2-x^{-2}y^2$

28. $\dfrac{15}{4}$ **29.** $(360-36\pi)\,\text{cm}^2 = 246.96\,\text{cm}^2$

30. $1200\,\text{m}^3$

practice   **a.** $5\sqrt{3}$ **b.** $10\sqrt{2}$ **c.** $3\sqrt{21}$ **d.** $\dfrac{1}{6}$

problem set 63   **1.** 4   **2.** 6000

Before, 100%   After

3. 36

Before, 100%   After

4. 93 lb   **5.** 4.02

6. $\dfrac{8(3)^3(12)^3(2.54)^3}{(100)^3}\,\text{m}^3$

7. $10\sqrt{3}$ **8.** $5\sqrt{2}$

9. (a) Rational   (b) Rational   (c) Irrational   (d) Rational

10. (a) Rationals, reals   (b) Naturals, wholes, integers, rationals, reals

11. $\sqrt{16.0000001}$ is greater than 4 because 16.0000001 is greater than 4^2.

12. (a) False. No irrational number is a member of the set of rational numbers.

   (b) False. Zero, a member of the set of whole numbers, is not a member of the set of natural numbers.

13. (a) 10 (b) 10 **14.** 7 and 8 **15.** 5.3852

16. (−2, −5) **17.** (2, 4) **18.** −1 < x ≤ 5

19.

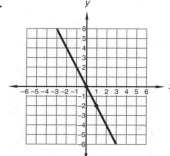

20.

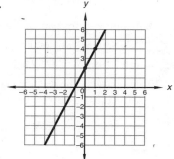

21. $a(a + b)$ **22.** $\dfrac{x^2}{x + y}$ **23.** $2x^5 - 3x^4 + 5x^3 - 25x^2 - 39x + 14$

24. $5m^2xk^4(3x^4 - m^4x^5k^2 + 4m^2k)$ **25.** $2x^4m^6$ **26.** $\dfrac{x^{12}}{9y^{18}}$ **27.** $\dfrac{x^2 + m^3y}{m^2yx}$

28. −1 **29.** $(96 - 8\pi)$ in.^{2} = 70.88 in.^{2} **30.** 1824 ft^2

practice

a.

b.

c.

d.

problem set 64

1. 114,000

of 30,000 | Before, 100%
114,000 is 380% | After

2. 6000

of 6000 | Before, 100%
2400 is 40% / 3600 is 60% | After

3. 460

of 460 | Before, 100%
184 is 40% / 276 is 60% | After

4. $900 **5.** Range = 9; median = 7; mode = 5 and 11; mean = 7.1

6. 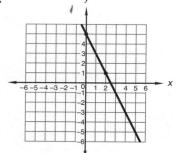 **7.** x > −4; D = {Integers}

8. $6\sqrt{2}$ **9.** (a) 4 and 5 (b) 4.796

10. (a) Rationals, reals (b) Irrationals, reals (c) Rationals, reals **11.** 16

12. (a) True. Every natural number is a member of the set of whole numbers.

(b) False. Zero, a member of the set of whole numbers, is not a member of the set of natural numbers.

13. (3, −3) **14.** (4, 4)

15.

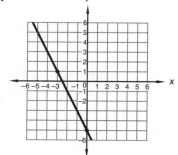

16.

17. -40 **18.** $48x^2 - 28x - 6$ **19.** $15x^2 - 16x + 4$ **20.** y **21.** $\dfrac{a + bx^3}{x^2 y}$

22. $20xym(2x^3m^6z - x^4y^4mz + y)$ **23.** $1 + x$ **24.** p **25.** $9m^5y^7$ **26.** $-\dfrac{3}{x^{-4}}$

27. $\dfrac{3}{x^4 y^8}$ **28.** -5 **29.** $(28 + 8\pi)$ cm = 53.12 cm   **30.** 560 m^3

practice   **a.** $8\sqrt{3} - 2\sqrt{2}$ **b.** $-2\sqrt{7}$ **c.** $6\sqrt{3}$ **d.** 90

problem set 65

1. 87.1   **2.** 250

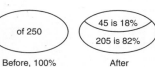

3. 700

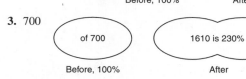

4. $6\sqrt{5} + 2\sqrt{3}$
5. $5\sqrt{7} + 3\sqrt{11}$ **6.** 12
7.

8. $x < 0$; $D = \{\text{Reals}\}$

9. (a) Rational   (b) Irrational   (c) Rational   **10.** (a) Irrationals, reals   (b) Rationals, reals

11. (a) False. None of the natural numbers are irrational.   (b) True. Every whole number is an integer.

12. $(5, 5)$ **13.** $(2, 1)$

14. 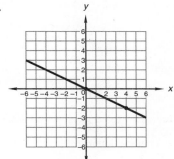   **15.**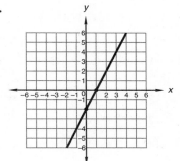

16. $\dfrac{ax^2 + 5(x + y)}{x^2(x + y)}$ **17.** $\dfrac{b^2 + ab - a^3}{b^2}$ **18.** $\dfrac{x^3 + x + 1}{x^2}$ **19.** $\dfrac{cx^3 + dz^2}{zx}$

20. $\dfrac{a^3}{x}$ **21.** $6p^2 + 7p - 20$ **22.** $-3 - 12y^3 + \dfrac{6}{x}$ **23.** $1 - x$ **24.** x^8

25. $16x^{-6}y^2p^{-6}$ **26.** $\dfrac{4a^2 x}{m}$ **27.** $\dfrac{319}{16}$ **28.** -57 **29.** 260 in.^{2} **30.** 900 ft^2

practice   **a.** $2\sqrt{6} + 4\sqrt{3}$ **b.** $6\sqrt{2} - 3\sqrt{3}$ **c.** $5000\sqrt{2}$

problem set 66

1. -2 **2.** 75

3. 111   **4.** 94%

5. Range = 36; median = 89; mode = 92; mean = 84.57   **6.** $1\dfrac{3}{4}$ **7.** $\dfrac{133}{85}$ **8.** 1

9. $10\sqrt{5} - 24\sqrt{2}$ **10.** 0   **11.** $1000\sqrt{70}$ **12.**

13. (a) Naturals, wholes, integers, rationals, reals　　(b) Integers, rationals, reals

14. (a) True. Every integer is a rational number.　　(b) False. Negative integers are not whole numbers.

15. $(-4, 2)$　　　**16.** $(-4, -2)$　　　**17.** $\dfrac{a(x + y) + bx^2y}{x^2y(x + y)}$　　　**18.** $\dfrac{m^3 + 1}{m^2}$

19.

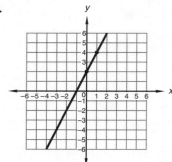

20.

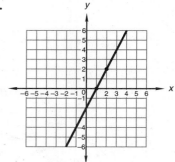

21. $16x^2 + 40x + 25$　　**22.** $15x^2 - 14x + 3$　　**23.** $\dfrac{pq^2 + x^2y}{xq^2}$　　**24.** $x(xy + b)$

25. ax　　**26.** $4x^2y^2p^4\left(3y - xp^2 + 4x^2y^2\right)$　　**27.** -4　　**28.** $9y^{12}m^4$

29. $(40 + 12\pi)\,\text{cm} = 77.68\,\text{cm}$　　**30.** $1100\,\text{m}^3$

practice　　**a.** $(3, -4)$　　**b.** $(1, -4)$

problem set 67

1. 2040　　**2.** 2,875,000　　**3.** 91.33　　**4.** $\dfrac{200(100)^3}{(2.54)^3}\,\text{in.}^3$　　**5.** 20　　**6.** $(3, 1)$　　**7.** $(2, 1)$

8. $(4, 3)$　　**9.** $18\sqrt{5} + 300\sqrt{2}$　　**10.** $-8\sqrt{2}$　　**11.** $4\sqrt{3} - 9\sqrt{2}$

12.
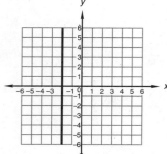
13. (a) Rational　(b) Irrational　(c) Rational　(d) Rational

14. (a) True. Every natural number is also a rational number.

(b) False. No integer is a member of the set of irrational numbers.

15. (a) 12　(b) 12.0416　　**16.** $(5, 5)$

17.

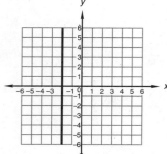

18.

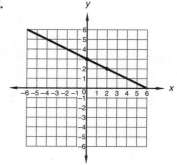

19. -5　　**20.** $\dfrac{m(a + x) + 3x^2}{ax^2(a + x)}$　　**21.** $\dfrac{4xy + 1}{y}$　　**22.** $\dfrac{1}{a^2}$　　**23.** $\dfrac{a + b}{a}$　　**24.** $1 + y$

25. $64y^9p^{12}$　　**26.** $\dfrac{1}{x^4y^{10}} - \dfrac{3}{x^4p} + 1$　　**27.** -1　　**28.** 10, 14　　**29.** $90\,\text{in.}^2$　　**30.** $900\,\text{ft}^2$

practice　　**a.** $\dfrac{(1 + c)c}{w}$　　**b.** $\dfrac{1 + 5m}{2 - x}$　　**c.** $\dfrac{ay + bx}{y}$

problem set 68

1. 5   **2.** 150

of 150
Before, 100%

345 is 230%
After

3. 3000

of 3000
Before, 100%

1110 is 37%
1890 is 63%
After

4. 7.6

5. Range = 51; median = 134; mode = 134; mean = 137.71

6. $\dfrac{12{,}000(100)^3}{(2.54)^3(12)^3(3)^3}$ yd^3 **7.** $\dfrac{16}{315}$ **8.** $\dfrac{3b - a}{1 + b^2}$ **9.** $\dfrac{y + x}{y}$ **10.** $8\sqrt{2} + 94\sqrt{3}$

11. $-26\sqrt{3}$ **12.** $\dfrac{25}{324}$ **13.** $\dfrac{5}{2}$ **14.** $(2, -3)$ **15.** $(4, 5)$ **16.**

17. (a) False. Some real numbers are not members of the set of irrational numbers.

(b) True. Every whole number is a member of the set of real numbers.

18. $(5, 5)$ **19.**   **20.**

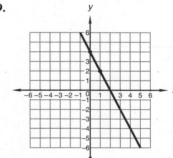

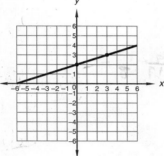

21. $\dfrac{xy + m + cx^3}{x^3 y}$ **22.** $\dfrac{2ab - b + a^2}{a^2}$ **23.** $\dfrac{x^4}{16y^3 m^2}$ **24.** $\dfrac{x^{10}}{y^{10}}$ **25.** $x^2 y^2 p^6$

26. 19   **27.** -6 **28.** $-9x^2 y$ **29.** $(16 + 2\pi)$ cm = 22.28 cm   **30.** 72 m^3

practice   **a.** $(x - 7)(x + 6)$ **b.** $(x + 7)(x - 6)$ **c.** $(x - 8)(x + 2)$

problem set 69

1. 4000

of 4000
Before, 100%

720 is 18%
3280 is 82%
After

2. 86%

3. (a) Rational. Every repeating decimal number is a rational number.

(b) Rational. Every whole number is a rational number and $\sqrt[3]{27}$ equals 3, which is a whole number.

(c) Irrational. The square root of any whole number that is not a perfect square is an irrational number.

4. $(x + 8)(x - 2)$ **5.** $(x - 3)(x - 3)$ **6.** $(x - 9)(x + 3)$ **7.** $(p - 5)(p + 4)$

8. $(x - 5)(x + 3)$ **9.** $(p - 7)(p + 3)$ **10.** $(p + 5)(p - 4)$ **11.** $(k - 8)(k + 5)$

12. $(m + 5)(m + 4)$ **13.** $(x + 11)(x + 3)$ **14.** $(p - 9)(p - 4)$ **15.** $(m - 6)(m + 5)$

16. $(n + 9)(n + 2)$ **17.** $(x + 9)(x + 3)$ **18.** $(x - 9)(x - 10)$ **19.** $y + 1$

20. $\dfrac{a - 4b}{x - b^2}$ **21.** $11\sqrt{5} - 30\sqrt{2}$ **22.** $-10\sqrt{7} + 40\sqrt{3}$ **23.** $14\sqrt{5} - 20$

24. $(3, -4)$ **25.** $(4, 5)$ **26.** $(2, 3)$ **27.** $-\dfrac{2a^2}{b^2}$ **28.** $\dfrac{80}{9}$ **29.** 800 in.^{2}

30. 144π ft^2 = 452.16 ft^2

practice   **a.** $\frac{1}{8}$ **b.** $\frac{1}{2}$ **c.** $\frac{5}{36}$ **d.** $\frac{6}{13}$ **e.** $\frac{1}{64}$

problem set 70

1. $\frac{1}{3}$ **2.** (a) $\frac{1}{12}$ (b) $\frac{1}{6}$ **3.** $\frac{1}{8}$ **4.** $\frac{1}{16}$ **5.** $\frac{5}{14}$ **6.** 82.31

7. (a) 10   (b) 9.9499   **8.** $(m - 2)(m + 1)$ **9.** $(y + 5)(y - 3)$ **10.** $(p + 5)(p - 1)$

11. $(a - 9)(a - 1)$ **12.** $(b - 3)(b + 1)$ **13.** $(p - 10)(p - 1)$ **14.** $(a + 16)(a + 2)$

15. $(b + 9)(b + 3)$ **16.** $(x + 8)(x + 2)$ **17.** $(x + 5)(x + 10)$ **18.** $(x + 9)(x + 2)$

19. $(x + 6)(x - 3)$ **20.** $(x - 5)(x - 4)$ **21.** $(x - 7)(x - 6)$ **22.** $(x - 3)(x + 1)$

23. -34 **24.** $-4\sqrt{2} + 35\sqrt{5}$ **25.** $(1, 1)$ **26.** $(5, 5)$ **27.** $\frac{m - y^2}{1 - y}$

28. $\frac{1 + yx}{xy^2}$ **29.** $\frac{a + 1}{a - 1}$ **30.** $864\pi \text{ cm}^3 = 2712.96 \text{ cm}^3$

practice   **a.** $-4x(x + 4)(x + 3)$ **b.** $-(x - 6)(x + 4)$ **c.** $N_N = 8; N_Q = 13$

d. $N_D = 18; N_N = -6$

problem set 71

1. $\frac{1}{2}$ **2.** $\frac{1}{64}$ **3.** $\frac{3}{13}$ **4.** (a) $\frac{1}{6}$ (b) $\frac{5}{12}$

5. Range = 6; median = 6; mode = 6; mean = 5.43   **6.** 84

7. $\frac{10,000(1000)^2 (100)^2}{(2.54)^2 (12)^2 (5280)^2} \text{ mi}^2$ **8.** $2(x + 3)(x + 2)$ **9.** $5(x + 4)(x + 2)$

10. $x(x - 5)(x + 4)$ **11.** $a(x + 3)(x + 3)$ **12.** $-b(b - 8)(b + 3)$

13. $-3(m + 8)(m + 2)$ **14.** $N_D = 10; N_N = 7$ **15.** $N_N = 8; N_Q = 12$

16. $(x - 5)(x + 2)$ **17.** $(x + 3)(x + 4)$ **18.** $(x - 2)(x - 2)$ **19.** $(x + 7)(x + 2)$

20. $(x + 6)(x + 2)$ **21.** $(x - 6)(x + 3)$ **22.** $\frac{mz^3 + nx}{xz^3 y}$ **23.** $\frac{a + x^2}{1 - x}$

24. $-53\sqrt{3} + 66\sqrt{2}$ **25.** 0, 1, 4, 9, 16, 25, 36, 49, 64, 81, 100, 121, 144, 169, 196, 225

26. (a) Irrational   (b) Rational   (c) Rational   (d) Irrational

27. (a) True. Every whole number is a member of the set of rational numbers.

(b) True. Every natural number is an integer.

28. 2   **29.** $(220 - 25\pi) \text{ in.}^2 = 141.5 \text{ in.}^2$ **30.** 320 ft^2

practice   **a.** $(a + b)(x + 5)(x + 3)$ **b.** $c(m - b)(x - 6)(x + 4)$ **c.** 320 cm^3

d. $216\pi \text{ m}^2 = 678.24 \text{ m}^2$

problem set 72

1. $\frac{1}{64}$ **2.** $\frac{7}{15}$ **3.** $\frac{1}{2}$ **4.** (a) $\frac{1}{9}$ (b) $\frac{13}{18}$ **5.** 8.50

6. 248 lb

of 248 lb   310 lb is 125%

Before, 100%   After

7. $(x - 1)(x + 2)(x + 5)$

8. $m(y + 1)(x + 2)(x + 2)$

9. $(z - 5)(x + 2)(x + 3)$

10. $(x + y)(m + 7)(m + 5)$

11. $2x(x + 3)(x + 5)$ **12.** $ab(x - 8)(x + 3)$ **13.** $(m + 8)(m + 2)$ **14.** $(n - 12)(n + 4)$

15. $(y - 8)(y - 7)$ **16.** $(p - 11)(p + 5)$ **17.** $(t + 7)(t + 5)$ **18.** $(y + 50)(y + 1)$

19. -2000 **20.** $-5 < x \le 2; D = \{\text{Reals}\}$ **21.** $\frac{m + p^2}{1 - px}$ **22.** $\frac{a^2 + b}{1 - 4a}$

23. $y + x$ **24.** 6   **25.** $(3, 3)$ **26.** $N_D = 7$; $N_Q = 17$

27. (a) Irrational   (b) Rational   (c) Rational   (d) Rational   **28.** $14\sqrt{2}$

29. $(32 + 4\pi)$ cm $= 44.56$ cm   **30.** 112 m^3

practice   **a.** $(8x - 9y)(8x + 9y)$ **b.** $(10m - 5)(10m + 5)$ **c.** $\left(y^2x - 13z^5\right)\left(y^2x + 13z^5\right)$

d. (1) $\dfrac{16}{49}$ (2) $\dfrac{2}{7}$ **e.** (1) $\dfrac{30}{121}$ (2) $\dfrac{3}{11}$

problem set 73

1. $\dfrac{1}{3}$ **2.** $\dfrac{10}{49}$ **3.** $\dfrac{1}{8}$ **4.** (a) $\dfrac{1}{18}$ (b) $\dfrac{1}{36}$

5. 360

 of 360

Before, 100%

 900 is 250%

After

6. 176 lb   **7.** $(2px - k)(2px + k)$

8. $(5px - 2m)(5px + 2m)$

9. $(2y - 3x)(2y + 3x)$

10. $(3ka + 7)(3ka - 7)$

11. $(p + 2k)(p - 2k)$ **12.** $(6ax + k)(6ax - k)$ **13.** $(x - 5)(x + 4)$

14. $4(x - 5)(x + 4)$ **15.** $2(b - 8)(b + 3)$ **16.** $3(x - 15)(x + 2)$

17. $(a + b)(x + 2)(x + 5)$ **18.** $p(m + 5)(m + 4)$ **19.** $5(k + 3)(k + 2)$

20. $-(x + 7)(x + 1)$ **21.** ———•—•—•—•—•—•—•—•—•—
                    −7 −6 −5 −4 −3 −2 −1 0 1 2 3 4

22. (a) Irrational   (b) Rational   (c) Irrational   (d) Rational

23. $\dfrac{25{,}000(5280)^2 (12)^2 (2.54)^2}{(100)^2 (1000)^2}$ km^2 **24.** $(1, 1)$ **25.** $N_N = 75$; $N_P = 100$

26. $\dfrac{2x + y - yx}{x(x + y)}$ **27.** $-79\sqrt{5}$ **28.** $\dfrac{x + 1}{y + x^2}$ **29.** $\dfrac{6}{5}$ **30.** 12π in.^{3} $= 37.68$ in.^{3}

practice   **a.** 4.99×10^4 **b.** 4.99×10^{-7} **c.** 4.99×10^{-1}

problem set 74

1. (a) $\dfrac{1}{4}$ (b) $\dfrac{3}{11}$ **2.** $\dfrac{7}{26}$ **3.** $\dfrac{1}{16}$ **4.** 1200   **5.** \$88,800   **6.** 9.16

7. ———•—•—•—•—•—•—•—•—•—•—
      −1 0 1 2 3 4 5 6 7 8   **8.** 4.78×10^{-4} **9.** 4.78×10^2

10. 4.78×10^{-12} **11.** $5(x + y)(x - y)$ **12.** $5(3x + 2m)(3x - 2m)$

13. $(2a - 3b)(2a + 3b)$ **14.** $a^2(7p + 1)(7p - 1)$ **15.** $(x + 5)(x + 4)$

16. $(x + 5)(x - 4)$ **17.** $(a + b)(x + 7)(x + 4)$ **18.** $(x - a)(y - 4)(y + 7)$

19. $x(x + 6)(x + 4)$ **20.** $a(x - 5)(x + 3)$ **21.** $\dfrac{c + x + bc + 5xc - 2x(c + x)}{xc(c + x)}$

22. $(-2, -4)$ **23.** $N_D = 35$; $N_Q = 5$ **24.**

25. $40\sqrt{5} + 84\sqrt{3}$ **26.** $\dfrac{1}{x^2 y^4}$

27. $-x^4 y + 2x^4 a^6$ **28.** 10

29. 51 cm^2 **30.** 144 m^2

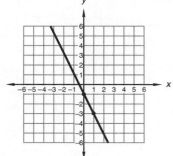

practice   **a.** $y = -3$ **b.** $y = -\frac{1}{2}x + 3$ **c.** $x = 3$ **d.** $y = \frac{1}{2}x + 3$

e.
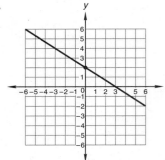

f.
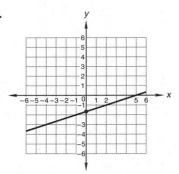

problem set 75

1. $\frac{35}{144}$ **2.** $\frac{1}{256}$ **3.** $\frac{36}{91}$ **4.** 4000

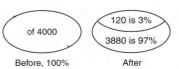

5. 1632
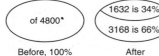

6. 56%

7. $x = -3$ **8.** $y = -x + 2$

9.
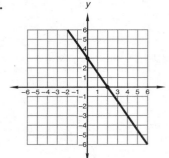

10.
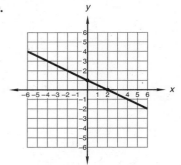

11. 1.23×10^{-8} **12.** 1.23×10^{5} **13.** $b^3(x + 2)(x - 2)$ **14.** $(4x - a)(4x + a)$

15. $(3p + m)(3p - m)$ **16.** $(x + 5)(x - 2)$ **17.** $(x + 7)(x - 3)$ **18.** $5(x - 5)(x + 2)$

19. $x(x - 2)(x - 1)$ **20.** $(x + y)(z + 6)(z + 3)$ **21.** $(m + a)(x + 6)(x - 3)$

22. $(1, 1)$ **23.** $N_D = 11$; $N_Q = 14$ **24.** $50\sqrt{3} - 90\sqrt{2}$ **25.** -43 **26.** $x^{12}y$

27. $b + a$ **28.** -1 **29.** 24 in.^{2} **30.** 36π ft^2 = 113.04 ft^2

practice   **a.** 70, 71, 72   **b.** 9, 10, 11, 12

problem set 76

1. 10, 11, 12, 13   **2.** 14,352   **3.** $\frac{4}{15}$

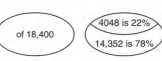

4. (a) $\frac{7}{12}$ (b) $\frac{5}{18}$ **5.** (a) $x = 5$ (b) $y = -x$

6.

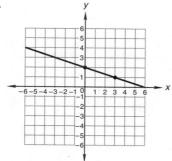

7.

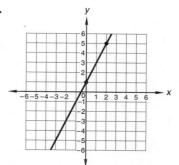

8. 4.3×10^3 **9.** 4.3×10^{10} **10.** $(m + 3x)(m - 3x)$ **11.** $(2x + 3m)(2x - 3m)$

12. $5(5m + x)(5m - x)$ **13.** $2(x + 6k)(x - 6k)$ **14.** $(x - 7)(x + 2)$

15. $-x(x - 6)(x + 2)$ **16.** $a(x + 5)(x + 2)$ **17.** $2(x + 7)(x + 5)$ **18.** $3(x + 8)(x + 1)$

19. $p(x - 2)(x + 1)$ **20.** $N_N = 30$; $N_Q = 15$ **21.** $(2, 5)$

22. (a) False. Some rational numbers are not integers.   (b) False. No integer is an irrational number.

23. $\dfrac{a^3x + 2ax + ba^2 - x^3}{a^2x^3}$ **24.** 5 **25.** $-2\sqrt{5}$ **26.** 21 **27.** $\dfrac{2a^2x^5}{y} - \dfrac{3a^2x^3}{y^3}$

28. $\dfrac{3x^6}{ay^4} - 6x + 12$ **29.** -2 **30.** 336 cm^3

practice   **a.** $-16, -14, -12$ **b.** 216 yd   **c.** 4480

problem set 77   **1.** 19, 21, 23, 25   **2.** 7.2   **3.** 48,000   **4.** $\dfrac{1}{6}$

5. $\dfrac{16}{121}$ **6.** $\dfrac{1}{32}$ **7.** 165

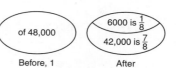

8. (a) $y = \dfrac{1}{2}x + 3$ (b) $x = 3$

9.

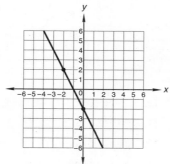

10.

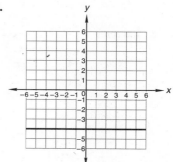

11. 7.0×10^{-4} **12.** 7.0×10^{-9} **13.** $(2x + 7)(2x - 7)$ **14.** $x^2(1 - 3y)(1 + 3y)$

15. $3(p + 2k)(p - 2k)$ **16.** $(k + 2m)(k - 2m)$ **17.** $(x - 3)(x - 3)$

18. $2(x - 2)(x - 2)$ **19.** $2(x + 2)(x + 2)$ **20.** $2(x + 5)(x + 5)$ **21.** $3(x - 5)(x - 5)$

22. $a(x - 6)(x - 6)$ **23.** $(4, 4)$ **24.** $N_D = 100$; $N_N = 400$

25. (a) Integers, rationals, reals   (b) Rationals, reals   **26.**

27. $\dfrac{xy + 1}{x^2 - 5y}$ **28.** $92\sqrt{3}$ **29.** $\dfrac{12}{5}$ **30.** $768\pi \text{ in.}^2 = 2411.52 \text{ in.}^2$

practice   **a.** $-\dfrac{4}{3}$ **b.** 16

problem set 78

1. $-10, -8, -6$ **2.** 3, 5, 7, 9   **3.** $\dfrac{40}{153}$ **4.** $\dfrac{2}{3}$ **5.** 3953

6. 4000

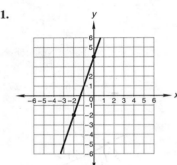

Before, 100%   of 4000   9120 is 228%   After

7. 6000

Before, 1   of 6000   1800 is $\dfrac{3}{10}$ 4200 is $\dfrac{7}{10}$ After

8. $\dfrac{161}{11}$ **9.** $\dfrac{4}{3}$

10. (a) $y = -3$ (b) $y = -\dfrac{1}{2}x + 3$

11.

12. 3.0×10^{-7} **13.** 4.0×10^{7}

14. $(x - 4)(x - 5)$ **15.** $2a(x - 7)(x - 3)$

16. $m(x + 6)(x + 7)$ **17.** $2(4x - 3a)(4x + 3a)$

18. $a^2(5m + 2)(5m - 2)$

19. $9(my - 2k)(my + 2k)$

20. $N_D = 20$; $N_Q = 320$ **21.** $(-3, -3)$

22. (a) Irrationals, reals   (b) Rationals, reals

23. $\dfrac{axy^2 + bxy + cx - d}{x^3 y^3}$ **24.** $76\sqrt{6}$

25. $x^8 y^4$ **26.** 8   **27.** $\dfrac{2a}{y^4} - \dfrac{6}{x^2 y^4} + 4$ **28.**

$-4 \quad -3 \quad -2 \quad -1 \quad 0$

29. 142 cm   **30.** $648\pi \text{ m}^3 = 2034.72 \text{ m}^3$

---

practice   **a.** 130   **b.** $T_R = 20$; $T_T = 10$

problem set 79

1. $-8, -6, -4, -2$ **2.** $\dfrac{35}{132}$ **3.** (a) $\dfrac{1}{9}$ (b) $\dfrac{13}{18}$ **4.** 3200   **5.** 82.64

6. 400 acres

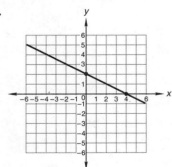

of 400 acres   132 acres is 33%   268 acres is 67%   Before, 100%   After

7. 55   **8.** $T_X = 3$; $T_H = 6$ **9.** -152

10. $\dfrac{21}{2}$ **11.** $\dfrac{2}{3}$

12.

13. 1.35×10^{-21} **14.** 1.35×10^{-12}

15. $(x + 2)(x - 15)$ **16.** $2(m - 7)(m - 5)$

17. $-x(x - 10)(x - 4)$

18. $n^2(2m + 7xp)(2m - 7xp)$

19. $(r + 2)(x + 2)(x + 5)$

20. $z(x + y)(z + 7)(z - 3)$ **21.** $(4, 4)$

22. $N_D = 5$; $N_N = 17$

23. (a) Irrational   (b) Rational

     (c) Rational   (d) Rational

24. $\dfrac{a(x + y) + 4y - x(x + y)}{xy(x + y)}$ **25.** $\sqrt{5}$ **26.** $\dfrac{\sqrt[4]{7}}{3} - 1$ **27.** $\dfrac{23{,}000(100)^3}{(2.54)^3 (12)^3} \text{ ft}^3$

28. $-\dfrac{3}{4}$ **29.** 54 in.^{2} **30.** $(1780 + 186\pi) \text{ ft}^2 = 2364.04 \text{ ft}^2$

practice   **a.** 1.4×10^9 **b.** 1×10^8

problem set 80

1. $34, 36, 38$ **2.** (a) $\dfrac{2}{5}$ (b) $\dfrac{1}{3}$ (c) $\dfrac{4}{15}$ **3.** $\dfrac{1}{32}$ **4.** 200 **5.** $10{,}725$ pounds

6. 1.2×10^{13} **7.** 6×10^{-21} **8.** $R_S = 80$; $R_F = 96$ **9.** $T_M = 1$; $T_R = 4$

10. $T_G = 5$; $T_B = 8$ **11.** $\dfrac{52}{11}$ **12.** $\dfrac{11}{2}$ **13.** $\dfrac{476}{125}$

14.

15.

16. $x(x + 8)(x + 1)$

17. $-a(x + 16)(x - 3)$ **18.** $bc(x + a)(x - a)$

19. $(x - a)(y + 4)(y - 4)$ **20.** $N_D = 30$; $N_N = 42$

21. $(3, -2)$

22. (a) Irrationals, reals (b) Integers, rationals, reals

23. $\dfrac{3a(a + x) + 4(a + x) + 7 - a}{a^2(a + x)}$

24. $1 + a^2b^2$ **25.** $\dfrac{y^{30}}{x^6}$ **26.** $\dfrac{4y^2 + 1}{xy + m}$

27. $\dfrac{1}{a^4} + \dfrac{3a^3}{x^6} - 1$ **28.** 5 **29.** $(40 + 20\pi)$ cm $= 102.80$ cm   **30.** 570 m^3

practice   **a.** $(2, 1)$ **b.** $(4, 4)$ **c.** Inconsistent

problem set 81

1. $14, 16, 18$ **2.** $-3, -2, -1, 0$ **3.** (a) $\dfrac{1}{36}$ (b) $\dfrac{1}{12}$ **4.** 60% **5.** 420 lb   **6.** 300

7. $\dfrac{20}{3}$ **8.** $(3, -3)$ **9.** $(-1, 0)$ **10.** Inconsistent   **11.** 2×10^{15} **12.** 1×10^{-5}

13. $T_G = 10$; $T_B = 8$ **14.** $T_K = 8$; $T_N = 16$ **15.** $\dfrac{21}{17}$ **16.** $\dfrac{8}{5}$ **17.** $a(x - 6)(x - 1)$

18. $-m(x + 4)(x + 2)$ **19.** $m(x - 3a)(x + 3a)$ **20.** $(x + a)(b + 6)(b - 4)$

21. $(2, 3)$ **22.** $N_D = 20$; $N_N = 10$ **23.** $-5\sqrt{7}$

24. (a) $-10, 16$ (b) $-3, 21$ (c) $-17, 21$ **25.** $\dfrac{x - y}{x + my}$ **26.** $2x^6y^6$

27. -21 **28.** 13 **29.** $\dfrac{x^2a^3}{y^2} - \dfrac{3a^2}{x^6} + 1$ **30.** 1020 in.^{3}

practice   **a.** $2m^4 + 3m^2 - 5$ **b.** $m^2 + 4m$ **c.** $D = \{x \in \mathbb{R}\}$; $R = \{y \in \mathbb{R}\}$
d. $D = \{x \in \mathbb{R}\}$; $R = \{2\}$
e. $D = \left\{x \in \mathbb{R} \mid -1 < x \le 5\right\}$; $R = \left\{y \in \mathbb{R} \mid -1 \le y \le 3\right\}$ **f.** $\left\{x \in \mathbb{R} \mid x \le 3\right\}$

problem set 82

1. $-3, -1, 1, 3$ **2.** $\dfrac{95}{203}$ **3.** (a) $\dfrac{5}{36}$ (b) $\dfrac{7}{12}$ **4.** 45 cm

5. Range $= 4$ mi; median $= 5$ mi; mode $= 5$ mi; mean $= 4.29$ mi   **6.** 3400

7. $x^2 + 2x + 2$ **8.** $\left\{x \in \mathbb{R} \mid x \le 4\right\}$ **9.** $D = \{x \in \mathbb{R}\}$; $R = \{-1\}$

10. $D = \left\{x \in \mathbb{R} \mid -4 \le x < 4\right\}$; $R = \left\{y \in \mathbb{R} \mid -1 \le y \le 3\right\}$ **11.** $T_M = 4$; $T_S = 3$

12. $(-1, 3)$ **13.** $(-3, 2)$ **14.** Consistent   **15.** 7×10^{-36} **16.** $-\dfrac{5}{2}$ **17.** $\dfrac{9}{7}$

18. $4(a + 8)(a - 5)$ **19.** $m(k + m)(k - m)$ **20.** $x^2(y + 1)(x + 1)(x + 1)$

21. $N_D = 40$; $N_N = 10$ **22.** $(1, -1)$ **23.** (a) Rational (b) Rational (c) Rational

24. $\dfrac{x(c + x) + bxc^2 + 5(c + x)}{x^2c^2(c + x)}$ **25.** $\dfrac{4ax + 6a(x + y) - 4(x + y)}{ax(x + y)}$

26. $8\sqrt{5} - 20\sqrt{2}$ **27.** $\dfrac{a^5}{x^3y^4} - \dfrac{3a^2}{y^4}$ **28.** $\dfrac{x^2 + y^2}{ay - x}$ **29.** 100π cm^2 = 314 cm^2

30. 1300 m^2

practice **a.** $N_D = 22$; $N_N = 14$ **b.** $N_D = 12$; $N_Q = 21$

problem set 83

1. $N_D = 31$; $N_N = 20$ **2.** $N_D = 35$; $N_Q = 5$ **3.** \$800 **4.** 6800 **5.** $\dfrac{5}{21}$ **6.** $\dfrac{1}{64}$

7. 29 **8.** $a^2 + 2ab + b^2 - 7a - 7b$ **9.** $\{x \in \mathbb{R} \mid x \leq 9\}$

10. $D = \{x \in \mathbb{R}\}$; $R = \{-5\}$

11. $D = \{x \in \mathbb{R} \mid -4 \leq x \leq 4\}$; $R = \{y \in \mathbb{R} \mid -3 \leq y \leq 3\}$

12. (a) $x = 4$ (b) $y = 2x$ **13.** $(-1, 1)$ **14.** Consistent **15.** 4×10^{-8} **16.** 100

17. $T_P = 4$; $T_M = 12$ **18.** $R_P = 85$; $R_G = 40$ **19.** $\dfrac{21}{4}$ **20.** 2

21. $x(x + 7)(x + 4)$ **22.** $x(2a + y)(2a - y)$ **23.** $(z + 1)(x + y)(x - y)$

24. $(5, -2)$ **25.** [number line from −4 to 3, closed dot at −3, open dot at 2]

26. (a) False. Zero, a member of the set of whole numbers, is not a member of the set of natural numbers.

(b) True. Every integer is a rational number.

27. $\dfrac{4a + 5b}{4a^3}$ **28.** $\dfrac{abc - 1}{c^2(4 - ac^2)}$ **29.** $\dfrac{33}{16}$ **30.** $\left(4140 + \dfrac{575\pi}{2}\right)$ in.^{3} = 5042.75 in.^{3}

practice **a.** 120 **b.** $12\sqrt{6} + 30\sqrt{3}$ **c.** Function **d.** Not a function **e.** $\{a, 6, 7\}$

f. $\{p, a, 7\}$ **g.** (2), (4)

problem set 84

1. $N_N = 75$; $N_P = 100$ **2.** $N_N = 42$; $N_D = 30$ **3.** 160 **4.** $-6, -4, -2$ **5.** 0, 1, 2

6. (a) $\dfrac{1}{18}$ (b) $\dfrac{5}{6}$ **7.** (a), (d) **8.** (b), (c), (d) **9.** $2a^2 + a + 1$

10. $\{x \in \mathbb{R} \mid x \leq 11\}$ **11.** $D = \{x \in \mathbb{R} \mid -4 \leq x \leq 4\}$; $R = \{y \in \mathbb{R} \mid -1 \leq y \leq 2\}$

12. (a) $y = 4$ (b) $y = -2x - 2$ **13.** $(1, -4)$ **14.** $(-2, -2)$ **15.** Dependent **16.** 40

17. $\dfrac{1}{x^{13}}$ **18.** $x \geq -3$; $D = \{\text{Integers}\}$ **19.** $T_M = 4$; $T_K = 12$ **20.** -51 **21.** 1.6

22. $x(x + 5)(x + 4)$ **23.** $ab(x + 3)(x - 2)$ **24.** $\dfrac{x - a - 3ax^2 - 2x(x - a)}{x^2(x - a)}$

25. $x^3 + 6x^2 + 11x + 12$ **26.** $\sqrt[3]{26.981}$ is less than 3, because 26.981 is less than 3^3.

27. -38 **28.** $\dfrac{9}{25}$ **29.** 252 cm^2 **30.** 648 in.^{2}

practice **a.**

STEM	LEAF
11	1, 8
12	8, 3, 7, 9
13	2, 6, 0, 5, 9
14	2, 5, 8, 9, 2, 9
15	1, 0, 0

b. 40 **c.** 137.5 **d.** 142, 149, 150 **e.** 136.7

f.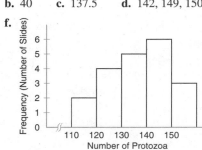

g. 15 **h.** 30%

problem set 85

1. $N_N = 250$; $N_P = 200$ **2.** Original price = \$4000; price reduced by \$560

3. 32, 34, 36, 38   **4.** 18   **5.** $\dfrac{1}{16}$

6. (a)

STEM	LEAF
3	5, 8, 1, 9
4	1, 3, 8, 5, 7, 2, 0
5	2, 1, 4, 4, 3, 9
6	3, 5, 2

(b) Range = 34
(c) Median = 47.5
(d) Mode = 54
(e) Mean = 48.1

7. (a)

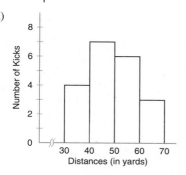

(b) 40–50 interval   (c) 55%

8. $\dfrac{40}{153}$ **9.** (a), (c), (d)

10. $6\sqrt{6}$ **11.** $30\sqrt{6} - 96$

12. $D = \{x \in \mathbb{R} \mid -3 \le x \le 3\}$; $R = \{y \in \mathbb{R} \mid -2 \le y \le 2\}$

13. (2, 2)   **14.** (4, 5)   **15.** $N_D = 7$; $N_Q = 17$

16. Inconsistent. Using the elimination method yields a false equality, so the equations have no points in common.

17. 2.8×10^{-17} **18.** $R_K = 38$; $R_M = 87$ **19.** $-2(p - 11)(p + 5)$ **20.** $(t + 7)(t - 7)$

21. $15ab^3c^4(2a - bc + 3b)$ **22.** $-\dfrac{122}{13}$ **23.** $\dfrac{29}{35}$

24. (a) Naturals, wholes, integers, rationals, reals   (b) Integers, rationals, reals

25. (a) -27 (b) $-\dfrac{1}{27}$ (c) $\dfrac{1}{27}$ **26.** $\dfrac{1}{x^3} - 4y^5 + 1$ **27.**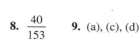

28. -58 **29.** a **30.** 216 cm^3

practice

a. $5x^2 - 9x + 1$ **b.** $6x^2 + 9x + 19 - \dfrac{2}{x - 2}$ **c.** $x^2 + 2x + 4 + \dfrac{3}{x - 2}$

d. $3x^2 + 12x + 43 + \dfrac{176}{x - 4}$

problem set 86

1. 151   **2.** 20   **3.** 12, 13, 14   **4.** 228   **5.** 4

6. (a) Range = 52; median = 82; mode = 85; mean = 80.2

(b)

STEM	LEAF
4	6
5	
6	8, 5
7	9, 5, 3
8	5, 5, 7, 2, 1
9	3, 5, 1, 8

(c)

(d) 80–90 interval

7. $4x^3 + x^2 - 2x + 6$ **8.** $x^2 - 5x + 12 - \dfrac{19}{x + 2}$ **9.** $x^2 - 3x + 9 - \dfrac{28}{x + 3}$

10. $-5x^2 + 24x - 49 + \dfrac{108}{x + 2}$ **11.** (a), (b), (d)   **12.** $864\sqrt{3}$ **13.** $42 - 6\sqrt{3}$

14. $\{x \in \mathbb{R} \mid x \le 11\}$ **15.** $x^2 + 6x + 11$ **16.** (a) $y = -2x + 4$ (b) $x = -3$

17. (1, 1)   **18.** (−4, 2)   **19.** Consistent. The equations intersect at only one point.

20. 6×10^{-5} **21.** $T_M = 6$; $T_D = 2$ **22.** $a(x + 2)(x + 2)$ **23.** $(x − 5)(x + 2)$

24. $a(3 + 2x)(3 − 2x)$ **25.** $x(x + 10)(x + 2)$ **26.** $\dfrac{11}{3}$ **27.** $\dfrac{6x^2y + 3y^2 − 2x^4}{x^2y(x^2 + y)}$

28. $\dfrac{3}{2}$ **29.** 54 cm^2 **30.** $(60 + 16\pi) \text{ m}^2 = 110.24 \text{ m}^2$

practice   **a.** $T_1 = 40$; $T_2 = 20$ **b.** $R_O = 1$; $R_S = −2$ **c.** Function   **d.** Not a function
e. Function

problem set
87

1. $N_N = 400$; $N_D = 100$ **2.** $N_N = 30$; $N_Q = 15$ **3.** 11, 12, 13, 14   **4.** 1737

5. (a) $\dfrac{100}{289}$ (b) $\dfrac{45}{136}$

6. (a)

Stem	Leaf
4	9, 8
5	7, 7, 7, 8, 7, 4, 1, 0
6	1, 1, 8, 4, 5

(b)

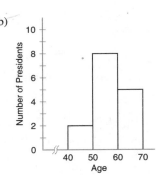

(c) Range = 20;
median = 57;
mode = 57;
mean = 57.13

7. $R_J = 10$; $R_T = 10$

8. (a) Function   (b) Function   (c) Not a function   (d) Function   **9.** $x^2 − 4x + 8 − \dfrac{12}{x + 2}$

10. $2x^2 + 3x + 11 + \dfrac{29}{x − 3}$ **11.** $8x^3 + 4x^2 − x + 2$ **12.** (a), (b)   **13.** $24 + 36\sqrt{3}$

14. $6 − 4y − y^2$ **15.** $D = \{x \in \mathbb{R} \mid −5 \le x \le 5\}$; $R = \{y \in \mathbb{R} \mid −3 \le y \le 3\}$

16. (a) $y = 3$ (b) $y = −\dfrac{1}{3}x − 4$ **17.** (0, −2)   **18.** (4, 4)

19. Consistent. The only ordered pair that is a solution to both equations is (0, 0).

20. 1.2×10^{19} **21.** $ma(x + 2)(x + 7)$ **22.** $−x(x + 7)(x + 5)$ **23.** $−\dfrac{17}{4}$

24. −56, −42   **25.** (a) 3.31662   (b) 4.12311   (c) 7.34847   (d) 5.47723

26. $\dfrac{x − y}{a + yb}$ **27.** $\dfrac{y^6}{x^5}$ **28.** $\dfrac{1}{x^4y^2} + 1 − \dfrac{3a}{x^6y^2}$ **29.** $(28 + 14\pi) \text{ in.} = 71.96 \text{ in.}$

30. $128\pi \text{ ft}^3 = 401.92 \text{ ft}^3$

practice   **a.** −8, 3   **b.** −12, 4

problem set
88

1. $N_N = 30$; $N_P = 120$ **2.** $N_P = 90$; $N_N = 36$ **3.** 31,200   **4.** 7, 9, 11, 13

5. $\dfrac{4}{11}$ **6.** 99.2   **7.** Answers will vary.   **8.** −4, 7   **9.** −5, 5   **10.** −2, 3

11. −4   **12.** $R_K = 30$; $R_P = 40$ **13.** (a), (c), (d)   **14.** $2x^2 − 4x + 3 − \dfrac{2}{x + 2}$

15. $3x^2 + 15x + 75 + \dfrac{371}{x − 5}$ **16.** $2x^3 − 3x^2 + 2x − 1$

17. $\{x \in \mathbb{R} \mid x \ge −1\}$ **18.** (a) $y = −2$ (b) $y = −\dfrac{1}{2}x + 3$ **19.** $50\sqrt{2} − 15\sqrt{15}$

20. $56 - 84\sqrt{2}$ **21.** $-3x^2 - 4x + 6$ **22.** $(-3, -3)$ **23.** $(2, 2)$ **24.** 6×10^{-2}

25. 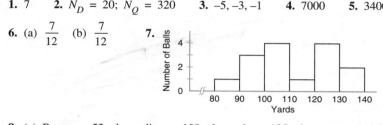   **26.** $\dfrac{7}{32}$ **27.** $\dfrac{4a^2 + ax + 2a + 2x}{a^2(a + x)}$ **28.** $-2, 0$ **29.** -5

30. 384 yd^2

practice   **a.** 13   **b.** $N_A = 112$; $N_C = 63$

problem set 89

1. 7   **2.** $N_D = 20$; $N_Q = 320$ **3.** $-5, -3, -1$ **4.** 7000   **5.** 3400

6. (a) $\dfrac{7}{12}$ (b) $\dfrac{7}{12}$ **7.**

8. (a) Range = 52 yd; median = 109 yd; mode = 125 yd; mean = 111.87 yd   (b) 26.67%

9. 5, 7   **10.** $-\dfrac{3}{2}, \dfrac{3}{2}$ **11.** $-\dfrac{7}{3}, \dfrac{7}{3}$ **12.** $-12, -5$ **13.** 4, 8   **14.** $-\dfrac{2}{3}, \dfrac{2}{3}$

15. $T_M = 5$; $T_T = 2$ **16.** (b), (c), (f)

17. (b) $D = \{x, y, m\}$; $R = \{p, 5\}$ (f) $D = \{1, 3, 6\}$; $R = \{-2\}$

18. $x - 3$ **19.** $3x^2 - 12x + 48 - \dfrac{193}{x + 4}$ **20.** $3a^2 - 6a + 20$

21. (a) $y = 4$ (b) $y = -\dfrac{1}{2}x - 2$ **22.** $(2, 2)$ **23.** $(4, 4)$ **24.** $75\sqrt{2} - 30$

25. (a) Irrational   (b) Rational   (c) Rational   (d) Rational   **26.** 2×10^{-40} **27.** $\dfrac{xy^2 + a}{xa - y}$

28. -19 **29.** (a) -9 (b) 9   (c) $-\dfrac{1}{9}$ **30.** 9120 cm^3

practice   **a.** $L = 69$; $S = 29$ **b.** $N_G = 24$; $N_B = 13$

problem set 90

1. $L = 36$; $S = 12$ **2.** $N_G = 22$; $N_B = 14$ **3.** $L = 44 \text{ m}$; $S = 32 \text{ m}$ **4.** 80   **5.** 90

6. Answers will vary.   **7.** $\dfrac{1000(3)^3(12)^3(2.54)^3}{(100)^3} \text{ m}^3$ **8.** -5 **9.** $-6, -5$ **10.** $-3, 3$

11. $-3, 3$ **12.** $T_M = 10$; $T_B = 8$ **13.** (a), (d), (f)   **14.** $3x^2 - 3x + 1 - \dfrac{5}{x + 1}$

15. $2x^2 - 4x + 4 - \dfrac{8}{x + 1}$ **16.** 147   **17.** $9\sqrt{3} + 36$ **18.** $180\sqrt{2}$

19. (a) $y = -2x$ (b) $y = -3$ **20.** $(3, -1)$ **21.** $(3, 1)$ **22.** 3×10^{-5}

23. (a) Naturals, wholes, integers, rationals, reals   (b) Integers, rationals, reals

24.   **25.** 46   **26.** $-\dfrac{2}{31}$ **27.** -7 **28.** $\dfrac{2x^2 - 2(x + 1)}{x(x + 1)}$

29. (a) $-\dfrac{1}{9}$ (b) $\dfrac{1}{9}$ (c) $-\dfrac{1}{9}$ **30.** $384\pi \text{ in.}^2 = 1205.76 \text{ in.}^2$

practice   **a.**   **b.**   **c.**

d. $\dfrac{256\pi}{3} \text{ in.}^3 = 267.95 \text{ in.}^3$ **e.** $100\pi \text{ ft}^2 = 314 \text{ ft}^2$

problem set 91

1. $N_F = 360$; $N_S = 270$ **2.** 30   **3.** $N_D = 15$; $N_Q = 20$ **4.** 2000

5. Range = 7; median = 50; mode = 50; mean = 50   **6.**

7.   **8.**   **9.** $3, 7$ **10.** $-\dfrac{7}{2}, \dfrac{7}{2}$

11. $-8, -4$ **12.** $R_H = 76; R_O = 9$ **13.** (b), (c)

14. (b) $D = \left\{ x \in \mathbb{R} \mid -5 \le x \le 3 \right\}; R = \left\{ y \in \mathbb{R} \mid -2 \le y \le 4 \right\}$

     (c) $D = \{3, 4, 9\}; R = \{2, 7\}$

15. $x^3 - 2x^2 + 2x - 4 + \dfrac{4}{x + 2}$ **16.** (a) $y = -3$ (b) $y = \dfrac{1}{2}x + 3$

17. $23\sqrt{3}$ **18.** $36 - 24\sqrt{2}$ **19.** $(-1, 2)$ **20.** $(2, -2)$ **21.** 2×10^{25}

22. (a) Rationals, reals   (b) Rationals, reals   **23.** 9 **24.** $\dfrac{1}{4}$ **25.** $-6, 8$

26. $\dfrac{3x - 2y}{ay - 4}$ **27.** $\dfrac{a^2 + b}{b^2}$ **28.** (a) $\dfrac{1}{8}$ (b) -8 **29.** $\dfrac{4\pi}{3}$ cm^3 $= 4.19$ cm^3

30. 780 m^3

practice   **a.** 18 mi   **b.** 360 mi

problem set 92

1. $R_F = 30$ mph; $R_P = 70$ mph   **2.** 40 km   **3.** 3000.04   **4.** 15   **5.** 19   **6.** $\dfrac{7}{40}$

7.   **8.**   **9.** $-4, -2$ **10.** $-\dfrac{3}{2}, \dfrac{3}{2}$

11. $-8, -4$ **12.** $D = \left\{ x \in \mathbb{R} \mid -8 \le x \le -2 \right\}; R = \left\{ y \in \mathbb{R} \mid -2 \le y \le 6 \right\}$

13. (a) $x = -3$ (b) $y = \dfrac{1}{3}x + 2$ **14.** $x^2 + 5x + 25 + \dfrac{121}{x - 5}$ **15.** $-3\sqrt{5} + 400\sqrt{2}$

16. $24\sqrt{10} - 18$ **17.** $(3, -2)$ **18.** $(5, 5)$ **19.** 2×10^{-20}

20. (a) False. Some real numbers are not members of the set of rational numbers.

     (b) False. Zero, a member of the set of whole numbers, is not a member of the set of natural numbers.

21. $\dfrac{10{,}000(3)^3 (12)^3 (2.54)^3}{(100)^3}$ m^3 **22.** $\dfrac{195}{2}$ **23.** $\dfrac{5}{2}$ **24.** $\dfrac{10}{7}$ **25.** 18   **26.** -10

27. (a) $-\dfrac{1}{4}$ (b) -8 (c) $-\dfrac{1}{4}$ (d) -2 **28.** $\dfrac{a^4 y^2}{x^5} + y^2 - \dfrac{a^6 y^2}{x^7}$

29. 16π in.^{2} $= 50.24$ in.^{2} **30.** 1350 ft^2

practice   **a.** $\dfrac{x + 5}{x}$ **b.** $\dfrac{x - 3}{x - 4}$

problem set 93

1. $T_C = 4$ min; $D = 1200$ cm   **2.** $R_1 = 33$ mph; $R_2 = 44$ mph   **3.** 22

4. $N_B = 96; N_G = 83$ **5.** 20%   **6.** 650   **7.** $\dfrac{1}{32}$ **8.** $\dfrac{x + 3}{x - 3}$ **9.** $x - 5$

10.   **11.**   **12.** $-10, -4$ **13.** $-2, 2$

14. (a), (b), (c), (d), (e)   **15.** $3x^2 - 9x + 27 - \dfrac{85}{x + 3}$ **16.** $4\sqrt{30}$ **17.** $24\sqrt{6} - 96$

18. $D = \left\{ x \in \mathbb{R} \mid -2 < x \le 4 \right\}; R = \left\{ y \in \mathbb{R} \mid -2 \le y < 3 \right\}$

19. (a) $x = -5$ (b) $y = -2x$ **20.** $(2, 0)$ **21.** $(-3, -1)$ **22.** 3×10^{-12} **23.** $\dfrac{34}{11}$

24. -4 **25.** -14 **26.** $9x^2 + 18xy + 9y^2$ **27.** $\dfrac{xy + xa - 3ay - a^2}{a^2 y^2}$

28. (a) -27 (b) -27 (c) $\dfrac{1}{27}$ (d) -4 **29.** $(10 + 15\pi)$ cm $= 57.1$ cm   **30.** 9660 m^3

practice **a.** $R_E = 50 \frac{km}{hr}$; $R_W = 50 \frac{km}{hr}$ **b.** $165 \frac{km}{hr}$

problem set 94

1. $R_1 = 50$ mph; $R_2 = 20$ mph **2.** $T_W = 15$ hr; $D_W = 60$ mi **3.** $N_B = 90$; $N_P = 102$

4. 900 **5.** 80 **6.** 4000 **7.** (a) $\frac{5}{12}$ (b) $\frac{13}{18}$ **8.** 9 **9.** $\frac{16}{(x+6)(x-7)}$

10. 4 **11.** $D = \{x \in \mathbb{R} \mid -4 \leq x < 4\}$; $R = \{y \in \mathbb{R} \mid -4 < y \leq 3\}$

12. (a) $y = -2$ (b) $y = \frac{3}{2}x + 3$ **13.** [number line from −5 to 2 with points at −4, −3, −1, 0] **14.** −3, 10

15. $-\frac{10}{3}, \frac{10}{3}$ **16.** $\left\{x \in \mathbb{R} \mid x \leq \frac{17}{2}\right\}$ **17.** $10x^2 - 47x + 57$ **18.** $x^2 + 2x - 1$

19. $60\sqrt{2} + 2\sqrt{5}$ **20.** $24\sqrt{6} - 144$ **21.** (−3, −3) **22.** (−3, −2) **23.** 1×10^{63}

24. (a) Rationals, reals (b) Wholes, integers, rationals, reals **25.** $-\frac{15}{2}$ **26.** $-\frac{3}{2}$

27. 20 **28.** $4 - 12y^3 - 8x^4$ **29.** 36π in.^{3} = 113.04 in.^{3} **30.** 972π ft^2 = 3052.08 ft^2

practice **a.** (1) $k(x) = \sqrt{x}$ (2) $h(x) = x^3 + 1$ (3) $g(x) = -|x| - 1$ (4) $f(x) = x^2 + 2$
b. (1) $k(x) = -(x + 1)^2$ (2) $h(x) = \sqrt{x}$ (3) $f(x) = |x|$ (4) $g(x) = -x^3 + 1$

problem set 95

1. $T_G = 10$ hr; $T_S = 15$ hr **2.** $R_F = 55$ mph; $R_S = 45$ mph **3.** $N_L = 21$; $N_S = 9$

4. −13, −11, −9, −7 **5.** 1200 **6.** 2610 **7.** (a) $\frac{90}{361}$ (b) $\frac{5}{19}$

8. (a)

STEM	LEAF
1	7, 8
2	4, 5, 7, 5, 9, 6
3	2, 1

(b)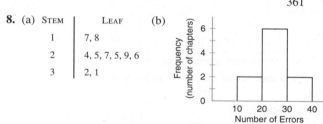

(c) Range = 15;
median = 25.5;
mode = 25;
mean = 25.4

9. (a) $f(x) = -x^2 + 5$ (b) $k(x) = x^3$ (c) $g(x) = |x| + 5$ (d) $h(x) = \sqrt{x}$
10. (a) $k(x) = (x - 5)^2$ (b) $f(x) = -|x|$ (c) $h(x) = -x^3$ (d) $g(x) = -\sqrt{x}$ **11.** $-(x + 3)$

12. $\frac{x(x-3)}{(x+2)(x-2)}$ **13.** [number line from 1 to 5 with points at 3, 4] **14.** −6, −4

15. $-\frac{2}{3}, \frac{2}{3}$ **16.** $-x^2 + 22x - 79$ **17.** $x^3 + x^2 + x - \frac{4}{x-1}$

18. $D = \{x \in \mathbb{R} \mid -3 < x \leq 4\}$; $R = \{y \in \mathbb{R} \mid -2 \leq y \leq 3\}$
19. (a) $y = -2$ (b) $y = -x + 5$ **20.** $288 - 3\sqrt{2}$
21. $30\sqrt{6} - 108\sqrt{2}$ **22.** (−1, 1) **23.** (6, 6) **24.** 1×10^{15}

25. (a) Irrationals, reals (b) Naturals, wholes, integers, rationals, reals **26.** $\frac{xy^2 - 1}{x - 4y}$

27. (a) −9 (b) 9 (c) $-\frac{1}{4}$ **28.** $\frac{13}{8}$ **29.** 36π cm^2 = 113.04 cm^2 **30.** 864 m^3

practice **a.** ±13 **b.** $\pm\sqrt{23}$ **c.** $\pm\sqrt{14}$

problem set 96

1. 9 p.m. **2.** 1 p.m. **3.** 24 km **4.** $N_H = 100$; $N_Q = 90$ **5.** $34\overline{0}$

6. $N_E = 300$; $N_H = 2700$ **7.** (a) $\frac{1}{12}$ (b) $\frac{5}{6}$

8. (a) ±7 (b) $\pm\sqrt{39}$ (c) $\pm\sqrt{11}$

9. (a) $b(x) = x^2 + 5$ (b) $a(x) = 3x + 2$ (c) $d(x) = |x| + 4$ (d) $e(x) = -x^3$ (e) $c(x) = \sqrt{x}$

10. 1   **11.**   **12.** –8, –7   **13.** $-\dfrac{9}{2}, \dfrac{9}{2}$

14. $\left\{ x \in \mathbb{R} \mid x \geq \dfrac{3}{2} \right\}$ **15.** (a) $x = -5$ (b) $y = -\dfrac{3}{2}x + 3$

16. $x^2 - 2x + 2 - \dfrac{4}{x + 1}$ **17.** 360   **18.** –24   **19.** (–1, –2)   **20.** (4, –5)

21. 3×10^{-17} **22.** (a) Irrational (b) Irrational (c) Rational (d) Rational   **23.** 54

24. $\dfrac{7}{40}$ **25.** 12   **26.** (a) $1 + ax$ (b) $-\dfrac{1}{9}$ **27.** –34   **28.** 79

29. $(960 - 50\pi)$ in.^{2} = 803 in.^{2} **30.** $(1056 + 180\pi)$ ft^2 = 1621.2 ft^2

practice   **a.** $\sqrt{61}$ **b.** $10\sqrt{2}$ **c.** 5   **d.** 8

problem set 97

1. T_D = 6 hr; T_W = 5 hr; D = 300 mi   **2.** 300 mi   **3.** N_F = 700; N_T = 550   **4.** –18

5. –5, –4, –3, –2   **6.** 132   **7.** 160   **8.** (a) 5 (b) 10 (c) 13 (d) 17   **9.** $2\sqrt{5}$

10. (a) $x = -2$ (b) $y = \dfrac{1}{3}x - 2$ **11.** (a) ±6 (b) $\pm2\sqrt{6}$ (c) $\pm\sqrt{17}$

12. (a) $L(x) = -2x + 3$ (b) $f(x) = -x^2 + 5$ (c) $g(x) = x^3$ (d) $p(x) = \sqrt{x}$ (e) $h(x) = -|x|$

13. $\dfrac{x + 5}{x - 2}$ **14.** 5, 20   **15.** $9 - 4(x + h)^2$ **16.** (a), (b), (c), (e)

17. $x^2 - 2x + 3 - \dfrac{6}{x + 2}$ **18.** $30\sqrt{6}$ **19.** $30\sqrt{3} - 60\sqrt{2}$ **20.** (1, 3)

21. 4×10^4 **22.** $\dfrac{20}{3}$ **23.** $-\dfrac{5}{4}$ **24.** (a) $4m^2 + 8mp + 4p^2$ (b) $4m^2 - 8mp + 4p^2$

25. –2, $-\dfrac{1}{2}$ **26.** $1 - \dfrac{4x^2y^2}{a^4} - \dfrac{1}{a^4x^6}$ **27.** $\dfrac{p - 4k}{k^2 - 1}$ **28.** (a) $-(1 + x)$ (b) 16

29. 24π cm = 75.36 cm   **30.** 2880π m^3 = 9043.2 m^3

practice   **a.** $2\sqrt{17}$ **b.** –1   **c.** $\dfrac{19}{18}$

problem set 98

1. 4 p.m.   **2.** T_W = 10 hr; D = 40 mi   **3.** –7   **4.** 28, 30, 32, 34   **5.** 630   **6.** 40 hr

7. (a) $\dfrac{1}{36}$ (b) $\dfrac{35}{36}$ **8.** (a) 3 (b) 6 (c) 5 (d) 15   **9.** $\sqrt{55}$

10. (a) $-\dfrac{1}{3}$ (b) $2\sqrt{10}$ **11.** (a) $-\dfrac{1}{2}$ (b) $4\sqrt{5}$ **12.** (a) ±7 (b) $\pm2\sqrt{3}$ (c) $\pm\sqrt{3}$

13. (a) $g(x) = \sqrt{x}$ (b) $k(x) = x^3 + 1$ (c) $p(x) = x^2 - 5$ (d) $h(x) = |x|$ (e) $f(x) = 3x + 1$

14. $\dfrac{x}{4}$ **15.** $36\sqrt{3} - 24\sqrt{6} + 6\sqrt{2}$ **16.** –7, 2

17. $D = \left\{ x \in \mathbb{R} \mid -3 \leq x < 4 \right\}$; $R = \left\{ y \in \mathbb{R} \mid -1 \leq y < 5 \right\}$

18. (a) $y = 3$ (b) $y = -\dfrac{1}{3}x - 1$ **19.** $x^2 + x + 1$ **20.** (4, –4)   **21.** 6.3×10^{-8}

22.   **23.** $\dfrac{39}{2}$ **24.** –2   **25.** 9   **26.** 0

27. (a) $x - 1$ (b) 9   **28.** $\dfrac{3xy - 1}{2x - 4y}$ **29.** $\dfrac{32\pi}{3}$ in.^{3} = 33.49 in.^{3} **30.** 540 ft^2

practice   **a.** $8 \frac{km}{hr}$ **b.** 2 hr

problem set 99

1. 25   **2.** 75 mph,   **3.** 7   **4.** $N_N = 250$; $N_Q = 200$ **5.** 5000   **6.** –7, –6, –5, –4

7. $\sqrt{65}$ **8.** $3\sqrt{7}$ **9.** $2\sqrt{10}$ **10.** (a) $-\frac{5}{3}$ (b) $\sqrt{34}$ **11.** (a) $-\frac{5}{6}$ (b) $\sqrt{61}$

12. (a) $h(x) = x$ (b) $f(x) = x^3$ (c) $p(x) = -x^3$ (d) $g(x) = x^2$ (e) $k(x) = -x^2$

13. (a) ± 8 (b) $\pm 4\sqrt{2}$ (c) $\pm\sqrt{11}$ **14.** $-\frac{(x + 7)(x + 2)}{x - 3}$ **15.** $-\frac{9}{2}, \frac{9}{2}$

16. (a) Rational (b) Rational (c) Irrational (d) Rational   **17.** $\left\{ x \in \mathbb{R} \mid x \geq \frac{4}{3} \right\}$

18. (a) $y = 4$ (b) $y = -x - 3$ **19.** $x^2 + 4x + 16 + \frac{60}{x - 4}$ **20.** $364\sqrt{2}$

21. $30 - 24\sqrt{21}$ **22.** $(3, -1)$ **23.**
   24. 5×10^{-9}

25. $\frac{x^3 + 2x^2 + 6x - 8}{x^2(x + 4)}$ **26.** –10   **27.** –19   **28.** (a) $2a + 1$ (b) 81

29. 64π cm^2 = 200.96 cm^2 **30.** 960 m^3

practice   **a.** 59,740,000   **b.** 513.1293   **c.** 63.014915

problem set 100

1. 10 seconds   **2.** $T_R = 8$ hr; $T_W = 6$ hr   **3.** $P_1 = 50$ ft; $P_2 = 10$ ft   **4.** –11, –9, –7, –5

5. 700   **6.** $\frac{1}{6}$ **7.** (a) 104.0625 (b) 400 (c) 0.29   **8.** (a) 4 (b) 8 (c) 12 (d) 8

9. $2\sqrt{5}$ **10.** (a) $x = 5$ (b) $y = -\frac{4}{3}x - 2$ **11.** (a) $-\frac{5}{3}$ (b) $\sqrt{34}$

12. (a) $k(x) = 1 + x^3$ (b) $f(x) = -x^3 + 1$ (c) $g(x) = -(x + 1)^2$ (d) $p(x) = 2x$ (e) $h(x) = x^2$

13. (a) ± 13 (b) $\pm 4\sqrt{3}$ (c) $\pm\sqrt{2}$ **14.** $x - 4$ **15.** –7, –5   **16.** (a), (b), (d), (e)

17. $x^2 - 2x + 16 - \frac{27}{x + 2}$ **18.** $240\sqrt{3}$ **19.** $48 - 18\sqrt{6}$ **20.** $(2, 4)$

21.
   22. 8×10^{48}

23. (a) Irrationals, reals (b) Naturals, wholes, integers, rationals, reals

24. $\frac{-9x^3 - 4x^2 + 13x + 16}{4x^2(x + 1)}$ **25.** 52   **26.** 8   **27.** $1 - a - 3x$ **28.** –634

29. 81π in.^{2} = 254.34 in.^{2} **30.** 400 ft^2

practice   **a.** $\frac{2x - 21}{(x + 3)(x - 7)}$ **b.** $\frac{-x + 45}{x(x - 1)(x - 9)}$

problem set 101

1. 5 seconds   **2.** 15 mi   **3.** $N_T = 600$; $N_O = 750$ **4.** –8, –6, –4   **5.** 480

6. (a) $\frac{6}{11}$ (b) $\frac{9}{16}$ **7.** Range = 56; median = 179.5; mode = 172; mean = 178

8. $\frac{p + 2x + 6}{(x + 3)(x - 3)}$ **9.** $\frac{8x^2 - 9x - 28}{(x - 2)^2(x - 4)}$ **10.** (a) 1.4142 (b) 0.67 (c) 4000

11. $4\sqrt{5}$ **12.** (a) $y = -2$ (b) $y = -2x$ **13.** (a) $-\frac{5}{8}$ (b) $\sqrt{89}$ **14.** (b)

15. (a) ± 15 (b) $\pm 6\sqrt{2}$ (c) $\pm\sqrt{29}$ **16.** $\frac{x + 10}{x + 7}$ **17.** $-\frac{9}{2}, \frac{9}{2}$

18. (a) Irrational (b) Irrational (c) Rational (d) Rational   **19.** $260\sqrt{6}$

20. $18\sqrt{15} + 15$ **21.** $(1, -2)$ **22.**
   23. $\frac{69}{7}$

24. $\dfrac{3}{4}$ **25.** (a) $1 + 2a$ (b) $-\dfrac{1}{81}$ **26.** $\dfrac{5p - 4x}{3 - x^2}$ **27.** -176 **28.** $\dfrac{a^9}{x^2}$

29. 12π cm $= 37.68$ cm   **30.** 288 m^3

practice   **a.**   **b.**

problem set 102

1. 6 p.m.   **2.** $N_R = 40$; $N_W = 12$ **3.** 490   **4.** $-10, -9, -8, -7$ **5.** 4800

6. $\dfrac{1}{16}$ **7.**   **8.**

9.   **10.** $\dfrac{4x + 21}{(x + 4)(x - 4)}$ **11.** $\dfrac{-3x + 1}{(x + 1)(x + 1)}$

12. (a) 2.236   (b) 3000   (c) 572.06   **13.** (a) 5   (b) 13   (c) 10   (d) 17

14. $\sqrt{146}$ **15.** (a) $\dfrac{1}{2}$ (b) $\sqrt{5}$

16. (a) $g(x) = -|x| + 1$ (b) $k(x) = |x|$ (c) $h(x) = 2x - 1$

(d) $p(x) = -\dfrac{1}{2}x + 1$ (e) $f(x) = x^2$

17. (a) $\pm\sqrt{5}$ (b) $\pm 2\sqrt{2}$ (c) $\pm\sqrt{19}$ **18.** $x + 10$ **19.** $-10, -8$

20. $D = \{x \in \mathbb{R} \mid -4 \le x < 5\}$; $R = \{y \in \mathbb{R} \mid -2 \le y \le 3\}$

21. (a) $x = -4$ (b) $y = \dfrac{5}{2}x - 3$ **22.** $x^2 - x$ **23.** $2506\sqrt{6} - 30$ **24.** $(2, 5)$

25. $\dfrac{64}{23}$ **26.** 2×10^{62} **27.** (a) $1 + 3x$ (b) $-\dfrac{1}{16}$ **28.** $\dfrac{3}{5}$ **29.** 580 in.^{2}

30. 660 ft^2

practice   **a.** 5   **b.** $\dfrac{24}{13}$

problem set 103

1. 8 hr   **2.** 8 mi   **3.** -4 **4.** $N_C = 15$; $N_D = 10$ **5.** \$10   **6.** 460

7. (a) $\dfrac{5}{18}$ (b) $\dfrac{7}{12}$ **8.** 6   **9.** 1   **10.**

11.   **12.** $\dfrac{10a + 8}{(a - 2)(a + 2)}$ **13.** $\dfrac{5x - 13}{(x + 4)(x - 2)}$

14. (a) 1.7321   (b) 0.167   (c) 1100   **15.** $2\sqrt{5}$ **16.** (a) $y = 4$ (b) $y = -\dfrac{1}{3}x - 3$

17. (a) -3 (b) $3\sqrt{10}$ **18.** (b)   **19.** $x - 2$ **20.** $-\dfrac{9}{2}, \dfrac{9}{2}$ **21.** (b), (c)

22. $x^2 - 7x + 49 - \dfrac{347}{x + 7}$ **23.** $-382\sqrt{6} - 6$ **24.** $(2, 0)$

25. (a) Rationals, reals   (b) Integers, rationals, reals   **26.** (a) $1 - x$ (b) $\dfrac{1}{4}$ **27.** $\dfrac{a^3 + 1}{a^2 x + b}$

28. 48   **29.** $(12 + 22\pi)$ cm $= 81.08$ cm   **30.** 7020 m^3

practice   **a.** $\dfrac{nm}{fm - 3z}$ **b.** $\dfrac{ky}{xy + sy - 3a}$

problem set 104

1. 4 hr   **2.** 240 mi   **3.** $-1, 1, 3$ **4.** 5   **5.** 270,500   **6.** $\dfrac{143}{570}$

7. $\dfrac{ax}{yx + mx - 5k}$ **8.** $\dfrac{ab}{2c - ax}$ **9.** 2   **10.** 3   **11.** $\dfrac{15}{2}$ **12.** -2

13.   **14.**

15. $\dfrac{3x^2 + 6x + 4}{(x - 2)(x + 2)}$ **16.** $-\dfrac{x^2 + x}{(x + 5)(x - 2)}$ **17.** (a) 5.10   (b) 3.141593   (c) 5250

18. $2\sqrt{10}$ **19.** (a) $y = 3$ (b) $y = \dfrac{3}{2}x - 3$ **20.** (a) $-\dfrac{2}{3}$ (b) $2\sqrt{13}$ **21.** (d)

22. $-9, -7$ **23.** $\left\{ x \in \mathbb{R} \mid x \le \dfrac{1}{4} \right\}$ **24.** $355\sqrt{2} + 24$ **25.** $-2, \dfrac{1}{2}$ **26.** 7   **27.** 44

28. (a) $x - 1$ (b) $-\dfrac{1}{4}$ **29.** $(54 - 4\pi)$ in.^{2} = 41.44 in.^{2} **30.** 2400 ft^2

practice   **a.** $(a + n)(mb - 7)$ **b.** $(s + 3x)(n + 2c)$

problem set 105

1. 12 km   **2.** 25 seconds   **3.** 30   **4.** 4, 6, 8, 10   **5.** 600   **6.** $\dfrac{1}{2}$

7. $(c - d)(a + b)$ **8.** $(b + 4)(a + 2)$ **9.** $(b + c)(a + x)$ **10.** $(2x - 3)(m + pc)$

11. $(4 - xy)(k + pc)$ **12.** $(c - xy)(a + d)$ **13.** $\dfrac{ca}{cd - 1}$ **14.** $\dfrac{cda - xd}{xc}$ **15.** 8

16. 44   **17.**   **18.**

19. $\dfrac{13 - 3x}{(x + 3)(x - 3)}$ **20.** $\dfrac{2x + 15}{(x + 3)(x + 2)}$ **21.** (a) 3.61   (b) 6.28319   (c) 58,000

22. $2\sqrt{5}$ **23.** $(3, 0)$

24. (a) $g(x) = x^2 + 2$ (b) $f(x) = |x + 3|$ (c) $p(x) = -(x + 2)^2$ (d) $h(x) = -|x|$

25. (a) $\dfrac{4}{3}$ (b) 10   **26.** $-50\sqrt{5} + 125$ **27.** $\dfrac{1}{x}$ **28.** $-\dfrac{1}{3}, 1$

29. $(8 + 12\pi)$ cm = 45.68 cm   **30.** 512 m^3

practice   **a.** $y = -4x + 7$ **b.** $y = \dfrac{8}{9}x - \dfrac{1}{3}$

problem set 106

1. 11 a.m.   **2.** 3 hr   **3.** $N_Q = 21$; $N_D = 43$ **4.** $-20, -18, -16$ **5.** 22,500

6. (a) $\dfrac{1}{36}$ (b) $\dfrac{35}{36}$ **7.** $y = \dfrac{4}{3}x + \dfrac{7}{3}$ **8.** $y = x$ **9.** $(a + 3)(b + 5)$

10. $(a + x)(y + c)$ **11.** $(3x - 2)(m + p)$ **12.** $(x - 5)(k + 3)$ **13.** $(x + c)(pc + 4)$

14. $(b - k)(ac + 2)$ **15.** $\dfrac{mx}{mp - 1}$ **16.** $\dfrac{m}{mx - k}$ **17.** $\dfrac{x}{xy - k}$ **18.** $\dfrac{cy}{cx - yb}$

19.   **20.** $\dfrac{7}{4}$ **21.** 9   **22.** $\dfrac{4 - x(x + 5)}{(x - 5)(x + 5)}$

23. $-\dfrac{6}{(x + 2)(x - 3)}$ **24.** (a) 3.317   (b) 50,000   (c) 0.6   **25.** $275\sqrt{3} + 30$

26. (a) $x + 1$ (b) $-\dfrac{1}{36}$ **27.** $5\sqrt{5}$ **28.** $\sqrt{106}$ **29.** 1, 2   **30.** 972 in.^{2}

practice   **a.** $y = -3x - 1$ **b.** $y = -\dfrac{3}{2}x - 6$ **c.** $y = -\dfrac{2}{5}x + \dfrac{19}{5}$ **d.** $y = \dfrac{1}{4}x + \dfrac{31}{4}$

problem set 107

1. 80 mi   **2.** 24 mph   **3.** \$50   **4.** $N_D = 500$; $N_Q = 100$ **5.** $-11, -9, -7$

6. $y = 2x + 7$ **7.** $y = -\dfrac{1}{2}x + 1$ **8.** $y = -\dfrac{1}{8}x - \dfrac{19}{8}$ **9.** $y = -\dfrac{1}{5}x$

10. $2\sqrt{10}$ **11.** $(m^2 - c)(k - 2)$ **12.** $(a + b)(6 - xy)$ **13.** $(x - 2y)(ab + c)$

14. $(n - m)(4x + ab)$ **15.** $\dfrac{xa}{xb + 1}$ **16.** $\dfrac{yk}{py - x}$ **17.**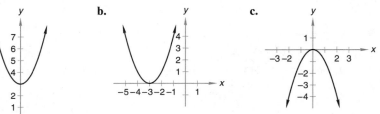

18. $\dfrac{7}{5}$ **19.** $\dfrac{35}{4}$ **20.** (a) 5.48   (b) 4300   (c) 0.4286   **21.** (c)   **22.** $\dfrac{9 - x(x + 9)}{(x - 9)(x + 9)}$

23. $-12, -10$ **24.** 7×10^{-25} **25.** $5\sqrt{15} + 30$ **26.** $\dfrac{3}{4}$ **27.** $-\dfrac{1}{4}, \dfrac{1}{18}$

28. (a) -3 (b) $1 + y$ **29.** $\dfrac{500\pi}{3}$ cm^3 = 523.33 cm^3 **30.** $\dfrac{275\pi}{3}$ m^3 = 287.83 m^3

practice   **a.** 15   **b.** 6

problem set 108

1. 30 mi   **2.** 8 mph   **3.** $N_G = 52; N_P = 71$ **4.** 85   **5.** (a) $\dfrac{2}{9}$ (b) $\dfrac{1}{4}$

6. 85   **7.** $-\sqrt{70}, \sqrt{70}$ **8.** 19   **9.** 3   **10.** 8   **11.** $y = -3x - 1$

12. $y = x - 2$ **13.** $(m + r)(t^2 + 3)$ **14.** $(c + d)(6 - xy)$ **15.** $\dfrac{cx}{ck + 1 + cd}$

16. $-\dfrac{39}{2}$ **17.** (a) 0.524   (b) 0.0374   (c) 10   **18.** $2\sqrt{14}$

19. (a) $y = -4$ (b) $y = \dfrac{3}{4}x + 2$ **20.** $\dfrac{4(x + y) - 2xy}{xy(x + y)}$ **21.** $\dfrac{3x^2 + 12x + 8}{(x - 4)(x + 4)}$

22. $(1, 3)$ **23.** $\dfrac{x + 5}{x - 2}$ **24.** $2x^2 + 5x + 10 + \dfrac{14}{x - 1}$

25. $D = \{x \in \mathbb{R} \mid -4 < x \le 6\}; R = \{y \in \mathbb{R} \mid -3 \le y \le 3\}$

26. $\dfrac{zx - 1}{az - 3x}$ **27.** -7 **28.** $-\dfrac{1}{14}, \dfrac{1}{2}$ **29.** $\left(36 + \dfrac{9\pi}{2}\right)$ in.^{2} = 50.13 in.^{2} **30.** 864 ft^2

practice   **a.** $(2x + 3)(x - 7)$ **b.** $(3x - 1)(x + 2)$

problem set 109

1. 24 mi   **2.** 2 p.m.   **3.** $N_L = 50; N_S = 75$ **4.** $-5, -3, -1$

5. $N_B = 1855; N_M = 725$ **6.** 12%   **7.** $(3x + 1)(x - 5)$ **8.** $2(x + 4)(x + 1)$

9. $(2x - 3)(x - 6)$ **10.** $(2x - 3)(x + 5)$ **11.** $2(x + 6)(x - 2)$ **12.** $2(x - 6)(x + 2)$

13. $2(x - 2)(x - 1)$ **14.** $(2x - 3)(x + 6)$ **15.** $2(x + 2)(x + 1)$ **16.** 6   **17.** 5

18. $y = -2x + 5$ **19.** $y = \dfrac{4}{3}x + \dfrac{7}{3}$ **20.** $\dfrac{c}{ck - a}$ **21.** $(t - 4)(y^2 + 3m)$

22. $(m + y)(x + 4)$ **23.** $6\sqrt{2}$ **24.** (a) $y = -4$ (b) $y = -x$

25. 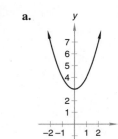   **26.** $(-1, 0)$ **27.** 16   **28.** $\dfrac{x - 3}{x^2(x + 8)}$

29. $-\dfrac{1}{2}, 2$ **30.** $(1584 + 144\pi)$ cm^3 = 2036.16 cm^3

practice   **a.**   **b.**   **c.**   **d.** (3)

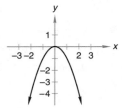

problem set 110

1. 5 mph **2.** 4 p.m. **3.** –4, –3, –2 **4.** –9, –7, –5, –3 **5.** $20,000 **6.** 4500; 7500

7. (a) 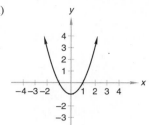 (b) 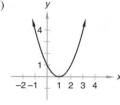 (c)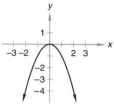

8. (d) **9.** $3(2y + 3)(y - 4)$ **10.** $(2z - 1)(z - 3)$ **11.** $(2y + 1)(y - 3)$ **12.** 23

13. 67 **14.** $y = \dfrac{2}{5}x + \dfrac{29}{5}$ **15.** $y = -\dfrac{1}{5}x - \dfrac{17}{5}$ **16.** $(b - 2c^3)(a^2 + m)$

17. $(a + 2d^3)(6x + 7m^3)$ **18.** $\dfrac{d(bx - a)}{b}$ **19.** 12 **20.** (a) 28.3 (b) 1 (c) 0.92308

21. (a) 4 (b) 8 (c) 6 **22.**  **23.** –76

24. $\dfrac{3x^2 + 12x - 6}{(x + 2)(x + 5)^2}$ **25.** (a), (d) **26.** 1 **27.** $\dfrac{x^3}{y^5}$ **28.** $-\dfrac{9}{10}, -\dfrac{1}{2}$

29. 144π in.^{2} = 452.16 in.^{2} **30.** 182π ft^2 = 571.48 ft^2

practice **a.**   **b.**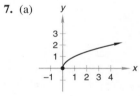

problem set 111

1. 14 mph **2.** 48 mi **3.** N_A = 11; N_P = 40 **4.** 10 **5.** $135 **6.** $\dfrac{1}{2}$

7. (a) 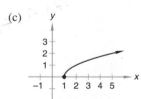 (b)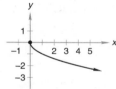

(c) 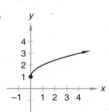 (d)

8. (a) **9.** $y = \dfrac{9}{5}x + \dfrac{7}{5}$ **10.**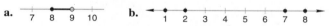

11.   **12.** $(3x - 1)(x + 5)$ **13.** $3(x + 9)(x - 1)$

14. $(2x - 1)(x + 5)$ **15.** $(3x + 1)(x - 7)$ **16.** 25 **17.** 68 **18.** $(a^2 + b)(c + 3)$

19. $\dfrac{acd}{c + d}$ **20.** –9, 5 **21.**   **22.** $\sqrt{145}$

23. $\{x \in \mathbb{R} \mid x \le 6\}$ **24.** (a) Irrational (b) Rational (c) Rational (d) Irrational

25. $40 - 16\sqrt{6}$ **26.** $-\dfrac{1}{27}$ **27.** $-\dfrac{3a^4}{x^4y^2}$ **28.** –5, 3 **29.** $(24 + 6\pi)$ cm = 42.84 cm

30. 900 m^3

practice   **a.** $19 + 13\sqrt{2}$ **b.** $-7 - 2\sqrt{5}$ **c.** $7 + 2\sqrt{10}$ **d.** $2x^2 + 2\sqrt{14}xy + 7y^2$

problem set 112

1. 4 hr   **2.** 90 km   **3.** $N_F = 163; N_T = 13$ **4.** $\dfrac{3}{4}$ **5.** 165   **6.** $\dfrac{5}{18}$

7. (a)   (b)   (c)   (d)

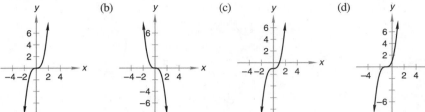

8. (b)   **9.** (a) $-66 - 10\sqrt{3}$ (b) $2a - 2\sqrt{6ap} + 3p$ **10.** $y = x - 2$

11. $y = -\dfrac{2}{3}x - \dfrac{13}{3}$ **12.** 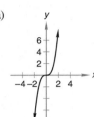   **13.**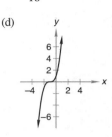

14. $2(x - 3)(x + 1)$ **15.** $(3x - 4)(x + 1)$ **16.** $(3x - 2)(x + 10)$ **17.** $\dfrac{49}{4}$ **18.** 20

19. $(r + a)(x - b)$ **20.** $(x + 3)(y - x)$ **21.**

22.   **23.** $\dfrac{bcx}{bcp + b - ac}$ **24.** $(5, -2)$

25. $D = \{x \in \mathbb{R} \mid -4 < x \le 4\}; R = \{y \in \mathbb{R} \mid -4 < y \le 3\}$

26. (a) $y = -2$ (b) $y = -2x$ **27.** $x^2 - 2x + 2 - \dfrac{8}{x + 2}$ **28.** $\dfrac{5x^2 + 15x + 4}{(x + 3)(x - 3)}$

29. 180 in.^{2} **30.** $(188 + 22\pi)$ ft$^2 = 257.08$ ft^2

practice   **a.** 13 liters   **b.** 75 K   **c.** 45 liters

problem set 113

1. 4 hr   **2.** 10.5 liters   **3.** 40 km   **4.** 50 km   **5.** $N_R = 15; N_W = 12$ **6.** 1500

7. (a)   (b)   (c)   (d)

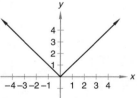
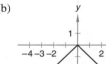
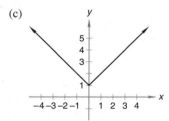
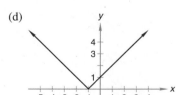

8. (c)   **9.** $-22 - 16\sqrt{3}$ **10.** $-4 - 8\sqrt{2}$ **11.** $-26 - 28\sqrt{6}$

12.   **13.**

14. $12(x + 3)(x + 2)$ **15.** $5(x - 4)(x - 2)$ **16.** $3(r - 13)(r + 10)$ **17.** $\dfrac{9}{4}$ **18.** 68

19. $\dfrac{cx}{ck + cm - 1}$ **20.** $-\dfrac{5}{2}$ **21.** $\sqrt{145}$ **22.** $(x - 3)(y - 2)$ **23.** $-1, 8$

24. $y = 2x - 1$ **25.** $\sqrt{39}$ **26.** 7×10^{-56} **27.** $x^2 y^3$ **28.** $\dfrac{-3 \pm \sqrt{6}}{6}$ **29.** 9 cm^2

30. $S.A. = (90 + 40\pi) \text{ m}^2 = 215.6 \text{ m}^2$; $V = \left(72 + \dfrac{75\pi}{2}\right) \text{ m}^3 = 189.75 \text{ m}^3$

practice   **a.** (1) 15.6250   (2) 0.7071   (3) 1.4643   **b.** (1) 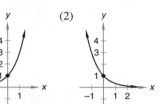 (2)

           c. $A_n = \$900(1.08)^n$; $\$2266.35$; $\$1366.35$

problem set 114

1. (a) $A(t) = 1000(4)^t$ (b) 2.81×10^{17}

2. (a) $A(n) = \$700(1.09)^n$ (b) $\$1806.30$ (c) $\$1106.30$

3. (a) 97.2117   (b) 17.4713   (c) 0.5000   **4.**

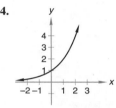

5. 35   **6.** 300   **7.** 40 mi

8. (a)   (b)

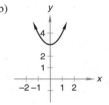

(c)   (d)

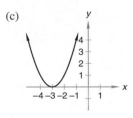
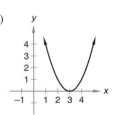

9. $y = -\dfrac{1}{4}x$ **10.** $y = -x + 3$ **11.** $y = -3x - 4$ **12.** $\dfrac{160{,}000(100)^3}{(2.54)^3} \text{ in.}^3$

13. 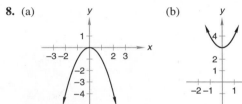   **14.** $-11 - \sqrt{5}$ **15.** $5 + 3\sqrt{2}$ **16.** -2 **17.** $-\dfrac{7}{90}$

18. $7x^2 - 14x + 26 - \dfrac{54}{x + 2}$ **19.** $(5x + 2)(x + 3)$ **20.** $(2x + 1)(2x + 1)$

21. $(l + 3)(2x^2 - 5)$ **22.** $\dfrac{xm}{p + am - km}$ **23.** 32   **24.** $(-4, -4)$ **25.** $\dfrac{mp^2 x - z}{y - 5ax}$

26. $\sqrt{29}$ **27.** $-\dfrac{28}{9}$ **28.** 1434   **29.** 136 in.^2

30. $S.A. = (300 + 100\pi) \text{ ft}^2 = 614 \text{ ft}^2$; $V = (500 + 125\pi) \text{ ft}^3 = 892.5 \text{ ft}^3$

practice

a.

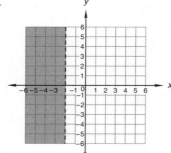

b.

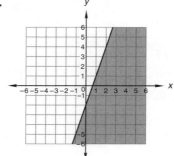

c.

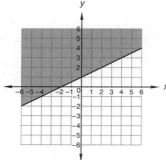

**problem set
115**

1. (a) $A_n = 17(2)^n$ (b) 1.83×10^{10} 2. 500 liters   3. 20

4. 42 miles   5. $N_D = 20$; $N_N = 14$ 6. $\dfrac{7}{44}$

7.

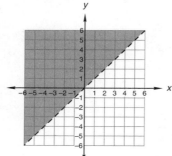

8.

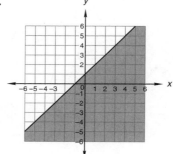

9.

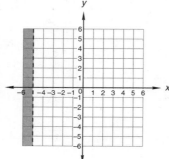

10.

11.

12.

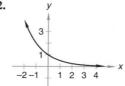

13. $y = -\dfrac{7}{5}x + \dfrac{11}{5}$

14. $y = -\dfrac{1}{3}x + \dfrac{13}{3}$

15. [number line with points]

16. [number line]

17. $3 + \sqrt{2}$ 18. $-4 - 14\sqrt{3}$ 19. $(3x + 1)(3x + 1)$ 20. $(5x + y)(5x - y)$

21. $(5z + 7)(z - 1)$ **22.** $\dfrac{25}{4}$ **23.** $\dfrac{8}{3}$ **24.** $\dfrac{dx}{d^2 + c}$ **25.** (a), (c), (e), (f)   **26.** 31

27. $\dfrac{y^2}{x^4}$ **28.** 5×10^{-88} **29.** 288π cm^3 = 904.32 cm^3 **30.** 450 m^3

practice   **a.** $\dfrac{\sqrt{138}}{23}$ **b.** $\dfrac{4\sqrt{3} + \sqrt{15}}{3}$

problem set 116

1. (a) $A(n) = \$10{,}000(1.08)^n$ (b) \$14693.28   (c) \$4693.28

2. (a) $A(n) = \$1100(1.06)^n$ (b) \$3527.85   (c) \$2427.85   **3.** 40   **4.** 30 km

5. \$6.00   **6.** $N_C = 20$; $N_E = 5$ **7.** $\sqrt{2} + 3\sqrt{3}$ **8.** $\dfrac{\sqrt{10}}{5}$ **9.** $\dfrac{4\sqrt{5} + 10\sqrt{2}}{5}$

10. 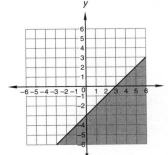   **11.**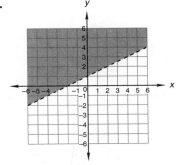

12. 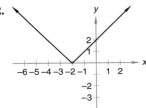   **13.** 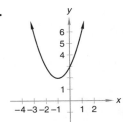   **14.**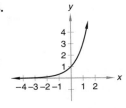

15.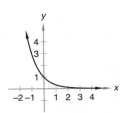

16. $y = -3x + 13$ **17.** $y = -5x - 23$

18.

19. $-10 - 8\sqrt{2}$ **20.** $-5 + 4\sqrt{3}$ **21.** 52

22. $(3x - 2)(x + 9)$ **23.** $(3x - 4)(x + 1)$

24. $(b + 5)(a + 3)$ **25.** $(a + x)(y + c)$ **26.** $\dfrac{mx}{a + bx - kx}$

27. (a) 7.3875   (b) 1.9994   (c) 23.0963   **28.** -1152 **29.** 256π in.^{2} = 803.84 in.^{2}

30. $S.A. = 2952$ ft^2; $V = 8640$ ft^3

practice   **a.** 2880 lb

problem set 117

1. 1568 m   **2.** 2704 ft   **3.** 36   **4.** 100

5. (a) $A_n = 2^n$ (b)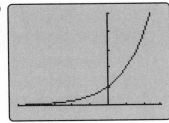
(c) 512

6. $R = 9800$; $S = 7000$

7. $\dfrac{\sqrt{21}}{3}$ **8.** 3

9.

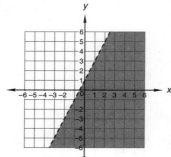

10.

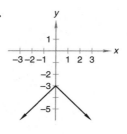

11.

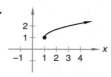

12.

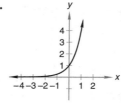

13.

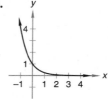

14. $y = -\dfrac{7}{5}x + \dfrac{11}{5}$ **15.** $y = -\dfrac{1}{4}x + \dfrac{9}{2}$ **16.** $y = -\dfrac{1}{3}x + \dfrac{13}{3}$

17. (number line: open circles at -2 and 2)   **18.** (number line: closed dots at 2, 3, 4)

19. (number line: closed dot at 3, open circle at 5)   **20.** 23 **21.** $(2x + 5)(x + 5)$ **22.** $2(3x - 2)(x + 10)$

23. $(k + 3)(x - 5)$ **24.** $(3x - 2)(m + p)$ **25.** $\dfrac{kcx}{km + c}$ **26.** $\dfrac{50}{9}$ **27.** 13

28. $-2, \dfrac{1}{2}$ **29.** $\left(150 - \dfrac{25\pi}{2}\right) \text{cm}^2 = 110.75 \text{ cm}^2$ **30.** 630 m^2

practice   **a.** $-\dfrac{7}{2} \pm \dfrac{\sqrt{85}}{2}$ **b.** $-1, 6$

problem set 118

1. 4000 **2.** (a) 3 (b) $64{,}093.53$ **3.** $R_E = 60$ mph; $R_F = 40$ mph

4. $N_O = 530$; $N_T = 237$ **5.** $2, 4, 6, 8$ **6.** $\dfrac{1}{4}$

7. (a) $A(n) = \$50{,}000(1.12)^n$ (b) $\$155{,}292.41$ (c) $\$105{,}292.41$

8. $-1 \pm \sqrt{5}$ **9.** $-\dfrac{3}{2} \pm \dfrac{\sqrt{41}}{2}$ **10.** $-1 \pm \sqrt{6}$

11. $-2 \pm \sqrt{11}$ **12.** $\dfrac{\sqrt{14}}{7}$ **13.** $\dfrac{\sqrt{15}}{6}$ **14.** $\dfrac{4\sqrt{6} + 3\sqrt{2}}{6}$

15.

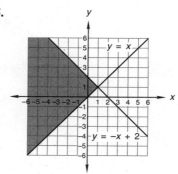

16.

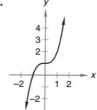

17.

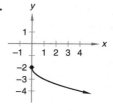

18. (a) 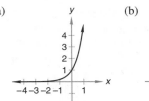 (b)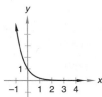

19. $y = \frac{1}{5}x + \frac{18}{5}$

20. $y = -\frac{5}{8}x + \frac{1}{8}$

21.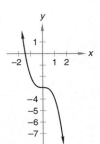

22.

23. 24. $(3x + 5)(x - 7)$ 25. $(3x - 5)(x + 1)$

26. $(2x + 3)(x - 4)$ 27. $(c + b)(p^2 - a)$ 28. $(m + 2)(x^3 + y)$ 29. 2

30. $S.A. = 360$ in.^{2}; $V = 400$ in.^{3}

practice   a. $\dfrac{3 \pm \sqrt{65}}{4}$ b. $\dfrac{-3 \pm \sqrt{17}}{4}$

problem set 119

1. 24,000 lb   2. (a) $A(n) = \$19,000(1.11)^n$ (b) \$43,786.22   (c) \$24,786.22   3. 125

4. $R_E = 50$ mph; $R_F = 40$ mph   5. \$120   6. $N_G = 42$; $N_S = 40$

7. 23, 25, 27   8. $\dfrac{3 \pm \sqrt{89}}{4}$ 9. $1 \pm \sqrt{6}$ 10. $-1 \pm 2\sqrt{3}$ 11. $\dfrac{3 \pm \sqrt{29}}{5}$

12. $-2, 5$ 13. $1 \pm \sqrt{6}$ 14. $-1 \pm 2\sqrt{3}$ 15. $12 + 8\sqrt{2}$ 16. $\dfrac{\sqrt{6}}{4}$ 17. $\dfrac{2 + \sqrt{2}}{2}$

18.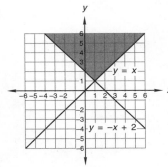

19.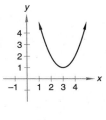

20.

21. (a) 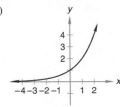 (b) 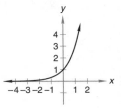 (c)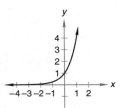

(d) $(0, 1)$

22. $y = \frac{1}{3}x + \frac{11}{3}$ 23. $y = -x + 4$ 24.   25. $(2x + 5)(x - 5)$

26. $(b - k)(ac + 2)$ 27. $-8, -7$ 28. 4   29. $\dfrac{3xy + 4x}{6ax + 12y}$

30. $S.A. = 90\pi$ cm^2 = 282.6 cm^2; $V = 100\pi$ cm^3 = 314 cm^3

practice   a. (1) Range = 45; median = 70; The mode and mean cannot be determined.

(2) Least = 45; Greatest = 90; Median = 70. Approximately one fourth of the scores lies between each of the following intervals: 45–60, 60–70, 70–85, and 85–90.

b.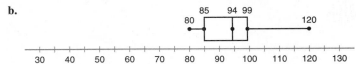

problem set 120

1. (a) Range = $18,000; median = $32,000; The mode and mean cannot be determined.

   (b) Least = $22,000; greatest = $40,000; median = $32,000. Approximately one fourth of the salaries (in thousands of dollars) lies between each of the following intervals: 22–28, 28–32, 32–35, and 35–40.

2.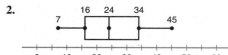

3. 5,904,900   4. 10,000,000 lb

5. $R_p = 12 \frac{km}{hr}$; $D = 72$ km   6. 10   7. (a) $A(n) = \$500(1.05)^n$ (b) $578.81   (c) $78.81

8. 34,000   9. 6   10. $-3 \pm \sqrt{7}$ 11. $-\frac{1}{2}, 4$ 12. $\frac{7}{2} \pm \frac{\sqrt{29}}{2}$ 13. $-1, 4$

14. $-\frac{2}{3}, \frac{2}{3}$ 15. $-5, -1$ 16. 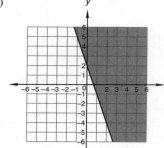   17.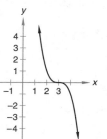

18.
```
◄─┼──┼──┼──┼──┼──┼──┼─►
 -3  -2  -1   0   1   2   3
```

19. (a) $y = 4$ (b) $y = -\frac{2}{3}x - 2$

20. (a)   (b)

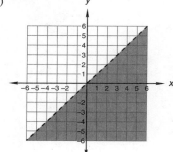

21. $y = \frac{1}{3}x + \frac{10}{3}$ 22. (a) $\frac{\sqrt{10}}{4}$ (b) $\frac{5 + 3\sqrt{5}}{5}$ 23. $-36\sqrt{2} + 60\sqrt{6}$

24. $3(x + 11)(x - 1)$ 25. $(x^2 + 5)(a - 4)$ 26. (a) Irrational   (b) Rational   (c) Rational

27. (a), (d), (g)   28. $x^2 + 2x + 3$ 29. $\frac{10}{x^{-2}y^2} - \frac{3}{x^{-6}y^{-2}}$

30. $S.A. = (64 + 264\pi)$ in.^{2} = 892.96 in.^{2}; $V = 544\pi$ in.^{3} = 1708.16 in.^{3}

Index